कलातत्त्वकोश
KALĀTATTVAKOŚA

कलातत्त्वकोश
KALĀTATTVAKOŚA

A LEXICON
OF FUNDAMENTAL CONCEPTS
OF THE INDIAN ARTS

कलातत्त्वकोश खण्ड – ६
KALĀTATTVAKOŚA VOL. – VI

APPEARANCE/SYMBOLIC FORM
ĀBHĀSA

KALĀTATTVAKOŚA
VOLUME – VI

Editors
Sukumar Chattopadhyay
&
Narasingha Charan Panda

Associate Editor
Pranati Ghosal

INDIRA GANDHI NATIONAL CENTRE FOR THE ARTS
NEW DELHI
and
MOTILAL BANARSIDASS PUBLISHERS PVT. LTD
DELHI

First Published 2008

Published by
INDIRA GANDHI NATIONAL CENTRE FOR THE ARTS
Central Vista, Janpath, New Delhi - 110001

in association with
MOTILAL BANARSIDASS PUBLISHERS PVT. LTD.
Bungalow Road, Jawahar Nagar, Delhi - 110007

ISBN: 978-81-208-3286-2 (Vol.
VI) ISBN: 978-81-208-1045-7
(Set)

Typeset by
The Indira Gandhi National Centre for the Arts,
Varanasi Office: B-1/3, E-7, Lane No. 2,
Ravindrapuri Extension, Varanasi - 221005.

Printed in India
at Shri Jainendra Press
A-45, Naraina Industrial Area, Phase-I,
New Delhi-110028

CONTENTS

INTRODUCTION

जात्याभासं चलाभासं वस्त्वाभासं तथैव च ।
अजाचलमवस्तुत्वं विज्ञानं शान्तमद्वयम् ।।

Māṇḍukya Kārikā IV.45

Consciousness which appears to be born or to move or to take the form of matter, is really ever unborn, immovable and free from the character of materiality; it is all peace and non-dual.

I. General Background

Indian tradition both in theory (*śāstra*) and practice (*prayoga*) evolves from the vision of 'Absolute Reality' that governs the whole universe at all levels and states of existence. The Vedas are revelations from a supreme state of consciousness. Upaniṣads, Brāhmaṇas and Purāṇas unravel the mysteries of the phenomena at various levels of perception. Various systems of thought, including the Buddhist and Jaina emerge. So do the disciplines – Āyurveda, Astronomy, metaphysics, philosophy and the arts. Fundamental conceptions of the cosmos, space, time, body, mind, and self pervade almost all theories and disciplines making each of them interrelated and interdependent just like a *sūtra* (thread) that holds (invisibly) all beads together (*sarvamidaṃ protaṃ sūtre maṇigaṇā iva* – Bhagavad Gītā VII.7).

In this framework the wide range of Indian art-forms can never be understood in isolation. For a fuller comprehension of the system of interrelatedness and interpenetration Indira Gandhi National Centre for the Arts identified approximately 250 important terms representing fundamental concepts occurring in various Indological schools and disciplines. This was done after considerable research and deliberations with the scholars. By selecting the groups of terms under particular categories and thereby concentrating upon each category in a single volume of the **Kalātattvakośa** while focussing upon their occurrence and significance in the arts, has given rise to an important modern device to grasp the essential thought and knowledge underlying in Indian tradition.

The criteria for selecting the terms and their grouping in the previous five volumes has been elaborately discussed by the editors of those volumes. The main purpose of the **Kalātattvakośa** is to concentrate on textual traditions principally drawn from Sanskrit, Pali and Prakrit sources covering a span of nearly 3500 years starting from the Vedas. An indepth investigation into the primary sources will and has hopefully already facilitated the reader to learn about the interlocking of different disciplines. The groupings in the first five volumes relate to:

a. pervasive and perennial terms (Category: *vyāpti*);

b. terms relating to notions of space and time (Category: *deśa* and *kāla*);

c. the primal elements (Category: *mahābhūtas*);

d. manifestation of nature (Category: *sṛṣṭivistāra*);

e. form/shape (Category: *ākāra/ākṛti*).

Following the same process of enquiry into the fundamental concepts, the present volume deals with the concepts of abstract or symbolic form grouped together as *ābhāsa*, signifying appearance, reflection, shining principle, semblance and convisibility for illuminating the creation.

Volume VII will be devoted to **Substratum/Abode** – *Āyatana*. Subsequently another volume concentrating on the related technical terms specific to the Indian arts is envisaged.

II. Method and Use

The system followed here in the method and use corresponds almost completely with that introduced in the previous volumes. The same is given as under:

1. The list of terms has been organised thematically by concepts. Groups of related terms are assembled in each volume, and the logic of their arrangement is explained in the introduction. Alphabetical reference is facilitated by the **List of Terms** which gives a complete list of entries for the whole series, mentioning the volume in which an article has already appeared. The **Index** directs the reader to the occurrence of the terms throughout, and also refers him to other significant terms in Sanskrit and English.

2. Within a desirable flexibility of structure, the content of an entry generally follows this sequence as under:

Overview
Etymology and Related Terms
Layers of Meaning
Development of the Concept
Manifestation in the Arts
Classification
Process
Conclusion

Quick identification of a section which may interest the reader specifically is thus facilitated.

In some cases where a concept has a distinct meaning in different fields, an article has been divided into two or three parts assigned to different authors.

3. All Sanskrit, Pali and Prakrit quotations are given in Devanāgarī with a full English translation; Sanskrit words or phrases occurring in the running text are transliterated and accompanied by a translation at least once. This is designed to provide access to the content of the quote for those having limited knowledge of Sanskrit, and for non-readers of the Devanāgarī script.

4. Text references are abbreviated; full titles appear only in the running text of the entry (in bold face). The **List of Abbreviations** provides the full titles, and the **General Bibliography** notes the text editions and translations used.

5. A **Select Bibliography** is appended to each article. This contains references to secondary literature to which the author refers. These references are not exhaustive but are relevant to tracing further information about the concept.

6. The etymologies, whether traditional or based on modern linguistics, represent the opinion of the author.

7. All translations are acknowledged, whether published (see **Bibliography**) or unpublished. If a translator's name is not given, the text has been translated by the author. Where the author has amended a previous translation, this also is indicated.

8. The volume is illustrated with a minimum number of essential line-drawings of fundamental diagrams. Full photographic illustration of art-historical developments and variations falls outside the purview of these volumes.

III. Concepts of Appearance/Symbolic Form (*Ābhāsa*)

Entire world or creation is actually the reflection of the Supreme Being, an inherent nature or appearance of Absolute Reality where some invisible or symbolic forms do appear as the primal factor to unravel the mystery of nature.

The concepts or key-terms of Indian arts as recorded in the previous **Kalātattvakośa** volumes ((I–V) clearly show the manifestation of a unified vision to multidimensional aspects within the periphery of various Indological disciplines from the Vedas to modern art and architecture – a journey in the field of eternal wisdom through the spheres of specific disciplines like epics, grammar, linguistics, politics, astronomy, mathematics, philosophy, *kāvya*, poetics, dramaturgy, sculpture, architecture, etc. Thus, the pentateuch of **Kalātattvakośa** attempts to touch the concepts of almost all schools of Indian thought and disciplines related to pervasiveness (*vyāpti*), space and time (*deśa-kāla*), primal elements (*mahābhūtas*), manifestation of nature (*sṛṣṭivistāra*) and form or shape (*ākāra/ākṛti*). The present volume is a complementary to the previous volume (V) on *ākāra/ākṛti*, as it deals with the abstract or symbolic forms containing closely-related eight fundamental terms: *ābhāsa, sādṛśya/sārūpya, anukaraṇa/anukṛti/anukīrtana, chāyā, bimba-pratibimba, liṅga, pāda* and *vṛtti-rīti*. In all these terms the basic concept of *ābhāsa*, appearance or seemliness or reflection is inherent. Where the form is invisible or symbolic, only *ābhāsa* helps there to realise the structure. *Sādṛśya* or convisibility and *sārūpya* or conformity also stand for semblance or *ābhāsa* persisting between original or model and the replica. *Ābhāsa*, again is basis of all forms of imitation – *anukaraṇa, anukṛti* and *anukīrtana*. Imitation presupposes a model, of which it is a reflection.

Chāyā is a related concept interlinking with all other terms of this volume bearing the sense of reflection, appearance, convisibility, imitation, sign or symbol and an unmanifest state as a reflection of the Supreme Being. The technical term *bimba-pratibimba* (*bhāva*) clearly denotes a model and a semblance of it. *Liṅga* is a symbolic representation of a godhead or an idea.

Pāda is also related with *liṅga* or *cihna*, especially when we worship a footprint of *mahā-puruṣa* like Rāma, Buddha, etc. and various deities like Viṣṇu, Śiva, Lakṣmī, etc. it indicates an *ābhāsa, sādṛśya, anukṛti* of the original person or god where a *rīti* or style of worship is reflected. Hence *pāda* is not only measurement but also a symbol for keeping a mark in the permanent memory of being. Different marks on the foot-sole of a great person symbolise many mysteries of his personality and creation.

Likewise, *vṛtti* and *rīti* signify the basic concept of status and its mode. As such, all these related terms, come within the purview of the keyterm of this volume, *ābhāsa*.

Acknowledgements

We are greatly indebted to Dr. Kapila Vatsyayan, Chairperson, Board of Trustees, IGNCA, for planning and determining the guiding-principles of preparing entire Kalātattvakośa series. Her illuminating guidance, encouragement and supervision are the main source of our inspiration in the preparation of this volume. Prof. K.K. Chakravarty, Member Secretary; Prof. Indra Nath Choudhuri, Academic Director and Prof. G.C. Tripathi, Head, Kalākośa

Division, IGNCA, were readily available for kind support and overall supervision. Mere words are insufficient to express our sincere gratitude to them. We are deeply beholden to them for their constant encouragement. Dr. Advaitavadini Kaul, Editor at our Head Office in New Delhi, was closely associated with the entire work and its progress. We are sincerely thankful to her.

We are highly grateful to our two consultant-guides, Prof. Bishwanath Bhattacharya and Prof. P.K. Agrawala for their constant guidance in preparing the volume at various stages. Our grateful thanks are also due to Prof. R.C. Sharma, former Coordinator, IGNCA, Varanasi for rendering his valuable suggestions from time to time, specially for the selection of illustrations. Padmabhushan (Late) Prof. Vidya Nivas Misra deserves our special mention for his scholastic advice and proper guidance. He is one of the contributors also. Similarly, we are obliged to Pt. H.N. Chakravarty for rendering guidance whenever sought. Sincere thanks are due to all the other contributors as they are the columns of present volume. Special thanks are credited to the Institute Jñāna Pravāha for supplying the materials of illustrations. We sincerely thank all the associates of Varanasi branch particularly, Dr. Pranati Ghosal, who laboured hard in going through the text and helping us at various stages of editing and preparing index, etc. Names of two Research Fellows, Dr. Parvati Banerjee and Dr. Rama Dubey deserve special mention for lending their active cooperation in this stupendous work. Similarly, the entire text is efficiently composed by Shri Gautam Kumar Chatterjee (IGNCA, Varanasi), who remained busy throughout in carrying out our instructions and correcting them in the computer repeatedly. We are thankful to our artist Sri Madanlal for preparing sketches of most of the illustrations. Moreover, we owe an enormous debt of gratitude to all those scholars and institutions/universities that have made the illustrations accompanying the volume possible.

Since this volume deals apparently with the invisible and symbolic forms, it may be apt here to conclude with a verse in glory of Lord Śiva, the Primal Source of *liṅga* as symbol.

> शूलिने त्रिदशेशाय त्र्यम्बकाय महात्मने ।
> भस्मदिग्धोर्ध्वलिङ्गाय तस्मै रुद्रात्मने नमः ।।
>
> MBh XII.47.52
>
> The one who bears the trident, is the Lord of celestials, has three eyes and is generous and noble. The one whose body is always besmeared with ashes and whose phallic emblem is always turned upwards. Salutations to Him in His form of Rudra.

Sukumar Chattopadhyay

Narasingha Charan Panda

December, 2005

ABBREVIATIONS

General principles in forming abbreviations, concerning the last part of the title:

Ā	Āgama
Ār	Āraṇyaka
Bh	Bhāṣya
Br	Brāhmaṇa
Ca	Carita
Dh	Dharma (e.g. DhŚ Dharmaśāstra)
Edn	Edition
Ed	Editor
G	Gītā
H	Hṛdaya
Ins	Inscription
Kā	Kārikā
K	Kathā
Ko	Kośa
L	Lakṣaṇa
Ms	Manuscript
Nik	Nikāya
P	Paddhati
Pari	Pariśiṣṭa
Prad	Pradīpikā
Pr	Prakaraṇa
Prak	Prakāśa
Prāt	Prātiśākhya
Pur	Purāṇa
R	Ratnākara
Sam	Saṃhitā
Samu	Samuccaya
Saṅg	Saṅgraha
Sā	Sāra
Ś	Śāstra
Śa	Śataka
Sm	Smṛti
Sū	Sūtra
T	Tantra

Ṭī	Ṭīkā
Up	Upaniṣad
Vā	Vārttika
V	Veda
Vim	Vimarśinī
Vi	Vivaraṇa
Vṛ	Vṛtti
Y	Yāmala

Sections of Agamic Texts:

cp	caryāpāda
jk	jñānakhaṇḍa
kp	kriyāpāda
vp	vidyāpāda
yp	yogapāda

Sections of Ayurvedic Texts:

CiSthā	Cikitsā Sthāna
ISthā	Indriya Sthāna
KaSthā	Kalpa Sthāna
NiSthā	Nidāna Sthāna
ŚāSthā	Śārīra Sthāna
SiSthā	Siddhi Sthāna
SūSthā	Sūtra Sthāna
UtT	Uttara Tantra
ViSthā	Vimāna Sthāna

List of commentators/commentaries:

Kṣ	Kṣīrasvāmī
Rāmā	Rāmāśramī

Major Texts

AbhiCi	Abhidhāna Cintāmaṇi
AbhidhKo	Abhidharma Kośa
AbhidhSamu	Abhidharma Samuccaya
AbhŚāk	Abhijñānaśākuntala
Abhil	Abhilaṣitārtha-Cintāmaṇi (also Mānasollāsa of Someśvara)

AbhiBhā	Abhinava Bhāratī (on Nāṭya-Śāstra)
AbhDar	Abhinaya Darpaṇa
Abhis	Abhisamayālaṅkāra
AbhNāṭ	Abhiṣeka Nāṭaka
ĀcD	Ācāra Dinakara
AdhSū	Adhyayana-Sūtra
AghŚP	Aghoraśivācārya Paddhati
AgPur	Agni Purāṇa
AhSam	Ahirbudhnya Saṃhitā
AitĀr	Aitareya Āraṇyaka
AitBr	Aitareya Brāhmaṇa
AitUp	Aitareya Upaniṣad
AjKo	Ajaya Kośa
AjitĀ	Ajitāgama
ĀlP	Ālāpa Paddhati
AmKo	Amara Kośa
Amṛto	Amṛtodaya (Gokulanātha)
AneSaṅg	Anekārtha Saṅgraha
AṅgNik	Aṅguttara Nikāya
AniSam	Aniruddha Saṃhitā
AnnaUp	Annapūrṇopaniṣad
AparPṛ	Aparājita Pṛcchā
ĀpDhSū	Āpastamba Dharma-Sūtra
ĀpGṛhSū	Āpastamba Gṛhya-Sūtra
ĀpŚrSū	Āpastamba Śrauta-Sūtra
ĀpŚulSū	Āpastamba Śulba-Sūtra
ArthŚ	Artha-Śāstra
ArthViSū	Arthaviniścaya-Sūtra
ArthaViSūNib	Arthaviniścayasūtranibandhana (Vīryaśrīdatta)
Ārya	Āryabhaṭīya
ĀryaMS	Āryamañjuśrīnāmasaṅgīti (with Amṛtakaṇikānāma... comm.)
ĀśCū	Āścaryacūḍāmaṇi (Śaktibhadra)
AṣṭH	Aṣṭāṅga-Hṛdaya (Vāgbhaṭa-I)
AṣṭSaṅg	Aṣṭāṅga-Saṅgraha (Vāgbhaṭa-II)
AṣṭPrPār	Aṣṭasāhasrikā Prajñā Pāramitā
ĀśvaGṛhSū	Āśvalāyana Gṛhya-Sūtra
ĀśvaŚrSū	Āśvalāyana Śrauta-Sūtra
AV	Atharvaveda (Śaunaka)
AV(P)	Atharvaveda (Paippalāda)
AVPari	Atharvaveda Pariśiṣṭa
AtSam	Atri Saṃhitā
Aṭṭh	Aṭṭhasālinī (on Dhammasaṅgaṇi)

Aucitya	Aucityavicāracarcā (Kṣemendra)
AvaŚa	Avadānaśataka
AvK	Avantisundarī Kathā
ĀNi	Āvassaya Nijjuti (Āvaśyaka Niryukti)
Avim	Avimāraka
BālCa	Bālacarita
BDhSū	Baudhāyana Dharma-Sūtra
BGṛhSū	Baudhāyana Gṛhya-Sūtra
BŚrSū	Baudhāyana Śrauta-Sūtra
BŚulSū	Baudhāyana Śulba-Sūtra
BhG	Bhagavad-Gītā
BhGŚBh	Bhagavad-Gītā Śaṅkara Bhāṣya
BhāgPur	Bhāgavata Purāṇa
BhSi	Bhaktirasāmṛtasindhu (Rūpa Gosvāmin)
BhRas	Bhaktirasāyana (Madhusūdana Sarasvatī)
BhārGṛhSū	Bhāradvāja Gṛhya-Sūtra
BhārSam	Bhāradvāja Saṃhitā
BhārŚrSū	Bhāradvāja Śrauta-Sūtra
BhaBh	Bharata Bhāṣya (Nānyadeva)
BhāCam	Bhārata Campū
BhāT	Bhārgava Tantra
BhāPari	Bhāṣāpariccheda
BhaKā	Bhaṭṭi Kāvya
BhPrak	Bhāva Prakāśana (Śāradātanaya)
BhoPra	Bhoja Prabandha
BhṛSam	Bhṛgu Saṃhitā
BhuPr	Bhuvana Pradīpa
BoPā	Bodha Pāhuḍa
BoCar	Bodhicaryāvatāra
BoBhū	Bodhisattvabhūmi
BraPur	Brahmāṇḍa Purāṇa
BrPur	Brahma Purāṇa
BrSū	Brahma-Sūtra
BrSūŚBh	Brahma-Sūtra Śaṅkara Bhāṣya
BṛUp	Bṛhadāraṇyaka Upaniṣad
BṛD	Bṛhaddeśī (Mataṅga)
BṛDev	Bṛhaddevatā (Śaunaka)
BṛJā	Bṛhat Jātaka
BṛSaṅg	Bṛhatkathāśloka Saṅgraha
BṛSam	Bṛhat Saṃhitā (Varāhamihira)
BudCa	Buddhacarita
CaRām	Campū Rāmāyaṇa

CāVyā	Cāndra Vyākaraṇa
CarSam	Caraka Saṃhitā
Cāru	Cārudatta
ChāgUp	Chāgaleya Upaniṣad
ChaSū	Chandaḥ-Sūtra
ChUp	Chāndogya Upaniṣad
Chan	Chandomañjarī
CiL	Citra-Lakṣaṇa
Cit	Citsukhī
DakMūSt	Dakṣiṇāmūrtistotra
DaPā	Darśana Pāhuḍa
DBhūSū	Daśabhūmika-Sūtra
DaśCa	Daśakumāra Carita
DUVṛ	Daśapādī Uṇādi Vṛtti
DaRū	Daśarūpaka
DaSū	Daśavaikālika-Sūtra
Datti	Dattilam (Dattila)
DBhāgPur	Devī Bhāgavata Purāṇa
DPur	Devī Purāṇa
DhPad	Dhammapada
DhSaṅ	Dhammasaṅgaṇi
Dhav	Dhavalā (comm. on ṢaṭĀ) (Vīrasenācārya)
Dhū	Dhūrtaviṭasaṃvāda
DhvĀl	Dhvanyāloka
DhvĀlLoc	Dhvanyāloka-Locana (Abhinavagupta)
DBUp	Dhyānabindu Upaniṣad
DīghNik	Dīgha Nikāya
DīĀ	Dīptāgama
Divyāv	Divyāvadāna
DSaṅg	Dravyasaṅgraha (Nemicandra)
DSaṅgVṛ	Dravyasaṅgraha Vṛtti (Brahma Deva)
DuSapta	Ḍurgā Saptaśatī
Dūta	Dūtaghaṭotkaca
Dūt	Dūtavākya
EpInd	Epigraphica Indica
GāSa	Gāhā Sattasai (Gāthā Saptaśatī)
Gaṇar	Gaṇaratnamahodadhi
GanT	Gandharva Tantra
GarbhUp	Garbhopaniṣad
GarPur	Garuḍa Purāṇa
GauDhSū	Gautama Dharma-Sūtra
Gīta	Gītagovinda

GGṛhSū	Gobhila Gṛhya-Sūtra
GomJīv	Gommaṭasāra Jīvakāṇḍa (Nemicandra)
GoBr	Gopatha Brāhmaṇa
GuhyaT	Guhyasamāja Tantra (with Guhyasamāja-Pradīpa ... comm.)
HaiKo	Haima Kośa
HalKo	Halāyudha Kośa
Har	Haravijaya
HBVil	Haribhaktivilāsa
HarPur	Harivaṃśa Purāṇa
HaCa	Harṣacarita
HyPrad	Haṭhayoga Pradīpikā
HayaPāñc	Hayaśīrṣa Pāñcarātra
HT	Hevajra Tantra
Hit	Hitopadeśa
ĪśGP	Īśānaśivagurudeva Paddhati
ĪśUp	Īśa Upaniṣad
ĪPraKā	Īśvara Pratyabhijñā-Kārikā (Utpaladeva)
ĪPraVim	Īśvara Pratyabhijñā Vimarśinī (Abhinavagupta)
ĪPraVivVim	Īśvara Pratyabhijñā Vivṛti Vimarśinī
ĪśSam	Īśvara Saṃhitā
JaimBr	Jaiminīya Brāhmaṇa
JaimUpBr	Jaiminīya Upaniṣad Brāhmaṇa
Jā	Jātaka
Jāmā	Jātakamālā
JāUp	Jābālopaniṣad
JaySam	Jayākhya Saṃhitā
JinSam	Jina Saṃhitā
JīvPradṬī	Jīvatattvapradīpikā Ṭīkā (on GomJīv)
Jñān	Jñānārṇava (Śubhacandra)
Kād	Kādambarī
KāCaT	Kālacakra Tantra
KāPur	Kālikā Purāṇa
KāmKVil	Kāma Kalā Vilāsa
KāNīSā	Kāmandakīya Nīti Sāra
KāmSū	Kāma-Sūtra
KāmĀ	Kāmikāgama
KāVṛ	Kāśikā Vṛtti
KāśSam	Kāśyapa Saṃhitā
KāśŚi	Kāśyapa Śilpa
KāVyā	Kātantra Vyākaraṇa
KāṭhSam	Kāṭhaka Saṃhitā
KaṭhUp	Kaṭha Upaniṣad

KātBhāSū	Kātyāyana Bhāṣika-Sūtra
KātŚrSū	Kātyāyana Śrauta-Sūtra
KātŚrSūBh	Kātyāyana Śrauta-Sūtra Bhāṣya (Karka Bhāṣya)
KātŚulSū	Kātyāyana Śulba-Sūtra
KaJNi	Kaula Jñāna Nirṇaya
KauśSū	Kauśika-Sūtra
KauṣUp	Kauṣītaki Upaniṣad
Kāvyād	Kāvyādarśa
Kāvyāl	Kāvyālaṅkāra (Bhāmaha)
KāvyālSū	Kāvyālaṅkāra-Sūtra (Vāmana)
KāMīm	Kāvya-Mīmāṃsā
KāSā	Kāvyānuśāsana
KāPrak	Kāvya Prakāśa
KeUp	Kena Upaniṣad
KhGṛhSū	Khādira Gṛhya-Sūtra
KhudNik	Khuddaka Nikāya
Kir	Kirātārjunīya
Kod	Kodaṇḍamaṇḍana
KulT	Kulārṇava Tantra
Kum	Kumārasambhava
Kund	Kuṇḍamālā
KūrPur	Kūrma Purāṇa
Kuva	Kuvalayānanda
LYVās	Laghu Yoga-Vāsiṣṭha (Abhinanda)
LT	Lakṣmī Tantra
Lalitā	Lalitā-Sahasranāma (with Bhāṣya)
LVi	Lalitavistara
LaSū	Laṅkāvatāra-Sūtra
LaṭSrSū	Lāṭyāyana Śrauta-Sūtra
Līlā	Līlāvatī (Bhāskarācārya)
LPur	Liṅga Purāṇa
Lok	Lokavibhāga
MāDhā	Mādhavīyā Dhātuvṛtti
MVy	Madhyamavyāyoga
MāKā	Mādhyamaka-Kārikā
MBh	Mahābhārata
Mahābh	Mahābhāṣya
MNUp	Mahānārāyaṇa Upaniṣad
MNPrak	Mahānaya Prakāśa
MNT	Mahānirvāṇa Tantra
MPur	Mahā Purāṇa
MaMa	Mahārtha Mañjarī

MSSaṅg	Mahāsubhāṣita Saṅgraha (Ed. L. Sternbach)
MVas	Mahāvastu
MaCa	Mahāvīracarita
Mahāv	Mahāvyutpatti
MSūAl	Mahāyāna Sūtrālaṅkāra
MSūSaṅg	Mahāyāna-Sūtra Saṅgraha
MaV	Mahāyānaviṃśaka
MahāUp	Mahopaniṣad
MaitSam	Maitrāyaṇī Saṃhitā
MaitUp	Maitrāyaṇī Upaniṣad (Maitrī Upaniṣad)
MajNik	Majjhima Nikāya
MālMā	Mālatīmādhava
Māla	Mālavikāgnimitra
MVT	Mālinīvijayottara Tantra
MāMey	Mānameyodaya
MāSā	Mānasāra
Mānas	Mānasollāsa
MānŚrSū	Mānava Śrauta-Sūtra
MānŚulSū	Mānava Śulba-Sūtra
MāṇḍKā	Māṇḍūkya-Kārikā
MāṇḍUp	Māṇḍūkya Upaniṣad
MMK	Mañjuśrīmūlakalpa
Manu	Manu Smṛti
MarSam	Marīci Saṃhitā (Vaikhānasa Āgama)
MārkPur	Mārkaṇḍeya Purāṇa
MPĀ	Mataṅgapārameśvara Āgama
MatPur	Matsya Purāṇa
Mayam	Mayamata
MedKo	Medinī Kośa
Megh	Meghadūta
MilPañ	Milinda Pañha
MīmNyPrak	Mīmāṃsānyāya Prakāśa (Āpodeva)
MīmSū	Mīmāṃsā-Sūtra (with Śābara Bhāṣya)
MKā	Mokṣa-Kārikā
Mṛcch	Mṛcchakaṭika
MṛgĀ	Mṛgendra Āgama
Mudrā	Mudrārākṣasa
MuktUp	Muktikopaniṣad
Mūl	Mūlācāra (Ācārya Vaṭṭakera)
MūMāKā	Mūla Mādhyamaka-Kārikā
MuṇḍUp	Muṇḍaka Upaniṣad
NādaKā	Nāda-Kārikā (Bhaṭṭa Rāmakaṇṭha)

Nāgā	Nāgānanda
NaiCa	Naiṣadhīyacarita
NāMa	Nānārtha Mañjarī
Ṇāsā	Ṇāṇasāra (Jñānasāra) (Padmasingh Munirāja)
NārBhSū	Nārada Bhakti-Sūtra
NārPur	Nārada Purāṇa
NārSm	Nārada Smṛti
NārŚik	Nāradīya Śikṣā
NārŚiŚ	Nārada Śilpa-Śāstra
NN	Nartana Nirṇaya
NLRKo	Nāṭakalakṣaṇaratna Kośa (Sāgaranandin)
NŚ	Nāṭya-Śāstra
Nay	Nayacakra (Mailladhavala)
NT	Netra Tantra
Nigh	Nighaṇṭu
Nir	Nirukta (Yāska)
NīŚa	Nītiśataka
NiṢo	Nityaṣoḍaśikārṇava
NiSā	Niyamasāra (Kundakundācārya)
NṛpūUp	Nṛsiṃhapūrvatāpanīyopaniṣad
NṛKo	Nṛtyaratna Kośa
NṛtRat	Nṛttaratnāvalī (Jayasenāpati)
NyDīp	Nyāyadīpikā (Dharma Bhūṣaṇa)
NyKu	Nyāyakusumāñjali
Nyā	Nyāyamañjarī
NySū	Nyāya-Sūtra
NySūBh	Nyāya-Sūtra Bhāṣya
Pādtāḍ	Pādatāḍitaka
PadMa	Padmānanda Mahākāvya
PPrā	Padma Prābhṛtaka
PPur	Padma Purāṇa
PSam	Padma Saṃhitā (Pāñcarātra School)
Pañcad	Pañcadaśī
Pañ(P)	Pañcādhyāyī (Pūrvārdha) (Rājamalla)
Pañ(U)	Pañcādhyāyī (Uttarārdha) (Rājamalla)
Pañca	Pañcarātra
PkāSā	Pañcāstikāya Sāra (Kundakundācārya)
Pañc	Pañcarātra
Pā	Pāṇini Aṣṭādhyāyī
PāDhā	Pāṇinīya Dhātupāṭha
PāŚik	Pāṇinīya Śikṣā
PPraṬī	Parama Prakāśa Ṭīkā

ParSā	Paramārthasāra
PPra	Paramātma Prakāśa (Yogīndu Deva)
ParSam	Parameśvara Saṃhitā
PāSū	Pārānanda-Sūtra
PārāŚik	Pārāśara Śikṣā
PārGṛhSū	Pāraskara Gṛhya-Sūtra
PTrī	Parātrīśikā (Tantra)
Paribh	Paribhāṣenduśekhara
PāśuSū	Pāśupata-Sūtra
PauṣSam	Pauṣkara Saṃhitā
PSā	Pavayaṇasāra (Pravacanasāra) (Kundakundācārya)
PiṅgUp	Piṅgalopaniṣad
PraCan	Prabodhacandrodaya
PraPañ	Prakaraṇapañcikā
PramMīm	Pramāṇamīmāṃsā (Hemacandrācārya)
PraRat	Prameya Ratnāvalī (Baladeva Vidyābhūṣaṇa)
PSāT	Prapañcasāra Tantra
PP	Prasannapadā
PrSam	Praśna Saṃhitā
PraUp	Praśna Upaniṣad
PrR	Prasthāna-Ratnākara
PraYau	Pratijñā Yaugandharāyaṇa
PraNāṭ	Pratimā Nāṭaka
PLSSamu	Pratiṣṭhālakṣaṇa-sāra-samuccaya
Prati	Pratiṣṭhātilaka (Nemicandra)
PrH	Pratyabhijñā-Hṛdaya
PrKā	Pratyabhijñā-Kārikā
PravBh	Pravacana Bhāṣya (on SāṃSū) (Vijñānabhikṣu)
PraBr	Pravargya Brāhmaṇa
Pri	Priyadarśikā
Pug	Puggalapaññatti
Rāga	Rāgavibodha (Somanātha)
Ragh	Raghuvaṃśa
RāNigh	Rāja Nighaṇṭu
RājTar	Rājataraṅgiṇī
RāVā	Rājavārttika (Bhaṭṭa Akalaṅkadeva)
RāmPUp	Rāmapūrvottaratāpinī Upaniṣad
Rām	Rāmāyaṇa
RāmCam	Rāmāyaṇa Campū
RāmUttUp	Rāmottaratāpinī Upaniṣad
RasGa	Rasagaṅgādhara (Jagannātha)
RP	Ratna Parīkṣā (Īśvara Dīkṣit)

RaPa	Ratnatraya-Parīkṣā
Rat	Ratnāvalī
RauĀ	Raurava Āgama
RauUtĀ	Rauravattara Āgama
Rāya	Rāyapasenīya-Sutta
ṚV	Ṛgveda
ṚVPrāt	Ṛgveda Prātiśākhya
Ṛtu	Ṛtusaṃhāra
Rūp	Rūpamaṇḍana (Maṇḍana)
ŚaKal	Śabdakalpadruma
ŚaRa	Śabdaratnāvalī
SaddhPuSū	Saddharma Puṇḍarīka-Sūtra
ṢaḍBr	Ṣaḍviṃśa Brāhmaṇa
SāDar	Sāhitya-Darpaṇa
ŚĀPM	Śaivāgama Paribhāṣāmañjarī
ŚPar	Śaiva Paribhāṣā
Sakala	Sakalādhikāra (Agastya)
SamāRājSū	Samādhirāja-Sūtra
SamSūt	Samarāṅgaṇa-Sūtradhāra (Bhoja)
SV	Sāmaveda
SViBr	Sāmavidhāna Brāhmaṇa
ŚāmPañcā	Śāmba Pañcāśikā
SāṃKā	Sāṃkhya-Kārikā
SāṃSū	Sāṃkhya-Sūtra
Samū	Samūrtārcanādhikaraṇa
SaṃNik	Saṃyutta Nikāya
SanSam	Sanatkumāra Saṃhitā
SDām	Saṅgīta-Dāmodara
SDar	Saṅgīta-Darpaṇa
SMak	Saṅgīta-Makaranda
SRāj	Saṅgītarāja
SR	Saṅgīta-Ratnākara (Śārṅgadeva)
SUpSā	Saṅgītopaniṣat-sāroddhāra
SaṅkSūr	Saṅkalpasūryodaya (Veṅkaṭanātha)
ŚāṅkhĀr	Śāṅkhāyana Āraṇyaka
ŚāṅkhBr	Śāṅkhāyana Brāhmaṇa
ŚāṅkhŚrSū	Śāṅkhāyana Śrauta-Sūtra
ŚāTil	Śāradā-Tilaka
Sark	Sarasvatīkaṇṭhābharaṇa (Alaṅkāra-Śāstra)
SākāT	Sārdhatriśatīkālottara Tantra
ŚārP	Śārṅgadhara Paddhati
SarDSaṅg	Sarvadarśana-Saṅgraha

Sar	Sarvānukramaṇī
SaSi	Sarvārthasiddhi (on TaSū) (Ācārya Pūjyapāda Devanandī)
ŚBr	Śatapatha Brāhmaṇa
ṢaṭĀ	Ṣaṭkhaṇḍāgama (Puṣpadanta & Bhūtabali)
ṢaṭSan	Ṣaṭsandarbha (Śivagosvāmin)
SātSam	Sātvata Saṃhitā
Saun	Saundarananda
SLah	Saundaryalaharī
SeṬī	Sekoddeśaṭīkā
SiKau	Siddhānta Kaumudī
SiddhSaṅg	Siddhāntaleśa-Saṅgraha
SiddhŚir	Siddhānta-Śiromaṇi
SiSiSaṅg	Siddhasiddhānta-Saṅgraha
ŚikSamu	Śikṣāsamuccaya
ŚiL	Śilpalakṣaṇa
ŚiPrak	Śilpa Prakāśa (Rāmacandra Kaulācāra)
ŚiRa	Śilparatna
ŚiRaKo	Śilparatnakośa (Sthāpaka Nirañjana Mahāpātra)
Śiśu	Śiśupālavadha
ŚDṛ	Śiva Dṛṣṭi
ŚMSt	Śivamahimnastotra
ŚPur	Śiva Purāṇa
ŚSam	Śiva Saṃhitā
ŚSto	Śiva Stotrāvalī
ŚSū	Śiva-Sūtra
ŚSūVā	Śiva-Sūtra Vārttika (Varadācārya)
ŚSūVim	Śiva-Sūtra Vimarśinī (Kṣemarāja)
SkaPur	Skanda Purāṇa
ŚlVā	Ślokavārttika
SP	Somaśambhu Paddhati
SpKā	Spanda-Kārikā
SpNir	Spanda Nirṇaya
ŚrīBh	Śrī Bhāṣya (on Brahma-Sūtra)
ŚHMu	Śrīhasta Muktāvalī
ŚrīkBh	Śrīkaṇṭha Bhāṣya (on Brahma-Sūtra)
ŚrīSam	Śrīpraśna Saṃhitā
ŚTaCi	Śrītattvacintāmaṇi
ŚṛKa	Śṛṅgāramañjarī Kathā
ŚṛPrak	Śṛṅgāra Prakāśa
ŚṛSa	Śṛṅgāra Śataka
SuRat	Subhāṣita Ratnāvalī
ŚNSā	Śukranītisāra

SupĀ	Suprabheda Āgama
SūrSiddh	Sūrya-Siddhānta
SuSam	Suśruta Saṃhitā
SutNip	Sutta Nipāta
SuSū	Suvarṇaprabhāsa-Sūtra
SvT	Svacchanda Tantra
Svap	Svapnavāsavadattam
ŚvUp	Śvetāśvatara Upaniṣad
Syād	Syādvādamañjarī
TĀr	Taittirīya Āraṇyaka
TBr	Taittirīya Brāhmaṇa
TSam	Taittirīya Saṃhitā
TUp	Taittirīya Upaniṣad
TāṇḍMBr	Tāṇḍya Mahābrāhmaṇa (Pañcaviṃśa Brāhmaṇa)
TĀl	Tantrāloka (Abhinavagupta)
TSāSaṅg	Tantrasāra Saṅgraha
TVā	Tantra Vārttika
TSamu	Tantrasamuccaya
TSā	Tantrasāra (Abhinavagupta)
TaBhā	Tarka Bhāṣā
TarkSaṅg	Tarka-Saṅgraha
TaKau	Tattva Kaumudī
TaPrak	Tattva Prakāśa
TaSū	Tattvārthādhigama-Sūtra (Tattvārtha-Sūtra)
TaSā	Tattvārthasāra (Amṛtacandra)
TaVā	Tattvārtha Vārttika
TaSaSū	Tattvasamāsa-Sūtra
TaSaṅg	Tattva-Saṅgraha (Śāntarakṣita)
TaVai	Tattva Vaiśāradī
Til	Tilakamañjarī
TiPa	Tiloya Paṇṇattī (Vṛṣabhācārya)
Trik	Trikāṇḍaśeṣa
TRa	Tripurārahasya
UbhSā	Ubhayābhisārikā
UjNīl	Ujjvalanīlamaṇi
UDVṛ	Uṇādi Dhātu Vṛtti
UṇSū	Uṇādi-Sūtra
Urbh	Urubhaṅga
USū	Uttarādhyayana-Sūtra
UttCa	Uttararāmacarita
VaiKo	Vaijayantī Kośa
VaiĀ	Vaikhānasa Āgama

VaiGṛhSū	Vaikhānasa Gṛhya-Sūtra
VaiŚa	Vairāgyaśataka
VaiśSū	Vaiśeṣika-Sūtra
VaiśSūBh	Vaiśeṣika-Sūtra Bhāṣya
VaitSū	Vaitāna-Sūtra
VaJī	Vakroktijīvita
Vāk	Vākyapadīya
VāPur	Vāmana Purāṇa
VaCam	Varadāmbikā Campū
VarPur	Varāha Purāṇa
VŚrSū	Vārāha Śrauta-Sūtra
VaCa	Varāṅga Carita
VaRa	Varivasyā-Rahasya
VŚ	Vāstu-Śāstra (Viśvakarman)
VSUp	Vāstusūtra Upaniṣad
VVid	Vāstuvidyā (Viśvakarman)
Vasu	Vasudevahiṇḍī
VPur	Vāyu Purāṇa
VedPar	Vedānta-Paribhāṣā
VedSā	Vedānta-Sāra
Veṇī	Veṇī Saṃhāra
Vibh	Vibhaṅga Pāli
ViMu	Vidagdha Mukha Maṇḍana
ViŚāl	Viddhaśālabhañjikā
ViBhai	Vijñāna Bhairava
ViCa	Vikrama Carita
ViDCa	Vikramāṅkadeva Carita
Vik	Vikramorvaśīya
VinPiṭ	Vinaya Piṭaka
Vīrmi	Vīramitrodaya
VirPañcā	Virūpākṣa Pañcāśikā
VDhPur	Viṣṇudharmottara Purāṇa
ViPur	Viṣṇu Purāṇa
ViSahasrBh	Viṣṇu-Sahasranāma Bhāṣya
ViSam	Viṣṇu Saṃhitā
ViSm	Viṣṇu Smṛti
ViMag	Visuddhimagga
VPark	Viśvakarmā Prakāśa
ViśKo	Viśva Kośa
VSam	Viṣvaksena Saṃhitā
ViśSam	Viśvāmitra Saṃhitā
ViKo	Viśvaprakāśa Kośa

VivR	Vivādaratnākara
ViPSaṅg	Vivaraṇaprameya Saṅgraha
ViCū	Vivekacūḍāmaṇi
VṛĀyu	Vṛkṣa Āyurveda (of Surapāla)
VyVive	Vyaktiviveka (Mahimabhaṭṭa)
YājŚik	Yājñavalkya Śikṣā
YājSm	Yājñavalkya Smṛti
YV	Yajurveda (Vājasaneyi Saṃhitā)
YSāSaṅg	Yogasāra Saṅgraha
YSū	Yoga-Sūtra
YSūBh	Yoga-Sūtra Bhāṣya (Vyāsa)
YVās	Yoga-Vāsiṣṭha
YYāj	Yogi Yājñavalkya
YoH	Yoginī-Hṛdaya
YuDīp	Yuktidīpikā (on Sāṃkhya-Kārikā)

LIST OF TERMS

aṃśa
agni (agni-soma) (Vol. III)
aṅga-aṅgin
adhikaraṇa/ādhāra
adhikāra
adhibhūta-adhidaiva-adhyātma (Vol. IV)
adhiṣṭhāna
anukaraṇa/anukṛti/anukīrtana (Vol. VI)
antaḥkaraṇa
ap/udaka/jala (Vol. III)
abhinaya
abhiprāya
amṛta
arcā (Vol. V)
artha-vācya-lakṣya-vyaṅgya
alaṅkāra
avatāra
avadhāna
avasthā
avyakta-vyakta-vyaktāvyakta
asura
ahaṃkāra
ākāra/ākṛti (Vol. V)
ākāśa (kha, vyoman) (Vol. III)
ākhyāna
āgama-nigama
ātman (Vol. I)
ānanda
ābhāsa (Vol. VI)
āyudha/āyudha-puruṣa
ālambana/āśraya
āsana
indriya (Vol. IV)
īśvara
ugra-saumya
ucita/aucitya
utsava
uddhata-sukumāra
upacāra
upamā
upāya
ṛta-anṛta
ojas
karaṇa-aṅgahāra
karaṇa/kāraṇa
karuṇā
karman
kalaśa (kumbha, ghaṭa)
kalā
kalpanā
kavi
kāma
kāla (Vol. II)
kāvya
kīrtimukha/grāsa
kuṇḍa
kuśala/kauśala
koṇa/aśra/vṛtta
krama (Vol. II)
kriyā/kṛti
kṣaṇa (Vol. II)
kṣetra (Vol. II)
gandharva-apsaras -yakṣa
garbha/garbha-gṛha
gavākṣa
guṇa-doṣa (Vol. IV)
guru/guru-laghu
cakra-paridhi (Vol. II)
catura/cāturya
camatkāra/camatkṛti
cāru/cārutā
cit/caitanya

citi/caitya/stūpa
citta
citra
citrakara
chandas-mātrā
chāyā (Vol. VI)
jāti-vyakti
jīva
jñāna-vijñāna
jyotis/tejas/prakāśa (Vol. III)
tattva
tantra
tāla (Vol. II)
triratna
tīrtha
darśana
dik/dikpāla
dīkṣā
dṛṣṭa-adṛṣṭa (phala)
deva/devatā
deśa (Vol. II)
dravya (Vol. IV)
dharma-dharmin
dhātu (Vol. IV)
dhyāna
dhvaja
dhvani
nandyāvarta
nāṭya
nāḍī
nāda
nābhi (Vol. II)
nāma(-rūpa)
nāyaka-nāyikā
nṛtta/nṛtya
nyāsa
paṅkti/avali/mālā
patra-racanā
pada
padma/kamala
pariṇāma
pāda (Vol. VI)
pāpa-puṇya
pīṭha
puruṣa (Vol. I)
puruṣārtha
pūjā/upāsanā/saparya
pūrṇa (Vol. II)
pṛthivī/bhūmi/bhūmikā (Vol. III)
prakṛti (Vol. III)
praṇava
pratibhā
pratimā-pratikṛti (Vol. V)
pratīka
pratīti/anumiti
pramāṇa
prayoga
pravṛtti-ṇivṛtti
prasāda
prastāra
prāṇa (Vol. I)
prāsāda (Vol. V)
preman/prīti
bandha-prabandha (Vol. V)
bahumukha/bahubhuja
bindu (Vol. II)
bimba-pratibimba (Vol. VI)
bīja (Vol. I)
buḍdhi/dhī/prajñā
brahman (Vol. I)
bhakti
bhagavān
bhāva-vibhāva/anubhāva
bhāvanā
bhūta-mahābhūta (Vol. III)
bhoga
makara/mīna
maṅgala
maṇḍapa
maṇḍala
madhura/mādhurya
manas/mānasika
mantra
marman

sāhitya/sahita
siddhi-vibhūti
sukha-duḥkha
sundara/saundarya
sūtra/sūtradhāra (Vol. II)
sṛṣṭi-sthiti-saṃhāra (Vol. IV)
skandha
skambha/stambha
sthāna/āyatana
sthāpatya/sthapati
sthūla-sūkṣma-para (Vol. IV)
spanda
sphoṭa
svatantra/svātantrya
svar/svarga
svara-vyañjana
svarūpa/svabhāva
svastika/nandyāvarta
haṃsa
hasta
hṛdaya

LIST OF ILLUSTRATIONS

ĀBHĀSA

Overview

The term *ābhāsa* (m.) being formed from the root *bhās-* to shine, to glow, etc. with prefix *ā*, appears already ingrained in the expressions of the Vedic Saṃhitās and allied texts to signify the entity illuminating the creation, the principle of light, appearance, reflection, as well as glimpse, illusion and seemliness. It conveys the sense of light, effects of light as well as an image reflected due to light rays. Diverse ideas regarding aspects of light in Vedic metaphysics are often conveyed by the root *bhās-* in its several word formations and derivatives. In all such conceptual assumptions the word seems to continue in the post-Vedic literature, Pali texts, and later in the context of philosophical deliberations evolved in the Nyāya school, Buddhist as well as Jaina logic, Vedānta, Kashmir Śaivism, Pāñcarātra Vaiṣṇavism, etc. Even as a concept of Sanskrit poetics, *ābhāsa* denotes that there does not exist any real identity in the illusory appearance of the object. It has also been recognised as an *alaṅkāra*, being defined as involving the poetic charm evoked through statements apparently incongruous to each other. It is also connected with varied deliberations on the nature of divine entities, even the highest truth.

Etymology and Related Terms

The term *ābhāsa* is etymologically explained from the root *bhās-* (*bhās dīptau* – PāDhā XVI.23) by adding verbal suffix *ac*, besides the prefix *ā* being added as signifying from the top, from all sides, etc. the root *bhās-* means to shine, to blaze, to appear, to appear as mere semblance; in causative, *ābhāsayati* denotes to illuminate, to make apparent, to reflect; to show as a semblance.

The notion conveyed by the word (*ābhāsate iti ābhāsaḥ*) in its several usages is related with light, effects of illuminating, glow or reflection, similitude, an image reflected from or due to refraction of light rays. Certain phrases allied in concept and etymology include *bhās, bhā, ābhā, prabhā, pratibhā, avabhāsa, ābhāsana, avabhāsana;* besides there are several synonyms that occur in specific contexts such as: *bimba, pratibimba, chāyā, chavi,* and so on. According to the **Amara Kośa**:

स्युः प्रभारुग्रुचिस्त्विड्भाभाश्छविद्युतिदीप्तयः ।
रोचिः शोचिरुभे क्लीबे ... ॥

AmKo I.3.34

These terms are synonymous, viz. *prabhā* (light), *ruk* (shining), *ruc* (lustre), *tviṭ* (blaze), *bhā* (radiance), *bhās* (splendour), *chavi* (complexion), *dyuti* (brightness), *dīpti* (glow), *rocis* (splendour) and *śocis* (radiance)– the last two being in neuter.

The term is not directly traceable to early Vedic texts. However, the following usage in the **Maitrāyaṇī Saṃhitā** would appear significant:

आदित्यः शुक्र उदगात् पुरस्ताज्ज्योतिः कृण्वन् वि तमो बाधमानः ।
आभासमानः प्रदिशो नु सर्वा भद्रस्य कर्ता रोचमाना आगात् ॥

MaitSam IV.14.14

The shining sun has arisen as creating the light in front (i.e. East), putting away the darkness and verily illuminating all the directions. The maker of auspicious forms has come here as shining.

A passage of the **Nirukta** is found to hint the etymology as well as meaning of this term in an interesting manner:

आ यो द्यां भात्या पृथिवीम् । इति । एष हि द्यावापृथिव्यावाभासयति ।

Nir VII.23

(The *mantra* addressed to Vaiśvānara, the sun, as:) who illumines heaven and earth. He indeed illuminates both heaven and earth. (Tr. L. Sarup)

Layers of Meaning

Primary notions about light (*jyotis, prakāśa, dhāman, bharga, tejas, bhāḥ, bhās,* etc.) and its shining presence or glow, illuminating feature, and its reflection would be found alluded to in many a passages of Vedic literature, no doubt including varied contexts of deliberations on metaphysical matters and as common analogy used for the shining ones (*devas*, stars, etc.) as well as the highest truth. However, attention may be drawn here to an Upaniṣadic verse using the root *bhās-*, and its several derivatives (*bhāsa, vibhāsa, anubhāsa*) in a specific context of spiritual enquiry:

न तत्र सूर्यो भाति न चन्द्रतारकं नेमा विद्युतो भान्ति कुतोऽयमग्निः ।
तमेव भान्तमनुभाति सर्वं तस्य भासा सर्वमिदं विभाति ॥

KaṭhUp V.15; MuṇḍUp II.2.11

The sun shines not there, nor the moon and stars,
These lightnings shine not, much less this (earthly) fire!
After Him, as He shines, doth everything shine,

This whole world is illumined with His light. (Tr. R.E. Hume)

The **Bhagavad-Gitā** seems to utilise the related ideas in its two verses:

न तद्भासयते सूर्यो न शशाङ्को न पावकः ।
यद्गत्वा न निवर्तन्ते तद्धाम परमं मम ॥
यदादित्यगतं तेजो जगद्भासयतेऽखिलम् ।
यच्चन्द्रमसि यच्चाग्नौ तत्तेजो विद्धि मामकम् ॥

BhG XV.6; XV.12

The sun does not illumine that,
Nor the moon, nor fire;
Having gone to which they return not;
That is My highest station.
The splendour that belongs to the sun,
Which illumines the whole world,
And that which is in the moon and in fire,
Know that to be My splendour. (Based on the tr. by F. Edgerton)

Or, we find a similar strain in the Buddhist **Udāna**:

न तत्थ सुक्का जोतन्ति आदिच्चो न प्पकासति ,
न तत्थ चंदिमा भाति तमो तत्थ न विज्जति ।

Udāna I.10

Nor do the luminaries shine there neither glows the sun there;
nor do the moon illumine there and no darkness prevails there.

The term is used in the **Śvetāśvatara Upaniṣad** as expressing a semblance or glimpse of an idea or experience:

सर्वेन्द्रियगुणाभासं सर्वेन्द्रियविवर्जितम् ।

ŚvUp III.17ab

Seeming to possess the quality (*guṇa*) of all the senses,
It is devoid of all the senses! (Tr. R.E. Hume)

From this evolved meaning suggesting illusion or falsity of a thing or notion:

भास्वरं शक्रकोदण्डं यथा नानेव शून्यकम् ।
आभासमात्रमेवायं तथा दृश्यात्मको भ्रमः ॥

YVās VI.2.125.65

As the shining bow of Indra (=rainbow) though appears (to men) in a variety (of changing forms) is (in actuality) just a void, (so is this manifestation) is just a mere *ābhāsa*, apparition, that is just an illusion (*bhrama*) of the visual kind.

Thus, in view of its conveying the duplex idea of manifestation and illusionistic appearance, the word came to acquire a unique contextual unfoldment in its significance in the metaphysical vocabulary, e.g. of Vedānta, Trika and other schools.

आभास एव च ॥

BrSū II.3.50

And (the individual soul is) an appearance (reflection) only. (Tr. G. Thibaut)

इयत्तया परिनिष्ठिता आभासाः ।

ĪPraVim II.1.3

Manifestations are defined in themselves by the principle of limitation (*iyattā*).

स हि आत्मनि नीलादीन् आभासान् आभासयन् चित्रतया अपरिमेयया भासयति ।

ĪPraVim II.1.4

The Self, manifesting the external objects of the world, such as blue etc., manifests them in innumerable variety. (Tr. K.C. Pandey)

Both the verbal forms and nouns derived thereof are commonly found in the above deliberations.

Development of the Concept

The root *bhās-* in its several dẹclensions, prefixed with *ā*, is often found utilised by several Vedic seers by way of rather a proverbial expression conveying the concept of 'shining', and even of 'manifesting'.

व्युच्छन्ती हि रश्मिभिर्विश्वमाभासि रोचनम् ।

ṚV I.49.4ab

Thou dawning with thy beams of light illumest all the radiant realm. (Tr. R.T.H. Griffith)

आ भात्यग्निरुषसामनीकम् .... ।

ṚV V.76.1a

Agni, the bright face of the Dawns, is shining. (Tr. R.T.H. Griffith)

सद्यो जज्ञानो वि हीमिद्धो अख्यदा रोदसी भानुना भात्यन्तः ॥

YV XII.6cd

At once, when born, he looked about, enkindled: he shineth forth between the earth and heaven. (Tr. R.T.H. Griffith)

तरणिर्विश्वदर्शतो ज्योतिष्कृदसि सूर्य ।

विश्वमा भासि रोचनम् ॥

ṚV I.50.4; AV XIII.2.19; XX.47.16; YV XXXIII.36

Swift and all beautiful art thou, O Sūrya, maker of the light,

Illumining all the radiant realm. (Tr. R.T.H. Griffith)

स्तवाम सूर्यं भुवनस्य गोपां यो रश्मिभिर्दिश आभाति सर्वाः ॥

AV XIII.2.2cd

Let us laud him, the whole world's Herdsman, Sūrya, who with his rays illumines all the regions. (Tr. R.T.H. Griffith)

सं दिव्येन दीदिहि रोचनेन विश्वा आ भाहि प्रदिशश्चतस्त्रः ॥

AV II.6.1cd

Flash forth with thy celestial effulgence: illumine all four regions of the heavens. (Tr. R.T.H. Griffith)

The **Atharvaveda** describes sun in multiple forms and in different ways:

स उपहूतः पृथिव्यां भक्षयत्युपहूतस्तस्मिन् यत् पृथिव्यां विश्वरूपम् ।

पृथिव्यां तपति पृथिव्याम् आ भाति स्वर्गलोको भवति य एवं वेद ॥

AV (P) XVI.117.1

He [the ascetic guest] being invited on the earth, eats – as being invited there – that multiform which is on the earth.

He blazes (or, undergoes penance) on the earth, shines forth on the earth, he who knows this becomes (like a denizen) of the heaven.

The entity illumining the worlds is also identified as Agni:

विश्वा आ भाहि प्रदिशः पृथिव्या इत्याह तस्मादग्निः सर्वा दिशोऽनु वि भाति ।

TSam V.1.8.6

Illuminate all the quarters of the earth, he says, therefore Agni illuminates all the quarters. (Tr. A.B. Keith)

We find the expression *ā-bhāti* thus explained by Brāhmaṇa texts:

"आ रोदसी भानुना भात्यन्तः"(वा॰ सं॰ XII.6) इति। इमे वै द्यावापृथिवी रोदसी।

तेऽएष भानुनाऽऽभाति ।

ŚBr VI.7.3.2

With his light he shineth between the two worlds, – the two worlds, doubtless are the heaven and the earth, and these two he indeed illumines by his light. (Tr. J. Eggeling)

"विश्वा आभाहि प्रदिशश्चतस्रः" (वा॰ सं॰ XXVII.1) इति । सर्वा आभाहि प्रदिशश्चतस्र – इत्येतत् ।

ŚBr VI.2.1.26

Lighten up the whole four regions! that is lighten up all the four regions. (Tr. J. Eggeling)

"आ या द्यां भास्या पृथिवीमोर्वन्तरिक्षम्" (वा॰ सं॰ XV.63) इति । एवं ह्येष इमांल्लोकानाभाति ।

ŚBr VIII.7.3.13

Thou that illumines the sky, the earth and wide air – for thus, indeed does he (the sun) illumines these worlds. (Tr. J. Eggeling)

In the great epics, the term *ābhāsa* as well as various usages of the root *bhās-* without a prefix or with *ā* prefix, occur sometime as implying the concept of appearance or semblance, besides the basic sense of 'shining'. For example:

ततः क्रुद्धो गदां तस्मै चिक्षेप रजनीचरः ।
ज्वलन्तीं भास्कराभासां सुग्रीवाय महोदरः ॥

Rām VI.97.20

Then the enraged demon Mahodara hurled on Sugrīva a flaming club that was shining like the sun.

निर्विकाराङ्गनाभासामपश्यद् रावणो नदीम् ॥

Rām VII.32.10cd

Rāvaṇa saw there the river (Narmadā) which gave an appearance like woman with no agitation.

शरबद्धमिवाभाति द्वितीयं भास्वदम्बरम् ।

Rām VI.107.24ab

(During the war of Rāma and Rāvaṇa) the firmament (was seen) as appearing like a second sky covered with arrows.

ततस्ताश्चञ्चलाभासश्चेरुरभ्रेषु विद्युतः ॥

MBh III.143.18cd

And there in clouds moved darting flashes of lightning.

The age-old Vedic concept of visualising the divine light principle as reflected or manifested in worldly bodies would be found charmingly reproduced in the following Puranic passage:

यस्मिन्न भासते विद्युन्न च सूर्यो न चन्द्रमाः ॥
यस्य भासा विभातीदं जगत्सर्वं समन्ततः ।
सर्वैश्वर्येण सम्पन्नो नाम्ना सर्वेश्वरः स्वयम् ॥
यो वै मुमुक्षुभिर्ध्येयः शम्भुराकाशमध्यगः ।
सर्वव्यापी प्रकाशात्मा भासरूपो हि चिन्मयः ॥

ŚPur VI.12.9cd-11

Which neither the lightning nor the sun nor the moon does illuminate; by whose splendour this entire universe is resplendent all round; he who is endowed with prosperity himself in the name of Sarveśvara; who is worthy of being meditated upon by those who are desirous of salvation; he who is the cause of welfare; who is in the middle of the firmament; who is omnipresent, whose soul is light, who is in the form of splendour, knowledge and consciousness; whose splendid Śakti is comprehensible only through emotion and who is both *nirguṇa* and *saguṇa*, unsullied and auspicious.

One of the false presumptions of one's duty is referred to as *ābhāsa*, i.e. *ābhāsa* of *dharma*:

विधर्मः परधर्मश्च आभास उपमा छलः ।
अधर्मशाखाः पञ्चेमा धर्मज्ञोऽधर्मवत्त्यजेत् ॥

BhāgPur VII.15.12

Unrighteous activities, conduct codes of other community, substandard actions (or heresies, *upamā*), semblance (*ābhāsa*) of righteousness, and deceptive practices are the five branches of irreligious following. The knower of *dharma* should give up these as (aspects of) non-righteousness (*(adharma*).

For conveying the concept of a semblance of the real, this term has been thus aptly used:

आबाधितोऽपि ह्याभासो यथा वस्तुतया स्मृतः ।
दुर्घटत्वादैन्द्रियकं तद्वदर्थविकल्पितम् ॥
क्षित्यादीनामिहार्थानां छाया न कतमापि हि ।
न संघातो विकारोऽपि न पृथङ्नान्वितो मृषा ॥

BhāgPur VII.15.58–59

As the unrestricted semblance (*ābhāsa*) is taken up (in proxy of) the real, so are the goals of sense-organs taken up (as real) due to the perceptible difficulty in their arbitrary alternatives. There may not be in them even a shadow of those principles pertaining to the earth, etc. (viz. to the five great elements); for the falsity is not (their) collection, neither (their) emanation nor their implication even singly.

The general sense conveyed by the word *ābhāsa* refers to a shining appearance or to a mere glimpse of some form. We may take here only one or two more Puranic illustrations:

नवीननीरदाभासधामैकं श्यामविग्रहम् ॥

DBhāgPur IX.2.17cd

His (the Lord's) dark form is the sole splendour-body giving semblance of a new rain-cloud.

In the Pāli canon this word occurs simply to imply a semblance or false appearance of something. As we read the words of Buddha in his discourse on the fourfold analysis of *kamma* (deeds):

इति खो, आनन्द, अत्थि कम्मं अभब्बं अभब्बाभासं, अत्थि कम्मं अभब्बं भब्बाभासं,
अत्थि कम्मं भब्बं चेव भब्बाभासं च, अत्थि कम्मं भब्बं अभब्बाभासं ति ।
इदमवोच भगवा । अत्तमनो आयस्मा आनन्दो भगवतो भासितं अभिनन्दी ति ।

MajNik (III.215, PTS) V.4.36.2

So, Ānanda, there is the deed that is inoperative, apparently inoperative; there is the deed that is inoperative apparently operative; there is the deed that is both operative and apparently operative; there is the deed that is operative, apparently inoperative.

Thus spoke the Lord. Delighted, the venerable Ānanda rejoiced in what the Lord had said. (Tr. I.B. Horner)

In Buddhist logic also, *ābhāsa* implies 'fallacy' of a statement, as it is noted in the **Sarvadarśana-Saṅgraha**:

एवं चायम् अभेदसाधको हेतुर्गोमयपायसीयन्यायवद् आभासतां भजेत् ।

SarDSaṅg p. 35

In this way, the argument put forth to show that there is non-difference (between subject and object), turns out to acquire mere fallacious nature through the opposite illustration of associating cowdung and milky preparation (i.e. as if arguing their relationship as both being derived from the cow).

The concept of *bhāvābhāsa* underlines the falsity of things or beings which may be taken as real only by an ignorant:

दर्पणे उदके नेत्रे भाण्डेषु च मणीषु च ।
बिम्बं हि दृश्यते तेषु न च बिम्बोऽस्ति कुत्रचित् ॥
भावाभासं तथा चित्तं मृगतृष्णा यथा नभे ।
दृश्यते चित्ररूपेण स्वप्ने बन्ध्यौरसो यथा ॥

LaSū X.186–187, cf. II.157–158

In a mirror, in water, in an eye, in a vessel, and on a gem, images are seen; but in them there are no images (i.e. realities) anywhere to take hold of.

Like a mirage in the air, so is a variety of things mere appearance; they are seen in diversity of forms, but are like a child in a barren woman's dream. (Tr. D.T. Suzuki)

The highest knowledge is thus defined to be above any duality of understanding:

तत्र लोकोत्तरतमं ज्ञानं बुद्धबोधिसत्त्वानां निराभासधर्मप्रविचयादनिरोधानुत्पाद-दर्शनात्सदसत्पक्षविगतं तथागतभूमिनैरात्म्याधिगमात्प्रवर्तते ॥

LaSū III.37 (prose) (p. 64)

Transcendental knowledge which is free from the dualism of being and non-being, belongs to the Bodhisattvas and takes its rise when they thoroughly examine things of imagelessness, see into the state of non-birth and no-annihilation, and realise egolessness at the stage of Tathagatahood. (Tr. D.T. Suzuki)

For the *yogī* the realm of *nirābhāsa* is explained as the imageless state of pure being reached in meditation away from all trammels of mundane binding as well as mental operations:

आर्याणां दर्शनं शुद्धं विमोक्षत्रयसंभवम् ।
उत्पादभङ्गनिर्मुक्तं निराभासप्रचारिणाम् ॥
निराभासो हि भावानामभावे नास्ति योगिनाम् ।
भावाभावसमत्वेन आर्याणां जायते फलम् ।

LaSū III.55–56

The insight of the wise, who move about in the realm of imagelessness, is pure, is born of the triple emancipation, is released from birth and destruction.

Where all things are wiped away, even a state of imagelessness ceases to exist for the yogins; in the sameness of existence and non-existence, the fruit (of wisdom) is born to the wise. (Tr. D.T. Suzuki)

All logicians are commonly found to have employed *ābhāsa* and its cognate terms under study as conveying the concepts of appearance, manifestation, shining, etc., besides their handy understanding of a fallacy or forced argument or false proposition through the expression *ābhāsa.* For example, the great Jaina logician Siddhasena Divākara observes:

प्रत्यक्षप्रतिपन्नार्थप्रतिपादि च यद्वच: ।
प्रत्यक्षं प्रतिभासस्य निमित्तत्वात्तदुच्यते ॥

Nyāyāvatāra 12

A statement expressive of the object ascertained by perception is also called perception: it is so called being the cause of the object's manifestation. (Tr. S.C. Vidyabhusana)

वैधर्म्येणात्र दृष्टान्तदोषा न्यायविदीरिता: ।
साध्यसाधनयुग्मानामनिवृत्तेश्च संशयात् ॥
वाद्युक्ते साधने प्रोक्तदोषाणामुद्भावनम् ।
दूषणं निरवद्ये तु दूषणाभासनामकम् ॥
सकलावरणमुक्तात्मकेवलं यत्प्रकाशते ।
प्रत्यक्षं सकलार्थात्मसततप्रतिभासनम् ॥
प्रमाता स्वान्यनिर्भासी कर्ता भोक्ता विवृत्तिमान् ।
स्वसंवेदनसंसिद्धो जीव: क्षित्याद्यनात्मक: ॥

Nyāyāvatāra 25–27, 31 (P.L. Vaidya edn)

Logicians have declared that fallacies (being of six kinds) of example in the heterogeneous form arise when the absence of the major term (*sādhya*) or the middle term (*sādhana* or *hetu*) or both is not shown or when there is a doubt about them.

Refutation (*dūṣaṇa*) is the pointing out of the aforesaid fallacies in the reasoning of an opponent; but it is called a semblance of a refutation (*dūṣaṇābhāsa*) when the reasoning is really devoid of defects.

That which is characterised as free from all obstructions and shines as the Absolute is called (Supreme or Transcendental) perception; it uninterruptedly illumines the nature of all objects.

The spirit (soul or *jīva*) is the knower, doer and enjoyer, illumines (*nirbhāsī*) itself and others, undergoes changes of condition, is realised only in self-consciousness and is different from the earth, etc. (Tr. S.C. Vidyabhusana)

As it is observed by Hemacandra in his **Pramāṇamīmāṃsā**:

प्रमाणान्तरानपेक्षया प्रतिभासो वैशद्यम् । इदन्तया प्रतिभासो वा वैशद्यम् ।

PramMīm I.1.14

Lucidity is awareness that is independent of the other types of valid knowledge.

Lucidity is (to be expressed as awareness expressible in the form) 'this is such and such an object'.

Several concepts conveyed through the word *ābhāsa* have been usefully handled by certain philosophical schools. In the context of its denoting light, the Yoga philosophy has its own viewpoint. It is argued that a self-luminary or sole light principle cannot be 'seen' or 'known' in itself since for the sake of any activity the perceiving eye or such other physical agencies essentially require a means of reflected light (*ābhāsa*) or energy. Thus we find it stated:

न तत् स्वाभासं दृश्यत्वात् ॥

YSū IV.19

It (the mind) is not self-illumined for it is quite perceivable.

यथेतराणीन्द्रियाणि शब्दादयश्च दृश्यत्वान्न स्वाभासानि तथा मनोऽपि प्रत्येतव्यम् ।

YSūBh IV.19

As the other organs and objects like light and sound, being knowable are not self-illuminating, so is the mind.

That is to say, in other words, that the self-effulgence or light itself cannot be "seen", we see objects through refracted light-rays only.

Superimposition is thus explained by Śaṅkara in his gloss on the **Brahma-Sūtra**:

स्मृतिरूपः परत्र पूर्वदृष्टावभासः ।

BrSūŚBh Intro., p. 10

(Superimpostion) is an awareness, similar in nature to memory that arises on a different (foreign) basis as a result of some past experience. (Tr. Gambhirananda)

In this context *avabhāsa* is further commented upon as follows:

अवसन्नोऽवमतो वा भासोऽवभासः । प्रत्ययान्तरबाधश्चास्यावसादोऽवमानो वा । एतावता मिथ्याज्ञानमित्युक्तं भवति ।

Bhāmatī on BrSūŚBh Intro., p. 11

Avabhāsa is an awareness which is somewhat dispirited or disregarded. *Avasāda* (exhaustion) or *avamāna* (disregard) is actually its annulment by another proof. Hence it can be called as erroneous knowledge. (Tr. P. Ghosal)

As it has been deliberated from the logical viewpoint:

एवं सर्वत्र तर्कौघैरर्थाभासनिरासतः ।
वाक्यार्थस्थापनी सर्वा मीमांसा तर्करूपिणी ॥

MāMey Pramāṇa, sec. on anumāna, verse 22

Thus in all cases, by the refutation of the fallacious meanings through a flood of counter-arguments, the entire investigation of the nature of counter-argument establishes the meanings of sentences. (Tr. C.K. Raja and S.S.S. Sastri)

आभाससङ्करे तावत् पुरःस्फुरितदूषणम् ।
उद्भाव्यमिति सर्वेषां निर्विवादं हि वादिनाम् ॥

MāMey Pramāṇa, sec. on anumāna, verse 80

When there is an intermixture of fallacies, the defect that shines in the forefront is what is to be taken up – this is incontestible in the case of all disputants. (Tr. C.K. Raja and S.S.S. Sastri)

अङ्गवैकल्ये च तर्काभासत्वं भवति ।

MāMey Pramāṇa, sec. on anumāna,after verse 11

If any of these elements be wanting, there is a fallacy of counter-argument. (Tr. C.K. Raja and S.S.S. Sastri)

The fallacious *sādhana* or merely the semblance of a *sādhana* (instrumental cause) has been thus commented upon elsewhere:

साधनाभासता चात्र पूर्वपक्षार्थगोचरा ।
अन्यसाधनमन्यस्य साधनाभास उच्यते ॥

ŚlVā Pratijñā-sūtra 122

The "semblance of means" will be found herein in the arguments used by the *pūrvapakṣī* (the questioner or objector). The means of one thing applied to the case of another constitutes what is called the "semblance of means". (Tr. G.N. Jha)

As says the **Prakaraṇapañcikā**:

येन च वचनेन सन्नपि साध्यसाधनयोस्संबन्धनियमो नाभिधीयते, तदप्याभास एव ।

PraPañ p. 222

> That statement is also regarded as a mere *ābhāsa* (faulty or fallacious argument) by which the existent rule of connection between the probandum and probans is not expressed.
> (Tr. R.S. Bhattacharya)

The **Brahma-Sūtra** under the topic *ābhāsa* preaches apparently the doctrine of taking the *jīva* as mere "reflection" in the ultimate reference of the Great Light, Brahman: *ābhāsa eva ca* (II.3.50).

However, teacher Gauḍapāda in his **Māṇḍūkya Kārikā** often employs the word *ābhāsa* (other words used by him to indicate the illusory nature of the world are *māyā, mithyā, viparyaya, kalpita,* etc.) to signify mere appearance or phenomenon, illusion of a thought or thing (MāKā III & IV) as opposed to the real knowledge or the reality (which is called *vijñāna, citta, manas, brahman,* etc.). But another aspect of *ābhāsa* as the attribute of Supreme Light has ever been in view of the metaphysical tradition. Thus, we read in the **Viṣṇu-Sahasranāma Bhāṣya** of Śaṅkara: *paraṃ prakṛṣṭaṃ mahat bṛhat tejaḥ caitanya-lakṣaṇaṃ sarvāvabhāsakam* (I.9). The notion of *māyā* came to be defined, redefined, modified or qualified according to the viewpoint held or evolved by various thinkers professing *advaita* (non-duality), *dvaita* (duality), *viśiṣṭādvaita* (conditioned non-duality), *dvaitādvaita* (dual-nonduality), *bhedābheda* (difference and non-difference), *acintya-bhedābheda* (inconceivable difference and non-difference), etc.

According to the non-dualist Vedānta, *māyā* is the principle of "measure" or "covering" which stays as enveloping Brahman, who is beyond every concept or attribute. The agency of *māyā* as a female *śakti,* potential power that is a positive principle on a lower order is said to receive as if in a mirror a reflection of the Intranscendental Self-contained Brahman and thereby projecting and bringing forth the universe. Thus the Absolute Brahman descends to the level of Phenomenonal Brahman, or personal lord, *īśvara, saguṇa.*

In some works of later Vedānta a doctrine of thought, named *ābhāsa-vāda,* is detailed in accordance to which the *jīva* is an illusory reflection of Brahma-intelligence in *avidyā.* It is variant of the theory of *pratibimba-vāda,* or *vivarta-vāda.*

As has been observed by T.M.P. Mahadevan, "From the standpoint of reasoning, *māyā* is uncharacterisable either as real, or as unreal, or as both real and unreal. The world of plurality appears in Brahman on account of *māyā,* even as a snake appears in what is a rope. This is known as *vivarta,* transfiguration... Bhāratītīrtha Vidyāraṇya, who follows mainly the Vivaraṇa tradition, teaches a modified form of the reflection-theory or *pratibimba-vāda* which is referred to as *ābhāsa-vāda.* While the Vivaraṇa view regards the reflection as real and as identical with the prototype, the theory sponsored in the **Pañcadaśī** holds that the reflection (*ābhāsa*) is mere appearance, an illusory manifestation. The apposition between the *jīva* and Brahman, according to this view, is through sublation (*bādha*), and not through identification (*aikya*)" (*The Pañcadaśī*, Madras, 1975, Intro., pp. 25–26).

A beautiful analogy based on a painted canvas has been drawn in the **Pañcadaśī** (ch. VI) by Vidyāraṇya to explain the nature of *jīva* (intelligent, individual self), *kūṭastha* (or *ātman*, immutable self at large), *īśvara* (the lord, as *māyin*), and Brahman (the Highest, Supreme Reality). There are four stages to be discerned of the Supreme Self as are four stages of a painted canvas, which is by nature white, firstly, it is bleached, then it is stiffened with starch, thirdly, sketched with outlines, and then filled in with paint. All created beings from Brahman down to a blade of grass are like the painted figures on the canvas, are but the shadows (*ābhāsa*-s) of the intelligent Self which is immutable and impartite.

पृथक् पृथक्चिदाभासाश्चैतन्याध्यस्तदेहिनाम् ।
कल्प्यन्ते जीवनामानो बहुधा संसरन्त्यमी ॥

Pañcad VI.7

As superimposed on the self the *ābhāsas*-reflections or shadows – of sentiency namely intelligent beings (like gods and men) appear to be so many and are variously subject to transmigration.

आत्माभासस्य जीवस्य संसारो नात्मवस्तुनः ।
इति बोधो भवेद्विद्या लभ्यतेऽसौ विचारणात् ॥

Pañcad VI.11

The recognition that the transmigration is of the *jīva* who is but a reflection of the Self (*ātmā-ābhāsa*) and not of the (immutable and eternal). *Ātman* is knowledge, which is acquired through inquiry.

As it has been put by T.M.P. Mahadevan, "According to the *ābhāsavāda*, in an act of perception there are four facts involved: (a) the intelligence qualified by the internal organ together with the *cidābhāsa* is the perceiving agent; (b) the intelligence qualified by the mental mode together with the *ābhāsa* (reflection) is the means of valid knowledge; (c) the intelligence limited by adjuncts like pot, etc. is the object-intelligence; (d) the reflection of intelligence which is generated by the relation of the mental mode with pot etc., is the fruit-intelligence (*phalacetanā*). If a pot is to be known, there must result in it the reflection of intelligence brought about by the contact of the mental mode with the pot. The intelligence which is in the intellect and which has assumed the form of the pot makes known the pot. But the known-ness of the pot is caused by Brahman-intelligence" (*ibid.*, p. 137).

According to the doctrine, there are two intelligences, one is the original and the other a reflection; the one as *cidābhāsa* is a reflection, having no reality of its own and subject to the wheel of life and death, while the other, *kūṭastha*, is unchanging, eternal, flawless intelligence. The preceptors of old have defined the *kūṭastha* as the witness of the mind and its modifications. Scriptures declare the immutable to be existence, knowledge, and bliss. In the **Upadeśasāhasrī**, Śaṅkara distinguishes the *kūṭastha* from the *ābhāsa*. He compares the latter to the reflection of a face in the mirror and the former to the original countenance.

The concept of *cidābhāsa* is thus explained in the **Pañcadaśī**:

चेतनाचेतनभिदा कूटस्थात्मकृता न हि ।
किंतु बुद्धिकृताऽऽभासकृतैवेत्यवगम्यताम् ॥
यथा चेतन आभासः कूटस्थे भ्रान्तिकल्पितः ।
अचेतनो घटादिश्च तथा तत्रैव कल्पितः ॥

Pañcad VI.45–46

It is not by the immutable *kūṭastha* or *ātman* that the difference between the animate and the inanimate is made; it is the *jīva*, the reflection of *kūṭastha* in the intellect, which makes the difference.

Just as in the conscious *jīva* an illusion of the *kūṭastha* is maintained due to a resembling of understanding (*bhrānti*), so are even on It (*kūṭastha*) the inanimate objects such as the pitcher and so on.

साभासमेव तद्बीजं धीरूपेण प्ररोहति ।
अतो बुद्धौ चिदाभासो विस्पष्टं प्रतिभासते ॥

Pañcad VI.154 (cf. Pañcad VII.91)

In association with a reflection of consciousness (which is not grasped) this seed (of the *māyā*) develops into the intellect and then in this very intellect, a reflection of the consciousness becomes further manifested plainly (in the form of ego).

नायं दोषश्चिदाभासः कूटस्थैकस्वभाववान् ।
आभासत्वस्य मिथ्यात्वात्कूटस्थत्वावशेषणात् ॥

Pañcad VII.15

This reflection of the consciousness (*cidābhāsa*) is not a defect for that is in the own sole nature of the *kūṭastha*. However, the reflection of it (*kūṭastha*) is only due to a (distinct) unreality (*mithyātva*), for there remains only the *kūṭastha* when all such factors are dispensed with.

Vidyāraṇya has shown the necessity of postulating *cidābhāsa* to explain the process of cognition:

ईषद्भासनमाभासः प्रतिबिम्बस्तथाविधः ।
बिम्बलक्षणहीनः सन्बिम्बवद्भासते स हि ॥

Pañcad VIII.32

Ābhāsa denotes a little of reflection (of the original). *Pratibimba* is also like that (i.e. a counter-image of the original). It does not have the properties of the Reality but bears a reflected semblance to it.

From the Vedānta point of view, manifestations are assumed by the Supreme Self through the effectuation of ignorance acting as his deluding Nature and as if by way of a reflection in the mirror he descends to the level of Īśvara-with-attributes (*saguṇa*):

अविद्यागताभासाविविक्तचित्त एवेश्वरत्वस्योक्तत्वात् साभासाविद्यायामीश्वरोपाधित्वम् ।

Nyāyaratnāvalī cited in Kālasiddhāntadarśinī, p. 38

From the fact stated in this doctrine of knowledge called *sābhāsa-vidyā*, namely that the Overlordship (*īśvaratva*) is Consciousness (*citta*) itself joined by manifestations coming from ignorance (*avidyā*), even the nature of *īśvara* is defined from its having attributes.

According to the Nātha Siddha preceptor Gorakhanātha, the mystery of pure consciousness called Śiva can be thus epitomised:

परमपदमिति स्वसंवेद्यं अत्यन्ताभासाभासकमयम् ।

Siddhasiddhāntapaddhati V.2

The Supreme Notion is thus to be self-realised as consisted of a reflection (*ābhāsaka*) of transcendent luminosity (*ābhāsa*).

According to the Siddha doctrines as summarised by Balabhadra, in his **Siddhasiddhānta-Saṅgraha**, the *śakti* of Supreme Śiva is His-self, itself, which when descends to the act of manifestation is called both *kula* and *akula*:

कुलाकुलस्वरूपोऽसौ सामरस्यस्वभूमिका ।
सत्ताहन्ता परा भासा स्फुरत्ता च कुलाकुलम् ॥
परस्परनिराभासभासि सम्यक्प्रकाशिका ।
पराभासैकमेवास्तीत्येका सत्ता निरुच्यते ॥

SiSiSaṅg IV.6–7

She is of the form of *kula* and *akula* for which there is their own substratum of Union (*sāmarasya*). *Kula* is (fivefold): *parā, bhāsā, sattā, ahantā,* and *kalā*. She is explained as the sole Being (*sattā*), and who is alone the Supreme Refulgence (*parābhāsā*); is the All-illuminating, and reveals together in the glory of the light which is beyond all light (*nirābhāsa*).

प्रसरं भासयेच्छक्तिः संकोचं भासयेच्छिवः ।
तयोर्योगस्य कर्ता यः स भवेत् सिद्धयोगिराट् ॥

Gorakṣa Siddhānta VI.63

The Śakti represents the principle of expansion. Śiva represents the principle of contraction. He, who is capable of inducing their union is king of Siddha Yogis.

In the Śaiva philosophy of Kashmir, Parama-Śiva is the Supreme Reality that is both the Universal Self as well as the all-pervading innermost true self of every being. This world is a manifestation of the Supreme Lord's immanent aspect which is His Śakti – Creative Nature, female power – in no way distinct or independent of Him, it being His Self-consciousness. Thus He is understood as an undivided coalescence of *prakāśa* (pure sentiency) and *vimarśa* (self-consciousness) – Śiva and Śakti. The Supreme Lord blossoms forth with the descent of His Śakti (*śaktipātonmiṣita-pārameśvara* – PrH Intro. comm. on sūtra 1, by Kṣemarāja).

As it is given in the **Pratyabhijñā-Hṛdaya**:

चितिः स्वतन्त्रा विश्वसिद्धिहेतुः ॥ स्वेच्छया स्वभित्तौ विश्वमुन्मीलयति ॥ तन्नाना अनुरूपग्राह्यग्राहकभेदात् ॥ चितिसंकोचात्मा चेतनोऽपि संकुचितविश्वमयः ॥

PrH 1–4

By her own free impulse the absolute *cit* (consciousness) causes worldly effectuation. By her own will she unfolds the world on her own canvas from Sadāśiva down to the earth. That world appears manifold being differentiated into objects and subjects, reciprocally complemented to one another. As the great Lord has in Himself the contracted (i.e. not differentiated) consciousness so his body is consisted of the contracted world.

As it is put forth in the **Mālinīvijayottara Tantra**:

निष्प्रपंचो निराभासः शुद्धः स्वात्मन्यवस्थितः ।
सर्वातीतः शिवो ज्ञेयोऽयं विदित्वा विमुच्यते ॥

MVT II.42

One gains redemption by knowing the Lord Śiva, who is to be

known as free from mundane activity, without *ābhāsa*, pure, staying in His own being and transcending all.

Elsewhere, the manifestation of world is thus indicated:

एष चानन्तशक्तित्वादेवमाभासयत्यमून् ।
भावानिच्छावशात् ... ।

SarDSaṅg Pratyabhijñādarśana 196

He (the Lord Maheśvara) thus manifests, by his infinite power, such worldly beings or object owing to his will (and not under any other effecting cause).

The **Netra Tantra** states:

साभास: कथ्यते देवि शिव: परमकारणम् ।

NT VIII.36ab

O Goddess! Śiva, the Supreme Cause is said to be having *ābhāsa* (His own refulgence).

स साभास इति प्रोक्तो निराभासस्तु कथ्यते ॥

NT VIII.38cd

[Owing to multiple manifestations being shone forth from him] He is called *sa-ābhāsa* 'having *ābhāsa*', (though) He is indeed stated to be without *ābhāsa* (*nirābhāsa*).

In creative revelation or expansion (*prasara*) His Śakti assumes an infinite number of definitions of which five primary ones are: 1) *cit*, power of Sentiency; 2) *ānanda*, power of Bliss; 3) *icchā*, power of Will; 4) *jñāna*, power of Knowledge; 5) *kriyā*, power of Creation. First two of the above aspects are, however, nothing else in definition but the principles of the Supreme and His Nature, viz. *śiva-tattva* and *śakti-tattva* in the creative state. He the pure Sentiency (*prakāśa* or *cit*) stays in union with Her, the perfect Beatitude (*ānanda*). Will, Knowledge and Action are the aspects that are instrumental for the union – revealed through them for the creative order, thus the Lord Śiva enjoys His own Glory or Śakti.

As it is explained by the teacher Kṣemarāja (PrH comm. on *sūtra* 1–4, etc.), Paramaśiva, the Highest Śiva, desiring to manifest the universe, which lies in Him as identical with Himself, in the form of Sadāśiva and other appropriate forms flashes forth at first as not different from the light of consciousness (*prakāśa*) but not experiencing the unity with it, and being more void than the void itself. Then He unfolds Himself in the totality of manifestations, namely worlds, entities and their respective experients which are only a solidified form of *cit*-essence. Thus, as the Lord is universe-bodied so is the individual experient also, because of consciousness being contracted, has the body of the entire universe in a contracted form even as the *vaṭa* tree appears in a contracted form in its seed. So does the established doctrine says, "one body and the embodied one really represent all the bodies and the embodied." This is the mode of *ābhāsana* or manifesting. In view of the ultimate reference, whatever appears through the successive functioning of the goddess, representing sight and other perceptual functions, is emanated.

In this system of philosophy known as Pratyabhijñā or Trika Darśana, which is analysed to present a synthesis of Realism and Idealism and hence nicknamed "Realistic Idealism" – the process of universal manifestation is thus technically explained by the concept of *ābhāsa* or *ābhāsana*, "shining forth", which is in essence not much different from the Vedantic theory of *vivarta-vāda* or the *pratibimba-vāda* excepting the point that the exponents of the *ābhāsavāda* maintain the worldly appearance to be not absolutely non-existent and unreal for they are experiences of the Ultimate Reality, and thus are of the nature of Reality in their essential character.

क्रमो भेदाश्रयो भेदोऽप्याभास-सदसत्त्वत: ।
आभाससदसत्त्वे तु चित्राभासकृत: प्रभो: ॥
मूर्त्तिवैचित्र्यतो देशक्रममाभासयत्यसौ ।
क्रियावैचित्र्यनिर्भासात्कालक्रममपीश्वर: ॥
सर्वत्राभासभेदोऽपि भवेत्कालक्रमाकर: ।
विच्छिन्नभास: शून्यादेर्मातुर्भातस्य नो सकृत् ॥
देशक्रमोऽपि भावेषु भाति मातुर्मितात्मन: ।
स्वात्मेव स्वात्मना पूर्णा भावा भान्त्यमितस्य तु ॥

ĪPraVim II.1.4–7

Succession depends upon difference, the latter on the existence of a certain manifestation and non-existence of another, and the existence of some manifestation and non-existence of another are brought about by the Lord Himself; who manifests the variety of manifestations.

The Lord makes the spatial succession manifest by means of variety of manifestations of bodies (*mūrti vaicitrya*) and the temporal succession by means of manifestation of the variety (of forms) in action (*kriyāvaicitrya*).

The variety of manifestations of forms, which is the basis of (the idea of) temporal succession in all things, shines to the limited subject only, such as *'śūnya'*. It does not shine to the universal subject, whose light is eternal.

The spatial succession also in things shines to the limited subject only. To the universal subject the objects shine as identical with itself and, therefore, as beyond all limitations, like the Self itself. (Tr. K.C. Pandey)

Both the root *ā-bhās-* and the abstract noun *ābhāsa* as allied word-forms derived thereof are found employed as conveying the idea of manifestations, outward emanations, or the act of shining forth:

संवित्स्वभाव आत्मा स्वप्नसंकल्पादौ आभासवैचित्र्यनिर्माणे प्रभुः प्रभविष्णुः इति स्वसंविदितस्तत एव तौ भवतः, स हि आत्मनि नीलादीन् आभासान् आभासयन् चित्रतया अपरिमेयया भासयति । तथा हि - लोहिताभासं घटाभासमुन्नताभासं दृढाभासं च सामानाधिकरण्येन घटाभासं पटाभासं च पृथक्त्वावभासेन अन्योन्यत्र आभासाभावेन, स्वात्मनि तु एकरसेनाभासेन .... ।

ĪPraVim II.1.4

Therefore, that very self, whose essential nature is consciousness and which is known through one's own experience, as capable of bringing about various manifestations in dream and in imagination, is the cause of these manifestations also. The Self, manifesting the external objects of the world, such as blue etc. manifests them in innumerable variety: viz. He manifests manifestation such as jar, red, tall, hard as having common basis. And He manifests manifestations such as 'cloth' and 'jar' as having different bases, as mutually exclusive, each one as negation of the other. But when He manifests them within Himself they are identical with Him. (Tr. K.C. Pandey)

स च यतः प्रमाता अहंभावसमावेशनात् अपरिपूर्णात् अतएव उद्रिक्तकालक्रमवत्त्वात् भावेष्वपि कालक्रममाभासयति, 'योऽहं बालोऽभवं तत्सहभावी घटाभासोऽपि अभवत्' इति, न तु यः 'सकृद् विभातः' इति अनया वाचोयुक्त्या अविच्छिन्नभासनः प्रमाता संविद्रूपः, तस्य स्वात्मनि कालक्रमः, नापि तदपेक्षया वेद्ये भावजाते, तद्धि तत्र अभेदेन भाति इति ।

ĪPraVim II.1.6–7

Because the empirical subject is identified with the limited I-consciousness, 'therefore, the temporal succession is evident in it. It is such a subject which is responsible for the appearance of temporal succession in external objects, e.g. 'I was a boy and a jar also had simultaneous existence with me as such'. There is no temporal succession in the eternal subject, who is essentially consciousness and, therefore, is ever-shining, as has been asserted in, 'The Self is ever shining' nor is there such a succession even in the object, related to Him. For, they shine as one with Him. (Tr. K.C. Pandey)

तत्र आभासरूपा एव जडचेतनलक्षणाः पदार्थाः ।

ĪPraVim III.1.1

Then the inanimate and the animate *padārthas* (objects, existences) are really of the form of appearances.

लौकिक्याः क्रियायाः सक्रमत्वं कालशक्तेः आभासविच्छेदनप्रदर्शनसामर्थ्यरूपात् पारमेश्वरात् शक्तिविशेषात् घटते .... ।

ĪPraVim II.1.2

But the successiveness of the worldly action is possible because of the particular power of the Highest Lord, the power to manifest the manifestables as cut off from one another, which is known as the 'Power of Time'. (Tr. K.C. Pandey)

It can thus be summarised that in Kashmir Śaivism, all the objects shining forth as worldly entities and principles are known as *ābhāsas*, manifestations; they shine externally in succession as distinguished from one another and appear as distinct owing to the efficacy of temporal (time-bound) unfoldment or expansion.

As K.C. Pandey explains: "All that emanates from or is manifested by the absolute is called *ābhāsa*, appearance or manifestation, ... it is all that appears; all that is within the reach of external senses or internal mind.... everything is a configuration of *ābhāsa* or limited manifestation. The subject is no less a configuration than the object. Both are unity in multiplicity... The *Abhasavadin* holds that the ordinary object of cognition is a collocation or configuration of a certain number of *ābhāsas*, each of which requires a separate mental process to cognise. Each constituent as it is apprehended separately is an *ābhāsa*, which marks the farthest limit of the cognitive activity.

The subject also is a similar configuration. It is made up of the limiting conditions or forms of cognition and action, *kāla* or time, etc. purposiveness, tendencies, intellectual background, body, vital airs, senses and intellect. But none is its permanent aspect. Its constituents differ in the case of every distinct experience. The inner being, the self-consciousness, with the impurity, called *āṇava-mala*, alone is the persisting element in the flux" (*History of Philosophy: Eastern and Western*, London, 1952, Vol. I, p. 390).

It is so simply expressed in a strain of one devotional verse:

लिखते जगत्त्रितयचित्रमद्भुतप्रतिभा - परिस्फुरितसंशिते नमः ।
सुसितैकसूक्ष्मनिजशक्तिवर्तिका- रचितावभास-शतशोभि शंभवे ॥

Cited in SpKā Vivṛti I.1

Homage to you, O Śambhu, who draws out as imagined and expressed with the wonderful *pratibhā* (splendour or intellect) the three worlds like pictorial representation, which shines forth with a hundredfold manifestations (*avabhāsa*) rendered by the painting-brush of your own sole nature of pure white.

Ābhāsa is the name of one of the netherworld, (*pātāla*) or hells (*narakas*), as described by the Śaivāgama tradition.

तन्नामतोऽधिपतित उच्यमानं निबोध मे ।
आभासं परतालाख्यं त्रितलं च गभस्तिमत् ॥
महातलं रसाङ्कं च पातालं सप्तमं मुने ।

MṛgĀ vp XIII.27–28ab

Listen to me, O sage, what I am stating: the names of hells are Ābhāsa, Paratāla, Tritala, Gabhastimat, Mahātala, Rasāṅka (i.e. Rasātala) and Pātāla, the seventh.(Tr. H.N. Chakravarty)

This list of hells also occurs in the **Svacchanda Tantra** (X.96). This aspect is further to be noted in the **Parākhya Saṃhitā**:

समन्तात्सर्वरत्नानां भासो यस्माद् विभान्त्यलम् ।
तद्धर्म्याणां च तत्स्त्रीणामाभासं तेन तत्स्मृतम् ॥
आभासे शंकुकर्णाख्यः कुटिलो विकलः पतिः ।

Parākhya Sam (as cited by SvT comm. on X.97cd and X.113, cf. NārSam IX.53)

From the reason that there are lights of all kinds of jewels shining forth on all sides copiously and there are women with shining beauty of that definition, so it is known as the Ābhāsa (netherworld). At Ābhāsa stays its regent Śaṅkukarṇa ("spike-eared") by name, a crooked and deformed person.

Besides the word *ābhāsa* of rare occurrence in classical poetry, various verb forms of the root *bhās-* ("to shine", "to appear") also with several prefixes are found to have presented useful poetic idiom. For instance:

प्रवृत्तमात्रेण पयांसि पातुमावर्तवेगाद्भ्रमता घनेन ।
आभाति भूयिष्ठमयं समुद्रः प्रमथ्यमानो गिरिणेव भूयः ॥
दूरादयश्चक्रनिभस्य तन्वी तमालतालीवनराजिनीला ।

आभाति वेला लवणाम्बुराशेर्धारानिबद्धेव कलङ्करेखा ॥

Ragh XIII.14–15

This ocean on account of the cloud which as soon as it begins to drink water from it is made to turn round (and round) by the force of the whirlpool, appears in a great way to be, as it were, churned again by the mountain (Mandāra).

The strand of the briny ocean resembling an iron-wheel which is dark on account of the row of Tamāla and Tālī forests, and which appeared like a slender line owing to distance, looks like a thin coating of rust formed on the edge of a steel-wheel. (Tr. G.R. Nandargikar)

अजिनदण्डभृतं कुशमेखलां यतगिरं मृगशृङ्गपरिग्रहाम् ।
अधिवसंस्तनुमध्वरदीक्षितामसमभासमभासयदीश्वरः ॥

Ragh IX.17

The god presiding over (lit. dwelling in) his body that had undergone the initiative ceremony of the sacrifices, with his speech restrained, holding the antelope hide and a staff, wearing a waistband of *kuśa*-grass and furnished with the horn of a deer, made it shine with matchless splendour. (Tr. G.R. Nandargikar)

Also, as we see in the contemporary inscriptions:

कैलासतुङ्गशिखरप्रतिमानि चान्यान्याभान्ति दीर्घवलभीनि सवेदिकानि ।
गान्ध्वर्व्वशब्दमुखराणि निविष्टचित्रकर्म्माणि लोलकदलीवनशोभितानि ॥

Mandasor Ins (of Kumāragupta) V.11

And other long buildings on the roofs of the houses, with arbours in them, are beautiful, being like the lofty summits of (the mountain) Kailāsa; being vocal with songs (like those) of the Gandharvas; having pictured representations arranged (in them); (and) being adorned with groves of waving plantain-trees. (Tr. J.F. Fleet)

Like philosophers, classical poets also favoured the word *ābhāsa* being quite handy as conveying the concept of a false experience or mere semblance of some object or emotion. As is the following example coming from the pen of poet-astronomer Varāha-mihira:

जात्यं मनोभवसुखं सुभगस्य सर्वमाभासमात्रमितरस्य मनोवियोगात् ।

BṛSam LXXV.1

The man who captivates the heart of damsels enjoys all kinds of erotic pleasures of a high order, while one who is not attractive gets only sham pleasures because the woman's mind is not fixed on him. (Tr. M.R. Bhat)

तदपि साहसाभासमित्यनुपदेष्टव्यमेव ।

MālMā II, after verse 7

It be thus advised that this act, moreover, looks like wantonness.

The concept of *ābhāsa* is found evolved in a specific context of Sanskrit poetics also. A rare usage of this word in the **Agni Purāṇa** is as follows:

आभासोपमशक्तिश्च सर्गे यद्भिन्नवृत्तता ।

AgPur CCCXXXVII.38ab

It is the writing of several chapters in various stanza-compositions that is called the *ābhāsopamaśakti*, i.e. the poetic capacity to render semblance (of ideas).

For conveying the impression of a notion in its outward appearance but not in reality the term *ābhāsa* as well as allied concepts of *avabhāsa* and *pratibhāsa* have been of special utility with the ancient writers on poetics and aesthetic theories. As observes the teacher Kuntaka:

अर्थयोरेकमुल्लेखि पदं शब्दतदर्थयो: ।
एकावभासयो: साम्यं तन्त्रत्वादत्र जृम्भते ॥

VaJī III.46

One and the same word will be denoting two meanings here; between the word and the two meanings so denoted as if they were identical, similarity will be found to be the ruling principle behind such unique technique of the poet.
(Tr. K. Krishnamoorthy)

In view of Rājaśekhara:

न च प्रतिभासस्तादात्म्येन वस्तुन्यवतिष्ठते । यदि तथा स्यात्तदा सूर्याचन्द्रमसोर्मण्डले दृष्ट्या परिच्छिद्यमानद्वादशाङ्गुलपरिमिते पुराणाद्यागमनिवेदितधरावलयाधिकमात्रे न स्त इति यायावरीय: ।

KāMīm IX, p. 112

And, there in the object the apparent (illusory) appearance does not exist by way of its real identity (*tādātmya*). Were it of that kind, then, the orbs of the sun and the moon should not have been mentioned to be of the measure of twelve *aṅgula* digits by distinctness of perception, in the traditional lores such as the Purāṇas, and would not be greater than the measure of the earth's orb. This is the opinion of the wandering teacher (i.e. Rājaśekhara himself).

In the highly developed tradition of *alaṅkāras* or the figures of speech, *ābhāsa* assumed a specific definition as involving the concept of poetic charm evoked through statements apparently incongruous or inconsistence to each other:

अनौचित्यप्रवृत्तत्व आभासो रसभावयोः ॥

SāDar III.241

When brought about in an improper manner, there occurs (only) *ābhāsa* (a semblance) of both the sentiment (*rasa*) and its inherent mood (*bhāva*, i.e. *sthāyībhāva*, constant stay of emotion).

The *ābhāsa* of a sentiment has been explained as follows:

हीनपात्रेषु तिर्यक्षु नायकप्रतियोगिषु ।
गौणेष्वेव पदार्थेषु तमाभासं विजानते ॥

Sark V.30

When a sentiment is described as situated in the inferior characters, animals, competitors to the hero, and in secondary objects only, it is known to be a fallacious form (of that sentiment; just its semblance indirectly or remotely induced).

As it is defined with reference to the figure of speech *virodhābhāsa*:

आभासत्वे विरोधस्य विरोधाभास इष्यते ।
विनापि तन्वि ! हारेण वक्षोजौ तव हारिणौ ॥

Kuva 76

When there is alluded to only a semblance of contradiction it is regarded *virodhābhāsa*. (For instance) 'Without even overhanging necklaces (*hāra*), O damsel, your bosom is bewitching the heart'.

The illustration given by Appaya Dīkṣita for this figure of speech is from the famous epic of Śrī Harṣa:

प्रतीपभूपैरिव किं ततो भिया विरुद्धधर्मैरपि भेतृतोज्झिता ।
अमित्रजिन्मित्रजिदोजसा स यद्विचारदृक्चारदृगप्यवर्तत ॥

NaiCa I.13

Just as hostile kings gave up creating disaffection among his subjects for fear of him, similarly did even mutually conflicting attributes give up their contrast out of fear for him? For by virtue of his power he was both conqueror of enemies and conqueror of friends; he saw through spies, and at the same time did not see through spies. (Tr. K.K. Handiqui)

At first there appears to be a contradictory statement conveyed through the words used but subsequently that is reconciled by the different connotations of the same expressions through various poetic techniques, that are said to be rendering this *alaṅkāra* into ten types referring to aspects opposite to origin, action, quality or riches (Śiva-Tattva-Ratnākara VII.5.62–63).

Another instance of the *ābhāsa* kind of figure of speech is *niṣedhābhāsa* or *ākṣepa*:

> निषेधाभासमाक्षेपं बुधाः केचन मन्वते ।
> नाहं दूती तनोस्तापस्तस्याः कलानलोपमः ॥
>
> Kuva 74
>
> The *ākṣepa alaṅkāra* is considered by certain scholars as *niṣedhābhāsa* (i.e. a semblance of denial or refusal). [For example, in the statement that] 'I am not her she-messenger; [but I must convey that] the heat of her body is as it were like the all-consuming fire'.

The concepts such as *rasābhāsa* are quite frequently used. As we see in the present citation:

> प्रतिबिम्बस्तथा छाया रत्याभासो द्विधा मतः ।
>
> BhSi I.3.25
>
> The *rati-ābhāsa,* i.e. semblance of *rati* is of two kinds, viz. (1) *pratibimba* or a direct reflection of form or image; and (2) *chāyā,* i.e. a shadowy or indirect reflection.

Manifestation in the Arts

The term *ābhāsa* has been amply discussed in the scriptures dealing with performing and visual arts. As a preamble to ch. 46 of the **Yoga-Vāsiṣṭha** (VI.1), the commentator Ānandabodhendra Sarasvatī has put forth the following stanza:

> इह शिल्पिमनोदृष्टपद्मिनीखण्डमण्डितम् ।
> शिलोदरमिव ब्रह्म प्रपञ्चाभासमीर्यते ॥
>
> YVās VI.1.46
>
> Just like the hidden interior of a piece of stone, which the sculptor sees, through his mind's eye, is revealing (to him) the possible decoration of a lotus vegetation, so is Brahman (stated to) cause these illusory manifestations (*prapañca-ābhāsa*) to appear.

Thus, reproducing so nicely a sampling of the metaphysical exposition found in the original that it gives – by way of an express analogy from the artist's creative activity – summary contents of the whole section elaborating Vedantic viewpoint on the formless nature of absolute Brahman in relation to the empirical definition of the worlds manifested through the active agency of *māyā* (= illusion; also crafty or magical acts).

Ābhāsa or *citra-ābhāsa* came specially to evolve in the Āgama-Tantra tradition of South India as a concept of art portrayal in painted medium. In this context the threefold classification of *citra* or art representation has been explained thus in the following Śaiva Āgama passages:

> एवमृज्वागतं विश्वदृश्यं चित्रमिति स्मृतम् ।
> भित्त्याश्लिष्टं ह्यर्धचित्रं दृष्टचित्रमिति स्मृतम् ॥
> आभासं भित्तिलेख्यं स्यादेतत्सामान्यमीरितम् ।
>
> KāmĀ LXV.132–133ab
>
> In this way (described above), the figure in which the form is seen in its entirety, as conceived in an upright posture, is called the *citra.* It is known as the *ardha-citra* which shows the visible figure as attached to the wall (or background). *Ābhāsa* is the (name for a) painting done on a wall (or surface, i.e. two-dimensional surface). This is what is known in general.

> एतानि सकलादीनि त्रिविधानि मयोच्यते ॥
> चित्रं चित्रार्धमेवं तु चित्राभासं तथैव च ।
> सर्वावयवसम्पूर्णं दृश्यं तच्चित्रमुच्यते ॥
> अर्धावयवसंदृश्यमर्धचित्रं तथैव च ।
> पटे भित्तौ च यो लेख्यं चित्राभासमिहोच्यते ॥
>
> SupĀ I.34.2cd–4
>
> By me these three kinds of *sakala* and other representations of the deity are being stated now. They are *citra, citrārdha* and *citrābhāsa.* Visible as complete in all the bodily part is called the *citra.* Likewise, that is *ardhacitra* (partial figure) in which only the half of bodily limbs are properly to be seen. In this context (of the Āgamas), that which is to be depicted as drawn on a piece of cloth or on a wall is called the *citrābhāsa.*

A passage almost similar to the above verses of the **Suprabheda Āgama** has been quoted by Vedajñāna in his **Śaivāgamaparibhāṣāmañjarī** (III.140–141).

Thus, the *citrābhāsa* is defined in the **Śilparatna** as a painted or pictorial representation:

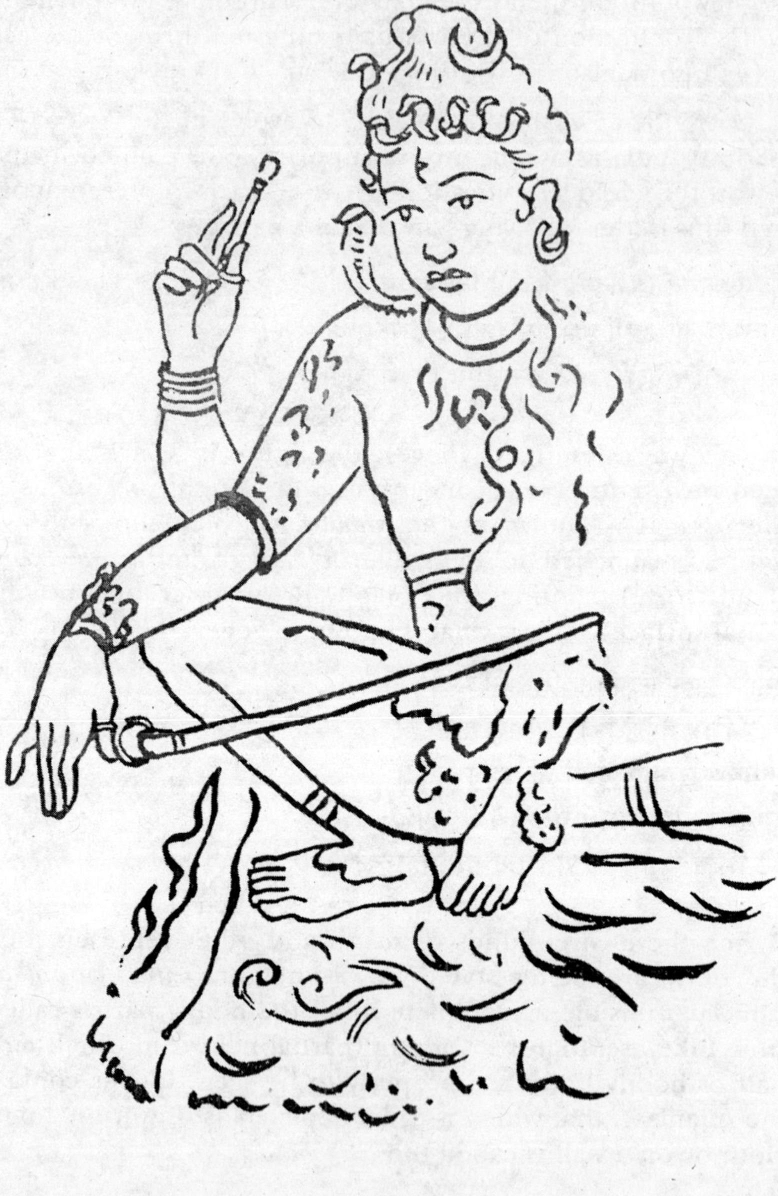

Figure 1: Yoga Dakṣiṇāmūrti as a painted representation (*ābhāsa*), Chola, Rājarājeśvara Temple, Tanjavur, 1000 AD.

तदेव चित्रमर्धाङ्गदर्शनं त्वर्धचित्रकम् ।
चित्राभासं तथालेख्यमुत्तमादिक्रमेण तु ॥

ŚiRa II.2.8

That is *citra* (already elaborated). And indeed in which only half side of the body is seen, is the *ardhacitra.* Likewise, the *citrābhāsa* is a painting (*ālekhya*). (These three are considered) in order of sequence as the best (the middling and the inferior).

This set of nomenclature also appears to have been well favoured by both the Pāñcarātra and the Vaikhānasa scholars:

चित्रं वाप्यर्धचित्रं वा चित्राभासमथापि वा ।
चित्रं सर्वाङ्गदृष्टं स्याद् अर्धचित्रं तु सार्धकम् ॥
आभासं पट-भित्तिस्थं त्रिविधं परिकीर्तितम् ।

AniSam XII.8–9

There are three categories (of representation): *citra, ardhacitra* and *citrābhāsa. Citra* is that which is (so carved in the round) as seen from all sides. *Ardhacitra* is the one that has half depiction (being in relief). *Ābhāsa* (i.e. *citra* of the *ābhāsa* kind) is the one which is executed on a cloth (or canvas) or a wall-surface.

Apparently, the word '*citra*' is employed here to indicate both sculpture as well as painting, with '*citra-ābhāsa*', abbreviated in this context as '*ābhāsa*' also, being applicable to painting done either on the flat surface of a cloth or of a wall.

या स्थितालेख्यरूपेण लिखितापि (चैव ?) शिल्पिभिः ॥
मानप्रमाणसंयुक्ता सा चित्राभास उच्यते ।
उत्तमं तु फलं चित्रं मध्यमं चार्धचित्रकम् ॥
आलेख्यमधमं प्रोक्तं प्रतिष्ठाकर्मणि क्रमात् ।

VSam X.34cd–36ab

The (image) which exists in the form of a painting (*ālekhya* or *lekhya*), or is drawn in outline (or incised) by the artists, as having proper proportions of measurements is called *citrābhāsa. Citra* is of excelling results; *ardhacitra* of middling merit while the painted one is said to be of inferior bearing in the rituals of the image-consecration.

Having elaborately described the installation ceremonies for the full-fledged statues sculptured in the round, the **Viṣvaksena Saṃhitā** has to thus indicate certain specific details of *pratiṣṭhā* rituals prescribed for the other two kinds of images:

स्थापनं संप्रवक्ष्यामि चित्राभासार्धचित्रके ।
आभासं त्रिविधं प्रोक्तं भित्तौ च फलके पटे ॥
फलके च पटे चैव विशेषं कथयाम्यहम् ॥
मण्डपं पूर्ववत् कृत्वा वेदिं कुर्यात्तु पूर्ववत् ।
कृत्वा सुलोचने दिव्ये शयने संनिवेशयेत् ॥
जलाधिवासनं चैव नेष्यते स्नपनं बुधैः ।
मूर्तिहोमं ततः कृत्वा दिशाहोमविवर्जितम् ॥

VSam XVII.14; 18cd–20

I would relate the installation rites of the *ardhacitra* and the *citrābhāsa* representations. The *ābhāsa* is said to be of three kinds being on a wall, a wooden (or stone) board or on a piece of cloth. The specifications with respect to the board and the cloth paintings are being told by me (now). Having prepared the pavilion as before, he should make the altar as formerly enjoined. Having done this, O beautiful-eyed one, he should make the depiction lie on a couch worthy of a divinity. However, in this case no ritual of consecration under water nor the ritual of bathing is desired to be actually performed by the learned. Then the oblations to be made in fire on behalf of the image are undertaken though without performing fire oblations to the direction-guardians.

One of the main rituals of image-installation is known as the 'eye-opening' ceremony (*akṣimocana, nayanonmīlana*) which includes the final handling of an image by the artist under strict direction of the priests. The eyes (and other limbs) of the deity, hitherto left unrevealed, are fully marked by the priest and accordingly carved in fine by the chief-artist:

ज्योतिर्मण्डलमालिख्य नेत्रमोचनमाचरेत् ।
तथैवोन्मीलनं शिल्पी वज्रकाञ्चनसूचितः ॥
पुष्पायोनिर्मितेनैव टङ्केनैव त्रिलोचने ।
नासिकाकर्णवक्त्राणि लिङ्गं पायुं च मोचयेत् ॥
तत्तद्देवाङ्गभूतानां नयनोन्मीलनं नयेत् ।
चित्राभासादि देवानां तत्तद्वर्णैस्समाचरेत् ॥

KāmĀ LXVIII.37–39

Having sketched the circle of the gaze (the ritualist) should perform the 'eye-opening', and following him the sculptor carries out the work of 'opening' (or finishing up). For the three-eyed god, also such parts as the nose, ears, mouth, phallus and rectum what have been marked (first by the priest) with a diamond or gold needle, (the artist) should render free by using his chisel, made of brass or iron, and carry out the act of eye-opening for each of these limbs of the god. However, in case of deity's representations that are in painted or pictorial medium (*citra, ābhāsa*) or the like, he should perform this ceremony using proper colours for each of these limbs.

It seems further alluded to that a painting may not be normally consecrated as the principal deity-figure in the sanctum of a public temple although a painting may be worshipped in the household ritual by an individual.

For a temple-banner of Vaiṣṇava shrine painted with the Garuḍa figure, the consecration enjoined in the **Viṣvaksena Saṃhitā** is as follows:

चित्राभासप्रतिष्ठां तु कारयेन्मन्त्रवित्तमः ।
छायाधिवासनं कुर्यात् जलं संहृत्य देशिकः ॥

VSam XXVI.47

The *pratiṣṭhā* of even such a *citrābhāsa* should be performed, duly with the ritual of preliminary consecration in water (*adhivāsana*) to be done in this case only through the proxy of its 'shadow' in the water collected for the purpose; the same being called '*chāyādhivāsana*', shadow consecration.

Details of the procedure can be found enumerated elsewhere for main images of the god and his consort (VSam XXVIII.52–57), while it is specifically enjoined that the *jalādhivāsa* of a painted representation and the like must be done on the 'image' (*bera*) placed or reflected on a mirror (*darpaṇa samsthite bere citrādīnāṃ viśeṣataḥ* – VSam XXVIII.55). There is another directive given as an alternative that for painted or clay icons the ritual of its 'water-stay' (*jalādhivāsana*) may be dispensed with (VSam XVII.20).

Likewise, we may remark, as indicated in the above passage just cited, a significant aspect regarding the tradition of ritual 'bathing' of painted deity-figures, whether in a temple cult or in a domestic shrine, or for individual's daily worship, which is not done directly by pouring water on the cult-object but rather through the agency of a reflected image or some symbolical representation, such as a pot, or *kūrca* (bunch of *kuśa*).

Sometimes a text appears categorically prohibiting worship of a painted or *ābhāsa* figure:

आभासमधमं प्रोक्तमाभासे तु न चार्चयेत् ।

दानहोमजपेष्वेव भावनार्थमिदं स्मृतम् ॥

Samu XVIII.14

Ābhāsa is the lowest kind of representation, and one should not worship that one. For it is regarded to be of use only in case of gift, *homa* (oblation) and *japa*.

But in a special case the very same authority may be found ordaining its worship.

The *ābhāsa* or pictorial representation of the Lord as Viśvarūpa is described to be of the last or lowest type of images, while the best one is carved in the round and the middling one is in half-carving or relief-work (*ardhacitra*):

मध्यमा विश्वमूर्तिः स्यात् जघन्यामपि संशृणु ॥
आभासेनैव कुड्यस्था देव्यौ पूजासने स्थिते ।
चतुर्भिर्बाहुभिर्युक्तः वासुदेवश्च शाश्वतः ॥
मुख्याभ्यां धारयन् सव्यदक्षिणाभ्यां गदाम्बुजे ।
ऊर्ध्वाभ्यामितराभ्यां तु शङ्खचक्रे यथातथम् ॥
अथवा दक्षिणो हस्तो वरदोऽभयदोऽपि वा ।
गदां विना वामहस्तः कटिदेशावलम्बितः ॥
द्विभुजो वा बहुभुजो युक्तोऽनेकैस्तथाननैः ।
एकेन वा सितो वर्णो वासुदेवस्सनातनः ॥

PSam kp XVI.24cd–28

(As described above) it should be the middling type of Viśvarūpa image. Now listen about the lowest type (of the same). It is in painted representation done on the wall, with the two goddesses poised on worshipful seat (on either side). He is the eternal god Vāsudeva, endowed with four arms, carrying in the main left and right (hands) a mace and a lotus and in the upper two hands a conch and a discus in proper order. Else, the (main) right hand may be held in the *varada* or the *abhaya* attitude. The left hand being without the mace may be placed akimbo. He may be two-armed or many-armed, have many faces or only one head. He is (thus) in the form of eternal god Vāsudeva, of white complexion.

It is quite remarkable to see the term *ābhāsa* as denoting a concept related to specific class of temple constructions based on the relative series of dimensions, taken as model by the practising architects. In temple constructions there are four relative series of model dimensions (breadth and height) which have been detailed by certain Vāstu treatises belonging to the south Indian tradition. *Ābhāsa* as such represents the last group of model-dimensions in the fourfold division as made for the types of *prāsādas*, viz.: (i) *jāti*, (ii) *chanda*, (iii) *vikalpa*, and (iv) *ābhāsa*.

A standard ratio to be maintained between the width and the height of a temple is 7:10; and thus the most ambitious dimension suggested to be normally practicable for the smaller temples below *tritala* (=three storeyed) and from eleven *hasta*-units are given largely to be imagined as per one's own discretion and means. But, the first series of the *jāti vimānas* from the above-stated three conditions can further be calculated by reducing two-digits (*dvi-kara*) with respect to each *tala* (=storey). With these figures there are suggested from 3 *talas* to 12 *talas* some sixty types based on even and odd numbers of measure=units, reduced at each stage by 2 units, both having three types, namely *uttama, madhyama* and *adhama* in each number group. The scheme may be put as under:

11–13–15–17 ... 65–67–69/ - 30 in all

12–14–16–18 ... 66–68–70/ - 30 in all

In each class, *madhyama* is less by 2 digits and *adhama* is further less by 2 digits or units; if *uttama* is 15 units, then *madhyama* is 13 units, and *adhama* is 11 units.

The odd number pair of units going together with the height and the width ratio units is 99:69; and with the even number pair is 100:70.

Likewise, along the self same consideration of the *jāti vimānas,* there are enumerated the *chandas vimāna* series, having 54 varieties; *vikalpa vimāna*-series having 48 varieties; and lastly, the *ābhāsa vimāna*-series of 38 varieties belonging, as specified, to the temple-buildings in the three latter series – from the *catustala* to *dvādaśatala*.

Thus, the *ābhāsa prāsāda* of 38 kinds would be found to have the following series of 4 *tala* to 12 *tala vimānas*; i.e. 9 groups from the *tala* (or storey) consideration. But, as it is stated in the texts, only the last group of 12-storeys can have the best, the middling and the lowest varieties; the eight preceding groups have only the *adhama* kind and the *uttama* kind of measurements. We get an excellent summary of the entire theory of the *jāti* etc. *vimānas* in the **Tantrasamuccaya** of Nārāyaṇa and so exhaustively studied and exposed by N.V. Mallayya in his work (*Studies in Sanskrit Texts on Temple Architecture: with special reference to Tantrasamuccaya*, pp. 67, 302–314).

On the *chanda, vikalpa* and the *ābhāsa* kinds of temples the above treatise says:

The courts for *Ābhāsa* and *Vikalpa* may likewise be drawn with the absolute measurement given in the text. The height of a court wall should extend up to the neck of the main edifice or otherwise if specified.

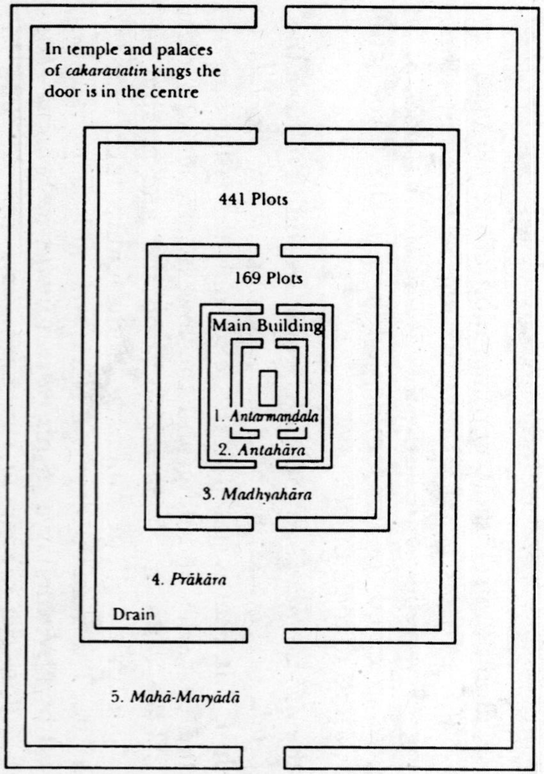

Courts for *Jāti* buildings

The number of the courts may even be seven in very large buildings such as palaces (Mānasāra Chap XI.), but the text does not give any description here.

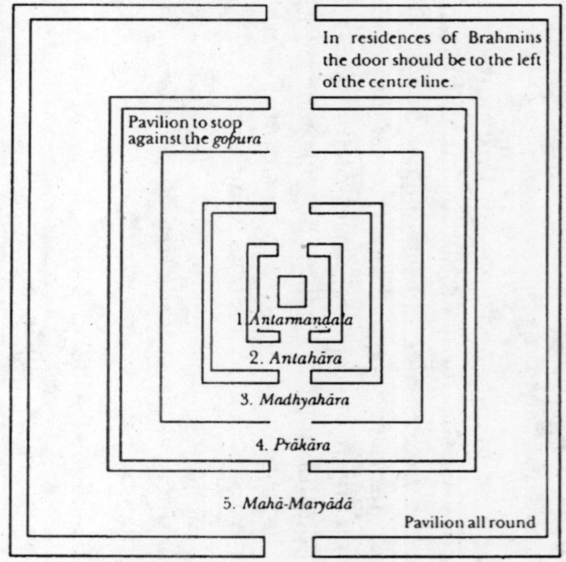

Courts for *Chanda* buildings

The courts for *jāti* has been drawn with rectangular units and those for *chanda* with square units.

Figure 2: Ground Plan of Ābhāsa Prāsāda

विश्वेन्द्राद्येषुषट्षष्ट्यसमसमकरैरब्धिभौमादयः स्यु-
श्छन्दा हस्तैर्नवाशादिभिरिषुरसपञ्चाशदन्तैर्विकल्पाः ।
पञ्चक्ष्माद्याश्च सर्वे प्रतितलमृतुभिन्ना विवस्वत्तलान्ता
रुद्राद्येकोनतानावधिभिरुदधिभूम्याद्यथाभाससंज्ञाः ॥
आभासेऽत्र चतुस्तलादिशिवभूम्यन्तं पृथग् वेदभे-
दाढ्यं द्वादशमन्तिमं द्व्यधममध्यादिक्रमात् षड्भिदम् ।
षष्टिर्जातिगृहे भिदाः करवशाच्छन्दे षडूनास्ततः
षट्कोनाश्च विकल्पधामनि तथाभासे दशोनास्ततः ॥

TSamu II.63–64

Beginning with the odd and even measures of thirteen and fourteen and ending with sixty-five and sixty-six cubits respectively, the temples of four *tala*s etc. form the '*chanda-prāsādas*'; beginning with (the odd and even measures of) nine and ten cubits and ending with fifty-five and fifty-six, *prāsādas* with five *tala*s, etc. constitute the '*vikalpa*' class. All these, ending with twelve *tala*s, in each instance of *tala* admit of a classification into six different kinds. Now, those which have odd and even measures beginning with eleven and twelve and ending with forty-seven and forty-eight cubits, and which have four *tala*s etc. are known as *ābhāsa*.

Here, in the '*ābhāsa*' class which has *tala*s beginning with four and ending with eleven, each case will have four varieties; the last case, which has twelve *tala*s, will have six varieties by reason of the order of '*adhama*' '*madhyama*' and '*uttama*' for both (odd and even types of its measure). Thus, from the point of view of (the different types of) cubit measures, in the '*jāti prāsāda*' there are sixty different kinds, in the '*chandas*' six less (i.e. fifty four), in the '*vikalpa*' six more less (i.e. forty-eight) and in the '*ābhāsa*' still ten less (i.e. thirty-eight). (Tr. N.V. Mallayya)

The **Īśānaśivagurudeva Paddhati** provides the further elaboration:

एकादशकरात् सप्तचत्वारिंशत्करातते: ।
द्विहस्तवर्धनात्प्राग्वदूनविंशतिसंख्यया ॥
चतुर्भौमाद्यार्कभौमादाभासाख्यानि तानि वै ।

ĪśGP III.2.30. 17–18ab

Beginning with eleven *hasta*-units and extending up as increasing two *hasta*-units at each next stage, thus ending with forty-seven units, they are as seen in the above demonstration, nineteen varieties in total specification of the numbers. They are applicable in

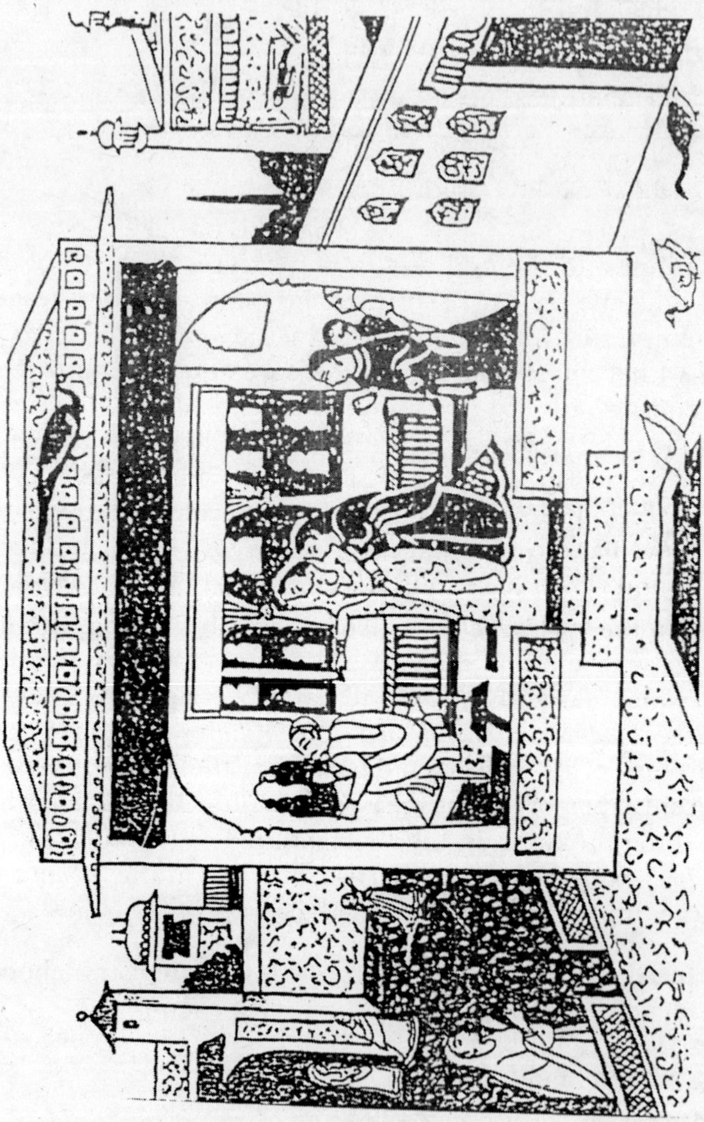

Figure 3: Ābhāsa Prāsāda

case of the shrine types called *ābhāsa* with reference to their having 'storey' (*bhūmi* or *tala*) specification ranging from four up to eleven storeys.

The details of various *ābhāsa* types of buildings are recorded in the **Aṃśumatkāśyapa**, an important and rare text which is yet to be published.

त्रिचतुर्हस्तमारभ्य द्विद्विहस्तविवर्धनात् ।
नवपङ्क्तिकरान्तं तु आभासैकतलं भवेत् ।।
एवमष्टविधं मानं युग्मायुग्मं चतुश्चतुः ।
पञ्चषड्ढस्तमारभ्य द्विद्विहस्तविवर्धनात् ।।
रुद्रभानुकरान्तं तु आभासद्वितलेऽष्टधा ।
सप्ताष्टहस्तमारभ्य द्विद्विहस्तविवर्धनात् ।।
तिथिकलाकरान्तं तु आभासत्रितले दश ।
ग्रहकर्म समारभ्य सप्ताष्टाधिकपङ्क्तयः ।।
चतुष्पञ्चतलं वाथ युग्मायुग्माश्च ते दश ।
विस्तारं सप्तषट्पञ्चभागं कृत्वा द्विजोत्तम ।।
रसभूतयुगांशं तु विस्ताराद्रोपयेत्क्रमात् ।
विस्तारद्विगुणं चैव तस्मादष्टांशमाधिकम् ।
पञ्चधाभ्युदितं तुङ्गमाभासे सदने द्विज ।
शान्तिकं पौष्टिकं चैव जयदं चाद्भुतं तथा ।।
सार्वकामिकमित्येतदभिधानं क्रमाद्भवेत् ।
हस्तैरेतैस्तु वृद्ध्या वा हान्या वा पूर्णमाचरेत् ।।
आभासं हर्म्यमाख्यातम् .... ।

Aṃśumatkāśyapa XXII.37ab–58a

Beginning with the three and four *hasta*-units and adding at each stage two *hasta*-units ending up in nine and ten *hasta*-units there are (obtained the standard width measurements) for the one-storeyed (*ekatala*) *ābhāsa* building. Thus, there are eight standard *mānas*, four each with respect to even and odd number series.

The two-storeyed (*dvitala*) *ābhāsa* building is likewise of eight types, as beginning with the five and six *hasta*-units going up to eleven and twelve digits respectively by increasing two-units at successive stages. There are ten varieties of a three-storeyed (*tritala*) *ābhāsa* building similarly beginning with the seven and eight *hasta*-units and going up to fifteen and sixteen digits respectively. Beginning with the nine and ten *hasta*-units and likewise going (by adding two digits at each stage) up to seventeen and eighteen digits are obtained the four-storeyed or five-storeyed (*catustala* and *pañcatala*) *ābhāsa* shrines of ten varieties with respect to even and odd number-series.

For an *ābhāsa*-type abode, there are five modes of the height stated (to be arrived at alternatively) as having divided the width into seven, six or five equal parts, and O twice-born, adding to that (select) width six, five or four parts (of its own measure) respectively; or by taking the width twice as much (for the height); or by taking twice the width increased by adding its one-eighth part. They are in sequence (to be employed) for the purpose of raising the abodes in case of *śāntika, pauṣṭika, jayada, adbhuta* and *sārvakāmika* rituals. This *hasta*-unit ratio can be (sometimes) modified (a bit) by increasing or decreasing, or (normally) used in full application. It is the *ābhāsa* type of building, thus, described.

Some of the significant observations, found in the **Mayamata**, an early Dravidian treatise of architecture, may also be noticed here further:

.... आभासं तद्विमिश्रितम् ।
क्षुद्राल्पमध्यमोत्कृष्टं हर्म्याणामेवमीरितम् ॥

Mayam XXII.88bcd

The *ābhāsa* mode (of the temple-type) can be identified when these two arrangements are employed together and is suitable for very small buildings, small, medium and large ones. (Tr. B. Dagens)

आभासमष्टहस्तेनाधिक्यं दैर्घ्यमिति स्मृतम् ॥
अष्टभागाधिकं व्यासादाभासं स्यात् तदायतम् ।
षडंशेन विशाले तु नेष्टमाभासदैर्घ्यकम् ॥

Mayam XXVI.69cd, 72

If the length is eight cubits (more than the width), it is *ābhāsa* (the length of house may be calculated in another way).

If the length is longer than eight (cubits than the width) goes by the name *ābhāsa*. When the width is six units (or less), *ābhāsa* mode is not to be used. (Based on the tr. by B. Dagens)

There are also the rules given for constructing *ābhāsa* kind of pavilions (*maṇḍapas*):

मण्डपानां तु विस्तारादायामं प्रविधीयते ।
... त्र्यंशकं प्रोक्तमाभासं ... ।

Mayam XXV.170ab, 171ab

The method for calculating the length of pavilions from their width is now indicated.

... in the *ābhāsa* three (unit more than the width should be used). (Tr. B. Dagens)

एकैकभागवृद्ध्या तु भवत्युक्तेतरा सभा ।
छन्दं विकल्पमाभासं तत्तन्नाम्ना विधीयते ॥

Mayam XXV.228

Other varieties of halls are arrived at by adding one unit each time (to the above given dimensions) and are called accordingly *chanda, vikalpa* and *ābhāsa.* (Tr. B. Dagens)

Yet again, there is an *ābhāsa* variety of a house mentioned in this work:

अधिष्ठानादिवर्गाढ्यं प्रासादवदलङ्कृतम् ।
नासिकातोरणाद्यङ्गैर्युक्तं वातायनादिभि: ॥
चतुर्मुखमिदं नाम्ना आभासमिति कल्पितम् ।

Mayam XXVI.42–43ab

This house has levels of elevation, the first being the base; it is disposed like a temple and has false dormer windows, arcatures and other similar elements as well as windows etc. .... It is called *caturmukha* and is in *ābhāsa* mode. (Tr. B. Dagens)

Conclusion

The evolving nature of the notion of *ābhāsa* is to be further seen as occurring in a varied contexts of its usage with respect to the concept of glowing light, shining principle, divine manifestation, and reflection even the semblance of a Reality. It came further to denote a 'fallacy' and a reflection in logic, *māyā* in Vedānta and as manifestation of the Absolute on a lower order of the creation (*ābhāsavāda*) in Kashmir Śaivism. It came also to be used as a compound word, *citrābhāsa* signifying painting in South Indian Āgama and Śilpa texts. In a classification of the temple superstructures in the South specifically, there is a type of *ābhāsa vimāna* as well as *ābhāsa maṇḍapas.*

Prithvi Kumar Agrawala

Select Bibliography

Bhattacharya H.C.: Kālasiddhāntadarśinī, Varanasi: Sampurnananda Sanskrit University, 1984.

Chatterjee, J.C.: Kashmir Shaivism, Srinagar: Research & Publication Department, Jammu & Kashmir Govt., 1914, reprint, 1962.

Dasgupta, Surendranath: A History of Indian Philosophy, Vol. V, 1922, reprint, Delhi: Motilal Banarsidass, 1997.

Mahadevan, T.M.P.: Pañcadaśī, Madras: Madras University, 1975.

— "Śaivism", in The Age of Imperial Kanauj, edited by R. C. Majumdar & A. D. Pusalker, Bombay: Bharatiya Vidya Bhavan, 1955.

Mallayya, N.V.: Studies in Sanskrit Texts on Temple Architecture: with special reference to Tantrasamuccaya, Calicut, Kerala, 1949.

Pandey, K.C.: History of Philosophy: Eastern and Western, Vol. I, London: George Allen & Unwin Ltd, 1952.

Radhakrishnan, S.: Indian Philosophy, London: George Allen & Unwin Ltd, 1923–27.

SĀDṚŚYA-SĀRŪPYA

Overview

The concept of *sādṛśya* (n.) convisibility, a word coined by A.K. Coomaraswamy is one of the most significant projections of typically Indian world-view. Seeing two things seemingly variant in both form and nature together, with the discerning eye is a feature which fits in the things with the hypothesis that there is not a single thing which is not related to the other. Convisibility is a very special relationship through which similarity is marked out between non-identical phenomena. This relationship is an evidence of a well designed interrelated scheme of the Universe where equilibrium is ensured through harmonious dynamism. In other words, it presupposes that while establishing such a relationship one looks at diversity and unity simultaneously and is taken by the striking property shared by the both. This looking at things has a bearing on man's perception of his environment. Both the philosophical and the creative perceptions of life reject uniformity. A lotus in art, especially in sculpture, is a replica which is supposed to create an illusion of a real lotus. And though the lotus in art creates an illusion, success of the artist depends on the verisimilitude of the replica with the original. Then only it can be placed in juxtaposition with the lotus.

Sādṛśya or convisibility has been accepted especially in Sanskrit Aesthetics as a similarity of quality (*guṇa*) and function (*kriyā*) between two separate things. For example, when it is said 'this man is a lion' it does not mean that the man is a four footed animal but means only that the man is endowed with the prowess of the lion. Physical similarity is not demanded in *sādṛśya*. Technically the basis of *sādṛśya* is noted as the common property (*sādhāraṇa dharma*), persisting between two separate things.

In the philosophical context, the concept of *sālokya, sāyujya, sāmīpya* and *sārṣṭi* may be taken to reflect the idea of *sādṛśya.*

Etymology and Related Terms

The word *sādṛśya* is etymologically explained as an abstract noun signifying the property of being *sadṛśa. Sadṛśa,* in turn, is that which looks alike (*sama* + *dṛś-*). In other words, it may be explained as: one considering at the same time a beautiful face and a beautiful full moon and is thereby delighted by the common property of both of them, i.e. pleasingness or charm. In almost all the figures of speech based on some sort of similitude, the perception of an abstract unity in two things, concrete or abstract, is therefore *sādṛśya.* The verbal root *dṛś-* by extension means not only visual perception but all perceptions by other senses as well as by the mind itself, mind being included in the category of senses. Even in a figure of speech like *rūpaka,* where one thing is superimposed on the other, identity is not the intended meaning, because, superimposition is not identity. Even, the explicit nullification of the superimposed is not intended to give a sense of identity. When one says that 'he is a lion', both the superimposed and the superimposition are brought together or perceived. The superimposition is intended to enhance the degree of similitude. Similarly, when one remarks of a person, "look here, a lion is there", the three things are still separate in the mind. The person who is referred to as a lion, the superimposition, i.e. a lion as well as the property of physical strength and undauntedness, common to both. This way of expression is intended to focus on the intensity of that property in a particular person.

Layers of Meaning

The concept *sārūpya,* i.e. taking of the same form is different from the concept of convisibility. The difference between *sādṛśya* and *sārūpya,* convisibility and uniformity, is quite obvious. While convisibility is a very important aspect in aesthetic perception, the uniformity is more notional oneness.

There is another word *sama* or *samāna* which is bracketed together with *sādṛśya.* Mostly *sama* is taken to mean equal while it means in reality just being coexistent and by implication in harmony with the other. Therefore *samadṛṣṭi* is not egalitarianism, but is harmony. This fits in well with definition of *yoga* in the **Bhagavad-Gītā** (II.48d): '*samatvaṃ yoga ucyate*' – communion is harmony. It is not just yoking of mind to something unrelated or without purpose. It is the yoking to something which connects both in a harmonious relationship. It is not an assimilation of two things, nor is it coalescence of two things, rather it is a search for the running thread which joins them together.

The concept denotes five layers: (1) likeness, (2) resemblance, (3) similarity, (4) portrait, and (5) image.

The earliest Lexicon **Nirukta** has defined these terms as follows:

अथात उपमाः । यदतत्तत्सदृशमिति गार्ग्यः । तदासां कर्म । ज्यायसा वा गुणेन प्रख्याततमेन वा कनीयांसं वाप्रख्यातं वोपमिमीते । अथापि कनीयसा ज्यायांसम् ॥

Nir III.13

Now, therefore, the similes. When an object bears (some) resemblance to another which is otherwise dissimilar, (it is denoted by a simile), says Gārgya. With reference to this, their function is to compare an inferior quality, or an unknown object, with a higher quality, or a very well known object. Further, (there is also the comparison of) the higher with the inferior. (Tr. L. Sarup)

अनु इति सादृश्यापरभावम् ।

Nir I.3

The word *anu* (a preposition) is used in the sense of 'similarity' and 'succession'. (Tr. L. Sarup)

In the **Vaijayantī Kośa** and **Medinī Kośa** (CVI.6) the meaning of *sādṛśya* is as follows: the indication of *sannibha* and *nibha*:

... सादृश्ये सन्निभं निभम् ॥

VaiKo III.9.21d

Sannibha and *nibha*, these two terms are used to mean similarity (*sādṛśya*). (Tr. P. Ghosal)

Development of the Concept

The different uses of these words may be given in a chronological order. Perception of analogous frames in the cosmic phenomenon is an oft-repeated theme in the Saṃhitā literature. Something perceived outside is visualized in the likeness of something conceived within and a look established between what is out and what is within, is always of the nature of similitude (*sādṛśya*). In passages after passages the external and internal perceptions are brought together through the process of convisibility. Likeness is also perceived as a thread of continuous cognition of a phenomenon which is changing and yet which is the same. For example, in the passage below Varuṇa's eternity is a continuous cognition of likeness:

सदृशीरद्य सदृशीरिदु श्वो दीर्घं सचन्ते वरुणस्य धाम ।
अनवद्यास्त्रिंशतं योजनान्येकैका क्रतुं परि यन्ति सद्यः ॥

ṚV I.123.8

The same in form today, the same tomorrow, they still keep
Varuṇa's eternal statute.
Blameless, in turn they traverse thirty regions,
and dart across the spirit in a moment. (Tr. R.T.H. Griffith)

Similarly, the ever-fresh splendour of the Dawn is perceived as the same ancient one and yet newly observed unique one:

क्व स्विदासां कतमा पुराणी यया विधाना विदधुर्ऋभूणाम् ।
शुभं यच्छुभ्रा उषसश्चरन्ति न वि ज्ञायन्ते सदृशीरजुर्याः ॥

ṚV IV.51.6

Which among these is eldest, and where is she through whom they fixed the Ṛbhus' regulations?

What time the splendid Dawns go forth for splendour, they are not known apart, alike, unwasting. (Tr. R.T.H. Griffith)

Vedic world-view distinguishes between uniformity and sameness and always emphasizes on the sameness aspect, rather on the unchanging uniformity. Agni (the presiding deity over the fire element) is perceived in different shapes as the same. It is not the uniform splendour for fire, it is the multimorphous aspect of fire which is recognised as same in all its aspects:

पुरुत्रा हि सदृङ्ङसि विशो विश्वा अनु प्रभुः ।
समत्सु त्वा हवामहे ॥

ṚV VIII.11.8

Thou art the same in many a place: mid all the people thou art Lord.

In fray and fight we call on thee. (Tr. R.T.H. Griffith)

ईदृङ् चान्यादृङ् च सदृङ् च प्रतिसदृङ् च ।
मितश्च सम्मितश्च सभराः ॥

YV XVII.81

(O Agni!) Such, other-looking, equal, similar, measured, commensurate, jointly-bearing up (be present today in our sacrifice). (Tr. R.T.H. Griffith)

A similar convisibility is visualized in different Maruts, deities presiding over different courses and speeds of the wind.

ईदृक्षास एतादृक्षास ऊ षु णः सदृक्षासः प्रतिसदृक्षास एतन ।
मितासश्च सम्मितासो नो अद्य सभरसो मरुतो यज्ञे अस्मिन् ॥

YV XVII.84

Today in this our sacrifice be present, such,

Looking-thus, same, similar in appearance.

Measured, commensurate, joint-bearers, Maruts !
(Tr. R.T.H. Griffith)

In fact, the entire divine phenomena is multi-form and yet every form shares the quality of earned merit and the inherent desire to be held in respect of likeness to Agni, Indra and Sūrya – the deities of the earth, the mid-region and the heaven.

> सर्वे ह वै देवा अग्रे सदृशा आसुः – सर्वे पुण्याः । तेषां सर्वेषां सदृशानां सर्वेषां पुण्यानां त्रयोऽकामयन्त 'अतिष्ठावानः स्याम' इति- अग्निः इन्द्रः सूर्यः ॥
>
> ŚBr IV.5.4.1
>
> Now, at first the gods were all alike, all good. Of them, being all alike, all good, three desired, 'May we be superior!' – Agni, Indra and Sūrya. (Tr. J. Eggeling)

Like other gods Indra is co-sharer of offering as follows:

> इन्द्रो वै सदृङ् देवताभिरासीत् स न व्यावृतमगच्छत् स प्रजापतिमुपाधावत् तस्मा एतमैन्द्रमेकादशकपालं निरवपत् तेनैवास्मिन्निन्द्रियमदधात् ... ॥
>
> TSam II.2.8.5
>
> Indra was equal with the gods, he did not attain distinction, he had recourse to Prajāpati, for him he offered this (offering) to Indra on eleven potsherds, and thereby he bestowed power upon him. (Tr. A.B. Keith)

It should be noted that this co-sharing property is not an indication of equality as comprehended in totality, equality is not the intended meaning. An inherent harmonious sharing is the intended meaning. Indra is placed at the head, it is just with the purpose of picking out one to ensure proper distribution and not to be overlord. This view is in consonance with the origin of kingship in the Indian political thought. King is just a corporate body having different parts, none of them being less important than the other. Not hierarchy but the interdependence is the basis of categorization. When we extend the significance of this view to the phenomena of creative activity, every activity has its own place, neither less nor more important. And each one of them is independent of the other. Such a harmony can be maintained only by sharing on the basis of every sharer being a part of a whole and not being equal.

In one of the passages even the demons have been perceived like the gods in as much as they are progenies of the same creator and they are products of their own earned merits. There is neither any perception of equality between them nor inequality. They are not mutually exclusive and opposites. This only emphasizes the anti-dichotomic Vedic position rather more clearly the wholeness of the Vedic view point.

देवाश्चासुराश्चोभये प्राजापत्याः प्रजापतेः पितुर्दायमुपेयुः - वाचमेव सत्यानृते । सत्यं चैवानृतं च । त उभय एव सत्यमवदन्, उभयेऽनृतम् । ते ह सदृशं वदन्तः सदृशा एवासुः ॥

ŚBr IX.5.1.12

The gods and the *asuras*, both of them sprung from Prajāpati, entered upon their father Prajāpati's inheritance, to wit, speech – truth and untruth, both truth and untruth: they, both of them, spake the truth, and they both spake untruth; and, indeed speaking alike, they were alike. (Tr. J. Eggeling)

The parts have their own roles but they will remain parts of one whole. So they have to be realised in relationship with the whole. Sharing of common properties in certain respects brings them together but it is their attitude towards the whole which make them different. This is well brought out by an epical metaphor of the Universal Being, Virāṭ visualized in the likeness of a Person, where *dharma* (good) is viewed as the chest of the Person and *adharma* (evil) as the back (BhāgPur II.6.8cd).

This metaphor, when understood properly, is intended to point out that when you do something with your attention centred on the wholeness of things, is good; and the same thing which is performed irrespective of the whole, is evil. In any case, evil is not antonym of good. It is rather a wrong turning of something which can be good. This explains as to why the total life is depicted in full vividity in all arts and all rituals.

In Epic and Puranic literature, we find a set of ideas for comparison. For example, they are oft-repeated in Puranic as well as classical literatures:

विष्णुना सदृशो वीर्ये सोमवत्प्रियदर्शनः ।
कालाग्निसदृशः क्रोधे क्षमया पृथिवीसमः ॥
धनदेन समस्त्यागे सत्ये धर्म इवापरः ।

Rām I.1.18–19ab

The peer of Viṣṇu's power and might,
And lovely as the Lord of Night:
Patient as Earth, but, roused ire,
Fierce as the world-destroying fire;
In bounty like the Lord of Gold,
And justice self in human mould. (Tr. R.T.H. Griffith)

In a passage of the **Mahābhārata**, *sādṛśya* denotes the meaning of almost equal. In other words, it is not only a word of comparison but also measuring status:

तस्मात् प्रहेष्याम्यद्य त्वां हीनः प्रजननात् स्वयम् ।
सदृशाच्छ्रेयसो वा त्वं विद्ध्यपत्यं यशस्विनि ॥

MBh I.111.32

O glorious lady! because I myself have become unable to procreate, therefore am requesting you to conceive a son from some one equal (to our status and race) or superior to us. (Tr. P. Ghosal)

इदं ज्ञानमुपाश्रित्य मम साधर्म्यमागताः ।
सर्गेऽपि नोपजायन्ते प्रलये न व्यथन्ति च ॥

BhG XIV.2

With this wisdom as their bulwark they reached a rank (in the order of existence) equivalent to my own, and even when (the universe is once again) engendered, they are not born (again) and when (again) it is dissolved, they know no trepidation.
(Tr. R.C. Zaehner)

आढ्योऽभिजनवानस्मि कोऽन्योऽस्ति सदृशो मया ।
यक्ष्ये दास्यामि मोदिष्य इत्यज्ञानविमोहिताः ॥

BhG XVI.15

I am rich and well-born. Who else is equal to me? I will sacrifice, I will give, I will rejoice. Thus deluded by unwisdom.
(Tr. A. Mahadeva Sastry)

न हि ज्ञानेन सदृशं पवित्रमिह विद्यते ।
तत्स्वयं योगसंसिद्धः कालेनात्मनि विन्दति ॥

BhG IV.38

Verily, there exists here no purifier equal to wisdom. He who is perfected by *yoga* finds it in time in himself by himself.
(Tr. A. Mahadeva Sastry)

In other passages, *sādṛśya* means befitting as in the following:

साधु साधु महाबाहो वत्स चित्राङ्गदात्मज ।
सदृशं कर्म ते दृष्ट्वा प्रीतिमानस्मि पुत्रक ॥

MBh XIV.78.25

Well done, O strong armed! dear son of Citrāṅgadā! I have been immensely pleased to see your feats (which is) befitting you.
(Tr. P. Ghosal)

कुले जातस्य वीरस्य क्षत्रियस्य विशेषतः ।
सदृशं मरणं ह्येतत्तव पुत्रस्य मा शुचः ॥

MBh VII.54.13

Such a heroic death is befitting for a valiant person, specially born of a noble Kṣatriya family. Therefore, don't mourn for your son's death. (Tr. P. Ghosal)

The passages after passages use *sādṛśya* in the sense of similar. A few are given below:

मरीचिरत्र्यङ्गिरसौ पुलस्त्यः पुलहः क्रतुः ।
वसिष्ठश्च महाभागः सदृशा वै स्वयंभुवा ॥

MBh XII.201.4

(The seven sons of Svayambhū Brahmā) Marīci, Atri, Aṅgirā, Pulastya, Pulaha, Kratu and revered Vasiṣṭha – were similar to the self born (*svayambhū*). (Tr. P. Ghosal)

In the Purāṇa literature, *sādṛśya* and *sārūpya* have connotations other than similarity and identity. *Sādṛśya* and *sārūpya* are two stages of achievement, *sādṛśya* being the lower ladder because *sārūpya* indicates full control of the cosmos as of the worship of deity while *sādṛśya* is merely some likeness:

तदा तु शिवसायुज्यमायुधाद्यैः क्रियादिभिः ।
महाप्रसादलाभे च बुद्धिश्चापि वशा भवेत् ॥

ŚPur I.18.20

Then he attains similarity with Śiva by means of weapons and activities. This is called *sāyujya.* When the devotee acquires the great favour, the cosmic intellect too comes under control.
(Tr. J.L. Shastri)

कायव्यूहं ततः कृत्वा भोजयित्वा स्वकर्मकम् ॥
तस्मै ददामि सारूप्यं करोमि तं च पार्षदम् ।

DBhāgPur IX.11.58cd–59ab

I get many bodies for him where he can enjoy the fruits of his *karma* and then I give him My *sārūpya* (form resembling mine) and make him My attendant. (Tr. Vijnanananda)

अन्यत्र वा त्यजेत् प्राणांस्त्वन्नामस्मृतिपूर्वकम् ॥
तस्मै ददामि सारूप्यमसंख्यं प्राकृतं लयम् ।

DBhāgPur IX.11.61cd–62ab

And if he remembers Thee with devotion, and quits his mortal coil at another place, I give him *sārūpya* (form resembling mine) for a period of endless *prākṛtika layas.* (Tr. Vijnanananda)

In other passages, the words, e.g. *saṅkāśa, sannibha* (the synonyms of *sadṛśa*), occur to denote simile as in:

विचित्रविविधाकल्पा कम्बुसंकाशकन्धरा ।

DBhāgPur XII.12.23ab

Her neck is shining like a conchshell decorated with artistic designs. (Tr. Vijnanananda)

जलबुद्बुद्वत् सर्वं विश्वसङ्घमनित्यकम् ॥

DBhāgPur IX.3.15cd

All are temporary like bubbles of water. (Tr. Vijnanananda)

शुद्धसत्त्वस्वरूपा च सुशीला श्रीहरिप्रिया ।
हिमचन्दनकुन्देन्दुकुमुदाम्भोजसन्निभा ॥

DBhāgPur IX.1.34

Her (of the Great Devī) nature is purely *sāttvika* (*śuddha sattva*); modest and very loving to Śrī Hari. Her colour is white like ice-clad mountains, like that of the white sandal, like that of the Kunda flower, like that of the moon, or white lotus. (Tr. Vijnanananda)

दृष्ट्वा तु देवि कुपितं भृकुटीकरालमुद्यच्छशाङ्क सदृशच्छबि यन्न सद्यः ।
प्राणान् मुमोच महिषस्तदतीव चित्रं कैर्जीव्यते हि कुपितान्तकदर्शनेन ॥

MārkPur LXXXI.13

But after seeing thy wrathful face,
O goddess, terrible with its frowns,
And sheeny in hue like the rising moon, that Mahiṣa
Did not forthwith yield up his life,
It was passing wonderful!
For who can live after beholding the
King of death enraged? (Tr. F.E. Pargiter)

मिथुनानि प्रसूयन्ते समकालस्थितानि वै ।
अन्योन्यमनुरक्तानि चक्रवाकोपमानि च ॥

MārkPur LVI.21

They (mankind) are born in pairs; the pairs abide an equal time, and are as fond of each other as Cakravākas. (Tr. F.E. Pargiter)

भ्राजसेऽस्मिन् वनोद्देशे विद्युत् सौदामिनी यथा ।

DBhāgPur VII.4.44ab

In this solitary forest you are shining like a steady lightning. (Tr. Vijnanananda)

The passages which denote the meaning 'equivalent' are also quite a few:

ध्येयालम्बनसंस्थस्य सदृशप्रत्ययस्य च ।
प्रत्ययान्तरनिर्मुक्तः प्रत्ययो ध्यानमुच्यते ॥

AgPur CCCLXXIV.3

If the *pratyaya* (awareness) of a person, who is established in the object of meditation and the flow of whose mental modification relates to the same object, gets uninterrupted by any other awareness then it is called meditation. (Tr. R.S. Bhattacharya)

स्वात्मन्यवस्थितेऽव्यक्ते विकारे प्रतिसंहृते ।
प्रकृतिः पुरुषश्चैव साधर्म्येणावतिष्ठतः ॥

MārkPur XLIII.4

When the imperceptible subsists within itself and when all modification is suspended, Nature and the Soul subsist with sameness of character. (Tr. F.E. Pargiter)

The **Agni Purāṇa** and **Viṣṇudharmottara Purāṇa**, give an aesthetic definition of *sādṛśya* as relevant to works of art and literature. The **Viṣṇudharmottara Purāṇa** (III.42.48) propounds that the entire creation is a sort of metaphor as two things can never be identical in creation, yet they are similar.

The **Agni Purāṇa** gives a definition relevant to poetics. It further supports the idea that all creation is a similitude.

सादृश्यं धर्मसामान्यमुपमा रूपकं तथा ।
सहोक्त्यर्थान्तरन्यासाविति स्यात्तु चतुर्विधः ॥

AgPur CCCXLIV.5

Sādṛśya occurs where equality of the common property (existing in the *upamāna* and *upameya*) is described. It has four varieties, namely *upamā, rūpaka, sahokti* and *arthāntaranyāsa.*
(Tr. R.S. Bhattacharya)

किञ्चिदादाय सारूप्यं लोकयात्रा प्रवर्त्तते ।

AgPur CCCXLIV.7ab

(Though *upamāna* and *upameya* are two distinct things, yet there lies similarity between them.) On this similarity all worldly behaviour is established. (Tr. R.S. Bhattacharya)

The concept of simile or metaphor, *sādṛśya* and *sārūpya* are further developed in the philosophical systems as follows.

In Buddhist literature, the concept of *sādṛśya* is recorded in different context. The production of thought or mind (*citta*) has twenty-two similes. Sometimes it is compared with a cloud.

मेघसदृशश्च कथितश्चित्तोत्पादो जिनात्मजानां हि ।
तस्मात्तथा गुणाढ्यं चित्तं मुदितैः समुत्पाद्यम् ॥

MSūAl IV.20

The production of thought is said to be like a cloud, or like the followers of the victorious (*jina*). It, therefore, produces joyous thought which is endowed with virtues. (Tr. S.V. Limaye)

To show the unequalled status and the absoluteness of Lord Buddha, the **Vinaya Piṭaka** records the view of Buddha. Lord Buddha advised to his disciples that he has no teacher and no one is like him, i.e. he is the highest teacher and the Absolute one.

न मे आचरियो अत्थि सदिसो मे न विज्जति ।

VinPiṭ I.8

I have no *ācārya* (teacher) and no one similar (equal) to me exists (in this world). (Tr. N.C. Panda)

The term *sādṛśya* is also used in the sense of equal or similar, in the context of solving a problem before Lord Buddha. Two brahmins came to ask Buddha whether one becomes *brāhmaṇa* by birth or by action (*karma*) and one brahmin addressed the blessed one with the following verse where some of the brahmins are compared with the well versed teachers of Vedic recitation.

तेविज्जानं यदक्खातं तत्र केवलिनोऽस्मसे ।
पदकस्मा वेय्याकरणा जपे आचरियसादिसा ॥

SutNip 595

Whatever is proclaimed by those who are versed in the three Vedas, therein we are fully accomplished. We are philologists, grammarians, like our teachers in Vedic recitation.
(Tr. K.R. Norman)

For identification or similarity in the basic nature, the existence of particular difference is unavoidable. It is also noticed even in the identical nature of being knowable entities like *puruṣa* (sensate) and *prakṛti* (insensate). It is reflected in the following verse of the **Bodhicaryāvatāra**.

चेतनाचेतने चैक्यं तयोर्येनास्तिता समा ।
विशेषश्च यदा मिथ्या कः सादृश्याश्रयस्तदा ॥

BoCar IX.68

So also (it would follow from your argument) that the sensate (*puruṣa*) and the insensate (*prakṛti*) would also become one because they are identical (being knowable entities). However, when even the special characteristics of these two *viśeṣas* or particular consciousnesses are *mithyā* or unreal how can they have similarity of basis? (Tr. P.N. Sharma)

The Sāṃkhya system defines similarity as something depending upon dissimilarity and vice-versa. The two similar things must possess a few dissimilar characteristics:

वैरूप्यापेक्षं हि सारूप्यं, सारूप्यापेक्षं च वैरूप्यम् इति ।

YuDīp on SāṃKā 10

Similarity is in relation to dissimilarity and vice-versa.
(Tr. R.S. Bhattacharya)

The **Yuktidīpikā** treats it as a common property (*sāmānya*) not different from the substance:

न हि वः सामान्यं द्रव्यादर्थान्तरभूतमस्ति । सारूप्यमात्रे सामान्यपरिकल्पनात् ।

YuDīp on SāṃKā 15

In your own view, *sāmānya* (generality) is not distinct from the substance, for generality can only be conceived where there is *sārūpya* (similarity). (Tr. R.S. Bhattacharya)

The **Nyāya-Sūtra** defines *sādharmya*, a related term of *sādṛśya*, as sharing of common properties which constitute the concept of the *sādharmya* (having common characteristics) depends upon *sāmānya* (*jāti*):

सामान्यात् साधर्म्यम् ।

NySūBh V.1.34

Sādharmya constitutes the 'similarity' (among things).
(Tr. G.N. Jha)

प्रसिद्धसाधर्म्यात् साध्यसाधनमुपमानम् ॥

NySū I.1.6

Analogy is that which accomplishes its purpose through similarity to a known object. (Tr. G.N. Jha)

सारूप्यं तु सामान्ययोगः ।

NySūBh I.1.3

By 'approximation' here is meant the presence of common properties, i.e. similarity. (Tr. G.N. Jha)

साधर्म्यम् समानधर्मता ।

NySūBh I.1.36

Similarity consists in the presence of the same property in both. (Tr. G.N. Jha)

All these definitions and clarifications have one thing in common that similarity is always between two substances overlapping each other in some respect and in the overlapping part lies the similarity of common properties. The Vaiśeṣika philosophy is almost identical with the Nyāya system, as explained in the relevant passages:

... पदार्थानां साधर्म्यवैधर्म्याभ्यां तत्त्वज्ञानान्निःश्रेयसम् ॥

VaiśSū I.1.4

The Supreme Good (results) from the knowledge of the essence of the predicables by means of their resemblances and differences. (Tr. N.L. Sinha)

द्रव्यगुणयोः सजातीयारम्भकत्वं साधर्म्यम् ॥

VaiśSū I.1.9

The resemblance of substance and attribute is the characteristic of being the originators of their congeners. (Tr. N.L. Sinha)

एवं सर्वत्र साधर्म्यं विपर्ययाद् वैधर्म्यञ्च वाच्यमिति द्रव्यासंकरः ।

VaiśSūBh p. 68

In this way we may describe the similarities of all things, and contrariwise, also their dissimilarities; and thus there would be no intermixture (or confusion) among the various substances. (Tr. G.N. Jha)

Among the neologicians, there are some scholars, who consider *sādṛśya*, as a separate *padārtha* (the category). But Viśvanātha in his auto-commentary on the **Bhāṣāparicchedа** has raised a question on its propriety. In order to refute *sādṛśya* as a separate *padārtha* he has defined it as something which inspite of being different, possesses some common attributes simultaneously.

सादृश्यमपि न पदार्थान्तरं किन्तु तद्भिन्नत्वे सति तद्गत-भूयोधर्मवत्त्वम् ।

Comm. on BhāPari 2

Likewise, similarity also is not a separate category, but it means the possession, by a thing which is different from some other thing, of many of the attributes of the latter. (Tr. Madhavananda)

Viśvanātha further continues that for instance the similarity of a face with the moon consists in its being different from the moon and at the same time possessing the gladdening and other attributes of the latter.

However, in later days Annambhaṭṭa considered this *sādṛśya* as an instrument of *upamāna,* the comparison:

> उपमितिकरणमुपमानम् ... तत्करणं सादृश्यज्ञानम् ।
>
> TarkSaṅg 47
>
> *Upamāna* (the comparison) is instrumental cause of *upamiti* (actual act of comparing). A clear notion of similarity is considered to be the instrument of comparison. (Tr. P. Ghosal)

To sum up, the Nyāya-Vaiśeṣika position, *sādṛśya* (similitude) is a tool of comprehension of things so that distinctiveness of a thing is comprehended along with the partial commonness of properties between them.

As regards Mīmāṃsā system the component of recollection is the concept of similarity. It is borne out by the following passages:

> उपमानमपि सादृश्यम् असन्निकृष्टे अर्थे बुद्धिम् उत्पादयति ।
>
> MīmSūBh I.1.5 (p. 44)
>
> The *pramāṇa* called *upamāna* (analogy) is similarity. It brings about the cognition of a thing which is not in contact with the sense organs. (Tr. R.S. Bhattacharya)

It further adds another component of structural correspondence:

> इकारसादृश्यं च यकारस्य उपलभ्यते, तेनापि तयोः प्रकृतिविकारभावो लक्ष्यते ।
>
> MīmSūBh I.1.10
>
> Similarity of the letter *i* is found in the letter *y*; the relation of cause and effect (*i* – the cause; *y* – the effect) between these two letters is noticed in this way. (Tr. R.S. Bhattacharya)

According to the Mīmāṃsā system, similarity has nothing to determine any ritual or part of ritual as original (*prakṛti*) or imitiation (*vikṛti*):

> न च सादृश्यमात्रं दृष्ट्वा प्रकृतिर्विकृतिर्वा उच्यते ।
>
> MīmSūBh I.1.16
>
> Nothing is regarded as the cause (of something) or the effect (of something) by observing mere similarity (existing in two things). (Tr. R.S. Bhattacharya)

Mīmāṃsā further treats similarity as a process of comprehending language and proceeding from the direct meaning to the intended meaning. One has to largely take resort to juxtaposition of two situations which are related to two different contexts but which have in common a similar relationship:

... गुणवादेन प्ररोचनार्थतां ब्रूमहे गौणत्वात् संवादः । किं सादृश्यं, यथाऽन्नं प्रीतेः साधनम् एवमिदमपि प्रीतिसाधनशक्तियुक्तं प्रशंसितुं प्रशंसावाचिना प्रीतिसाधनशब्देन उच्यते ... ।

MīmSūBh I.2.22

... this figurative interpretation would reconcile the Vedic declaration with ordinary facts – "But what is the similarity (on which the figurative signification would be based)?" – The similarity is this – Just as food is the means of satisfaction, so this (post of Udumbara wood) also has the power to bring about satisfaction, and it is on this basis that the post is being commended and spoken of by means of a word ('*ūrk*', essence of food) denoting a means of satisfaction. (Tr. G.N. Jha)

In Mīmāṃsā view, similarity plays another important role in becoming one of the epistemological tools:

को गुणः ? सारूप्यम् । किं सारूप्यम् ? ऊर्ध्वता, तेजस्विता च ।

MīmSūBh I.4.22

What is the quality (on the basis of which the figurative statements are used)? It is similarity. What is the similarity here? Tallness and brightness. (Tr. R.S. Bhattachartya)

To sum up, the Mīmāṃsā position holds similarity as a very important process of human cognition and its relevance to the total understanding of things as well as to the total understanding of language.

Further, similarity has a reality of its own, inherent in the nature of things:

अस्मन्मते तु गुणावयवसामान्यानाम् अल्पसंख्याभाजां सादृश्याल्पत्वं बहुसंख्याभाजां सादृश्यबहुत्वमिति विवेकः सुकरः । तस्माद् द्रव्यादिष्वेव सादृश्यस्याप्यन्तर्भावः ।

MāMey (Prameya) sec. on abhāva, para - 7

But according to our view, it is easy to make a distinction thus: there is smallness in similarity for qualities, parts and generality, when they are smaller in number, and greatness in similarity when they are larger in number. Therefore, similarity is certainly to be included in substance, etc. (Tr. C.K. Raja and S.S.S. Sastri)

अपि च सादृश्यस्य तत्त्वान्तरत्वे गवयेन गौर्बहुसदृशः, वराहेण पुनरल्पसदृश इत्यादिप्रत्ययानां कथमुपपत्तिः ? न हि भवन्मते सादृश्यस्याल्पत्वबहुत्वे सम्भवतः ... ।

MāMey (Prameya) sec. on abhāva, para – 7

Further, if similarity be a distinct reality, how can there by intelligibility for the cognition like 'a cow is very similar to a *gavaya,* but

slightly similar to a boar?' Indeed, according to your view, smallness and greatness are not possible for similarity ......
(Tr. C.K. Raja and S.S.S. Sastri)

गवयस्थितसादृश्यदर्शनं करणं भवेत् ।
फलं गोगतसादृश्यज्ञानमित्यवगम्यताम् ॥

MāMey (Pramāṇa) sec. on upamāna, para – 1

The instrument should be the knowledge of the similarity present in the *gavaya*; the effect is the knowledge of the similarity present in the cow: so must it be understood.
(Tr. C.K. Raja and S.S.S. Sastri)

दृश्यमानार्थसादृश्यात् स्मर्यमाणार्थगोचरम् ।
असन्निकृष्टसादृश्यज्ञानं ह्युपमितिर्मता ॥
यथा गवये गोसादृश्यदर्शनानन्तरं स्मर्यमाणे गवि गवयसादृश्यज्ञानम् ।

MāMey (Pramāṇa) sec. on upamāna, para – 1

The knowledge of the similarity of what is not in contact, having as its sphere an object that is remembered, and arising from the similarity to an object that is seen – this, indeed, is recognised to be Analogy.

For example, after seeing the similarity to a cow in a *gavaya* an image of cow appears in mind stored in memory and there arises authentic knowledge (*pramāṇa*) of the similarity between the two.
(Tr. based on C.K. Raja and S.S.S. Sastri)

उपमानपदं लोके सादृश्ये सति विश्रुतम् ।

MāMey (Pramāṇa) sec. on upamāna, para – 12

In the world, the word 'analogy' is found used when there is similarity. (Tr. C.K. Raja and S.S.S. Sastri)

अत्र सादृश्यविषये गुरुणा कलहोऽस्ति नः ।
पदार्थान्तरमेवेदं सादृश्यं मन्यते गुरुः ॥
वयं गुणादिसामान्यसमाहारं वदामहे ।
पदार्थावसरे किञ्चित् तत्प्रकारो वदिष्यते ॥

MāMey (Pramāṇa) sec. on upamāna, para – 13

Here, in respect of similarity, we have a quarrel with the *guru* (Prabhākara). The *guru* considers this similarity even as a distinct category. We speak of it as the assemblage of common features like quality, etc. When we have occasion to deal with the categories, the mode of this will be declared to some extent.
(Tr. C.K. Raja and S.S.S. Sastri)

Prabhākara school of Mīmāṃsā makes the issue of *sādṛśya* further more complex. It is best expressed by the **Prakaraṇapañcikā** which states that similarity is a step towards the realization of identity:

स्पष्टे हि शुक्तिका-रजतयोर्भेदावसायिनि प्रमाणे सादृश्याद् भेदानवबोधाद् अभेदप्रतीतिरिति कल्प्यते ।

PraPañ p. 361

When the difference between oyster-shell and silver is clearly proved, then it should be conceived that the notion of non-difference is on account of the non-realization of difference caused by similarity. (Tr. R.S. Bhattacharya)

It further takes on the component of recollection which again leads to the identification of the person who recollects and who perceives:

दृष्टा शुक्तिकायां तदेवेदं रजतमिति मतिः । सा च सादृश्यवशेन भेदाग्रहणनिबन्धनैवेति ।

PraPañ p. 373

We find the notion that 'this silver in the mother-of-pearl is the same as that (silver seen previously)'. It is quite reasonable to hold that this notion is based on similarity and is verily caused by the non-apprehension of the difference. (Tr. R.S. Bhattacharya)

Coming to the Vedānta system, the position is that, sometimes similarity is a basis for illusory identification and so is an important aspect of perception – *kiṃ ca kādācitke vibhrame sārūpyāpekṣā* (SarDSaṅg p. 393). But there is no invariable rule that all illusory perceptions are based on similarity – *na hi sārūpyanibandhanā sarve vibhramā iti vyāptirasti* (SarDSaṅg p. 393). But overall, similarity consists only in not observing difference – *bhedāgrahaṇam eva sārūpyam* (SarDSaṅg p. 427). Further, similarity is partially based on correspondence of one relationship in one situation and the same relationship in another situation.

The Bhakti texts have mostly confined themselves to the concept of *sārūpya* which in that context is having the same form as the deity. *Sārūpya* is one of the four types of *mukti*, deliverance, the other three being *sālokya, sāyujya* and *sārṣṭi*. The **Bhaktirasāmṛtasindhu** states:

सालोक्य-सार्ष्टि-सामीप्य-सारूप्यैक्यत्वमप्युत ।
दीयमानं न गृह्णन्ति विना मत्सेवनं जनाः ॥

BhSi I.2.28

Lord Kapiladeva further tells His mother Devahūti: "Mother, My genuine devotees besides serving Me alone for My delight do not accept *sālokya-mukti*, i.e. liberation in the sense of living together with Me in My Realm, *sārṣṭi-mukti*, i.e. liberation in the sense of possessing some of the majestic powers equal to Mine, *sāmīpya-mukti*, i.e. liberation or *mukti* as close proximity to Me, *sārūpya-mukti*, i.e. liberation as possession of beauty equal to My beauty and *ekatva* or *sāyujya-mukti*, i.e. liberation as identity with Me, even if I offer all these to them; what to speak of their asking for them? My devotees never ask for any such salvation or anything else whatsoever. They find their delight in serving Me alone for My delight. (Tr. Bon Maharaja)

But most of the Bhakti texts prefer being in the presence of the deity rather than assuming his form or immersion in the deity.

मोक्षसालोक्य-सारूप्यान् प्रार्थये न धराधर !
इच्छामि हि महाभाग ! कारुण्यं तव सुव्रत ॥

BhSi I.2.51

Oh Lord Ananta (Holder of the Universe)! Oh Lord of noble resolves! Oh Repository of all wealth! I do not pray for *mokṣa*, *sālokya* and *sārūpya* and other forms of *mukti*, but my only longing is for Thy compassion. (Tr. Bon Maharaja)

Before we take up the dimensions of these concepts in art and literature, we would like to sum up the fundamental philosophical observations.

1. Similarity is always between two substances overlapping each other in some respect, and in the overlapping part lies the similarity of common properties. The stand of the Vaiśeṣika system is also in agreement with the Nyāya system.

2. As regards Mīmāṃsā, the component of recollection is the concept of similarity. It holds similarity as a very important process of human cognition and its relevance to the total understanding of things as well as to the total understanding of language.

3. According to Vedānta system, similarity is a basis for illusory identification and so is an important aspect of perception.

4. In almost all the realistic system, similarity is a step towards the realization of identity.

The works on poetics have dealt at length with the figures of speech, especially simile and metaphor. Therein the writers have gone into the depth of the concepts of similarity (*sādṛśya*) and uniformity (*sārūpya*) . In both the concepts, one thing is clear: the referents of comparison are not identical. They share certain common properties and these properties are more known to be inherent in the item to which comparison is made and less so in the item which is compared to. The mode of expression varies for the sake of emphasis. For example: (1) when it is said the face is like the moon, it is a simile and thereby one intends to communicate that two objects are to be visualized coevally, (2) they share certain common properties, (3) the item to which comparison is made is more well-known for inhering these common properties than the other ones, (4) the objective of this phrase is to emphasize the fact that both items are to be taken seriously. On the other hand, when one says, her face is moon or her face is lotus, he wants to communicate all the three points enumerated above but instead of the fourth he intends to communicate that: (1) there are two items, (2) similarity is highly striking between them, so much so that they appear to be identical, (3) though the very purpose of a metaphor is defeated if they are absolutely identical, appearance of identity is itself a mode of close similarity.

Basis of these two *arthālaṅkāras* is *sādṛśya* (resemblance) and this resemblance is two fold: that which is conveyed by the meaning of a group of words, i.e. simile and the one which comes to fore by the repetition of same letters or sounds. The former is called *upamā* (simile) and the latter is called *anuprāsa* (alliteration).

The second common point is the perception of a resemblance which is also simultaneously different, so that in the figures of speech like *bhrānti* (illusion) and *sandeha* (doubt), the perception of difference does not disappear. It has to be kept in the mind that all perceptions meant here are figurative perceptions:

> वर्णसाम्यमनुप्रासः ॥
>
> स्वरवैसादृश्येऽपि व्यञ्जनसदृशत्वं वर्णसाम्यम् ।
>
> KāPrak IX.79
>
> Alliteration (*anuprāsa*) consists in the similarity of letters.
>
> The 'similarity of letters' meant here is the sameness of consonants, even though vowels may be different. (Tr. G.N. Jha)

Here the term *sāmya* does not stand for the similarity as is intended in the case of *upamā* and *rūpaka*. It is only the repetetion of the same letter or sound. The **Kāvyādarśa** defines first point of difference though similarity is expressed throughout the words:

> सरूपशब्दवाच्यत्वात् सा समानोपमा ... ।
>
> Kāvyād II.29ab
>
> That is called *samānopamā*, as because the similarity is expressed there throughout the words, similar in form (even if there is difference of meaning). (Tr. P. Ghosal)

So, in the case of second point the resemblance is emphasised, as the basic factor of *upamā* is resemblance.

यथाकथञ्चित् सादृश्यं यत्रोद्भूतं प्रतीयते ।
उपमा नाम सा ... ॥

Kāvyād II.14abc

When the resemblance is manifested (in a poetic composition) in any way, it (the figure of speech) will go by the name simile (*upamā*). (Tr. P. Ghosal)

For the definition of *vakrokti* the **Kāvyālaṅkāra-Sūtra** stresses the scope of resemblance to indicate meaning:

सादृश्याल्लक्षणा वक्रोक्तिः ॥

KāvyālSū IV.3.8

Where the indication (of things) is based upon similarity, we have the *vakrokti* (homonym). (Tr. G.N. Jha)

Sādṛśya (resemblance) is sometimes known as inference. All the concepts of *sādṛśya* are extended:

संभावनानुमानेन सादृश्येनोभयेन वा ।
निर्वर्ण्यातिशयोद्रेक प्रतिपादनवाञ्छया ॥

VaJī III.24

Either by way of fancying or by way of similarity or by way of both, when the poet desires to convey the extraordinary nature of the subject under description. (Tr. K. Krishnamoorthy)

This can also be realised through an evasive and indirect speech.

यत्रोक्तिभङ्ग्या वाक्यार्थे सादृश्यमवगम्यते ।
वाक्यार्थयोर्विस्तरतः सा प्रपञ्चोपमेष्यते ॥

Sark IV.19

In the meaning of a sentence where a similarity in the meaning is realised through the evasive speech, there is accepted the *prapañcopamā*. (Tr. K.N. Mishra)

It is clearly articulated – the points of similitude and the perception of true sites, *upamāna* and *upameya*.

उपमा यत्र सादृश्यलक्ष्मीरुल्लसति द्वयोः ।
हंसीव कृष्ण ! ते कीर्तिः स्वर्गङ्गामवगाहते ॥

Kuva 6

Upamā 'the simile' occurs (there) where similitude between the two, i.e. standard of comparison (*upamāna*) and subject of comparison (*upameya*) manifests, graciously; e.g. O Kṛṣṇa! thine fame is swimming in the celestial Ganges (milky way) just like a swan. (Tr. P. Ghosal)

The **Rasagaṅgādhara** further elaborates this point by adding the conditional marvel and wonder, otherwise a simile will be very flat. The same text has defined *rūpaka* (metaphor) where identity is imposed on simile and further elaborates *rūpaka*. The additional element indicates precise resemblance.

सादृश्यं सुन्दरं वाक्यार्थोपस्कारकमुपमालङ्कृतिः ।

RasGa II.1

When similarity is charming and enhances the beauty of the meaning of the sentence it becomes an *alaṅkāra* and is called *upamā*.

In *upamālaṅkāra*, similarity presents difference also but in *rūpaka* it shows sameness (absence of difference).

So, there are two kinds of similarity: (i) similarity together with difference, and (ii) similarity without difference. For example:

चन्द्रमिव मुखं पश्य (उपमा), मुखचन्द्रं पश्य (रूपक) ।
See face like moon and see moon-face, respectively.

उपमेये उपमानस्य तादात्म्यं रूपकम् । अथाभेदप्रधानेषु रूपकं तावन्निरूप्यते. । किञ्च रूपके सादृश्यातिरिक्तोऽपि सम्बन्धो भवति । यथा मनोरमा रामा सुखम् इत्यत्र कार्यकारणभावसम्बन्धः ।

RasGa II (p. 297)

The metaphor (*rūpaka*) is complete identification of *upamāna* (standard of comparison) with *upameya* (object of comparison). Hence, metaphor is being analysed, where identification or non-difference is emphasized. Further, in (case of) metaphor, in addition to the resemblance, other relations also are noticed. For example, a beautiful lady is bliss. Here the relationship is cause and effect. (Tr. P. Ghosal)

However, Coomaraswamy in his "Imitation, Expression and Participation" observes: "Likeness (*similitudo*) may be of three kinds, either (1) absolute, and then amounting to sameness, which cannot be either in nature or works of art, because no two things can be alike in all respects and still be two, i.e., perfect likeness would amount to identity, (2) imitative or analogical likeness, *mutatis mutandis* and judged by comparison, e.g., the likeness of a man in stone, and (3) expressive likeness, in which the imitation is neither identical with, nor comparable to the original but is an adequate symbol and reminder of that which it represents, and to be judged only by its truth, or accuracy." (*Traditional Art and Symbolism*, p. 278).

The **Kuvalayānanda** defines *sārūpya* as similarity – cause and effect relationship.

> सारूप्यमपि कार्यस्य कारणेन समं विदुः ।
>
> Kuva 92ab
>
> Similarity in the cause and effect should be designated as the *samālaṅkāra*, the figure of speech known as sameness.
> (Tr. P. Ghosal)

In other words it is similar to the definition given in the **Rasagaṅgādhara**. The **Ujjvalanīlamaṇi** further distinguishes *abhirūpatā* from *sārūpya*.

When a person through his own excellence in qualities transforms the things lying near him into his own form, this transformation is known as *abhirūpatā* by the wise.

> यदात्मीयगुणोत्कर्षैर्वस्त्वन्यन्निकटस्थितम् ।
> सारूप्यं नयति प्राज्ञैराभिरूप्यं तदुच्यते ॥
>
> UjNīl X.33
>
> The ability of an object to turn the thing lying near into its own form due to the excellence of its qualities, is called *abhirūpatā* by the scholars. (Tr. S. Punjani)

The **Rasagaṅgādhara** designates this word-similitude when the two objects under comparison are distinctly realised.

> सारूप्यं शब्दाकारसाम्यम् ॥ सादृश्यम् ॥
>
> RasGa II (p. 659)
>
> Similitude (*sārūpya*) is conformity of letters (*śabdākāra sāmya*) or similarity. (Tr. P. Ghosal)

Whenever the points of resemblance are not realised, it cannot be called a perfect resemblance and such unrealised resemblances are deemed faulty. Now, to juxtapose the concept *sādṛśya*, it is very close to the concept of *sārūpya*. In a definition of alliteration in the *kāvyālaṅkāra*, arrangement of identical letters is *anuprāsa*. *Sārūpya* is the same form. In such alliteration the same letter is repeated, irrespective of different vowel sounds. This quality of alliteration is enhanced.

क्वचिदव्यवधानेऽपि मनोहारिनिबन्धना ।
सा स्वराणामसारूप्यात् परां पुष्णाति वक्रताम् ॥

VaJī II.3

Sometimes alliteration without any interval too, employed artistically by the poet, contributes to high poetic charm because of variation in vowels. (Tr. K. Krishnamoorthy)

In short, all these discussions on poetics the resemblance and identity are related concepts and they share the core idea of perceiving two dissimilar objects coevally through very emphasis on presentation.

These texts also make it clear that this perception must have added sense of wonder and strikingness, otherwise it could not become figure of speech.

Manifestation in the Arts

The concept of *sādṛśya* has been construed as the concept of likeness. In painting and sculpture likeness has been over-emphasised. Such pictures have been designated as *viddhacitra.* In the words of C. Sivaramamurti:

"The **Abhilaṣitārtha-Cintāmaṇi** defines this type of picture as looking faithful to the original like the reflection in a mirror: *sādṛśyaṃ dṛśyate yat tu darpaṇe pratibimbavat, taccitraṃ viddham ityāhur viśvakarmādayo budhāḥ.* The **Viddhaśālabhañjikā** is a drama primarily centred on a portrait of a beautiful princess. The word is used in several other passages from literature, as in *dvīpāntararājakanyakābhir anudivasam apahāryamāṇacitraphalakāropitaviddharūpaḥ* (Tilakamañjarī, p. 133). *Sādṛśya* or perfect semblance as in a mirror in a pictorial representation intended to be a portrait is mentioned by Hemachandra: *te viśvakarmaṇo mūrtyantarāṇīvātikauśalāt, tam ālikhaṃ yathāvastham ādarśapratibimbavat* (Sthavirāvalīcarita I.184). It is also a semblance like that of the moon reflected in still waters as her companions reassure a princess on the faithful likeness of the prince painted in a picture: *nṛpasya citre madhureyam ākṛtir na bhidyate candramaso yathāmbhasi, sakhījanas tām iti narmapeśalais śanais trapānamramukhīm abhāṣata* (Navasāhasāṅkacarita 7)" (C. Sivaramamurti, *Citrasūtra,* pp. 118–119).

According to A.K. Coomaraswamy *sādṛśya* has wider meaning where *sādṛśya* is not veristic but analogical, particularly in *āviddhacitra* – "It is in fact obvious that the likeness between anything and any representation of it cannot be likeness of nature, but must be analogical or exemplary or both of these. What the representation imitates is the idea or species of the thing, by which it is known intellectually, rather than the substance of the thing as it is perceived by the senses." It is also noted in the **Viṣṇudharmottara Purāṇa**:

दृष्टं सुसदृशं कार्यं सर्वेषामविशेषतः ।
चित्रे सादृश्यकरणं प्रधानं परिकीर्तितम् ॥

VDhPur III.42.48

What can be easily observed and studied should be so sketched and painted as to lay stress on their proper semblance to the original without difference. In a picture the most essential factor is to bring out prominently the semblance of the portrait to portrayed. (Tr. C. Sivaramamurti)

यद्यत्साधु न चित्रे स्यात्क्रियते तत्तदन्यथा ।
तथापि तस्यां लावण्यं रेखया किञ्चिदन्वितम् ॥

AbhŚāk VI.14

Whatever could not be depicted properly is being improved by me. And yet her beauty cannot be properly reflected by any picturization. (Tr. G.C. Tripathi)

It follows from this that the manifestation in art is not intended to create an illusion, on the contrary, the very concept of sharing property is always between two different objects, that is why A.K. Coomaraswamy coined the new word convisibility for *sādṛśya* which is very apt in an aesthetic situation. Hence, *sādṛśya* has been described as one of the limbs of painting:

रूपभेदाः प्रमाणानि भावलावण्ययोजनम् ।
सादृश्यं वर्णिकाभंग इति चित्रं षडङ्गकम् ॥

Yaśodhara on KāmSū I.3.15

Painting has six limbs, viz. the variety of forms, measures or proportions, *bhāva* (psychic feeling), *lāvaṇya* (lit. the quality of salt; grace and beauty), *sādṛśya* (similitude) and *varṇikābhaṅga* (dark and light shades of colour).

Conclusion

To sum up the discussion, *sādṛśya* in essence is convisibility. Looking at two different objects simultaneously with a purpose to see an inherent relationship between them is a normal frame of Indian thought. Its use in art is derived from the central idea of looking closely at connections. Even when we express convisibility in terms of identity and even going beyond that we express in terms of complete merger of the one into the other. This fact is never lost sight of that there are two different objects of reference and they sometimes get apart and sometimes get consumed by each other.

A.K. Coomaraswamy in "*The Transformation of Nature in Art*" (pp.8–9) states: "Now as to *sādṛśya*: literal meanings are sym-visibility, con-similarity; secondary meanings co-ordination, analogy. That aesthetic *sādṛśya* does not imply naturalism, veri-similitude, illustration or illustration in any superficial sense is sufficiently shown by the fact that in Indian lists of factors essential to painting it is almost always mentioned with *pramāṇa* 'creation of truth'".

Both convisibility (*sādṛśya*) and uniformity (*sārūpya*) are two ways of looking at the process of unfolding of the cosmic phenomena. Uniformity exists at the level of appearance and so does convisibility. One-ness of form at the level of manifestation or at the level of observation is not identity. A whole is not a summation of parts, rather, it is a connectedness of different collections.

These concepts are very focal to the understanding of Indian art and literature inasmuch as they neither aim at differentiation in absolute terms nor they aim at similarity or identity in absolute terms. Their main objective is to provide ways and means to give an incomplete (perhaps which can never be completed and for this reason which is always a challenge to go deeper and deeper into the reality of the Reality) picture of the manifested world and its inherent manifestable property.

Vidya Nivas Misra

Select Bibliography

Coomaraswamy, A.K.: The Transformation of Nature in Art, edited by Kapila Vatsyayan. New Delhi: IGNCA & Sterling Publishers, 1995.

— Traditional Art and Symbolism, Princeton: Princeton University Press, 1977.

Sivaramamurti, C.: Chitrasūtra (of the Viṣṇudharmottara Purāṇa), New Delhi: Kanaka Publications, 1978.

ANUKARAṆA/ANUKṚTI/ANUKĪRTANA

Overview

The history of *anukaraṇa/anukṛti/anukīrtana* (fn.) could be traced from the period of the Brāhmaṇas. These stand for various meanings according to their occurrence, perspective and period. Several interesting theories of Indian art, aesthetics, drama and philosophy not only revolve around these terms, they are even evolved through them. A study of the Indian tradition from the Epics to the Purāṇas brings out a hoard of the terms bearing the same sense. They are derived from the same root '*kṛ-*' and prefix '*anu*' like *anukṛti, anukaraṇa, anukīrtana, anukāra, anucikīrṣaṇa,* etc.

This is to be explored whether *anukaraṇa/anukṛti/anukīrtana* could be simply taken as their English translation 'imitation' and whether the Indian view of art is confirmed to the concept of 'art as imitation' (*anukaraṇa*). The study delineates that these terms should not be taken by their literal meaning but on a much broader canvas. Thus the term not only conveys the meaning imitation, but also stands for re-creation, re-statement representation so far as art, aesthetics and drama are concerned. On a wider perspective the terms also connote 'following' 'recitation' and 'similarity'.

Art as *anukṛti* (imitation) brings before us a copy of divine as well as human world. It also leads to an aesthetic experience – from *anukṛti* to *anukīrtana,* a fascinating journey from mundane to the philosophical world. They involve the philosophers, thinkers and sages like Śaṅkara, Abhinavagupta, Bhartṛhari, etc. Their writings bring forth the inner meaning and historical significance of the word. Actually the beauty does not lie so much in the scholarly debate of the different schools, but rather in the experience of the '*rasa*' it projects.

Etymology and Related Terms

Anukṛti and *anukaraṇa* have been used as synonyms. *Anukṛti* is derived from the root *kṛ-* 'to do' followed by the suffix *ktin* with the prefix '*anu*' meaning after, subsequent.

Similarly, *anukaraṇa* comes from the same root preceded by *anu* and followed by *lyuṭ*. Both the terms have been interpreted as imitation. Thus the **Aitareya Brāhmaṇa** (I.27) explains it in the sense of acting. The **Aṣṭādhyāyī** takes *anukaraṇa* in the sense of imitation.

अनुकरणं चानितिपरम् ।

Pā I.4.62

A word imitative of a sound is also called *gati*, when it is not followed by the word *iti*. (Tr. S.C. Basu)

The **Mahābhāṣya** relates *anukaraṇa* as following:

अनुकरणं हि शिष्टस्य साधु भवति, अशिष्टाप्रतिषिद्धस्य वा, नैव तद् दोषाय भवति नाभ्युदयाय । यथा लौकिकवैदिकेषु ।

Mahābh I.1.2 (p. 20)

The imitation of an enjoined act becomes valid (*sādhu*), or the imitation of that act which is neither enjoined nor prohibited becomes valid. This second imitation, however neither does harm nor affords benefit as is found in the Vedic and secular acts. (Tr. R.S. Bhattacharya)

In the **Āpastamba Dharma-Sūtra** (II.2.5.8) the term *anucikīrṣan* is used to denote imitation. Both the words are derived from the same root here and have the same prefix- *anu* + *kṛ-* + *san* + *śatṛ* = *anucikīrṣan* and *anu* + *kṛ-* + *ktin* = *anukṛti.*

The synonyms not only betray an interesting development of the concept but also lead to different meaning. Thus the '*anukīrtana*' (*anu* + *kīrt-* + *lyuṭ*) delineates representation and portrayal according to **Nāṭya-Śāstra** (I.107), while the **Bṛhaddevatā** (II.21) explains it in the sense of recitation.

Anukāra (*anu* + *kṛ-* + *ghañ*) is appearance, resemblance, and a symbol according to the **Vākyapadīya** (I.5).

Anuhāra (*anu* + *hṛ-* + *ghañ*), though the word has a different root it has the same meaning as *anukāra.* It is used for resemblance and imitation.

अनुहारोऽनुकारः स्यात् ।

VaiKo V.2.17c

Actually *anukāra* and *anuhāra* (both these synonyms) are used to denote imitation or resemblance. (Tr. P. Ghosal)

Anukāriṇaḥ (*anu* + *kṛ-* + *ghañ* + *ini*) occurs in the **Mārkaṇḍeya Purāṇa**:

सेनानुकारिणः प्राणान् मुमुचुस्त्रिदशार्दनाः ।

MārkPur LXXXII.59

Following the manner of an army, the afflictors of the gods gave up their life. (Based on the tr. by F.E. Pargiter)

Layers of Meaning

Anukaraṇa

Anukaraṇa and *anukṛti* bear the same meaning:

(a) *Anukaraṇa* as imitation of sound (Pā I.4.62),

(b) in the onomatopoetic sense (Nir IX.12),

(c) in the sense of following (Mahābh I.1.2).

Anukṛti

(a) Imitation as acting (AitBr I.27),

(b) imitation as re-producing (AitBr VI.27),

(c) following and imitation in the sense of divine musical instrument (ŚāṅkhĀr VIII.9),

(d) it is used as compliance in the Upaniṣads (TUp I.8),

(e) *anukṛti* is also an onomatopoetic word (Nir III.18).

Anukīrtana

(a) Reciting (BṛDev II.21),

(b) restatement or portrayal (NŚ I.107; IV.11),

(c) followed or result of (ŚSto XIV.16).

Anukāra

(a) Similarity (AmKo III.2.17),

(b) an act of resemblance (AbhiBhā on NŚ I.117),

(c) resemblance and similarity (Vāk II.7).

Anukāriṇa

(a) Following (MārkPur LXXXII.59),

(b) apprehension of (PraPañ p. 96).

Anucikīrṣan

It occurs as imitation in the **Āpastamba Dharma-Sūtra** (II.2.5.8).

Thus *anukaraṇa/ anukṛti* is similar to *anucikīrṣaṇa, anukāra, anukāriṇa* and *anukīrtana.* All these terms collectively mean – imitation, reproduction, following, representation, restatement and portrayal.

Development of the Concept

From the Vedic to the Epic period *anukaraṇa* and *anukṛti* have been used as synonyms. In the beginning they signify simply 'imitation and acting'. The actor as well as the spectator both were aware of imitations. Such an early example of *anukṛti* as *abhinaya* (acting) could be found in the **Aitareya Brāhmaṇa:**

तामनुकृतिमस्कन्नां वत्सतरीमाजन्ति सोमक्रयणीं ... ।

AitBr I.27

In imitation (of this precedent) they drive away an immaculate cow of one year's age, being the price at which they purchase the king Soma. (Tr. M. Haug)

The same text takes it in the sense of copy or imitation also.

शिल्पानि शंसन्ति । देवशिल्पान्येतेषां वै शिल्पानामनुकृतीह शिल्पमधिगम्यते– हस्ती कंसो वासो हिरण्यमश्वतरीरथः शिल्पम् ।

AitBr VI.27

They recite the *śilpas.* These are the works of art of the gods; in imitation of these works of art here is a work of art accomplished; an elephant, a goblet, a garment, a gold object, a mule chariot are works of art. (Tr. A.B. Keith)

In the Upaniṣads, there is a stark difference from what has been established so far. The **Taittirīya Upaniṣad** applies it in the meaning of compliance.

ओमित्येतदनुकृतिर्ह स्म वा अप्यो श्रावयेत्याश्रावयन्ति ।

TUp I.8

Om – that is compliance as also verily, it is well known – upon the words 'O' call forth! they call forth. (Tr. R.E. Hume)

In the later Vedic period, *anukīrtana* occurs as recitation:

अध्यापयन्नधीयानो मन्त्रं चैवानुकीर्तयन् ।
स्थानं सालोक्यं सायुज्यम् एतेषामेव गच्छति ॥

BṛDev II.21

Teaching, studying and reciting a formula (addressed to them), a man attains to the sphere of, to identity of world (and) intimate union with, these same (gods). (Tr. A.A. Macdonell)

In the Mauṣalaparva of **Mahābhārata** the concept of *anukaraṇa* has been recorded. After the devastation of Kurukṣetra war, Lord Kṛṣṇa noticed different portentuous phenomena:

अन्वकुर्वन्नुलूकानां सारसा विरुतं तथा ।
अजा: शिवानां विरुतमन्वकुर्वत भारत ॥

MBh XVI.3.5

O descendant of Bharata, the cranes started to imitate the screaming of owls so did the goats, the howling of Jackals. (Tr. P. Ghosal)

The **Mahābhāṣya** strengthens this by stating that the imitation of a word is exactly like the original. If the original words are imitated, the same will be treated as the original words so far as the grammar is concerned *(prakṛtivad anukaraṇaṃ bhavati* – Mahābh I.1.2, p. 21).

A similar concept of imitation of the word was appreciated at a much later stage. The **Śṛṅgāra Prakāśa** of Bhojarāja vividly describes that statement of a word or sound exactly in the same way, is called *anukaraṇa* 'imitation'.

शब्दस्य ताद्रूप्येणाभिधानमनुकरणम्। यदाह – व्यक्ताव्यक्तवर्णपदवाक्यसादृश्योक्तयोऽ-
नुकरणानि ।

ŚṛPrak I, p.20

Anukaraṇa is the statement of a word or sound exactly in the same manner. Now, this *anukaraṇa* (becomes sixfold) on account of similar presentation of letters, words and sentences (once) distinctly and (once) indistinctly. (Tr. P. Ghosal)

There is yet another text by Bhojarāja, i.e. the **Sarasvatīkaṇṭhābharaṇa**, in which the imitation of other's words is called *chāyā.*

अन्योक्तीनामनुकृतिश्छाया सापीह षड्विधा ।
लोकच्छेकार्भकोन्मत्तपोटामत्तोक्तिभेदत: ॥

Sark II.39

The imitation of other's words is *chāyā,* that too is of six types here on the basis of utterance of a lay man, a wise, the children, a mad, a masculine woman and a drunkard. (Tr. K.N. Misra)

Unlike the Upaniṣads and Epics these terms occur in the Purāṇas in a totally different way so far as the art is concerned. It is not an imitation of the divine art, rather a reproduction or representation of the affairs of the world. It was not only confined to the Śilpa (art) only, even in the dance and painting these tendency could be seen.

> यथा नृत्ते तथा चित्रे त्रैलोक्यानुकृतिः स्मृता ॥
>
> VdhPur III.35.5cd
>
> In dance as well as in *citra* the imitation of the three worlds is enjoined by tradition. (Tr. S. Kramarisch)

The development and meaning of *anukāra/anukāriṇa* have been intriguing as the **Viṣṇu Purāṇa** uses it to suggest imitation. But it also signals resemblance in the **Viṣṇu Purāṇa**.

> अक्षाणि योगवित् ... कुर्याच्चित्तानुकारीणि ॥
>
> ViPur VI.7.43
>
> The Yogin should direct the sense organs to imitate the mind. (Tr. R.S. Bhattacharya)

Thus imitation could be from mundane to supermundane. Usually the Purāṇas from the **Viṣṇudharmottara** to the **Matsya** use the term as imitation in art.

Anukṛti as imitation or acting was not limited to the drama or in the wordly affair. The **Brahma-Sūtra** uses *anukṛti* to explain the realization of the self.

> अनुकृतेस्तस्य च ॥
>
> BrSū I.3.22
>
> Because of "acting in accordance". (Tr. Gambhirananda)

Śaṅkara, while commenting on the same clarifies:

> कस्मात्, अनुकृतेः । अनुकरणमनुकृतिः । यदेतत् तमेव भान्तमनुभाति सर्वम् इत्यनुभानं, तत्प्राज्ञपरिग्रहेऽवकल्पते । ... न तु तेजोधातुं कंचित्सूर्यादयोऽनुभान्तीति प्रसिद्धम् । समत्वाच्च तेजोधातूनाम् ... । नहि प्रदीपः प्रदीपान्तरमनुभाति। यदप्युक्तं समानस्वभावकेष्वनुकारो दृश्यत इति। नायमेकान्तो नियमः । भिन्नस्वभावकेष्वपि ह्यनुकारो दृश्यते । यथा सुतप्तोऽयःपिण्डोऽग्न्यनुकृतिरग्निं दहन्तमनुदहति ।
>
> BrSūŚBh I.3.22
>
> Because of 'acting in accordance' which phrase means imitation. This shining in imitation as implied in; 'the shining all those shines', fits in exactly if the conscious self is accepted, ... For it is not a matter of experience that the sun and other things shine in accordance with some other shining substance. The luminaries

like sun etc. are similar in nature. .... For a lamp does not shine in imitation of another lamp. As for the assertion that acting in imitation is seen in the case of things of the same nature, there is no such hard and fast rule for action in imitation is seen in the case of things of the dissimilar things as well. For instance a red-hot ball of iron stimulates fire and burns things in accordance with the fire's doing so. (Tr. Gambhirananda)

The **Prakaraṇapañcikā** explains the last instance in a same way.

दृष्टा हि सन्तापसंचारित-दहनपरमाणुसंवलितायोगोलके दहनाकारानुकारिणी प्रतीतिरिति ।

PraPañ p. 96

There is the apprehension of fire in the iron-ball associated with the atoms of fire characterized by heat. (Tr. R.S. Bhattacharya)

But *anukāra* as similarity or resemblance has been vividly described in the early medieval period. Thus, the **Vākyapadīya** uses the term *anukāra* as a symbol and similarity.

प्राप्त्युपायोऽनुकारश्च तस्य वेदो महर्षिभिः ।
एकोऽप्यनेकवर्त्मेव समाम्नातः पृथक् पृथक् ॥

Vāk I.5

A means of attainment and a symbol of that one is the Veda, which though one, has been handed down as though in many recensions by the sages. (Tr. K.A.S. Iyer)

The **Vākyapadīya** again cites it as supposition, the same.

भेदानुकारो ज्ञानस्य वाचश्चोपप्लवो ध्रुवः ।
क्रमोपसृष्टरूपा वाग् ज्ञानं ज्ञेयव्यपाश्रयम् ॥

Vāk I.86

The appearance of diversity in knowledge and the word is surely an illusioṇ. The word is coloured by sequence and knowledge is coloured by the known. (Tr. K.A.S. Iyer)

The **Vākyapadīya** explains *anukāra* as similarity. It seems as if the word *anukāra* is cited in order to explain it in the next sentence but, actually, the text of the *paddhati* is as follows:

अनुकार इति व्याख्येयमुत्थापयति ।
वस्तुतो भेदाभावादनुकार इव वेदो ब्रह्मणः ॥

Paddhati comm. on Vāk I.5

The word *anukāra* is cited here, in order to elucidate it. As a matter of fact, as because there is no difference, Vedas are (something like) resemblance of *brahman*. (Tr. P. Ghosal)

Anukāra in the similar sense occurs in the Bhāṣya of Śaṅkara on **Brahma-Sūtra**.

न च विवक्षितार्थभेदेऽवगम्यमाने वाक्यच्छायानुकारमात्रेण समानार्थत्वमध्यवसातुं युक्तम् ।

BrSūŚBh III.3.7

And if we understand that the text intends to convey a difference of matter we have no right to conclude from merely apparent similarities of expression that only one matter is intended to be expressed. (Tr. G. Thibaut)

Gradually, it is established that the very foundation of imitation is similarity. Thus, when *anukaraṇa* and other words mean similarity only, imitation is suggestive.

The term *anukaraṇa/anukṛti* suggests a simple as well as deep meaning. Initially, it was taken in the sense of simple imitation. The **Aitareya Brāhmaṇa** (I.27) gives a very beautiful example of imitation or *abhinaya*. The brahmin, who sold the *soma* (creeper) would not be given the cow, instead, money or price of the cow.

In the beginning the imitation was merely acting. It was also copying someone else for amusement. Here the spectator was capable of distinguishing between the real character and the action. There is no illusion of reality. Such instance is found in the **Mahāsubhāṣita Saṅgraha**.

अप्राप्तवल्लभसमागमनाधिकायाः सख्याः पुरोऽत्र निजचित्तविनोदबुद्ध्या ।
आलापवेषगतिहास्यविकत्थनाद्यैः प्राणेश्वरानुकृतिमाकलयन्ति लीलाम् ॥

MSSaṅg 2183

The friend finding the companion full of worry due to the delay in her lover's return played the role of the lover for amusement by imitating him in his speech, dress, gait, laughter, jokes and other characteristics. (Tr. A.A. Ramanathan)

Here *anukṛti* means imitation in the sense of *abhinaya* (acting) for amusement – *līlā*. The audience is fully aware that *līlā* is being played *and* the *ābhāsa* – manifestation becomes futile.

There is yet another word, used in the similar sense *viḍambayantaḥ*. The

Viṣṇu Purāṇa states that the gods are enacting as human being for pastime.

मनुष्यलीलां भगवन् भजता भवता सुराः ।
विडम्बयन्तस्त्वल्लीलां सर्व एव सहासते ॥

ViPur V.7.39

The gods, to partake of thy pastimes as man have all descended under a like disguise. (Tr. H.H. Wilson)

The **Āpastamba Dharma-Sūtra** narrates the imitation of conduct of a teacher by his student. Here the term used, '*anucikīrṣan*' means imitation or acting .

स्थानासनचङ्क्रमणस्मितेष्वनुचिकीर्षन् ॥

ĀpDhSū II.2.5.8

He shall imitate (his teacher) in rising, sitting, walking about and smiling. (Tr. G. Bühler)

All these references use imitation in the same way, where the subject and object both were aware of the dividing line of the act.

Manifestation of the Arts

Now so far as the drama or acting is concerned, the question arises whether *anukṛti* is merely imitation or this English term has its own limitations. The Western notion attached to this word is inadequate to express the totality of the concept.

'Imitation' – the way it is used among western aesthetes becomes irrelevant in Indian context.

What is drama?

अनुकृतिरिति नाट्यम् ।

AbhiBhā on NŚ I.57

Anukṛti (? imitation) is drama.

Thus Bharata has understood entire *nāṭya* or drama as *anukṛti.* In the above reference the term *anukṛti* has been technically used, which stands for *nāṭya* as *anukṛti.*

The *nāṭya* or drama has its origin in the Vedic tradition. The **Nāṭya-Śāstra** narrates that after *nāndī* of eight *padas*, the *anukṛti* was arranged, e.g. the victory of gods over demons.

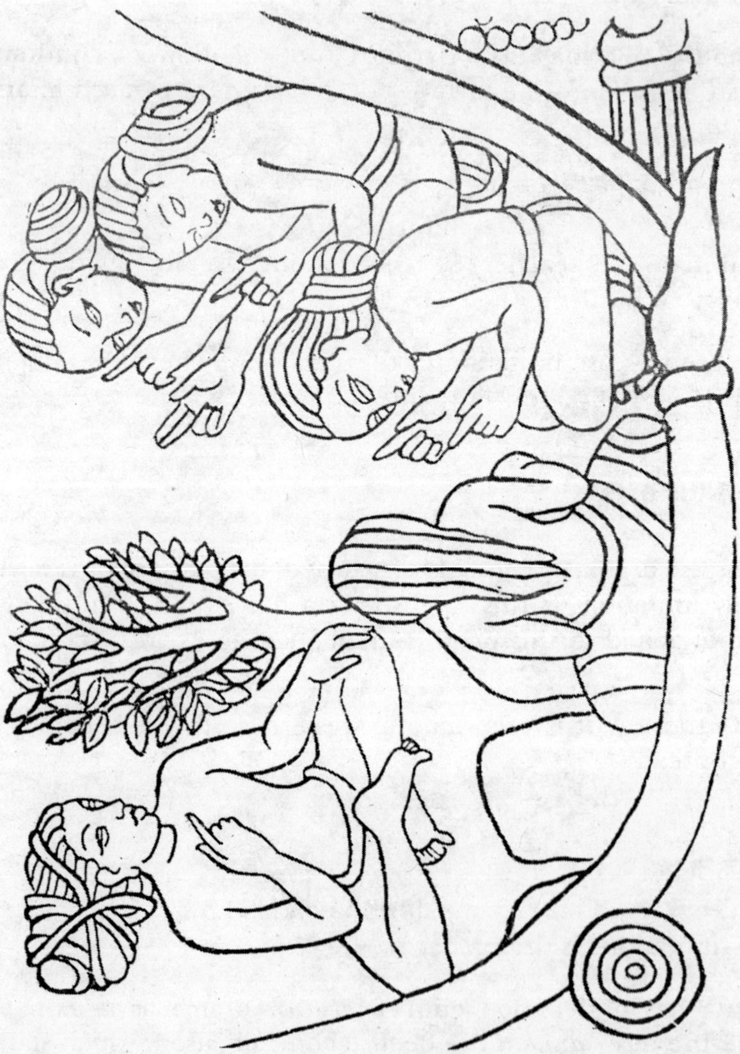

Figure 4: Students following instructions of *guru*, Bharhut Sculptures (c. second century B.C.)

अष्टाङ्गपदसंयुक्ता विचित्रा वेदनिर्मिता ।
तदन्तेऽनुकृतिर्बद्धा यथा दैत्याः सुरैर्जिताः ॥

NŚ I.57

In the Vedic tradition (this) beautiful (*nāndī*) is of eight *padas*. After that (*nāndī*) the *anukṛti* (*nāṭya*) was arranged just as the demons were defeated by the gods. (Tr. S. Das)

Anukṛti here denotes '*nāṭya*' (drama). The *anukaraṇa* is also *nāṭya* (drama). Either of these represents the various *bhāvas* (mental states) and the totality of human life.

The myth of the origin of *nāṭya* begins with *anukaraṇa*. The Asuras and Dānavas (demons) took the scenes of ocean churning too literally and created troubles during the first dramatic performance. The first performance was in the nature of '*anukṛti*'.

The position is not so simple as it appears. It has led aesthetes to an interesting debate. The perplexing question was if *anukaraṇa* was merely 'imitation', then how could it produce '*rasa*'? Bhaṭṭa Lollaṭa has maintained that '*rasa*' lies both in the represented personage and in the imitating action. He says that the actor manages very well in experiencing the same feeling and then representing it by virtue of *anusannidhi* or *anusannidhāna*. Bhaṭṭa Lollaṭa's main concern was the correspondence or dialogue between the form of an idea of artist and the rise of that concept or idea. Bhaṭṭa Lollaṭa uses the term *anusannidhāna* where Bharata employs '*anukaraṇa*'. He picks up the thread from Śaiva philosophy specially in the **Īśvara Pratyabhijñā-Kārikā**. Vatsyayan (1996, 140) has rightly pointed out that "Bhaṭṭa Lollaṭa furthers it by saying that there is a causal relationship between idea or image and sensation or emotion. It is the same as the unseen, unexpressed, *amūrta* experience and its manifestation through symbols. This entire process evolves through three individual stages: when artist experiences the idea or image or form. The second stage is marked with acceptance of that abstract idea or image and the last stage shows creation of that stage.

Bhaṭṭa Lollaṭa says that the realisation is power through which the actor becomes, for the time being the represented or imitated personage and feels himself as Rāma, the faculty through which he does not forget his real nature of action. To the objection that being it so, the actor would fail to maintain ...". Bhaṭṭa Lollaṭa answers that on the contrary the actor can manage very well by virtue of *anusannidhi* or *anusannidhāna*.

रसभावानामपि वासनावेशवशेन नटे सम्भवादनु ।

AbhiBhā on NŚ VI.11

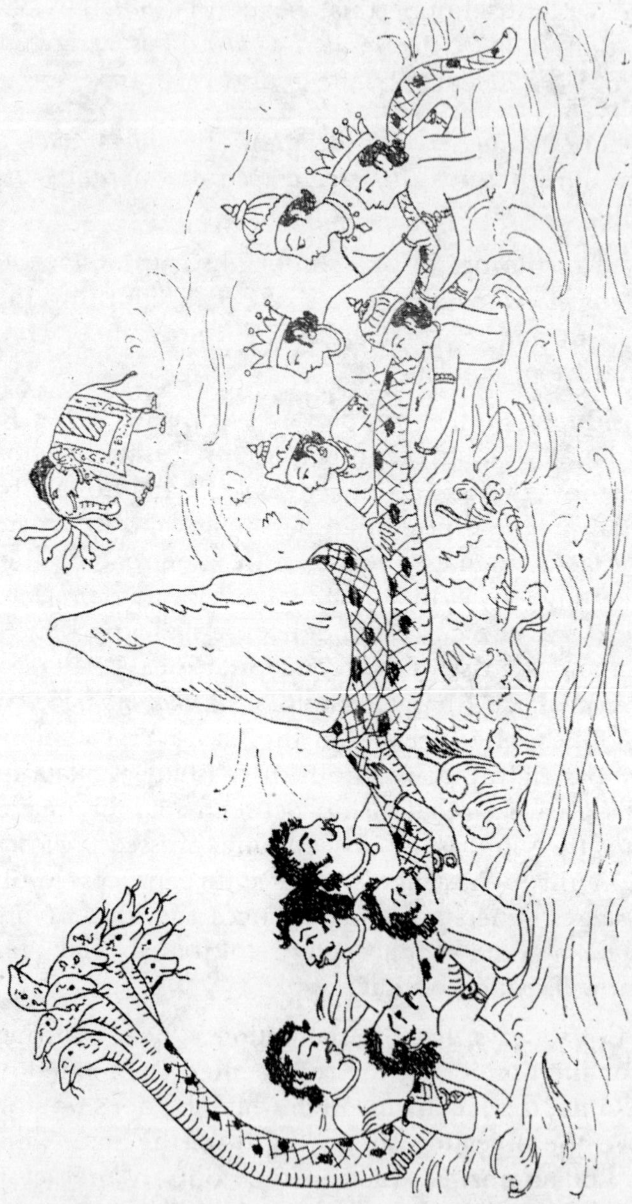

Figure 5: Airāvata coming out of churning of ocean

> Existence of (both) flavour (*rasa*) and mood (*bhāva*) is possible in the actor because of its being aroused by previous impression (*vāsanā*). (Tr. P. Ghosal)

Though Bhaṭṭa Lollaṭa based his argument on Śaiva philosophy as *pūrvapakṣa* he faced criticism for having ignored the problem of how the spectators do relish *rasa*. It did not probe into the experience of the audience. Moreover, the severe objection was raised as to how a symbol can create the impression of real thing.

Śrī Śaṅkuka accelerated the theory of *rasa* and he was the chief opponent of Bhaṭṭa Lollaṭa's theory. He says that *rasa* is not an intensified stage, but an imitated stage. He extended Bhaṭṭa Lollaṭa's theory and tried to overcome his shortcoming. He said that *rasa* was not only a representation or re-creation of an image or idea or of a particular character but also of experience or emotions it generates among the audience. Thus the greatest contribution of Śrī Śaṅkuka, if we can borrow Vatsyayan's words (1996, 141) "... pointing out explicitly that *rasa* was not an aesthetic object but an aesthetic experience in the receptors', spectators' consciousness". The successful imitation by the actor of characters and their experience, is no doubt Śaṅkuka says artificial and unreal but is not realised to be so by the spectators, who forget the difference between the actor and the character themselves. He explores the possibility of an identical similarity in the emotions (*bhāva*) of actor and spectator.

He cites the example of creating the emotive stage through cognition. Just as the painting of the horse is only the idea of horse and yet it leads to the cognition of the horse. This artificial artistic creation can arouse the same experience of the real.

Obviously Śrī Śaṅkuka's theory was put to doubt and criticism. His interpretation was taken as simple imitation only. Hemachandra analysed his theory and he described that a horse imitated by a painter seemed to the onlookers neither real nor false and is nothing but an image which precedes any judgement of reality or unreality (Gnoli R., *The Aesthetic Experience*, Introduction, p. XIX).

Here a veiled sceptical notion is also brought forth, the significance of not only *anukaraṇa* or representation but also the process or stages or method of creating that re-narration.

Subsequently, Abhinavagupta rejects the theory of imitation as drama and *rasa*. He asks where the original is not available, how can one recognise the imitation. If one fails to identify with the drama and in place of appreciating or enjoying the *rasa* and takes it as a deformed or distorted copy (*vikiraṇa*) he will feel comic jealousy or amusement in place of aesthetic experiences.

The fascinating query remains perplexing. What is *anukaraṇa, anukṛti* and *anukīrtana* so far as drama (*nāṭya*) is concerned? Abhinavagupta says that simple imitation *anukaraṇa* or *anukṛti* cannot be drama or *nāṭya* as it cannot produce *rasa.* It is only an amusing copy of real and it cannot create the concept of real from the spectator or beholder's point of view. He tries to explain *anukaraṇa* in a different way. '*Anukaraṇa*' should be justified by cognition. '*Anukāra*' can be accepted only through evidence.

किंचिद्धि प्रमाणेनोपलब्धं तद् अनुकरणम् इति ॥

AbhiBhā on NŚ VI.31 (p. 268)

Representation indeed can be said to be only something perceived by means of cognition. (Tr. R.N. Misra)

Abhinavagupta takes the term *anukīrtana* instead of *anukṛti.* He says that drama is in fact re-narration or re-production of mental states. He says that imitation of mental states like grief, anger are not possible. The actor's emotions are his own. He cannot feel the grief of Rāma, because the intensity of Rāma's grief is totally missing here.

Thus the *nāṭya* (drama) is not imitation or *anukṛti* it is rather portrayal of mental states *anukīrtana.* The *anukaraṇa* is justified as following or as recitation and is rightly placed for *līlā* or amusement or for miracle. Thus the *nāṭya* is neither *anukṛti* nor *anukaraṇa,* it is *anukīrtana* re-statement of the mental states. The term has occurred in the **Nāṭya-Śāstra** in the same sense.

त्रैलोक्यस्यास्य सर्वस्य नाट्यं भावानुकीर्तनम् ॥

NŚ I.107cd

Nāṭya is in fact statement of the mental states of the three world.

Śāgaranandī, author of the **Nāṭakalakṣaṇaratna Kośa** defines on the line of Bharata and Abhinavagupta and uses the term *anukaraṇa*:

नाट्यमनुकरणम् ।

NLRKo after verse 38

Nāṭya is actually the representation. (Tr. P.Ghosal)

The **Bhāva Prakāśana,** a later text, explains *anukṛti* as a characteristic of drama. Here the argument has been accelerated from the player and audience's point of view. It is the representation of the state, thus it is drama and it is being viewed by the spectators, so it is called *rūpa.*

अवस्थानुकृतिर्नाट्यमिति सामान्यलक्षणम् ।

रामादि तादात्म्यापत्तिर्नटे या नाट्यमुच्यते ।
रूपकं तद्भवेद्रूपं दृश्यत्वात्प्रेक्षेकैरिदम् ।

BhPrak VII.1 (line 2–4)

Nāṭya is the representation of states (and this is) general feature of drama. Identification of Rāma etc. with the dramatic person, is called *nāṭya*. Because of its being viewed by the audience, it is called *rūpa*, and the same *rūpa* is called *rūpaka*. (Tr. P. Ghosal)

The Avaloka comm. on **Daśarūpaka** also emphasises the above comment almost in a similar manner, while explaining the *avasthānukṛtirnāṭyam.*

काव्योपनिबद्धधीरोदात्ताद्यवस्थानुकारश्चतुर्विधाभिनयेन तादात्म्यापत्तिर्नाट्यम् ।

Avaloka on DaRū I.7

Nāṭya is the re-enactment (*anukāra*) of *dhīrodātta* hero etc. described in the drama, that is harmonization of the actor with *dramatis personae* through four types of acting. (Tr. P. Ghosal)

Abhinavagupta has drawn a dividing line between '*anukaraṇa*' a simple imitation and *anukīrtana* (statement). The drama is the re-statement of the affairs of the world. It is the re-telling of the mental state, which is created by the artist and grasped by the viewers. It is a dialogue of the emotive state between the narrator and the beholder and this is where the *rasa* lies. What did Bharata mean by the term? The problem has been explored by Bhaṭṭa Lollaṭa, Śrī Śaṅkuka, Bhaṭṭanāyaka, and Abhinavagupta. According to Bhaṭṭa Lollaṭa it is *anusannidhāna* where the artist communicates through symbols and images. For Śrī Śaṅkuka it is imitation but Abhinavagupta rejects the theory of imitation, because here the spectator was missing and puts forward the notion that it is the re-telling of the mental state.

It could be summarised in the writings of **Nāṭya-Śāstra**, where *nāṭya* is the representation of the various emotions and portrays the totality of human actions and world.

नानाभावोपसम्पन्नं नानावस्थान्तरात्मकम् ।
लोकवृत्तानुकरणं नाट्यमेतन्मया कृतम् ॥

NŚ I.112

This *nāṭya* (drama) has been created by me which is rich with various *bhāvas* (mental states), is full of many situations and is representational of the totality of human life (*loka-vṛtta*).
(Tr. P.L. Sharma)

The theory of art or art experience should not limit itself with only one

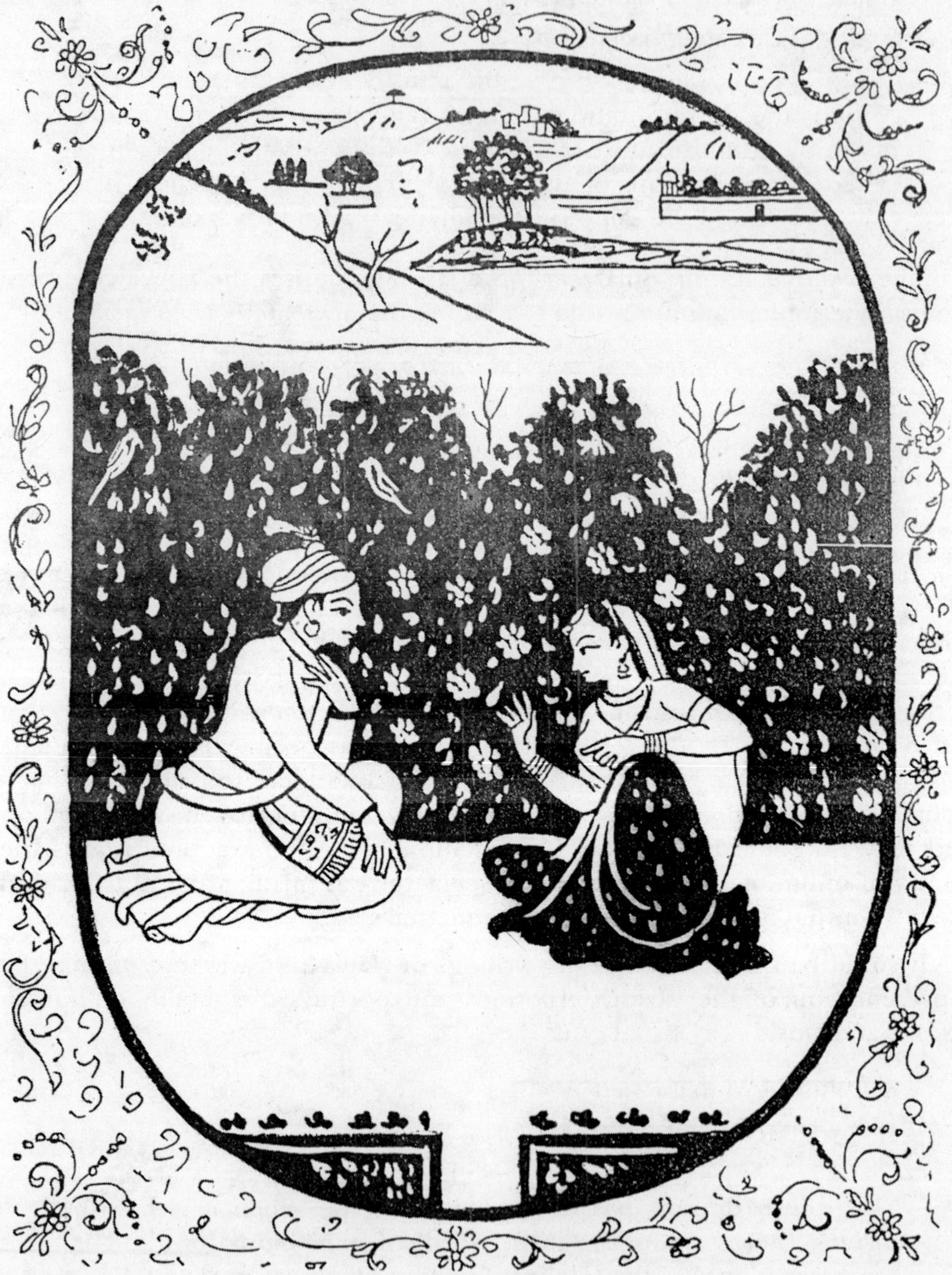

Figure 6: Drama-dialogue between *nāyaka* and *nāyikā*

dimension but should try to see entire humanity as artistic expression. Unfortunately history of aesthetics is full with the doctrines of fractional theories like art as dialogue or art as imitation. In drama or theatre it may not be imitation so far as aesthetic experience is concerned but in art it is the reproduction or imitation. It is Hofstaderian view of aesthetics. In fact in western world the art has been taken as the imitation or mirroring of the world, which is copy of god's creation. It is both Platonic and Aristotalian view of all art.

Plato rejects the meaning and significance of imitation at human level but he says that the material world is an imitation of God's perception. Imitation in art is only a poor copy of that imitation. Aristotle has totally revised Plato's concept and thus in his analysis 'imitation' does not have any place rather it is the representation of the artist's attitudes. The stark contrast between the two may be delineated like this. For Plato, all the arts without exception are imitation. The Aristotalian school so far as the 'imitation', application and upsurgance are concerned, believes that the poet or artist receives inspiration from the material world. He imitates or follows his inner inspiration and reaction. Coomaraswamy (1984–27) has hit the right chord, while assessing these views. He quotes Irdell Jenkins and says that Irdell Jenkins has by pointing out that art is expression added nothing new to the older doctrine that art is imitation. The older view had been that the art is demonstration of the invisible form whether human or divine. "A beautiful imitation could never be produced unless from a beautiful pattern and that no sensible object could be faultless unless it were made in the likeness of an archetype visible only to the intellect. God when He willed to create the visible world, first fully formed the intelligible world, in order that He might have use of a pattern, wholly divine and incorporeal" (*Selected papers*, Coomaraswamy, p. 277).

These views are not new to Indian tradition, where all the works of art is an imitation of heavenly body. There is no argument that the *śilpa* of this world is based on the divine model. Here the idea of *śilpa* begins with the imitation (*anukṛti*). Thus the **Aitareya Brāhmaṇa** (VI.27) regards *śilpa* as imitation of divinity.

> शिल्पानि शंसन्ति । देवशिल्पान्येतेषां वै शिल्पानामनुकृतीह शिल्पमधिगम्यते - हस्ती कंसो वासो हिरण्यमश्वतरीरथ: शिल्पम् ।
>
> AitBr VI.27
>
> They recite the *śilpas.* These are the works of art of the gods; in imitation of these works of art here is a work of art accomplished an elephant, a goblet, a garment, a gold object, a mule chariot are works of art. (Tr. A.B. Keith)

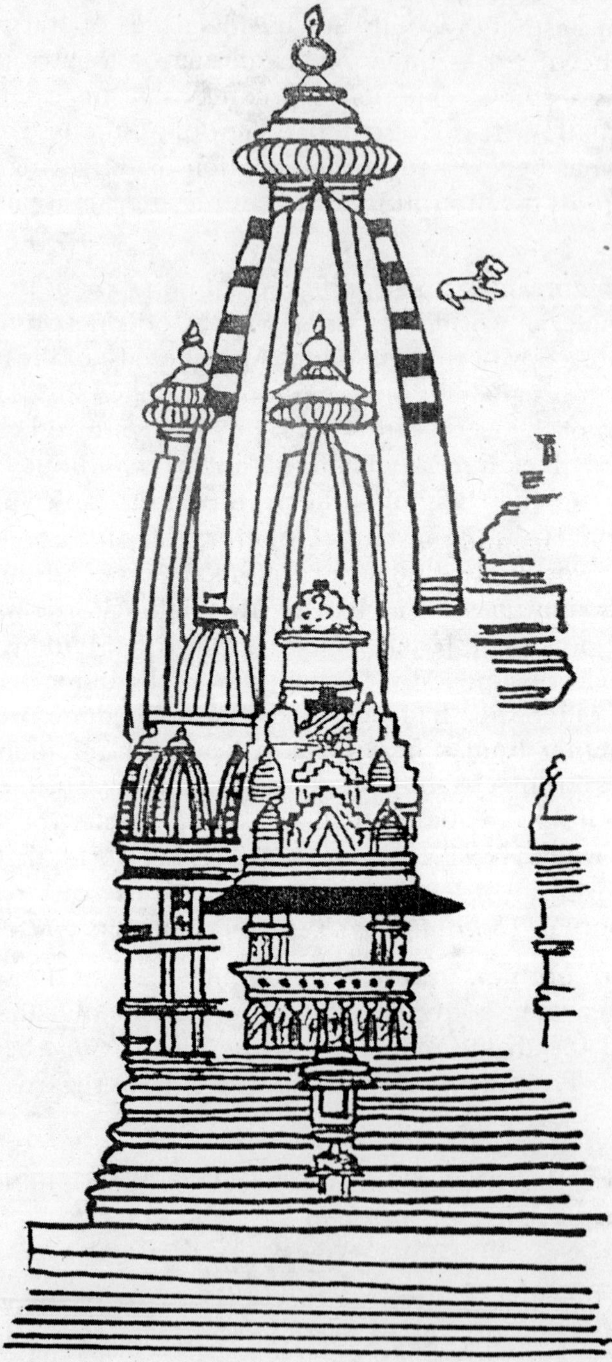

Figure 7: Temple (*devāyatana*) – an imitation of *devaśilpa*

The imitation here does not mean merely reflection or mirror or a copy of the divine world. It is implied here that the divine art has ascended into this material world. The human effort is in fact imitation, representation and portrayal of God's creation. It is like a mirror of whatever is there above it.

The dimensions of art does cease with the bringing down divine art to this material world. If it imitates the divine world it also reflects the affairs of the three worlds. Thus, the **Viṣṇudharmottara Purāṇa** says that the painting and the canon of dance, project the affairs of this world.

> विना तु नृत्तशास्त्रेण चित्रसूत्रं सुदुर्विदम् ।
> जगतोऽनुक्रिया कार्या द्वयोरपि यतो नृप ॥
>
> VdhPur III.2.4
>
> It is very difficult to know the canon of painting without the canon of dance because O King! in both of them the world is to be imitated. (Tr. P. Shah)

Here the imitation is not reproduction, it is rather copy of an already existing model or archetype. Here this copying is based on another concept that is similarity, resemblance or *sādṛśya.* The successful imitation addresses a hidden likeness with the already existing model.

The imitation and likeness are the essential nature of art. In the words of Coomaraswamy (1986, p. 276), "In the catholic view of art imitation, expression and participation are three predications of the essential nature of art". Here along with imitation and likeness we come across a strong view of imagination as well. The operation of God and human beings are linked together. God creates from void absolute and man copies it or uses his imagination, but he is not the creator or God so he does not work on his free will.

Then what is common between the original and imitated world? The work of art and its models are different things, but likeness in different things is to some extent common to both. Coomaraswamy (1986, p. 21) has cited similar concept in the western philosophy. The imitation or representation of a model involves indeed a likeness but hardly what we usually mean by 'Verisimilitude'. Art is iconography, the making of images or copies of some model whether visible or invisible. Indian works of art are called counterfeits or commensurations (*anukṛti, tadākāra, pratikṛti, pratibimba, pratimāna*), where likeness (*sārūpya, sādṛśya*) is demanded. Actually imitation constitutes one of the three components of likeness.

Coming back to the very basis of *anukṛti* or *anukaraṇa* one may assert that the likeness is one of the characteristics of imitation. This similarity leads the work of art from a mere imitation to the reflection (*pratibimba*).

The **Citra-Lakṣaṇa** says:

> सादृश्यं दृश्यते यत्तु दर्पणे प्रतिबिम्बवत् ।
> तच्चित्रमिति विख्यातं नालमाकारमात्रकम् ॥
>
> CiL 147
>
> That painting is well known as *citra* (i.e. *rasacitra*) which is not merely a sketch in outline, but shows the resemblance (of a figure) as truly as the reflection on a mirror. (Tr. A. Bhattacharya)

If *anukaraṇa* implies representation it betrays or presents only through the similarity. Similarity justifies the presentation even of an absolute object or concept. Abhinavagupta also explains *lakṣaṇa*, known as *sārūpya.*

> अपदेशस्तु परोक्षो यस्मादुत्पद्यतेऽनुकरणेन ।
> लक्षणसमानकरणात्सारूप्यं तत्तु विज्ञेयम् ॥
>
> AbhiBhā on NŚ XVI.15
>
> When the indirect (thing or meaning) is pointed out through representation, it is known as *sārūpya* (identity of form) on account of the creation of similar *lakṣaṇa* (signs).

Thus resemblance is not merely a part of imitation or representation. The existence of one presupposes the other. The process of *anukaraṇa/ anukṛti* will be incomplete without similarity or likeness. Thus, the **Amara Kośa** (III.2.17) takes the two terms as synonyms.

Anukaraṇa is not directly relevant to music because music does not present or re-present any situation from life. Music, being a cultural evolute, does not obtain a natural model. The music forming part of dramatic presentation does highlight the situation presented by the later. It can be non-referential when it is independent of drama.

Pitch level and temporal modulation are the two basic factors that provide a bridge between life and music. Unregulated variations of pitch and tempo occur in speech and in music they attain a regularised form. Higher pitch and faster speed go with excitement and turbulence of various kinds; and lower pitch and slower speed go with depression and peace. Music when forming part of drama highlights the different emotive situations in consonance with the other components of drama. By itself, music can and does suggest in a subtle manner mental states without presenting any specific situations. *Anukaraṇa* or 're-doing' of life could be said to operate in music through the above bridge.

Anukaraṇa within music itself has been accorded a position by accepting *anukāra* (one who is adept in imitating another singer) as one of the five categories of singers:

> शिक्षाकारोऽनुकारश्च रसिको रञ्जकस्तथा ।
> अनुकार इति प्रोक्तः परभङ्गयनुकारकः ॥
>
> SR III.19ab–20cd
>
> Five types of vocalists are recognised by the vocal experts, viz. *śikṣākāra, anukāra, rasika, rañjaka,* and *bhāvaka.* ... The imitator of another's style is called *anukāra* (the imitator).
> (Tr. R.K. Shringy and P.L. Sharma)

Thus, *anukaraṇa* does not operate directly in music unless it pertains to music itself.

In oriental view the *anukṛti* did not cease with the *śilpa,* even the dance is considered to be an imitation. But unlike the *śilpa* it is a re-production of the affairs of the world.

The concept of music is based upon the following, i.e. accompaniment (*anukaraṇa* or *saṅgati*) of the different instruments. It is an idea of divine imitation. The **Śāṅkhāyana Āraṇyaka** states:

> अथ खल्वियं दैवी वीणा भवति, तदनुकृतिरसौ मानुषी वीणा भवति ।
>
> ŚāṅkhĀr VIII.9
>
> Again, there is this divine lute that human lute is an imitation of it. (Tr. A.B. Keith)

The *anukaraṇa* is rather 'following' and the musical instruments are named according to the sound they make. The **Nirukta** (IX.12) says that the word *dundubhi* (drum) is onomatopoetic. Here it is not imitation, it is rather following – *dundubhiriti śabdānukaraṇam.*

Śabdabrahma echoes and the sound it creates, is 'following' according to the **Taittirīya Upaniṣad** (I.8), the compliance is *anukṛti.*

It echoes Buddhist view. He who sees the word sees me (SaṃNik III.120). The iconic and aniconic imitations are different. The aniconic is the imitation of the unspoken word – Brahma body, not of the alive human body or of the stone.

In soem cases the birds are named as per their sound they make. Thus the **Nirukta** again uses the term in the onomatopoetic sense.

> काक इति शब्दानुकृतिः । तदिदं शकुनिषु बहुलम् ।
>
> Nir III.18
>
> The word *kāka* (crow) is an onomatopoetic word. The onomatopoeia is mostly found in the names of birds. (Tr. L. Sarup)

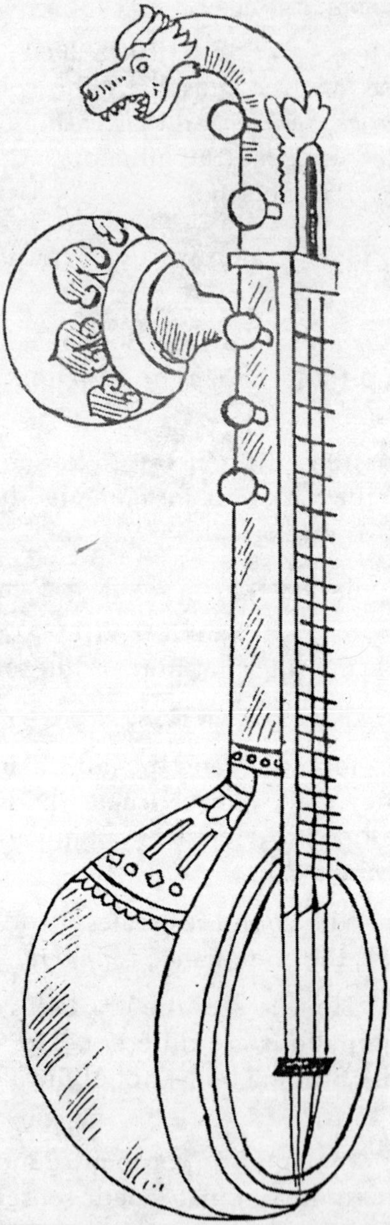

Figure 8: *Vyālamukhī vīṇā*

Durgācārya comments on the same – *anukaraṇam anukṛtiḥ śabdasyānukṛtiḥ śabdānukṛtiḥ, yādṛśamevāsau tayaivānukṛtyā śabdaṃ karoti tasya nāmāpi bhavati.*

The gestures in dance follows the words or the harmony on instrument. The different expressions are nothing but the imitation of the theme. Thus the **Viṣṇudharmottara Purāṇa** (III.2.4, III.35.9) says that in dance the affairs of the three worlds are to be represented.

Thus art as imitation' is either the imitation of the divinity or the copy of this material world. Art as imitation has its own aesthetic value. As an imitation it does not stop to be original or it diminishes its significance as an art object. It is both imitative and expressive of its themes by which it is constituted.

Conclusion

The concept of *anukaraṇa* or *anukṛti* originally conveyed the simple meaning 'imitation or acting'. Gradually the terms like *anukīrtana, anucikīrṣaṇa, anukāra* have become synonyms.

Anukaraṇa or *anukṛti* could be simple imitation, but imitation is not *nāṭya. Nāṭya* or drama is the representation of emotive states that is *anukīrtana.* If drama is simple *anukṛti* it cannot produce *rasa,* as the audience cannot identify the actor with the original character. In the words of Biswanath Bhattacharya: "Drama is an imitation of action which is meant for presentation before an audience. This presentation must not be narrative but should be capable of interpretation. A drama as a distinct literary form must then have these features. There should be imitation of life and action, capable of being interpreted by the actors through acting (*abhinaya*) in order to please an audience (*Sanskrit Drama & Dramaturgy,* p. 5).

"The term *anukṛti* which occurs in the **Viṣṇudharmottara Purāṇa** several times is yet another fundamental term which requires volumes of explanations and qualifications before it can be translated into an equally simple but complex and loaded term imitation. From the **Nāṭyaśāstra** to the Abhinavabhāratī and numerous other commentators and interpreters, the terms *anukaraṇa* and *anukṛti* have a fascinating history. The theory of aesthetics rests squarely on it. In recent scholarship 're-narration', 're-creation', 're-shaping' are the close approximations offered" (Kapila Vatsyayan, The Citrasūtra, Foreword, p. xvi).

A very different canvas is protrayed so far as the art is concerned. This interesting debate becomes irrelevant and one is rather exposed to a world of oriental and occidental views. Whether the art is an imitation of God's cre-

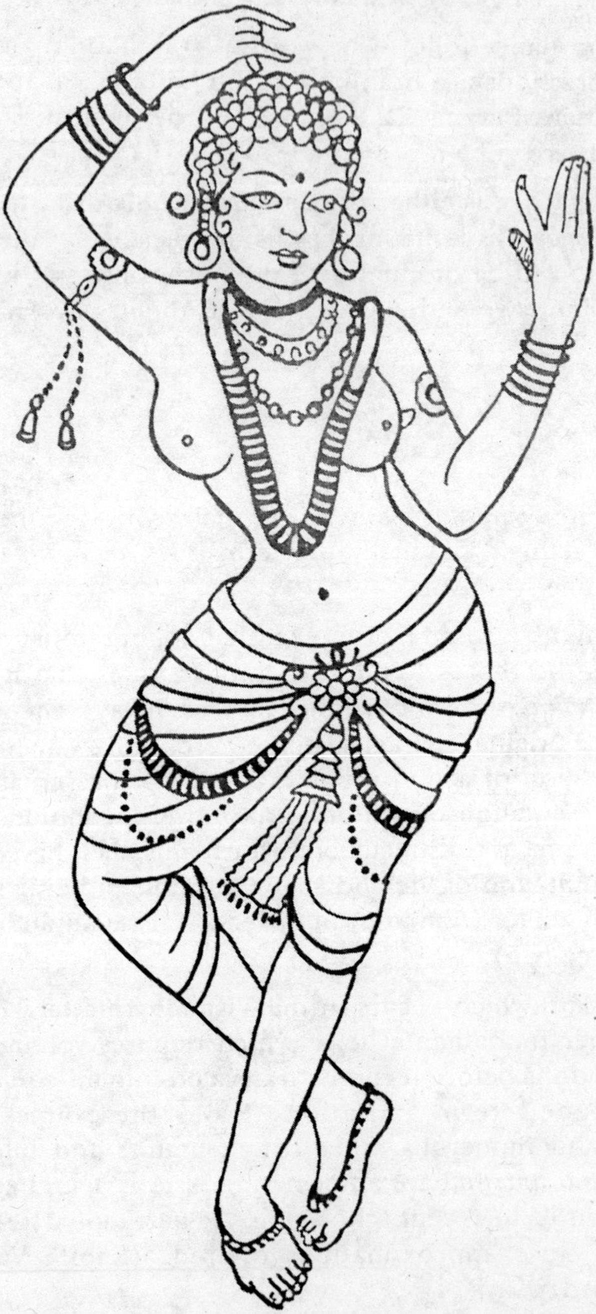

Figure 9: Dancing lady

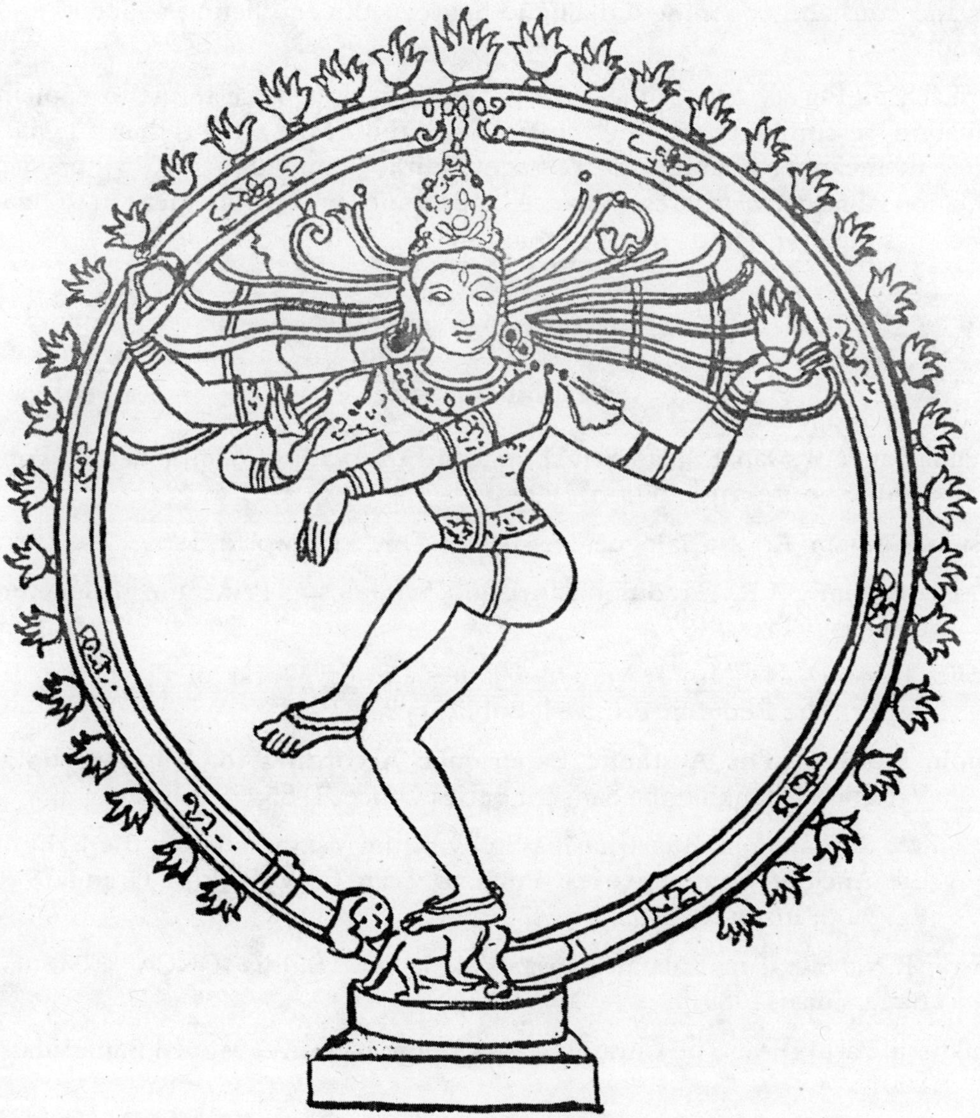

Figure 10: Naṭarāja – dance of creation

ation or the human mind and hands are also exercising their power here. The art is an imitation of human and divine world. The western view that art is imitation, expression and participation is not so strongly expressed here. The art is rather imitative and for this it seeks resemblance. Though the terms go through a fascinating journey from the period of the Brāhmaṇas to the early medieval period, in each epoch and text it delineates a different meaning and constantly opening a dialogue between the conflicting concepts and schools.

Each and every text of the different periods uses these terms to explain imitation, resemblance and following. The beauty of the term is that it signals different meaning through the passage of time – imitations of divine *śilpa,* imitation of *śabdabrahma,* resemblance, appearance and re-statement in drama, which has made the study more enchanting.

Anamika Roy

Select Bibliography

Bhattacharya, Biswanath: Sanskrit Drama and Dramaturgy, Delhi: Sarada Publishing house, 2nd edition, 1994.

Biswas, Gautam: Art as Dialogue, New Delhi: D.K. Printworld, 1955.

Coomaraswamy, A.K.: Traditional Art and Symbolism, Princeton: Princeton University Press, 1977.

Devies Lekwely, N. John & Vanghan James Davies: Works of Plate, Vol. II, Jaipur: The Republic Printwell Publications, 1988.

Gnoli, Raniero: The Aesthetic Experience According to Abhinavagupta, Varanasi: Chaukhamba Sanskrit Series Office, 1985.

Iyer, K.A. Subramania: Bhartṛhari: a Study of the Vākyapadīya in the light of the Ancient Commentaries, Pune: Deccan College, Post Graduate & Research Institute, 1992.

Misra, R.N.: Śilpa, in Kalātattvakośa, Vol. I, New Delhi: IGNCA & Motilal Banarsidass, 1980.

Mukherji, Parul Dave: The Citrasūtra, New Delhi: IGNCA & Motilal Banarsidass, 2001.

Singhal, R.L.: Aristotle and Bharat, Hoshiarpur: V.V. Research Institute, 1977.

Vatsyayan, Kapila: Bharata: The Natyas, New Delhi: Astra Sahitya Akademy, 1996.

Walimbe, Y.S.: Abhinavagupta on Indian Aesthetic, Delhi: Ajanta Publication, 1980.

CHĀYĀ

Overview

The term *chāyā* (f.) primarily denotes 'shadow' and secondarily reflection and likeness. In Indian tradition, *chāyā* is treated as a multi-dimensional concept bearing the connotations of *pratirūpa, bimba-pratibimba-bhāva,* image, reflection, shadow, likeness, darkness, etc. But being compounded with *ātapa* as a twin concept of natural dualism and an intertwined basic concept of Indian culture and artistic tradition it is widely known as *chāyātapa* 'light and shade'. Mutuality of this pair emerges to develop a mighty system of interdependence of the balance of active and passive outlook.

Both primary and secondary senses of the term *chāyā* are interrelated. Generally shadow denotes a relative darkness over some area caused by the interception of light waves by an opaque mass. But reflection emerges when a ray of light or other radiant energy strikes a surface and is thrown back into the medium through which it has come.

Shadow is the absence of light and so it has no motion, but motion is attributed to it on the basis of the movement of the object which shuts off the light and causes the shadow. So *chāyā* (shadow or reflection) is interrelated with form, shape, figure, body, appearance or the objects which has a shape '*ākāra*'. Light (*ātapa*) is associated with life whereas shadow or darkness (*chāyā*) with death. Actually, life is not the opposite of death and shadow is also not the opposite of light. It is also not that light means good and shadow means bad or evil; it is due to our partial vision that we divide one unified or uniaxial concept into two, like day and night.

From the *adhidaivata* outlook, the deity is light but the image is shadow or reflection. Light symbolizes activity, shadow represents inertia and regression indicating concealment and obstruction of activities. Light and white colour have a positive connotation, whereas in the system of binary oppositions, *chāyā* or darkness and black colour just form the opposite element. This natural dualism is also associated with spirit and matter; body (*śarīra*) and soul (*ātman*). Shadow has a shape but darkness has no shape. The shadow is interrelated with darkness as colour of shadow is dark. Light is truth whereas *chāyā* is untruth or false. In a Ṛgvedic cosmogonical *mantra* '*tama āsīt tamasā gūḷham agre*' (ṚV X.129.3), it is discussed that 'there was darkness in the beginning, concealed by darkness' and out of this darkness light appeared. As light arises from darkness (colour of shadow), life arises from death; similarly from the shadow of ignorance (*tamas* in the Sāṃkhya philosophy) generated the insight. Thus *chāyā* (shadow), *tamas* (darkness) and *mṛtyu* (death) are equivalent; they are not synonymous but simultaneous and eternal concept of creative process.

Chāyā is a fundamental concept of visual and performing arts as it deals with the basic idea of *praticchāyā* or *pratirūpa*, a reflection, though secondarily it is interlinked with the various Indological concepts like *bimba-pratibimba* 'reflection', *ābhāsa* 'appearance', *sādṛśya* 'convisibility', *anukṛti* 'imitation', *vyakta-avyakta* 'manifest-unmanifest', etc. The Vedic concept of *śilpa*: '*yad vai pratirūpaṃ tacchilpam*' (ŚBr III.2.1.5) is reflected in *chāyā* as *praticchāyā*. This is the basic idea of painting. Practically we see in a *chāyā* or shadow of an object a reflective, convisible and imitative appearance from visible to invisible or manifest to unmanifest state. As a multidimensional concept of Indian art the term *chāyā* is widely associated with the various Indological disciplines being in its various forms such as shade, shadow, image of the divinities or gods, colour of the face, resemblance, reflection, light, lustre, protection, darkness, hallucination, etc. An inter-disciplinary approach around the concept of *chāyā* revolves in all streams of Indian thought – Vedas, Epics and Purāṇas, philosophy, Buddhist and Jaina literature, Āyurveda, metaphysics, astronomy, politics, visual and performing arts for exploring the best physical, material, metaphysical and spiritual levels.

Etymology and Related Terms

The term *chāyā* is derived from the root *cho-* 'to cut, pierce' with the suffix *ya* (UDVṛ IV.118). So etymologically *chāyā* means 'one that cuts or checks heat'. Keeping this idea, the term denotes the wife of the sun, beauty, a reflected image and a shade (cf. *chāyā sūryapriyā kāntiḥ pratibimbam anātapaḥ*– AmKo III.3.157). As a second part of a compound it is used as a synonym of *pratimā, praticchāyā*, a reflected image (cf. AmKo II.10.35). These basic connotations are also noted in other lexicons (cf. MedKo XXVI.22b, VaiKo VI.2.13). All the four connotations: (i) absence of heat of the sun, fire, etc., i.e. shade, (ii) reflection or likeness, (iii) radiance, and (iv) the wife of the sun, bear clearly the etymological sense.

In the Kṣīrasvāmin's comm. (on AmKo III.3.157) examples for each meaning are given: *chāyākhyā arkabhāryā, kāntau yathā - vicchāyaḥ puruṣa bhavet, pratibimbe yathā – saṃkrāntacchāya ādarśaḥ, ātapābhāve yathā – naṣṭacchāyo madhyāhnaḥ*, where in *vicchāya, saṃkrāntacchāya* and *naṣṭacchāya*, the concept is used as the last part of the compound. *Chāyā* is opposite or *viparyaya* to sunrays or light which seems that oppositon is shown by cutting or preventing. It is also the lustre which follows leaves (*chāyā ātapaviparyayaḥ, parṇānugatā dīptiśca* – UDVṛ IV.118).

Some compounds with *chāyā* (beginning of the compound) are: *chāyākara* 'a parasol bearer', *chāyāgraha* 'a mirror' (RājTar III.154), *chāyāgrāha* 'depriving of the shadow' (Rām I.3.28), *chāyāṅka* 'the moon', *chāyātanaya, chāyātmaja*, 'the planet Saturn', *chāyātapa* 'light and shade', *chāyātaru* 'an umbrageous tree' (Megh I.1), *chāyātman* 'one's shadow or reflected image' (Megh I.40), *chāyādruma* (AbhŚāk IV.11), *chāyādvitīya* 'alone' (MBh III.57.25), *chāyānaṭṭa* 'name of a *rāga* (in music), *chāyānāṭaka* 'a small drama or one imitative of another', *chāyāpatha* 'the milky way', *chāyāpuruṣa* '*puruṣa* in the form of a shadow', *chāyābhartṛ* 'husband of Chāyā, the sun', *chāyābhinna* 'reflecting light from various surfaces', *chāyābhṛt* 'the moon', *chāyāmaya* 'shadowy' (ŚBr XIV.5.1.12), *chāyāmāna* 'a measure of a shadow', *chāyāmitra* 'a parasol', *chāyāyantra* 'a sun-dial' (BṛSam II.3), etc.

As a second part of *tatpuruṣa* compound the term *chāyā* is also noticed in many places of Sanskrit literature specially in the works of Kālidāsa: *ratnacchāyā* (Megh I.15; 38), *pāṇḍucchāyā* (Megh I.24), *kṣāmacchāyā* (Megh II.20), *vaktracchāyā* (Megh II.44), *ikṣucchāyā* (Ragh IV.20), *dhvajacchāyā* (Ragh VII.4).

The **Uṇādi Dhātu Vṛtti** gives a very clear etymological explanation of the term *chāyā*:

> माच्छाससिसूभ्यो यः ॥
>
> एभ्यो यः प्रत्ययो भवति ।... छो छेदने, छ्यति छायते वा छाया प्रतिरूपम् । कर्ता कर्म च ।
>
> UDVṛ VIII.12
>
> The suffix *ya* is used with the roots *mā*- etc. *Chāyā* is derived from the root *cho*- 'to cut' with the suffix *ya* in the sense of agent (*kartā*) and object (*karma*). 'That which cuts or which is cut' is (the derivative meaning of) *chāyā*, meaning *pratirūpa* 'image, likeness or reflection'.

Similarity or likeness in morphological and phonological features of letters is also treated as *chāyā* in the **Kāśikā Vṛtti:**

> वर्णेषु ये वर्णैकदेशा वर्णान्तरसमानाकृतयस्तेषु तत्कार्यं न भवति । तच्छायानुकारिणो हि ते, न पुनस्त एव ।
>
> Kā on Pā Pratyāhāra Sū 4
>
> In the alphabets, the grammatical operation (e.g. *sthānyāśrayaṃ kāryam*, an operation resting on the primitive form as opposed to the *ādeśa* or substitute) of a letter is not applicable in a part of the letters which are similar in form with other letters (i.e. the former

ones). Because they are similar in (morphological and phonological) feature but not the exact ones.

Most of the words for *chāyā* are used in Indo-European languages to denote shadow, shade, image as reflection, etc. The term is also used in the sense of 'disembodied spirit' in a figurative sense.

Some of the phonologically similar Indo-European synonyms of *chāyā* are: Greek *σκιά*, Avestan *saya* (*a-saya* 'without shadow'), 'New Persian *sāya* from Indo-European **skāi-*, **ski-* 'to shine'. The term is interconnected through a notion of 'faint light' (*ābhāsa*) or 'reflection' (*pratibimba/praticchāyā*) as noticed in old English *scima*, 'shadow, gloom' beside *scīma* 'light, brightness'. In colloquial New Greek *ἥσκλος* from *ἥσκια* with influence of the opposite *ἥλιος* 'sun, sunshine'. Latin *umbra*, Italian *ombra*, French *ombre*, Spanish *sombra* 'shade', French *sombre* 'dark, gloomy, Greek *σκοτος* 'darkness', where the basic concept of light and shade is reflected.

Another range of meaning of the concept *chāyā* is shelter as noticed in some Indo-European languages, like Russian *ten' seni*, Polandish *sien*'entrance room', etc. as room without light', New Iranian *scāth* 'shelter', etc. follows one Vedic concept of *chāyā* as home.

The term *chāyā* is so popular in Indology that more than twenty texts of different disciplines like Yoga, Tantra, Jyotis, , Dharmaśāstra, Gṛhyasūtra, etc. are stated with this term as recorded in the *New Catalogus Catalogorum*: *chāyā, chāyāgaṇita, chāyādānavidhi, chāyādvāra, chāyānāṭaka, chāyāpātradāna, chāyāpuruṣa, chāyāpuruṣaprakaraṇa, chāyāpuruṣamāhātmya, chāyāpuruṣalakṣaṇa, chāyāpuruṣavidhi, chāyāpuruṣāvabodhana, chāyālakṣaṇa, chāyāviṃśati-stotra, chāyāvidhi, chāyāvihārakāvya, chāyāṣṭaka*, etc.

Layers of Meaning

The term *chāyā* primarily denotes shadow but in secondary sense it indicates a number of meanings like reflection, likeness, etc. In Indian tradition this multilayered concept indicates various meanings as recorded by Indian lexicographers Amarasiṃha etc. (cf. AmKo III.3.157). The **Nānārtha Mañjarī** gives different shades of meaning from which the semantical development of the concept could be known:

छाया स्त्री सूर्यभार्यायां प्रतिबिम्बे अनातपे ।
पालनोत्कोचयोः कान्तिसच्छोभाकाव्यपङ्क्तिषु ।

NāMa 1288–1289

The term *chāyā* (in feminine gender) is used to denote sun's wife, reflection, shade, protection, bribe, lustre, beauty, a Sanskrit version of the Prakrit and a series.

Chāyā is also recorded in the **Rāja-Nighaṇṭu** as a synonym of *kānti* 'lustre' (RāNigh XXI.26) and *tamas* 'darkness' (RāNigh XXI.27). The same text also records the property of shadow as coolness and pleasantness (*chāyā madhuraśītalā* – RāNigh XXI.28).

The different meanings of the term may be grouped as follows:

(i) Shade cast by the interception of light by an object, shadow, umbra, a faint shadow or mere appearance or slight influence (*ābhāsa*),

(ii) likeness (*sādṛśya*), semblance, resemblance (BhāgPur VII.15.59),

(iii) reflection, a reflected image (*chāyā na mūrchati malopahata prasāde* ... AbhŚāk VII.32),

(iv) an inseparable or constant companion (MBh IV.35.10), a spy or detective who follows one,

(v) a shadowy fancy, a spectre, hallucination, an apparition, a ghost, spirit (BhāgPur VIII.3.14),

(vi) colour (MālMā VI.5), colour of the face, complexion (*kevalaṃ lāvaṇyamayī chāyā* ... AbhŚāk III, after 7),

(vii) darkness (metaphorically *avidyā*, cf. *chāyātapau yatra* ... BhāgPur VIII.5.27), the dark part of a picture, the dark figure so projected on a surface, mimicking the object,

(viii) lustre, light, glow, shine (Rām II.69.20, Ragh IV.5, Megh XV.35),

(ix) beauty (*kṣāmacchāyaṃ bhavanam* – Megh II.20),

(x) protection, shelter (*pādacchāyā* ... Rām II.48.17, VII.47.15–17), protective shade,

(xi) a row, line, series (*paṅkti*), e.g. beads of lustre (Pañc I.379),

(xii) name of goddess Durgā (*chāyārūpeṇa saṃsthitā* – MārkPur LXXXII.17),

(xiii) name of wife of the Hindu sun-god,

(xiv) name of a *rāga* (BhPrak VII.50),

(xv) name of a *śabdālaṅkāra* 'embellishment of a sound' (Sark II.39), and

(xvi) a Sanskrit version of a Prakrit text.

As an adjective the term denotes feigned, unreal, existing only in skeleton, only partly active or inactive, etc. As a verb it is used in the causative as *chāyayati* to denote 'cut or cut off' (cf. *śācchāsāhvāvyāvepāṃ yuk* – Pā VII.3.37).

In the modern society the term *chāyā* is closely related with picture widely known as *chāyācitra* 'a cinematographic file', silhouette or shadow figure, shadowgraph or a radiograph, i.e. an image produced by shadow throwing a shadow on a screen originated from the concept of *chāyānāṭaka* 'the shadow play' in Sanskrit literature.

The term *chāyā* covers a large range of meanings relating to various levels, physical and metaphysical, astronomical and spiritual. Interconnectedness and merging of different meanings of this term are very clearly reflected in the Indian tradition. In early Vedic literature the connotation of this term was mainly used in the sense of shelter, home (*chāyā iti gṛhanāma* – Nigh III.4), but in later Sanskrit literature the term appears in various senses through different semantic changes like expansion of meaning, contraction of meaning and transference of meaning. Hence the term *ābhāsa*, *pratibimba*, etc. are sometimes synonyms of *chāyā*. Grassman also suggests three meanings of this term in the Vedas: non-existence of the sun's heat, picture and shadow "Widerschein, Abbild, Schatten" (*Wörterbuch Zum Rigveda*) but in the Vedic literature it is mostly used in the sense of shelter instead of picture.

Development of the Concept

In the **Ṛgveda**, two basic senses of *chāyā* are noticed – shadow or shelter and reflection or likeness. These two senses are closely related and hence it may be said that shadow is the manifested likeness of a deity and a temporal shelter of a being. Both the immortality and death or mortality are the shadow of the Supreme Creator. It means ignorance, displeasure, cold shadow or darkness of Brahman is death and the reflected shadow or *praticchāyā* is the knowledge of his bright glory. In the context of the knowledge of the Supreme Spirit, the **Ṛgveda** records *chāyā* as a pervasive concept.

यस्य च्छायामृतं यस्य मृत्युः कस्मै देवाय हविषा विधेम ॥

RV X.121.2cd

Whose shadow is immortal life and death –
What God shall we adore with our oblation ? (Tr. R. Panikkar)

Here perhaps the sun is denoted by the Supreme Spirit – '*yasya chāyā amṛtam*' means all beyond the sun is immortal and '*yasya* (*chāyā*) *mṛtyuḥ*' means all that is under the sun is death. Death does not die. It is only by the conquest of the one and union with the other of his aspects that an immortality can be attained. Hence *chāyā* and *ātapa* are basic units of eternal creative process of the universe. This Ṛgvedic *mantra* denotes the shadow of sun as a symbol of immortality and death. Actually the entire universe lies in the shelter (*chāyā*) of the Supreme Soul (cf. *etasya hīḍaṃ sarvaṃ chāyāyām* – ŚBr VII.7.3.13). Since the very outset of Vedic literature the term *chāyā* is used to denote shelter or shadow. Agni, the source or representative of light is associated with the whole world like shadow (*chāyeva viśvaṃ bhuvanaṃ sisakṣi* – ṚV I.73.8). Agni has the power of giving shelter to the entire world as the umbrella averts the distress of oppressive heat of the sun. The whole world is averting distress as the shade of a great rock or tree wards off the oppressive heat of the sun. This simile is perhaps in case of avoiding cold with fire. The same idea is further noticed in the **Ṛgveda**:

उप च्छायामिव घृणेरगन्म शर्म ते वयम् ।
अग्ने हिरण्यसंदृशः ॥

ṚV VI.16.38

To thee for shelter are we come, as to the shade from fervent heat,
Agni, who glitterest like gold. (Tr. R.T.H. Griffith)

Shadow or shelter gives refreshment to the creative being from fervent sunlight and it is used as simile in the **Ṛgveda**.

घृणीव च्छायामरपा अशीया विवासेयं रुद्रस्य सुम्नम् ॥

ṚV II.33.6cd

As he who finds a shade in fervent sunlight may I, uninjured, win
the bliss of Rudra. (Tr. R.T.H. Griffith)

It is by means of *chāyā* ('shadow' or reflection) that the whole light is brought forth in the world of experience. A Ṛgvedic *mantra* indicates the reflection of nature, expressed by the seers, the manifestation of unchangeable nature, whose reflection is also noticed in the water.

यादृगेव ददृशे तादृगुच्यते
सं छायया दधिरे सिध्रयाप्स्वा ।

ṚV V.44.6ab

Like as he is beheld such is he said to be.
They with effectual splendour in the floods have made.
(Tr. R.T.H. Griffith)

Here the form of deity or nature is reflected in flood of waters, the manifested light in the world. Reflection of self in water is a recurrent motif in Vedic literature which is explicitly the intellectual activity in the vision of the Vedic seers. So the term *chāyā* is not only used in a figurative sense of shelter in the **Ṛgveda** but also in the sense of reflection of the manifested light or deity in the world of waters. This idea is more explicitly noticed in the **Gopatha Brāhmaṇa** (I.3).

A Vedic seer sees a *mantra* in a *sattvic* stage. Knowledge or intuition is light and reflection of anything is possible on light or white surface and not in the dark surface. The seer sees the *mantra* expressing the original form of natural phenomenon and it comes in the mind of poet through intuition, i.e. light. So light is the original and reflection is the secondary matter.

In the **Yajurveda** the term *chāyā* is mostly used in the sense of shelter or shade related with the sacrificial work. The sacrificer touches the *udumbara* post and addresses the branch or post by uttering the following *mantra* where the term *chāyā* conveys the universal shelter.

ध्रुवासि ध्रुवोऽयं यजमानोऽस्मिन्नायतने प्रजया पशुभिर्भूयात् ।
घृतेन द्यावापृथिवी पूर्येथामिन्द्रस्य छदिरसि विश्वजनस्य छाया ॥

YV V.28

Firm-set art thou. Firm be this Sacrificer

within this home with offspring and with cattle.

O Heaven and Earth, be ye filled full of fatness.

Indra's mat art thou, shelter of all people. (Tr. R.T.H. Griffith)

Here the heaven and earth is compared with the Indra's mat, the shelter of all people. Almost same concept is noticed in the **Taittirīya Saṃhitā** (I.3.1) in the event of Soma-sacrifice where the erection of the *sadas* is going on: *indrasya sado'si viśvajanasya chāyā* 'thou art the seat of Indra, the shade of all folk' (tr. A.B. Keith). According to Baudhāyana (BŚrSū VI.27) the *mantra* accompanies the placing on the roof of the midmost of the nine coverings (*chadis*).

The sacrificer lays the *svayamātṛṇṇā* brick in the fifth layer of the sacrificial altar keeping the idea in his mind that it is laying in the shadow or shelter of the protector in the heart of ocean.

आयोष्ट्वा सदने सादयाम्यवतश्छायायां समुद्रस्य हृदये ।
रश्मीवतीं भास्वतीमा या द्यां भास्यापृथिवीमोर्वन्तरिक्षम् ॥

YV XV.63

In Āyu's seat I (the sacrificer) set thee (*svayamātṛṇṇā* brick) in the shadow of the protector in the heart of Ocean,

Thee luminous, bright with eyes, thee who illumest the sky, the earth and air's broad realm between them. (Tr. R.T.H. Griffith)

In the context of laying down three offering spoons by Adhvaryu in

Darśapūrṇamāsa sacrifice Agni's shade is praised as Viṣṇu's mansion, i.e. the place of the personified sacrifice. It indicates that shade was the first shelter or place of refuge or home of living being.

अस्कन्नमद्य देवेभ्य आज्यं संभ्रियासमङ्घ्रिणा विष्णो मा त्वावक्रमिषं वसुमतीमग्ने ते छायामुपस्थेषं विष्णो स्थानमसीत इन्द्रो वीर्यमकृणोदूर्ध्वोऽध्वर आस्थात् ॥

YV II.8

May I (i.e. the Adhvaryu) today offer Gods unsplit butter.
Let me not with my foot offend thee, Viṣṇu.
Agni, may I approach thy shade abounding in store of riches.
Thou art Viṣṇu's mansion.
Hence Indra wrought his deed (*vṛtravadha*) of manly vigour.
The sacrifice stood firmly elevated. (Tr. R.T.H. Griffith)

In the **Taittirīya Saṃhitā** the shadow of the gods are symbolized as the immortality and the sun is the supreme energy of this luminous world.

ऋतस्य पन्था असि देवानां छायाऽमृतस्य नाम तत् ।

TSam VII.1.20.1

Thou art the path of holy order, the shadow of the gods, the name of immortality. (Tr. A.B. Keith)

Gods are shadowless and luminous due to the power of sun but here the part *devānāṃ chāyā* is used in the sense of shelter of the gods. The same Saṃhitā also records the union of light and shade in connection with sprinkling of *vasatīvarī* water on *soma* altar.

छायायै चाऽऽतपतश्च सन्धौ गृह्णात्यहोरात्रयोरेवास्मै वर्णं गृह्णाति, ... ।

TSam VI.4.2.4

He takes (them) at the union of shade and light; verily for him he secures the colour of day and night .... (Tr. A.B. Keith)

The **Atharvaveda** records the term *chāyā* in the sense of shadow, shelter, likeness or simile, phantom, etc. some of which are related with the black magic. A plotter or conspirator against brahmin should be driven out even from the sheltering under the shade of a tree.

तं वृक्षा अप सेधन्ति छायां नो मोपगा इति ।

AV V.19.9ab

The very trees repel the man and drive him from their sheltering shade. (Tr. R.T.H. Griffith)

This Vedic *mantra* means that if somebody forcibly captures the wealth of brahmin, he is not allowed even by a tree to take shelter under its shade. *Chāyā* is also recorded as a playful war-tactics of Lord Indra.

यैरिन्द्रः प्रक्रीडते पद्घोषैश्छायया सह ।
तैरमित्रास्त्रसन्तु नोऽमी ये यन्त्यनीकशः ॥

AV V.21.8

With which noise of footsteps and shadowy troops (i.e. unseen army) Indra plays battle let those our enemies be feared (in the same way) who go yonder in the battle as marching army in a row.

In the **Atharvaveda** *chāyā* is also prescribed for the person who follows good conduct or moral and who misbehaves like kicking a cow with the foot, urinating towards the sun, keeping somebody under one's shadow and causing disturbances by staying between the sacrificer and fire, he should be punished in a shadowless state for ever (... *tasya vṛścāmi te mūlaṃ na cchāyāṃ karavo'param* – AV XIII.1.56). The term *chāyā* is recorded also in the sense of darkness as a comparison in the context of guarding a pregnant woman from demons.

छायामिव प्र तान्त्सूर्यः परिक्रामन्ननीनशत् ॥

AV VIII.6.8cd

... them the circling (*pari-kram*) sun hath made to vanish away like a shadow. (Tr. W.D. Whitney)

It is very ineresting to note that the idea of phantom was current in the period of **Atharvaveda** where the term *chāyaka*, cognate word of *chāyā* is recorded alongwith other evil spirits (*chāyakāduta nagnakāt* – AV VIII.6.21).

The Brāhmaṇa literature also treats *chāyā* in the sense of shadow and reflection both. In the context of some penances for mishaps to the performer of the Agnihotra, the **Aitareya Brāhmaṇa** compares the shadow of darkness with death.

पुरा संभेदाच्छायानामाहवनीयमुद्धरेन्मृत्युर्वै तमश्छाया, तेनैव तज्ज्योतिषा मृत्युं तमश्छायां तरति, सा तत्र प्रायश्चित्तिः ॥

AitBr VII.12

He (the performer of the Agnihotra) shall take out (of the Gārhapatya) the Āhavanīya before the shadows are cast together (before it has grown completely dark). For the shadow of darkness is death. By means of this light (the silver) he overcomes death, which is the shadow of darkness. This is the penance. (Tr. M. Haug)

Chāyā is also compared with vice (*pāpa*) as an inseparable aspect of a being. In the context of *punarādheya* or re-establishment of the sacred fires, the **Śatapatha Brāhmaṇa** records the smallest shadow of a person (at mid-day) as a simile of smallest evil of a person.

> छाययेव वा अयं पुरुषः पाप्मनानुषक्तः । सोऽस्यात्र कनिष्ठो भवति - अधस्पद-
> मिवेयस्यते तत् कनिष्ठमेवैतत् पाप्मानमवबाधते । तस्मादु मध्यन्दिन एवादधीत ।
>
> ŚBr II.2.3.10
>
> Verily, this man is affected with evil, as with a shadow. But then (at mid-day) that (evil) of his (like his shadow) is smallest, and shrinks, as it were, beneath his foot; hence he thereby crushes that evil, when it is smallest. For this reason also he should establish his fires (the second time) at mid-day. (Tr. J. Eggeling)

The whole universe lies in the shelter of Brahman. The same text records this concept in the context of laying down the *svayamātṛṇṇā* brick.

> "छायायाम्"-इति, एतस्य हीदं सर्वं छायायाम् ।
>
> ŚBr VIII.7.3.13
>
> .... 'in the shadow', – for in his shadow all this universe is.
> (Tr. J. Eggeling)

The same concept is also found in the **Jaiminīya Brāhmaṇa.**

> अवतश् छायायाम् इति । यज्ञो वा अवतिः । तस्यैषा छाया क्रियते यत् सदः ।
>
> JaimBr I.70
>
> (I set thee) in the shadow of the protector (YV XV.63). Sacrifice is verily the protector. It is of the sacrifices that the sacrificial shelter is shaded.

In a creation myth of the **Gopatha Brāhmaṇa** the term *chāyā* is explicitly used in the sense of reflection. Prajāpati tormented his self, the waters came forth as a stream of his sweat and they were given the status of *jāyā* (wife), female-principle, in which the creator found his reflection.

> ता अपः सृष्ट्वान्वैक्षत । तासु स्वां छायामपश्यत् । तामस्येक्षमाणस्य स्वयं
> रेतोऽस्कन्दत् । तदप्सु प्रत्यतिष्ठत् ।
>
> GoBr I.1.3
>
> He, the creator-god (Brahma), having created the waters (as his female-principle), saw his reflection (*chāyā*) in them; thereby the own seed or self-essence (*retas*) of him, who perceived, dissipated and that became borne on the waters. (Tr. P.K. Agrawala)

Here the water is an effulgent entity, as liquid with reflective power which takes shadow and mingles it where shadow itself identified with liquid effulgence (*taralatā*).

The **Śāṅkhāyana Āraṇyaka** records the position of shadow of a being at the time of death.

> अथाप्यादर्शे वोदके वा जिह्मशिरसं वाऽशिरसं वाऽऽत्मानं पश्येन्न वा पश्येत्तदप्येवमेव विद्यादथापि च्छिद्रा छाया भवति न वा भवति तदप्येवमेव विद्यात् ... ।
>
> ŚāṅkhĀr VIII.7
>
> Again, if he sees himself in a mirror or water with a crooked head or without a head, or cannot see himself, he should know that it is so. Again, if his shadow is pierced, or he throws no shadow, he should know that it is so. (Tr. A.B. Keith)

The same text again explains that the crooked shadow is an indication of death.

> अथायं पुरुषः प्रेष्यन् पुरा संवत्सरात् संवत्सरस्य दृष्टीः पश्यति च्छिद्रा छाया भवति न वा भवति ... ।
>
> ŚāṅkhĀr XI.3
>
> Now, a man, when he is to die before the year's end, sees visions of the year. His shadow is crooked or is not seen at all. (Tr. A.B. Keith)

In the Upaniṣads also the use of the term *chāyā* is noticed in the sense of shade and reflection. The **Kaṭhopaniṣad** gives the simile of light and shade for presenting universal and individual soul to distinguish the attained and attainer or the goal and the goer. The knowers of Brahman speak of these two as different like shade and light, because of their worldliness and freedom from worldliness (*chāyātapau brahmavido vadanti* – KaṭhUp III.1). Again, the same Upaniṣad treats '*chāyā*' as a mixture of both shade and reflection in the following *mantra*.

> यथाऽऽदर्शे तथाऽऽत्मनि यथा स्वप्ने तथा पितृलोके ।
> यथाऽप्सु परीव ददृशे तथा गन्धर्वलोके छायातपयोरिव ब्रह्मलोके ॥
>
> KaṭhUp VI.5
>
> As in a mirror, so is it seen in the body (*ātman*);
> As in dream, so in the world of the fathers;
> As if in water, so in the world of the Gandharvas (*genii*),
> As if in light and shade, so in the world of Brahma.
> (Tr. R.E. Hume)

As one sees oneself distinctly reflected in a mirror similarly in one's spotless intellect springs a vision of the self. Only in the world of Brahman which is difficult to attain, the vision is very distinct as it is in the case of shade and light.

In the narrative of Gārgya-Bālāki, and Ajātaśatru, king of Kashi, the **Bṛhadāraṇyaka Upaniṣad** shows that Gārgya worshipped a being identified with shadow as Brahman. The person consists of shadow is actually the deity of Death.

> स होवाच गार्ग्यः - य एवायं छायामयः पुरुष एतमेवाहं ब्रह्मोपास इति ।
>
> BṛUp II.1.12
>
> Gārgya said: the person here who consists of shadow – him indeed I worship as Brahman. (Tr. R.E. Hume)

Ajātaśatru made him realise that there is a god in the external darkness or shadow and internal ignorance (seated in the heart inseparably) where this person identified with shadow is death. The nature of this shadowy (*chāyāmaya*) state is expressed more distinctly in the story of Yājñavalkya and Śākalya where Brahman's abode is darkness and it is the very being who is identified with shadow cum ignorance (*ya evāyaṃ chāyāmayaḥ puruṣaḥ sa eṣaḥ* – BṛUp III.9.14).

The **Chāndogya Upaniṣad** also explains this concept of *chāyā* as reflection in the narrative of Indra-virocana and Prajāpati. Prajāpati taught them that reflection of this body is seen in the eyes, in water and in the mirror etc. Indra and Virocana felt satisfied and left the place but afterwards Indra felt that this reflection considered as soul in subject to destruction. Actually Prajāpati intended to teach them that the person reflected in eye is considered as self.

The term *chāyā* is very closely related with the term *ābhāsa*. Śaṅkara, while expounding *trivṛtkaraṇa prakriyā* (process of triplication in the Bhāṣya of Chāndogya Upaniṣad) has described individual soul as reflection of the deity (*jīvo hi nāma devatāyā ābhāsamātram* – ŚBh on ChUp VI.3.2). It is like a reflection of a being in a mirror and the reflection of the sun etc. in water. It does not itself become connected with physical happiness, sorrow, etc. as the deity enters merely as a reflection in the form of an individual soul (*chāyāmātreṇa jīvarūpeṇānupraviṣṭatvād devatā na daihikaiḥ svataḥ sukhaduḥkhādibhiḥ sambadhyate* – ŚBh on ChUp VI.3.2). So deity remains unaffected inspite of its contact with the individual soul.

The term *chāyā* is also noticed in the **Praśna Upaniṣad** in the context on discussion on two questions on the source of a person's life and its embodiment: (i) from where is this *prāṇa* (life) born? And, (ii) how does it comes into this body ? In reply Pippalāda says:

> आत्मन एष प्राणो जायते । यथैषा पुरुषे छायैतस्मिन्नेतदाततम् ।
> मनोकृतेनायात्यस्मिञ्शरीरे ॥
>
> PraUp III.3
>
> From the self this life is born. It is same as in the case of a person there the shadow is extended, so this *prāṇa* is fixed on the self. It comes into this body by the actions of the mind.

Appearance of Yakṣa, a momentary appearance of light, before the gods in the **Kena Upaniṣad** gives us an idea of *chāyā* as phantom, flashing upon the sight, manifestation of something, normally invisible. This indistinct figure of Yakṣa is Brahman, inexpressively manifested (*prādur babhūva*) before the deities and it also disappears (cf. KeUp ch. 3–4). It also indicates that due to the disappearance of light, shadow or momentary appearance also disappears.

Extension of shadow is a natural aspect. It remains with a person as an inseparable relation. The relation between *vṛkṣa* and *chāyā* is also manifested in the **Dhyānabindu Upaniṣad**:

> वृक्षं तु सकलं विद्याच्छाया तस्यैव निष्कला ।
> सकले निष्कले भावे सर्वत्रात्मा व्यवस्थितः ॥
>
> DBUp 8
>
> Know the tree as the whole (i.e. possessed of parts), while its shadow is partless. In (both) whole or (possessed of parts) and non-whole (partless) states, everywhere the self pervades.

In the Sūtra literature the term *chāyā* is mainly used to denote shadow. The **Baudhāyana Śrauta-Sūtra** prescribes to collect *vasatīvarī*-water, in the Agniṣṭoma sacrifice, from the nearest flowing water during twilight, a conjunction of day and night.

> छायायै चातपतश्च संधौ गृह्णाति ॥
>
> BŚrSū VI.32
>
> One should take up (water) at the conjunction of shade and sunshine. (Tr. R.N. Dandekar)

The **Āśvalāyana Gṛhya-Sūtra** records the importance of shadow of a round apartment in the context of a ritual for preventing any disturbance or danger during conception. Shadow of a circular building is auspicious for a pregnant woman.

अथास्यै मण्डलागारच्छायायां दक्षिणस्यां नासिकायामजीतामोषधीं नस्तः करोति ।

ĀśvaGṛhSū I.13.5

He then inserts into her right nostril in the shadow of a round apartment (the sap of) an herb which is not faded. (Tr. H. Oldenberg)

The Dharmasūtras use the term *chāyā* in the context of prescribing some ethical rules.The **Āpastamba Dharma-Sūtra** shows that beside fruits, shadow and fragrance of mango tree are also the examples of worldly benefits (*tad yathāmre phalārthe nirmite chāyā gandha ityanūtpadyete, evaṃ dharmaṃ caryamāṇam arthā anūtpadyante* – ĀpDhSū I.7.20–3). The same text also prescribes to avoid urination in the shadow of a tree.

छायायां मूत्रपुरीषयोः कर्म वर्जयेत् ॥
स्वां तु छायामवमेहेत् ॥

ĀpDhSū I.11.30.16-17

One should avoid ejecting urine or faeces in the shadow of trees.
But he may urinate in his own shadow. (Tr. P. Ghosal)

The **Gautama Dharma-Sūtra** prescribes to avoid ejecting faeces in the shade of a tree along with other places or objects like ashes, cow-dung, ploughed field, beautiful site, etc. (*na bhasma-kariṣa-kṛṣtacchāyāpathikāmyeṣu* – GauDhSū IX.45). The **Nāradīya Śikṣā** shows the intertwined concept of *chāyātapa* (shade and sunlight) in the context of movement from one musical note to another.

स्वरात् स्वरं संक्रमस्तु स्वरसन्धिरनुल्बणम् ।
अविच्छिन्नं समं कुर्यात् सूक्ष्मछायातपोपमम् ॥

NārŚik I.6.18

(While) going from one musical note to another the joint between the two notes should be indistinct, unbroken and *sama.* It should be made to resemble the faint shade and sunlight. (Tr. U.R. Bhise)

In Paninian grammatical system the word *chāyā* is used in the sense of shadow and mostly noticed as a second part of *tatpuruṣa* compound. A *tatpuruṣa* compound not co-occurring with *nañ* or a *karmadhāraya* compound is neuter in gender when it ends with the word *chāyā* 'shadow' to express abundance of the preceding member of the compound (*chāyā bāhulye* – Pā II.4.22). Here the nature of preceding member is abundance. For example, *śalabhacchāyam* 'shadow cast by a huge cloud of locusts'; *ikṣucchāyam* 'shadow cast by a thick grove of sugar-cane'. But as an optional rule of this regular aphorism (*chāyā bāhulya*), Pāṇini has made a rule (*vibhāṣā ... chāyā* – Pā II.4.25) by which the term ending with *chāyā* is used in neuter or feminine gender. For example, *kuḍyacchāyam, kuḍyacchāyā* 'shadow of a wall'. In case of Vedic accent the term *chāyā* has some influence. In a *tatpuruṣa* compound occurring in the neuter gender (*napuṃsaka*) the first member retains its original accent when co-occurring before the nominal stems *mātrā* 'measure', *upajñā* 'invention', *upākrama* 'initiation' and *chāyā* 'shadow' (*mātropajñopakramacchāye napuṃsaka* - - Pā VI.2.14). The **Kāśikā** has given the example *iṣucchāyam* 'shadow cast by a mass of arrows'. In this *tatpuruṣa* compound the term *chāyā* helps to retain the original accent of first member.

The basic meanings of the term *chāyā*, shadow and reflection are recorded in the **Vākyapadīya** in different context. Some philosophers opine that the atoms (*aṇu*) called words (*śabda*) as they have the power of transforming themselves into light and shade.

अणवः सर्वशक्तित्वाद्भेदसंसर्गवृत्तयः ।
छायातपतमःशब्दभावेन परिणामिनः ॥

Vāk I.110

Because the different kinds of atoms have all powers, they, in combination or otherwise, transform themselves into shadow, sunlight, darkness and sounds. (Tr. K.A.S. Iyer)

In the context of discussing on direction (*dik*), **Vākyapadīya** records that in mountain, division is very clear as it is based on light and shade on account of direction. Mountains seem to be illuminated by the light of the sun on one side and to be covered with darkness on another (*chāyābhābhyāṃ nagādīnāṃ bhāgabhedaḥ prakalpate* – Vāk III.6.12). In the context of explaining impossibility of birth and destruction according to Monism, Bhartṛhari, compares the same with the movement of shadow (*chāyāyāścalanaṃ yathā* – Vāk III.7.111). Shadow is motionless but motion is attributed to it, on the basis of the movement of the object which obstructs light and causes shadow. In the world we see the shadow caused by the sun-rays. Day (a symbol of light) and night (a symbol of darkness) are possible due to the movement of the earth. By the changes in light and shade, time, the abode of the seasons is determined (*chāyādi pariṇāmaiśca ṛtudhāmā nirūpyate* – Vāk III.9.45cd). In the sense of reflection the term *chāyā* is also used in the **Vākyapadīya.**

अथास्मान्नियमादूर्ध्वं जातयो याः प्रयोजिकाः ।
ताः सर्वा व्यक्तिमायान्ति स्वच्छे छाया इवाम्भसि ॥

Vāk III.9.19

Further, after the determination of the effect all the prompting universals, manifest themselves in it, like reflections in clear water. (Tr. K.A.S. Iyer)

Two popular Indian epics record the term *chāyā* basically in the sense of shadow or shelter. To denote the inseparable companion of Rāma and Sītā, the **Rāmāyaṇa** gives a nice description of *chāyā* through the saying of Sutīkṣṇa.

अरिष्टं गच्छ पन्थानं राम सौमित्रिणा सह ।
सीतया चानया सार्धं छाययेवानुवृत्तया ॥

Rām III.8.11

Oh Rāma ! safely proceed on your journey with the son of Sumitrā (Lakṣmaṇa) and this Sītā, who is your follower like a shadow.

The term *chāyā* is recorded in the **Rāmāyaṇa** to glorify the beauty of nature. Around the sacrificial pits, bushy and shady trees may be planted for cool shade and beauty (*viropyantāṃ bahuvidhāś chāyāvantaśca gulminaḥ* – Rām VII.54.11ab). Again, in the description of beautiful Citrakūṭa mountain, the term *chāyā* occurs with pleasant and shady trees laden with flowers and fruits (*puṣpavadbhiḥ phalopetaiśchāyāvadbhirmanoramaiḥ* – Rām II.94.10ab). In the context of pathetic scene of Lakṣmaṇa's lamentation with a heavy heart, thinking of Sītā's future in the vicinity of Vālmīki's hermitage, the term *chāyā* is used in the sense of shelter which is very close to the Vedic concept of *gṛha* (Nigh III.4). Lakṣmaṇa requests Sītā to dwell in the shelter of Vālmīki with happiness, observing fasts and with attachment to Rāma (*pādacchāyāmupāgamya ... vasa tvaṃ janakātmaje* – Rām VII.47.15–17). Śrī Rāma's feet is the best shelter to the devotees of Rāma and it is their only goal and happiness.

पादच्छाया सुखं भर्तुस्तादृशस्य महात्मनः ।
स हि नाथो जनस्यास्य स गतिः स परायणम् ॥

Rām II.48.17

The shelter of the feet of such a high-souled master (as Śrī Rāma) is our only joy (or happiness); in fact he is the protector of us (all); he is our goal, he is our supreme asylum. (Tr. Gita Press edn)

In the description of dreams in different contexts the **Rāmāyaṇa** records the term *chāyā* in the sense of lustre or splendour. Bharata describes a bad dream, dreamt at the night where his lustre has departed (*chāyā cāpagatā mama* – Rām II.69.20d). Trijaṭā, an ogress speaks of a dream to her companion that misfortune and adversity come in the life of Sītā like the shadow of an eclipse, only in the shape of diminution of splendour occasioned by want of bath, toilet, etc. (*chāyāvaiguṇyamātraṃ tu śaṅke duḥkham upasthitam* – Rām

V.27.48). Importance of giving shadow (*chāyā*) in the Vājapeya sacrifice is found in the **Rāmāyaṇa** following the Vedic rules 'who performs a Vājapeya sacrifice must be supplied with a white canopy' (*śvetacchatrī ha bhavatīti vijñāyate* – ĀpŚrSū XVIII.7.18). The priests of Vājapeya sacrifice bear or use white umbrellas which are permitted to kings only. But in the state of resigning claim to kingship, Rāma is being offered white umbrellas by the following Brahmins, which they have obtained on their performing Vājapeya.

> वाजपेयसमुत्थानि च्छत्राण्येतानि पश्य नः ।
> पृष्ठतोऽनुप्रयातानि मेघानिव जलात्यये ॥
> अनवाप्तातपत्रस्य रश्मिसंतापितस्य ते ।
> एभिश्छायां करिष्यामः स्वैश्छत्रैर्वाजपेयकैः ॥
>
> Rām II.45.22–23
>
> Look at these canopies obtained by us during the performance of a Vājapeya sacrifice and following at your heels like (white) clouds appearing in autumn (marking the end of the monsoon). With these canopies of ours, obtained during a Vājapeya sacrifice, we shall give shade to you, who have got no canopy and (as such) are being scorched with rays (of the sun). (Tr. Gita Press edn)

In ancient times, some magical power of seizing shadow was known to the giants and ogresses. The powerful Hanumān was also captured by Surasā in the Indian Ocean. A giantess named Aṅgārakā, lived in the middle of Indian Ocean and used to procure her prey by seizing the shadow of those flying in the air (*aṅgāraketi vīkhyātā chāyāmākṣipya bhojinī* – Rām IV.41.26). On his shadow being seized, Hanumān thought that he has been rendered powerless like a big bark retarded in its course by an adverse wind, being clutched by someone all of a sudden (*chāyāyāṃ gṛhyamānāyām* ... Rām V.1.187). The size of shadow of any object may be increased or decreased depending on the light. A picturesque description of the increased shadow of Hanumān is noticed in the **Rāmāyaṇa**, which is due to the rapidity and distance from the sea level to the sky level. It was also very charming like a row of clouds sailing in the clear sky. The size of Hanumān's shadow was ten *yojanas* (approx. 80 miles) in width and thirty *yojanas* (approx. 240 miles) in length, appearing lovelier due to the rapidity of movement (*daśayojanavistīrṇā triṃśadyojanam āyatā, chāyā vānarasiṃhasya .. tasya sā śuśubhe chāyā patitā lavaṇāmbhasi* – Rām V.1.76–77).

The **Mahābhārata** also records a number of occurrences on the concept *chāyā* with its multidimensional nature of shadow and reflection. Close relation between trees and shades, is mentioned in the several verses of the **Mahābhārata**. The tree serves all, i.e. to deities by their flowers, the departed manes by their fruits and the guests by providing shades (*chāyayā cātithīṃstāta* *pūjayanti mahīruhāḥ* – MBh XIII.99.28).

In the episode of Jamadagni and Reṇukā, the term *chāyā* is used to denote both shade and shelter. Reṇukā got tired in the terrible sunlight and took shelter under the shade of a tree (*sā gacchantyantarā chāyāṃ vṛkṣamāśritya bhāminī ... sūryatejo nirudvāhaṃ vṛkṣacchāyāṃ samāśritā* – MBh XIII.97.11ab, 15cd). Traveller also prefers to take rest under the shade of some tree (*yathā hi pathikaḥ kaściccāyām āśritya viśramet* – MBh XIII, app. 20.250). To avoid getting wet from rain Arjuna takes shelter under the shade of a banyan tree (*chāyāyāṃ vaṭavṛkṣasya* – MBh I, app. 113.32–33). Shade of a mango tree is accepted as a place of meditation (*āmra vṛkṣasya chāyāyām* – MBh II.16.27cd). The shade of a Yoga-tree is praised in the **Mahābhārata** as a goal of liberation. It means the super mundane knowledge which comes through reflection (*chāyā*) and practice of eight yogic systems. Through this yogic practice one can overcome the threefold pains — physical, metaphysical and supernatural.

योगवृक्षस्य या छाया तापत्रयविनाशिनी ।
धर्मज्ञानसुपुष्पस्य स्वर्गमोक्षफलस्य च ।
दुःखत्रयार्कसंतप्तश्छायां योगतरोः श्रितः ।
न बध्यते पुनर्दुःखैः प्राप्य निर्वाणमुत्तमम् ।

MBh XIII, app. 20.409–12

The shade of Yoga-tree removes the three-fold pains *ādhibhautika* - - physical, *ādhidaivika* – supernatural and *ādhyātmika* – metaphysical or belonging to personal plain and bestows the flower of righteous knowledge and fruit of heaven and liberation. The person, who being scorched by the heat of three-fold pain has taken shelter to this yogic tree, attains excellent Bliss and is no more bound by any type of sufferings. (Tr. P. Ghosal)

Description of a beautiful shadowy bamboo-clump on the both side of a river reminds a poet, the natural beauty (*kīcakaveṇūnāṃ chāyām* – MBh II.48.2). The way to *yamaloka* is described by Mārkaṇḍeya as shelterless.

न तत्र वृक्षच्छाया न वा पानीयं केतनानि च ।

MBh III, app. 21A.100

There is neither any shade of a tree nor any drink nor abode or shelter (*ketana*). (Tr. P. Ghosal)

It is a natural fact that in the summer people feel comfort in shady place, air and water (*chāyāyām apsu vāyau ca sukham uṣṇe'dhigacchati* – MBh XII.73.23). In the description of Nala-Damayantī's *svayambara* it is noticed that *chāyā* helps a lot in recognising the king Nala from the deities (*chāyādvitīya* – MBh

III.54.24). Regarding the shadowlessness it is said that '*jyotisvarūpa ṛṣi* or *sādhaka*' has also no shadow because he exists in the domain of light possessing equal status of a deity. *Pretātmā* is *vāyubhūta*, hence its shadow is unmanifested (*avyakta*). Shadows of *gandharvas* and *rakṣases* are recorded as enormous (*chāyāśca vipulā dṛṣṭvā devagandharva-rakṣasām* – MBh IX.36.10).

In the narrative of Vipula and his preceptor's wife it is described that one great ascetic remains there just like a shadow, i.e. the position of ascetic is imitative. Here imitation is indicated by *chāyā* (MBh XIII.40.57). Idea of shadowy form is also noticed in the **Mahābhārata** (XII.124.45). In the narrative of Prahlāda, it is recorded that while he was in deep thought, a flame of light came out of his person which had a shadowy form (*chāyābhūtam*) of great effulgence and huge proportions. In the description of battle between Kuru army and Arjuna the sky is also noticed as umbrageous (*chāyābhūta*) by the shower of arrows from all directions (MBh IV.54.3). The term *chāyābhūta* is also used to denote the constant accompaniment like one's shadow. In the context of explaining the conduct of a disciple to his teacher it is said that he should follow his preceptor like a shadow (*chāyābhūta* – MBh XIV.35.10; XIII, app. 15.3898, etc.). Again, Bhīṣma advises Yudhiṣṭhira how to serve a teacher-cum-preceptor in the following verse.

उपतिष्ठति तिष्ठन्तं गच्छन्तमनुगच्छति ।
करोति कुर्वतः कर्म छायेवानुविधीयते ॥

MBh XII.174.9

The student or disciple should sit while his teacher is seated, while going he should follow him and while doing any work he should serve him, just like his shadow. (Tr. P. Ghosal)

Similarly, a queen, a wife, and a servant should follow her king, her husband and her or his Lord like a shadow. Bhadrā, queen of king Vyuṣitāśva, told her departing husband that she will follow him like a shadow (*chāyevānapagā rājan satataṃ vaśavartinī* – MBh I.112.23). Damayantī laments to the mother of Chedi king and sought shelter to her place. Then she also says how she follows her husband like a shadow (*bhartāramapi taṃ vīraṃ chāyevānapagā sadā* – MBh III.62.27). It is also said that resident of a royal campus should always be loyal to the king just like his shadow (*chāyevānapagaḥ sadā* – MBh IV.4.37). In the world hereafter one's own action follows him like his shadow (*svakṛtaṃ karma chāyevānugataṃ sadā* – MBh III.181.25). King's intelligence follows the course of virtue like a man's shadow (*buddhiḥ satatam anveti chāyeva puruṣaṃ nijā* – MBh III.31.8). Own shadow is also dependent on one's body. It is dependent like wife, son and daughter (MBh XII.235.18). After the departure of liberated Śuka, Vedavyāsa was overwhelmed with grief.

Lord Śiva appeared there and consoled him with the blessings of finding his son's reflection everywhere in this world and Vedvyāsa also pleased to see his son's reflection in all direction (*chāyāṃ paśyan samāvṛttaḥ sa muniḥ parayā mudā* – MBh XII.320.38cd). The intertwined concept *chāyātapa* is recorded in the several verses of **Mahābhārata**. To attain the liberation one should impartial to both shade and sunlight (*chāyāyāmātape caiva samadarśī* – MBh XII.312.31). Sunshine and shade are inseparable. Creation of day and night etc. is possible due to the inseparable relation of light and shade (*chāyātapavilekhaṃ ca* ... MBh XIV.45.4). Lord Śiva is also praised as *chāyātapa* (one of his 1008 names), as He provides both light and shade (*chāyāyātapanāya ca* – MBh XII, app. 28.213).

The concept of *chāyā-stambha* is also noticed in the **Māhābhārata**. While describing to Śakuni, Duryodhana felt jealous of the wealth and palace of Yudhiṣṭhira at Indraprastha. That place had the capacity to perplex a person as its shadowy places are looked like pillars due to illusion.

> छायाः स्तम्भा इवातिष्ठञ्शतशोऽथ सहस्रशः ।
>
> MBh II, app. 32.16
>
> In that hall there were hundreds and thousands of shadowy places which looked like pillars. (Tr. P. Ghosal)

Besides the four principal lexicographic connotations of *chāyā*, i.e. (i) the wife of the sun, (ii) lustre or beauty, (iii) a reflected image, and (iv) a shade, the Puranic literature deals with other shades of meaning: replica, resemblance, imitation, etc. As the first part of compound it is also recorded in the Puranic literature, e.g. *chāyāpuruṣa* (ŚPur V.28.3–7), *chāyāsītā* (DBhāgPur IX.16.31b–32a), etc.

Denoting the idea of shadow, intertwined with *ātapa* or light, the term *chāyā* is nicely recorded in the **Kūrma Purāṇa** (II.2.11) in the context of the *yoga* of Īśvara where it is mentioned that the *ātman* is neither *māyā* nor the vital breath, the relation between *prapañca* and the supreme soul is like the relation between light and darkness.

> छायातपौ यथा लोके परस्परविलक्षणौ ।
> तद्वत् प्रपञ्चपुरुषौ विभिन्नौ परमार्थतः ॥
>
> KūrPur II.2.11
>
> Just as shadow and the sunlight are mutually distinct and different in this materialistic world, in the same way the world and the puruṣa are intrinsically and factually different.
> (Based on the tr. by G.V. Tagare)

From the astronomical point of view, *chāyā* or shadow is very essential in the field of eclipses. In the **Kūrma Purāṇa** a piquant description of the evil planet Rāhu and the shadow of the earth is noticed. The evil planet Rāhu is named as Svarbhānu and it assumes a size equal to sun and moon.

> उद्धृत्य पृथिवीच्छायां निर्मितो मण्डलाकृतिः ।
> स्वर्भानोस्तु बृहत् स्थानं तृतीयं यत् तमोमयम् ॥
>
> KūrPur I.39.15
>
> (The evil planet Rāhu) is created with a spherical shape after extracting the shadow of the earth. The extensive third abode of Rāhu is full of darkness. (Tr. G.V. Tagare)

The term *chāyā*, to denote shadow, is also recorded as an attribute or aspect of fire in the **Agni Purāṇa** along with other forms:

> अग्ने रूपं दर्शनं स्याद् ऊष्मा पङ्क्तिश्च पित्तकम् ।
> मेधा वर्णं बलं छाया तेजः शौर्यं शरीरके ॥
>
> AgPur CCCLXIX.29
>
> The forms or aspects of fire are the following: vision, bodily heat, cooking, bile, retentive faculty, complexion, strength, shadow, lustre, and valour. (Tr. R.S. Bhattacharya)

Prohibition of urinating on different shadows is also mentioned in the **Viṣṇu Purāṇa** (III.11.10) as: '*ātmacchāyāṃ tarucchāyām ... budho nādhimehet kadācana*', 'a wise man will never void urine on his own shadow, nor on the shadow of a tree'.

The term is also very popular as an inherent nature in the Durgā Saptaśatī, a part of the **Mārkaṇḍeya Purāṇa**, where we find the reverence to the goddess Durgā:

> या देवी सर्वभूतेषु छायारूपेण संस्थिता ।
> नमस्तस्यै नमस्तस्यै नमस्तस्यै नमो नमः ॥
>
> MārkPur LXXXII.17
>
> To the goddess who among all created beings stands firm with the form of shadow, reverence to her. (Tr. F.E. Pargiter)

According to Śāntanavī commentary *chāyā* denots reflection (*chāyā pratibimbarūpā sarvabhūteṣu tiṣṭhati*).

In the sense of *kānti* or lustre or brilliance, '*chāyā*' has been used with the several jewels.

क्वचिद् विद्रुमसंकाशं क्वचिन्मरकतच्छवि ॥
विद्युद्भानुसमच्छायं मध्यसूर्यसमं क्वचित् ।

DBhāgPur XII.12.56cd–57ab

At some places the lustre is like *vidruma maṇi*; some places are illumined like the lustre of *marakata maṇi*; some like *sūryakānta maṇi* and some places are rendered brilliant like numerous lightnings. (Based on the tr. by Vijnanananda)

In the eulogy of Viṣṇu in his *brahman* aspect, *chāyā* has been used to denote lustre in the expression '*asnehacchāyam*' as an epithet of Parama Brahman 'Supreme Soul' (cf. ViPur I.14.39).

To denote image, *chāyā* is recorded in the **Viṣṇu Purāṇa** where it is noted that the energy or reflection of Viṣṇu is never disjoined from the sun's car which is like the stand of the mirror, but remains eternally in the sun as in the mirror, which is stationed there:

स्तम्भस्थदर्पणस्येव योऽयमासन्नतां गतः ।
छायादर्शनसंयोगं स तं प्राप्नोत्यथात्मनः ॥

ViPur II.11.19

In the same manner as a man approaching a mirror, placed upon a stand, beholds in it his own image. (Tr. H.H. Wilson)

Intrinsic relation of shade and light is symbolically described in the **Viṣṇu Purāṇa** in the legend of *arka* (sun) and *chāyā* (shadow) where *chāyā* is used to denote the shadow of the image of Saṃjñā, wife of sun. The legend is:

असहन्ती तु सा भर्तुस्तेजश्छायां युयोज वै ।
भर्तृशुश्रूषणेरण्यं स्वयं च तपसे ययौ ॥
संज्ञेयमित्यथार्कश्च छायायामात्मजत्रयम् ।
शनैश्चरं मनुं चान्यं तपतीं चाप्यजीजनत् ॥
छायासंज्ञा ददौ शापं यमाय कुपिता यदा ।
तदान्येयमसौ बुद्धिरित्यासीद्यमसूर्ययोः ॥

ViPur III.2.3–5

Unable to endure the fervours of her lord, Saṃjñā gave him Chāyā as his handmaid, and repaired to the forests to practise devout exercises. The sun, supposing Chāyā to be his wife Saṃjñā, begot by her three other children, Śanaiścara (Saturn), another Manu (Sāvarṇi), and a daughter Tapatī (the Tapti river). Chāyā, upon one occasion, being offended with Yama, the son of Saṃjñā denounced an imprecation upon him, and thereby revealed to

Yama and to the sun that she was not in truth Saṃjñā, the mother of the former. (Tr. H.H. Wilson)

In the sense of replica the term *chāyā* is nicely mentioned in the **Devī Bhāgavata Purāṇa** where Mahā Lakṣmī is appeared as a replica in different *yugas*:

कृते युगे वेदवती कुशध्वजसुता शुभा ।
त्रेतायां रामपत्नी च सीतेति जनकात्मजा ॥
तच्छाया द्रौपदी देवी द्वापरे द्रुपदात्मजा ।

DBhāgPūr IX.16.52–53ab

She (Mahālakṣmī) was Vedavatī, the daughter of Kuśadhvaja in the Satya-yuga; Sītā, the wife of Rāma and the daughter of Janaka in Tretā-yuga; and Draupadī, the daughter of Drupada, in Dvāpara-yuga was her replica. (Tr. Vijnanananda)

The term *chāyā* is also recorded as a figure of speech, one of the nine *śabdālaṅkāras* in the **Agni Purāṇa**. Nine *śabdālaṅkāras* are: *chāyā*, *mudrā*, *ukti*, *yukti*, *gumphanā*, *vākovākya*, *anuprāsa*, *citra* and *duṣkara*.

तत्रान्योक्तेरनुकृतिः छाया सापि चतुर्विधा ।
लोकच्छेकार्भकोक्तीनाम् मत्तोक्तेरनुकारतः ॥

AgPur CCCXLII.21

Imitation of other's speech is called *chāyā*. It is of four kinds: *lokokti* 'popular saying', *chekokti* 'clever speech', *arbhakokti* 'childish utterance' and *mattokti* intoxicated raving'.
(Tr. R.S. Bhattacharya)

As an actual nature of *ābhāsa*, resemblance, the term *chāyā* is manifested through the psycho-physical organism, which is popularly believed to be a combination of the five gross elements, but it is deceptive appearance:

क्षित्यादीनामिहार्थानां छाया न कतमापि हि ।
न संघातो विकारोऽपि न पृथङ् नान्वितो मृषा ॥

BhāgPur VII.15.59

The resemblance of earth and so on, is indeed none of the following possibilities: it is neither their collection nor compound nor even modification for it is neither distinct from them nor pervaded by them.

As the first part in a compound the term *chāyā* is interestingly recorded in the purāṇas to remind several figures of Indian tradition. Two of such compound forms are *chāyāpuruṣa* and *chāyāsītā*.

श्रृणु देवि प्रवक्ष्यामि छायापुरुषलक्षणम् ।
यज्ज्ञात्वा पुरुषः सम्यक् सर्वपापैः प्रमुच्यते ॥
सूर्यं हि पृष्ठतः कृत्वा सोमं वा वरवर्णिनि ।
शुक्लाम्बरधरः स्रग्वी गन्धधूपादिवासितः ॥
संस्मरेन्मे महामन्त्रं सर्वकामफलप्रदम् ।
नवात्मकं पिण्डभूतं स्वां छायां संनिरीक्षयेत् ॥
दृष्ट्वा तां पुनराकाशे श्वेतवर्णस्वरूपिणीम् ।
स पश्यत्येकभावस्तु शिवं परमकारणम् ॥
ब्रह्मप्राप्तिर्भवेत्तस्य कालविद्भिरितीरितम् ।
ब्रह्महत्यादिकैः पापैर्मुच्यते नात्र संशयः ॥
शिरोहीनं यदा पश्येत्षड्भिर्मासैर्भवेत्क्षयः ।
समस्तं वाङ्मयं तस्य योगिनस्तु यथा तथा ॥

ŚPur V.28.3–8

Śiva said to Devī: O goddess, listen. I shall explain the characteristics of the *chāyāpuruṣa*, on knowing which man becomes released from all sins. The aspirant wears garlands and white cloth. He makes himself fragrant with scents, incense and other things. O fair lady, he then sits with his back to the sun or the moon remembering the great *mantra* that bestows the benefits of all desires and that consists of the nine units solidified into one. He then glances at his own shadow.

If he can see the shadow in the sky in a white-coloured form and beings to meditate on Śiva, the great cause with single-minded attention, he attains Brahman then. This has been mentioned by the experts. In this state he is rid of Brahminicide and other sins.

If he finds the shadow person headless, the entire power of oral expression of practising Yogin becomes eliminated within six months. (Tr. J.L. Shastri)

This beautiful description of shadowy person practically creates a thrill in the mind of Yogins.

Another interesting compound is *chāyāsītā*, very popular because of epical influence, noticed also in the later Sanskrit works of Bhavabhūti, the **Uttararāmacarita** finds its place in the **Devī Bhāgavata Purāṇa** when Agni said to Rāma to give over his Sītā, the world mother to fire and to keep the false *chāyāsītā* with Rāma. At the time of Sītā's ordeal by fire, Agni will give her back to Rāma.

जगत्प्रसूं मयि न्यस्य छायां रक्षान्तिकेऽधुना ॥
दास्यामि सीतां तुभ्यं च परीक्षासमये पुनः ।

DBhāgPūr IX.16.31cd–32ab

So give over your Sītā, the World Mother to me and keep with you this *chāyā* Sītā (the shadow Sītā; the false Sītā). When the time of Sītā's ordeal by fire will take place, I will give Her back to you. (Tr. Vijnanananda)

So *chāyā*, shadow, an intrinsic part of light, finds its place with the diversified layers of meaning and richly presented in the Puranic literature with its various aspects.

In the context of prescribing rules for a *snātaka*, Manu records the term *chāyā* in his law-book. One twice-born *snātaka* should not step on the shadow of gods etc.

देवतानां गुरो राज्ञः स्नातकाचार्ययोस्तथा ।
नाक्रामेत्कामतश्छायां बभ्रुणो दीक्षितस्य च ॥

Manu IV.130

Let him not intentionally step on the shadow of (images of) the gods, of a *guru*, of a king, of a *snātaka*, of his teacher, of a reddish-brown animal, or of one who has been initiated to the performance of a Śrauta sacrifice. (Tr. G. Bühler)

The same text also compared the relation of a slave with his master as the shadow with a person. Master should bear the offence of a slave as he follows his master like a shadow (*chāyā svo dāsavargaśca* – Manu IV.185). For voiding urine etc. there is no hard and fast rule for a brahmin *snātaka*. According to Manu, he can void urine etc. in the shade or in darkness both by day and night (*chāyāyāmandhakāre vā rātrāvahani vā dvijaḥ* – Manu IV.51).

The **Yājñavalkya Smṛti** follows the same rules of Manu on the prohibition of voiding urine etc. (*natu mehen nadīchāyā* ... – YājSm I.6.134) and stepping over the shadow of divinities etc. (*devartvik* ... *chāyāṃ* ... *nākrāmed* – YājSm I.6.152). The same text also prescribes to recite a particular *mantra* for removing impurity due to seeing one's own reflection in water.

मयि तेज इति च्छायां स्वां दृष्ट्वाऽम्बुगतां जपेत् ।
सावित्रीमशुचौ दृष्टे चापल्ये चानृतेऽपि च ॥

YājSm III.5.279

One should recite (the hymn) '*mayi teja* ...' etc. on seeing his own reflection in water, and he should mutter Savitri hymn in order to remove the impurity of casting a glance at impure objects (of) falsehood and unsteadiness (of limbs). (Tr. P. Ghosal)

The **Nārada Smṛti** also records the term *chāyā* in the context of treating innocent person by Manu if he remains free from convulsions caused by poison.

छायानिवेशितो रक्ष्यो दिनशेषमभोजनः ।
विषवेगक्लमातीतः शुद्धोऽसौ मनुरब्रवीत् ।

NārSm (Vyavahārapāda) I.326

Let the man be kept in shadowy place without taking food, for the whole remainder of the day. If he remains free from convulsions such as are generally caused by poison, he is declared innocent by Manu. (Tr. Julius Jolly)

In the Nīti Śāstras also the term *chāyā* is recorded in the sense of shadow and reflection. While prescribing the nature of devoted and faithful wife the **Śukranītisāra** says that she should follow her husband like a shadow.

मनोवाक्कर्मभिः शुद्धा पतिदेशानुवर्त्तिनी ।
छायेवानुगता स्वच्छा सखीव हितकर्मसु ।
दासीव दिष्टकार्य्येषु भार्य्या भर्त्तुःसदा भवेत् ॥

ŚNSā IV.4.12

A virtuous wife should always remain pure in mind, speech and deeds, obedient to her husband, following like a shadow, clean like a friend in auspicious works, as a maid-servant in performing the works assigned by her husband.

The **Kāmandakīya Nīti Sāra** records the inseparable relation between the king and his dependents. Prosperity remains with an ever-energetic good-ruler like his own shadow.

उद्योगादनिवृत्तस्य सुसहायस्य धीमतः ।
छायेवानुगता तस्य नित्यं श्रीः सहचारिणी ॥

KāNīSā V.91 (ka)

A ruler who never lacks initiative in taking proper actions (i.e. ever-energetic) and who is always attended by intelligent and reliable counsellors, invariably attains prosperity (*śrī*) that always keeps close to him like his own shadow (*chāyeva ... sahacāriṇī*).
(Tr. S.K. Mitra)

The same text also treats the shadow of a gnomon or any object is temporary. It should be kept in mind that the frail human body is temporary like a shadow and vanishes like a bubble of water (*chāyāmātrakamevedaṃ paśyedudakabinduvat* – KāNīSā III.10). *Chāyā* as reflection takes an important role to protect the princes from poison etc.

> छायाऽतिरिक्ता हीना वा स्याद्रसे विषदूषिते ।
> दृश्यते राजिरूर्ध्वा च फेनमण्डलमेव च ॥
>
> KāNīSā VII.19
>
> Liquids (soups, etc.) mixed with poison show one's own reflection unusually enlarged or shortened and appear bright on surface but fringed with streaks. (Tr. S.K. Mitra)

The **Artha-Śāstra** (I.7.8) of Kauṭilya records the term *chāyā* as one of the mediums of ascertaining time. Kauṭilya goes on to describe elaborately, the different measurement of the shadow of the gnomons in different time and seasons.

> छायायामष्टपौरुष्यामष्टादशभागश्छेदः, षट्पौरुष्यां चतुर्दशभागः, चतुष्पौरुष्यामष्टभागः, द्विपौरुष्यां षड्भागः, पौरुष्यां चतुर्भागः, अष्टाङ्गुलायां त्रयोदशभागाः, चतुरङ्गुलायाम् त्रयोऽष्टभागाः, अच्छायो मध्याह्न इति । परावृत्ते दिवसे शेषमेवं विद्यात् । आषाढे मासि नष्टच्छायो मध्याह्नो भवति । अतः परं श्रावणादीनां षण्मासानां द्व्यङ्गुलोत्तरा माघादीनां द्व्यङ्गुलावरा छाया इति ।
>
> ArthŚ II.20.39–42
>
> When the shadow (of the gnomon) is eight *pauruṣas*, one eighteenth part (of the day) is past, when six *pauruṣas*, one fourteenth part (is past), when four *pauruṣas*, one eighth part, when two *pauruṣas*, one sixth part, when one *pauruṣa*, one fourth part, when eight *aṅgulas*, three-tenth part (is past), when four *aṅgulas*, three eighth part, (and) when there is no shadow, it is midday, when the day has turned, one should understand the remaining parts in like manner. In the month of Āṣāḍha, the midday loses shadow. After that, in the six months beginning with Śrāvaṇa, the shadow (at midday) increases by two *aṅgulas* in each month and in the six months beginning with Māgha, it decreases by two *aṅgulas* in each month. (Tr. R.P. Kangle)

The Āyurveda clearly shows that our body consists of both materials shade (*chāyā*) and lustre (*bhā*). *Chāyā* means the shade based on lustre and complexion (*chāyā varṇaprabhāśrayā* – CarSam ISthā VII.9). Being a kind of lustre, a sort of splendour it is closely associated with night which has the capacity to defend shadow due to darkness (*chāyāṃ pāntu niśāstava* 'may the night defend thy shadow' – SuSam SūSthā V.27). It is more clear in 'the commentary of Ḍalhaṇa as:

> छाया प्रभाभेदः तदुक्तम् - आसन्ना लक्ष्यते छाया प्रभा दूरात् प्रकाशते ।
>
> Ḍalhaṇa on SuSamSūSthā V.27
>
> *Chāyā* 'shadow' is a different kind of *prabhā* 'radiance' or lustre. Hence it is said that shadow is observed from proximity but the radiance or lustre (*prabhā*) shines from a distance.

This close relation between *chāyā* and *prabhā* is reflected in the **Caraka Saṃhitā** as a source of Ḍalhaṇa's idea on the same. In the presence of light or shade, original complexion of a body is not clear. A yellowish body looks very lustrous due to the illuminative power of lustre while in darkness or shadow it looks dark-yellow or black.

> वर्णमाक्रामति च्छाया भास्तु वर्णप्रकाशिनी ।
> आसन्ना लक्ष्यते च्छाया भाः प्रकृष्टा प्रकाशते ॥
> नाच्छायो नाप्रभः कश्चिद्विशेषाश्चिह्नयन्ति तु ।
> नृणां शुभाशुभोत्पत्तिं काले छायाप्रभाश्रयाः ॥
>
> CarSam ISthā VII.16–17
>
> *Chāyā* (shade) invades complexion while '*bhā*' (lustre) illumines the same. *Chāyā* is observed from nearby while *bhā* shines from a distance. There is none who is devoid of *chāyā* and *prabhā;* the different features of *chāyā* and *prabhā* arisen in certain times indicate the auspiciousness or otherwise for the person.
> (Tr. P.V. Sharma)

The **Suśruta Saṃhitā** (SūSthā XXXI.1) treats *chāyā* in a chapter called '*chāyāvipratipatti*', i.e. the prognosis to be gathered from the altered condition of features: The Ayurvedic physicians observe a clear distinction between *chāyā* 'shade of complexion', *prabhā* 'healthful glow of the complexion' and *varṇa* 'natural colour of the complexion. The shade of one's complexion may be easily distinguished as clear, rough or cool, etc. *Chāyā* is a very important factor to a physician to diagnose a diseased person. The person, who fails to see his own image reflected in a mirror, in the moonlight, or in hot water, is an indication of dying stage (*jyotsnā darśoṣṇatoyeṣu chāyāṃ yaśca na paśyati* – SuSam SūSthā XXX.21).

The **Caraka Saṃhitā** (ISthā I.3) treats lustre (*chāyā*) as one of the essential entities for examining the remaining span of life with perception, inference and authoritative statements. From the complexion of man, physical condition of a person could be guessed. The man should take rest whose complexion suddenly assumes a brown, red, blue or yellow shade. It is an indication of sickness as recorded in the **Suśruta Saṃhitā** (SūSthā XXXI.3): *śyāvā lohitikā nīlā pītikā vā'pi mānavam, abhidravanti yaṃ chāyāḥ sa parāsurasaṃśayam.*

Chāyā 'shade' gives contrary results of *ātapa* 'sun' in the body of creative being. It is aptly recorded in the **Suśruta Saṃhitā**:

आतपः पित्ततृष्णाग्निस्वेदमूर्च्छाभ्रमास्रकृत् ।
दाहवैवर्ण्यकारी च छाया चैतानपोहति ॥

SuSam CiSthā XXIV.86

An undue exposure to the sun (*ātapa*) aggravates the *pitta*, but increases the power of digestion. It agitates the blood and begets thirst, perspiration, faintness (sun stroke), vertigo and a burning sensation in the body attended with a discolouring of the complexion, etc.; whereas the contrary results are produced by a (cool) shade (*chāyā*). (Tr. K.L. Bhishagratna)

Others take *chāyā* (shade) as a product of the fraction of darkness (*anye chāyāmapi tamaḥ paramāṇujāmāhuḥ* – Ḍalhaṇa on the same).

The **Suśruta Saṃhitā** also deals with the general rules of conduct regarding the crossing over a shadow as a sign of paying regards.

देवगोब्राह्मणचैत्यध्वजरोगिपतितपापकारिणां च छायां नाक्रमेत ।

SuSam CiSthā XXIV.92

Even the shadow of a fallen, degraded and sick persons as well as of a cow, brahmin, divine image, banner of a *caitya* (tree growing on a cremation ground) should not be trodden upon.
(Tr. K.L. Bhishagratna)

The **Aṣṭāṅga Hṛdaya** records the utility of shade for drying a reed of *kuśa*, smeared with fat material.

वर्तिरङ्गुष्ठकस्थूला यवमध्या यथा भवेत् ।
छायाशुष्कां विगर्भां तां स्नेहाभ्यक्तां यथायथम् ॥

AṣṭH SūSthā XXI.20

The thickness of a reed of *iṣikā* (*kuśa*) should be that of the middle portion of a thumb. It should be dried in shade, removed of its reed, smeared with any suitable fat material.
(Tr. K.R. Srikantha Murthy)

Āyurveda records the classification of *chāyā* relating the same with five gross elements and hence it is mostly of five types (*chāyā bhautikī pañcarūpā* –

Cakrapāṇidatta on CarSamISthā I.3). The **Caraka Saṃhitā** explains these five types of *chāyā* with their different salient features.

खादीनां पञ्चपञ्चानां छाया विविधलक्षणाः ।
नाभसी निर्मला नीला सस्नेहा सप्रभेव च ॥
रूक्षा श्यावारुणा या तु वायवी सा हतप्रभा ।
विशुद्धरक्ता त्वाग्नेयी दीप्ताभा दर्शनप्रिया ॥
शुद्धवैदूर्यविमला सुस्निग्धा चाम्भसी मता ।
स्थिरा स्निग्धा घना श्लक्ष्णा श्यामा श्वेता च पार्थिवी ॥

CarSam ISthā VII.10–12

According to five *mahābhūtas*, there are five types of *chāyā* having different features such as – the *chāyā* predominant in *ākāśa* is pure, blue, unctuous and lustrous. That predominant in *vāyu* is rough, blackish, reddish and lustreless. The *chāyā* predominant in *agni* (*tejas*) is pure red, brilliant and charming. That predominant in *ap* is clear like pure *vaidūrya* (cat's eye) and much unctuous. The *chāyā* predominant in *pṛthivī* is stable, unctuous, solid, smooth, sky-colour or white. (Tr. P.V. Sharma)

Ḍalhaṇa, in his commentary on the **Suśruta Saṃhitā** summarises the basic concept of *chāyā* in the Āyurveda:

वर्णप्रभाश्रिता या भवति सा छायाशब्देनोच्यते । छाया पञ्चविधा - स्निग्धा, विमला, रूक्षा, मलिना, संक्षिप्ता, इति ।

Comm. on SuSam SūSthā XXXI.1

Chāyā is lustre depending on complexion and splendour. It is of five types – unctuous, clean, rough, dirty and decrease.
(Tr. P.V. Sharma)

In the works on Jyotiṣa, the term *chāyā* is used mostly in the sense of shadow with its multidimensional aspect. Time can be calculated by means of the shadow of the gnomon. Despite differences of opinion among the astronomical systems on the ending time of solstice (*ayana*), the astronomers prefer to calculate the same by observing the circle drawn on the ground by means of the shadow of the gnomon as well as water-appliances (*chāyājalayantradṛgganitasāmyena pratipādanakuśalaḥ* – BṛSam II.8). The sun's change of course can be detected by watching and marking the entry and exit of the shadow of the gnomon planted at the centre of a big circle drawn on the ground (*chāyāpraveśanirgamacihnair vā maṇḍale mahati* – BṛSam III.3). Effect of an omen is also guessed in case of arrival of a person. An omen situated in the shade indicates the arrival of a person holding an umbrella (*chāyāsthe chatrasaṃyutaḥ* – BṛSam LXXXVI.74b). The natural calamity like drought, excessive rain, untimely rain, etc. also could be guessed from different types of shadows.

> यद्यमलेऽर्के छाया न दृश्यते दृश्यते प्रतीपा वा ।
> देशस्य तदा सुमहद्भयमायातं विनिर्देश्यम् ॥
>
> BṛSam XLVI.44
>
> If trees etc., do not cast their shadow even when the sun shines brightly, or if the shadow is in the same direction as the sun, it should be predicted that great calamity is in store for the country. (Tr. M.R. Bhat)

The bodily lustre or complexion (*chāyā*) of a person, an animal or a bird suggests both good and bad effects (*chāyā śubhāśubhaphalāni nivedayantī* – BṛSam LXVIII.89a). The **Bṛhat Saṃhitā** gives importance on this science of complexion or bodily lustre and related the same with five elements (BṛSam LXVIII.90–94). The physical lustre born of the element earth indicates wealth and progress in life, of the element water is bright, white and indicates happiness and prosperity; of the element fire indicates brilliance, valour and prowess; of the element air causes diseases, disasters or loss of income; and of the element ether is a bestower of good fortune. Thus, the text completes the delineation of five kinds of bodily lustres born of five elements, viz. earth, water, fire, air and ether (*chāyāḥ krameṇa kujalāgnyanilāmbarotthāḥ* – BṛSam LXVIII.94).

The **Sūrya-Siddhānta** discusses this concept of *chāyā* in details specially on the aspects of the shadow of gnomon – its names, base or north and south projection of the same, path of its extremity, equinoctial shadow, noon shadow and various calculations, other shadows, and shadows cast by any planet or star. It is also very interesting to note that generally the term *chāyā* is used to denote shadow but the terms *prabhā* and *bhā* are also used to denote the same which are actually the very opposite of shadow namely light, radiance, etc., which are used mainly to denote the shadow of the gnomon (*dattairiṣṭa prabhā smṛtā* – SūrSiddh III.5d). This astronomical text records the process of setting up a gnomon upon ground for exhibiting the shadow.

> छायाभूमौ विपर्यस्ते स्वच्छायाग्रे तु दर्शयेत् ।
> ग्रहः स्वदर्पणान्तःस्थः शङ्क्वग्रे सम्प्रदिश्यते ॥
>
> SūrSiddh VII.15
>
> Exhibit, upon the shadow-ground, the planet at the extremity of its shadow reversed: it is viewed at the apex of the gnomon in its mirror. (Tr. E. Burgess)

This process helps to calculate and lay off from the base of the gnomon, but in the opposite to the true direction of the planet, a time could be fixed by the shadow. By placing a horizontal mirror at the extremity of the shadow, the reflected image of the planet's disc will be seen in it at the given time through an eye placed at the apex of the gnomon.

In eclipse (*grahaṇa*) *chāyā* takes a very important role. True theory of lunar eclipse is – the moon is the eclipser of the sun, coming to stand underneath it, like a cloud; the moon moving eastward, enters the earth's shadow (*bhūcchāyā*) and the latter becomes its eclipser (SūrSiddh IV.9). The earth's penumbra (*upacchāyā*) is not taken into account in calculating eclipse according to Hindu process of calculation. Primitive theory on the cause of eclipse is:

> भानोर्भार्धे महीच्छाया तत्तुल्येऽर्कसमेऽपि वा ।
> शशाङ्क पाते ग्रहणं कियद्भागाधिकोनके ॥
>
> SūrSiddh IV.6
>
> The earth's shadow is distant half the signs from the sun: when the longitude of the moon's node is the same with that of the shadow, or with that of the sun or when it is a few degrees greater or less, there will be an eclipse. (Tr. E. Burgess)

In the same text also discusses on the hypotenuse (*karṇa*) of the shadow in a mathematical way. In a right-angled triangle the square of the hypotenuse is equal to the sum of the squares of the other two sides, to the triangle produced by the gnomon as perpendicular, the shadow as base and the hypotenuse of the shadow, the line drawn from the top of the gnomon to the extremity of the shadow, as hypotenuse (SūrSiddh III.8). The mid-day base is invariably the midday shadow (*mādhyāhniko bhujo nityaṃ chāyā mādhyāhnikī smṛtā* – SūrSiddh III.25ab). To find out the hypotenuse of different types of shadows, the **Sūrya-Siddhānta** gives a very clear view. When the sun is upon the prime vertical, the shadow falls directly eastward or westward. Hence its extremity lies in the east and west axis of the dial and its measure of amplitude is equal to the equinoctial shadow (SūrSiddh III.25–27). From the shadow of a given time, the sun's attitude and Zenith distance could be calculated by a contrary process (*abhīṣṭacchāyayā* – ŚūrSiddh III.37).

Various instruments are recorded in the **Sūrya-Siddhānta** for ascertaining or measuring time with the help of shadow, e.g. *yaṣṭiyantra, narayantra, chāyāyantra*, etc. Among these *chāyāyantra* (SūrSiddh XIII.20) takes a very important role. When used a wheel (*cakra*) as an instrument for measuring time, its edge is turned toward the sun, so that the shadow of the peg falls upon the graduated periphery and the distances of the point where it meets the latter from the horizontal and lowest points of the wheel respectively are the required altitude and Zenith-distance of the sun. In the *narayantra*, the term *nara* means a simple gnomon. In the day-time when the sun is clear, the best determination of time could be said by means of the shadow of a gnomon (SūrSiddh. XIII.24). The sun during *uttarāyaṇa* and *dakṣiṇāyana* revolves directly over a fifteenth part of the earth's circumference. Between those limits, the shadow is cast both southward and northward depending on latitudes and zones (SūrSiddh XII.68–69).

Varāhamihira has also used the term *chāyā* in his **Bṛhat Jātaka**, in the sense of lustre or shade of the colour the person possesses. Generally, man has good or bad charm or fascination about his personality which is represented by lustre (*chāyā*). The planets give such colour or personal charm of the gross elements (*mahābhūtas*) which they represent.

> छायां महाभूतकृतां च सर्वेऽभिव्यञ्जयन्ति स्वदशामवाप्य ।
> क्ष्म्ब्वग्निवाय्वम्बरजान् गुणांश्च नासास्यदृक्त्वक्छ्रवणानुमेयान् ॥
>
> BrJā VIII.21
>
> The different planets give their lustre of the *mahābhūtas* in their periods. This lustre or shade has to be identified by the nose, face, eyes, skin and ear obtained by or through the earth, water, fire, air and space. (Tr. B. Suryanarain Rao)

The same text also used the term *chāyāṅgula* 'shadow measurement', supposed to be of five *aṅgulas*, in the context of birth star where Varāhamihira gives a method to identify the birth constellation of the querist. Taking the *mātrās* (measure of time) of the real name of the querist, multiplying the same by two and adding to the result the number of *chāyāṅgulas* obtained at the time and the total number is to be divided by 27. Then taking the remainder and counting it from Dhaniṣṭhā the birth constellation of the querist is to be obtained (*saṃskāranāmamātrā dviguṇā chāyāṅgulaiḥ samāyuktaḥ* – BṛJā XXVI.15).

In the field of ancient mathematics also the term *chāyā* plays an important role to find the height of a lamp and to calculate the distance between the base points. Bhāskarācārya, a renowned mathematician and astronomer of Vedic tradition, has given various formulae on the length of shadow calculated from different aspects in his **Līlāvatī**. He explains the process of calculating length of shadow where pole is fixed and string is tied to its top.

> छाययोः कर्णयोरन्तरे ये तयोः वर्गविश्लेषभक्ता रसाद्रीषवः ।
> सैकलब्धेः पदघ्नं तु कर्णांतरं भान्तरेणोनयुक्तं दले स्तः प्रभे ॥
>
> Līlā XXXII.241

Obtain squares of the (given) difference of hypotenuses and that of shadows. Divide 576 by the difference of these two squares. Add one to this quotient and then take the (positive) square-root. Multiply this result by the difference of hypotenuses, and write the product in two places. Add the difference of shadows to one place and subtract the same from the other place. The outcomes divided by two are lengths of shadows.
(Tr. K.S. Patwardhan, S.A. Naimpally & S.L. Singh)

Diagram:

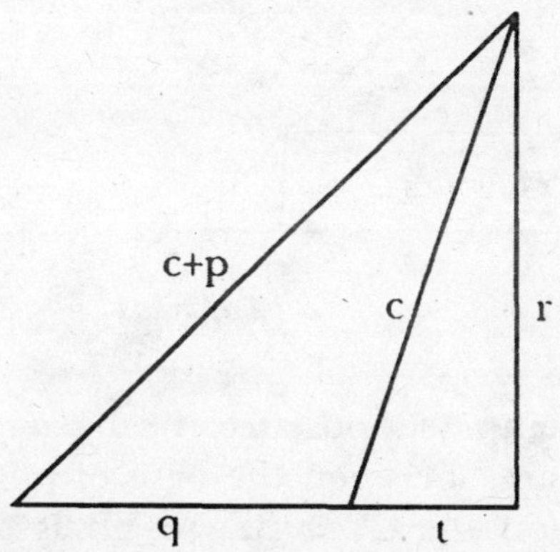

[Height of the vertical pole = **r**, its shadows are: **t**, **t+q** and corresponding hypotenuses are: **c**, **c+p.** We are given **r**, **p**, **q** and we have to find **t** when **q > p**.

$t=\frac{1}{2}\left(-q+p\sqrt{1+\frac{576}{q^2-p^2}}\right)$ The other shadow is **t + q**]

If the altitude of the sun and the height of the vertical pole are known, the length of the pole's shadow fallen on the ground may be calculated. For this marks are made on the ground where the shadows fall and the corresponding lengths.

Calculation of length of shadow is also reflected in the following verse:

शङ्कुः प्रदीपतलशङ्कुतलान्तरघ्नः ।
छाया भवेद्विनरदीपशिखौच्च्यभक्तः ॥

Līlā XXXII.242

(To find out the shadow of a gnomon) the area between the base of a lamp and base of a gnomon is to be multiplied by the size of gnomon. Then the *guṇaphala* (product) is to be divided by the height of the lamp minus gnomon.

This may be illustrated through a diagram (Līlā XXXII.243).

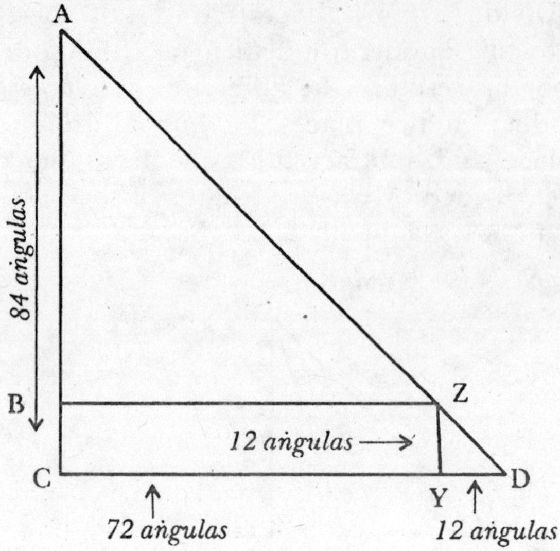

Here the height of the lamp (supposed to be 84 *aṅgulas*) is **AC**; gnomon is **YZ** (12 *aṅgulas*), the area between the base of a lamp and the base of a gnomon is **CY**(72 *aṅgulas*). As **CY** = **BZ**, so **YD** is the shadow of the gnomon. To find out this result a process is given: height of the lamp – gnomon = **AC** – **YZ** = **AC** – **BC**. By similar triangles **ABZ** and **ZYD** the proportion is:

$$\frac{\text{difference between base of lamp and gnomon} \times \text{gnomon}}{(\text{height of lamp - gnomon})} = \text{length of the shadow}$$

$$\left[(CY \times YZ) / (AC - YZ) = (CY \times YZ) / (AC - BC) = (CY \times YZ) / AB = YD\right]$$

Or $(72 \times 12) / (84 - 12) = (72 \times 12) / 72 = 12$ *aṅgulas.*

It indicates that the concept of 'Basic Proportionality Theorem' was known to the period of **Līlāvatī** (12th Cent. A.D.).

From the calculation of lengths of shadows and the distances of their tips from that of lamp a scientific principle is known that the light travels in a straight line. Bhāskarācārya has explained the use of shadow in calculating the height of lamp and difference between the base points in the last of this chapter (Līlā XXXII.246–249).

This discussion on shadows gives an idea of movable and immovable shadows. In case of movable shadows two aspects are noticed: (i) object and light both are movable, and (ii) object (earth) is movable and light (sun) is fixed. But in immovable shadow, light and object both are fixed. Hence shadow is also fixed and easy to calculate the length, height, base, etc. through mathematical process.

In the Buddhist literature *chāyā* is used in the sense of image or *pratikṛti*. In the story of Rudrayāna Avadāna, Buddha is said to have cast his image on a canvas or cotton-cloth (*paṭa*) which was to be coloured by Rudrāyaṇa's painters (*citrakara*):

> भगवानाह – महाराज, खेदमापतस्यन्ते, न शक्यते तथागतस्य निमित्तमुद्ग्रहीतुम् । अपि तु पटकमानय । तेन पटक आनीतः । तत्र भगवता छाया उत्सृष्टा, उक्ताश्च – रङ्गैः पूरयत ।
>
> Divyāv (PTS 547) XXXVII before 1
>
> Lord told - Oh King, distress would come, it is now possible to raise the mark of Tathāgata, but you can bring a canvas (cotton cloth). Cotton-cloth is being brought by him. His (Tathāgata's) image (*chāyā*) have cast on a canvas and he also said the artist to colour the same.

Shadow is an essential quality of a tree as it casts its shadow over the being without any distinction who comes to it and takes shelter beneath it, i.e. without making any distinction it affords shadow (*rukkho chāyāvemattaṃ na karoti* – MilPañ VII.6, PTS 409–410).

The term *chāyā* is used in the sense of reflection, in the context of age (*āyus*), where Nāgasena explains the number of years to the king Milinda by giving the examples of *chāyā* or *pratibimba* and reality.

> तेन खो पन समयेन मिलिन्दस्स रञ्ञो सब्बाभरणपटिमण्डितस्स अलङ्कतपटियत्तस्स पथवियं छाया दिस्सति, उदकमणिके च छाया दिस्सति । अथ खो आयस्मा नागसेनो मिलिन्दं राजानं एतदवोच – "अयं ते, महाराज, छाया पथवियं उदकमणिके च दिस्सति ॥ किं पन, महाराज, त्वं वा राजा, छाया वा राजा" ति? "अहं, भन्ते नागसेन, राजा, नायं छाया राजा । मं पन निस्साय छाया पवत्तती" ति । "एवमेव खो, महाराज, वस्सानं गणना सत्त । न पनाहं सत्त । मं पन निस्साय सत्त पवत्तति छायूपमं, महाराजा" ति ।
>
> MilPañ II.1.2
>
> Now that moment the figure of the king, decked in all the finery of his royal ornaments, cast its shadow on the ground and was reflected in a vessel of water. And Nāgasena asked him: your figure, O king, is now shadowed upon the ground, and reflected in the water, how now, are you the king, or is the reflection the king?

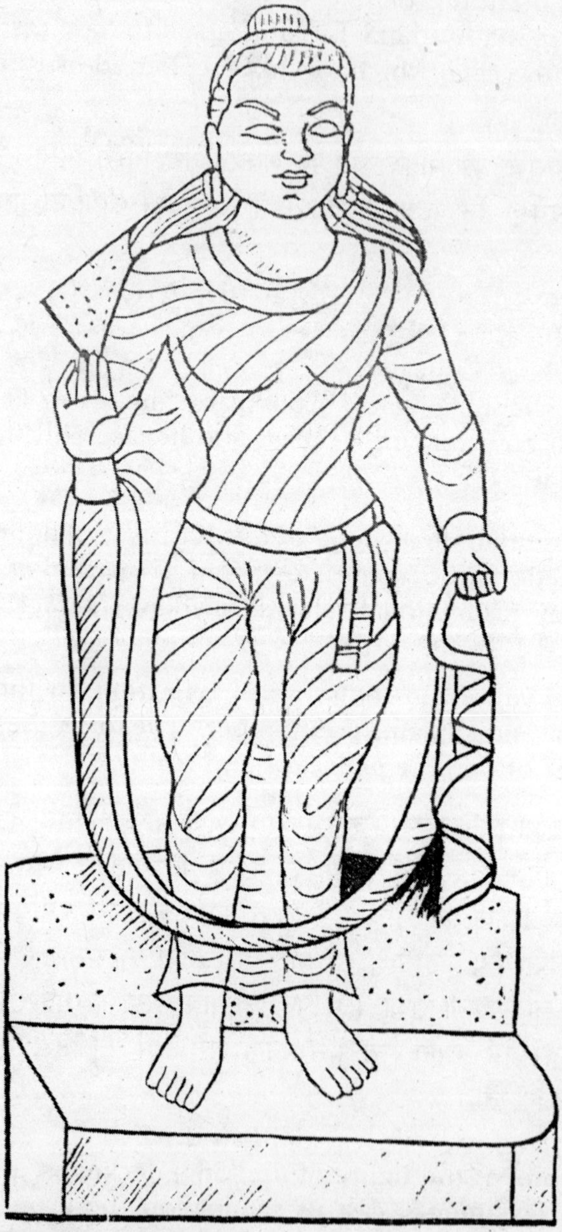

Figure 11: Image of Buddha

'I am the king, Nāgasena, but the shadow comes into existence because of me.' Just even so, O king, the number of the years is seven, I am not seven. But it is because of me, O king, that the number seven has come into existence; and it is mine in the same sense as the shadow is yours. (Tr. T.W. Rhys Davids)

This example of *chāyā* and *pratibimba* for identifying the age of a person is noticed also in the practical world. The **Dhammasaṅgaṇi** treats *chāyā* as a shape of that material form which is the sphere of visible shape and derived from the great five elements. Such type of form, may be of different colours (like blue, red, green, etc.) and different sizes of visible shapes (*rūpāyatana*) like long, short, big, little, circular, oral, square, etc. and low, high, shady, glowing, light, etc. or like in colour to the disc of moon (*candra maṇḍala*), sun, stars, a mirror, etc. (DhSaṅ rūpakhaṇḍa 617). So *chāyā* is treated here as a material form in the sphere of visible shape alongwith its essential companion like *ātapa* (glow) and *āloka* (light) denoting reflection and shade. The basic concept *chāyātapa* occurs also in the **Aṭṭhasālinī** (p. 317) in connection with the discussion of *rūpāyatana* 'locus of form' or 'sphere of visible shape' defined as 'coloured appearance', it shines (*nibbhāti*), hence appearance. In the **Abhidharma Kośa** of Vasubandhu the term bears rather the general meaning 'pairs of opposites' than the literal meaning 'light and shade' it is nevertheless actually the immediate equivalent of 'chiaroscuro'. The smallest part of the visible object termed *chāyā* includes odour, taste, tangible *ātapa* (glow) and *āloka* (light) denoting reflection and shade.

छायातपज्वालाप्रभासु तेषां कथमाहारत्वम् ?

AbhidhKo III.39

But how does one attribute the quality of food to odours etc. which are also found in shade (*chāyā*) and warm light (*ātapa*), inflames (*jvālā*) and in the light (of gems etc.) ? (Tr. L.M. Pruden)

The same concept is also discussed in the context of Bodhisattva's *āsphānaka* meditation.

न च आतपात्तु छायां छायाया नातपं गतश्चासौ ।
मेरुरिव निष्प्रकम्प्यो ध्यायत्यास्फानकं ध्यानम् ॥

LVi XVII.29

(Bodhisattva) meditates upon *āsphānaka* meditation in a state of motionless great mountain where he does not go to shadow from the sun or vice versa, i.e. not from shadow to the sun.

Without changing the place of meditation Bodhisattva fixed his mind in meditation. During the severe meditation for six years, Bodhisattva did not go to shadow from the sun nor did he go to the sun from shadow (*nātapācchāyāmagaman na chāyāyā ātapam* – LVi XVII, 322, PTS). In the **Laṅkāvatāra-Sūtra** this concept is elaborately discussed showing the interrelatedness with the reflection in a mirror or own shadow in the water where Rāvaṇa is asking for instruction bearing the importance of self-realization against the futility of the verbal teaching.

तद्यथा दर्पणान्तर्गतं स्वबिम्बप्रतिबिम्बं जले वा स्वाङ्गच्छाया वा ज्योत्स्नादीपप्रदीपिते वा गृहे वा अङ्गच्छाया प्रतिश्रुत्कानि । अथ स्वविकल्पग्रहणं प्रतिगृह्य धर्माधर्मं प्रतिविकल्पयन्ति । न च धर्माधर्मयोः प्रहाणेन चरन्ति । विकल्पयन्ति पुष्णन्ति, न प्रशमं प्रतिलभन्ते ।

LaSū I.43

It is like seeing one's own image reflected in a mirror, or one's own shadow in the water, or in the moonlight, or seeing one's shadow in the house, or hearing an echo in the valley. People grasping their own shadows of discrimination uphold the discrimination of *dharma* and *adharma* and, failing to carry out the abandonment of the dualism, they go on discriminating and never attain tranquillity. (Tr. D. T. Suzuki)

In the **Jātakamālā**, Bodhisattva advises a king that he should be like a tree who provides shelter and shadow to all beings without any discrimination through which a king could receive gratitude from his subjects.

छायाद्रुमेष्विव नरेषु कृताश्रयेषु
तावत्कृतज्ञचरितैः स्वयशः परीप्सेत् ।
नार्थोऽस्ति यावदुपभोगनयेन तेषां
कृत्ये तु यज्ञ इव ते पशवो नियोज्याः ॥

Jāmā XXIII.21

You must avail yourself of men, as of shady trees, considering them fit objects to resort to. Accordingly, endeavour to extend your glory by showing them gratitude only as long, until your policy ceases to want their use. They are to be appointed to their task in the manner of victims destined for the sacrifice.
(Tr. J.S. Speyer)

Gratitude should be extended towards the trees for their shadow.

In the same text the concept of reflection in the disc of the moon is narrated in the context of naming of moon as *śaśāṅka.*

सम्पूर्णेऽद्यापि तदिदं शशबिम्बं निशाकरे ।
छायामयमिवादर्शे राजते दिवि राजते ॥

Jāmā VI.37

At full-moon even now that image of the hare (*śaśa*) appears in the moon's disc in the sky, as a reflected image shines in a silver mirror. (Tr. J.S. Speyer)

The **Sutta Nipāta** gives a nice simile where essential need of a shade to a heat-burnt or sun stroked person is shown. A thirsty man to cool water is like one sun-stroked person to shade.

तसितो वुदकं सीतं महालाभंऽव वाणिजो ।
छायं घम्माभितत्तोऽव तुरिता पब्बतमारुहुं ॥

SutNip 1014

Like a thirsty man (going) to cool water, like a merchant (going) to great profit, like one burned by heat (going) to shade, quickly they climbed the mountain. (Tr. K.R. Norman)

In the **Tattva-Saṅgraha** of Śāntarakṣita, a text of Buddhist philosophy, records the term *chāyā* in the sense of reflection in the context of momentariness and non-momentariness of things. The mirror-surface cannot contain the reflection as it is indivisible and non-momentary (*bibharti darpaṇatalaṃ naiva cchāyāṃ kadācana* – TSaṅg 259). The mirror, when connects with an object like blue lotus, creates illusion regarding its reflection (*chāyāvibhrama*) as the things reflect in different type from different position (TSaṅg 257–258).

In Jain philosophy, the term *chāyā* is treated as a modification of *pudgala*, material object or the soul. A number of Jain texts have discussed on this concept of *chāyā* as an inherent quality of *pudgala* or material substance. The **Tattvārtha-Sūtra** records the term *chāyā* as a synonym of *pudgala*:

शब्दबन्धसौक्ष्म्यस्थौल्यसंस्थानभेदतमश्छायातपोद्योतवन्तश्च ॥

TaSū V.24

(The material substances or *pudgala*s are possessed of) sound, union caused by man or otherwise (*bandha*), subtleness, grossness, figure (*saṃsthāna*), splitting, darkness, shade (*chāyā*), sunshine (*ātapa*) and *udyota* 'moon light.'
(Based on the tr. by J.L. Jaini)

The **Sarvārthasiddhi** elaborates this idea, treating *chāyā* as of two kinds: (i) inverted images as seen in the mirror etc., where the left side becomes right and vice versa, (ii) non-inverted images.

छाया प्रकाशावरणनिमित्ता । सा द्वेधा, वर्णादिविकारपरिणता प्रतिबिम्बमात्रात्मिका चेति ॥

SaSi on TaSū V.24

An image (shadow) results from obstruction of light by an object. It is of two kinds, images as seen in a mirror and uninverted images like shadows. (In the first of these, the left side becomes right and the right side becomes left.) (Tr. S.A. Jain)

The **Tattvārthavārttika** (V.24.16–17) gives a more clear idea on the same: *chāyā prakāśāvaraṇanimittā, sā dvedhā tadvarṇādivikāra pratibimbamātra grahaṇavikalpāt.* The **Rājavārttika** commentary on the same says: *prakāśāvaraṇaṃ śarīrādi yasyā nimittaṃ bhavati sā chāyā*, i.e. 'obstruction of light by body' etc. creates shadow. The **Tattvārthavārttika** in this context shows the difference between two lights *ātapa* 'heat caused by the sun' and *udyota* light resulting from the moon, fire-fly, jewels, etc. Both these lights are interrelated with *chāyā* :

The basic idea of *chāyā* is two-fold: (i) shelter as tree etc., and (ii) reflection as the image of man etc. (cf. *vṛkṣādyāśrayarūpā manuṣyādi pratibimbarūpā ca chāyā vijñeyā* – DSaṅg Vṛ 16.) As modification of substance, *chāyā* (image) is listed in the **Dravyasaṅgraha** with *tamas* (darkness) (... *tamaśchāyā* .. *pudgala dravyasya paryāyāḥ* – DSaṅg 16).

Adharma is compared with *chāyā*. As shadow assists the staying of the travellers so *adharma* assists the staying of the *pudgala*s and immovable *jīva*s. *Dharma* is the support or holding of motion but *adharma* is the support of rest. The **Dravyasaṅgraha** explains this idea as follows:

ठाणजुदाण अधम्मो पुग्गलजीवाण ठाणसहयारी ।
छाया जह पहियाणं गच्छंता णेव सो धरई ॥

स्थानयुतानां अधर्म्मः पुद्गलजीवानां स्थानसहकारी ।
छाया यथा पथिकानां गच्छतां नैव स धरति ॥

DSaṅg 18

As shadow (assists the staying of) the travellers, (so) *adharma* assists the staying of the *pudgala*s and *jīva*s which are stationary. But that (i.e. *adharma*) does not hold back moving (*pudgala*s and *jīva*s). (Tr. S.C. Ghoshal)

Here *adharma* is said to be like shadow which does not forcibly stop the travellers scorched by the rays of the sun from moving, but assists in their rest, while they of their own accord to sit in the shade.

In the Jaina **Harivaṃśa Purāṇa** the term *chāyā* is noticed as a compound form – *chāyāsaṃkrāmiṇī*, one of the sixteen *vidyās*, presumably referring to a magical charm invoked for the purpose of entering into a different body through the shadow–essence of one's being.

महाश्वेतापि मायूरी हारी निर्वज्ञशाड्वला ।
सा तिरस्करिणी विद्या छायासंक्रामिणी परा ॥

HarPur XXII.63

Mahāśvetā, Māyūrī, Hārī, Nirvajñaśāḍvalā, Tiraskariṇī and Chāyā-saṃkrāmiṇī – these are treated as the *vidyās*.

In Indian philosophic schools of theistic system the term *chāyā* has been discussed as a multidimensional concept denoting shadow, darkness, reflection, etc. The **Sāṃkhya-Kārikā** records the term *chāyā* in the context of proving the impossibility of *liṅga* or *sūkṣma-śarīra* (subtle-body) without the gross body (*sthūla-śarīra*). As shadow is impossible without an object like post etc. similarly subtle body cannot subsist without gross-body.

चित्रं यथाश्रयमृते स्थाण्वादिभ्यो विना यथाच्छाया ।
तद्वद् विना विशेषैर्नतिष्ठति निराश्रयं लिङ्गम् ॥

SāṃKā 41

As, a picture cannot exist without a support or substrate (like a wall), or a shadow without a post, so the *liṅga* (defined in SāṃKā 40) cannot subsist without the *viśeṣas* (three varieties of *viśeṣas* described in SāṃKā 39) being supportless. (Tr. R.S. Bhattacharya)

In the **Nyāya Siddhānta Muktāvalī**, commentary on **Bhāṣāpariccheda** (I.3), *chāyā* is treated as the property of earth. To support this, a line is quoted by the commentator from **Tantrarahasya** – '*apavāritāloka kevalaṃ bhūbhāgādikam eva chāyā*', i.e. *chāyā* or darkness is nothing but the empty spot from where light has been veiled.

The Mīmāṃsā school also discussed on the same idea. The **Prakaraṇa-pañcikā** (a text of the Prabhākara school) comments:

तेन मन्यामहे - अपवारितालोकभूभागादिकम् एव छायेति ।

PraPañ p. 322

Therefore we are of the opinion that *chāyā* (shadow) is nothing but the ground and the like from which light has got concealed. (Tr. R.S. Bhattacharya)

Again the same text opines on the idea that darkness is verily the same as shadow (*chāyaiva tamaḥ*) which possesses the qualities like movement, non-movement, greatness, non-greatness, remoteness, proximity, etc. and as such a positive entity. This is however baseless on account of the impossibility of accomplishment, i.e. the connection of the aforesaid qualities with *chāyā* is not established.

Chāyā is compared with darkness (*tamaḥ*) in the **Mānameyodaya** (a work of Kumārila school). Darkness is black like the shade of the *kalāya* flower (*kalāyakomalacchāyaṃ ... tamaḥ kṛṣṇaṃ vijānīyāt* – MāMey sec. on *dravya*, para 20).

Śaṅkara has clearly described the nature of *chāyā* as reflection in his **Bhāṣya** on the **Brahma-Sūtra**, following the Upanisadic concept. The person in the eye is the reflected self, i.e. the image of a person reflected in the eye of another (*chāyātmā puruṣapratirūpa iti* – BrSūŚBh I.2.13). It is more clear in the following passage:

> यदैव हि कश्चित् पुरुषश्चक्षुरासीदति तदा चक्षुषि पुरुषच्छाया दृश्यते, अपगते तस्मिन् न दृश्यते ।
>
> BrSūŚBh I.2.17
>
> For when some person approaches the eye the reflection of that person is seen in the eye, but when the person moves away the reflection is seen no longer. (Tr. G. Thibuat)

The same text also quotes the views of *paurāṇikas* who designate the colour (*chāyā*) of the earth as dark night, where the term *chāyā* is used in the sense of colour (*paurāṇikā api pṛthivīcchāyāṃ śarvarīm upadiśanti, sā ca kṛṣṇābhāsā* – BrSūŚBh II.3.12).

The **Pañcadaśī** of Vidyāraṇya, a comprehensive manual of Advaita Vedānta, also takes *chāyā* as reflection. *Māyā*, derives its power from *brahman*. *Brahman* is omniscient because this power of consciousness is associated with the reflection of *brahman* (*cicchāyāveśataḥ śaktiścetaneva vibhāti sā* – Pañcad III.40). When the essence of *brahman* is reflected on the intellect of some objects they exhibit a state of animation. The mind turns inward and becomes calm, when an object is being enjoyed. In that state of mind, the bliss or the self is reflected. The **Pañcadaśī** supports this idea as follows:

> खानिलाग्निजलोर्व्यण्डलोकप्राणिशिलादिका: ।
> विकारा: प्राणिधीष्वन्तश्चिच्छाया प्रतिबिम्बिता ॥
>
> Pañcad XIII.91
>
> *Ākāśa*, air, fire, water, earth, the universe, the different *lokas* and animate and inanimate objects are appearances, produced by *māyā*. Pure consciousness appears as a reflection in the intellects of living beings. (Tr. Swahananda)

In Vaiṣṇva philosophy also the term *chāyā* is used in the sense of lustre, reflected image, etc. In the context of defining *lāvaṇya*, the **Ujjvalanīlamaṇi** records the term *chāyā*. Beauty (*lāvaṇya*) is the subtle effulgence exuding from the body in the manner of lustre emanating from pearl.

मुक्ताफलेषु छायायास्तरलत्वमिवान्तरा ।
प्रतिभाति यदंगेषु लावण्यं तदिहोच्यते ॥

UjNīl XI.26

That is called beauty (*lāvaṇya*) which reflects on the body like the glittering of lustre (*chāyā*), in the pearls.

The **Bhaktirasāmṛtasindhu** records the term *chāyā* as a kind or type of *ratyābhāsa*. The *rati-ābhāsa*, i.e. semblance of a *rati* is of two kinds, viz. (i) a direct reflection of form or image (*pratibimba*), and (ii) a shadow (*chāyā*) or indirect reflection (*pratibimbastathā chāyā ratyābhāso dvidhā mataḥ* – BhSi I.3.25). The indirect reflection or *praticchāyā* is clearly noticed in the *pūjā* ritual. For example, image of Durgā is reflected primarily on a mirror then on the water surface.

The Tantra and Āgama school also discusses on the concept of *chāyā* from its two dimensional aspect, (i) shadow, and (ii) reflection. The **Tantrāloka** records these two aspects in the context of describing different kinds of bodies – *para* 'transcendent', *sūkṣma* 'subtle', *sthūla* 'gross' and *chāyā* 'the nature of reflection'.

पिण्डः परः कलात्मा सूक्ष्मः पुर्यष्टको बहिः स्थूलः ।
छायात्मा स पराङ्मुख आदर्शादौ च सम्मुखो ज्ञेयः ॥

TĀl XXIX.265

The aggregate of all is the beyond, while the subtle is characterised by *kalā* (implying six sheathes), the gross body consisting of eight components (viz. the mind, intellect, egoism and five subtle elements) is the exterior one. It is by nature, shadow turned away from light while in the mirror etc., it is known as the front (on which the reflection is seen). (Tr. H.N. Chakravarty)

Again, in the sense of reflection the term *chāyā* is used in the same text to denote the interchangeable letters among the vowel and consonants. *Bindu* or *anusvāra* is actually a reflection of the consonant *m* (cf. *mo'nusvāraḥ* – Pā VIII.3.23). Similarly, *ṛ*, *ḷ* and *visarga* (:) are the reflection of the consonants *r*, *l*, and *h*.

मकारादन्य एवायं तच्छायामात्रधृद्यथा ॥
रलहाः षण्ठवैसर्गवर्णरूपत्वसंस्थिताः ।

इकार एव रेफांशच्छाययान्यो यथा स्वरः ॥

TĀI III.134cd–135

The letter *m* holds only the shadowy structure (with the sound) of *bindu,* i.e. *anusvāra* or dot; similarly the letters *r, l,* and *h* bear the phonemic concept of *ṛ, ḷ* and *visarjanīya* (:). The consonant *r* becomes vowel *ṛ* only with the appearance (*chāyā*) of vowel *i* (i.e. *r* + *i* = *ṛ*).

Kṣemarāja in his Uddyota commentary on the **Netra Tantra** quotes a verse from the **Trika Hṛdaya** which shows that shadow of a person's head is unattainable by his feet for comparing the unattainability of unlimited consciousness.

स्वपदा स्वशिरश्छायां यथा लंघितुमीहते ।
पादोद्देशे शिरो न स्यात्तथेयं बैन्दवी कला ॥

Kṣemarāja on NT after verse I.47

Just as a person while trying to cross the shadow of his head by his feet and finds the head absent under his feet, in the same way the unlimited consciousness *samvid* remains unattainable.
(Tr. H.N. Chakravarty)

It is also noticed that the term *chāyā* is used as a compound with *chidra* to denote shadow-hole for casting glance badly by the evil spirits. The ghosts can harm even through the hole of the shadow of a being.

छायाच्छिद्रेण भूताश्च मातरो बलवत्तराः ।
दृष्टिपातं प्रकुर्वन्ति लब्धच्छिद्रा हि हिंसकाः ॥

NT XIX.46

Being the opportunist and noxious animal, the ghosts are stronger than the mothers as they look through the shadow-hole or even through the most insignificant loop-hole.

The **Mahānirvāṇa Tantra** describes a compound with *chāyā* from its ritual viewpoint. In the *upanayana saṃskāra*, a *chāyāmaṇḍapa* (i.e., a clean space with an awning over it) is noticed, covered with cloth. The child for taking sacred thread should sit on a *chāyā-maṇḍapa.* In an open space, *upanayana saṃskāra* cannot be performed. So the covered *maṇḍapa* is known as *chāyāmaṇḍapa.*

छायामण्डपमानीय समुद्भवहुताशितुः ।
समीपे चात्मनो वामे संस्थाप्य विमलासने ॥

MNT IX.190

The boy should then be taken to the *chāyāmaṇḍapa* near fire under his name of *samud-bhava,* and there made to sit on a clean seat to the left (of his father or *guru*). (Tr. John Woodroffe)

The same text also uses the term *chāyā* in the sense of *guru*'s (preceptor's) mercy. The disciple should come to a teacher or preceptor for protection also. The preceptor will then cast the shadows of his lotus like feet to his disciple (*tvatpadāmbhoruhacchāyāṃ dehi* – MNT III.130).

The **Mṛgendra Āgama** tries to relate the elemental complexion with fire forms of Lord Śiva which are mostly considered in correspondence with the nature and their evolutes, subtle and gross elements.

निस्पृहा गगनच्छाया: सूक्ष्मकाया: सुबुद्धय: ।
साधयन्त्यभियोगेन लघुनैवेशदैवतम् ॥
गौरास्तत्पुरुषस्कन्धमिष्टच्छायासमाश्रया: ।
तृतीयं तैजसच्छाया: कृष्णपिङ्गदृश: खरा: ॥
क्षीबाक्षा रक्तगौराभा वामदेवपरिग्रहम् ।
वारिच्छाया दृढस्निग्धदेहा: सद्यपरिग्रहम् ॥

MṛgĀ kp VIII.222–224

Those who are non-attached have pure and transparent complexion like the clear sky. Their bodies are slender but their intellect is keen and goes to the right direction. By means of slight effort they are able to propitiate Lord Īśāna. They who are blessed with desirable complexion of whiteness belong to the family of Tatpuruṣa (therefore they can propitiate the superintending deity easily by the mantra of Tatpuruṣa. Those belonging to third kind are possessed by Aghora and hence they can propitiate the god easily. Their eyes are dark-red and their figures are cruel. Those whose eyes are dull as if in intoxication and figures are brownish-white should be known as possessed by Vāmadeva, hence they can easily fulfil their aims by means of *mantras* belonging to Vāmadeva class. Those who are possessed by Sadyojāta have the complexion of water. Their bodies are well-built and compact.
(Tr. H.N. Chakravarty)

In Kaula tradition, yogin and his *śakti* are treated as unseperable, specially during some tantric practices. This inseparable nature is compared with the nature of tree and its shadow or fire and smoke (*agnidhūmau*) in the **Kaula Jñāna Nirṇaya** (XVII.9).

न वृक्षरहिताच्छाया न छायारहितो द्रुम: ।
शक्त्याभ्यासरतो योगी कुले सामान्यतां व्रजेत् ॥

KaJNi XVII.9

Just as there is no tree without its shadow, nor the shadow of a tree without the tree itself, so in kula practice one should think of the *yogi* and his *śakti* as inseparable. (Tr. Michael Magee)

The **Pauṣkara Saṃhitā** records the term *chāyā* in the context of explaining the gnomon of shadow from astronomical viewpoint. The shadow of the gnomon plays an important role in establishing shrines or townships or the residence and the ritual performance of *maṇḍala*-worship of the householders. One has to be very careful for the observation of the shadows. For finding out a place of conjunction, shadow should be taken at midday eastward and westward (PauṣSam III.21–22). The same text also describes the measurement and division of the shadow of a gnomon.

... छायाभागं चतुर्विधम् ।
पूर्वभागाधिके देशं विधेयं तेन गृह्यते ॥
मेषे माध्याह्निकी छाया विज्ञेयाऽष्टाङ्गुला तथा।
संयुक्ताद्यङ्गुला षड्भिर्वृषे पञ्चाङ्गुला भवेत् ॥
चतुर्भिरङ्गुलैरूना मिथुने त्र्यङ्गुला भवेत्।

PauṣSam III.24–26ab

The division of the actual shadow is fourfold; the surplus portion of demarcation of the east is calculated thereof. During the period of the zodiac-*meṣa* the noon-shadow is to be known as equivalent to eight *aṅgulas*, i.e. two plus six. In the zodiac *vṛṣa*, the shadow is five *aṅgulas* (minus four *aṅgulas*). In the zodiac sign *mithuna*, the shadow is three *aṅgulas* . (Tr. P.P. Apte)

To pay respect to his preceptor a disciple should not surpass even his shadow. As **Prapañcasāra Tantra** says:

छायाज्ञापादुकोपानद्दण्डांश्च शयनासने ।
यानं मनोगतं चाऽन्यदन्तेवासी न लङ्घयेत् ॥

PSāT XXXVI.52

A disciple should not cross the shadow of his spiritual director or *guru*, nor his order, slipper, shoe and staff in sleeping position or sitting position; and not in the state of leading or concealed in the mind.

Chāyā is recorded in the **Dakṣiṇāmūrtistotra Bhāṣya** to support the inseparable nature between the lordship and the state of the Lord.

ऐश्वर्यमीश्वरत्वं हि तस्य नास्ति पृथक्स्थिति : ।

पुरुषे धावमाने हि छाया तमनुधावति ॥

DakMūStBh X.4

Lordship and the state of the Lord do not indeed have two distinct entities. A person while running, the shadow definitely follows him. (Tr. H.N. Chakravarty)

Jīva and Śiva are compared with the intertwined concept of light and shade in Śaivism. As records the **Anubhava-Sūtra**:

छायातपौ जीवशिवावसौ गुरुः
शिवोऽस्य शिष्यः खलु जीवसंज्ञिकः ।
लिङ्गं परं हृद्गगनं तदङ्गकं
प्राणानिलोऽयं शिवसूत्रमुच्यते ॥

Anubhava Sūtra V.35

Jīva and Śiva are treated as shade and light respectively where Lord Śiva is known as preceptor and *jīva* as disciple. This (theme) is called Śivasūtra as it deals with the Supreme Cause as the cavity of the heart and His parts as breath and air.

The term *chāyā* is widely used in the Sanskrit literature whether audible poems (*śravya*) or visible plays (*dṛśya*) touching the inmost cords of human mind, presenting a sense of delight and reflecting the mirror of life. Kālidāsa, the great poet of aesthetic beauty and sensuous emotion, uses the term *chāyā* in the sense of shadow, reflection, radiance, etc. The shade of divine wish-fulfilling tree is described in the **Raghuvaṃśa**:

आसीत् कल्पतरुच्छायामाश्रिता सुरभिः पथि ॥

Ragh I.75cd

There was on your way the divine cow Surabhi lying under the shade of the Kalpa tree. (Tr. G.R. Nadargikar)

Similarly, shade of the forest-trees suitable for ascetics is indicated (*munivanatarucchāyām* – Ragh III.70). Trees remove the fatigue of journey by offering their shade (*chāyāvinītādhvapariśrameṣu* – Ragh XIII.46). Rāma has the divine power of fixing a shadow, i.e. motionless state (*prabhāva-stambhitacchāyam* – Ragh XII.21). The shade of Nameru trees are described as the best resting places for the soldiers (*namerūṇāṃ chāyāsvadhyāsya sainikāḥ* – Ragh IV.74). The same text records a number of illustrations with the term *chāyā*, e.g. *ikṣucchāyā*, *dhvajacchāyā*, *gṛdhracchāyā*, *chāyāpatha*, *chāyāmaṇḍala*, etc. Kālidāsa uses the term *ikṣucchāyā* to denote the thickness (*bāhulya*) of shade of sugarcanes presenting a natural scene of northern part of Uttar Pradesh – watching the crops of *śāli* corn by women, shattering themselves under the deep shade of sugarcanes (Ragh IV.20). Again, in the description of *dhvajacchāyā* Kālidāsa depicts a custom of raising flags and banners by the citizen in front of their houses to show respect to their kings and the shades of those banners are sufficient to keep off the heat (*dhvajacchāyā-nivāritoṣṇam* – Ragh VII.4). The expression '*suṣvāpa gṛdhracchāye*' (Ragh XII.50) 'fell asleep under the shade of vulture (carrion birds)' indicates the death of army.

In the **Raghuvaṃśa** some universal concepts are noticed where the term *chāyā* is used to denote radiance related with light and shade. Kālidāsa compares a foaming ocean divided by means of a bridge with a galaxy (*chāyāpatha*) in a clear autumnal sky displaying beautiful stars (*chāyāpatheneva* ... Ragh XIII.2). Presence of a divine power could be guessed from the halo of radiance around an object or person known as *chāyāmaṇḍala* (Ragh IV.5).

The term *chāyā* is used in the sense of reflection in different places of **Raghuvaṃśa**: *chāyāmivādarśatalaṃ* ... (XVI.6) 'as a reflection does the surface of a mirror', *nepathyadarśinacchāyā tasyādarśe hiraṇmaye...* (XVII.26) 'his image shone in the mirror that was made of gold', *chāyā hi bhūmeḥ śaśino malatvenāropitā* ... (XIV.40) 'the reflection of the earth is attributed as a spot of the pure moon'. The same text also records a dramatic charm with reflection as follows:

दर्पणेषु परिभोगदर्शिनीर्नर्मपूर्वमनुपृष्ठसंस्थितः ।
छायया स्मितमनोज्ञया वधूर्ह्रीनिमीलितमुखीश्चकार सः ॥

Ragh XIX.28

Standing behind a youthful damsel by way of jest he by means of his reflection charming on account of his sweet smiling made her hang down her face with shame while she was looking at the marks of enjoyment on her body in a mirror.
(Tr. G.R. Nandargikar)

King Dilīpa is compared as a shadow of the cow Nandinī as he follows her blindly (*chāyeva tāṃ bhūpatiranvagacchat* – Ragh II.6). Impression of feet of god, is also worshipped with flowers, etc. in the world even today. It is called *chyāyāpūjā*. Raghu's feet were worshipped symbolically after placing on a golden foot-stool (*ratnapuṣpopahāreṇa chāyāmānarca pādayoḥ* – Ragh IV.84). Kālidāsa has described different types of aesthetic charm in the **Raghuvaṃśa** related with *chāyā*, e.g. clouds with shade (*chāyayā ca jaladāḥ* – XI.11), embracing Lakṣmī by Raghu under the disguise of the shade of his umbrella (*ātapatracchāyā* – XVIII.47).

In the **Meghadūta**, Kālidāsa has dealt with the term *chāyā* in various places and it is used mostly as a second part of *tatpuruṣa* compound, e.g. *ratnacchāyā*, *kṣāmacchāyā*, *pāṇḍucchāyā*, *vaktracchāyā*, etc. At the very outset of **Meghadūta** the term *chāyātaru* is used in the sense of tree affording thick shade over which the position of the sun had no effect (*snigdhacchāyātaruṣu* ... Megh I.1). The same text describes the streaming light or rays of gems by the term *ratnacchāyā*. The lustre of each gem is meant as blending with that of another in the following verse:

रत्नच्छायाव्यतिकर इव प्रेक्ष्यमेतत्पुरस्ताद्
बल्मीकाग्रात्प्रभवति धनुःखण्डमाखण्डलस्य ।
येन श्यामं वपुरतितरां कान्तिमापत्स्यते ते
बर्हेणेव स्फुरितरुचिना गोपवेषस्य विष्णोः ॥

Megh I.15

Here appears to view in front, from the top of an ant-hill, a fragment of Indra's bow (a fractional rain-bow), attractive like an intermingling of the streaming rays of gems by which your dark body will attain an exceedingly charming splendour, like that of Viṣṇu in his cowherd's character (Kṛṣṇa) by peacock's featheres with their glowing splendour. (Tr. M.R. Kale)

Again, it is noticed in the description of ornamental hook of the handles of dancing girls as the glittering rays of sparkling lustre of the gems set in their bracelets (*ratnacchāyākhacitavalibhiścāmaraiḥ klāntahastāḥ* – Megh I.38b). To present a glomy appearance due to separation is expressed by the term *kṣāmacchāyā* (*kṣāmacchāyaṃ bhavanamadhunā madviyogena nūnam* – Megh II.20c) and the beauty of one's face is described as *vaktracchāyā* comparing with moon (*vaktracchāyāṃ śaśini* – II.44b). The term *chāyā* is also used in the sense of colour as depicted by Kālidāsa to describe the gardens of Daśārṇa country with white coloured Ketaka flowers (*pāṇḍucchāyopavanavṛtayaḥ ketakaiḥ* – Megh I.24a). The shade of the heavenly Mandāra trees on the banks of the Mandakini river are treated as cool and pleasant because of their capacity of keeping off heat (*mandārāṇāmanutaṭaruhāṃ chāyayā vāritoṣṇāḥ* – Megh II.6b). The shade of a tree is very pleasant after suffering from heat. The **Vikramorvaśīya** records:

यदेवोपनतं दुःखात्सुखं तद्रसवत्तरम् ।
निर्वाणाय तरुच्छाया तप्तस्य हि विशेषतः ॥

Vik III.21

The happiness which waits upon one after misery is the sweeter (more savoury) for the shade of a tree is the more refreshing to him who has been oppressed with heat. (Tr. M.R. Kale)

In the **Kumārasambhava**, the concept of *chāyā* and *ātapa* is recorded in a verse where *chāyā* means shadow '*anātapa*' and '*ātapavanti*' means perpetually exposed to the sun, being above the region of clouds.

आमेखलं संचरतां घनानां छायामधःसानुगतां निषेव्य ।
उद्वेजिता वृष्टिभिराश्रयन्ते शृङ्गाणि यस्यातपवन्ति सिद्धाः ॥

Kum I.5

To whose sunny peaks the siddhas repair (for comfort) when troubled by showers, after having enjoyed the shadow, fallen on the peaks below, of the clouds floating round the mountain's zone. (Tr. M.R. Kale)

The same text also shows that the shades of heavenly Santānaka trees are favourite to *vidyādharas* (*santānakatarucchāyā* – Kum VI.46). The **Ṛtusaṃhāra** also records that people like the shade of trees (*chāyāṃ janaḥ samabhivāñchati-pādapānām* – Ṛtu VI, after verse 9).

Aśvaghoṣa has nicely described the term *chāyā* in the context of a lotus like face of a lady. Here the term *chāyāmaya* is used in the sense of radiance:

तस्याः मुखं पद्मसपत्नभूतं पाणौ स्थितं पल्लवरागताम्रे ।
छायामयस्याम्भसि पङ्कजस्य बभौ नतं पद्ममिवोपरिष्टात् ॥

Saun VI.11

Her (Sundarī's) lotus like face, lying on hands, red coloured like a young twig was adorned like a reflected lotus on water from the above befallen lotus.

Bhāravi has used the term *chāyā* to denote shadow in his **Kirātārjunīya** showing how the effulgence of Lord Śiva disperses the dark shadow.

छायां विनिर्धूय तमोमयीं तां तत्त्वस्य संवित्तिरिवापविद्याम् ।
ययौ विकासं द्युतिरिन्दुमौलेरालोकमभ्यादिशती गणेभ्यः ॥

Kir XVI.32

As the essence of true knowledge removes the darkness of ignorance, the effulgence of the Lord Śiva, who bears the crescent on his crown having repelled that dark shadow (of the form of slumber caused by the *prasvāpana* arrow of Arjuna) expanded far and wide as directing the path of light to the *gaṇas*. (Tr. P.K. Agrawala)

Harṣa has depicted a natural scene of drinking wine in the shades of Candana trees by Vidyādharas (a class of demi-gods) in the **Nāgānanda**.

सार्धं सिद्धजनैर्मधूनि दयितापीतावशिष्टान्यमी ।
मिश्रीभूय पिबन्ति चन्दनतरुच्छायासु विद्याधराः ॥

Nāgā III.9cd

The Vidyādharas mingling with the Siddhas drink the wine left over by their loving women after tasting it, in the shades of the sandal trees. (Tr. Bak Kun Bae)

After the completion of wedding ceremony, all the Siddhas and Vidyādharas are enjoying a hearty banquet with their beloved by drinking liquor, in the shade of sandal trees.

In the **Naiṣadhīyacarita**, Śrīharṣa has used the term *chāyā* in different senses like the wife of the sun, shadow, reflection, etc. Both the wives of the sun, Saṃjñā and Chāyā are mentioned in the **Naiṣadhīyacarita** (XIII.17). In a nice description of meeting of lovers and their beloved in moonlight under trees having discarded blue clothing in the guise of shadows (*chāyācchalā-dujjhitanīlacelā* – NaiCa XXII.41). The borders of the trees enveloped in darkness at night prior to moonrise are fancied as young women secretly coming to meet their lovers, wearing blue clothing which makes them invisible in the darkness. After moonrise the borders shining with moonlight are imagined as the maidens returning home with scarves on, which makes them invisible in the moonlight. The shadows cast by the trees are imagined to the blue clothing discarded by the maidens when they changed for white. The same text also gives some other references of *chāyā* in the sense of shadow as follows: *chāyā mayā puṃsa iva vyaloki* (VI.47) 'I saw something like the shadow of a man', *chāyaiva vāmatha ... adhvajaśramaharā makaradhvajasya* (XXI.136) 'Nala's shadow remove cupid's fatigue from journeying', *chāyā vidhāya ... andhakāraḥ* (XXII.38) 'the darkness had employed shadows', etc. In the sense of reflection, the term *chāyā* is nicely used by Śrīharṣa in the description of attractive reflection of king's beauty on the floor.

पुंसि स्वभर्तृव्यतिरिक्तभूते भूत्वाप्यनीक्षानियमव्रतिन्यः ।
छायासु रूपं भुवि वीक्ष्य तस्य फलं दृशोरानशिरे महिष्यः ॥

NaiCa VI.43

The queens (in the harem), though they were devoted to the austerity of not looking at any man except their own consorts, obtained the supreme joy of their eyes, by looking at his beauty in his reflections on the floor. (Tr. K.K. Handiqui)

In ancient times, the queens of inner apartment or harem looked only the shadow of their consort reflected on the floor.

In the **Bhaṭṭi Kāvya** the term *chāyā* is profusely used to denote different types of shadows of tree, weapon, etc. and resemblance. Hence, shadow of lofty trees (*tuṅgatarucchāyā* – XIII.34), of huge Tamāla trees (*mahātamāla-cchāyam* – XIII.32), (*haritamālacchāyam* – XIII.8), thick shadow of Kesara, Bakula and Hintāla trees (XIII.33), shadow of any tree (*pādapacchāyām* – VII.32), cool shadow of tall, massive and radiant trees (*taruvarahimacchāyam* – XIII.6), etc. Bhaṭṭi also gives a nice description of spreading a thick shadow of weapons on the battlefield, strewn over by the darkness produces by dust (*akārṣṭām āyudhacchāyaṃ rajaḥ santamase raṇe* – BhaKā V.2).

In Sanskrit dramas the term *chāyā* is used widely. In the **Pratimānāṭaka**, Bhāsa shows the same honour even to a shadow like a person. Rāma honours the shadow of Rāvaṇa, ought to the body which casts shadow and therefore superior to it (*chāyāṃ parihṛtya śarīraṃ na laṅghayāmi* – PraNāṭ V, after 8). The same text has also used the term to describe an immediate follower. Lakṣmaṇa follows Rāma as a shadow in the forest (*chāyevānugamyate* – PraNāṭ II.10). Sītā is also noticed as *chāyā* of Rāma.

सूर्य इव गतो रामः सूर्यं दिवस इव लक्ष्मणोऽनुगतः ।
सूर्यदिवसावसाने छायेव न दृश्यते सीता ॥

PraNāṭ II.7

Rāma has departed like the sun; Lakṣmaṇa has followed him as day-light does the sun; Sītā is not seen like a shadow at the disappearance of the sun and daylight. (Tr. M.R. Kale)

In the **Abhijñānaśākuntala** this concept is treated mainly for shade and shadows. It records how the tree suffers burning heat with its head, but by its shade it allays the pain of those resorting to it (*śamayati paritāpaṃ chāyayā saṃśritānām* – AbhŚāk V.7). Trees affording thick shade are also recorded here (*chāyādrumaiḥ* – IV.11). The shadow of a Saptaparṇa tree is very pleasant for its density and coolness (*pracchāyaśītalāyāṃ saptaparṇavedikāyām* – after I.22). The same text also describes the shadows of demons are terrific and brown like evening clouds (*chāyāścaranti bahudhā bhayamādadhānāḥ* – III.25c). Kālidāsa has also shown the term *chāyā* to denote the reflection of an image.

छाया न मूर्च्छति मलोपहतप्रसादे शुद्धे तु दर्पणतले सुलभावकाशा ॥

AbhŚāk VII.32cd

An image takes no effect on the surface of a mirror having its transparency obscured by dust, but finds an easy access (has a clear reflection) when it is clean. (Tr. M.R. Kale)

By describing the shade of the leaves of the lotus-plants very nicely Kālidāsa depicts a beautiful picture of noon in the **Mālavikāgnimitra**.

पत्रच्छायासु हंसा मुकुलितनयना दीर्घिकापद्मिनीनां ।

Māla II.12a

The geese have their eyes half closed under the shade of the leaves of the lotus-plants in the pleasure-tank. (Tr. M.R. Kale)

Śūdraka has mentioned also this term in his **Mṛcchakaṭika** in the sense of shade and reflection. Suffering from summer's heat, one should have resort to shade under a tree (*chāyārthaṃ grīṣmasaṃtapto* – Mṛcch IV.18a). A nice description of the herd of bullocks, sleeping under shade is also depicted in the same text (*chāyāsu ... nidrāyate gokulam* – VIII.11a). Contrary reflection in a mirror is also denoted by the term *chāyā.*

> मम पुनर्ब्राह्मणस्य सर्वमेव विपरीतं परिणमति । आदर्शगतेव छाया वामतो दक्षिणा दक्षिणतो वामा ।
>
> Mṛcch I, after verse 16
>
> For, in the case of me a (poor) Brāhmaṇa, everything turns out in a contrary manner: just like the reflection in a mirror, the left appearing to the right and the right to the left. (Tr. M.R. Kale)

Diṅnāga's **Kundamālā**, the best resource on the concept of *chāyā* as reflection in the field of Sanskrit drama where the idea of *chāyāsītā* is hidden. The shadow is sometimes described here against the law of nature due to the divine influence of Rāma. Normally, in mid-day the shadow of any object goes very close to the object but in the following part of a verse it is described as opposite: *madhyāhne'pi na yāti gulmanikaṭaṃ chāyā tadadhyāsitā* (III.14c), i.e. 'the shade resorted to by him goes not close to the hedge though it is midday' (tr. S.D. Bhanot & Veda Vyas).

A natural scene with the concept of light and shade is beautifully depicted by Diṅnāga. The shade of a tree takes rest under the root of a tree at mid-day but with the lessening of the intensity of the sun's rays recedes more and more from the root.

> प्रविश्य तरुमूलानि नीत्वा मध्यन्दिनातपम् ।
> अध्वनीना इव छाया निर्गच्छन्ति शनैः शनैः ॥
>
> Kund III.16
>
> After having whiled away the mid-day heat by resorting to (lit. entering) the roots of the trees, the shade like the travellers, recedes slowly and slowly. (Tr. S.D. Bhanot & Veda Vyas)

The same text also describes the shade of a tree, embracing like a friend gratifies the heart (*sakhīva chāyeyaṃ ramayati pariṣvajya hṛdayam* – Kund I.7c). Some other important references on the term *chāyā* in the **Kundamālā** are: *viralacchāyā vanaspatayaḥ* (III, after 6) 'shade of less dense tree', *gulmapracchāyam atiramaṇīyam* (III, after 11) 'thick shadow', *sālapādapacchāyām* (II, after 1) 'the shade of Sāla tree', etc. Again, in the sense of reflection: *chāyāṃ ca devagaṇikā* (Kuṇd V.3), *chāyādi darśanavalād* (V.4), etc. where due to the revivification of the mind Rāma sees Sītā's reflection.

Viśākhadatta has also dealt with this concept in his **Mudrārākṣasa**. Here servants are compared with shades as they leave their master with declining prosperity like the motion of shadow with the sun; in forenoon shadow of the leaves of garden tree moves towards west in the path of sun but in afternoon it moves towards east in opposite direction (cf. *āvirbhūtānurāgāḥ ... parṇacchāyaiḥ* – Mudrā IV.22).

In the **Veṇīsaṃhāra** also Bhaṭṭanārāyaṇa records this concept in the sense of shade, shadow, etc.: *bhujavanacchāyāṃ* (II.16) 'under the shade of many arms for perfect safety' *kaścijjalacchāyāpradānena* (VI.14), i.e. 'shade and water gives refreshment to a tired being' etc. To touch one's shadow is an expression of showing prowess and brevity as Karṇa said: 'in his presence Bhīma has no power even to touch the shadow of Duḥśāsana (*mayi jīvati duḥśāsanasya chāyām apyākramitum* – III, after 47).

Harṣa has depicted a natural scene of summer in the **Priyadarśikā** where the term *chāyā* is used in the sense of shade:

छायाचक्रं तरूणां हरिणशिशुरुपैत्यालवालाम्बुलुब्धः ।

Pri I.12c

The fawn covetous of water in the basins seeks the circle of shades of the trees. (Tr. M.R. Kale)

Bhavabhūti has used the term *chāyā* in the depiction of a natural scene of scratching the insects etc. by birds in the shade of a tree for food (*chāyāpaskiramāṇa* – UttCa II.9). But the best example of *chāyā* lies in the concept of *chāyāsītā* – invisibility of Sītā to Rāma due to the favour of Gaṅgā (III act) and the golden image of Sītā (*hiraṇmayī sītāpratikṛti* III, after 45). In the **Mālatīmādhava**, a natural sence of the shadow of the wings of Cāṣa birds is depicted by the poet (*cāṣacchadacchāyā* – VI.5).

Rājaśekhara has also used the term *chāyā* in different senses in his **Viddhaśālabhañjikā** to denote beauty – '*kuvalayacchāyā*' (I.39) 'beauty of blue lotuses'; to denote likeness: *mauktikacchāyā* (II.15) 'comparable to rows of pearl', *kāñcanacchāyam* (II.16) 'comparable to bright and polished gold' and to denote elegance of poetry which depends upon the talent of poet (*yādṛśaḥ kavistādṛśī kāvyabandhacchāyeti* – I, after verse 35).

In the **Hitopadeśa** and **Pañcatantra** also the term *chāyā* is used to denote shadow, series, etc. The friendship to wicked man and that of good man is compared with the shadow of an object in the first half and second half of a day (*chāyeva maitrī khalasajjanānām* – Pañc II.38d; also cf. NīŚa 60). As shadow and light are inter-connected with each other so are action and its doer invariably linked to each other (*yathā chāyātapau nityaṃ susaṃbaddhau parasparam* – Pañc II.130cd-131). In the sense of *paṅkti* (series or multitude or bed) the term *chāyā* is recorded in the **Pañcatantra** (*kamalacchāyāsanātham sarah* – I.379, 'a lake beautiful with the beds of lovely lotuses'). The friendship of a wicked man, woman, etc. are compared with the momentariness of the shadow of the clouds (*abhracchāyā khalaprīti* – Hit I.178). The duty of a householder is to give shelter like a tree which does not withdraw its shade from its cutter (*chāyām nopasamharate drumah* – Hit I.59). Forest conservation is also essential for the shade as the **Hitopadeśa** records:

सेवितव्यो महावृक्षः फलच्छायासमन्वितः ।
यदि दैवात्फलं नास्ति च्छाया केन निवार्यते ॥

Hit III.10

A large tree, endowed with fruit and shade, should be resorted to:
if, through ill luck, there be no fruit who can take off the shade?
(Tr. M.R. Kale)

Anthological texts also record the concept of *chāyā* in the sense of shadow, reflection, etc. Some references from the **Mahāsubhāṣita Saṅgraha** (2207) are: *aphalasyāpi vṛkṣasya chāyā bhavati śītalā* 'the shade of even a tree devoid of fruit remains cool or pleasant', *chāyevānugatah sadā* (3206) 'ever in close attendance like a shadow', *ekaiva gacchet sādṛśyam svacchāyā darpaṇāśritā* (3974) 'there is only one thing fit to be compared and that is her own reflection on a mirror', *chāyā hi bhūmeh śaśino malatvenāropitā śuddhimatah prajābhiḥ* (3423) 'for the shadow or reflection of the earth is falsely supposed by the people to be the stain on the naturally spotless pure moon'. Shadow of lamp's flame flickering through the puff of the wings of a deluted moth is treated as unstable in the **Vairāgyaśataka** (80) ... '*dīpāṅkura chāyācañcalam* ...' etc.

In the Sanskrit Poetics and dramaturgy the term *chāyā* is mainly used in the sense of reflection, beauty, etc. to produce artistic charm. Rājānaka Kuntaka records the term to denote beauty in several places of his **Vakroktijīvita**: *yannātikomalacchāyam* (I.48), to denote 'medium to beauty'; *bandhacchāyā* (I.50), *chāyā vaicitryarañjake* (I.52); *citracchāyā manoharām* (II.34) to denote mixed beauty etc. Bhoja has recorded the term as one of the twenty four *śabdālamkāras* and denoted by the imitation of some other person's statement (*anyoktīnāmanukṛtiśchāyā* – Sark II.39). Six kinds of *chāyā* are mentioned in the same text: (i) *lokokti,* (ii) *chekoti,* (iii) *arbhakokti,* (iv) *unmattokti,* (v) *poṭokti,* and (vi) *mattokti.*

The germ of a play is to be introduced by various means, one of which is called *chāyā.* It is introduced by *sūtradhāra* using the similarity with the subject matter or dramatic plot of the original story (*bīja*). On the basis of similarity with the dramatic plot the *bīja* is introduced. This is called *chāyā* (prototype or similarity) because of its concordance with the main plot (*chāyā kathāsāmyam* - - NLRKo under 23).

As a technical name of musical unit the term *chāyā* is accepted by Śāradātanaya, as noticed in his **Bhāva Prakāśana**:

रागव्यक्तिकृतालापश्छायेति परिभाष्यते ॥

BhPrak VII.50

The span of melody (*ālāpa*) manifesting (real nature of) *rāga* (musical mode) has been termed as *chāyā.* (Tr. P. Ghosal)

Manifestation in the Arts

The concept of *chāyā* is very close with the terms *pratirūpa* 'prototype', *praticchāyā* and *bimba-pratibimba* 'reflection' in the field of art. The world is a model representation of the Supreme Brahman and all the imitations (*anukṛti*) are the *chāyā* of the prototype. This concept is revealed to the Vedic seers – '*yad vai pratirūpaṃ tacchilpam*' (ŚBr III.2.1.5). Reflection of this Vedic concept is noticed in various Indological disciplines of poetry, Purāṇa, art and architecture, etc. A semantic journey of this concept presents an artistic vision from the Vedas to classical Sanskrit literature.

Chāyā of a particular object can be imagined from the convisibility (*sādṛśya*) or *anurūpatā* of *pratirūpa* (prototype) and it is observed in various reflecting surfaces related with the capacity of seeingness (*dṛśyamānatā*) of form (*rūpa*), like mirror, water, eye or reflection in the dream, etc. (cf, BṛUp II.1.2–13; II.5.1–13; ChUp VIII.7.4–8; VIII.8.1).

Chāyā is a very wider concept of art where the whole world is entangled in a chain of appearance (*ābhāsa*), convisibility (*sādṛśya*), imitation (*anukṛti-anukaraṇa*), reflection (*bimba-pratibimba*), invisible form (*pratīyamānatā*), unmanifest to manifest (*avyakta-vyakta*), in the artistic vision of *rūpa-pratirūpa-anurūpa.* Without light we cannot realise the form. So light is the mediator of original and its shadow or reflection. Counterpart or shadow of any object is not as it is of the original but there is some likeness or convisibility from which the original and shadow or counterpart both could be traced.

Chāyā as reflection is an artistic creation bearing an indistinct or illegible form through the projection of original form with the help of light. Images emerge or come into view primarily in the sense of materialising the object's or the deities' reflection (*chāyā*) and secondly in the sense of incorporating the transcendental suggestive nature based on fact. *Chāyā* takes an important role in image-making. The idea of image rests in the mind of the image-maker for manifesting the unmanifestable idea in the manner of *ādarśa-pratirūpaḥ,* because the form or shape signifies *bhāvarūpa* and abides in the gross state merely as a reflection (*chāyā*) of something beyond and above. *Chāyā* or reflection is a conceptual form (*bhāvarūpa*) and not as the material form. This means that indistinct form or *chāyā* is reflected in *citra* as moon is reflected in water:

> पश्यन्ति भावरूपैश्च जले चन्द्रमसं यथा ।
> तद्वच्चित्रमयं सर्वं पश्यन्ति ब्रह्मवादिन: ॥
>
> ApPṛ CCXXIV.11
>
> The Vedantins or Brahmavadins (those who asserts that all things are to be identified with Brahman) see everything as picture or painting like the reflection of conceptual form as the refelction of moon in water.

The idea of such reflected deity-image is Vedic as well as Upanisadic which revolves round *chāyāpuruṣa*. The concept of *chāyā* could be realised and its ideal form, i.e. deity inasmuch as it involves the latter's latent power and the forms of concretisation. The deity or object reflected in the shadow (*chāyā*) of a mirror seems to be comprehended in terms of a subtle suggestion (*bhāva* or *pratīti* etc.).

Image is the reflection of *citramūla* (essence) or the original object. This idea is vividly described in the **Viṣṇudharmottara Purāṇa** (I.129.11–14 & III.35.1--3). But it is originally a Vedic concept (cf. *apsu tvā hastair duduhur manīṣiṇaḥ* -- ṚV IX.79.4) and the same idea is also noticed in the Buddhist literature, in the legend of the first image or figure of the Buddha drawn by an artist from his reflection in waters. The story occurs in the Rudrayāna Avadāna (ch XXXVII) of the **Divyāvadāna** (p. 466) where Buddha is said to have cast his image on a cloth (*paṭa*) and asked the artist to colour it: *tatra bhagavatā chāyā utsṛṣṭā, uktāśca – raṅgaiḥ pūrayata.*

Chāyā as an indistinct form is noticed in the incident of appearance of light in a female form in the **Abhijñānaśākuntala** (V.30), where it is expressed as *saṃsthāna*, an indistinct shape closely related with the primary concept of shadow. This imaginary shape (*avyākṛtā ākṛti*) is the combination of light and shade as an intermingled concept in the description of a flash of light appears in a female form (*strīsaṃsthāna*).

> स्त्रीसंस्थानं चाप्सरस्तीर्थमारादुत्क्षिप्यैनां ज्योतिरेकं जगाम ।
>
> AbhŚāk V.30
>
> And immediately in the vicinity of Apsarastīrtha, a flash of light in a female form lifted her (Śakuntalā) up and vanished.
> (Tr. M.R. Kale)

The term *saṃsthāna* is used here in the sense of an invisible and imaginary shape closely related with a shadow. Rāghavabhaṭṭa clearly explains it in his commentary: *strīsaṃsthāna lalanākāram, tejorūpatvena spaṣṭam adṛśyamānam ataeva saṃsthānaśabdaprayogaḥ.* Here Menakā is the *citramūla* or essence and *apsarā* in the indistinct form of light is only *chāyā*; they both typify light incarnated into a distinct corporeality. This incarnated light (*jyotiḥ*) is the essence here and the indistinct form of a female in its worldly shape is the reflection of incarnated light. Here one is *ādarśa*, 'ideal' while the other is *chāyā*. *Chāyā* is the reflection of form. In the words of R.N. Misra: "In these references it is the reflection of form (*rūpa*) in terms of its *chāyā* which is supposed to endow a *citra* with the quality of art. ... *citra* and *chāyā* are complementary and *rūpa* and *citra* are similarly conceived invariably as 'reflected' ('Indian Śilpa Tradition' by R.N. Misra in *Shastric Tradition in Indian Arts*, p. 180).

The reflection (*praticchāyā*) of the original object (*mūlaprakṛti*) is beautifully described in the **Kundamālā** of Diṅnāga where the subtle nature of *chāyā* is noticed. Rāma after killing Śambuka descended in a lake for water to quench his thirst and saw there the reflection (*chāyā*) of Sītā, without seeing her actual appearance. This incident of reflection in water of invisible being creates an artistic charm in the drama.

> (उदकमध्ये छायां निर्वर्ण्य ससम्भ्रमम्) कथं सीताप्यत्रैव! (हर्षविस्मयं नाटयति)।
>
> Kund IV, after 12
>
> (Seeing reflection in the midst of water, with confusion) Is it that Sītā is here? (expresses joy and surprise)
> (Tr. S.D. Bhanot and Veda Vyas)

The term *chāyā* is used here to denote the *rūpa-pratirūpa* (counter-reflection) or *ādarśa-pratirūpa* as Rāma has seen only Sītā's reflection.

> वैदेह्याः क्वापि गच्छन्त्या दीर्घिकातीरवर्त्मना ।
> अन्तर्गतजलच्छाया मया सैवेति वीक्षिता ॥
>
> Kund IV.14
>
> I (Rāma) saw in water only the reflection of Sītā going somewhere by the path along the bank of the lake.
> (Tr. S.D. Bhanot & Veda Vyas)

Without the presence of object reflection is impossible. *Chāyā* is a means by which the original object will be seen in its unmanifested and invisible form. But by the divine power of the sages due to austerity sometimes the invisibility of the original object and visibility of only shadow or reflection of the same is also possible.

तदस्याः प्रतिकृतेर्मूलप्रकृतिमन्वेषयामि । (अन्वेषणं नाटयति) निःसम्पातविविक्तमिदं दीर्घिकातीरम्, बिम्बेन च विना प्रतिबिम्बमित्यसम्भाव्यमेतत् । किमिदम् ?
सीता - प्रेक्षते प्रतिकृतिं कथं न प्रेक्षते मामार्यपुत्रः । (विचिन्त्य) भवतु, विज्ञातम्, मुनिप्रसाद एष तपोवनवासिनीनां स्त्रीणामेतस्मिन् दीर्घिकातीरे पुरुषनयनानामगोचरता। यदि प्रतिकृतेरप्यदर्शनं महर्षिणाऽऽदिष्टं भवेत् तदायं जनोऽनुगृहीतो भवेत् । अहमपि तावत् यथैषा प्रतिकृतिर्न दृश्यते तथापसरामि । (अपसरति) ।

Kund IV, after 14

I would, therefore, make a search for the original of this reflection. (Gesticulates search.) The bank is lonely on account of the absence of any habitation, but (at the same time) it cannot be (imagined) that there should be reflection without the type. What is it?
Sītā – How is it that my Lord sees the image but does not see me ! (Reflecting.) Yes, I understand it. The invisibility of the women, dwelling in the penance-grove to the eyes of man on this bank of the lake is due to the graciousness of the sage. If the invisibility of the shadow also had been ordained by the sage, this person (Sītā) would have felt obliged. I must just slip away in a manner that the reflected image is not seen (by Rāma) (goes away).
(Tr. S.D. Bhanot & Veda Vyas)

But after introspection Rāma opines:

तामेव तावत् प्रसन्नसलिलमध्यवर्तिनीं प्रतिमासीताम् अवलोकयामि ।

Kund IV, after 14

I would just see that very Sītā in image lying in midst of the transparent water. (Tr. S.D. Bhanot and Veda Vyas)

From the above citations of the **Kundamālā** on the *rūpa-pratirūpa* or *ādarśa-pratirūpa*, the main concept of *chāyā* could be understood. Manifested reflection (*chāyāpratimā*) of the suprasensual image is the counter part of the original unmanifested deity (*pratikṛter mūlaprakṛtim*). *Chāyā* is the medium through which the unmanifested and invisible *mūlaprakṛti* also manifests itself. It also suggests that image and even the original object may stand apart and beyond. Thus, "the conceptual image abiding in the *bhāvarūpa* (ideational form) or *citramūla* (essence) and reflected through *chāyā* helps in establishing the amorphous and transcendental character of deity in Indian tradition: but the problem still remains with regard to interpreting the phenomenon of its concretisation in art" ('Indian Śilpa Tradition' by R.N. Misra in *Shastric Tradition in Indian Arts*, p. 182).

The **Mayamata**, a treatise on housing, architecture and inconography, records the values of *apacchāyā* in the context of finding the orientation and fixing the cardinal points for the building site with the gnomon. The orientation is determined with the help of the shade of the gnomon. Here lies the concept of *chāyāyantra.* The position of sun in different Zodiac sign is also a major factor for the different values.

कन्यायां वृषभे राशावपच्छायात्र नास्ति हि ॥
मेषे च मिथुने सिंहे तुलायां द्व्यङ्गुलं नयेत् ।
कुलीरे वृश्चिके मत्स्ये शोधयेच्चतुरङ्गुलम् ॥
धनुःकुम्भे षडङ्गुल्यं मकरेऽष्टाङ्गुलं तथा ।
छायाया दक्षिणे वामे नीत्वा सूत्रं प्रचारयेत् ॥

Mayam VI.11cd–13

(When the sun) is in Tauras or in Virgo there is no *apacchāyā*; when it is in Aries, Gemini, Leo or Libra the (east-west axis) must be put back two digits; when it is in Cancer, Scorpio or Pisces it must be adjusted by four digits; when it is in Sagittarious or Aquarius (it must be adjusted) by six digits and when it is in Capricorn by eight digits. The east-west line is to be fixed after it has been moved to the right or to the left of the shadow.
(Tr. Bruno Dagens)

This *apacchāyā* actually gives a method of presenting the variation of the length of the noon shadows in a modified linear function, which is known to the astronomers and architects of ancient India.

But in the **Mayamata**, a systematic representation of oriental rules also records the universal truth – the radius of the circle being equal to the height of the gnomon, the shadow touches the circle when the sun is at 45^0, in the morning and in the afternoon (Mayam VI.8).

In the description of the bracket capital, the **Mayamata** shows how the measurement of the shadow or overhang (*chāyāmāna*) takes an important role.

तदुच्चत्रिचतुर्भागोच्चा वा स्वाग्रे तु पट्टिका ।
अर्धं त्रिद्व्यंशमङ्घ्र्यूनं छायामानं विधीयते ॥

Mayam XV.43

The top of the bracket capital is a string-course a third or a quarter its height and whose overhang (*chāyāmāna* i.e. the measure of the shadow) is half, two-thirds or three quarters (its width).
(Tr. Bruno Dagens)

The **Mānasāra** also records the term *chāyā* with the prefix *su* (*succhāyā*) as an attribute of tree while describing the good omens in a wood.

वनं संप्राप्य सुच्छायं सुशीतलतरुं तथा ॥
दृष्ट्वा निर्ज्येर्यतेच्छायां शृणुयाच्छाकुनस्वरान् ।

MāSā XV.142cd–143ab

After reaching the forest, they should find out some tree casting pleasant and cool shade, and should rest there and try to hear some auspicious sounds of birds. (Tr. P.K. Acharya)

But the Nāgārjunakoṇḍa Pillar Inscription (time of Vīrapuruṣadatta, year vijaya, 273–274 A.D.) gives a glorious example of artistic creation by using the term *chāyā* as an attribute of pillar (*chāyāstambha*). The term *chāyāstambha* denotes a memorial pillar raised in the memory of a dead king's image and this term occurs in many places of the pillar inscriptions discovered at Nāgārjunakoṇḍa (cf. EpInd XXX, p. 25). The depiction of cranes and creepers in blossom on the symbolic memorial pillar represents the beautiful artistic vision of the artists of third century A.D.

सरसिकाय कुसुमलताय च छायाथभो ।

सरसिकया कुसुमलतया च छायास्तम्भः = (स्वर्गगतराज्ञः मूर्तिसनाथः स्मृतिस्तम्भः) [समुत्थापितः]

Nāgārjuna Pillar Ins, verse 13

The memorial pillar is erected depicting cranes and creeper in blossom.

The concept of light and shade is vividly depicted in a figure (No. 15) of Bhājā cave as a glorious example of artistic creation of the Satvahana sculpture (2nd Cent. B.C.) which shows the sun (lord of daylight) in his chariot destroying the huge monster of darkness. This is one of the earliest representation of this theme. Here two consorts of Sūrya – Suvarcasā and Chāyā remain on either side of him as symbol of light and shade that automatically go with Sūrya.

The shade of the Kalpataru or wishfulfilling tree in heaven is depicted in the **Raghuvaṃśa** where some artistic imagination may be assumed:

पुरा शक्रमुपस्थाय तवोर्वीं प्रति यास्यतः ।
आसीत् कल्पतरुच्छायामाश्रिता सुरभिः पथि ॥

Ragh I.75

On a past occasion, when you were returning to the earth after waiting upon Indra, there was on your way the divine cow Surabhi lying (at her ease) under the shade of the Kalpa tree.
(Tr. G.R. Nandargikar)

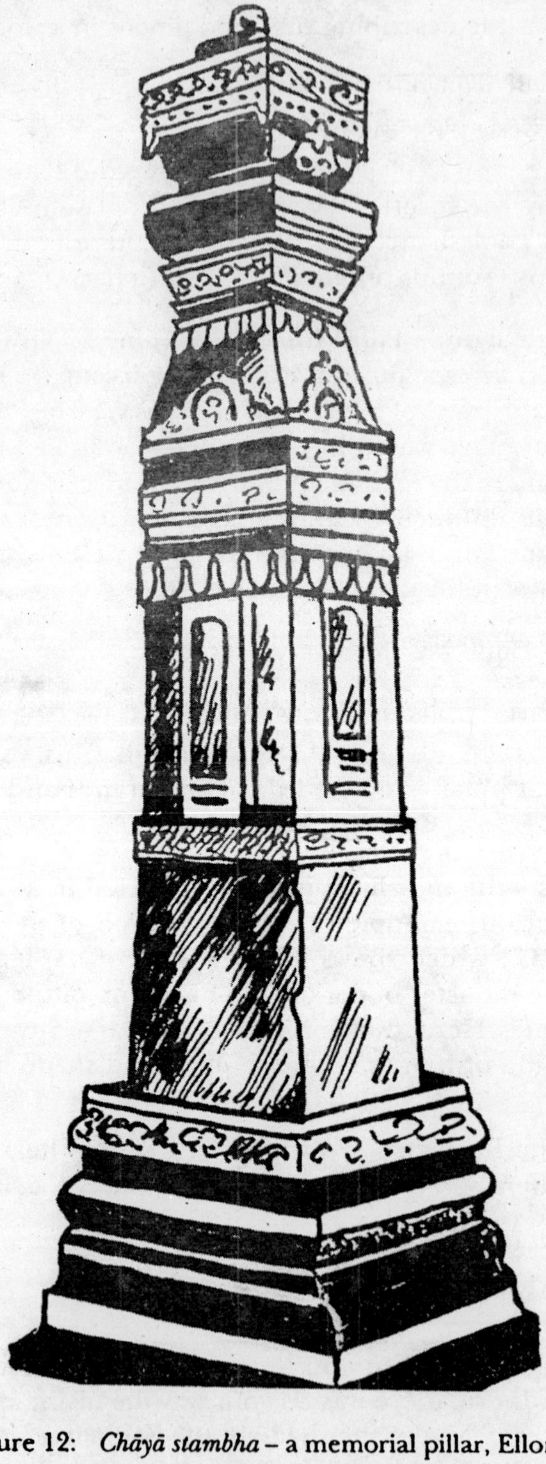

Figure 12: *Chāyā stambha* – a memorial pillar, Ellora

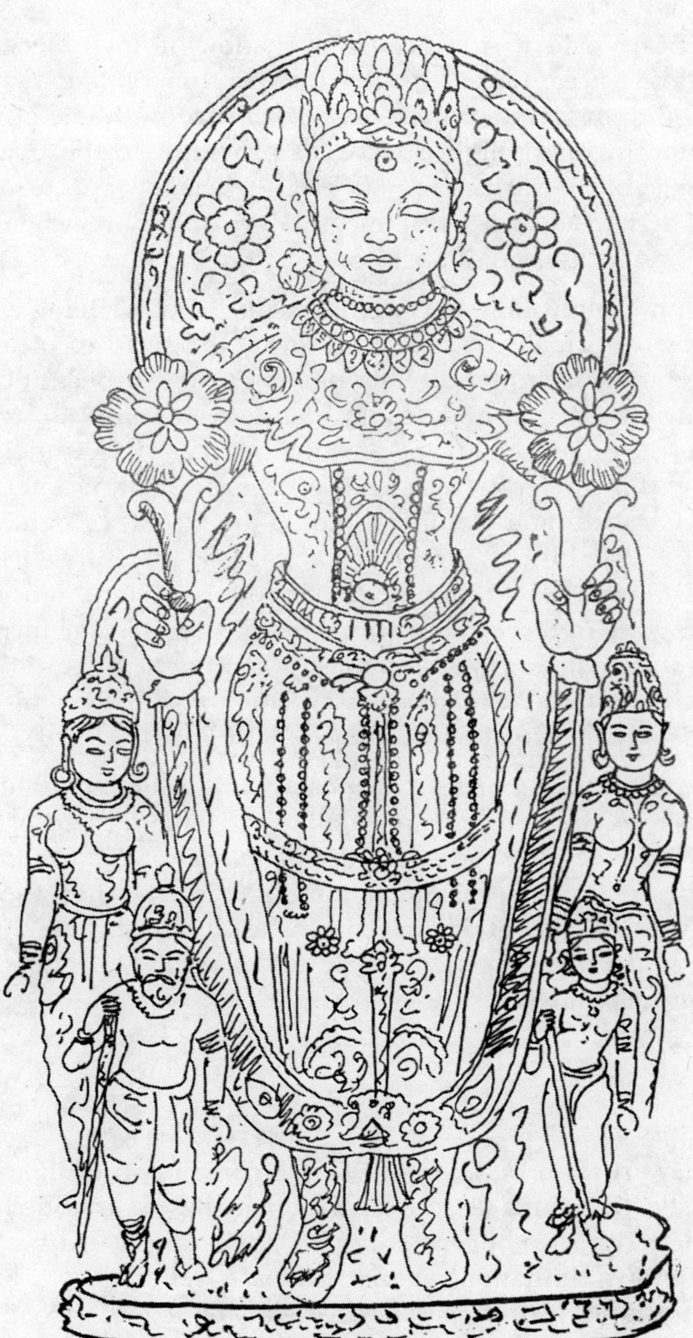

Figure 13: Sūrya on a chariot with Suvarcasā and Chāyā, as Symbol of Light and Shade

Process

In the practical world it is noticed that shadow of any object is relative darkness over some area caused by the interception of light waves by an opaque mass. Different factors work in casting of shadow. Some of which are: the size and intensity of the light source, its proximity to the opaque mass, angle and distance of the surface upon which the shadow appears. Complete interception of light causes a complete shadow or umbra whereas partial interception of light causes penumbra.

The reflection of light follows certain basic principles. Being a wave phenomenon it travels normally in straight lines by the surfaces of transparent medium through which light normally passes. By the process of light and shade the beauty or lustre of body could be drawn out and well represented in a picture of three dimensional type on a flat surface. The **Viṣṇudharmottara Purāṇa** describes this concept of *chāyā* as a process of painting where the term *vartanā* is used for shading a picture. It means the display of light and shade appreciated by the connoisseurs (*rekhāṃ praśaṃsantyācāryā vartanāṃ ca vicakṣaṇāḥ* – VDhPur III.41.11) methods of producing light and shade with lines in a painting are of three types: (i) *patraja* (i.e. lines in the form of leaves by crossing lines), (ii) *airika* (by stumping showing fineness), and (iii) *binduja* (by dots), which are treated as most essential to produce *chāyā* or picture (*tisraśca vartanāḥ proktāḥ patrāhairikabindujāḥ* – VDhPur III.41.5cd).

In a living and colouring picture (*vartanacchāyā*), the body or lustre of the body is noticed in a defined and well delineated manner. According to C. Sivaramamurti '*vartanā* gives both *chāyā* and *aujjvalya*' (cf. *Citrasūtra of the Viṣṇudharmottara Purāṇa* – C. Sivaramamurti, p. 125). He has also quoted a verse from **Kāvyānuśāsana** of Hemachandra as an illustration of *atiśayokti* (*chāyā*): *anyat saukumāryam anyaiva kāpi vartanacchāyā, ... syāmā sāmānya prajāpateḥ rekhaiva na bhavati.*

Conclusion

Thus, the key art term *chāyā*, an inevitable companion of light, an inherent power of reflection finds its source in Indian shastric tradition and practice, intermingled with the concept of *ābhāsa* 'appearance', *sādṛśya* 'convisibility', *anukaraṇa-anukṛti* 'imitation', *bimba-pratibimba* 'reflection', *avyakta-vyakta*, etc. Artistic concept lies in the *chāyāmayatā* of any basic ideas. Poetic charm is noticed in the description of a dark night with the lustre of stars like *ratnacchāyā*. An apparition is *vāyubhūta* and shadowless. *Jyotisvarūpa ṛṣi* or *sādhaka* is also shadowless due to his actual existence in the domain of light enjoying equal status of a deity (cf. king Nala – MBh III.54.24). *Chāyādhivāsana* is an alternative installation method *pratiṣṭhā* for icons of precious stones, clay or pictures to avoid wetting by the more conventional *jalādhivāsana* techniques. A *tripatrikā*, made of the blades of three *darbha*-grass, is used for sprinkling in the *chāyādhivāsana* (VSam XXVI.47). *Chāyāstambha* denotes a memorial pillar bearing image of the deceased. It is an important record of existence of a king or person.

From the above semantic journey it can be safely concluded that the term *chāyā* starting from the veda finds many connotation in its reaching to modern idea of a fundamental concept of Indian art. The entire world is a reflection of the Supreme Being so all the objects in this world are *chāyā* and not the eternal truth.

Sukumar Chattopadhyay

Select Bibliography

Misra, R.N.: "Indian Śilpa Tradition", in Shastric Tradition in Indian Arts, Stuttgart, Steiner Verlag Wiesbaden GMBH, 1989.

Shivaramamurti, C.: Chitra-Sūtra of Vishnudharmattora Purāṇa, Delhi: Kanak Publication, 1978.

BIMBA-PRATIBIMBA

Overview

Bimba-pratibimba (mn.) is a significant term used in Indian arts, aesthetics, religion and philosophy. It has two horizons – physical and metaphysical, i.e. philosophical. At physical level it means anything which shines or reflects (*bhāti*), circuit (*ābhoga*), disc (*maṇḍala*), shadow (*chāyā*), lustre (*kānti*), etc. All these meanings convey two basic elements intimately connected to each other: (1) light or lustre and (2) glow or reflection (*chāyā*). This suggests that somehow or the other the origin of this concept is intimately connected with the perception of sun or moon (*maṇḍala* – disc), i.e. reflected light (*kānti*), causing further formation of shadows of the objects falling on earth. Astronomical usage of the term also proves the above analogical origin of the concept. The most important use of this concept is seen in Indian art and aesthetics where it means *pratimā* (image), *arcā* (icon), *praticchāyā* (reflected image), *pratinidhi* (representative), *pratirūpa* (image), *pratiyātanā* (picture), *pratimāna* (model) and *pratikṛti* (likeness). Indian aesthetics as expressed in Kāvya and drama makes use of this concept as allegory, analogy, comparison or *upamāna*.

At philosophical level *bimba-pratibimba* has been used epistemologically and also as allegory and *upamāna* to explain the complexities of physical and metaphysical interrelatedness. Philosophers have accepted this term to suggest its core meaning: *bhāti* (to shine) and *chāyā* (reflection). Vedic philosophy describes the relationship of *paramātmā* and *jīvātmā* as *chāyātapau* (KaṭhUp I.3.1). In philosophical interpretations this concept has been explained through the analogy of *darpaṇavat pratibimba* (reflection in the mirror) for the existence of this world in pure consciousness or soul. Various philosophers have deliberated upon the nature of reality through the interpretation of *bimba* (as reflecting object) and its relationship *vis-a-vis pratibimba* (as reflection) and reflectors such as mirror, oil, etc. which are equated with Supreme Reality or Consciousness, physical world or universe and *avidyā* or *māyā* (*bimba* as *paramātmā, pratibimba* as *viśva* or *jagat, darpaṇa* as *avidyā* or *māyā*). This concept provides a very wide range of epistemological debate on the related issues.

Indian art and philosophy are closely connected. This is made clear by the use of term *bimba* and its synonyms in Indian iconography (Pratimāśāstra). In fact, without the proper understanding of the term *bimba-pratibimba* used in Indian thought and world view, one cannot follow the real meaning of this concept illustrated in Indian arts and aesthetics. Historical development of the concept makes it clear that *bimba* is used to convey the meaning of original *rūpa* or form as a reflecting object and also in the sense of a reflection or *pratibimba* where *bimba* becomes synonym of *pratibimba*.

Etymology and Related Terms

Bimba-pratibimba is a term of wide significance and has multilayered connotations. Derived from the root *bimba-* to shine, it means *ābhoga*, i.e. circuit, circumference, extension. The root *bimba-* is not included in the **Dhātupāṭha**, but is used in some *sūtras* of Pāṇini and by other grammarians.

Kṣīrasvāmin commenting on the **Amara Kośa** states:

बिम्बति भाति बिम्बम् आभोगः ।

AmKo I.2.16

Bimba is derived from the root *bimba-*, to shine – one that shines. *Bimba* means *ābhoga* (circuit, circumference, extension).
(Tr. R.S. Bhattacharya)

Bimba also written as *vimba* or *vimva*, is of doubtful origin but of *bī-* with the suffix *ban* forms *bimba* (*ulvādayaśca* – UṇSū IV.95), which means 'to move'. Thus formed, the word *bimba* means *pratirūpa* and *phala*, i.e. image and fruit. The word *bimba* in masculine gender means *pratibimba* (*prati* + *bī-* + *ban-*) 'reflection'. According to the **Amara Kośa** (III.3.133) the term *bimba* denotes solar or lunar orb, shape and a particular fruit named *bimba*. The **Medinī Kośa** (XIII.7a) also states that the term *bimba* is used in the sense of any round or disc-like surface, i.e. *maṇḍala*. It also means face, mark or type, shadow or reflected form (*pratibimba*) and an image while used in masculine and neuter gender but in feminine gender it means the *bimba* fruit (*Momordica Monadelpha*) (NāMa 1125–1126). The **Vaijayantī Kośa** (VI.5.55) further adds that in masculine and neuter gender it also means *sama* (similar), *pratimā* 'image' *mukha* 'face'and *lakṣma*, i.e. sign, distinctive feature and indication.

Layers of Meaning

The term *pratibimba* is enumerated as one of the eight synonyms of *pratimā* as given in the **Amara Kośa**:

प्रतिमानं प्रतिबिम्बं प्रतिमा प्रतियातना प्रतिच्छाया ॥
प्रतिकृतिरर्चा पुंसि प्रतिनिधिः ।

AmKo II.10.35cd–36ab

Pratimāna – 'a model' and *pratibimba* – 'a reflection' are used in neuter gender; *pratimā* – 'an image', *pratiyātanā* – 'a picture', *praticchāyā* – 'a reflected image', *pratikṛti* – 'a likeness' and *arcā* – 'an idol or image intended to be worshipped' are used in feminine gender while the term *pratinidhi* – 'a substitute or representative' is used in masculine gender. (Tr. S. Chattopadhyay)

The **Amara Kośa** (III.3.157) adds *chāyā* as another synonym of *pratibimba. Kṛkalāsa* a kind of lizard is described as '*kāmarūpī bimbaḥ*', i.e. having the power to assume any form or shape or *bimba* at will. Thus it can be summarized that in masculine and neuter genders *bimba-pratibimba* connotes the meaning of circuit, solar or lunar orb or disc, *pratimā* 'image or icon', *praticchāyā* 'a reflected image', *pratirūpa, mukha* 'face' and *lakṣma* 'sign or distinctive feature'. Only in feminine gender it conveys the sense of *bimba* fruit. The **Vaijayantī Kośa** (III.9.21c) makes it clear that *pratibimba* conveys the sense of *upamāna* or comparison. Hence, the terms like *pratimā, pratirūpa, praticchāyā, pratikṛti,* etc. also convey the sense of comparison '*upamāna*'. The main idea is to suggest that all these synonyms refer to original form and are nothing but the reflection of the original one.

The term *bimba-pratibimba* has been used in the sense of *upamāna* or simile or similitude in the poetics, dramas and the Purāṇas. The **Vaijayantī Kośa** clearly states that:

प्रतिबिम्बोपमाने च ... ॥

VaiKo III.9.21c

Pratibimba, the reflection conveys the sense of *upamāna* – the comparison. (Tr. P. Ghosal)

Development of the Concept

The term *pratimā,* a synonym of *pratibimba* is used in the **Yajurveda** in the sense of simile, though, in literal sense it could also be taken as image. While describing the characteristics of Brahman as the basic element, it is said that:

न तस्य प्रतिमा अस्ति यस्य नाम महद् यशः ।

YV XXXII.3ab

There is no simile of that (basic substance) whose very name is unparalleled fame.

Bimba-pratibimba and its related words occur in various Upaniṣads conveying multilayered meaning and thereby revealing macro and microcosmic, physical and metaphysical interrelatedness and ideational content of the concept. The **Śvetāśvatara Upaniṣad** uses the term *bimba* in the sense of a mirror or a jewel.

यथैव बिम्बं मृदयोपलिप्तं तेजोमयं भ्राजते तत् सुधौतम् ।
तद्वाऽऽत्मतत्त्वं प्रसमीक्ष्य देही एकः कृतार्थो भवते वीतशोकः ॥

ŚvUp II.14

Even as a mirror (or jewel) stained by dust
Shines brilliantly when it has been cleansed,
So the embodied one, on seeing the nature of the soul (*ātman*),
Becomes unitary, his end attained, from sorrow freed.
(Tr. R.E. Hume)

It suggests the core concept of the term – 'to shine' or 'to reflect'. Several other Upaniṣads have used terms related to or synonymous of *bimba-pratibimba* to explain the macro-microcosmic reality of *brahman* and *ātman*. The **Kaṭhopaniṣad** uses the core sense of the term, 'to shine', as follows:

न तत्र सूर्यो भाति न चन्द्रतारकं नेमा विद्युतो भान्ति कुतोऽयमग्निः ।
तमेव भान्तमनु भाति सर्वं तस्य भासा सर्वमिदं विभाति ॥

KaṭhUp II.2.15

There the sun does not shine, nor the moon nor the splendour of the stars!
Not even the lightnings flash, not to speak of the earthly fire,
He alone shines: all else takes its splendour from him, the whole world shines by his splendour. (Tr. V.M. Bedekar & G.B. Palsule)

The same text (I.3.1; II.3.5) has used the related term *chāyā* to convey the intimate relationship of *paramātmā* and *jīvātmā*. Thus, the description – '*chāyātapau brahmavido vadanti*', conveys the core concept of the term *bimba-pratibimba*, i.e. to shine, to reflect and *praticchāyā*, i.e. reflection. Here *jīvātmā* is described as the reflection of *paramātmā*. Reflection is not possible without light. Above description conveys two fold meanings: (1) shine, and (2) reflection – both intimately connected to each other.

Pratirūpa, a synonym of *bimba-pratibimba*, occurs in many verses of the **Kaṭhopaniṣad**:

वायुर्यथैको भुवनं प्रविष्टो रूपंरूपं प्रतिरूपो बभूव ।
एकस्तथा सर्वभूतान्तरात्मा रूपंरूपं प्रतिरूपो बहिश्च ॥

KaṭhUp II.2.10 (cf. II.2.9)

> As there is only one Vāyu which entering the whole cosmos assumes different forms and identical images, likewise, there is only one *antarātmā* which exists in every being and assumes different forms and images; and yet it is outside.

Here *pratirūpa* conveys the meaning of *pratibimba* (reflection) suggesting the sense of *upamāna* as stated in the **Amara Kośa** (III.9.21c).

The **Gautama Dharma-Sūtra** (XXII.21) uses the term *bimba* in the sense of a chameleon or lizard. As chameleon is associated with the change of colour or form, therefore, the term *bimba*, perfectly conveys the meaning of a chameleon. This is further explained in the **Vaijayantī Kośa** (IV.1.29), where it is stated that a lizard or chameleon may assume any form or shape (*bimba*) at will.

Logically, next question arises, how far an adjunct as a reflector of a reflected image is responsible for the qualitative change in the appearance of that reflection? It is explained in the **Vākyapadīya** as follows:

> प्रतिबिम्बं यथान्यत्र स्थितं तोयक्रियावशात् ।
> तत्प्रवृत्तिमिवान्वेति स धर्मः स्फोटनादयोः ॥
>
> Vāk I.49
>
> Just as a reflection, found elsewhere (as in water) seems to have movement because of the movement of water, such is the relation between *sphoṭa* and *nāda*. (Tr. K.A.S. Iyer)

Here water is held responsible for the movement of the reflection which is not there in the original object. As the movement of the reflected image exists independent of the original object, in the same, way *nāda* or sound is related to *sphoṭa* or word, i.e. *sphoṭa* takes on the properties of *prākṛtadhvani* and *vaikṛtadhvani* (*nāda*) which is not inherent in it.

This poses great difficulty in the realm of philosophy. There are three different views about the nature of reflection (*pratibimba*) *vis-a-vis* its original *bimba* (reflected object):

(i) Reflection is dependent upon various adjuncts like water, gem, mirror, etc. and apart from them there can't be any reflection. Presence of original (*bimba*) does not necessarily create reflection (*pratibimba*). It is created only when water, mirror, etc. is affected by the original. Hence, the affectation of water, mirror is the cause of reflection. Therefore, apart from it reflection does not exist.

(ii) Reflected object or original (*bimba*) is the material cause of the reflection or *pratibimba*. Therefore it can be said that reflection exists apart from water, mirror, etc. Reflection is dependent upon the original.

(iii) Reflection exists apart from its receptacle and the original object in the sense that the rays of the eyes turned back by shiny surfaces like those of a mirror, water, etc. are the material cause of the reflection. Therefore it is deduced that seeing is the reflection. The **Vākyapadīya** (I.99) posits all these different views to explain the relationship of *sphoṭa* and *nāda*. According to it the thing that is revealed follows the differences of the revealors in the same way as reflections differ according to the properties of the reflectors as oil, water, mirror, etc. In other words a thing can only be known according to the mode of the knower. For example (Vāk II.294) actual mountains and other such natural objects (tree, jungle, etc.) cover a wide area in reality, but their *pratibimba* covers only a small area. If one learns about them only through their reflections then due to the inherent differentiation between the original and reflection the true picture may not emerge. The **Vākyapadīya** (III.9.40) equates time with that of mirror in which is reflected *bhāvī rūpa*, i.e. form of objects yet to come. Time is the background of the cause of everything in the universe. In this way the **Vākyapadīya** explains that intellect reflects the light of self and this forms the basis of the use of words.

अचेतनेषु संक्रान्तं चैतन्यमिव दृश्यते ।
प्रतिबिम्बकधर्मेण यत्तच्छब्दनिबन्धनम् ॥

Vāk III.14.325

That which is projected on the insentient forms of the intellect as a reflection, it is that which is the basis of the use of words.
(Tr. K.A.S. Iyer)

The **Suśruta Saṃhitā** (ŚāSthā V.11)and its commentary have shown the usage of the term in the sense of buttock: *adhobhāgagatānāṃ bimbam* 'extended down to the buttocks'. Ḍalhaṇa comments on the same as: *bimbaṃ maṇḍalam arthān nitambasya.*

The **Goladīpikā**, an astronomical text, uses the term *bimba* and *maṇḍala* to illustrate the spherical shape of the orbs of the sun and the moon:

गोलाकारं मण्डलमर्कादीनां स्मृतं गणकमुख्यैः ।
दर्पणवृत्ताकारं दूरगतत्त्वात् प्रदृश्यतेऽस्माभिः ॥
शशिबिम्बे दर्पणवद् वृत्ते तस्यैकदेशसितलब्धिः ।
भानोः करसम्पाते व्यवधानाभावतो न संभवति ॥

Goladīpikā II.46–47

The shape of the orbs of the sun, etc. is said to be spherical by great astronomers. They appear to us in the shape of plane circular mirrors on account of their being at a (great) distance. If the orb of the moon is like a plane circular mirror, when the sun's rays fall on it, the phenonomenon of a part alone being lighted cannot happen, since there is no obstruction. (Tr. E. Burgess)

Chāyā, a related word of *bimba* is used in the **Sūrya-Siddhānta** to denote shadow:

स्फुटेन्दुभुक्तिर्भूव्यासगुणिता मध्ययोद्धृता ।
लब्धं सूची महीव्यासस्फुटार्कश्रवणान्तरम् ॥
मध्येन्दुव्यासगुणितं मध्यार्कव्यासभाजितम् ।
विशोध्य लब्धं सूच्यां तु तमो लिप्तास्तु पूर्ववत् ॥
भानोर्भार्धे महीच्छाया तत्तुल्येऽर्कसमेऽपि वा ।
शशाङ्कपाते ग्रहणं कियद्भागाधिकोनके ॥

SūrSiddh IV.4–6

Multiply the earth's diameter by the true daily motion of the moon, and divide by her mean motion: the result is the earth's corrected diameter (*sūcī*). The difference between the earth's diameter and the corrected diameter of the sun is to be multiplied by the moon's mean diameter, and divided by the sun's mean diameter: subtract the result from the earth's corrected diameter (*sūcī*), and the remainder is the diameter of the shadow; which is reduced to minutes as before. The earth's shadow is distant half the signs from the sun: when the longitude of the moon's node is the same with that of the shadow, or with that of the sun, or when it is a few degrees greater or less, there will be an eclipse. (Tr. E. Burgess)

In the **Rāmāyaṇa** the fair complexioned Sītā is described as: *hemabimbanibhā,* i.e. looking like an image of gold (Rām VI.12.14). Lava-Kuśa twin sons of Rāma are described as his reflections, born of same image, i.e. Rāma's body:

रूपलक्षणसम्पन्नौ मधुरस्वरभाषिणौ ।
बिम्बादिवोत्थितौ बिम्बौ रामदेहात् तथापरौ ।।

Rām I.4.11

Endowed with physical charm and auspicious marks on their body, they spoke in a sweet strain and, like two images made from the original, they looked like two other Rāmas sprung from the loins of Śrī Rāma. (Tr. Gita Press edn)

Here the first occurrence of the word *bimba* is in the sense of an image, like that of the sun, while the second occurrence means reflection. The idea conveyed by this usage is that Lava-Kuśa are identical to each other and to their father Rāma. They are like the twin reflection of the image of Rāma. Thus *bimba* here means image as well as its reflection. In fact instead of *bimba, pratibimba* would have been more appropriate in the second occurrence here but by using *bimba* to convey the idea of image and its reflection it is made clear that *bimba* and *pratibimba* (reflection) are synonymous and interchangeable.

In literature where *bimba-pratibimba* is used as comparison *(upamāna)* similitude *(anurūpatā* or *sādṛśya)* is implied. One of the core meanings of *bimba* is *maṇḍala* or *ābhoga*, i.e. anything circular disc-like object such as solar or lunar orb. Roundness of a beautiful face in general and roundness of *nāyikā*'s buttocks in particular are compared with a *bimba*. *Sādṛśya* between solar or lunar orb and a beautiful face is implied through comparison or exemplification. For example:

> ईषत्सहासममलं परिपूर्णचन्द्र -
> बिम्बानुकारि कनकोत्तमकान्तिकान्तम् ।
>
> MārkPur LXXXI.12ab
>
> Slightly smiling, spotless, resembling the full moon's orb, beautiful as the choicest gold, and lovely was thy face. (Tr. F.E. Pargiter)

It is an eulogy to the goddess Durgā where her lustrous and beautiful face is compared with the full moon's orb (*bimba*). *Sādṛśya* is based on the glow or *kānti* and rounded contour of the face and moon. *Arkabimba* is described as solar orb and is compared with the *cakra* or disc (*āyudha*) of the goddess in the **Mārkaṇḍeya Purāṇa** (LXXXVII.17). In the **Devī Bhāgavata Purāṇa** (VII.31.36) Devī in the form of *kumārī* is described as having *aṣṭamī candrabimba*, i.e. the half moon on her forehead. *Bimba* in the sense of an image also occurs in the **Agni Purāṇa** (XLIII.20) – *viṣṇu bimbārtham*, i.e. the image of Viṣṇu.

Illusion of duality is also explained through this concept. The **Devī Bhāgavata Purāṇa** states:

> यथा दीपस्तथोपाधेर्योगात्संजायते द्विधा।
> छायेवादर्शमध्ये प्रतिबिम्बं वा तथाऽऽवयोः ॥
>
> DBhāgPur III.6.5
>
> As a lamp, though one, becomes two by virtue of adjuncts; as a face, though one, becomes two, as reflected in a mirror; as one man becomes double by his shadow, so we become reflected into many. (Tr. Vijnanananda)

Here Devī is narrating the exact nature of *prakṛti* and *puruṣa* and explains the appearance of dualism as born of illusion (*mativibhramāt*). This is further explained by using the concept of earth and jar and it is said that everything exists in Supreme Brahman and this Eternal Substance Itself becomes dual at the time of creation, creating the illusion of separateness as in the case of a reflecting object (*bimba*) and its reflection (*pratibimba*). Only one who sees the oneness between *prakṛti* and *puruṣa* is capable of freeing himself from the bondage of *saṃsāra.* Adjuncts like mirror, water, etc. which cause the reflection are equated with impure *māyā* or *avidyā.* Causal theory is frequently used in Indian philosophy to interpret the causal nature or non-eternal nature of physical world (*avidyāyāṃ tu yatkiñcitpratibimbam* – DBhāgPur VII.32.45cd). *Ātman* or Supreme Self is the reflecting object in the mirror of *māyā* or *avidyā.* And *jīva* is the reflection of it in the form of *śarīra* or body.

> निद्रादयः शक्तयश्च ताः सर्वाः प्रकृतेः कलाः ।
> आत्मनः प्रतिबिम्बश्च जीवो भोगशरीरभृत् ॥
>
> DBhāgPur IX.41.10
>
> Sleep etc., all these things are powers of *prakṛti*; when these have been reflected on by the *ātman, jīva* is formed with a body for enjoyment, called *bhoga-śarīrabhṛt.* (Based on the tr. by Vijnanananda)

The **Artha-Śāstra** has used the term *bimba* in two different and distinct senses. Providing guidelines to the officials of mint to expose the makers of false coins the term *bimba* has been used for die (IV.4.20) from which coins are made. In this sense *bimba* is not used in later texts or lexicons. The idea behind this use of the term corresponds to the core concept of *bimba-pratibimba* as *rūpa-pratirūpa* or *ākṛti-pratikṛti* in the sense that die here is *bimba* (original *rūpa* or *ākṛti*) and coin made therefrom is *pratibimba* (reflection) or unfolding of the original form in exact likeness. This is very interesting use of the term because in the same way Indian works of art are called counterfeits or commensurations – *anukṛti, pratikṛti, pratibimba, pratimāna, tadākāratā* of the divine or original form and likeness is demanded. This likeness may be of two types: (1) exact likeness of the original or *ābhāsa* of a likeness in all respects as in case of a reflection of an image or object in a mirror or water etc., (2) likeness based on an equality as to the whichness and whatness (i.e. form and force) of the archetype. Here the sense of comparison (*upamāna*) is involved. Another sense in which *bimba* has been used in the **Artha-Śāstra** (IV.10.5) is exhibition (*pradarśanī*) of animals.

What is the exact relationship between the reflecting object and its reflection? What is the exact status of a reflection *vis-a-vis* the original object and different adjuncts? These are some of the questions which are the subject matter of philosophical deliberations in Indian texts. Quality of reflection depends upon the quality of receptacle or adjuncts like gem or water.

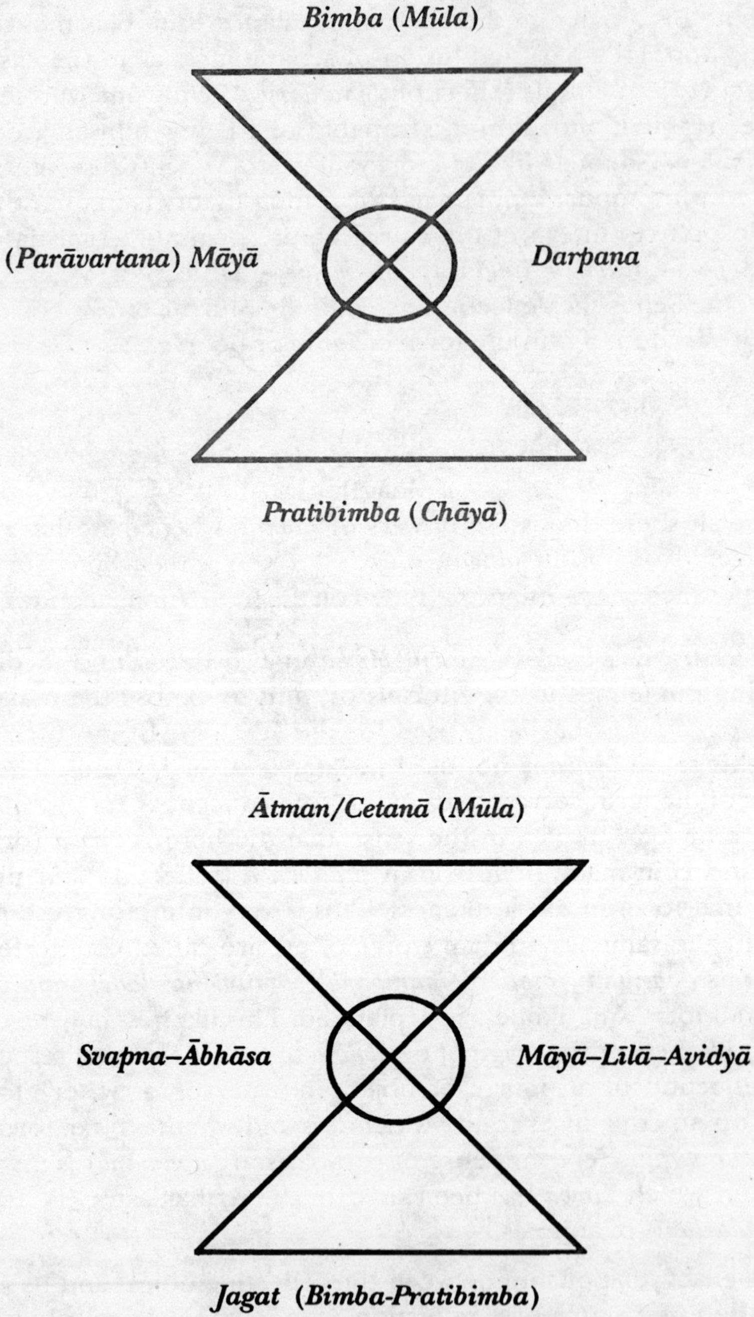

Figure 14: *Bimba-pratibimba*: Soul and Universe

In the realm of philosophy the development of the concept *bimba-pratibimba* and its cognates and synonyms are related to the explanation of abstract concepts like *ātman, brahman,* time, knowledge, existence or reality, etc. While using *bimba* and its cognates to elucidate abstract ideas and concepts the core meaning of *bimba-pratibimba* 'to shine, to reflect' is always kept in mind. There is an interesting passage in the **Milinda Pañha** (II.1.2) where the king Milinda tries to judge the knowledge of Nāgasena. In the field of science this relates to the question of time's independent existence and relativity. Nāgasena uses the analogy of body and its reflection (*chāyā*) to explain the relativity and dependent nature of time. He asks king Milinda – who is real king, he (standing beside a pool) or his shadow reflecting in the pool? ('*tvaṃ vā rājā, chāyā vā rājā' ti*? MilPañ II.1.2).

This is typical Indian view in philosophy where physical world is supposed to be reflection of Supreme Reality. It is in this sense that the **Kaṭha Upaniṣad** (I.3.1; II.3.5) describes the relationship of *jīvātmā* and *paramātmā* (*chāyātapau brahmavido vadanti*; also cf. PraUp III.3).

In Indian world view existence of any kind is not possible beyond the limit of consciousness, and consciousness in its purest form is supposed to be the Ultimate Reality. It is one of the reasons why one has to search within and not without to find *nirvāṇa* or *mokṣa.* Buddha after attaining *bodhi* (enlightenment) sees the whole world within himself:

> विश्वं स्वस्मिन् ददर्शासौ दर्पणे प्रतिबिम्बवत् ।
>
> BudCa XXVII.40ab
>
> He saw the whole world (reflected) within himself just like a reflection in a mirror. (Based on the tr. by E.H. Johnston)

In the **Laṅkāvatāra-Sūtra** (I.43) theory of dualism and its futility is explained by using the term *bimba-pratibimba* and its cognate *chāyā* in the sense of a shadow or reflection in a mirror or water (*darpaṇāntargataṃ svabimbapratibimbaṃ jale vā svāṅgacchāyā* – LaSū I.43). Here it is noteworthy that *bimba* is used as one's own body or *rūpa* and *pratibimba* as its reflection. The term *chāyā* explicitly connotes the meaning of shadow or reflection. In the same text (LaSū I.43) this physical world has been described merely as an appearance like figures painted on the wall or like an image magically transformed (*bhittikhacita vigrahasamaḥ nirmita pratimaḥ....*). *Pratimā* is another synonym of the term *bimba* (YV XXXII.3). *Vigraha* is used in the sense of *pratimā* or image. It is explained that just as shadows or appearances have no independent existence, therefore, *ekāgratā* or the feeling of oneness is essential to attain tranquility or *samādhi* which gives birth to wisdom realized in one's inmost self, i.e. within (... *sva pratyātmāryajñānagocara* ... – LaSū I.43). The

Mahāvastu also uses the term *pratibimba* in the sense of reflection to explain the nature of being:

सर्वे भावा: स्वभावेन प्रतिबिम्बसमा मता: ।

MVas 4ab

All things by nature are regarded as reflections. (Tr. V. Bhattacharya)

In the **Bodhicaryāvatāra** the term *bimba* has been used in the sense of actual body of Lord Buddha '*jinabimba*':

चिन्तामणि: कल्पतरुर्यथेच्छापरिपूरण: ।
विनेयप्रणिधानाभ्यां जिनबिम्बं तथेक्ष्यते ॥

BoCar IX.36

Just as the *cintāmaṇi* (wishfulfilling gem) and the *kalpataru* (wishfulfilling tree) fulfill all desires so is the physical body of the *jina* (Buddha) for those who are devoted (with their mind) to him (i.e. Buddha). (Tr. Paramananda Sharma)

This has been explained in the **Pañjikā** commentary as:

जिनस्य बुद्धस्य भगवत: बिम्बं द्वात्रिंशता महापुरुषलक्षणैर्विराजितं शरीरम् ।

Comm. on BoCar IX.36

Of Lord Buddha who has defeated evil forces has the body which is adorned with thirty two marks of a great person.
(Tr. H.N. Chakravarty)

In the **Jātakamālā** the term *śaśabimba* has been used as a mark, sign or a distinctive feature of the full moon.

अथ शक्रस्तत्कर्मातिशयविख्यापनार्थं लोकहितावेक्षी शशबिम्बलक्षणेन वैजयन्तस्य प्रासादवरस्य सुधर्मायाश्च देवसभाया: कूटागारकर्णिके चन्द्रमण्डलं चाभ्यलंचकार ।

सम्पूर्णेऽद्यापि तदिदं शशबिम्बं निशाकरे ।
छायामयमिवादर्शे राजते दिवि राजते ॥
तत: प्रभृति लोकेन कुमुदाकरहासन: ।
क्षणदातिलकश्चन्द्र: शशाङ्क इति कीर्त्यते ॥

Jāmā VI.37–38

Then, in order to glorify that extraordinary fact, and having in view the good of the world, Śakra adorned with the image of the hare as a distinctive mark both peaks on the top of the belvederes – one on his most excellent palace Vaijayanta and the other on Sudharmā, the hall of the *devas* – and likewise the disc of the moon.

> At full-moon even now that image of the hare (*śaśa*) appears in the moon's disc in the sky, as a reflected image shines in a silver mirror. From that time onward Candra (the moon), named also the ornament of the night and the cause of the brilliancy of the night-waterlilies, is famous in the world as the hare-marked (*śaśāṅka*). (Tr. J.S. Speyer)

The concept of Buddhabimba is nicely described in the **Guhyasamāja Tantra**:

> सर्वाकारवरोपेतं बुद्धबिम्बं विभावयेत् ।
> पाणौ च कायवाक्चित्तं अङ्कुशादीनि भावयेत् ॥
>
> GuhyaT XII.39
>
> He should contemplate a Buddha image endorsed with the best of all aspects. And he should contemplate in its hand the hook and so on (the differentiation of the hook) of body, speech and mind. Indeed, with this yoga he would be a performer of the rites of the 'place' (the rank of Vajrasattva). (Tr. Alex Wayman)

In the same philosophy seeing is the reflection and apart from seeing, reflection does not exist in the mirror. The **Tattva-Saṅgraha** contains detailed deliberation on the problem of *bimba-pratibimba*, i.e. their exact relationship. How *bimba* or original object, *pratibimba*, i.e. reflection and various reflectors such as water, mirror, etc. are interrelated to each other and how complex is their status *vis-a-vis* each other is clearly discussed in this text.

> आह केन निमित्तेन प्रतिपात्रं पृथक् पृथक् ।
> भिन्नानि प्रतिबिम्बानि गृह्यन्ते युगपत् तया ॥
> अत्र ब्रूमो यदा तावज्जले सौरेण तेजसा ।
> स्फुरता चाक्षुषं तेजः प्रतिस्रोतः प्रवर्त्तितम् ॥
>
> TaSaṅg 2215–2216
>
> The opponent says – 'by what cause are the reflected images perceived simultaneously as distinct in each vessel (of water) ?'
>
> Our answer to this is as follows: what actually happens is that by the light from the sun scintillating in the water, the light from the eye (striking the water) is turned back in the wake of the reflected solar light. (Tr. G.N. Jha)

Importance of perception is recognized in the discussion. Even if one accepts that the original object really exists simultaneously in the form of multiple reflections in different reflectors, this plurality is nothing but illusion (*ābhāsa*), because they are all apprehended by the same cognition. The idea of diversity is inferential whereas the idea of sameness or oneness is perception and it destroys the plurality. The **Tattva-Saṅgraha** (2585–90) tries to differentiate between a reflection and the original object on the basis of the differences caused in reflection due to different properties of the reflector and the rules of light refracting from shiny surfaces and coming back to eyes, thus changing the direction and size of the reflection as inverted trees in the water etc. The same view has been taken in the **Abhidharma Kośa** and its commentary (III.11) when it is said that *pratibimba* or reflection is not established or *siddha* because it entails the production of different qualities (*dharma*), therefore it cannot be quoted as a *pramāṇa* in philosophy.

In the **Prakaraṇa Pañcikā** (p. 346) the term *bimba-pratibimba* is used in literal sense to denote the meaning of reflecting object (*bimba*) and its reflection (*pratibimba*). It is explained here that *pratibimba* or reflection acquires the qualities of its own due to the nature of different adjuncts (a gem, sword, mirror, etc.) creating reflection which is not inherent in the *bimba* or the reflecting object itself and this may differentiate the reflection from that of reflecting object.

The **Brahma-Sūtra Śaṅkara Bhāṣya** states that:

> किमयं प्रतिबिम्बात्माऽक्ष्यधिकरणो निर्दिश्यते ।
>
> BrSūŚBh I.2.13
>
> The doubt here arises whether this passage (ChUp IV.15.1) refers to the reflected self which resides in the eye... (Tr. G. Thibaut)

Here it is implied that seeing is reflection. The **Brahma-Sūtra Śaṅkara Bhāṣya** (II.1.32) uses the term *bimba* with the *pūrvapada* (first member) *jagat* thus equating the world with the reflection: *yad uccāvacaprapañcaṃ jagadbimbaṃ viracayitavyam.*

Śaṅkarācārya, to prove the unreality of Universe and the reality of Brahman alone, gives a number of verses on the concept of reflection of the sun in the water of a jar through various illustrations in his **Vivekacūḍāmaṇi**, a treatise on the discrimination between real and unreal. *Jīva* is the reflection of Brahman.

> घटोदके बिम्बितमर्कबिम्बमालोक्य मूढो रविमेव मन्यते ।
> तथा चिदाभासमुपाधिसंस्थं भ्रान्त्याहमित्येव जडोऽभिमन्यते ॥
>
> ViCū 218
>
> Seeing the reflection of the sun mirrored in the water of a jar, the fool thinks it is the sun itself. Similarly the stupid man, through delusion, identifies himself with the reflection of the *cit* caught in the *buddhi*, which is Its superimposition. (Tr. Madhavananda)

In order to determine real nature of *jīva*, Vidyāraṇya in his **Pañcadaśī** has stated:

> ईषद्भासनमाभासः प्रतिबिम्बस्तथाविधः ।
> बिम्बलक्षणहीनः सन्बिम्बवद्भासते स हि ॥
>
> Pañcad VIII.32
>
> '*Ābhāsa*' means slight or partial manifestation, '*pratibimba*' is also like that, i.e. partial manifestation. It does not have the properties of the real entity but resembles it in having some of them. (Tr. Swahananda)

The **Dakṣiṇāmūrtistotra Bhāṣya** accepts the view that original is the material cause of reflection, but also accepts the power of *māyā* or adjuncts like mirror, etc. which create the illusion of duality and separateness as if the reflection comes from without having separate existence:

> अन्तरस्मिन्निमे लोकाः अन्तर्विश्वमिदं जगत् ।
> बहिर्वन्मायया भाति दर्पणे प्रतिबिम्बितम् ॥
>
> DakMūStBh 8
>
> This world abides inside (the self), these worlds also exist within but it shines as if externally by the power of *māyā* (ignorance) reflected in the mirror. (Tr. H.N. Chakravarty)

The same view has been taken in another example of the same text :

> विश्वं दर्पण दृश्यमाननगरीतुल्यं निजान्तर्गतं पश्यन् आत्मनि मायया बहिरिवोद्भूतं यथा निद्रया ।
>
> DakMūSt 1
>
> The universe similar to the city reflected in a mirror, though shining within one's own self yet by the overpowering influence of *māyā* it becomes clearly manifest as if externally like the objects seen externally in the state of dream. (Tr. H.N. Chakravarty)

This is the typical Advaita view preached by Ādiśaṅkarācārya.

Abhinavagupta in the **Tantrāloka** has also tried to explain the nature of reality through the concept of *bimba-pratibimba* and in the process has thrown light on the relationship of reflection, reflector and the thing reflected. He has equated the absolute freedom of the Lord with that of *bimba* which shines just like a face in the mirror:

> निर्मले मुकुरे यद्वद् भान्ति भूमिजलादयः ।

अमिश्रास्तद्वदेकस्मिंश्चिन्नाथे विश्ववृत्तय: ॥

TĀl III.4

Just as a stainless mirror catches the reflection of the earth, the water and others without being intermixed with one another, similarly in the sole Lord of consciousness all the various forms of the universe are reflected. (Tr. H.N. Chakravarty)

The **Tantrāloka** accepts that *pratibimba* has no independent existence from that of its reflector as mirror etc. *Tādātmya* or oneness with the mirror is necessary for the reflection.

अन्यव्यामिश्रणायोगात्तद्भेदाशक्यभासनम् ।
प्रतिबिम्बमिति प्राहुर्दर्पणे वदनं यथा ॥

TĀl III.56

The reflection is that which shines after becoming one with the other like the mirror which catches the reflection of the face. It (*pratibimba*) is not able to shine, when it is separated from it (the mirror). (Tr. H.N. Chakravarty)

सदृशं भाति नयनदर्पणाम्बर वारिषु ।
तथा हि निर्मले रूपे रूपमेवावभासते ॥

TĀl III.5

The thing which is similar (that is in possessing the quality of colour) is reflected in the void of the eye, the mirror and in the still water. If the image is clear, the reflection becomes flawless. (Tr. H.N. Chakravarty)

This world is the reflection of Supreme Being and it lies within that being as a reflection of different things lies in a mirror without being intermixed:

अन्यामिश्रं स्वतन्त्रं सद्भासमानं मुखं यथा ॥

TĀl III.53cd

Excluded from others the absolute freedom which abides in its own, is *bimba*. It shines in the way as the face shines (in the mirror). (Tr. H.N. Chakravarty)

Jayaratha gives the meaning of '*anyāmiśra*' as: '*sajātīya vijātīya vyāvṛtta*', which states that *bimba* has such an uniqueness of character that it is distinct from others and it cannot be classed under any group. It is the absolute freedom of the Lord which is *bimba* and none else.

The **Tantrāloka** (IV.207–208) equates meditation, worship and rituals with the reflection of Lord's *vikalpa* with which a devotee has to identify himself if he desires to become Bhairava, i.e. the Lord in the same way as one recognizes and identifies one's own face seeing it reflected in a mirror.

Pratyabhijñā darśana explains the whole world as the reflection of Supreme Lord in a mirror:

> ... परमेश्वरो ... स्वात्मदर्पणे भावान् प्रतिबिम्बवद् अवभासयतीति ।
>
> SarDSaṅg sec. on Pratyabhijñā, line 4–5
>
> ... this Supreme Lord, ... gives manifestation, in the mirror of one's own soul, to all entities as if they were images reflected upon it. (Tr. A.E. Gough)

The **Īśvara Pratyabhijñā Vivṛti Vimarśinī** (I.11.8) defines the rules of reflections. According to it reflection has its own limitations. It can not reflect touch or weight but only form and structure. For its clarity it solely depends upon the quality of the reflector. Echo of the sound in the void is just like a reflection. Void contains the property of sound and because of this it receives the echo just as mirror possesses the property of colours to reflect an image. The same text further explains the view of the Vaiśeṣikas as:

> स्वच्छेन द्रव्येण प्रतिहता नयनरश्मयः परावृत्य स्वमेव मुखं गृह्णन्ति, दर्पणे मुखमिति तु भ्रान्तिरियम् ।
>
> ĪPVivVim I.2.8, p. 160
>
> The rays of the eyes when struck against a clear object like a mirror come back again and see one's own face. The view that the face is in the mirror is false. (Tr. H.N. Chakravarty)

The **Mṛgendra Āgama** (vp XI.8) uses the term *bodha* (intelligence) in the sense of reflection which manifests in the bound soul.

The **Bodha Pañcadaśikā** (4), **Paramārthasāra** (9) and **Mahārtha Mañjarī** (verse 40) all use the term *pratibimba* and *bhāti* (to shine, cf. AmKo I.2.16) in the sense of a reflection in a mirror whose externality is illusion because the world as reality resides in the Supreme Lord or Devī:

> यस्यां हि भित्तिभूतायां मातृमेयात्मकं जगत् ।
> प्रतिबिम्बतया भाति नगरादीव दर्पणे ॥
>
> MaMa after verse 40
>
> In the base of whose the entire universe with the characteristics of the subject and the object shines as a city reflected in a mirror. (Tr. H.N. Chakravarty)

In this way the concept of *bimba* and *pratibimba* has been used and historically developed in different contexts such as religion, philosophy, art and lexicons. Throughout the course of its development it has retained its core meanings – to shine, to reflect, an image, shadow, etc. It is interesting to note that the term *bimba* has been used in the sense of a reflecting object and reflection both. It depends upon the context of the reference. Its interchangeability with *pratibimba* is without any doubt.

Kālidāsa is famous for the use of his similies. In the **Kumārasambhava** (VII.16) he has compared the grace of Pārvatī's face set off by her decorated tresses with that of lotus with bees adhering to it or with the moon's disc with streaks of dark clouds. In the present context lotus and moon resemble the face of Pārvatī, whereas bees and dark clouds resemble her tresses partially covering her face. Here likeness is suggested through analogy. The simile of the moon slightly visible from among the clouds is frequently used by Kālidāsa. For example:

एतन्मुनेर्मानिनि शातकर्णेः पञ्चाप्सरो नाम विहारवारि ।
आभाति पर्यन्तवनं विदूरान्मेघान्तरालक्ष्यमिवेन्दुबिम्बम् ॥

Ragh XIII.38

O lady of exalted mind, this is the pleasure-lake named *pañcāpsaras* of the sage Śātakarṇi (a tank where the *muni* used to sport), and which environed by woods looks from a great distance like the disc of the moon slightly visible from among the clouds.
(Tr. G.R. Nandargikar)

This description is similar to '*sameghalekhaṃ śaśinaśca bimbam*' used in the **Kumārasambhava** (VII.16). Here *sādṛśya* or likeness doesn't imply an illusion but only a real equivalence or adequacy. It is in this sense that art is an adequate symbolism, i.e. proper symbol of its referent. *Bimboṣṭhī* (Māla IV.14), *bimbaphalādharoṣṭhe* (Kum III.67), *pakvabimba oṣṭham* (DBhāgPur IX.12.6), *bimbādhara* (Kum III.56) are some of the conventional usages of the term *bimba* in the sense of a *bimba* fruit resembling ruddy lips or lower lip of the beautiful female characters.

Bimba is also used in the sense of shape or form as in the **Kumārasambhava**:

दरीगृहद्वारविलम्बिबिम्बास्तिरस्करिण्यो जलदा भवन्ति ॥

Kum I.14cd

Where the clouds, with their forms accidentally hanging over the entrances to the caverns serving as houses, become the screens ...
(Tr. M.R. Kale)

Bimba and *maṇḍala* both are used to indicate the region of buttocks :

नितम्बबिम्बैः सदुकूलमेखलैः स्तनैः सहाराभरणैः सचन्दनैः ।
शिरोरुहैः स्नानकषायवासितैः स्त्रियो निदाघं शमयन्ति कामिनाम् ।।

Ṛtu I.4

Women allay the heat felt by (their) lovers, by (their) round hips having (covering) silk-cloths and waist-bands, by (their) breasts having garlands and (other) ornaments, and smeared with sandal-paste, (and) by (their) hair fragrant with the cosmetics used in bathing. (Tr. M.R. Kale)

सैकतं च सरयूं विवृण्वतीं श्रोणिबिम्बमिव हंसमेखलम् ।
स्वप्रियाविलसितानुकारिणीं सौधजालविवरैर्व्यलोकयत् ।।

Ragh XIX.40

He saw through the holes of the windows of his palace the river Sarayū displaying its sandy-banks resembling the hip and loins with rows of flamingoes for its waist-bands and thus imitating the graceful and wanton gestures of his own beloveds.
(Tr. G.R. Nandargikar)

The **Amara Kośa** (III.3.133) makes it clear that the term *bimba* in masculine and neuter gender means a particular fruit named *bimba* (*momordica monadelphạ*) – *bimbo'strīmaṇḍale cākṛtau phale.* But the **Nānārtha Mañjarī** (1125-1126) records that – *striyāṃ syādbimbikāphale*, i.e. the term *bimba* if used in feminine gender means the fruit of *bimba.* This fruit is frequently used in literature as a simile to which the lips of women are often compared.

तन्वी श्यामा शिखरिदशना पक्वबिम्बाधरोष्ठी
मध्ये क्षामा चकितहरिणीप्रेक्षणा निम्ननाभिः ।
श्रोणीभारादलसगमना स्तोकनम्रा स्तनाभ्यां
या तत्र स्याद्युवतिविषये सृष्टिराद्येव धातुः ।।

Megh II.22

The lady, who will be found there, slender-framed, youthful, with pointed teeth and her lower lip resembling a ripe *bimba* fruit, thin in the middle (waist), possessed of eyes like those of a frightened doe, having a deep navel, of a gait slow on account of the weight of her hips, slightly stooping on account of her breasts and the first creation, as it were, of the Creator in the department of woman-kind. (Tr. M.R. Kale)

The **Nāgānanda** (IV.25a) and the **Naiṣadhīyacarita** (VII.77, XVIII.102) use the term *bimba* in the sense of lunar orb or disc resembling beautiful faces of *nāyaka* and *nāyikā* etc. The **Naiṣadhīyacarita** uses the term *pratibimba* in the sense of a halo made of the jasmine blossoms (VII.88) implying the core concept of the term *bimba-pratibimba* as *ābhoga* (circuit) and *maṇḍala* (orb). Solar disc is often described only as *bimba,* whereas in context of moon it (*bimba* or *maṇḍala*) is always preceded by various names of moon. For example:

> निर्गत्य बिम्बादिव भानवीयात्सौधाकरं मण्डलमंशुसङ्घः ॥
>
> NaiCa VI.7cd
>
> Just as a mass of rays, going out, the solar disc, enters the lunar orb ... (Tr. K.K. Handiqui)

Bimba here means solar orb and *sudhākaramaṇḍala,* conveys the meaning of lunar orb. The reference is to the astronomical fact that the moon reflects the light of the sun.

Bimba fruit is of red or crimson colour. This colour resembles the ruddy lips particularly lower lips of women in poetry and drama. Here likeness between the fruit and lips is provided by the deep red colour and ripeness or fullness of the shape common in both the objects, i.e. *upamāna* and *upameya.* The **Naiṣadhīyacarita** (IX.119) compares the lower lip of Damayantī which is red like a *bimba* fruit with the Bhūrja leaf having coloured letters written on it because of the red marks of biting left on lower lip by Nala (*dantakṣata-rājirañjanaiḥ sa bhūrjatāmarjatu bimbapāṭalaḥ* – NaiCa IX.119). Again in the same text Damayantī's lower lip on her moon-like face is said to be the fit image of *bimba* fruit grown in some nectar-fed soil:

> अस्या मुखेन्दावधरः सुधाभूबिम्बस्य युक्तः प्रतिबिम्ब एषः ।
>
> NaiCa VII.38ab
>
> This lower lip on her moon-like face is the fit image of *bimba* fruit of some nectar-fed soil ... (Tr. K.K. Handiqui)

The term *pratibimba* as reflecting the exact likeness of the original object is suggestive of illusion. It is explained in the **Nāgānanda** as follows:

> ईदृशं सौसादृश्यं येन न ज्ञायते किं तावदिहैव शिलातले भर्तृदारिकायाः प्रतिबिम्बं संक्रान्तमुत त्वमालिखितेति ।
>
> Nāgā II, after verse 12
>
> This likeness is so excellent that it cannot be known whether your image is now reflected here on the stone-slab or you are painted. (Tr. B.K. Bae)

Here *sādṛśya* or resemblance creates the illusion of reflected image being the person himself or that of his painted form.

In the **Uttararāmacarita** it is discussed that a teacher imparts knowledge to his disciples without discriminating whether they are bright or dull, but the result of his teaching varies according to the capacity of his disciples, talent for learning (*jñāna śakti*). A bright disciple is like a bright, lumnious gem reflecting the knowledge received from his teacher whereas a dull student is like a lump of earth unable to reflect that knowledge. An adjunct like gem, mirror is naturally empowered to reflect an image. The power of reflection resides in it and it is in this sense that a gem is described as *śucibimbagrāhe maṇi.*

वितरति गुरुः प्राज्ञे विद्यां यथैव तथा जडे ।
न च खलु तयोर्ज्ञाने शक्तिं करोत्यपहन्ति वा ॥
भवति च पुनर्भूयान्भेदः फलं प्रति तद्यथा ।
प्रभवति शुचिर्बिम्बग्राहे मणिर्न मृदां चयः ॥

UttCa II.4

The instructor imparts knowledge to the talented scholar just as he does to the dull; he does not, indeed, give them nor does he take away from them the talent for learning; and yet there is a very great difference as to the result. It happens thus (the explanation is this): – a bright gem can take in an image (reflection); not so a heap of earth. (Tr. M.R. Kale)

This is a conversation between Ātreyī (a female ascetic) and Vāsantī (goddess). *Bimba* here means *pratibimba* or *praticchāyā* or reflection.

The idea of *bimba-pratibimba* (reflection of type and prototype) plays an important role in the Alaṅkāra-Śāstra; because a vital portion of *arthālaṅkāra* (Dṛṣṭānta, Nidarśanā and Prativastūpamā) is based on the concept of *bimba-pratibimba,* e.g. when there is reflective representation of *upamāna* and *upameya* that is Dṛṣṭānta 'the exemplification'; when a possible or sometimes impossible connection of things implies a relation of type and prototype that becomes Nidarśanā 'the illustration', and when same attribute is expressed by different words (in the narration) that is a case of Prativastūpamā 'the typical comparison'.

The **Sāhitya-Darpaṇa** defines Dṛṣṭānta:

दृष्टान्तस्तु सधर्मस्य वस्तुनः प्रतिबिम्बनम् ।

SāDar X.71

Exemplification is the reflective representation of similar attributes. (Tr. J.R. Ballantyne & P.D. Mitra)

However, the Haimavatī commentary on the **Kāvya Prakāśa** has elucidated the phrase '*sādhāraṇadharmādīnām*' similar attribute, in wider sense; i.e. all the required factors namely standard of comparison (*upamāna*), object of comparison (*upameya*) and common attribute (*sādharmya*). The **Kuvalayānanda** has almost echoed the statement of Viśvanātha.

चेद्बिम्बप्रतिबिम्बत्वं दृष्टान्तस्तदलंकृतिः ।

Kuva 52ab

The figure of speech Dṛṣṭānta (the exemplification) is that when there is reflective representation (between standard of comparison and object of comparison). (Tr. P. Ghosal)

As regards Nidarśanā the **Sāhitya-Darpaṇa** states:

सम्भवन् वस्तुसम्बन्धोऽसम्भवन् वापि कुत्रचित् ।
यत्र बिम्बानुबिम्बत्वं बोधयेत् सा निदर्शना ॥

SāDar X.72

When a possible or as is sometimes the case even an impossible connection of things, implies a relation of type and prototype it is illustration. (Tr. J.R. Ballantyne & P.D. Mitra)

Regarding Prativastūpamā Viśvanātha says:

प्रतिवस्तूपमा सा स्याद्वाक्ययोर्गम्यसाम्ययोः ।
एकोऽपि धर्मः सामान्यो यत्र निर्दिश्यते पृथक् ॥

SāDar X.70

Typical comparison is when in sentences or descriptions, of which the correspondence is implied, the same common attribute is differently expressed. (Tr. J.R. Ballantyne & P.D. Mitra)

Manifestation in the Arts

Bimba-pratibimba in the sense of an image presuppose likeness or resemblance of the original form. *Pratibimba* or reflection is nothing but the *praticchāyā* or *pratikṛti* of the original form. There are two types of reflections: (1) reflection of the perceptible model as reflection of a person or object in a mirror or water and (2) reflection of an intelligible model through imitation or comparison, i.e. *anukaraṇa* and *upamāna* or *sādṛśya* – analogy. In Indian philosophy and art the first category is treated like *ābhāsa* in the sense of an illusion because of the exact likeness, whereas the second category belongs to the realm of art where artist creates through the process of *dṛṣṭvā dhyāyet, dhyātvā kuryāt,* i.e. the process of sensible perception through memory and intellect. The artist's perception of angelic prototypes is always considered superior to the mere observation of natural objects.

The term *bimba* has been used in sculpture and painting in the sense of an image or icon. The **Amara Kośa** (II.10.35–36) defines the term *pratibimba* as the synonym of *pratimā* and *arcā* (icon). The **Uṇādi Dhātu Vṛtti** (IV.535) uses

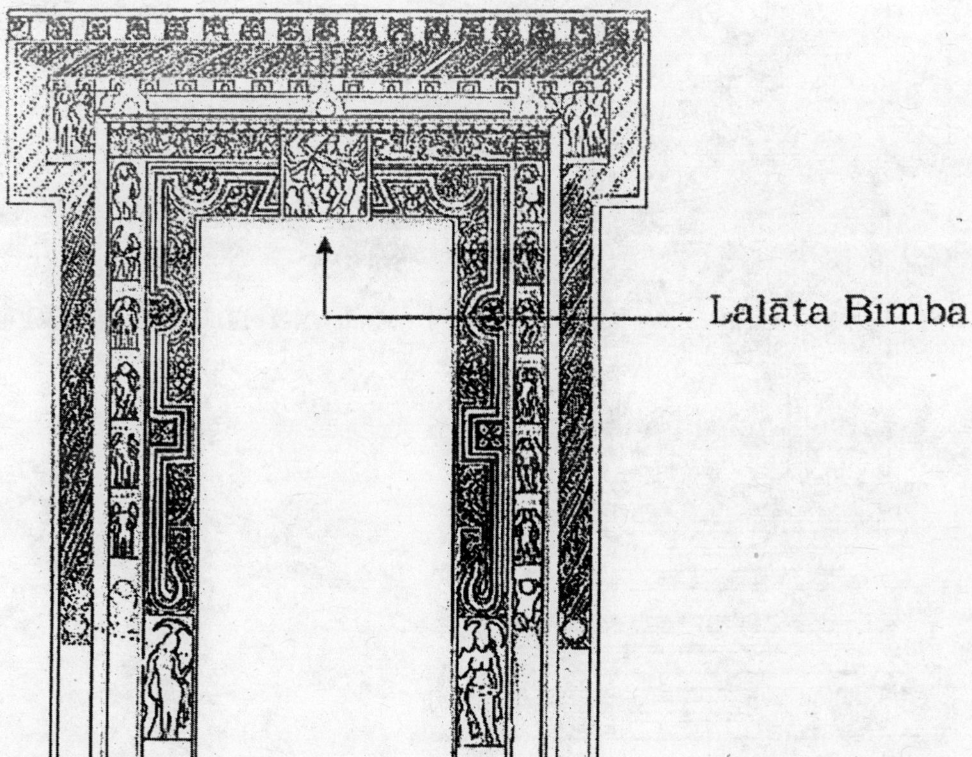

Figure 15: *Lalāṭa-bimba*

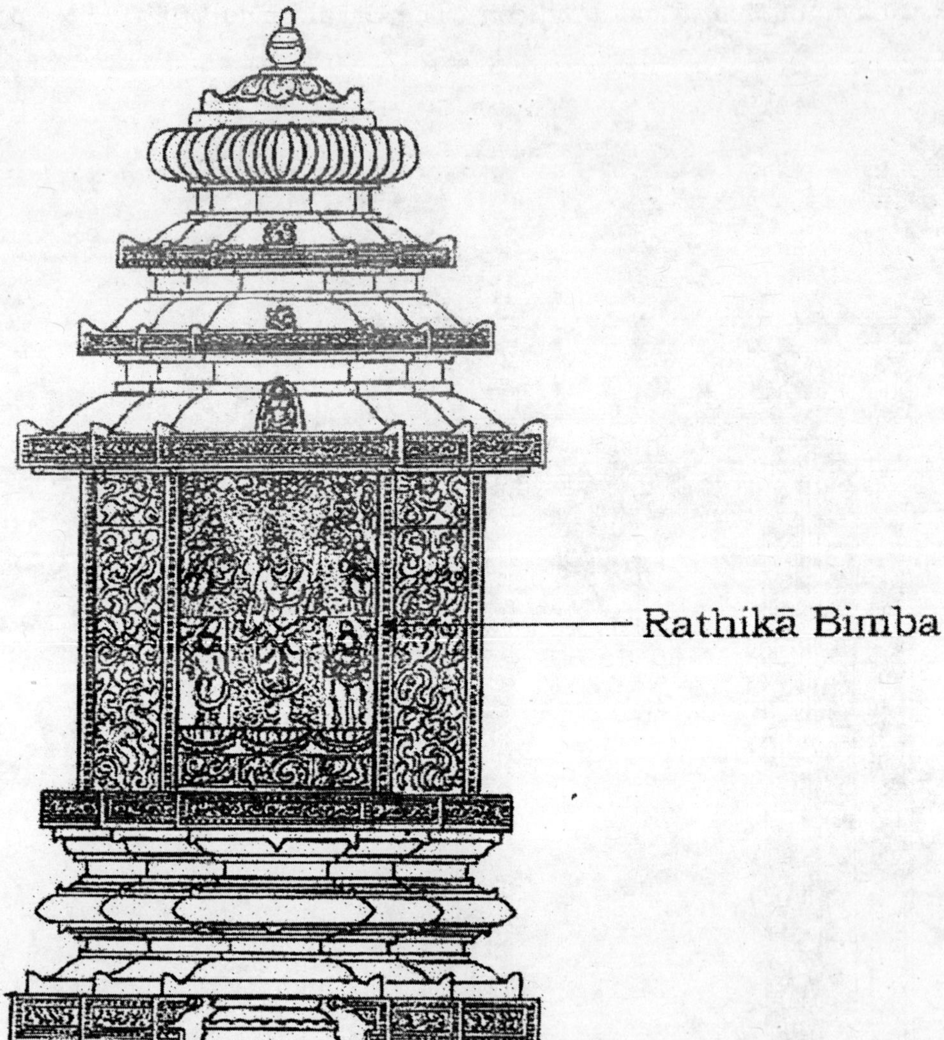

Figure 16: *Rathikā-bimba*

the term *bimba* to mean a *pratirūpa* that is explained as an image. The **Medinī Kośa** (XXIII.7a) makes it clear that *bimba* in the masculine gender means *pratibimba,* i.e. reflection. Canonical literature on Śilpa mentions the term *bimba* in the sense of an image or icon suggesting the core meaning of the term to shine or to reflect and thus equating the installed or carved or painted image being the reflection or *pratinidhi* or *praticchāyā* of the *iṣṭa devatā.*

Texts on temple architecture refer to the term *bimba* as *lalāṭa-bimba, rathikā-bimba,* etc. *Lalāṭabimba* is an image of the deity installed in the *garbhagṛha* carved in a niche on the outer face of the architrave of the sanctum, exactly in the middle or centre. This is an important element and suggests the reflection of the *garbhagṛha* deity. All major temples in India use mirrors to reflect the *pratibimba* of the installed deity on the mirror hanged above the entrance of the sanctum (Somanātha, Dvārakā, etc.). *Ratha* is a term used for vertical offsets or projections on the outer face of the walls of *garbhagṛha.* On these *rathas,* particuarly on *bhadra ratha,* i.e. central offset images of different gods and goddesses are carved. They are described as *rathikā-bimbas* or images carved in the niches of offsets.

Pratimā in Indian art does not mean portraiture or the exact copy of the model. Indian mind perceives individual forms as the manifestation of soul, therefore all arts (sculpture, painting, etc.) proceed from within – that follows the form or *rūpa* conceived in mind. Indian artist is the human counter part of divine artists like Tvaṣṭā, Viśvakarmā, etc. The term *bimba-pratibimba* in the context of Indian art follows the course of its development in Indian philosophy. Like a *yogī,* Indian sculptor or painter is also supposed to meditate upon the *rūpa* or form conceived in mind and imitate that form while externalizing it in desired mediums such as stone, metal, pigments, etc. Only that is sup-

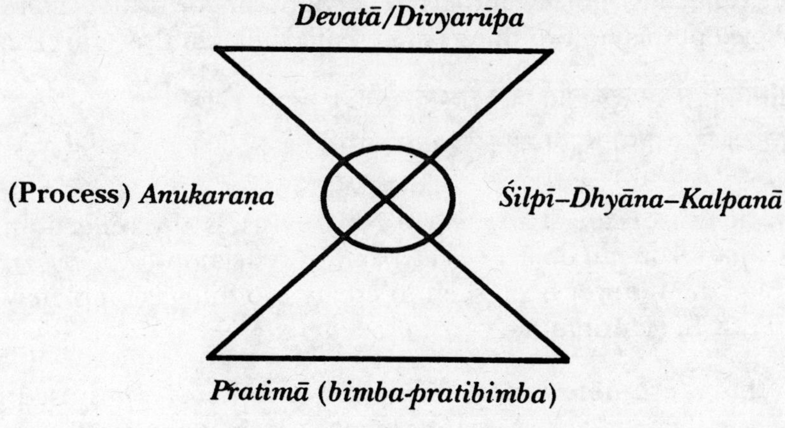

Figure 17: From *devatā* to *pratimā*

posed to be beautiful which is made in the likeness of an archetype or divine form visible only to the intellect. The **Śukranītisāra** states:

> देवानां प्रतिबिम्बानि कुर्य्याच्छ्रेयस्कराणि च ।
> स्वर्ग्याणि मानवादीनामस्वर्ग्याण्यशुभानि च ॥
>
> ŚNSā IV.4.74
>
> Anything created on the pattern of angelic prototype is a source of *śreya* and divine pleasure whereas anything created only on the pattern of external world or human world is undesirable and *aśubha*.

This is one of the reasons why Indian images are more like a symbol of their referents, i.e. divine form and negate the rules of visual or natural world by incorporating only its essentials and leaving the particulars. True *anukaraṇa* of the divine form or model is not a matter of illusory resemblance, but of proportion, true analogy or adequacy by which we are reminded of the intended referent. It is this view that makes it possible to see God in the image rather than merely seeing the image of the god. Sāyaṇa in his commentary on the **Aitareya Brāhmaṇa** (VI.27) has classified *śilpa* in two categories: (1) *devaśilpa* – divine or angelic prototypes and (2) *mānuṣaśilpa*. Through the process of '*anukaraṇa*' human artists try to create artefacts which have a likeness in form corresponding with the divine form. The **Aitareya Brāhmaṇa** makes it clear that one who imitates (*anukṛ-*) the divine arts (*devaśilpāni*), is said to be reintegrated in the metric mode (*chandobhīr ātmānaṃ saṃskurute* – AitBr VI.27). *Śādṛśya* or *tādātmya* (likeness, similitude) may be of three kinds:

(1) Absolute sameness which can not exist either in nature or art because no two things can be alike in all respects and still be two. This idea has been expressed in the **Naiṣadhīyacarita** where it is suggested that only *bimba* and *anubimba*, i.e. reflecting object and its reflection can be called completely identical and except this no two things are created alike in this universe:

> संसारसिन्धावनुबिम्बमत्र जागर्ति जाने तव वैरसेनिः ।
> बिम्बानुबिम्बौ हि विहाय धातुर्न जातु दृष्टातिसरूपसृष्टिः ॥
>
> NaiCa VIII.46
>
> I know, in this ocean of the world Nala exists as thy reflection; indeed, apart from an object (*bimba*) and its reflection (*anubimba*), the Creator hath never been seen to create two things completely alike. (Tr. K.K. Handiqui)

Here two things are noteworthy. Firstly the term *anubimba* is used in the sense of *pratibimba*. Secondly *bimba* stands for the original object.

(2) Imitative or analogical likeness are judged by comparison. This view is taken in the **Vaijayantī Kośa** (III.9.21c) – *pratibimbopamāne,* i.e. *pratibimba* conveys the sense of *upamāna* – the comparison.

(3) Expressive likeness in which the *anukaraṇa* is neither identical with nor comparable to the original but is an accurate symbol and reminder of that which tries to represent. The words are images of things. Imitative and expressive likenesses are not mutually exclusive categories. Ancient Indian art follows the precepts of these two categories and images or icons are made in likeness of divine forms conceived in mind. In this sense the term *bimba-pratibimba* and their cognates like *chāyā, pratimā, pratirūpa, pratikṛti, praticchāyā, pratinidhi* and *anukṛti,* reveal the theory and philosophy of Indian art. *Pratimā* or *bimba* is only a reminder of its intended referent. It is not an end in itself rather a means to an end, i.e. realization of the divine form or existence.

In the context of temple architecture it is this likeness with that of Supreme God which is spoken of in the **Śilparatnakośa**.

> विमानं पुरुषाकारं पीठात् ध्वजस्थलावधिः ।
>
> ŚiRaKo I.6
>
> The *vimāna* (temple) is in the form of the *puruṣa* (Man, Eternal Being), from the *pīṭha* (plinth) up to the flag (on the top). (Tr. B. Bäumer)

Here temple is conceived or built in the likeness of *puruṣa* or archetype of divine form. *Puruṣa* becomes *bimba* or original form and *vimāna* becomes *pratibimba* or *ākāra* of the *puruṣa.*

It is interesting to note that Śilpa texts use those terms for images and icons which are described as the synonyms of *bimba-pratibimba* such as: *pratimā, pratirūpa, ākṛti, mūrti, vigraha,* etc., thus conveying images (creations of art) to be reflections of *divya śilpa.* God→ *prakṛti*→ *avidyā* or *māyā* = *līlāśakti*→ *viśva* or creation = *bimba* or *rūpa* being reflection of God.

The **Citra-Lakṣaṇa** further explains:

> सादृश्यं दृश्यते यत्तु दर्पणे प्रतिबिम्बवत् ।
> तच्चित्रमिति विख्यातं नालमाकारमात्रकम् ॥
>
> CiL 147
>
> That painting is wellknown as *citra* which is not merely a sketch in outline, but shows the resemblance (of a figure) as truly as the reflection on a mirror. (Tr. A.K. Bhattacharya)

Here again mere approximation of the physical form is condemned as a piece of art which is supposed to portray or depict the likeness of the figure as

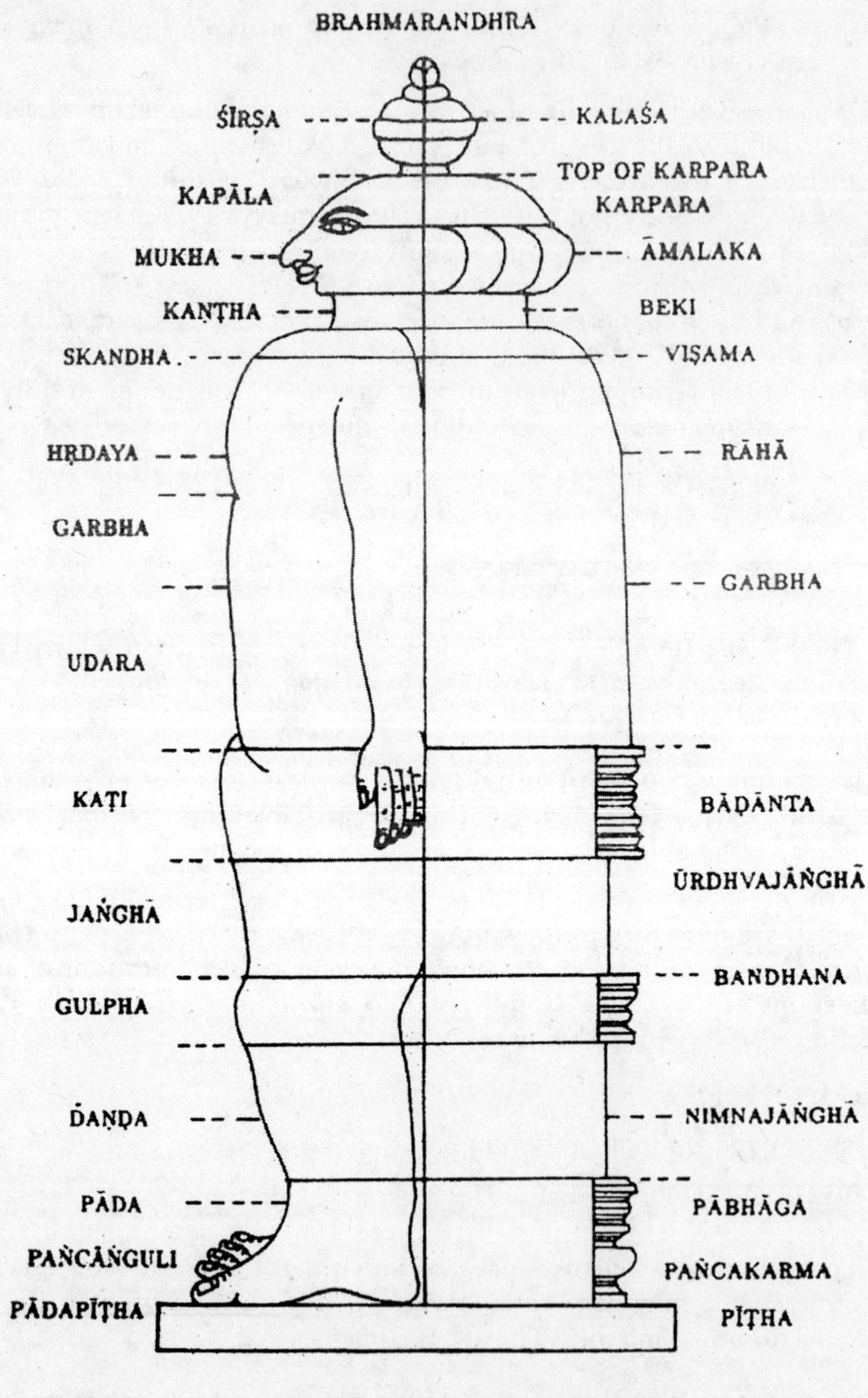

Figure 18: Temple as reflection of *puruṣa*

of a shadow in a mirror – this likeness is not that of a copy but of an image akin and equal to its model. For example the representation of a man must really correspond to the idea of the man or form, but it should not try to deceive the eye by being 'natural' in functional or biological sense.

There are several references in canonical literature pertaining to art and architecture where the term *bimba* has been used in the sense of an image or icon (cf. Mayam IX.126cd). The **Mayamata** makes reference to *bimba* in the sense of an image or icon to be installed or carved at the assigned place in a temple and also elaborates different modes of carving or fashioning *bimba* (images) out of stone such as – *jāti, chanda, vṛtta* and *ābhāsa*, etc.

इष्टायामविशालेन चतुरश्रीकृतं समम् ।
जातिरूपं तु तद् बिम्बं छेदनीयं यथोचितम् ॥
छन्दमष्टाश्रकं षोडशाश्रं नाम्ना विकल्पकम् ।
वृत्तमाभासकं लिङ्गं तच्छेद्यं स्यात् त्रयात्मकम् ॥

Mayam XXXIII.65–66

Jāti mode is to be adopted to fashion the image of god if it is of quadrangular shape. (In that case) at first (basic) stone should be shaped into a parallel piped dimension in length and breadth. If it is in the shape of an octagonal prism chanda-mode is adopted. If the prism has sixteen sides *vikalpa* mode and if cylindrical *ābhāsa* mode. That is the rough shape that should be sculpted, in a tripple natured *liṅga.* (Based on the tr. by B. Dagens)

The sizes of different *bimbas* also expounded in the **Mayamata** as:

चतुष्पदे च लोकेशाः स्थाप्याश्चाभ्यन्तराननाः ॥
षड्भिः पञ्चचतुस्त्रिद्विमात्रे बिम्बोदयं भवेत् ।
तदर्धं वाहनोत्सेधं स्थानकासनमेव वा ॥

Mayam IX.112cd–113

The lords of the cardinal points are installed facing the centre (of the casket) and in four compartments; their images are six, five, four, three or two digits high and their mounts half that height; they are either standing or seated. (Tr. B. Dagens)

It further explains: *bimba-mūrtiḥ śarīrābhā* (Mayam XXXIII.2) – the manifestation in the form of an image is analogous to a body.

Here it is made clear that the term *bimba* denotes not only image or *mūrti* but that *bimba* is a substitute for body or bodily representation of the desired deity (*iṣṭadevatā*). Interestingly the **Amara Kośa** (II.10.35–36) states that *pratikṛti,* *pratibimba, pratinidhi, pratimā,* etc. are synonyms of *arcā* (image to be worshipped), thus making it clear that *bimba* is visual or bodily *pratinidhi* of God, desired by the devotee to be worshipped. In this sense *bimba* is the visual reflection of *paramātmā* or Supreme Lord.

The term *bimba-pratibimba* in the sense of an image occurs in several texts. Art and iconography provide the use of this term either as sculpted image or as painted image or reflected image.

Bimba in the sense of an effigy occurs in the **Artha-Śāstra**:

प्रतिपन्नं बिम्बं कृत्वा शत्रुमावाहयित्वा निरुद्धे देशे घातयेत् ।

ArthŚ XIII.2.19

When he agrees, he should make an effigy and invoke the enemy and should kill the king in a secluded spot. (Tr. R. P. Kangle)

Painted images were differentiated from other types of images by using the term – *citra-bimba* or *paṭa-bimba.* The **Jayākhya Saṃhitā** has used this kind of differentiation.

पटे बिम्बविधानं तु सांप्रतं शृणु नारद । सर्वसिद्धिकरं रम्यं निर्दोषं नातिविस्तरम् ॥
द्विहस्तं चतुरस्त्रं तु हस्तमात्रं तु वा पटम् । कार्पासमथ वा क्षौमं नवं शुक्लमनाहतम् ॥

JaySam XX.3 (3)

O Nārada, listen to now regarding the method of preparing an image on a canvas. The canvas representation is the bestower of all attainments. It is beautiful and free from all faults. It should not be very long. The canvas should be two cubit square or may be one cubit square. The canvas is made of cotton or silk. It should be new, white and unbleached. (Tr. H.N. Chakravarty)

The text further adds:

हस्ताधिकेऽपि च कृते चित्रबिम्बे गृहस्थिते ।
न दोषः साधकानां तु दारुमृच्छैलजैर्विना ॥
बिम्बमानं तु नवधा प्रोच्छ्र्यात्संविभज्य च ।
भागं भागं तु तं भूयो भजेद्द्वादशधा मुने ॥
तदङ्गुलं तु बिम्बस्य तेनाङ्गावयवास्ततः ।
दर्शनीयाश्च गुरुणा शिल्पिकस्य समासतः ॥

JaySam XX.8–10

The painting representation of the deity which is in the house hold, if it is bigger than one cubit, there is no fault regarding the worshipper but it excludes the image made of wood, earth and stone.

> From the elevation of the *bimba* it should be divided into nine sections and then it, that is each section is to be divided into twelve parts. This part is the *aṅgula* of the image by (the measure of) which the limbs and the body is to be made. Only then it is nice looking to the wise and in short, to the painter.
> (Tr. H.N. Chakravarty)

Jain iconography also uses the term *bimba* and *pratimā* in the sense of an image or icon desired to be worshipped. For example in the **Ācāra Dinakara** (II.2–11) gives a detailed description of different materials to be used in the making of different *bimbas* or images. Some metals and other materials are prohibited for making the images to be worshipped at home by those who desire protection and prosperity.

Conclusion

Bimba-pratibimba is primarily a reflection which shines or extends from the original source. Corresponding to Indian world-view it conveys the meaning of *pratimā* (image), *pratiyātanā* (picture), *arcā* (icon) *pratinidhi* (representative), *pratirūpa* (image), suggesting that this world is the reflection of the Supreme Lord. Indian Philosophy – Brahmanic, Buddhist, Jain, etc. all have developed this concept to explain the complexities of the interrelatedness between physical and metaphysical. Through the imagery of *darpaṇavat – pratibimba*, philosophers have taken the epistemological view of this concept – *bimba-pratibimba* and on the other hand; in Indian poetry and drama this concept has been utilized to create the *śabda-citra* of natural scenes or physical beauty of *nāyaka-nāyikās.* Rarely it has been used to denote other meanings such as die in **Artha-Śāstra** and lizard or *bimba* fruit in others. *Bimba* has often been differentiated from *pratibimba* in the sense of reflecting object and its reflection. But in popular usage, drama, poetics, lexicons, aesthetics and philosophy the term *bimba* and *pratibimba* are taken as synonyms and are interchangeable terms. Even where they are differentiated the idea of *sādṛśya* or *anukaraṇa*, i.e. likeness and imitation intimately link them together. The pervasiveness and significance of this concept in Indian philosophy, arts and aesthetics is self-evident and have to be unfolded, so that the real purport becomes clear.

Pushpa Tiwari

Select Bibliography

Coomaraswamy, A.K.: "Imitation, Expression and Participation" in Traditional Art and Symbolism, Part I, ed. by Roger Lipsey, Princeton: Princeton University Press, U.S.A., 1977.

— Christian and Oriental Philosophy of Art, New York, 1956.

Kramrisch, S.: Indian Sculpture, Calcutta: Y.M.C.A. Publishing House & London: Oxford University Press, 1933.

Meister, M. W. (&others ed.): Encyclopaedia of Indian Temple Architecture North India, Vol. II, Part 1, New Delhi: American Institute of Indian Studies and Oxford University Press, 1988.

Rao, T.A. Gopinatha: Elements of Hindu Iconography, 4 Vols, Delhi: Motilal Banarsidass, reprint, 1993.

Ray, Niharranjan: Idea and Images in Indian Art, New Delhi, 1973.

Sivaramamurti, C.: Chitrasūtra of the Vishnudharmottara Purāṇa, New Delhi: Kanak Publications, 1978.

LIṄGA

Overview

The concept of *liṅga* (n.), signifying gender, underlies the whole complex of thought and its expression through the understanding of language, with respect especially to objects, notions and embodied entities or personification in terms of common behaviour as well as activity both on manifest and unmanifest planes. The notion of *liṅga* is primarily derived from the biological differentiation in nature, realised into its three possible aspects, namely male, female and neuter, the last being neither male nor female or something that is genderless or is beyond apparent male-female categories. Indeed, the first two symbols of the male and the female represent the bisexual categorization into the father and the mother, Puruṣa and Prakṛti.

The third aspect termed *napuṃsaka* denotes a negation of the masculine as well as the feminine gender, indicating something other than the two basic categories, beyond the male and the female attributes, but referring in cases to an inanimate, inert or genderless object or concept of which neither male nor female qualities are manifest or can be emphasised or identified.This specific aspect of the *liṅga* notion, however, plays a significant role in grammar, philosophical doctrines and many an allied definition of expressions.

Being one of the most significant terms of Indian thought and tradition, the word *liṅga* has been used in multiple contexts of its wide-range connotations from the later Vedic works throughout subsequent corpus of literary documents. It occurs and recurs as indicating many a subtle and general definitions according to the Śāstra or instruction of thought, branch of expert knowledge, or religious discipline and philosophy.

(1) One of the primary senses of the term to appear in Vedic texts, is gender, denoting collectively the three grammatical aspects of words into masculine, feminine and neuter.

(2) Sign or charactersing feature.

(3) Used in a specific manner to indicate a *mantra* dedicated to a deity by prefixing the initial phrase, name or ritual purpose to the word *liṅga* as its second element in a compound so formed.

(4) Male organ or symbol.

(5) Later in the Epics, the *liṅga*-emblem clearly gets defined for a Śaivite symbol of worship .

(6) In philosophical implications, the term has been freely used to mean a sign, feature, token, inner essence, unmanifest aspect, nature (*prakṛti, pradhāna*) or its symptomatic name and convincing reason (in the context of *anumāna*).

(7) There are several remarkable synonyms to be enlisted in the sense of which the word *liṅga* appears alternatively, such as: *cihna, lakṣma, lakṣaṇa, guṇa, saṃsthāna, pratīka,* Śiva-liṅga, male member (*śepha, śiśna*) and gender, etc. The variable contexts of wider perspectives indeed, go to specify such different meanings and connotations of the word *liṅga.*

Etymology and Related Terms

Beginning to occur, though in a limited usage, in the later strata of Vedic literature the term *liṅga* (in neuter gender) is widely used in several contexts and disciplines of Indian knowledge and wisdom. Its main connotation seems to be linked with the context of gender in the science of language and with male emblem or phallic symbol in religious understanding and following, besides its common useful nature in general consideration of a handy phrase to denote a sign, token, symbol, characteristic feature or aspect of an abstract thought as well as physical form or entity.

In his gloss on the **Amara Kośa,** Kṣīrasvāmī hints at the etymological derivation of the word *'liṅgam'* as understood by grammarians and exegesists in the following analysis: *līnaṃ gamayati liṅgati citrīkaroti vā liṅgam* (Kṣ on AmKo III.3.25).

According to Rāyamukuṭa, it is justified as per the rule *pṛṣodarādiḥ* (Pā VI.3.109). Bhānuji Dīkṣita in his Rāmāśramī commentary has thus given the derivation*: liṅgyate' nena, ligi gatau, 'halaśca'* (Pā III.3.121) *iti ghañ.*

According to the view given by the great polymath Ācārya Hemacandra:

> ... अथ पुंश्चिह्नं मेहनं शेपशेपसी ।
> शिश्नं मेढ्रः कामलता लिङ्गं च द्वयमप्यदः ॥
>
> AbhiCi III.274
>
> Now, the male sign, genital member, *śepa* (privy part), *śepas, śiśna, meḍhra,* sex vine (*kāmalatā*) and *liṅga*; the latter two words also denote female parts.

In his autocommentary, he further adds some variant words of general vocabulary for the same such as: *lāṅgulam, śaṅku, lāṅgūla, sepha* and *śephas* (*śeṣaścātra-śiśnetu śaṅku lāṅgūla śepha-śephasī*).

Metaphysical implications of the term *liṅga* are, however, spoken of thus by the **Śiva Purāṇa** while referring to its fundamental essence in an etymological understanding:

लिङ्गे प्रसूतिकर्तारं लिङ्गिनं पुरुषो यजेत् ।
लिङ्गार्थगमकं चिह्नं लिङ्गमित्यभिधीयते ॥

ŚPur I.16.106

A person should venerate the possessor of *liṅga* (*liṅgin*). The emblem (*cihna*) that leads to the idea of *liṅga* (i.e. the Absolute Abstraction) is styled as *liṅga* (on a common level).

In the Sāṃkhya thought the term *liṅga* has been semantically explained in several ways. The **Yuktidīpikā** on **Sāṃkhya-Kārikā** attempts to grasp its implications in several of its different expressions as follows:

(1) *Tallakṣaṇopapanna*, "possessing the characteristics of that (i.e. the material cause)" (SāṃKā 10).

(2) *Kāraṇaguṇātmakatvāt kāryasya*, "the effect being of the same nature as the cause" (SāṃKā 14).

It has been usually explained by the scholiasts in two specific ways: (1) *layaṃ gacchati*, i.e. that goes to absorption or destruction; (2) *liṅgayati jñāpayati iti liṅgaṃ jñāpakam*, i.e. the mark through which something is inferred.

According to the Agamic tradition as indicated in the **Ajitāgama** the word *liṅga* is to be understood as derived from the exegetical analysis of its two syllables allied to the roots *lī-* and *gam-*:

लयं गच्छन्ति भूतानि संहारे निखिलानि च ॥
निर्गच्छन्ति यतश्चापि लिङ्गोक्तिस्तेन हेतुना ।

AjitĀ kp III.17cd–18ab

During the period of great dissolution all beings dissolve therein and emerge from there, for this reason it is designated as *liṅga*. (Tr. H.N. Chakravarty)

Notion-based metaphysical definition of the *liṅga* doctrine has been thus remarked in the Kashmir Śaivism:

यत्तदव्यक्तलिङ्गं नृशिवशक्त्यविभागवत् ।
अत्र विश्वमिदं लीनमत्रान्तःस्थं च गम्यते ॥
इदं तल्लक्षणं पूर्णशक्तिभैरवसंविदः ।

TĀl V.113–114ab

That which is called Abstract Symbol (*avyakta-liṅga*), has no divisions (as yet) of Puruṣa, Śiva and Śakti, It is in It, that this world is known to have immersed as staying within. This is of the nature of complete unison of Śakti and Bhairava knowledge (*saṃvid*).

Based on variant expositions of the *liṅga* concept in Śaivite philosophy the **Śiva Purāṇa** has thus summarised their substance:

लिङ्गमर्थं हि पुरुषं शिवं गमयतीत्यदः ।
शिवशक्त्योश्च चिह्नस्य मेलनं लिङ्गमुच्यते ॥

ŚPur I.16.107

The intent of the word *liṅga* reaches to the Auspicious Person Śiva. Thus the unification of cognizances of Śiva and Śakti (into one symbol) is called a *liṅga*.

As it is explained from semantic viewpoint of Tantric understanding in the **Yoginī-Hṛdayadīpikā** by Amṛtānandayogin (I.44):

लीनं बाह्येन्द्रियागोचरं चिद्रूपमर्थं गमयन्तीति लिङ्गानि ।

Dīpikā comm. on YoH I.44

Those attributes (*liṅgāni,* i.e. features, aspects) which lead to the essence of life-form, not known otherwise by outer sense-faculties [are conveyed by the word *liṅga*].

Layers of Meaning

According to the **Amara Kośa**, the word *liṅga* stands for a sign or the male organ:

लिङ्गं चिह्नशेफसोः ॥

AmKo III.3.25d

The term *liṅga* means a sign or the male member.

The **Vaijayantī Kośa** also records:

लिङ्गं शेफसि वेषेंऽशे चिह्ने बुद्ध्यादिसंहतौ ।

VaiKo VI.3.30ab

The term *liṅga* (when it is used in neuter gender) refers to *śepha* (phallus/genital organ), *veṣa* (assumed appearance), *aṃśa* (portion), *cihna* (mark/spot) and for the combination of *buddhi,* etc. [components of a conscious entity.] (Tr. P. Ghosal)

Other lexicographers also opine almost same:

लिङ्गं संगमने चिह्ने माने शेफेशमूर्तिषु ।
सांख्योक्तप्रकृतौ हेम्नि शिवमूर्तौ प्रचक्षते ।

NāMa 274–275

The term *liṅga* is stated to denote union, sign, measure or pride, the male organ, *īśa* (Śiva), form, *pradhāna* or *prakṛti* stated in the Sāṃkhya philosophy, as well as gold and the image of God Śiva.

लिङ्गं चिह्नेऽनुमाने च सांख्योक्तप्रकृतावपि ॥
शिवमूर्तिविशेषेऽपि मेहनेऽपि नपुंसकम् ।

MedKo III.21cd–22ab

The word *liṅga* means sign or distinguishing mark (*cihna*), a means of proof or a proof (*anumāna*). In Sāṃkhya philosophy the term *prakṛti* is known as *liṅga*. It also means the genital organ of Śiva worshipped in the form of a phallus (*śivamūrti*) and again it means the sign of gender, or sex organ (*mehana*). In all these senses the term *liṅga* it is used in neuter gender. (Tr. S. Das)

Hemacandra records several of the connotations evolved around the word *liṅga* in various contexts:

.... लिङ्गं मेहनचिह्नयोः ॥
शिवमूर्तावनुमाने सांख्योक्तप्रकृतावपि ।

AneSaṅg II.47d–48ab

The term *liṅga* denotes male member, sign or emblem, an image of Śiva, inference or guess, and also the idea of change in form as taught in the Sāṃkhya.

A hypocrite is referred to by two specific words of common parlance:

धर्मध्वजी लिङ्गवृत्तिः ।

AmKo II.7.54a

The term *dharmadhvajin* denotes a religious follower whose assumption is merely up to the outward signs (of a sect).

चिह्नमङ्के पताकायां ... ।

VaiKo VI.3.8c

Cihna occurs to denote *aṅka* (sign/mark) as well as *patākā* (banner). (Tr. P. Ghosal)

For the spot visible in the lunar orb, the following terms are given by Yādavaprakāśa:

अङ्क श्चिह्नमभिज्ञानं लाञ्छनं लक्ष्म लक्षणम् ।

VaiKo II.1.29ab

Aṅka (mark), *cihna* (sign), *abhijñāna* (memento), *lāñchana* (stain), *lakṣma* (characteristic) and *lakṣaṇa* (characteristic feature) – all these are synonymous. (Tr. P. Ghosal)

The term *lakṣman* is also recorded as a synonym of *aṅka* (NāMa 55), *ketu* (NāMa 667), *bimba* (NāMa 1125) as well as *pradhāna* in the following:

लक्ष्म चिह्ने प्रधाने च ... ।

NāMa 972

The term *lakṣma* is used to denote a mark or sign and original source of the material world. (Tr. S. Chattopadhyay)

व्यञ्जनं लाञ्छने ... ।
स्यात्पद्मो लाञ्छने ... ।

NāMa 1033, 1197

The term *lāñchana* is used as a synonym of *vyañjana* to denote a mark or sign and a synonym of *padma* to denote a mark or mole on human body. (Tr. S. Chattopadhyay)

लक्ष्म लाञ्छनं चिह्नलक्षणे, अभिज्ञानं कलङ्कोऽङ्कोऽथ .... ॥

Siddhaśabdārṇava (of Sahajakīrti) II.60bc

(For the sign in the moon are used these words:) mark (*lakṣma*), sign (*lāñchana*), symbol (*cihna*), symptom or feature (*lakṣaṇa*), identity (*abhijñāna*), spot (*kalaṅka*) and mark (*aṅka*).

Development of the Concept

We do not find the term *liṅga* in the **Ṛgveda**. However, its one synonym seems to be mentioned in this hymnal anthology:

स वाजं यातापदुष्पदा यन्त्स्वर्षाता परि षदत् सनिष्यन् ।
अनर्वा यच्छतदुरस्य वेदो घ्नञ्छिश्नदेवाँ अभि वर्पसा भूत् ॥

ṚV X.99.3

Going to the battle, marching with easy gait, desiring the spoil, he set himself to the acquisition of all (wealth). Invincible, destroying the phallus-worshippers, he won by his prowess whatever wealth (was concealed in the city) with the hundred gates.
(Tr. H.H. Wilson)

न यातव इन्द्र जूजुवुर्नो न वन्दना शविष्ठ वेद्याभिः ।
स शर्धदर्यो विषुणस्य जन्तोर्मा शिश्नदेवा अपि गुर्ऋतं नः ॥

ṚV VII.21.5

Let not the Rākṣasas, Indra, do us harm: let not the evil spirits do harm to our progeny, most powerful (Indra): let the sovereign lord. (Indra), exert himself (in the restraint) of disorderly beings, so that the unchastes (*śiśnadeva*) may not disturb our rite. (Tr. H.H. Wilson)

The above *mantra* is explained by Sāyaṇa as: '*śiśnadevāḥ abrahmacaryā ityarthaḥ*', following Yāska (*śiśnadevā abrahmacaryāḥ, śiśnaṃ śnathateḥ* – Nir IV.19). Anyway, the sense referring to one who considers the *liṅga* for one's deity may not be altogether precluded.

Yet another term *śepa* signifying male member occurs in an interesting context of the **Atharvaveda**:

अभिक्रन्दन् स्तनयन्नरुणः शितिङ्गो बृहच्छेपोऽनु भूमौ जभार ।
ब्रह्मचारी सिञ्चति सानौ रेतः पृथिव्यां तेन जीवन्ति प्रदिशश्चतस्रः ॥

AV XI.5.12

Roaring on, thundering, the ruddy white-goer has introduced (*anu-bhṛ*) in the earth a great virile member: the Vedic student pours seed upon the surface (*sānu*), on the earth; by that live the four directions. (Tr. W.D. Whitney)

Presumably, the expression *bṛhat śepa* installed on the ground evinces a cult of the Phallic Symbol set up on an imminent base.

Defining the indeclinable phrases in a grammatical context the **Gopatha Brāhmaṇa** has thus observed:

सदृशं त्रिषु लिङ्गेषु सर्वासु च विभक्तिषु ।
वचनेषु च सर्वेषु यन्न व्येति तदव्ययम् ॥

GoBr I.1.26

(Grammatically) that which remains the same in three genders and undergoes no change in all of the case-endings as well as all the numbers is an *avyayam* (i.e. indeclinable word). (Tr. P. Ghosal)

The symbol of Śiva's generative organ seems to be indicated in the **Taittirīya Āraṇyaka** (*śivaliṅgāya namaḥ* – 'homage to the *liṅga* of Śiva' – TĀr X.16) wherein some dozen other compounds of divine attributes are paid homage as marked with the word *liṅga*, which can hardly be denied to imply the *mantra* or formula referring to that concept or aspect, such as: *hiraṇyaliṅga*, *divya-liṅga, bhavaliṅga, śarvaliṅga, ātmaliṅga, paramaliṅga,* etc.

This Vedic usage or mode of indicating a specific *mantra* or *sūkta* by its principal 'phrase' or initial part added with the word *liṅga* as its second element (for abbreviation) has been indeed a common technique throughout the literary tradition.

The concept of *liṅga* as sign or form is described in the **Śvetāśvatara Upaniṣad**:

वह्नेर्यथा योनिगतस्य मूर्तिर्न दृश्यते नैव च लिङ्गनाशः ।
स भूय एवेन्धनयोनिगृह्यस्तद्वोभयं वै प्रणवेन देहे ॥

ŚvUp I.13

As the form of fire is not seen when it lies (latent) in its source, and yet its latent form is not destroyed, and that (fire) is perceptible after repeated rubbing of its source, the fuel, – as in the case of those two (viz. fire and its subtle form) (similarly, the Self is realized) in the body with the help of *om.* (Tr. Gambhirananda)

Commenting on a famous stanza of the **Śvetāśvatara Upaniṣad**, R.G. Bhandarkar long ago observed, "I do not, however, deny the possibility that when the **Śvetāśvatara Upaniṣad** in IV, 11 speaks of the god Īśāna as presiding over every *yoni* and in V, 2 of the lord as presiding over all forms and *yonis*, the allusion to the physical fact of the *liṅga* and *yoni* connected together may have been meant as typifying the philosophical doctrine of gods presiding over every creative cause" [*Vaiṣṇavism, Śaivism and Minor Religious Systems*, p. 114].

न तस्य कश्चित् पतिरस्ति लोके न चेशिता नैव च तस्य लिङ्गम् ।
स कारणं करणाधिपाधिपो न चास्य कश्चिज्जनिता न चाधिपः ॥

ŚvUp VI.9

Of Him there is no ruler in the world,

Nor Lord; nor is there any mark (*liṅga*) of Him.

He is the cause (*kāraṇa*), Lord of the lords of sense-organs .

Of Him, there is no progenitor, nor Lord. (Tr. R.E. Hume)

As observed in the **Maitrāyaṇī Upaniṣad**:

प्राकृतमन्नं त्रिगुणभेदपरिणामत्वान्महदाद्यं विशेषान्तं लिङ्गम् ।

MaitUp VI.10

The food, derived from Nature through the transformation in the partition of the three qualities becomes the subtile body (*liṅga*), which includes from intellect up to the separate elements. (Tr. R.E. Hume)

अचित्तं चित्तमध्यस्थमचिन्त्यं गुह्यमुत्तमम् ।
तत्र चित्तं निधायेत तच्च लिङ्गं निराश्रयम् ॥

MaitUp VI.19

That which is non-thought, (yet) which stands
in the midst of thought,
The unthinkable, supreme mystery!
Thereon let one concentrate his thought
And the subtile body (*liṅga*), too, without support.
(Tr. R.E. Hume)

The sage (who is really a perfect *yogin*) bears no manifest mark (in his person) and also does not have some unmanifest import of his own. He behaves like an insane or a child, though a poet he remains dumb and thus he shows himself to people (*avyaktaliṅga*.... Nāradaparivrājakopaniṣad V.23).

The stanza mentioning presumably the ithyphallic aspect of Rudra-Śiva occurs for the first time in the **Mahānārāyaṇa Upaniṣad** (XII.1) which sometimes is given the status of an apocryphal section of the **Taittirīya Āraṇyaka** itself. This expression appears to afford indeed a parallel to the address Ūrdhvaliṅga for Rudra.

ऋतं सत्यं परं ब्रह्म पुरुषं कृष्णपिङ्गलम् ।
ऊर्ध्वरेतं विरूपाक्षं विश्वरूपाय वै नमः ॥

MNUp XII.1

Homage to Him, as cosmic order, truth, Supreme Brahman, dark brown Puruṣa, ithyphallic, having odd eyes and various forms.

Liṅga-worship was prevalent but worship of defective image was inauspicious as recorded in the **Atharvaveda Pariśiṣṭa**:

विहसन्ति निमीलन्ति लिङ्गानि विकृतानि च ॥
मासान्तरेण जानीयात् तत्र तत्र महद्भयम् ।

AVPari 70kha.7.19cd–20ab

Wherever damaged or broken *liṅgas* (images of deities) laugh and wink, it should be known that there will arise great terror within a month. (Tr. R.S. Bhattacharya)

Yāska has used the term *liṅga* in the sense of characteristic mark of deities.

इन्द्रं न त्वा शवसा देवता वायुं पृणन्ति (ṚV VI.4.7) इति । वायुलिङ्गं चेन्द्रलिङ्गं चाग्नेये मन्त्रे ।

Nir I.17

Like Indra, like Vāyu, the gods fill thee with strength (ṚV VI.4.7). Here is the characteristic mark of Indra and Vāyu in a stanza addressed to Agni (cf. BṛDev I.87). (Tr. L. Sarup)

As one finds it stated in the **Bṛhaddevatā**:

त्रीण्येव लोके लिङ्गानि पुमान् स्त्री च नपुंसकम् ।

BṛDev II.96ab

There are just the three genders in popular usage (*loke*) – masculine, feminine and neuter. (Tr. A.A. Macdonell)

Of those root-verbs (*dhātu*) which possess traditionally fixed usage, the sense as intended is known through them and from their secondary (grammatical) analysis.

यावतामेव धातूनां लिङ्गं रूढिगतं भवेत् ।
अर्थश्चाप्यभिधेयः स्यात् तावद्भिर्गुणविग्रहः ॥

BṛDev II.102

The analysis of the secondary elements (*guṇa*) may be (effected) by the aid of all roots (*dhātu*) which possess a traditional characteristic form (*liṅga*), and the sense of which can be stated. (Tr. A.A. Macdonell)

In the context of explaining the deities of the Nivids and of the Nigada *mantras* Śaunaka has stressed on the *liṅgas*, i.e. characteristic names (cf. BṛDev VIII.104; V.93; VII.108; IV.129, VII.65, etc.).

For the purpose of stating grammatical aphorisms in language the letters of the alphabet were given a workable gender-definition by the older worthies:

स्वरा विसर्जनीयाश्च यमाः पुँल्लिङ्गकाः स्मृताः ॥
प्रथमाश्च तथाऽन्तस्थाः स्त्रीलिङ्गाः परिकीर्तिताः ।
शेषाक्षराणि षण्ढानि प्राहुर्लिङ्गविवेचकाः ॥

YājŚik (sec. on varṇa) 6cd–7

The vowels, *visarga* and the *yamas* are masculine; the first letter of each of the five mutes, and the semi-vowels are feminine; the rest of the letters are neuter. This has been stated by those who know the nature of gender. (Tr. R.S. Bhattacharya)

Liṅga also connotes a determining factor as recorded in the **Kātyāyana Śrauta-Sūtra** (I.8.36): *ghṛtam ājye liṅgāt.* The expression '*ājya*' stands for ghee in general, since there are statements in the Śruti to identify this.

Further in the context of rendering remuneration in the Rājasūya the same text states in the absence of any specification (*liṅga*) a bull is to be understood as prescribed fees (*aliṅgagrahaṇe gauḥ sarvatra* – KātŚrSū XV.2.10).

A hymn or *mantra* belonging to a deity or personified entity is indicated by the expression using the phrase *liṅga*, i.e. token mark, through a compound defined with that name:

शय्यादेशे कामलिङ्गेन ॥
देहल्यामन्तरिक्षलिङ्गेन ॥

ĀpDhSū II.4.1–2

Near the bed (a *bali* must be offered) with a (*mantra*) addressed to Kāmadeva (Cupid). On the door-sill (a *bali* must be placed) with (a *mantra*) addressed to *antarikṣa* (the air).
(Tr. R.S. Bhattacharya)

In several other contexts implying the variant meanings of the word, such usages are quite commonly found throughout Indian literature:

सन्देहे लिङ्गतो दैवेनेति विचित्य ॥

ĀpDhSū II.29.6

In doubtful cases (they shall give their decision) after having ascertained (the truth) by inference, ordeals and the like (means).
(Tr. G. Bühler)

An extensive treatment of the subject of genders in grammatical works is noted which have by necessity the same, properly analysed and defined as to their far-reaching principles and assertions. For example:

परवल्लिङ्गं द्वंद्वतत्पुरुषयोः ॥

Pā II.4.26

The gender of a *dvandva* or *tatpuruṣa* compound is that of the final member (*paravalliṅgam*). (Tr. S.M. Katre)

The **Mahābhāṣya** has also discussed on *liṅga* from two aspects – worldly gender (*laukika*) and wordly gender (*śābdika*). The first one is defined as follows:

संस्त्यानप्रसवौ लिङ्गम् ।

Mahābh I.2.64

To become condensed or compact and giving birth are to be known as gender (feminine and masculine respectively).
(Tr. R.S. Bhattacharya)

स्तनकेशवती स्त्री स्याल्लोमशः पुरुषः स्मृतः ।
उभयोरन्तरं यच्च तदभावे नपुंसकम् ॥

Mahābh IV.1.3 (p. 196)

Woman is one who possesses breasts and long hair, while male is one whose body is full of hair. The one that is different from the both and the person who does not possess these elements is neuter. (Tr. H. N. Chakravarty)

In case of doubt about the attributes of a word Patañjali suggests to treat the same as neuter gender (Mahābh I.2.69). Therefore the grammarians have not accepted worldly gender, i.e. male, female and eunuch to be applicable to words. They require a separate suitable principle (Mahābh I.2.64). The same text also focuses on the gender of the words related with *jāti* (genus). Generic words have their definite genders and these words do not leave their genders till end (Mahābh I.2.52). But synonyms of a word may be of different genders.

In ancient times various marks (*liṅga*), viz. *aṅkuśa, svastika*, etc. were used in branding cows.

अवयवे कृतं लिङ्गं समुदायस्य विशेषकं भवति । तद्यथा - गोः सक्थिनि कर्णे वा कृतं लिङ्गं समुदायस्य विशेषकं भवति ।

Mahābh I.3.62

A characteristic sign marked on a component part qualifies the whole. As for example, a mark put on the thigh or the ear of a cow qualifies the cow (i.e. cow is said too possess that mark).

On the grammatical concept of the gender definition in language, Bhartṛhari has to specifically remark:

ते लिङ्गैश्च स्वशब्दैश्च शास्त्रेऽस्मिन्नुपवर्णिताः ।
स्मृत्यर्थमनुगम्यन्ते केचिदेव यथागमम् ॥

Vāk I.26

These have been described in this *śāstra* through indications and direct statements. These are only some which have been dealt with here according to tradition, in order that they may be fixed in memory. (Tr. K.A.S. Iyer)

For the clarity of meaning Bhartṛhari (Vāk II.73) also refers to *liṅga* as one of the six *pramāṇas* as laid down by Jaimini in his **Mīmāṃsā-Sūtra**.

The true essence concerning genders of words has been explained in the **Vākyapadīya** (*liṅga-samuddeśa*) by showing seven views (*liṅgānāṃ liṅgatattvajñair* *vikalpāḥ sapta darśitāḥ* – Vāk III.13.2cd): (1) that it is the relation of a thing with sex signs such as breast and hair, (2) that it is the sex-signs themselves characterised by the relation, (3) that it is the universal manifested by the sex-signs, (4) that it is the three conditions of the three *guṇa*s (*sattva, rajas* and *tamas*), (5) that it is the three *guṇa*s themselves in these conditions, (6) that it is an attribute created in objects by words, and (7) that it is an attribute of the words themselves.

Seven different ways in which gender is conveyed by words have been described and they are associated with words as alternatives or as restrictions. According to some, these are three universals, co-existing in things, without contradiction, with the universals cow-ness, buffalo-ness, etc. which are exclusive of one another. Just as a cognition in which water figures takes place in mirages even though there is no water there, through the former impression which is favourable to the perception of water. In the same way, distinctions of gender (*liṅga*) are understood from the words *tāraka* etc. even though the things which they denote have no distinctions of sex as from words denoting things having distinctions of sex. Manifestation, disappearance and continuity are eternal properties found in all things and they are what is called gender. Of the qualities *śabda* etc. which constitute the essence of everything, in each one are found the qualities, *sattva,* etc. (cf. Vāk III.13.1–4, 8–9, 13–14, tr. K.A.S. Iyer).

Some words in the language were said to be fixed in various contextual usages to be of a constant nature in reference particularly of their neuter gender. As stated by Helārāja:

> समप्रविभागेऽर्धशब्दो नपुंसकलिङ्गः पिप्पल्या अर्धमर्धपिप्पलीति । एकदेशमात्रे तु पुंल्लिङ्गः । सारशब्दो न्यायादनपेते नपुंसकलिङ्गः, नैतत् सारमिति । उत्कर्षे पुंलिङ्गः, चन्दनसारः खदिरसारः ।
>
> Comm. on Vāk III.13.22
>
> The term *ardha* when separated equally (from the whole) is neuter for example 'half of the fruit of the fig tree', while it denotes a part of it, is masculine. The term *sāra*, while anything is obtained improperly, it is neuter, namely, it is not proper, while it denotes excellence, it is masculine, for example this is the core of the sandal tree, and it is the core of the *khadira* tree. (Tr. H.N. Chakravarty)

In grammar as well as lexical references the form used essentially indicates the gender of a word:

> लिङ्गं तु नामपदानामधिकं वाच्यम् ।
>
> Helā comm. on Vāk III 13 (Intro.)

Gender is an additional notion expressed by nouns.
(Tr. K.A.S. Iyer)

As it is further remarked by Bhartṛhari:

स्थितेषु सर्वलिङ्गेषु विवक्षानियमाश्रयः ।
कस्यचिच्छब्दसंस्कारे व्यापारः क्वचिदिष्यते ॥

Vāk III.13.19

While all the genders are present everywhere only one of them is applied, in any particular case, for the correct formation of the word. (Tr. K.A.S. Iyer)

For characteristic tokens revealing the identity of a divine person, the word *liṅga* is used by Vālmīki:

देवलिङ्गानि दृष्टानि रामलक्ष्मणसंनिधौ ।
तानि दर्शय देवेन्द्र यदि त्वं देवराट् स्वयम् ॥
सीताया वचनं श्रुत्वा तथा चक्रे शचीपतिः ।
पृथिवीं नास्पृशत् पद्भ्यामनिमेषेक्षणानि च ॥
अरजोऽम्बरधारी च न म्लानकुसुमस्तथा ।
तं ज्ञात्वा लक्षणैः सीता वासवं परिहर्षिता ॥

Rām Interpolated canto (after III.56) 17–19

The distinguishing marks of gods have been seen by me in the presence of Rāma and Lakṣmaṇa. (Kindly) reveal them (to me), O ruler of gods, if you are Indra (the king of gods) himself. Hearing the request of Sītā, Indra (the spouse of Śachī) did the same. He did not touch the ground with his feet and his eyes did not wink. His clothes were free from dust and the flowers of his garland did not fade (even after his very long journey). Sītā greatly rejoiced to recognise him by his distinguishing marks to be (no other than) Indra. (Tr. Gita Press edn)

A list of characteristic tokens endowing the worthy persons are thus given by Vālmīki:

यानि रामस्य चिह्नानि लक्ष्मणस्य च यानि वै ।
लक्षितानि विशालाक्षि वदतः शृणु तानि मे ॥
विपुलांसो महाबाहुः कम्बुग्रीवः शुभाननः ।
गूढजत्रुः सुताम्राक्षो रामो नाम जनैः श्रुतः ॥
दुन्दुभिस्वननिर्घोषः स्निग्धवर्णः प्रतापवान् ।

समश्च सुविभक्ताङ्गो वर्णं श्यामं समाश्रितः ॥
त्रिस्थिरस्त्रिप्रलम्बश्च त्रिसमस्त्रिषु चोन्नतः ।
त्रिताम्रस्त्रिषु च स्निग्धो गम्भीरस्त्रिषु नित्यशः ॥
त्रिवलीमांस्त्र्यवनतश्चतुर्व्यङ्गस्त्रिशीर्षवान् ।
चतुष्कलश्चतुर्लेखश्चतुष्किष्कुश्चतुःसमः ॥
चतुर्दशसमद्वन्द्वश्चतुर्दंष्ट्रश्चतुर्गतिः ।
महोष्ठहनुनासश्च पञ्चस्निग्धोऽष्टवंशवान् ॥
दशपद्मो दशबृहत्त्रिभिर्व्याप्तो द्विशुक्लवान् ।
षडुन्नतो नवतनुस्त्रिभिर्व्याप्नोति राघवः ॥

Rām V.35.7, 15–20

Hear from me (even), as I speak, O large eyed lady of those (distinctive) marks which have been actually noticed by me on the person of Rāma as well as on that of Lakṣmaṇa. He has broad shoulders, mighty arms, a conch-shaped neck, a charming countenance and coppery eyes; he has his clavicle concealed (behind muscles) and is known by the people by the name of Rāma. He has a voice (deep) like the sound of a kettledrum and a glossy skin, is full of glory, square-built and of well-proportioned limbs and is endowed with a dark, brown complexion. He is ever stiff in three limbs (viz. the breast, wrist and fist), long in three (viz. the eyebrows, arms and the scrotum), uniform in three (viz. his locks, testicles, and knees), elevated in three (viz. the breast, the rim of the navel and the abdomen), coppery in three (viz. the rims of his eyes, nails and the palms as well as the soles), soft in three (viz. the end of the membrum virile, the lines on his soles and the hair), and deep in three (viz. the voice, gait and the navel). He has three folds (in the skin of his neck and belly) is depressed at three places (viz. the middle of his soles, the lines on his soles, and the nipples), undersized at four places (viz. the neck, membrum virile, the back and the shanks), endowed with three spirals in the hair of his head, four lines at the root of his thumbs (indicating his knowledge of all the four Vedas), and four lines on his forehead (indicating longevity) is four cubit high, and has four pairs of limbs (viz. the cheeks, arms, shanks and knees) equally matched. He has fourteen (other) pairs of limbs (viz. the eyebrows, nostrils, eyes, ears, the lips, nipples, elbows, wrists, the knees, the testicles, the loins, the hands, the feet and the thighs) equally matched. The four large teeth at both the ends of his upper and the lower jaws are very sharp. He walks in four (different) gaits (resembling those of a lion, a tiger, an elephant and a bull), is endowed with excellent lips, chin and nose, five glossy limbs (viz. the hair, eyes, teeth, skin and soles) and eight long limbs (viz. the arms, the fingers and the toes, the eyes and the ears, the nose, the backbone and the body). Rāma (a scion of Raghu) has ten lotus-like limbs (viz. the countenance, the mouth, the eyes, the tongue, lips, palate, breasts, nails, the hands and the feet), ten ample limbs (viz. the chest, the head, the forehead, the neck, the arms, the shoulders, the navel, the feet, the back and the ears), is spread through by reason of three (viz. splendour, renown and glory), has two white limbs (viz. the teeth and the eyes), is elevated in six limbs (viz. the flanks, the abdomen, the breast, the nose, the shoulders and the forehead), small, thin, fine or sharp in nine (viz. the hair, the moustaches and the beard, nails, the hair in the body the skin, the finger-joints, the membrum virile, acumen and perception), and pursues religious merit, worldly riches and sensual delight in three periods (viz. the forenoon, midday and afternoon). (Tr. Gita Press edn).

Lamenting on the death of Bālī, Sugrīva is found referring to the ill signs presaging prognostically one's fateful end:

अहं त्ववगतो बुद्ध्या चिह्नैस्तैर्भ्रातरं हतम् ।

Rām IV.9.19ab

By recourse to reason on the strength of the aforesaid indications I, for my part concluded my (elder) brother to have been killed. (Tr. Gita Press edn)

The term *liṅga* connotes a similar implication elsewhere in the text:

त्वं नराधिपतेः पुत्रः प्रतीतः प्रियदर्शनः ।
लिङ्गमप्यस्ति ते राजन् दृश्यते धर्मसंहितम् ॥
कः क्षत्रियकुले जातः श्रुतवान् नष्टसंशयः ।
धर्मलिङ्गप्रतिच्छन्नः क्रूरं कर्म समाचरेत् ॥

Rām IV.17.26–27

You are a sovereign's son, (hence) worthy of trust and pleasing of aspect (too). Emblems (too such as matted hair and the bark of trees for clothing) conformable to righteousness exist and are seen on your person, O prince. Who, born in the Kṣatriya race and possessed of sacred knowledge, whose doubts (regarding right and wrong) have been resolved (through such knowledge) and who is furnished with emblems of piety, will perpetrate a cruel deed (like the one perpetrated by you)? (Tr. Gita Press edn)

The inner soul is styled as *liṅgin* (i.e. possessing the *liṅga*s or all outer and subtle attributes):

> उपविष्टस्य वा सम्यग् लिङ्गिनं साधयिष्यतः ।
> शरीरं भक्षयिष्यन्ति वायसाः श्वापदानि च ॥
>
> Rām V.13.42
>
> Or crows and beasts of prey will eat up my body when I have sat down for fasting till death and am engaged in my attempt to extricate the soul (encased in the subtle body, which constitutes the *liṅga* or invariable concomitant of an embodied soul)from the body. (Tr. Gita Press edn)

A popular rule designating a country or a spot from its features is thus remarked in the **Mahābhārata**:

> येन लिङ्गेन यो देशो युक्तः समुपलक्ष्यते ।
> तेनैव नाम्ना तं देशं वाच्यमाहुर्मनीषिणः ॥
>
> MBh I.2.12
>
> The wise have declared that every country should be distinguished by a name significant of some circumstance which may have rendered it famous. (Tr. P.C. Roy)

In the sense of adoration for Śiva the word *liṅga* had well acquired currency for a divine statue or worshipful symbol.

> ताभ्यां लिङ्गेऽर्चितो देवस्त्वयार्चायां युगे युगे ॥
> सर्वरूपं भवं ज्ञात्वा लिङ्गे योऽर्चयति प्रभुम् ।
> आत्मयोगाश्च तस्मिन्वै शास्त्रयोगाश्च शाश्वताः ॥
>
> MBh VII.172.86cd–87
>
> By both of them (viz. Arjuna and Kṛṣṇa) as well as you the god in his phallic form had been adored aeon after aeon. In him, who worships in the Liṅga the Lord Bhava as knowing Him to be the all-form, the spiritual *yogas* and the *yogas* of knowledge (*śāstra*) come eternally to stay.

A clear-cut evidence for the prevalence of a *liṅga* symbol of Rudra-Śiva also appears in the Droṇa Parva in connection with the story of Upamanyu.

> सर्वभूतभवं ज्ञात्वा लिङ्गेऽर्चयति यः प्रभुम् ।
> तस्मिन्नभ्यधिकां प्रीतिं करोति वृषभध्वजः ॥
>
> MBh VII.172.90

Knowing the phallic form of Śiva to be the origin of all forms, who adores him, the god having the bull for his emblem (Śiva) entertains great respect for him. (Tr. M.N. Dutt)

शूलिने त्रिदशेशाय त्र्यम्बकाय महात्मने ।
भस्मदिग्धोर्ध्वलिङ्गाय तस्मै रुद्रात्मने नमः ॥

MBh XII.47.52

(Bhīṣma praises Lord Kṛṣṇa) 'Thou bearest the trident, thou art the lord of the celestials, thou hast three eyes and thou art high-souled. Thy body is always besmeared with ashes and thy phallic emblem is always turned upwards. Salutations to thee in thy form of Rudra. (Tr. P.C. Roy)

Regarding the source of knowledge of the Self it is said:

यदिदं ब्रह्मणो लिङ्गं क्षेत्रज्ञमिति संज्ञितम् ।
ग्रहीतुं येन तच्छक्यं लक्षणं तस्य तत् क्व नु ॥
अलिङ्गो निर्गुणश्चैव कारणं नास्य विद्यते ।
उपायमेव वक्ष्यामि येन गृह्येत वा न वा ॥

MBh XIV.34.4–5

About the symbol of Brahman, which is designated Kṣetrajña, where indeed, is its description by which it is possible to comprehend it?

He is without symbols and without qualities. Nothing exists that may be considered as his cause. I shall, however, tell you the means by which he can be apprehended or not. (Tr. M.N. Dutt)

It has been a perplexed problem to conceive the attributeless Absolute Person, preached in metaphysical ramblings; thus the **Bhagavad-Gītā** poses this eternal mystery in the following manner:

कैर्लिङ्गैस्त्रीन्गुणानेतानतीतो भवति प्रभो ।
किमाचारः कथं चैतांस्त्रीन् गुणानतिवर्तते ॥

BhG XIV.21

(Arjuna said:) What signs, Lord, mark him out, – (this man) who has transcended these three constituents? How does he behave? And how does he step out beyond these three constituents? (Tr. R.C. Zaehner)

The term *liṅga* has been widely discussed in the Purāṇas denoting the senses of sign, mark, symbol, emblem of Lord Śiva, etc.

न लिङ्गं धर्मकारणम् ॥

AgPur CLXI.11d

No (outward sectarian) sign is the cause of religious virtue.

That great God ((Maheśvara) himself created the names and forms of the *bhūtas* (living beings).

यावन्ति प्रतिलिङ्गानि नानारूपाणि पर्यये ॥
दृश्यन्ते तानि तान्येव तथा भावा युगादिषु ॥

KūrPur I.7.69cd–70

Whatever forms and functions are seen in the beginning of the *yugas* are definitely the same as are seen in the various cycles of ages. (Tr. G.V. Tagare)

In the sense of subtle seeds of universal manifestation the **Devī Bhāgavata Purāṇa** employs the word *liṅga* as follows:

एषा संहृत्य सकलं विश्वं क्रीडति संक्षये ।
लिङ्गानि सर्वजीवानां स्वशरीरे निवेश्य च ॥

DBhāgPur III.3.54

At dissolution, She (alone) sports as having destroyed the entire universe though withdrawing subtle elements (*liṅga*) of all living beings into Her own body.

ज्ञानेन्द्रियाणि पञ्चैव पञ्च कर्मेन्द्रियाणि च ।
प्राणादिपञ्चकं चैव धिया च सहितं मनः ॥
एतत् सूक्ष्मशरीरं स्यान्मम लिङ्गं यदुच्यते ।

DBhāgPur VII.32.41–42ab

My subtle body (*liṅga deha*) arises from the union of the five *jñānendriyas*, the five *karmendriyas* (organs of action), the five *prāṇas* and the mind and intellect, these seventeen elements.
(Tr. Vijnanananda)

In a fresh exegetical exposition of the Yoga and Tantra concept of human body with its scheme of spheres (*cakra*), the **Devī Bhāgavata Purāṇa** observes:

स्वशब्देन परं लिङ्गं स्वाधिष्ठानं ततो विदुः ॥

DBhāgPur VII.35.36cd

The word *sva* indicates the highest 'symbol' (*paraṃ liṅgam*), so they know this as *svādhiṣṭhāna* plexus.

This indeed, leads to specify *svādhiṣṭhāna* as the individual centre of Subtle Person's stay in his mystic body.

Liṅga or sign occurs yet in further implication of a sectarian marking:

श्रौतधर्मैकनिष्ठानां लिङ्गं तु श्रौतमेव हि ॥
अश्रौतधर्मनिष्ठानामश्रौतं लिङ्गमीरितम् ।
देवता वेदसिद्धा यास्तासां लिङ्गं तु वैदिकम् ॥
वेदसिद्धो महादेवः साक्षात् संसारमोचकः ॥
भक्तानामुपकाराय श्रौतं लिंगं दधाति च ।

DBhāgPur XI.15.112cd–113, 114cd–115ab

Only the *tilakas* (mark on the forehead) prescribed in the Vedas ought to be used by those who are devoted to the Vedas. Those who do not observe the duties of the Vedas would use *tilakas* approved by other Śāstras. Those should use marks approved by the Vedas whose Deity as that of the Vedas. For bestowing the grace upon his devotees He assumes the *liṅga* or sign as per Śrauta convention. (Based on the tr. by Vijnanananda)

As also elsewhere in the sense of external signs:

लिङ्गधारणमेवाश्रमहेतुः ।

ViPur IV.24.82

(In the Kali age) external types (as the staff and the red garb) will be the only distinctions of the several orders of life.
(Tr. H.H. Wilson)

आश्रमो वैष्णवो ब्राह्मो हराश्रम इति त्रयः ।
तल्लिंगधारी नियतं तद्भक्तजंनवत्सलः ॥
ध्यायेदथार्चयेदेतान् ब्रह्मविद्यापरायणः ।
सर्वेषामेव भक्तानां शम्भोर्लिङ्गमनुत्तमम् ॥

KūrPur I.2.101–102

There are three religious followings (*āśramas*), i.e. the Vaiṣṇava, Brāhma and the Śaiva who wear the tokens of a particular section invariably endearing oneself to the votaries of that. One who is devoted to the *brahmavidyā* or the knowledge of the Supreme Self should discern and venerate them. The excellent *liṅga* of Śambhu is worthy of all devotees.

As it imbibes the parts of all the three gods: Śiva part (top) Viṣṇu part (middle) and Brahmā (base).

Figure 19: *Tripuṇḍraka*

Those who resort to the Parameṣṭhin Brahmā, the seed of all worlds, should always bear the *tilaka* (seasame-seed like) mark on the forehead (KūrPur V.104–5).

> सितेन भस्मना कार्यं ललाटे तु त्रिपुंड्रकम् ।
> यस्तु नारायणं देवं प्रपन्नः परमं पदम् ॥
> धारयेत्सर्वदा शूलं ललाटे गन्धवारिभिः ।
>
> KūrPur I.2.103–104ab
>
> Thus the *tripuṇḍraka* (consisting of three horizontal parallel lines) is to be done by white ashes (for Śiva). One who resorts to the god Nārāyaṇa as the supreme station should always bear the mark of three vertical strokes (*śūla*-like mark) made by scented water.

According to the story narrated in the **Bhāgavata Purāṇa** (IV.19) once Indra felt jealous with Pṛthu's prosperity. With a desire to cause harm to the king, Indra determined to spoil his sacrifice and accordingly stole away the sacrificial horse. The ever-alert guards chased the thief; when he was about to be caught he assumed, various disguise to protect himself. Whatever disguise he assumed were mere aspects of his evil nature, which have been termed as *liṅga* in the **Bhāgavata Purāṇa** (*tāni pāpasya khaṇḍāni liṅgaṃ khaṇḍamihocyate* – IV.19.23cd).

In the **Agni Purāṇa** (XLVI.5) the symbolic design for the Śālagrāma for the Varāha incarnation is said to consist two unequal circles revealing as it were the shape of a *śakti* (head). *Śakti* is a variety of lance with its specific top, somewhat like a betel-leaf.

लिङ्गमूर्तिं शिवं स्तुत्वा गायत्र्या योगमास्तवान् ।
निर्वाणं परमं ब्रह्म वशिष्ठोऽन्यश्च शंकरात् ॥

AgPur CCXVII.1

He further reached the state of emancipation in Supreme Brahman from (the grace of) Śaṅkara.

For Śiva and his symbol, the word occurs in a metaphysical context:

शिव एव स्वयं लिङ्गं लिङ्गं गमकमेव हि ।
शिवेन गम्यते सर्वं शिवो नान्येन गम्यते ॥

Sūta Saṃhitā, yajña-vaibhavakāṇḍa XXXVIII.2

Śiva Himself is the *liṅga*, *Liṅga* decidedly is the indicator. Everything is caused to be known by Śiva but as He is self-luminous it does not need anything to be known by any other agent.
(Tr. H.N. Chakravarty)

लिङ्गे प्रतिष्ठितः शंभुर्भुक्तिमुक्तिप्रदायकः ॥
लिङ्गवेदिर्महादेवी लिङ्गं साक्षान्महेश्वरः ।
लयनाल्लिङ्गमित्युक्तं तत्रैव निखिलं जगत् ॥

ŚPur II.1.10.37cd–38

Śiva installed in the *liṅga* bestows (both) worldly weal as well as final emancipation. The great goddess serves as the pedestal of the *liṅga*. The *liṅga* is the Lord Śiva Himself. For everything finally merges into which the same is called the *liṅga*.

The devotees of Śiva are said to carry a *liṅga*-symbol on their head as a mark of intense dedication:

मूर्द्धन्याधाय तल्लिङ्गं शाम्भवं रागवर्जितः ।
निर्गत्य तु पुरात्तस्मात्तुष्टाव परमेश्वरम् ॥
संस्तुतो भगवानीशः शङ्करो नीललोहितः ।
गाणपत्येन बाणं तं योजयामास भावतः ॥

KūrPur I.18.6–7

Bearing that Liṅga of Śambhu over his head, he came out of the city and devoid of passion eulogised the Supreme ruler.

Lord Īśa, Śaṅkara, Nīlalohita, on being eulogised, (and propitiated) lovingly engaged Bāṇa in the chieftancy of the Gaṇas.
(Tr. G.V. Tagare)

सेतुमध्ये महादेवमीशानं कृत्तिवाससम् ॥
स्थापयामास लिङ्गस्थं पूजयामास राघवः ।

KūrPur I.21.46cd–47ab

In the middle of the bridge, Rāma, the descendant of Raghu, installed the *liṅga* of Mahādeva, Īśāna the elephant-hide-robed-god and worshipped him. (Tr. G.V. Tagare)

The mythical saga of *liṅgodbhava*, "emanation of the Arch-liṅga", is often detailed in the Puranic and Agamic works:

स्तूयमानः सुरैर्विष्णुः स्तौति देवं महेश्वरम् ॥
लिङ्गोद्भवकथा पुण्या सर्वपापप्रणाशिनी ।

VPur I.1.96cd–97ab

(Wherein) the Great Lord Śiva is eulogised by Viṣṇu who himself is lauded by the gods. That narrative of the '*liṅga*-origin' is holy as well as sin-destroyer.

छद्मना चरितं यच्च व्रतं रक्षांसि गच्छति ॥
अलिङ्गी लिङ्गिवेशेन यो वृत्तिमुपजीवति ।
स लिङ्गिनां हरेदेनस्तिर्यग्योनौ च जायते ॥
वैडालव्रतिनः पापा लोके धर्मविनाशकाः ।

KūrPur II.16.12cd–14ab

A vow practised in deceptive manner goes to the demons. One, who has not been initiated in a specific conduct, if plies such conduct by shamely assuming the outer marks (belonging to it), receives the sins committed by those sectarians and would be born as an animal. The sinful persons who lead a life like a hypocrite destroy the pious virtue in the world.

On the symbolical significance of *liṅga* and *liṅgin* (the Lord of *liṅga*), the **Kūrma Purāṇa** thus observes:

अव्यक्तं लिङ्गमित्याहुरानन्दं ज्योतिरक्षयम् ।
वेदा महेश्वरं देवमाहुर्लिङ्गिनमव्ययम् ॥

KūrPur I.26.63

The Unmanifest is called Liṅga, which is beatitude and unfading light. The Vedas speak of the god undecaying Maheśvara as possessing that *liṅga* (*liṅgin*).

सर्वं लिङ्गमयं ह्येतत्सर्वं लिङ्गे प्रतिष्ठितम् ॥

तस्माल्लिङ्गेऽर्च्चयेदीशं यत्र क्वचन शाश्वतम् ।
अग्नौ क्रियावतामप्सु व्योम्नि सूर्ये मनीषिणाम् ॥
काष्ठादिष्वेव मूर्खाणां हृदि लिङ्गं तु योगिनाम् ।

KūrPur II.11.97cd–99ab

This entire (creation) is permeated by the Liṅga. All is established in the Liṅga. Therefore, the eternal Lord Īśa should be worshipped in a *liṅga*-symbol. This symbolical *liṅga* is (seen) in fire and water by the ritualists; for the high-souled it is in the sky or the sun; to the ignorant it is only in (images of) wood and other materials. For the *yogins* the same is in their own heart.

यल्लिङ्गांकं त्र्यम्बकः सर्वमीशो
भगलिङ्गांकं यद्धयुमा सर्वधात्री ।
नान्यत् तृतीयं जगतीहास्ति किञ्चित्
महादेवात् सर्वसर्वेश्वरोऽसौ ॥

HarPur II.72.60

He who has the symbol of *liṅga* is Īśa the Lord of all. She who has the symbol of female member is Umā, bearing all. There is no third entity in this world other than the Great God. He is the Lord of all.

Speaking of the Śivaliṅga and its symbolical components, the **Liṅga Purāṇa** has thus enjoined:

मूले ब्रह्मा तथा मध्ये विष्णुस्त्रिभुवनेश्वरः ॥
रुद्रोपरि महादेवः प्रणवाख्यः सदाशिवः ।
लिङ्गवेदी महादेवी त्रिगुणा त्रिमयाम्बिका ॥
तया च पूजयेद्यस्तु देवी देवश्च पूजितौ ।

LPur I.74.19cd–21ab

At the root (of the Śivaliṅga) presides Brahmā, and over the middle part, Viṣṇu, the Lord of Universe. On the Rudra or top portion (resides) Mahādeva himself, who is called Praṇava (i.e. Oṃkāra) and Sadāśiva. The pedestal of *liṅga* is the Great Goddess Ambikā herself, being threefold and comprising the three qualities (i.e. *sattva, rajas* and *tamas*). He who worships (the *liṅga*) along with it (the pedestal), in fact worships the God and the Goddess together.

विशोध्य स्थापयेद्भक्त्या सवेदिकमनुत्तमम् ।

लिङ्गवेदी उमादेवी लिङ्गं साक्षान्महेश्वर ॥

LPur II.47.8

With devotion one should set up the all-excelling (*liṅga*) together with the foundation piece (*vedi*). This pedestal of the *liṅga* is the goddess Umā herself and the *liṅga* is the great Lord Śiva in manifest form.

One further finds in the **Viṣṇudharmottara Purāṇa** the following constituent features of the *liṅga* representation:

लिङ्गे हि पूजिते पूजा कृता तु जगतो भवेत् ।
भोगोऽस्य वृत्तः कर्तव्यो भागमष्टास्त्रमेव तु ॥
चतुरस्त्रं तथा भागं कर्तव्यं भूरिदक्षिणम् ।
वृत्तं दृश्यन्तु कर्तव्यमष्टास्त्रं पिण्डिकागतम् ॥
चतुरस्त्रं तु कर्तव्यं ब्रह्मपीठगतं तथा ।
अधस्ताद् भद्रपीठस्य ब्रह्मपीठं विदुर्बुधाः ॥
लिङ्गोपरिष्टात्तु गता पुरस्ताल्लेखा सुवृत्ता तु तथैव कार्या ।
ऊर्ध्वायता च द्विगुणा तथान्या या ब्रह्मसूत्रे विबुधैः प्रदिष्टा ॥

VDhPur III.74.2–5

On the *liṅga* being worshipped the worship of the whole world is brought about. Its 'hood' (top) part is to be made circular, the (next) portion is an octagon. (Then) there is the square part. The circular one is made as visible receiving ample offerings. The octagonal one is inside the *pīṭhikā* (base portion). The square portion is to be made inserted in the *brahma-pīṭha* (=*brahma-śilā* = slab). Underneath the auspicious base portion (of the *liṅga* itself) the learned know this *brahmapīṭha* (-*śilā*) as the set up.

On the uppermost (circular) part, on the front of *liṅga*, a circular mark in line is shown, and likewise another double upright line is carved, which the conversant propound on the *brahmasūtra* (=plumb-line or fulcrum).

The great physician Caraka defines *liṅga* as: *prādurbhūta lakṣaṇaṃ punarliṅgam* (CarSam NiSthā I.9), i.e. '*liṅga* consists of the manifested signs and symptoms of disease.' The same text enumerates six synonyms of *liṅga* – *ākṛti, lakṣaṇa, cihna, saṃsthāna, vyañjana* and *rūpa* (also cf. AṣṭH NiSthā I.5).

The necessity of the study of symptoms has also been expressed by Caraka:

हेतुलिङ्गौषधज्ञानं स्वस्थातुरपरायणम् ।

CarSam SūSthā I.24ab

Āyurveda providing knowledge of aetiology, symptomatology and therapeutics, best way for both the healthy and the sick.
(Tr. P.V. Sharma)

Cakrapāṇi Datta comments on the same:

लिङ्गग्रहणेन च व्याधेरारोग्यस्य च कृत्स्नं लिङ्गमुच्यते, तेन व्याध्यारोग्ये अपि लिङ्गशब्दवाच्ये, यतस्ताभ्यामपि हि तल्लिङ्गंमेव वक्ष्यति।

Comm. on CarSam SūSthā I.24

Here the word *liṅga* denotes the entire signs and symptoms of disease and health, thus disease and health also are denoted by the word *liṅga*.

Referring to imbalance or balance of the *tridoṣa*s (i.e. *vāta*, *pitta*, *kapha*) in body, it has been thus observed:

दोषाः प्रवृद्धाः स्वं लिङ्गं दर्शयन्ति यथाबलम् ।
क्षीणा जहति लिङ्गं स्वं, समाः स्वं कर्म कुर्वते ॥

CarSam SūSthā XVII.62

*Doṣa*s, if aggravated, show their symptoms according to the strength; if diminished, give up their normal character and if normal, perform their functions properly. (Tr. P.V. Sharma)

Adapting the concepts and vocabulary of Sāṃkhya philosophy, the **Caraka Saṃhitā** gives the following principles of Ayurvedic metaphysics:

अव्यक्तमात्मा क्षेत्रज्ञः शाश्वतो विभुरव्ययः ।
तस्माद्यदन्यत्तद्व्यक्तं, वक्ष्यते चापरं द्वयम् ॥
व्यक्तमैन्द्रियकं चैव गृह्यते तद्यदिन्द्रियैः ।
अतोऽन्यत् पुनरव्यक्तं लिङ्गग्राह्यमतीन्द्रियम् ॥

CarSam ŚāSthā I.61–62

The self which is the knower of the body, eternal, omnipresent and indestructible is the unmanifest. Contrary to that is the manifest one. Both will be described further. The manifest or *aindriyaka* (pertaining to sense organs) is that which is perceived by the sense organs. Contrary to that is unmanifest which can be known only by certain signs and transcends all senses. (Tr. P.V. Sharma)

As the same scheme of Samkhyan evolution theory regarding the life-entity is elaborated elsewhere in the Ayurvedic context:

समुदयकारणं तु ब्रूमः – अव्यक्तात् महान्, महतोऽहङ्कारः; अहङ्कारात् खादीनि, ता

अष्टौ भूतप्रकृतयः । चक्षुः श्रोत्रं घ्राणं रसनं स्पर्शनमिति पञ्चेन्द्रियाणि, तान्येव बुद्धीन्द्रियाणि; हस्तौ पादौ जिह्वा गुद उपस्थ इति पञ्च कर्मेन्द्रियाणि; शब्दस्पर्शरसरूपगन्धाः पञ्चेन्द्रियार्थाः; अतीन्द्रियं तु मनः; इत्येते षोडश विकाराः महदादि सर्वं क्षेत्रमव्यक्तमाचक्षते, क्षेत्रज्ञं तु शाश्वतमचिन्त्यमात्मानम् । अस्य लिङ्गानि – चेतनाहङ्कारप्राणापानोन्मेषनिमेषसुखदुःखेच्छाद्वेषस्मृतिधृतिबुद्धयः ... ।

KāśSamŚāSthā I.3

Now (I) will tell the process of evolution – from *avyakta* (primordial unmanifest) is *mahat* (intellect), from *mahat* is *ahaṃkāra* (ego), from *ahaṃkāra* is *ākāśa* etc. and from those (*ākāśa* etc.) eight *bhūta prakṛti*s (basic source of physical constitutions), eyes (opthalmic apparatus), ear (auditory apparatus), nose (olfactory apparatus), tongue (gustatory apparatus), and skin (sense of touch) are five *indriyas*, same are organs of perception; hands, feet, tongue, anus and genitals are five *karmendriyas* (organs of action); sound, touch, taste, vision and smell are five objects of *indriyas*; *manas* (mind) is trans-sensuous; there are sixteen *vikāra*s (products). *Mahat* etc. all unmanifest are termed as *kṣetra* (body); the knower of body, eternal and unthinkable is *ātmā* (self). Features (*liṅga*) of self are consciousness, ego, inspiration, expiration, open and closer (twinkling) of eyes, happiness, misery, desire, dislike, memory, power of retention and intellect. (Tr. P.V. Tewari)

The main signs (properties) of a living self are thus enlisted:

इच्छा द्वेषः सुखं दुःखं प्रयत्नश्चेतना धृतिः ।
बुद्धिः स्मृतिरहङ्कारो लिङ्गानि परमात्मनः ॥
यस्मात् समुपलभ्यन्ते लिङ्गान्येतानि जीवतः ।
न मृतस्यात्मलिङ्गानि तस्मादाहुर्महर्षयः ॥

CarSam ŚāSthā I.72–73

Desire, aversion, happiness, misery, will, consciousness, control, knowledge, memory and ego – these are the signs of the self. As these signs are found only in living beings and not in dead ones, the sages have said them as the signs of the self. (Tr. P.V. Sharma)

Features (*liṅgāni*) of properly uncted person are described elsewhere:

धृतिर्मृदुपुरीषत्वं मेधापुष्ट्यग्नितेजसां वृद्धिः ।
काले शरीरवृत्तिः स्निग्धस्य वदन्ति लिङ्गानि ॥

KāśSam SūSthā XXII.34

The features of properly uncted (person) are said to be (increase

in) retention power, softness of stool, increase in intellect, digestive fire and lustre and timely functions of the body.
(Tr. P.V. Tewari)

According to the Lakṣaṇa Śāstra (the science of bodily marks and attributes), as summarised by Varāhamihira, the shape of one's male organ, was believed to give certain results or consequences as follows:

लिङ्गेऽल्पे धनवानपत्यरहितः स्थूलेऽपि हीनो धनै-
र्मेढ्रे वामनते सुतार्थरहितो वक्रेऽन्यथा पुत्रवान् ।
दारिद्र्यं विनते त्वधोऽल्पतनयो लिङ्गे शिरासन्तते
स्थूलग्रन्थियुते सुखी मृदु करोत्यन्तं प्रमेहादिभिः ॥

BṛSam LXVIII.7

A man with a small genital organ becomes rich, but issueless; one with a stout organ, poor; with one bent towards the left, devoid of issue and wealth; with one turned towards the right, blessed with sons; with one bent on the lower side, poor, with one full of veins, father of few children, with one having a thick knot, happy; and with a soft one, dies of gonorrhoea and the like.
(Tr. M.R. Bhat)

Being synonymous of *cihna*, *lakṣaṇa*, etc. the word *liṅga* in the sense of characteristic signs frequently occurs in the Dharmaśāstra literature. Manu has compared *ṛtuliṅga*s with the course of action assigned to *jīva* in their new births.

यथर्तुलिङ्गान्यृतवः स्वयमेवर्तुपर्यये ।
स्वानि स्वान्यभिपद्यन्ते तथा कर्माणि देहिनः ॥

Manu I.30

As at the change of the seasons each season of its own accord assumes its distinctive marks, even so corporeal beings resume in new births) their (appointed) course of action. (Tr.G. Bühler)

Yājñavalkya opines that accompaniment of people is so powerful that it can influence his characteristic features even in the following births and manifests on his person as a consequent result.

ब्रह्महा क्षयरोगी स्यात्सुरापः श्यावदन्तकः ।
हेमहारी तु कुनखी दुश्चर्मा गुरुतल्पगः ॥
यो येन संवसत्येषां स तल्लिङ्गोऽभिजायते ।

YājSm III.5.209–210ab

A murderer of *brāhmaṇa* will become tuberculous, a drunk will have defective teeth, a gold-thief will have diseased nails, the violater of teacher's bed will be leprous and the persons (who are the associates of the said persons) will be born with the characteristics according to their companion. (Tr. P. Ghosal)

The same text also enumerates the characteristic marks of the Highest Lord which are actually the qualities only:

अहंकारः स्मृतिर्मेधा द्वेषो बुद्धिः सुखं धृतिः ।
इन्द्रियान्तरसंचार इच्छा धारणजीविते ॥
स्वर्गः स्वप्रश्च भावानां प्रेरणं मनसो गतिः ।
निमेषश्चेतना यत्न आदानं पाञ्चभौतिकम् ॥
यत एतानि दृश्यन्ते लिङ्गानि परमात्मनः ।
तस्मादस्ति परो देहादात्मा सर्वग ईश्वरः ॥

YājSm III.4.174–176

Egoism, remembrance, talent, jealousy, intellect, happiness, perseverance, capacity of shifting the functions of senses, desire, continuance of life, heavenly bliss, dreaming, to set forth senses (to respective actions), mobility of mind, twinkling of eyes, consciousness, effort, assimilation of (five) gross elements and their seizure – these are the characteristic marks of Great Lord. Hence, above this body existence of All-pervading Highest Lord (Almighty) is proved. (Tr. P. Ghosal)

For the sake of common understanding Supreme Lord has been elucidated as *savikāra* through the aforesaid properties (YājSm III.4.183).

The term *liṅgin* is also used in the same sense of a deceitful person; for example, without being a student who puts on such characteristic marks (*liṅga*) commits offence resulting into birth as animal (*tiryak yoni*):

अलिङ्गी लिङ्गिवेषेण यो वृत्तिमुपजीवति ।
स लिङ्गिनां हरत्येनस्तिर्यग्योनौ च जायते ॥

Manu IV.200

He, who without being a student, gains his livelihood by (wearing) the dress of a student, takes upon himself the guilt of (all) students and is born again in the womb of an animal.
(Tr. G. Bühler)

At the time of investigating criminal cases, the intention of accused are to be determined through the expression of their external signs or gestures:

बाह्यैर्विभावयेल्लिङ्गैर्भावमन्तर्गतं नृणाम् ।
स्वरवर्णेङ्गिताकारैश्चक्षुषा चेष्टितेन च ॥

Manu VIII.25

By external signs let him discover the internal disposition of men, by their voice, their colour, their motions, their aspects, their eyes, and their gestures. (Tr. G. Bühler)

Similarly, the **Kāmandakīya Nīti Sāra** throws light on the employees' expertness to interpret master's mood from his gestures or appearances.

रागापरागौ जानीयाद् भर्तुः कुशलकर्मकृत् ।
इङ्गिताकारलिङ्गाभ्यामिङ्गिताकार तत्त्ववित् ॥

KāNīSā V.34

An intelligent employee, capable of reading the mood of the master (whether pleased or displeased) expressed through gestures, like an expert in interpreting such gestures, appearances and movement of his master. (Tr. S.K. Mitra)

For denotation of a private organ, the term *liṅga* and its allied synonyms are used in the sexual context of criminal offences particularly.

लिङ्गस्य छेदने मृत्यौ मध्यमो मूल्यमेव च ।
महापशूनामेतेषु स्थानेषु द्विगुणो दमः ॥

YājSm II.19.226

If amputation of phallus causes the death of animal then fine should be equal to (that) which is implemented in case of *madhyama sāhasa.* If such brute action is done with big animals (like cow, horse, elephant, etc.) punishment should be double. (Tr. P. Ghosal)

The Śivaliṅgas of different kinds are mentioned with respect to their origin or medium in the **Śukranītisāra**:

बाणलिङ्गे स्वयंभूते चन्द्रकान्तसमुद्भवे ।
रत्नजे गण्डकोद्भूते मानदोषो न सर्वथा ॥
पाषाणधातुजातानां मानदोषो विचिन्तयेत् ।

ŚNSā IV.4.154–155ab

There is, on all counts, no deficiency to be (observed) in case of the Śiva *liṅga*s of the Bāṇa category, of self-born type, carved of the moon-stone, or made of precious stones, or produced in the Gaṇḍakī river.

But in case of those that are made in (ordinary) stones or cast in metals, one should consider if there are any defects of relative proportions (*māna-doṣa*).

According to the Buddhistic usages of the word *liṅga*: *liṅgati saṇṭhānam* (Aṭṭh IV.61, p. 258). The **Abhidharma Kośa Bhāṣya** has designated the characteristic mark as *liṅga* (*liṅgamiti vyañjanasyākhyā* – AbhidhKoBh IV.14).

Further, treating the context of gender, it has been thus observed:

लिङ्गतो नामसंचारात् ... ।

लिङ्गमिति व्यञ्जनस्याख्या येन स्त्रीपुरुषौ लिङ्ग्येते । लिङ्गतो हि भिक्षुभिक्षुण्यादीनां नामसंचारो भवति । (कथं कृत्वा) । परिवृत्ते हि व्यञ्जने भिक्षुर्भिक्षुणीत्युच्यते, भिक्षुणी च पुनर्भिक्षुः ।

AbhidhKoBh IV.14c

The name changes with the gender.

Liṅga is *vyañjana,* that which distinguishes men and women. It is by reason of gender that the names, Bhikṣu, Bhikṣuṇī, etc. differ. When their gender is modified, the Bhikṣu becomes a Bhikṣuṇī and the Bhikṣuṇī, a Bhikṣu. (Tr. L.M. Pruden)

A Puranic definition of the Śivaliṅga principle has been cogently cited by the **Mahāyāna-Sūtra Saṅgraha**, as follows:

आकाशं लिङ्गमित्याहुः पृथिवी तस्य पीठिका ।
आलयः सर्वभूतानां लीलया लिङ्गमुच्यते ॥

MSūSaṅg XVIII.4

The sky is the *liṅga,* as it is said. The earth is its pedestal. Being the residing place of all beings, it is styled as *liṅga* its sportive nature.

The five marks or attributes of a Bodhisattva are thus mentioned:

अनुकम्पा प्रियाख्यानं धीरता मुक्तहस्तता ।
गम्भीरसंधिनिर्मोक्षो लिङ्गान्येतानि धीमताम् ॥

MSūAl XX & XXI.1

Sympathy, sweet speech, intelligence, free hand, profound and serious detachment, not striving for *mokṣa;* these are the marks of a sage. (Tr. S.V. Limaye)

It is further noted, *liṅga vibhāge dvauślokau,* i.e. two *ślokas* on the marks (signs) of a sage.

परिग्रहेऽधिमुक्त्याप्तावखेदे द्वयसंग्रहे ।
आशयाच्च प्रयोगाच्च विज्ञेयं लिङ्गपंचकम् ॥

तत्र प्रथमेन श्लोकेन पंच बोधिसत्वलिङ्गानि दर्शयति । द्वितीयेन तेषां कर्म समास-संग्रहं च । तत्रानुकम्पा बोधिचित्तेन सत्त्वपरिग्रहार्थं प्रियाख्यानं सत्त्वानां बुद्धशासनाधिमुक्तिलाभार्थं धीरता दुष्करचर्यादिभिरखेदार्थं मुक्तहस्तता गम्भीरसंधिनिर्मोक्षणं च। द्वयेन संग्रहार्थमामिषेण धर्मेण च यथाक्रमम् । एषां पंचानां लिङ्गानाम् अनुकम्पा आशयतो वेदितव्या । शेषाणि प्रयोगतः ।

MSūAl XX-XXI.2

Acceptance induced by freedom, being without lassitude, collection of the two, which should be known to be the five marks of intention and its use (employment).

By the first verse are shown the five marks of Bodhisattva; by the second verse their acts and their whole burden in short, are indicated. The sympathy in the *artha* of collection of the beings by the illuminated mind; sweet speech, for those beings who obey the rule of the Buddha doctrine, and obtainment of their illumination; intelligence for being without lassitude for tests, free hand (generous), profound and serious detachment, not striving for *mokṣa*; by the two, for bringing together the beings by attracting and by *dharma* respectively. By these five marks, the sympathy in intention is to be known; the remaining by use. (Tr. S.V. Limaye)

The Pali canon has thus observed on the emergence of duplex nature of creative process (distinctive features of male and female):

(इत्थिपुरिसलिङ्गपातुभावो –)

यथा यथा खो ते, वासेट्ठ, सत्ता अकट्ठपाकं सालिं परिभुञ्जन्ता तम्भक्खा तदाहारा चिरं दीघमद्धानं अट्ठंसु तथा तथा तेसं सत्तानं भिय्योसोमत्ताय खरत्तं चेव कायस्मिं ओक्कमि, वण्णवेवण्णता च पञ्ञायित्थ । इत्थिया च इत्थिलिङ्गं पातुरहोसि पुरिसस्स च पुरिसलिंगं । इत्थी च पुरिसं अतिवेलं उपनिज्झायति पुरिसो च इत्थिं । तेसं अतिवेलं अञ्ञमञ्ञं उपनिज्झायतं सारागो उदपादि, परिळाहो कायस्मिं ओक्कमि । ते परिळाहपच्चया मेथुनं धम्मं पटिसेविंसु ।

ये खो पन ते, वासेट्ठ, तेन समयेन सत्ता पस्सन्ति मेथुनं धम्मं पटिसेवन्ते । अञ्ञे पंसुं खिपन्ति, अञ्ञे सेट्ठिं खिपन्ति, अञ्ञे गोमयं खिपन्ति 'नस्स असुचि, नस्स असुची ति । कथं हि नाम सत्तो सत्तस्स एव रूपं करिस्सती' ति! तदेतरहि पि

मनुस्सा एकच्चेसु जनपदेसु वधुया निब्बुय्हमाना अञ्ञे पंसुं खिपन्ति, अञ्ञे सेट्ठिं खिपन्ति, अञ्ञे गोमयं खिपन्ति, तदेव पोराणं अग्गञ्ञं अक्खरं अनुसरन्ति, न त्वेवस्स अत्थं आजानन्ति ।

DīghNik III.88–89, Aggañña Sutta

O Vāseṭṭha, then those beings feasting on this rice in the clearings, feeding on it, nourished by it, so continued for a long long while. And in measure as they, thus feeding, went on existing, so did the bodies of those beings become even more solid, and the divergence in their comeliness more pronounced. In the female appeared the distinctive features of the female, in the male those of the male. Then truly did woman contemplate man too closely, and man, woman. In them contemplating over much the one the other, passion arose and burning entered their body. They in consequence thereof followed their lusts. And beings seeing them so doing threw some sand, ashes, some cowdung, crying: Perish, foul one! perish, foul one. How can a being treat a being so? Even so now when men, in certain districts, when a bride is led away, throw either sand or ashes or cowdung, they do but follow an ancient enduring primordial form, not recognizing the significance thereof. (Tr. T.W. & C.A.F. Rhys Davids)

An important doctrine of *dvātrimśat-lakṣaṇas*, the thirty-two bodily signs of a Superman (*mahāpuruṣa*) is frequently mentioned in the teachings of the Nikāya literature (DīghNik III.142, Lakkhaṇa Sutta).

In reference to the sex-based genders the term *liṅga* has been significantly employed by Jaina thinkers also:

गतिकषायलिङ्गमिथ्यादर्शनाज्ञानासंयतासिद्धत्व-
लेश्याश्चतुश्चतुस्त्र्येकैकैकैकषड्भेदाः ॥

TaSū II.6

(These are) the conditions of existence, the passions, sex, wrong belief, wrong knowledge, non-restraint, non-attainment of perfection (imperfect disposition) and colouration, which are of four, four, three, one, one, one, one and six kinds. (Tr. S.A. Jain)

The celestial bodies called Sādhyas are described as follows:

संयमश्रुतप्रतिसेवनातीर्थलिङ्गलेश्योपपातस्थानविकल्पतः साध्याः ॥

TaSū IX.49

They are fit to be described (differentiated) on the basis of differences in self-restraint, spiritual knowledge, transgression, the period of Tīrthaṅkara, the sign, the colouration, birth and the state or condition. (Tr. S.A. Jain)

क्षेत्रकालगतिलिङ्गतीर्थचारित्रप्रत्येकबुद्धबोधितज्ञानावगाहनान्तरसंख्याल्पबहुत्वत: साध्या: ।

TaSū X.7

The emanicipated souls can be differentiated with reference to the region, time, state, sign, type of Arhat, conduct, self-enlightenment enlightened by others knowledge, stature, interval, number and numerical comparison. (Tr. S.A. Jain)

ते चैवास्तिकाया: त्रैकालिकभावपरिणता नित्या: ।
गच्छन्ति द्रव्यभावं परिवर्तनलिङ्गसंयुक्ता: ॥

PkāSā 6

These five *astikāyas* which though manifesting themselves diversely, maintain their permanency, constitute together with *kāla* or time which has the quality of permanence in change, the *dravyas*. (Tr. A. Chakravarti)

एवमभिगम्य जीवमन्यैरपि पर्यायैर्बहुकै: ।
अभिगच्छत्वजीवं ज्ञानान्तरितैर्लिङ्गै: ॥

PkāSā 123

Thus having seen the nature of *jīva* through the numerous and distinct characteristics, well do thou grasp the nature of non-life that is absolutely of non-thinking nature. (Tr. A. Chakravarti)

अरसमरूपमगन्धमव्यक्तं चेतनागुणमशब्दम् ।
जानीह्यलिङ्गग्रहणं जीवमनिर्दिष्टसंस्थानम् ॥

PkāSā 127

Understand that life has no sense qualities of taste, smell, colour, touch and sound. It has no form either. It has only thought or consciousness. (Tr. A. Chakravarti)

The term *liṅga* denoting identity (distinguishing mark), as the change is understood one of the characteristics of *dravya* (matter).

The **Sāṃkhya-Kārikā** explains the concept and activity implied around the expression *liṅga* for inference, characteristics in its own system of thought as follows:

लिङ्गम् । सावयवं परतन्त्रं व्यक्तम् ... ॥

SāṃKā 10

Vyakta (the manifest or evolved, i.e. the 23 modifications of *prakṛti* beginning with the *buddhi* and ending with the five *bhūtas*) is mergent (i.e. they get dissolved in their material causes) a combined component and dependant. (Tr. R.S. Bhattacharya)

Some commentator however, take this word in the sense of 'inferential mark', i.e. the evolutes of *prakṛti* are such as can indicate the existence of their material causes.

त्रिविधमनुमानमाख्यातम् तल्लिङ्गलिङ्गिपूर्वकम् .... ॥

SāṃKā 5

Inference (inferential knowledge) follows on the knowledge of the *liṅga* (the characteristic sign or mark) and *liṅgin* (that which bears the mark) and it is said to be of three kinds.
(Tr. R.S. Bhattacharya)

साध्यतेऽनेनेति साधनं लिङ्गम् ।

YuDīp on SāṃKā 6

That by which something is proved or established is called *sādhana*. (In the field of inference) *liṅga* (inferential mark) is the *sādhana* (because on the strength of *liṅga* something is proved).
(Tr. R.S. Bhattacharya)

तस्मात् तत्संयोगादचेतनं चेतनावदिव लिङ्गम् ।

SāṃKā 20ab

Therefore on account of its (Puruṣa's) association the non-intelligent *liṅga* becomes intelligent, as it were. (Tr. R.S. Bhattacharya)

A recourse to demonstrate Samkhyan thought has been taken by quoting several analogies from art activities:

चित्रं यथाऽऽश्रयमृते स्थाण्वादिभ्यो विना यथा च्छाया ।
तद्वद्विना विशेषैर्न तिष्ठति निराश्रयं लिङ्गम् ॥
प्रकृतेर्विभुत्वयोगान्नटवद् व्यवतिष्ठते लिङ्गम् ॥

SāṃKā 41–42cd

As a picture cannot exist without a support or substrate (like a wall), or a shadow without a post, so the *liṅga* (defined in SāṃKā 40) cannot subsist without *viśeṣa* (three varieties of *viśeṣa*s described in Kā 39) being supportless.

The *liṅga* acts like an actor on account of its association with the all-pervading power of *prakṛti* (as an actor takes the roles of many characters so the *liṅga* is born in various species one after another). (Tr. R.S. Bhattacharya)

The other orthodox systems of philosophy also employ the word in a more or less similar connotation with their specific phraseology.

इच्छाद्वेषप्रयत्नसुखदुःखज्ञानान्यात्मनो लिङ्गम् ॥

NySū I.1.10

Desire, aversion, effort, pleasure, pain and cognition are the indicatives (*liṅga*) of the Soul. (Tr. G.N. Jha)

Here the term *liṅga* is used in the sense of probans. (Also cf. NyBh III.2.41; VaiśSū II.1.8; II.1.18; IX.2.4.)

हेतुरपदेशो लिङ्गं प्रमाणं करणम् इत्यनर्थान्तरम् ।

VaiśSū IX.2.4

The words like *hetu, apadeśa, liṅga,* etc. are synonyms.

In the Mīmāṃsā vocabulary, the term *liṅga* occurs in similar contexts and doctrines:

लिंगदर्शनाच्च ॥

लिङ्गं चैव भवति, वाचा विरूपनित्ययेति । अन्यपरं हीदं वाक्यं वाचो नित्यतामनुवदति ।

MīmSūBh I.1.23, cf. also MīmSūBh III.2.8; III.2.20

Also because we find indicative texts.

We also find a Vedic text (ṚV VIII.75.6) indicating the eternality of word, e.g. by means of words which is eternal etc. Though this text relates to a different topic, yet it reiterates the eternality of the word. (Tr. G.N. Jha)

As stated in the **Ślokavārttika**:

तस्माच्छ्रुतार्थसिद्ध्यर्थं वृत्तं किमपि गम्यते ।
विशिष्टलिङ्गविज्ञानाद् विशिष्टे लिङ्गिनीक्षिते ॥

ŚlVā Pratijñā Sūtra 68

Therefore for the sake of the accomplishment of the direct meanings, a certain foregoing event has to be assumed; – the knowledge of the specified 'mark' (middle term) leading to the comprehension of the specified 'subject' (major term). (Tr. G.N. Jha)

As we find, defined in several other contexts of metaphysical analyses:

सामर्थ्यं लिङ्गम् । यदाहुः 'सामर्थ्यं सर्वभावानां लिङ्गमित्यभिधीयते' इति ।

MīmNyPrak 90 (p. 103)

Liṅga is the power (of words), as has been said, 'power of all entities (i.e. all words) is called *liṅga.* (Tr. R.S. Bhattacharya)

तादात्म्येनापि यदनुमानं तदपि न साधीयः । सिद्धं हि लिङ्गं, साध्यं हि लैङ्गिकम् ।
न च सिद्धस्य साध्यस्य च तादात्म्यम् उपपद्यते ।

PraPañ p. 201

The inference based on *tādātmya* (the relation of self-identity) is also not proper. An inferential mark is an established factor, while inferential knowledge is a matter to be established. It is not reasonable to hold that the relation of self-identity exists between a matter already established and a matter to be established.
(Tr. R.S. Bhattacharya)

स्वाभाविकी हि यस्य संबन्धव्याप्तिस्तस्य लिङ्गत्वम् ।

PraPañ p. 358

That thing is to be taken as *liṅga* (inferential mark), the concomitance of which is natural (i.e. without any condition).
(Tr. R.S. Bhattacharya)

The phrase *liṅga* denoting an indicative sign or symbol for the unknown occurs in the Vedantic vocabulary also:

आकाशस्तल्लिङ्गात् ॥

BrSū I.1.22

The *ākāśa,* i.e. ether (is Brahman) on account of characteristic marks (of the latter being mentioned). (Tr. G. Thibaut)

जीवमुख्यप्राणलिङ्गान्नेति चेन्नोपासात्रैविध्यादाश्रितत्वादिह तद्योगात् ॥

BrSū I.1.31

If it be argued that Brahman is not spoken of here on account of the indications of the individual soul and the chief vital force, then that cannot be so since this will lead to a threefold meditation. (Besides, *prāṇa*) is accepted (elsewhere) as meaning Brahman (because of the presence of Brahman's characteristics) (and these are) in evidence here. (Tr. Gambhirananda)

प्रतिज्ञासिद्धेर्लिङ्गमाश्मरथ्यः ॥

BrSū I.4.20

Āśmarathya thinks this (statement of non-difference between the individual soul and Supreme Self) to be a sign indicative of the fulfilment of the declaration. (Tr. Gambhirananda)

Giving the Buddhist viewpoint, Sāyaṇa-Mādhava summarised: *kāryaliṅgakam anumānam* (SarDSaṅg p. 19).

In viewpoint of the Raseśvara thought, the word refers to well-known Śaivite *liṅgas*:

केदारादीनि लिङ्गानि पृथिव्यां यानि कानिचित् ।
तानि दृष्ट्वा च यत् पुण्यं तत् पुण्यं रसदर्शनात् ॥

SarDSaṅg (Raseśvara) p. 208

Equal merit accrues from seeing mercury as accrues from seeing all the phallic emblems.

On earth, those at Kedāra, and all others whatsoever. (Tr. E.B. Cowell & A.E. Gough)

काश्यादिसर्वलिङ्गेभ्यो रसलिङ्गार्चनाच्छिवः ।
प्राप्यते येन तल्लिङ्गं भोगारोग्यामृतप्रदम् ॥

SarDSaṅg (Raseśvara) p. 208

The adoration of the sacred quicksilver is more beatific than the worship of all the phallic emblems at Kāśī and elsewhere.

Inasmuch as there is attained thereby enjoyment, health, exemption from decay, and immortality. (Tr. E.B. Cowell & A.E. Gough)

According to the Nakulīśa Pāśupata doctrine:

तत्र असुप्तस्यैव सुप्तलिङ्गप्रदर्शनं क्राथनम् ।

SarDSaṅg p. 170

Snoring is showing all the signs of being asleep while really awake. (Tr. E.B. Cowell & A.E. Gough)

As we find the same, stated in the **Pāśupata-Sūtra** itself:

लिङ्गधारी ॥

PāśuSū I.6

The follower of Pāśupata doctrine should bear the mark of Śiva. (Tr. H.N. Chakravarty)

Couched in a symbolic language the **Haṭhayoga Pradīpikā** has thus ordained:

दिवा न पूजयेल्लिङ्गं रात्रौ चैव न पूजयेत् ।
सर्वदा पूजयेल्लिङ्गं दिवारात्रिनिरोधतः ॥

HyPrad IV.41

Do not worship the *liṅga* by day, nor worship it at night. Stopping the night and the day, the *liṅga* should always be worshipped. (Tr. S. Iyangar)

Liṅga here means the Self (*ātman*), the originator of all creation: '*liṅgaṃ* :*arvakāraṇamātmānam* (comm. *ibid.*). The intended injunction seems to refer o the state of *samādhi* which can hardly be realised as an act of day or night.

The Agamic tradition centres around the primary notions of their phi-osophy as based on the term *liṅga*, indicating arch-symbol and formal repre-entative of the Lord Śiva:

वाच्यस्य देवदेवस्य लोकानुग्राहकस्य च ।
लिङ्गं चिह्नं शरीरं च कथ्यतेऽत्र जनार्दन ॥

AjitĀ kp XVIII.10

O Viṣṇu, I shall tell you here about *liṅga*, the mark and the body of the graceful Lord who is the signified meaning of *mantra*, and is the highest god. (Tr. H.N. Chakravarty)

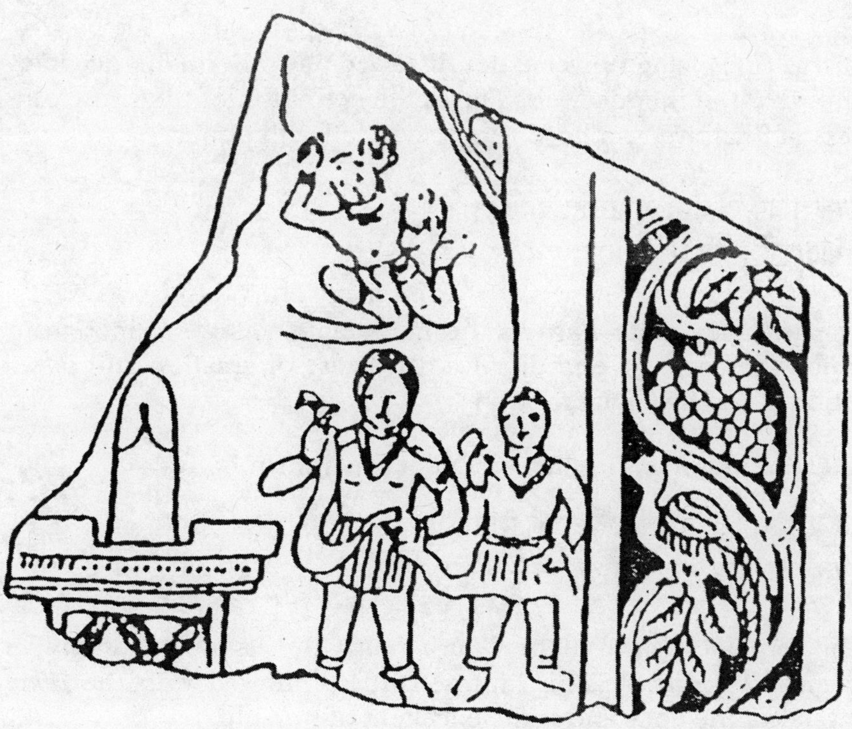

Figure 20: Installed Śiva-liṅga and its worship, Mathura Sculpture, Kuṣāṇa period

पुरुषस्य तु यच्चिह्नं पुरुषव्यक्तिकारणम् ॥
सदाशिवस्य तल्लिङ्गं शिवलिङ्गमिति स्मृतम् ।

AjitĀ kp III.1cd–2ab

The sign of man which is the cause to make him manifest as a man. That is the *liṅga* of Sadāśiva. It is known to be the *liṅga* of Śiva.

सर्वो लिङ्गभवो लोकः सर्वं लिङ्गे प्रतिष्ठितम् ।

AjitĀ kp XVIII under fn. 2
(cf. Śiradharmottara, 3ab)

Everything in the world and the world itself are born of *liṅga* and everything steadily abides in *liṅga*. (Tr. H.N. Chakravarty)

Referring to the etymological exegesis of word, Abhinavagupta puts as follows:

अत्र विश्वमिदं लीनमत्रान्तःस्थं च गम्यते ॥
इदं तल्लक्षणं पूर्णशक्तिभैरवसंविदः ।

TĀl V.113cd–114ab

In this (*liṅga*) the universe lies dissolved and where one becomes one with it, it is conceived. This is the definition of the consciousness of Bhairava, the Lord who is ever full with power.

लिङ्गशब्देन विद्वांसः सृष्टिसंहारकारणम् ।
लयादागमनाच्चाहुर्भावानां पदमव्ययम् ॥

Comm. on TĀl V.113

The wise designate *liṅga* as the immutable state of beings from which they emerge and dissolve, the cause of creation and dissolution. (Tr. H.N. Chakravarty)

It is further observed in the context of the human body:

देह एव परं लिङ्गं सर्वतत्त्वात्मकं शिवम् ।
देवताचक्रसंजुष्टं पूजाधाम तदुत्तमम् ॥

TĀl XXIX.171

The very body is the highest *liṅga*, being the essence of all *tattvas* (principles) and it is Śiva himself. It is endowed with the *cakra* (cycle) of the gods and is the excellent of worship.
(Tr. H.N. Chakravarty)

The worship of Śivaliṅga is stated to be of the highest merit:

लिङ्गार्चनसमो नास्ति धर्मोऽत्र भुवनत्रये ।

पूजा च त्रिषु लिङ्गेषु व्यक्ताव्यक्तोभयात्मसु ॥

AjitĀ kp XVIII.6

There is nothing equal in virtue in the three worlds than performing ritualistic worship on three types of *liṅga*, viz. (i) the manifest, (ii) the unmanifest, and (iii) manifest-unmanifest both. (Tr. H.N. Chakravarty)

Referring to the legend of Jyotir-liṅga its mythical significance has been thus summarised.

किमिदं न्विति संचिन्त्य तत्परीक्षासमुद्यतौ ॥
गतावूर्ध्वमधस्तात्तु लिङ्गरूपस्य तस्य हि ।
हंसक्रोडशरीरेण तत्पर्यन्तदिदृक्षया ॥
सर्वलोकेश्वरौ देवौ निवृत्तावकृतार्थकौ ।
नत्वा स्तुत्वाथ देवेशं युवां तत्पार्श्वयोः स्थितौ ॥

AjitĀ kp III.8cd–10

(Seeing the pillar of fire) what indeed it is: thinking thus the two (Brahmā and Viṣṇu) were engaged to examine it. They indeed went upward and downward of the form of *liṅga.* One assuming the form of a swan and the other as a hog in order to trace the end of the *liṅga,* but they returned being unfulfilled in their aim. Then paying homage to it and praising it both of them remained at its side. (Tr. H.N. Chakravarty)

With respect to the direction in which the Śiva-liṅga is set up, each bestows merit of specific nature.

ब्रह्मस्थानस्थितं लिङ्गं ब्रह्मक्षत्रहितावहम् ॥
ऐन्द्रे राज्यप्रदं प्रोक्तं याम्ये वृद्धिस्तथायुषः ।
आरोग्यं वारुणे चापि सौम्ये वित्तप्रदं भवेत् ॥
वह्निदेशे सुखं दद्यात् विजयं नैर्ऋते तथा ।
वायव्ये सम्पदं दद्यान्मोक्षमीशान गोचरे ॥

AjitĀ kp VI.24cd–26

The *liṅga* installed in the *brahmasthāna* is the bestower of good to *brāhmaṇas* and *kṣatriyas*. In east it is said to be the giver of kingdom and to the south it bestows longevity, while in the west it is the giver of freedom from illness, while in the north it is the giver of wealth, in the south-east happiness, victory in the south-west, in the north-west riches and liberation in the north-east. (Tr. H.N. Chakravarty)

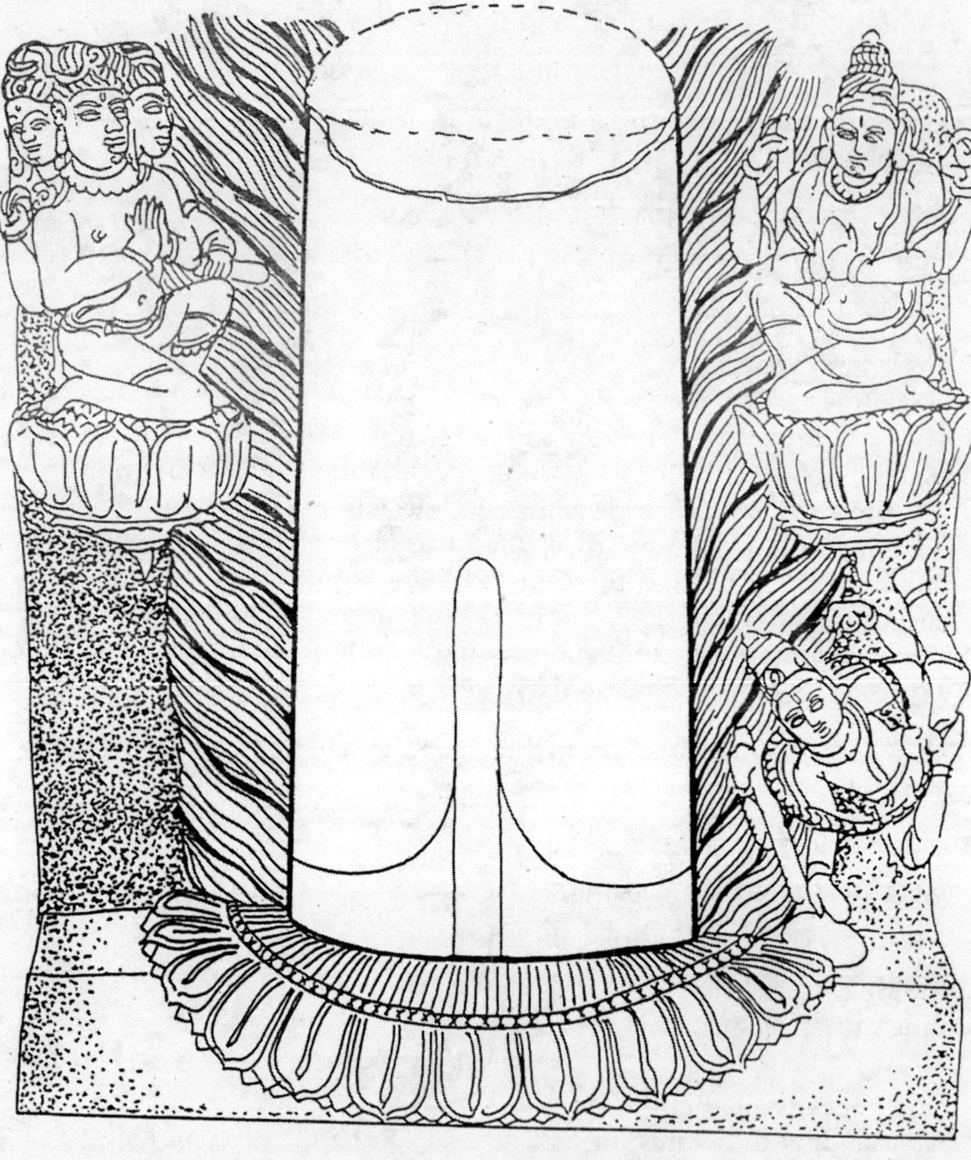

Figure 21: Jyotirliṅga

As based on its colour, the efficacy of a Bāṇa-liṅga is thus enumerated:

श्वेतवर्णं भवेद्विप्रे क्षत्रिये रक्तवर्णकम् ।
पीतवर्णं भवेत् वैश्ये कृष्णवर्णं तुरीयके ॥

RauUĀ XVIII.2

The characteristic colour of Bāṇa-liṅga is white for *brāhmaṇas*, for *kṣatriyas* it is red in colour, and yellow for *vaiśyas* and for the fourth it is black. (Tr. H.N. Chakravarty)

The procedure of *liṅga* worship and related Tantra-yogic practices have been commented as follows:

सर्वमन्यत्परित्यज्य चित्तमत्र निवेशयेत् ।
मृच्छैलधातुरत्नादिभवं लिङ्गं न पूजयेत् ॥
यजेदाध्यात्मिकं लिङ्गं यत्र लीनं चराचरम् ।
बहिर्लिङ्गस्य लिङ्गत्वमनेनाधिष्ठितं यतः ।

MVT XVIII.2–3 (cf. VIII.7, XVIII.9cd–11)

Leaving all aside concentrate your mind to it (to *liṅga*). One should not worship any *liṅga* made of soil, metals and gems and so on. One should worship the spiritual *liṅga* where the universe consisting of mobile and immobile objects remains dissolved. All superintendence, otherwise they are not all *liṅgas*.

यन्न्यक्कृतशिवाहन्तासमावेशं विभेदवत् ॥
विशेषस्पन्दरूपं तद् व्यक्तं लिङ्गं चिदात्मकम् ।

TĀl V.116cd–117ab

The (state) which having conquered the concept of "I am Śiva", being completely absorbed (into Self) and beyond differentiation, is the specific form of Spanda, that is (as it were) the revealed Sign, endowed of consciousness.

भैरवीयं च तल्लिंगं धरणी चास्य पीठिका ॥
सर्वे देवा निलीना हि तत्र तत्पूजितं सदा ।

TĀl VIII.45cd–46ab

The *liṅga* belonging to Bhairava has earth as its base. All the heavenly beings remain indeed merged there. It is always worshipped there. (Tr. H.N. Chakravarty)

Referring to the Svayambhu-liṅga, the **Yoginī-Hṛdaya** specifies thus:

स्वयंभुर्बाणलिङ्गं च इतरं च परं पुनः ।

पीठेष्वेतानि लिङ्गानि संस्थितानि वरानने ॥
हेमबन्धूककुसुमशरच्चन्द्रनिभानि तु ।
स्वरावृतं त्रिकूटं च महालिङ्गं स्वयंभुवम् ॥

YoH I.44–45

O lady with graceful face, the *liṅgas* which are stationed in these *pīṭhas* are named as: Svayambhu, Bāṇa, Itara and Para. Their colours are golden, the colour of *bandhūka* flower (red), white like the colour of the autumnal moon. The Svayambhu-liṅga is great, is surrounded by all the vowels and is constituted of three *bindus*.

A specific *mudrā* (hand-pose) has been described as denoting *liṅga* gesture or *liṅga-mudrā*:

पूर्वं कलशमारोप्य शस्त्रालुं तस्य वामतः ।
समग्रासनके कुम्भे यजेद् देवं स्थिरासने ॥
वार्धान्यां प्रणवस्थायामायुधं तदनु द्वयोः ।
भगलिङ्गसमायोगं विध्याल्लिङ्गमुद्रया ॥

Kriyā Kāṇḍakarmāvalī 406–407

Having placed the pitcher on the front, the spouted pot for *śastra* be placed to its left. On the frontally set-up pitcher one should give offering to the lord as fixed on his seat. On the spouted pot, set-up on *praṇava* (*oṃkāra*) should be (placed) the *āyudha* (part of the *mantra*, i.e. *phaṭ* vocation). Thereupon one is to bring about on them together the union of female and male symbols by showing the pose of *liṅga-mudrā*.

सव्यमुष्टिरुमा पिण्डी लिङ्गमंगुष्ठको हरः ।

ĪśGP kp 16, after 37

(Explaining the ritual union of Umā and Śiva) the left-hand posed in fist represents the goddess Umā as base-portion (*piṇḍī*) while the thumb (of the right hand united into it) represents Śiva and the *liṅga* itself.

In its several connotations the term *liṅga* frequently occurs in the classical Kāvyas and Poetics.

Taking cue from the list of thirty two *mahāpuruṣa* cognizances, as mentioned in the cannon, Aśvaghoṣa describes a few principles being seen on the body of the Śākya child:

चक्राङ्कपादं स ततो महर्षिर्जालावनद्धाङ्गुलिपाणिपादम् ।
सोर्णभ्रुवं वारणवस्तिकोशं सविस्मयं राजसुतं ददर्श ॥

BudCa I.60

Then the great seer with wonder saw the prince, whose soles of feet were marked with a wheel, who has webbed fingers and toes, the eyebrows bearing the *ūrṇā* mark, and endowed with the pelvis and scrotum like that of an elephant.

In the sense of sign or mark, the word has been used by the great poet Kālidāsa:

तमश्रुनेत्रावरणं प्रमृज्य सीता विलापाद् विरता ववन्दे ।
तस्यै मुनिर्दोहदलिङ्गदर्शी दाश्वान् सुपुत्राशिषमित्युवाच ॥

Ragh XIV.71

Sītā refraining from lamentation and wiping off the tears that obstructed her eye-sight, saluted him. The sage seeing the signs of pregnancy pronounced benediction, that she might get a good son and said .... (Tr. G.R. Nandargikar)

In a unique manner, the poet Bhavabhūti remarks proverbially:

गुणाः पूजास्थानं गुणिषु न च लिङ्गं न च वयः ॥

UttCa IV.11d

In the case of (or, with) the virtuous, merits are the objects of reverence; neither (their) sex nor (their) age. (Tr. M. R. Kale)

In a beautiful imagery, a Śivaliṅga has been thus described by poets:

अमलमुक्ताशिलाघटितलिङ्गम् अशेषत्रिभुवनवन्दितचरणं चराचरगुरुं चतुर्मुखं भगवन्तं त्र्यम्बकम् ।

Kād sec. 132, p.128

(He saw) the four-faced divine (image of the) three-eyed God (Śiva), ... with the *liṅga* (form) fashioned out of a bright pearl-slab, whose feet are saluted by the entire universe, (and) the preceptor of (all) movable and immovable (objects).
(Tr. R.D. Karmarkar)

Playing upon two senses of the word *liṅga*, Somadeva Suri employs an interesting pun:

... लिङ्गभेदः प्राकृतेषु ... ।

Yaśastilaka Campū (āśvāsa) II, p. 202

... variation of gender is found (only) in (the writings of) treatises ...

Śrutasāgarasūri comments on the same: *prākṛteṣu śāstreṣu liṅgabhedaḥ strīpuṃnapuṃsakaliṅgavyabhicāro vartate.*

The **Nāṭya-Śāstra** (Kāvyamālā edn)of Bharata frequently employs the phrases such as *liṅgin* (religious mendicants), *liṅga* (sign, feature, distinctive mark) etc.:

उत्तमानां भवेदेषा लिङ्गिनां ये महाव्रताः ।
एभिरेव विपर्यस्तैर्गुणैरन्येषु योजयेत् ॥

NŚ XII.77

The best asceties of the great vow are to be connected with these qualities or others contrary to them. (Tr. M.M. Ghosh)

लिङ्गिनां वासनविधिः कार्यो व्रतसमाश्रयः ।
बृषीमुण्डासनप्रायं वेत्रासनमथापि वा ॥

NŚ XII.175

The sitting posture of the sectarian hermits should be shown as they assume in practising specific vows. Normally that is a seat of mat, wicker-made settle or cane-work.

स्व (ख) स्थानां स्यन्दनस्थानां विमानस्थायिनामपि ॥
लिङ्गस्थानां व्रतस्थानां स्थानमेतत्तु कारयेत् ।

NŚ X.59cd–60ab

Persons in the sky, chariot and aerial car (*vimāna*) persons of marked sects (*liṅgastha*) and persons practising vows are also to assume this *sthāna.* (Tr. M.M. Ghosh)

नीचे मत्ते सलिङ्गे च प्राकृतं पाठ्यमिष्यते ।
परिव्राण्मुनिशान्तेषु वा (शा ?) क्येषु श्रोत्रियेषु च ॥
द्विजा ये चैव लिङ्गस्थाः संस्कृतं तेषु योजयेत् ।
राज्याश्च गणिकायाश्च शिल्पकार्यास्तथैव च ॥

NŚ XVII.36–37

Prakrit is used in recitation by persons of low birth, lunatics and phallus-worshippers. But in case of indifferent recluses, sages, Buddhists, Śrotriyas and the twice-born (*dvija*) initiated or observing religious vows (*liṅga-sthāḥ*) Sanskrit should be assigned. Similarly for a queen, a courtesan and also a female artiste (Sanskrit is befitting in special situations).

तथा वृत्तानुषङ्गेण शेषाणां लिङ्गिनां शिरः ।
मुण्डं वा कुञ्चितं वापि लम्बकेशमथापि वा ॥

NŚ XXI.146

And according to their (respective) sectarian doctrine (*vṛtta*) the remaining ascetics should have their heads shaven or should have cutting hairs or long hairs loosely hanging down. (Tr. M.M. Ghosh)

Writing on poetic decency, Vāmana gives arch instance of Śivaliṅga:

संवीतस्य हि लोकेन न दोषान्वेषणं क्षमम् ।
शिवलिङ्गस्य संस्थाने कस्यासभ्यत्वभावना ॥

KāvyālSū II.1.19

The practice accepted by the people nobody is likely to take objection. For in the design of the Śiva's *liṅga* who entertains obscene intentions.

The authors on Poetics thus comment in a different context of the word:

त्रिरूपाल्लिङ्गतो ज्ञानमनुमानं च केचन ।
तद्विदो नान्तरीयार्थदर्शनं चापरं विदुः ॥

Kāvyāl V.11

There are three kinds of *liṅgas* (middle terms). Knowledge resulting from them is *anumāna* (inference). Some are of opinion it is also *anumāna* where those people that are experienced in it (*tadvidaḥ*) perceive a thing as invariable associated with another. (Tr. P.V. Naganatha Sastry)

साध्येन लिङ्गानुगतिस्तदभावे च नास्तिता ।
ख्याप्यते येन दृष्टान्तः स किलान्यैर्द्विधोच्यते ॥

Kāvyāl V.27

Some say that Dṛṣṭānta is two-fold: that by which the co-existence of '*sādhya*' with '*liṅga*' is proved and also that by which the absence of the *liṅga* in the absence of the *sādhya* is proved. (Tr. P.V. Naganatha Sastry)

स च श्लेषच्छायामनोज्ञविशेषणवक्रभावाद् विशिष्टलिङ्गसामर्थ्याच्च ... ।

VaJī III.62

And that (Rūpaka, i.e. Allegory) through expressions of punserving as elegant adjectives featuring paronomasia and because of its efficacy of specific attributes.

Classification

A threefold classification of the *liṅga* form of Śiva has been thus given in a general way by the following authorities:

निष्कलं सकलं मिश्रं लिङ्गं चेति त्रिधा मतम् ।

Mayam XXXIII.1ab

It is said that there are three sorts of representation of the god, symbolic, iconic and mixed. (Tr. B. Dagens)

अथ लिङ्गं त्रिधा ज्ञेयं निष्कलं सकलं तथा ।
मिश्रं चेति च तल्लिङ्गमचलं च चलं द्विधा ॥
निष्कलं केवलं लिङ्गं सकलं प्रतिमा स्मृता ।
मिश्राख्यं मुखलिङ्गं स्यान्मिश्रलक्षणलक्षितम् ॥

ĪśGP kp XXXVI.1–2

Now *liṅga* should be known as threefold. They are *niṣkala* (partless), *sakala* (with parts) and *miśra* (mixed). There again *liṅga* is of two types, namely mobile and immobile. Niṣkala liṅga is the one which is only the *liṅga,* while *sakala* is with image-form (*pratimā*). The mixed type having faces is the one which is characterised by various characters. (Tr. H.N. Chakravarty)

The Niṣkala liṅga is still said to be sixfold with respect to the material employed:

शैलं रात्नं तथा लौहं दारवं मार्त्तिकं पुनः ।
क्षणिकं चेति षोढा स्यात् क्रमाल्लिङ्गं तु निष्कलम् ॥

ĪśGP kp XXXVI.3

The Niṣkala liṅga may be sixfold: made of stone, gem, iron, wood, clay and temporary materials. (Tr. H.N. Chakravarty)

From another point of view the Śivaliṅga has further classified into two main kinds:

स्थावरं जङ्गमं चैव द्विविधं लिङ्गमुच्यते ।
शैलजै रत्नलोहैश्च मृन्मयै नैव कारयेत्
शिलामयं तु यद्रूपमजविष्णुहरैर्युतम् ।

Kāraṇāgama I.9

Liṅgas are said to be of two types, the one is immovable and the other is movable. It should be made of stone, jewel, metals and

earth. The one which is processed with stone should be associated with the portion of Brahmā, Viṣṇu and Hara.
(Tr. H.N. Chakravarty)

As has been observed in the **Ajitāgama** about these types in a comprehensive way:

लिङ्गं तु त्रिविधं प्रोक्तं व्यक्ताव्यक्तोभयात्मकम् ॥
व्यक्तं यत्प्रतिमाव्यक्तं शिवलिङ्गमिति स्मृतम् ।
मुखलिङ्गं भवेदन्यत्तृतीयमुभयात्मकम् ॥

AjitĀ kp IV.1cd–2

Liṅga is said to be of three types. They are manifest, unmanifest and manifest-unmanifest both. The manifest is the image, the unmanifest is the Śiva's *liṅga* having the face of Śiva, the third has the feature of both. (Tr. H.N. Chakravarty)

The phallic emblems made in various gems are specified for varying merits:

माणिक्यं श्रीप्रदं प्रोक्तं यशसे नीलमुच्यते ।
हरितं फलदं प्रोक्तं दोषमुक्त्यै च मौक्तिकम् ॥
प्रवालं वशदं विद्याद् वज्रं राज्यप्रदं भवेत् ।
वैडूर्यं वैरिनाशार्थं सौभाग्ये पुष्परागकम् ॥
सर्वकामप्रदं प्रोक्तं स्फटिकं तु जनार्दन ।
उत्तमं स्वस्वयोनि स्यान्मध्यमं स्वर्णयोनिकम् ॥
अधमं रौप्ययोनि स्यात्तदभावे तु ताम्रजम् ।

AjitĀ kp IV.53–56ab

The *liṅga* made of ruby is the bestower of prosperity, for fame it is said to be made of sapphire. It is stated that emerald is fruitful, while *liṅga* made of pearl is for the purpose of get oneself released from defects. One should know that the coral one is for the achievement of bringing someone under control. The diamond one is the bestower of kingdom. The one made of cat's eye is for subduing enemies, for the attainment of good fortune it is made of topaz. O Viṣṇu, the one made of crystal is said to be the bestower of fulfilment of all desires. The best one is that in which the *yoni*, the *pīṭha*, is made of the same material. The better is that of gold, the inferior is that in which the *pīṭha* is made of silver – in the lack of that it should be made of copper.
(Tr. H.N. Chakravarty)

Manifestation in the Arts

Śiva's symbol of *liṅga*-shape is of outstanding significance in its representation in art forms. There is a great corpus of canonical texts which treat the manufacture of Śaivite *liṅga* in its numerous variant forms and plastic manifestations.

The **Bṛhat Saṃhitā**, being one of the earliest treatises extant on iconographic injunctions, describes the manufacture of a Śaivite *liṅga* in its strict Āgama-based conventions and symbolic components as frequently demon-

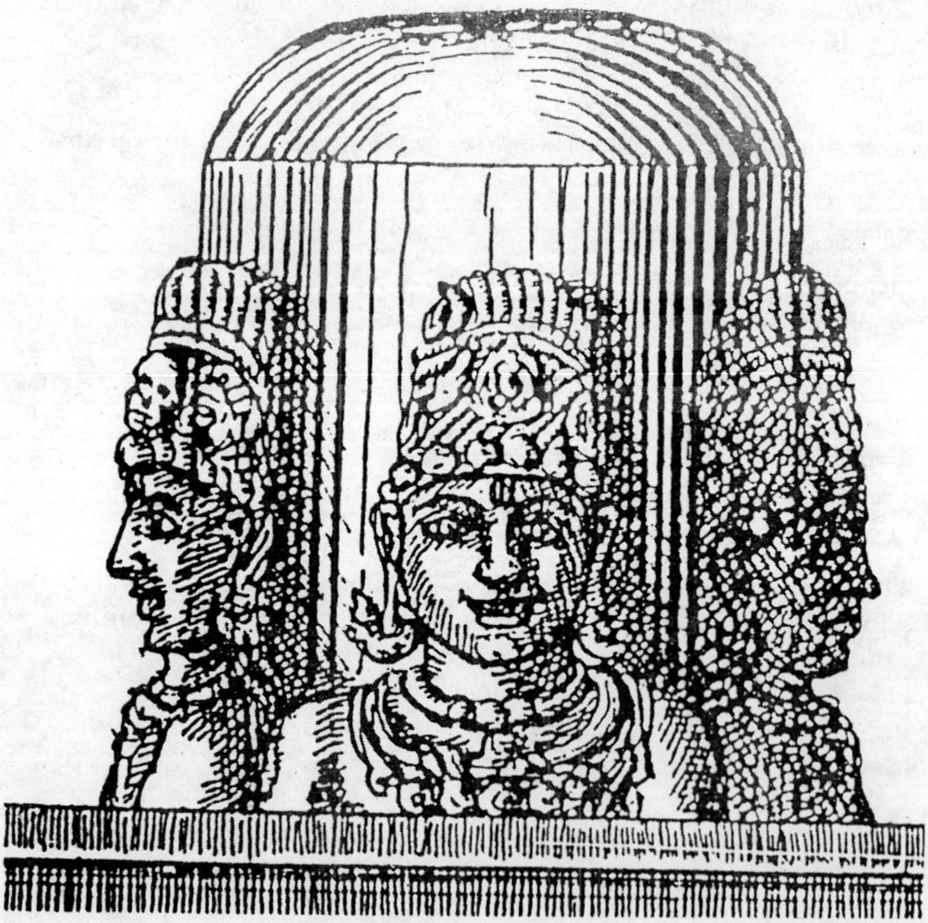

Figure 22: Mukhaliṅga

strated by Bhaṭṭa Utpala in his commentary:

लिङ्गस्य वृत्तपरिधिं दैर्घ्येणासूत्र्य तत् त्रिधा विभजेत् ।
मूले तच्चतुरस्रं मध्ये त्वष्टाश्रि वृत्तमतः ॥
चतुरस्रमवनिखाते मध्यं कार्यं तु पिण्डिकाश्वभ्रे ।
दृश्योच्छ्रायेण समा समन्ततः पिण्डिका श्वभ्रात् ॥

BṛSam LVIII.53–54

Treat the circumference of the round part of the Śivaliṅga as the height and divide it into three equal parts. The lowest part should be quadrilateral, that in the middle, octagonal, and the uppermost one, cylindrical. The quadrilateral part should be buried in the earth, the middle one in the pit of the pedestal, and the pedestal around the pit must be equal in extent to the visible height of the *liṅga.* (Tr. M.R. Bhat)

अनिमित्तभङ्गचलनस्वेदाश्रुनिपात जल्पनाद्यानि ।
लिङ्गार्चायतनानां नाशाय नरेशदेशानाम् ॥
लिङ्गं वा प्रतिमा वा द्रुमवत् स्थाप्या यथादिशं यस्मात् ।

BṛSam XLVI.8, LIX.7ab

The breaking, moving, sweating, shedding tears, falling, muttering and the like of Śiva's emblems, idols of gods and temples (or holy places), without any cause, forebode the destruction of kings and their countries. Since, an emblem of Śiva or any image should be installed according to the directions of the tree.
(Tr. M.R. Bhat)

The *liṅga* symbol or image should be installed as to the directions (of its top and bottom) originally belonging to the tree-source (out of the material of which it is carried):

अथातः संप्रवक्ष्यामि लिङ्गलक्षणमुत्तमम् ।
सुस्निग्धश्च सुवर्णश्च लिङ्गं कुर्याद्विचक्षणः ॥
प्रासादस्य प्रमाणेन लिङ्गमानं विधीयते ।
लिङ्गमानेन वा विद्यात् प्रासादं शुभलक्षणम् ॥

MatPur CCLXIII.1–2

Now we shall state the excellent features of a (Śaivite) *liṅga.* The expert should render the *liṅga* as having a smooth finish and pleasing colour. The size of the *liṅga*-symbol is enjoined according to the dimension of its temple or, the suitable temple (for it) is (governed) by the size of the *liṅga* (itself).

शिरसा च सदा निम्नं मनोज्ञं लक्षणान्वितम् ।
सौम्यन्तु दृश्यते लिङ्गन्तद्वैवृद्धिप्रदं भवेत् ॥
अथ मूले च मध्ये तु प्रमाणे सर्वतः समम् ।
एवम्विधन्तु यल्लिङ्गं भवेत्तत्सार्वकामिकम् ॥

MatPur CCLXIII.23–24

Its (phallus) lower part and its head is to be made always somewhat low, beautiful, and endowed with good qualities. The *liṅga* that looks elegant is the giver of prosperity. The phallus which is even at the base as well as in the middle is also the giver of all desires. The one that has not such a construction brings bad luck. (Tr. M.N. Dutt)

लक्षणोद्धरणं वक्ष्ये लिङ्गस्य सुसमाहितः ।
त्रिधा विभज्य पूज्यायां लक्षणं स्याद् विभाजकम् ॥
लेखात्रयं तु कर्तव्यं यवाष्टान्तरसंयुतम् ।
न स्थूलं न कृशं तद्वन्न वक्रं छेदवर्जितम् ॥
निम्नं यवप्रमाणेन ज्येष्ठलिङ्गस्य कारयेत् ।
सूक्ष्मास्ततस्तु कर्तव्या यथा मध्यमके न्यसेत् ॥
अष्टभक्तं ततः कृत्वा त्यक्त्वा भागत्रयं बुधः ।
लम्बयेत्सप्तरेखास्तु पार्श्वयोरुभयोः समाः ॥
तावत्प्रलम्बयेद्विद्वान् यावद्भागचतुष्टयम् ।
भ्राम्यते पञ्चभागोर्ध्वं कारयेत्सङ्गमन्ततः ॥
रेखयोः सङ्गमे तद्वत् पृष्ठे भागद्वयं भवेत् ।
एवमेतत्समाख्यातं समासाल्लक्षणं मया ॥

MatPur CCLXIV.35–40

The image should be divided into three parts and afterwards three lines at a distance of eight *yavas* from one another should be drawn which should be broad, thin and crooked. They should not be broken (i.e. should be continuous). In the *jyeṣṭha* phallus, the lowermost line should be of the dimension of one *yava*, the middle one is to be finer still. Then eight divisions should be made and three of them should be discarded. Then seven lines should be drawn on either side and four divisions are to be noted. Afterwards the lines should be allowed to meet at the top of the fifth line. This is the union of the lines; on the back of these lines, two divisions are to be made. These are in brief, the *lakṣaṇas* (character). (Tr. M.N. Dutt)

One finds a whole section dealing in detail the aspects of a Śaivite *liṅga* with respect to its sculptural formation, installation in a sort of holystead or shrine, its iconographic morphology and iconoplastic significance and traditional principles as well as ritual and religious activities connected with its worship and metaphysical relevance thereof. Referring to certain contexts of old and damaged stances of the *liṅga* representation it has been thus observed:

> तल्लिङ्गं तु निमग्नं कालज्ञातं त- [थ-] । वापि ।
> तदधोगतमित्युक्तं तल्लिङ्गं चो- [द्धरेत् समितम्] ॥
> तल्लिङ्गं तु निमग्नं कालाज्ञातमूर्ध्वगतम् ।
> तत्र स्थाप्यं [पुनरपि] निर्दोषकं यदिदम् ॥

Mayam XXXV.21–22

> A *liṅga*, buried for a known period of time, is a 'gone down' *liṅga*; it is to be reinstalled after it has been measured (to see if it has the prescribed dimensions). A *liṅga*, buried for an unknown period of time, is a 'gone up' *liṅga* and there is no error in reinstalling it in the same place. (Tr. Bruno Dagens)

> सरित्सरस्तटाकादि तीरजातां च कज्जलैः ॥
> क्षालितां च द्रुमच्छायागृहीतां सुसमां दृढाम् ।
> आयामपरिणाहाढ्यां शिलां लिङ्गार्थमाहरेत् ॥
> प्राच्यां शिरः प्रतीच्यां च मूलं तस्याः प्रकीर्तितम् ।
> उदीच्यां वा शिरो मूलं दक्षिणां दिशमाश्रितम् ॥
> अधोभागे मुखं तस्या लाञ्छयित्वा समुद्धरेत् ।

AjitĀ kp V.25cd–28ab

> One should procure a hard stone for the purpose of making a *liṅga*. The stone be procured from near the bank of a stream or a lake or a pool. One should select such a stone the length and the breadth of which are suitable for the purpose and is covered under the shade of the tree. It should be made smooth. The east of it is the face and the root of it is the west – it has been stated thus. If the stone lies north and south, the head portion is the north and the root portion is the south. The stone should be raised from the spot after making mark below where the face portion is to be curved. (Tr. H.N. Chakravarty)

Human manufactures of the *liṅga*-images are classified into several categories:

> प्रथमं सर्वतोभद्रं द्वितीयं वर्धमानकम् ।

शैवाधिक्यं तृतीयं तु त्रैराशिकं चतुर्थकम् ॥
एवं लिङ्गं चतुर्वर्गं महालिङ्गमितीरितम् ।
एकैकं तु चतुर्भेदमेकैकं तु चतुर्विधम् ॥
चतुःषष्टिविधं लिङ्गं समासात्संप्रकीर्तितम् ।

RauUĀ XV.3–5ab

Liṅgas are fourfold – of them the first is Sarvatobhadra, the second is Vardhamānaka, the third is Śaivādhikya and the fourth is Trairāśika. Thus these *liṅgas* are classified under four and are called *mahāliṅgas*. Each of the classes has four divisions each and each of them is of four types. Thus the *liṅgas* are briefly stated to be of sixty-four types. (Tr. H.N. Chakravarty)

नागरे सर्वतोभद्रं द्राविडे वर्धमानकम् ॥
शिवाधिकं वेसरे च त्रैराशिकं तु मिश्रके ।
क्रमाच्चतुर्विधं लिङ्गं स्थापयेद्विधिपूर्वकम् ॥

RauUĀ XV.6cd–7

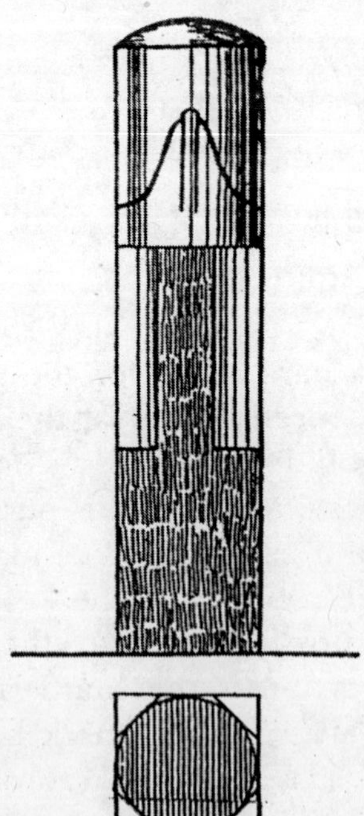

Figure 23: Trairāśika-liṅga

In the Nāgara type of temple the Sarvatobhadra, in the Drāviḍa the Vardhamānaka, in the Vesara the Sivādhika, in the Miśra the Trairāśika liṅgas respectively are to be installed according to the prescribed procedure. (Tr. H.N. Chakravarty)

A *liṅga* is described to consist triple portions:

लिङ्गोच्चे तु गुणांशे तु ब्रह्मविष्ण्वीश्वरान्तकम् ॥
तुङ्गं प्रत्येकभागेन वेदाश्राष्टाश्रवृत्तकम् ।
ब्रह्माद्यानां क्रमात्कल्प्य लिङ्गोच्चसमनाहकम् ॥

RauĀ kp XXVIII.7cd–8

When the height of the *liṅga* has three portions, named as the portion of Brahmā, Viṣṇu and Īśvara, height of the each should be shaped accordingly. It should be square (for Brahmā), octagonal (for Viṣṇu) and round (for Īśvara). After considering the height and width of Brahmā and others with equal measures, the *liṅga* should be made. (Tr. H.N. Chakravarty)

Writing on the form and symbolism of the Śivaliṅga, Abhinavagupta thus observes:

ऊर्ध्वं तु भवति रुद्रो वृत्ताकारः समन्ततः ।
मेरुः संजायते लिङ्गं, धरणी चास्य पीठिका ॥
आलयः सर्वदेवानां तेन लिङ्गत्वमागतम् ।
लीनमस्य जगत्सर्वं ब्रह्माद्यं सचराचरम् ॥

TĀl VIII, after verse 55

Rudra is the top (of Meru). It is round in every direction. The Meru has become the *liṅga* and the earth is its base. It (the Meru) is the abode the final resort of all heavenly beings. Therefore it is known by the name *liṅga*. The entire universe from Brahmā including movable and immovable objects remains dissolved in it. (Tr. H.N. Chakravarty)

A Śivaliṅga can be of three varieties with respect to the symbolical presentation of the god's symbol:

व्यक्तं-प्रतिमा, अव्यक्तं अनभिव्यक्ताङ्गम्, उभयात्मकं व्यक्ताव्यक्तं मुखलिङ्गमित्यर्थः ।

MṛĀ (Appendix) comm.

Manifest is the image, unmanifest is the one in which limbs are not manifest. With the characteristics of the both means Mukha liṅga, i.e. that is the *liṅga* in which the face is depicted. (Tr. H.N. Chakravarty)

As regards the dimension, and measurements the **Raurava Āgama** thus enjoins:

नवाष्टसप्तहस्तं चाप्युत्तमत्रयमानकम् ।
षट्पंचचतुर्हस्तं च मध्यमत्रयमुच्यते ॥
त्रिहस्तं द्व्येकहस्तं च कन्यसत्रयमानकम् ।
प्रासादे गर्भगेहस्य विशालं नवधा भजेत् ॥
श्रेष्ठान्तरकनिष्ठानां प्रत्येकं त्रित्रिमानकम् ।
एवं नवविधं ख्यातं लिंगमानं रुरो विदुः ॥

RauĀ kp XXVIII.3–5

The *liṅga* of Śiva measures nine, eight and seven cubits in height. This is of three types for the best. The median three types measure six, five and four cubit. In the temple of the (*garbhagṛha*), the inner sanctum, the largeness of the *liṅga* should be of nine types. The measurement of the best, the medium and the small have three measurement of the each. Thus according to *Ṛuru* the measurement of the *liṅga* is of nine types. (Tr. H.N. Chakravarty)

On the sacred zone around any installed *liṅga*, the following observation has been made:

लिङ्गाद्धस्तशतं क्षेत्रमाचार्यस्थापिते सति ।
स्वयम्भूते सहस्रं तु तदर्धमृषियोजिते ॥
तत्त्ववित्स्थापिते लिङ्गे स्वयम्भूसदृशं फलम् ।

ṬĀl XXVIII.252–253ab

When a *liṅga* has been installed by an *ācārya* (the spiritual teacher) the field hundred cubits from it is *kṣetra* (sacred spot). It is one thousand cubits from the *liṅga* if it is self-existing but the area is half of it if installed by a seer (*ṛṣi*). The *liṅga* installed by the knower of the Supreme Reality, the result is similar to that of the self-revealed one.

As a rule, the central image enshrined in the *garbhagṛha* of a temple dedicated to Śiva is enjoined to be a *liṅga*-form only. Nevertheless, the phallic emblem can be conceived and represented in a medium of material ranging from gems, jewels, stones, metals, wood, clay, painting, ivory or even in such ephemeral means as flowers, scents, pastes, etc.

The classical texts of Śilpaśāstra and temple rituals take immense care in detailing the religious principles and canonical rules with respect to the making of various types of Śivaliṅgas and their constituent-portions, their measurements and allied ratios of dimensions and symbolic shapes as it has been categorically stated in his Śaivite treatise by the teacher Vairocana (c. 10–11 cent. A.D.):

न वेदे त्रिविधं लिङ्गं न च प्रासादलक्षणम् ।
न द्वारं मण्डपादिश्च स्थापनं न शिवादिके ॥
शिवसिद्धान्त एवोक्तं लक्षणं शाङ्करादिकम् ।

PLSSamu II.156–57ab

In the Vedic lore, there is no ruling for the triple *liṅga*, nor are there (given) the injunctions for shrines, doors, pavilions and for installation. It is only in the texts of Śaiva doctrines, promulgated by Śiva (*śivādika*) himself that the features pertaining to Śaivite things are spoken of.

पिण्डिकां साम्प्रतं वक्ष्ये लिङ्गं च त्रिविधे शुभाम् ।
महत्याः प्रतिमायाश्च दिग्लिङ्गादेश्च साधने ॥

PLSSamu VIII.1

Now, I would describe the *piṇḍikā* (base-portion) which is befitting for the three types of *liṅga*. Also the pedestals, which are (used) in case of large images and those that are implemented for the (ten types of) *dik-liṅga*s (direction *liṅga*s).

In essence, a *liṅga*-form represents the composite of Śiva and Śakti:

पिण्डिका स्यादुमादेवी लिङ्गं च परमेश्वरः ।

PLSSamu VIII.2ab

The base-part is goddess Umā and the *liṅga* represents the great lord himself.

Likewise, Śivaliṅga stands as a cosmic symbol with reference to its enshrinement:

प्रासादं लिङ्गमित्याहु स्त्रि(ज)गल्लयनाद् यतः ॥
ततस्तदाधारतया जगती पीठिका मता ।

SamSūt LXVIII.3cd–4ab

The temple-building is called the *liṅga* for all the three worlds are merged (or represented) into it. Therefore, the socle is opined to be its pedestal (*pīṭhikā*) owing its serving as the foundation.

The same idea has been put as follows:

आकांशं लिङ्गमित्याहुः क्षितिः स्याज्जलहारिका ।

तन्मध्ये सर्वभूतात्मलयनाल्लिङ्गमुच्यते ॥
उच्छ्रयो लिङ्गमित्याहुः पृथिवी तस्य पीठिका ।
उमा तु पीठिका ज्ञेया शङ्करो लिङ्गमुच्यते ॥

ApaṛPṛ CXCVI.64–65

The sky is called the *liṅga* and the earth, its oblation-basin. As the soul of all beings merges inside it, that is named as *liṅga*. The 'elevation' is styled as *liṅga* and the earth as its pedestal. Thus the pedestal is known as the goddess Umā and the *liṅga*, as Śaṅkara.

पीठिका विष्णुरूपं स्याल्लिङ्गरूपी महेश्वरः ।
तस्माल्लिङ्गार्चनं श्रेष्ठं सर्वेषामपि वै द्विजाः ॥

SkaPur (Maheśvara, Kedāra) VIII.21

The base-stone is Viṣṇu's form and the *liṅga* represents the great lord Śiva himself. Therefore the worship of *liṅga* is also the best of all (worships).

The *liṅga*-form as having a partial representation of Śiva's image-form is conceived in several such varieties:

व्यक्ताव्यक्तं प्रवक्ष्यामि दशभेदैर्व्यवस्थितम् ।
पंचास्यादि यथा लिङ्गं भवेत्सुव्यक्तपंचकम् ॥

PLSSamu VII.1

One-faced, two-faced, three-faced, four-faced, five-faced Śivaliṅgas described in further details, and those five varieties as well which have bodies of fully developed images.

A full-fledged, ten-armed image of Śiva is marked by an ithyphallic attribute:

पीनांगं यौवनोद्भिन्नं दशबाहुं त्रिलोचनम् ।
ऊर्ध्वमेढ्रं महादीप्तं वैशाखकरणे स्थितम् ।
नृत्यन्तं तु महाहृष्टमायुधाकुलपाणिनम् ॥

PLSSamu VI.16ab, 18

The dancing lord (Śiva) having ten arms, with three eyes, endowed with stout limbs, developed in youth, shining with light and standing in the stance of Vaiśākha, being greatly delighted and bearing ten weapons in hands, and featured with the erect *liṅgam*....

Similarly, the Ardhanārīśvara image is defined:

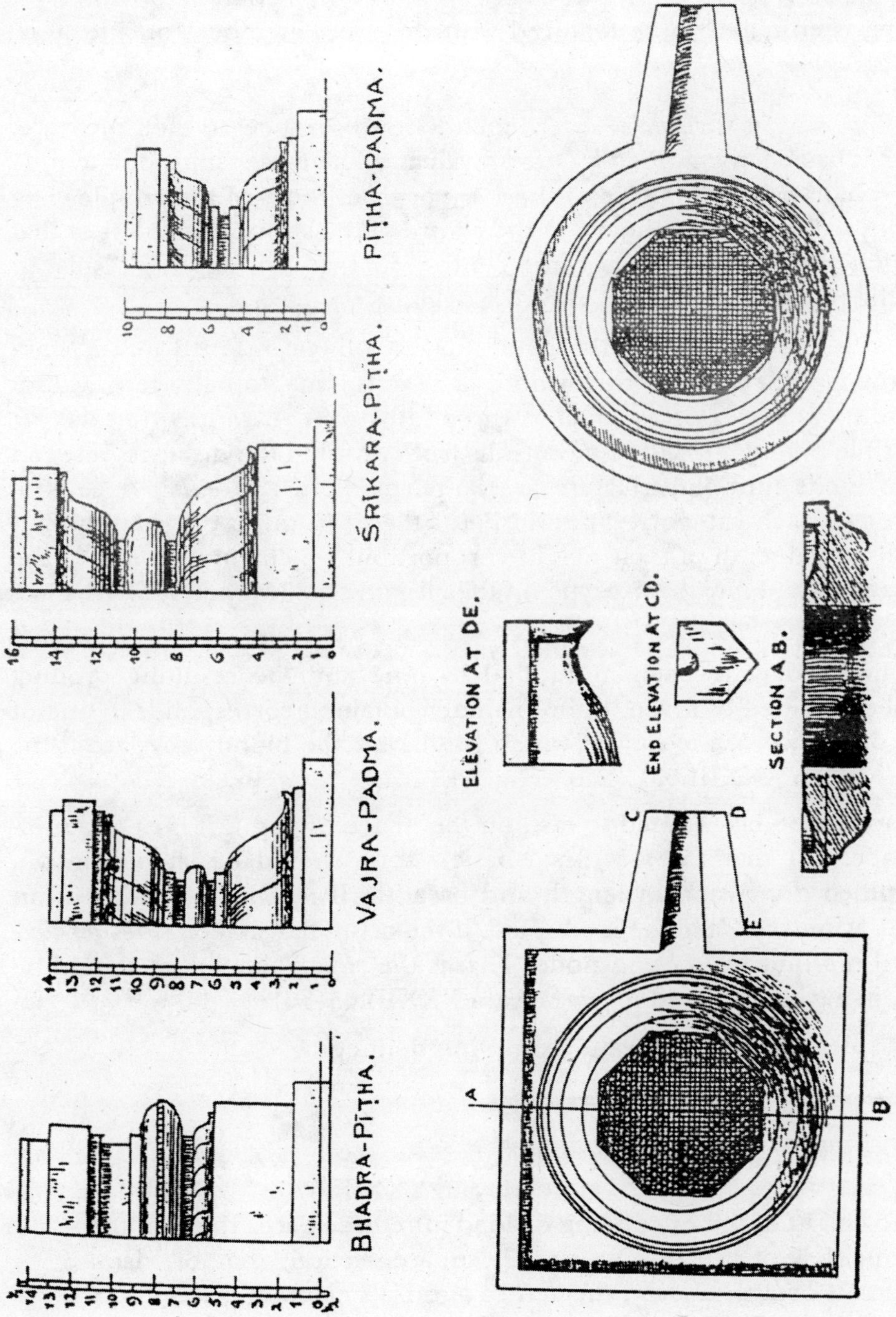

Figure 24: Some Varieties of *liṅga-pīṭhikā*

विधेयः शास्त्रविद्वद्भिरूर्ध्वलिङ्ग उमेश्वरः ॥

PLSSamu VI.50cd

By the conversant in scriptures the form of Īśvara combined with Umā is enjoined to be featured with the erect member (on the Śiva's side).

The *liṅga* and its shrine are interdependent with respect to their measurements. As it has been enjoined by the **Mayamata**. The dimensions of a temple (may be calculated) from those of the *liṅga* or from those of the temple. The sage places the *liṅga* or the image in the centre of the shrine to the left of that line (which passes through its exact centre) so that it is slightly displaced towards the north-east (Mayam XXXIII.37–38a).

Herewith appear the dimensions of a Nāgara liṅga installed in a Nāgara temple: the least height for (this symbol of) Śiva is equal to half the (width of the sanctum); the greatest is equal to three fifths (of that width); (a total of) nine possible heights) for the *liṅga* results from dividing the distance between these two limits into eight. There are large, medium and small ones and, thus, three of each category. The width (of these *liṅgas*) is respectively five, four or three-sixteenth of their height (proportions which correspond) to the *jayada, pauṣṭika* and *sārvakāmika* types in the Nāgara class (Mayam XXXIII.40cd-43ab).

The height having been multiplied by nine and the resulting product having been divided by seven, the remainder obtained corresponds to one of the days of the week, the first of which is Sunday; the bloody days are to be avoided (Mayam XXXIII.63).

Jāti-mode is to be adopted to fashion the image of god if it is of quadrangular shape. (In that case) at first (basic) stone should be shaped into a parallel piped dimension in length and breadth. If it is in the shape of an octagonal prism *chanda*-mode is adopted. If the prism has sixteen sides *vikalpa*-mode and if cylindrical *ābhāsa*-mode. That is the rough shape that should be sculpted, in a triple natured *liṅga* (Mayam XXXIII.65–66).

The triple sections of a Śivaliṅga are thus defined:

त्रिधा कृत्वायतं मूले ब्रह्मांशं चतुरश्रकम् ।
अष्टाश्रं वैष्णवं मध्ये वृत्तमूर्ध्वांशमैशकम् ॥

Mayam XXXIII.67

The height of the *liṅga* being divided into three parts, the Brahmā element is at the bottom and is square section, that of Viṣṇu which is octagonal, is in the centre and Īśa's element is the circular summit. (Tr. Bruno Dagens)

The Śivaliṅga is said to be of several types with definite names and forms:

लिङ्गं सुरार्चितं धारालिङ्गं साहस्रलिङ्गकम् ।
त्रैराशिकं तु सर्वेषां सर्वकामफलप्रदम् ॥

Mayam XXXIII.80

Liṅgas of the following varieties bring the satisfaction of all desires to everybody: Surārcita, Dhārāliṅga, Sāhasraliṅga and Trairāśika. (Tr. Bruno Dagens)

With their specific canonical names, formation of each one of them has been defined by the author of the **Mayamata** as follows:

त्रिंशद्भागे सर्वतोभद्रलिङ्गे मूले मध्येऽग्रे दशांशं क्रमेण ।
वृत्तं तुल्यं सर्वतः शम्भुभागं विप्राणां तद् भूपतीनां प्रशस्तम् ॥
वेदभूत रसभागिकैरधो भूतषण्मुनिपदैरधः परम् ।
षट्कसप्तवसु भागया ततः सप्तनागनवभागया पुनः ॥
वर्धमानमुदितं चतुर्विधं ब्रह्मविष्णुशिव भागतः क्रमात् ।
सर्वसम्पदुदयं जयप्रदं पुत्रवृद्धिदमिदं महीभृताम् ॥

Mayam XXXIII.74–76

The height of the Sarvatobhadra-liṅga is divided into thirty parts, ten of which are for the lower part; there are as many, for the median part and as many again for the top; Śambhu's element is perfectly circular and this *liṅga* is invariably suitable for brahmins. Herewith, that appropriate for princes: these are the four varieties of Vardhamāna-liṅga determined by the heights of the elements of Brahmā, Viṣṇu and Śiva; the proportions, starting from the bottom (of the *liṅga*) may be four parts (for Brahmā's element), five (for Viṣṇu's) and six for Śiva's, or there may be five parts, six parts and seven parts or six, seven and eight, or lastly seven, eight and nine. To princes, this *liṅga* brings escalating success, victory and an increase in the number of their sons. (Tr. Bruno Dagens)

सप्तसप्तवसु भागया ततः पञ्चपञ्चकषडंशकैरपि ।
वेदवेदशर भागया ततो बन्धबन्धयुग भागया पुनः ॥
उक्तमत्र हि मया चतुर्विधं तच्छिवाधिकमजादिभागिके ।
सर्ववस्तुदमिदं विशामलं सर्ववर्णयमिनामुदीरितम् ॥

Mayam XXXIII.77–78

I now present the four varieties of the *liṅga* [Śivādhika] where the

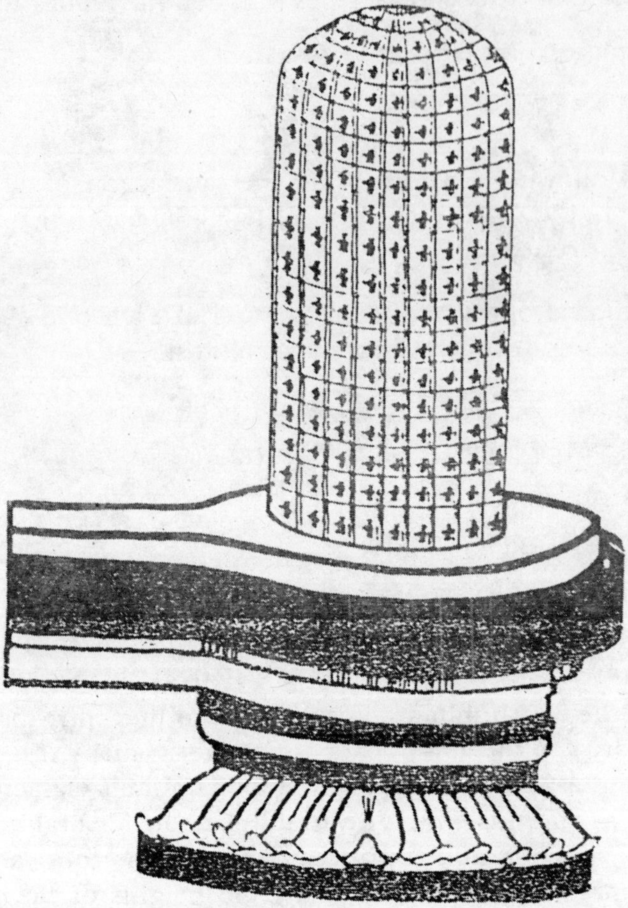

Figure 25: Sāhasra-liṅga

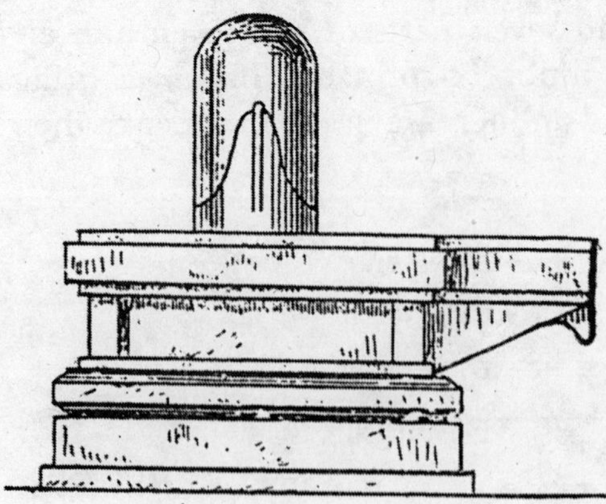

Figure 26: Dhārā-liṅga

element of Śiva is the largest; the three elements, beginning with that of *aja* (i.e. Brahmā) make, respectively, seven parts, seven parts and eight parts or five, five and six, or four, four and five or lastly, three, three and four. It is said that this *liṅga* brings all sorts of riches to *vaiśya* who have mastered their senses.
(Tr. Bruno Dagens)

इष्टायामसमोपेतं स्वायामार्धार्धविस्तरम् ।
शेषं पूर्ववदुद्दिष्टं नाम्ना सुरगणार्चितम् ॥

Mayam XXXIII.81

That *liṅga,* to which is given a width equal to a quarter of its height and the rest of which is as above, is called 'honoured by the host of gods' (*suragaṇārcita*). (Tr. Bruno Dagens)

धारालिङ्गं सर्वलिङ्गे मतं तन्मूलेऽष्टाश्रं वा कलाश्रं युगाश्रम् ।
तस्मादूर्ध्वं द्वैगुणं स्यात् सधारं धारालिङ्गं सर्ववर्णे प्रशस्तम् ॥

Mayam XXXIII.82

A faceted *liṅga* may be made on the same basis as a regular one; there are eight, sixteen or four faces on the bottom part and twice as many above that. This faceted Dhārā-liṅga is suitable for all classes. (Tr. Bruno Dagens)

पूजाभागे सर्वतोभद्रलिङ्गे धारा कार्या पञ्च पञ्चक्रमेण ।
एकैकस्यामष्टपञ्चोपरिष्टात् साहस्रं तद्रेखया लिङ्गमुक्तम् ॥

Mayam XXXIII.83

If twenty-five facets are cut, side by side, on the worshipped element of a Sarvatobhadra-liṅga and if forty superposed (*liṅga*) are drawn on each of these, a thousand *liṅga* result from this design and this is said to be a Sāhasra-liṅga. (Tr. Bruno Dagens)

सस्थूलमूललिङ्गं यवमध्यं वा पिपीलिकामध्यम् ।
लिङ्गं तु शिरः स्थूलं ह्यार्षं लिङ्गं चतुर्भेदम् ॥

Mayam XXXIII.85

There are four varieties of *liṅga* fitting for *ṛṣi*, depending upon whether the bottom is wider (than the other two elements) or whether the median element is (convex, like the middle of) a barley grain or (concave, like the middle of) an ant or, lastly, whether the upper element is the widest (of all).
(Tr. Bruno Dagens)

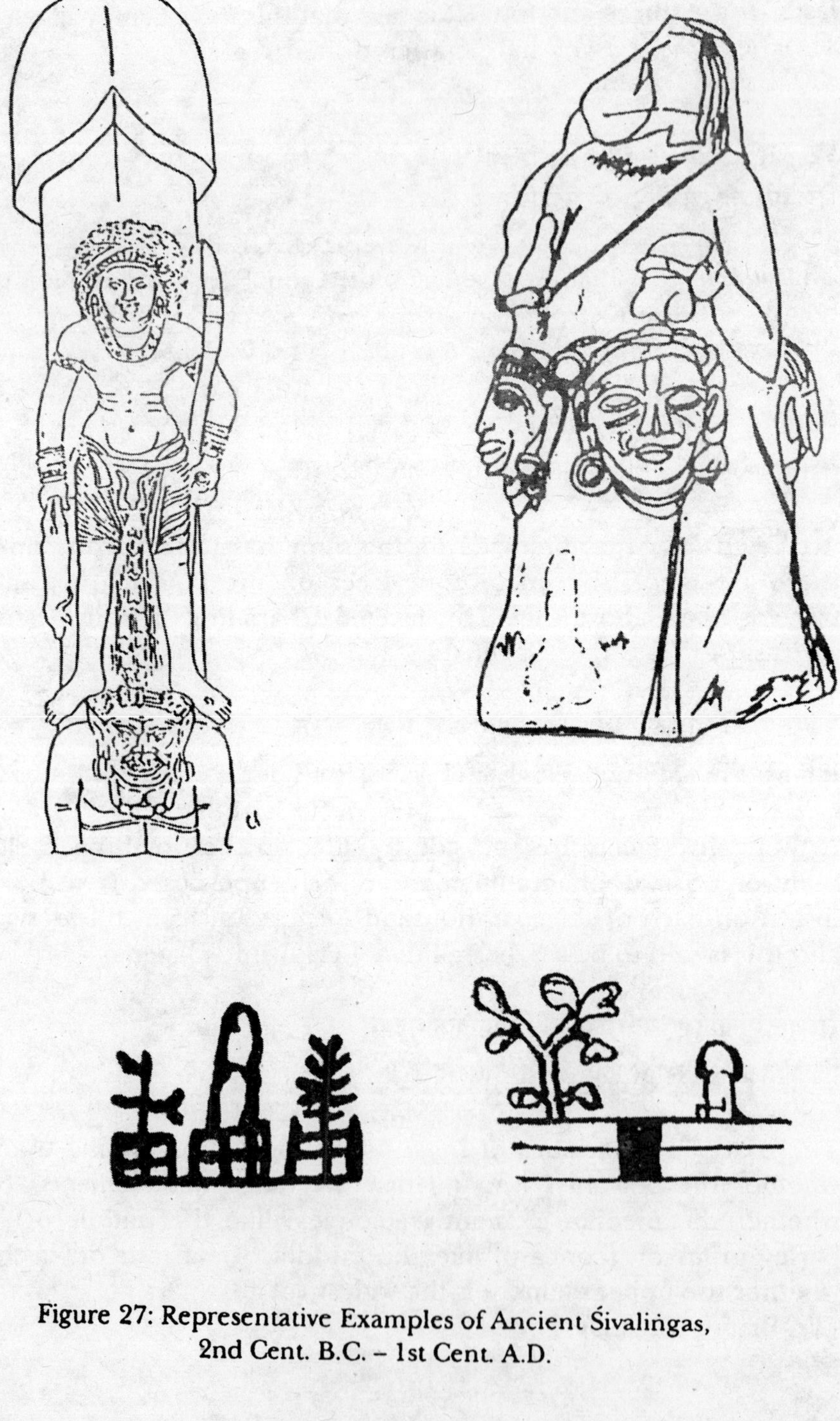

Figure 27: Representative Examples of Ancient Śivaliṅgas,
2nd Cent. B.C. – 1st Cent. A.D.

निजविपुलाष्टांशघ्नं मूले मध्ये तथा तदग्रे च ।
विष्ण्वजभागो सम्यक् चतुरश्रं चार्षके लिङ्गे ॥

Mayam XXXIII.86

Depending on the circumstance, the width of bottom, middle or top is to be decreased by an eighth of the chosen width. In the case of a *liṅga* fitting for *ṛṣi,* (Ārṣa-liṅga) both the Aja and Viṣṇu elements are square section. (Tr. Bruno Dagens)

लिङ्गं फलकाकारं द्व्यश्रं पञ्चाश्रकं त्रिकोणं च ।
एकादशनवषट्सप्ताश्रं च द्वादशाश्रं च॥
पूर्वोदितेतराश्रं शूलाग्रं शृङ्गसदृशशिरः ।
अन्यदपि भेदयुक्तं सशिरः सूत्रेतरं न मानयुतम् ॥

Mayam XXXIII.87–88

A self-generated *liṅga* (Svayambhu-liṅga) is shaped like a plank or it has two or five sides or is triangular or has eleven, nine, six, seven or twelve sides, or the number of its sides is different from those indicated above. It may also be pointed at the top or in the shape of a horn; it may be of one specific type and its rounded top drawn according to another type or it may not be in conformity with the prescribed dimension. (Tr. Bruno Dagens)

Yet another categorisation of Śivaliṅgas is with reference to the shape of its part or head:

शिरसो वर्तनमधुना लिङ्गानां वक्ष्यते क्रमशः ॥
छत्राभा त्रपुषाभा कुक्कुटकाण्डार्धचन्द्रसदृशाभा ।
बुद्बुदसदृशा पञ्चैवोद्दिष्टा वर्तना मुनिभिः ॥

Mayam XXXIII.92cd–93

The manner in which the top of the *liṅga* is to be rounded is now given. The sages say that this rounded part may have one of five profiles: parasol, cucumber, hen's egg, hemisphere and bubble. (Tr. Bruno Dagens)

About the rounded shape of the topmost portion of a *liṅga,* the **Mayamata** has thus enjoined:

सूत्राणां सर्वेषां कर्तव्या वर्तना तदग्रे तु ।
लिङ्गानां शिरसि यथा सामान्यं स्यात्तथा समुद्दिष्टम् ॥
अश्वत्थपत्रसदृशं कदलीमुकुलोपमं यवाभं च ।
अम्बुजकुड्मलसदृशं सामान्यं सर्वलिङ्गेषु ॥

सूत्राग्रमात्तभागैकांशं व्यासोन्नतं हि मतम् ।

Mayam XXXIII.136–138ab

A rounded contour must always be drawn at the top of the frenum. It may (be drawn) according to the shape of the summit of the *liṅga* or in accordance with the general rule. (Rounded) shapes, common to all *liṅga*, are those of the *aśvattha* leaf, *kadalī* bud and *ambuja* bud. The width and height of the frenum are equal to the fraction (of the Śiva element) chosen (as unit of calculation for the lines). (Tr. Bruno Dagens)

For installing a *liṅga* in its shrine there can be three modes of its practical handling:

लिङ्गं महत्त्वधिष्ठाने चार्धे स्थिते च मध्यमम् ।
समाप्ते च विमाने स्यात् कन्यसं स्थापयेद् बुधैः ॥
एवं स्थाप्यं लिङ्गमुक्तप्रकारं श्रीसौभाग्यारोग्यभोग्यप्रदायि ।
उक्तादन्यद् यत् कृतं तद् विपत्त्यै पत्युर्नित्यं रोगशोकप्रदं स्यात् ॥

Mayam XXXIII.161–162

The wise man installs a small *liṅga* in a finished temple; it is when a temple is half built that medium *liṅga* is to be installed and a large one is installed when the base has been constructed.

A *liṅga* of prescribed shape is to be installed; it brings good fortune, well-being, health and enjoyment. If not made according to the norm, it will be to the founder, a failure and a source of illness and of distress without end. (Tr. Bruno Dagens)

The *liṅga*-shape is employed in several other structural parts of a shrine. For example:

शिखराकृतिवत् कीलं लिङ्गच्छन्दमथापि वा ॥
एवं त्रिधा समुद्दिष्टं स्थूपिकाकीलमार्यकैः ।

Mayam XVIII.126cd–127ab

The axis of the finial may be in the shape of a pin, nail, or *liṅga*, these are the three shapes, the sages prescribe. (Tr. Bruno Dagens)

सर्वात्मीयं लिङ्गमाकाशरूपं तस्माल्लिङ्गं पौरुषं स्थापनीयम् ।
तज्ज्ञैर्युक्त्या सावकाशालये वा पश्चाद् बध्नीयात् तु वा मूर्धेष्टकां वा ॥
लिङ्गानां वै पौरुषाणां विमाने प्रोक्ते नीत्या स्थापना च क्रमेण ॥

Mayam XXXIV.73, 74cd

The universal *liṅga* is (formless like) ether; thus the *liṅga* which is

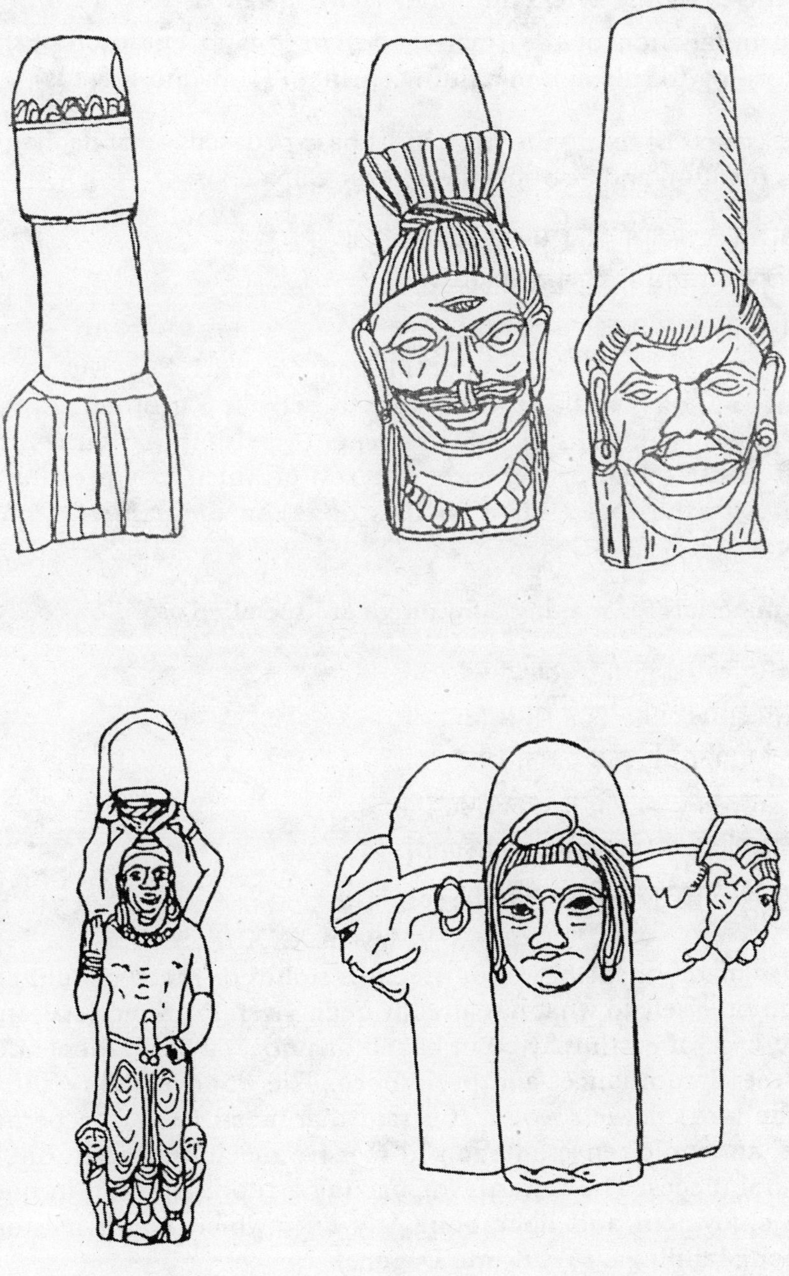

Figure 28: Early Śivaliṅgas from Mathura Relief, 1st – 3rd Cent. A.D.

to be installed, is a man-made one. According to circumstance, the sages install it in a sufficiently large temple and they do not fix the crowning bricks until they (have installed) (the *liṅga*). The installation of the (man-made) *liṅga* is to be accomplished according to rule and in a fitting shrine. (Tr. Bruno Dagens)

Some aspects of fixing the *liṅga* in its base-pedestal, or of its manufactures in various medium and also specified in the Śilpa texts:

बाणलिङ्गं यथालाभं तत्तत् सम्यग् निधापयेत् ॥
पञ्चत्रिभागमुच्चार्धं त्रिद्व्यंशं वार्चनार्हकम् ।
भागं शेषांशकं पीठबन्धं स्याद् बाणलिङ्गके ॥

Mayam XXXIII.158cd–159

A Bāṇa-liṅga is to be set (into its pedestal) in a manner fitting to the circumstance; its venerated element (is visible) on three-fifths, half or two-thirds of its height, the rest of which may provide the link with the socle(this is what is done) in the case of a Bāṇa-liṅga. (Tr. Bruno Dagens)

Such materials for making a Śivaliṅga are specified as follows:

मृद्वृक्षरत्नलोहैश्च कुर्यात् स्फाटिकवद् दृढम् ।
मृण्मयं युक्तितः पक्वमपक्वं वा यथेष्टतः ॥
वृक्षजं दोषनिर्मुक्तं लोहजं घनमिष्यते ।
घनं साङ्गमनङ्गं वा लोहेन सकलं मतम् ॥
लोहेन पूजितं कल्प्य भुक्तिमुक्तिफलप्रदम् ।
लिङ्गं शिलेतरं सर्वं मणिलिङ्गमिति स्मृतम् ॥

Mayam XXXIII.153–155

Liṅga made of earth, wood, precious stones or metal should conform precisely to what has already been given for the crystal ones. The *liṅga* of earth may be in baked or unbaked earth, depending on the circumstances and preference. The wooden *liṅga* (is to be made with) flawless wood. It is said that metal *liṅga* is to be massive; an iconic representation in massive metal may be in one or several pieces. The rewards for making a representation in metal are enjoyment and liberation. Any *liṅga* which is not in stone, called Maṇiliṅga. (Tr. Bruno Dagens)

As regards, the position of Śivaliṅga in the sanctum, it has been thus observed:

विभज्य नवधा गर्भं मध्ये लिङ्गस्य पीठिका ।
पादाष्टकं तु रुचिरं (सुषिरं) पार्श्वत: परिकल्पयेत् ॥

VPrak VI.69

Having divided the dimension of the *garbha* chamber into nine (equal parts), the central one is for the pedestal of the *liṅga*. (The remaining) eight units around it are employed for the (free) space on sides.

Other relevant specifications are further noteworthy:

लिङ्गदैर्घ्याङ्गुलैर्लिङ्गं विस्तारं गणयेद् बुध: ।
लिङ्गविस्तारमानेन त्रिगुणं पीठविस्तरम् ॥
गर्भगेहप्रविस्तारं त्रिभागं परिकल्पयेत् ।
तेषु भागेषु चैकेन पीठविस्तारमाचेरत् ॥
दीर्घं कुर्वन्ति पीठानां विष्णुभागावसानकम् ।
मूले मध्ये तथोर्ध्वे च ब्रह्मविष्णुहरांशकम् ॥

VPrak VI.108–110

The learned should calculate the width of the *liṅga* from the (ratio of) finger breadths of the length of it. From that *liṅga*-width the width of *pīṭha* is thrice in measure. One should divide the width of the sanctum into three parts, of which one is to be used for the *pīṭha*. They make the height of the *pīṭha* up to the end of the Viṣṇu-portion (of the *liṅga*), as there are its three sections at the base, the middle and the top belonging respectively to Brahmā, Viṣṇu and Hara.

बाणलिङ्गादिकं कुर्यात् सप्तांशं वा त्रिभागितम् ।
पञ्चभागं द्विभागं वा यथायोग्यं यथा स्थिरम् ।
सप्तभागकृते लिङ्गे चतुरंशान्निवेदयेत् ॥
पीठमध्यगते गर्ते त्रिभागं चैक (श) भागकम् ।
पञ्चभागे तु भागांस्त्रीन्द्विभागेऽर्धं यथाक्रमम् ॥

VPrak VI.114–115

The Bāṇa-liṅga and other types should be assumed as consisting of seven parts, or of three parts, five parts or of two parts as it is befitting and is ordained (in a specific case). When of seven (equal) parts four parts are inserted into the cavity in the centre of the pedestal while the Śiva-top (read *caiśabhāgam*) is three parts. In case of the five divisions three are (set in), and when of two divisions a half is (inserted in the pedestal-perforation), respectively.

अथान्यच्च प्रवक्ष्यामि प्रासादं लिङ्गमानतः ।
लिङ्गपूजाप्रमाणेन कर्तव्या पीठिका बुधैः ॥
पीठिकार्धेन भागे स्यात् तन्मानेन तु भित्तयः ।
बाह्यभित्तिप्रमाणेन उत्सेधस्तु भवेत् ततः ॥

VPrak VI.62–63

Of a variant scheme, now I speak about a temple measured according to the dimension of its enshrined *liṅga.* The pedestal is to be made as equal to the venerated top of the *liṅga.* Half that pedestal size are the walls (in thickness). The elevation of the shrine should be according to the space covered between the outer walls.

एवं बाणादिलिङ्गानां प्रवेशः शिवेनोदितः ।
स्थूलं शिरः कृशं मूलमुन्नते तन्मुखं शिरः ॥
निम्नपृष्ठमितिख्यातं बालगेहादिलिङ्गके ।
अज्ञातमुखपृष्ठानां कन्यास्पृष्टं मुखं शिरः ॥

VPrak VI.117–118

Thus is spoken by Śiva the insertion of the *liṅga* pertaining to the Bāṇa and other varieties. Its top is larger while the bottom is thin as its head-top is erected according to the original stones piece querried. The bottom is known as per the back (side, read *nimnaṃ pṛṣṭham*). In case the top and back is unknown, the side which is touched by a maiden is taken to form the face as well as the top.

With regards to the foundation-stone, the following rules are stated to be carefully followed:

लिङ्गायामसमव्यासा श्रेष्ठा ब्रह्मशिला स्मृता ।
पूजांशद्विगुणा नीचा तयोर्मध्येऽष्टभागिके ॥
प्राग्वन्नव प्रकाराः स्युः क्रमाद् ब्रह्मशिलाः शुभाः ।
स्वव्यासार्धोन्नता मुख्या नीचा वेदांशतो घनाः ॥
तयोर्मध्येऽष्टधा भक्ते घनाद् ब्रह्मशिला नव ।

ĪśGP kp 39.88–90ab

The best type width of Brahma-slab is known to be equal in height of the *liṅga.* The inferior kind is double in size to the *liṅga*-top part. In between them lie eight divisions, which make, as stated earlier, a total of nine auspicious Brahma-slabs. A Brahma-stone of the leading type has its thickness to be half the width while the inferior ones have the breadth as a fourth of the dimension. The mean difference, being divided into eight successive measures, (likewise) gives a total of nine sequences of the Brahma-stone thickness.

There can be numerous alternatives as to the size of a Śivaliṅga selected for the purpose of religious significance and aims:

लिङ्गानि सायककरादिपदोनिताश्विहस्तान्तिमानि चरणांशविमुक्तिक्लृप्त्या ।
स्युर्वर्णिनां मुखभुजोरुपदोद्भवानां पञ्चाग्निपावकजगत्परिसङ्ख्यकानि ॥

TSamu II.119

There are (fourteen sizes to be arrived at in sequence) for Śivaliṅgas beginning from five *hasta*-measure (downwards) to one-fourth one-and-three-fourth *hasta*-measure deducting a fourth *hasta* (i.e. six *aṅgulas*) successively. (Thus are arrived) first five sizes for the *brāhmaṇa* class, next three for the *kṣatriyas*, next three for the *vaiśyas*, and the last three for the *śūdras*, respectively.

आयामे दलिते दिवाकरयुजाभीष्टेऽष्टभिर्विस्तृतिः
कार्यांशैरथ पञ्चपञ्चयवयुक्तैः सप्तभिः पञ्चभिः ।
स्वायामार्कयुगांशतद्द्विरसनांशःस्याद् यवः केवलैः
पञ्चांशैरपि गर्भगेहनवमांशेनापि सा स्मर्यते ॥

TSamu II.123

Taking the desired height divided into twenty-four parts, eight of them make the width of the Śivaliṅga, also that width is alternatively of seven parts plus five *yavas*, or five parts plus five *yavas*. The *yava* unit (in the context) has to be of (one-eighth) portion of the twentyfourth division of the assumed height of the *liṅga*. Or, the width can be five parts only (of the twenty-four parts of the *liṅga* height). Also, the width (of the *liṅga*) is calculated to be one-ninth of the *garbhagṛha* dimension.

The four main types of popular Śivaliṅga worthy of installation in the shrine are thus summarized in the **Tantrasamuccaya**:

लिङ्गं सर्वसमं समोन्मितिविभक्तांशत्रयं तत्पुनः
स्वायत्या समनाहकं यदि समांशं चाथ वृद्ध्युत्तरम् ।
भक्ते भानुयुजोच्छ्र्येऽद्रिवसुनन्दांशै (स्तु) मूलादिषू-
पेतं दिग्दलिते त्रिलोकयुगसङ्ख्याभिस्तथेशाधिकम् ॥

TSamu II.122

The Sarvasama type Śivaliṅga has three equal divisions of its height

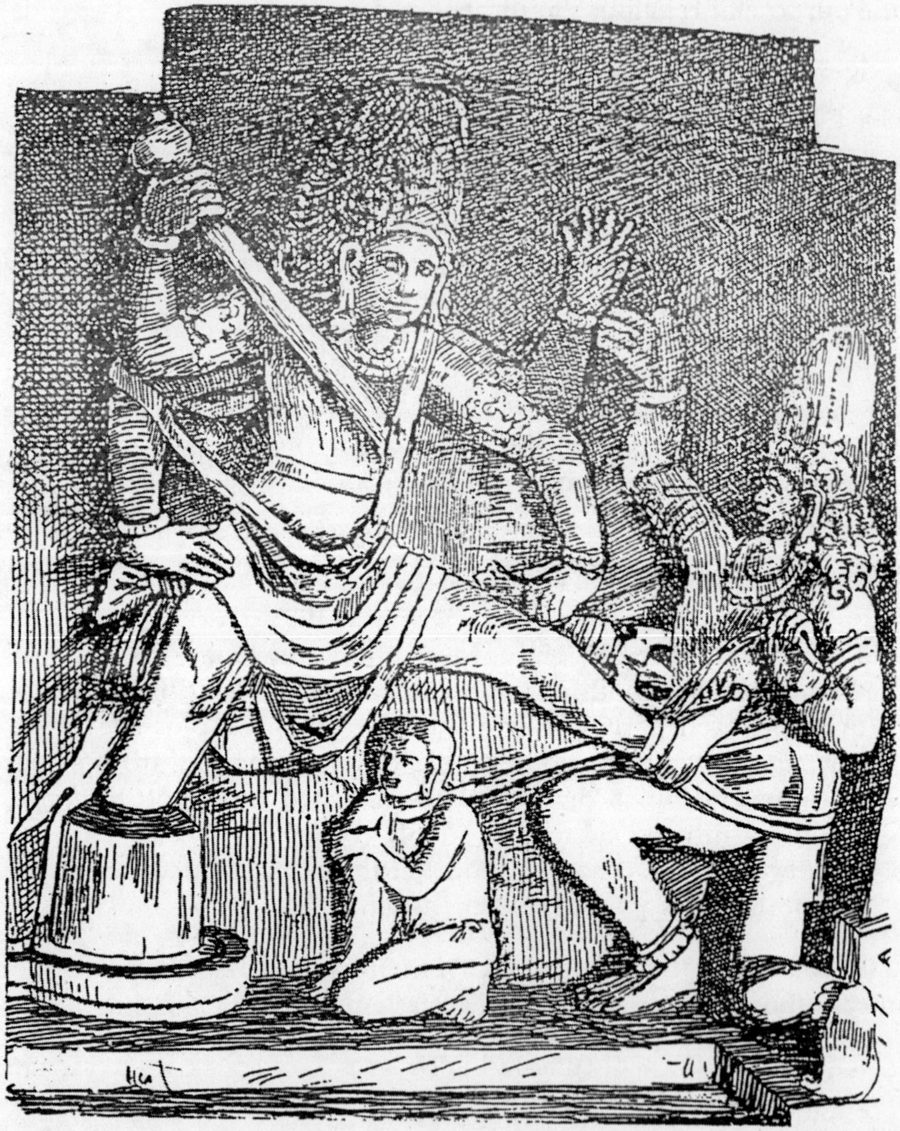

Figure 29: Kālārimūrti: Stone-panel – Daśāvatāra Cave: Ellora

(for the *pūjā-bhāga, viṣṇu-bhāga* and *brahmā-bhāga* respectively). The Samāṃśa type has (in each case of) its height-wise parts equal also in their width. Then, the Vṛddhyuttara (Vardhamāna) type has each of the above three parts as increasing in height, (from below) measuring seven, eight and nine units when that is assumed to carry total twentyfour divisions. The Īśādhika (=Śivādhika) kind is known as the total height is taken as divided into ten parts and the three sequences are of three, three and four units.

Conclusion

The phallic emblem and its worship seems to have assumed specific relevance in ancient Indian tradition with Śaivisim from hoary antiquity. Some phallic representations are now found from the protohistoric sites of Harappa cultures. However, early Vedic texts do not provide any clear-cut mention of a *liṅga*-symbol. The earliest evidence for such a Rudra-Śiva cult centred around a *liṅga* can be found in the Epics and in certain later Vedic texts.

In art context, certain uninscribed early coins have been identified to depict a phallic symbol as a sacred object of its own kind. Besides, a few Mathura reliefs, belonging to 1st Cent. B.C. to 2nd Cent. A.D. fully evince the cult of Śaivite emblem. Indeed, two of the earliest specimens of well developed Śiva-liṅga representation have been found from Gudimallam (Chitoor Dt., Andhra Pradesh) and Bhita (Allahabad Dt., U.P.), assigned roughly to the above antiquity. The former is a realistically carved phallus form with a two-armed epiphany of the god carved on its front. The latter is shaped to carry a bust of the deity with four other heads shown on the four sides below. Recent discoveries from Mathura area and some sites of Rajasthan now provide a variety of *liṅga* sculptures, which can largely be explained and defined as referring to the evolved cult of the Śivaliṅga, detailed in the Purāṇas, Āgamas and Tantra descriptions, and iconographic treatises some passages of which have already been culled and commented above. Thus, there are, extensively studied by many competent scholars and authorities, numerous aspects of the *liṅga* in Śaivite worship and philosophical-mythical visualisations, both in their art-iconographic developments as well as mystic symbolical contents.

Prithvi Kumar Agrawala

Select Bibliography

Agrawala, P.K.: Studies in Indian Iconography, Jaipur: Publication Scheme, 1994.

Agrawala, V.S.: Śiva-Mahādeva – The Great God, Varanasi: Prithivi Prakashan, 1966.

Banerjea, J.N.: Development of Hindu Iconography, Calcutta: University of Calcutta, 2nd edn, 1956.

Bhandarkar, R.G.: Vaiṣṇavism, Śaivism and Minor Religious Systems, Varanasi: Indological Book House, 1965.

Sharma, I.K.: The Development of Early Śaiva Art and Architecture, New Delhi: Sandeep Prakashan, 1982.

PĀDA

Overview

Pāda (mn.) literally and etymologically means foot. However, various other connotations got attached to it due to the processes of expansion and transference of meaning. All these connotations are interrelated and the primary meaning of *pāda* (i.e. foot) always remained as a base for the development of the conceptual frameworks which have been built over this term throughout the millennia.

Etymology and Related Terms

Pāda (Greek *pedon*, Latin *ped* (pl. *pedes*), German *Fuß* (*fuss*), Hindi *pāṃva* and *pāva* is a masculine *prātipadika* derived from the root *pad-* (to go) adding the suffix *ghañ*. The word *pada*, meaning a footstep, footpoint, a place or some abode is also derived from the same root:

> पादः पद्यतेः । तन्निधानात् पदम् । पशुपादप्रकृतिः प्रभागपादः ।
> प्रभागपादसामान्यादितराणि पदानि ।
>
> Nir II.7
>
> *Pādaḥ* (foot) is derived from (the root) *pad-* (to go); when it is placed down, (the same word in the neuter gender) means a footstep. The word (also signifies) a quarter of division from the analogy of a quadruped; and other quarters from the analogy of *pāda* of division. (Tr. L. Sarup)

The word *pad* is also used in place of *pāda*, in the Puruṣasūkta of **Ṛgveda**, in the sense of feet (*padbhyāṃ śūdro'jāyata* – ṚV X.90.12d).

Pāda (in neuter gender), *aṅghri* and *caraṇa* (both in masculine gender) are the synonyms of *pāda* in the sense of a foot (*pādaḥ padaṅghriścaraṇo'striyām* – AmKo II.6.71). The word *pāda* also denotes a part of the metre, verse or poem and subsequently a song. The **Chāndogya Upaniṣad** (III.12.5) calls the metre Gāyatrī as *catuṣpadā* and *ṣaḍvidhā*. Jayadeva's songs in the **Gītagovinda** are termed as *aṣṭapadīs* and the devotional songs of medieval poets related to the cult of Bhakti are also known as *padas*.

The word '*caraṇa*' is derived from root *car-* (to walk, to move). *Caraṇya* is a person who promotes his family or brings glory to his family. The **Gaṇaratna**

Mahodadhi says: Just as the feet give height to the body and carry it forward, in the same way one who promotes his family is called *caraṇya.*

> चरणौ इव चरण्यः । यथा चरणौ शरीरस्य प्रकर्षकौ तद्वत् कुलस्य प्रकर्षक एवमुच्यते ।
>
> Gaṇar III.190
>
> One who promotes a dynasty is called *caraṇya* (from the word *caraṇa* a foot). As the two legs (*caraṇas*) draw a body, so one who promotes (his dynasty) is called *caraṇya.* (Tr. R.S. Bhattacharya)

In the context of Vedic Saṃhitās the word *caraṇa* is related to a particular *śākhā* (branch) of a Saṃhitā. *Caraṇa* has been defined by Jagaddhara in the following way: *caraṇaśabdaḥ śākhāviśeṣādhyayanaparaikatāpannajanasaṅghavācī* (MālMā I.5). The word *caraṇa* denotes a group of persons devoted to the study of a particular *śākhā* of Veda. The meaning signified by *caraṇa* here is limited to a particular context and not to be attached with the word *pāda.*

However, a sense of sanctity remained attached to both the words *pāda* and *caraṇa* in Vedic and later Vaiṣṇava tradition. The word *pāda* is added after the name of a great man to denote reverence for him. The commentators and authors like Mammaṭa, a celebrated *ācārya* on Alaṅkāraśāstra refer to Abhinavagupta as Abhinavaguptapādāḥ, to suggest that even naming his feet is sufficient. Here the last part, i.e. *pādāḥ* is used in the plural as token of respect. The **Viṣṇu Purāṇa** describing the incarnation of Viṣṇu as boar (*varāhāvatāra*) says that the four Vedas dwell in his four feet (*pādeṣu vedāstava* – ViPur I.4.32). In the same Purāṇa the earth is said to be having abode in the feet of Viṣṇu in the form of a lady (*ibid.*, I.4.20).

Several words, phrases and idioms have been formed through *pāda. Pādakaṭaka* and *pādāṅgada* (the anklet), *pādakṛcchra* (a vow), *padātiḥ, pādātaḥ, pādātiḥ, pādātikaḥ* (a walker), *pādagaṇḍika* and *pādavalmīkaḥ* (a disease in feet), *pādagrahaṇa* (touching the feet out of respect), *pādacatura* (a person adept in walking), *pādaja* (a *śūdra*), *pādacārī* (synonymous to *cārī* described in texts on dance), *pādātam* (a group of walkers), *pādatrāṇa* (shoes), *pādapa* (*pādena mūlena pibati* – that which sucks water by roots), *pādaparuhā* (a creeper), *pādapā, pādukā, pādapradhāraṇam, pādarathī* and *pādavirajā* (the wooden footwear), *pādapāśaḥ* (a noose for tying a horse), *pādapāśī* (a chain), *pādapīṭha* (wooden footrest), *pādaprakṣālanam* (washing the feet), *pādaprahāra* (a kick), *pādabandhanam, pādarajjuḥ* (a cord for tying the buffalo's or cow's feet), *pādamūlaḥ, pādarakṣaṇam* (shoe), *pādarohaṇa* (Vaṭa tree), *pādāgra* (the toe), *pādāvartaḥ* (the water-wheel), *pāda* (one fourth) denoting a part, are some such words.

Layers of Meaning

The **Amara Kośa** accepts three meanings of the term *pāda*- 'rays, feet and one fourth':

> पादा रश्म्यङ्घ्रितुर्यांशाः ।
>
> AmKo III.3.89
>
> *Pāda* means a ray of light, a foot and a fourth part.
> (Tr. R.S. Bhattacharya)

These three may be taken as its basic meanings, and the term gathered some other meanings subsequently. Thus *pāda* came to denote the following meanings – the foot, the lowest part, a quarter (*pādasturīyo bhāgaḥ syāt* – AmKo II.9.89), the architrave, a pillar, a column, the foot of a cot or a chair, the root of a tree, a measurement, a part or a chapter of a book (*pādāḥ pratyantaparvatāḥ,* i.e. a hill near a mountain – AmKo II.3.7), ray of light, a quarter or one line of a verse.

Pāda in the **Atharvaveda** (XIV.1.60), **Aitareya Brāhmaṇa** (VIII.5.12), **Kauṣītaki Brāhmaṇa**(I.5) and **Śatapatha Brāhmaṇa** (XII.4.3.4) denotes the feet of an animal. The **Śatapatha Brāhmaṇa** (VI.5.3.2; VII.2.1.7; VIII.7.2.17) and **Āśvalāyana Śrauta-Sūtra** (VI.10) use the word *pāda* in the sense of a measurement. Again, the **Aitareya Brāhmaṇa** (I.4) and **Kauṣītaki Brāhmaṇa** (XXVI.5) use the word *pāda* to denote the quarter of a verse. The **Nirukta** (II.7 & VII.9) upholds the two meanings of *pāda*: 'the feet and quarter of a verse'.

The earliest use of *pāda* in sense of 'share' occurs in the **Ṛgveda**. It gives a touching portrayal of suffering and hunger of the deprived and the craving of the rich for wealth. The seer vividly describes the race for wealth:

> एकपाद्भूयो द्विपदो वि चक्रमे द्विपात् त्रिपादमभ्येति पश्चात् ।
> चतुष्पादेति द्विपदामभिस्वरे संपश्यन् पङ्क्तीरुपतिष्ठमानः ॥
>
> ṚV X.117.8
>
> He with one foot hath far outrun the biped, and the two-footed catches the three-footed. Four-footed creatures come when bipeds call them, and stand and look where five are met together.
> (Tr. R.T.H. Griffith)

The words *ekapāt, dvipāt, tripāt* and *catuṣpāt* occur here to denote persons having single, double, triple or fourfold shares of wealth. R.T.H. Griffith understands them as one-footed, biped, three-footed and four-footed creatures, but this rendering does not fit into the context. Sāyaṇa has given a very apt interpretation by remarking: "*atra pādaśabdo bhāgavacanaḥ*". Here the word *pāda* is used in the sense of share.

Kālidāsa has used the word *pāda* in the sense of the feet (*pādanyāsaiḥ kvaṇitaraśanāstatra līlāvadhūtaiḥ* – Megh I.38a) and also rays (*pādānindoramṛta-śiśirāñjālamārgapraviṣṭān* – Megh II.30a) in the same poem. In the **Vikramorvaśīya** (III.20), he uses the word *pāda* for the 'rays of moon' (*pādāsta eva śaśinaḥ sukhayanti gātram*).

Caraka has dealt with *pāda* as one of the motor organs of human body. But in the context of prescription of a doze of a medicine, the word *pāda* wherever used should be taken to mean one fourth part:

> यतश्च पादनिर्देशश्चतुर्भागस्ततश्च सः ।
>
> CarSam KaSthā XII.100
>
> If there is mention of '*pāda*' one-fourth should be taken.
> (Tr. P.V. Sharma)

The connotation of *pāda* in the sense of one fourth came to be correlated in the context of the sum of money, so that a coin of the value of one fourth of a unit in money was named as *pāda*. The earliest reference to *pāda* in the sense of a coin occurs in the **Bṛhadāraṇyaka Upaniṣad**. King Janaka is said to have got one thousand cows enclosed (in a pen) and to the horns of each cow, ten coins of gold were fastened. The word *pāda* has been used here for a coin.

> स ह गवां सहस्रमवरुरोध । दशदश पादा एकैकस्याः शृङ्गयोराबद्धा बभूवुः ।
>
> BṛUp III.1.1
>
> He had a thousand cows confined in a pen, and on the horns of each cow were fixed ten *pāda*s (of gold). (Tr. Gambhirananda)

Macdonnel and Keith interpret the use of *pāda* here in the sense of weight (*Vedic Index of Names & Subjects,* Vol. I, p. 516). S. Radhakrishnan however, understands here *pāda* as a coin of gold (*The Principal Upaniṣads,* p. 211).

Pāṇini (IV.1.8; V.4.1) uses the term *pāda* to denote the foot of a verse, and also to denote one-fourth in *paṇapādamāṣaśatādyat* (V.1.34.). As the word *pāda* here has occured with *paṇa* (coin), V.S. Agrawala interprets it to mean a particular kind of coin (*India as Known to Pāṇini,* p. 259). At least in two places Pāṇini uses the word *pāda* in the specific sense of a part of Vedic *mantra* only (Pā VI.1.115, VI.1.134).

Pāda technically came to denote a particular unit for measurement, because the word Puruṣa also meant a unit for measurement, equal to five *aratnis* or 120 *aṅgulas* (90 inches). As a unit of measurement *pāda* thus will be equal to 30 *aṅgulas* or $22^{1/2}$ inches.

The **Yajurveda** in the context of rituals, uses the word *caritra* as synonymous to *pāda* (TSam I.3.9.1); it also uses the word *pāda* to denote the waves of the sea (*ibid.*, III.2.2.1).

Both the words, *pāda* and *caraṇa* came to be used in the sense of steps or stages in a serial order. Yājñavalkya describes a legal dispute or lawsuit with four stages:

> चतुष्पाद् व्यवहारोऽयं विवादेषूपदर्शितः ।
>
> YājSm II.1.8
>
> In the legal dispute it has been shown that the legal procedure consists of four stages (*pāda*). (Tr. H.N. Chakravarty)

These four stages are: *bhāṣāpāda* (plaint), *uttarapāda* (reply or defence of the accused), *kriyāpāda* (rejoinder of the plaintiff) and *sādhyasiddhipāda* (judgement or decision).

In the Vedic view every concept has three aspects– *ādhibhautika* (physical), *ādhidaivika* and *ādhyātmika* (the inner or spiritual). *Pāda* too is described with these three aspects in the **Mahābhārata** as under:

> पादावध्यात्ममित्याहुर्ब्राह्मणास्तत्त्वदर्शिनः ।
> अधिभूतं तु गन्तव्यं विष्णुस्तत्राधिदैवतम् ॥
>
> MBh XIV.42.33
>
> Accordingly, the destination to be reached by feet is its *ādhibhautika* aspect, Viṣṇu the presiding deity is its *ādhidaivika* aspect and the foot is *ādhyātmika.*

Development of the Concept

The word *pāda* basically denotes the feet. It is one of the five *karmendriyas* (motor organs) in human body. Caraka has given the measurement of the feet just as a biological part of human body. Accordingly the feet should be four *aṅgulas* in height, six *aṅgulas* in breadth and ten *aṅgulas* in length.

The feet are related to movement. Therefore, *pāda* naturally came to signify measuring the space and spatio-temporal motion. As the **Taittirīya Upaniṣad** says by the way of comparison: "one should think that Brahman pervades everything as movement pervades the feet"– *gatiriti pādayoḥ* (TUp III.10.2). The feet thus became the metaphor for movement and also for the goal to be reached. The **Bṛhadāraṇyaka Upaniṣad** says that feet are the goal of all paths (*evaṃ sarveṣāmadhvānāṃ pādāvekāyanam* – BṛUp IV.5.12).

The tendency to employ the word *pāda* in a metaphorical sense is evinced for the first time in the **Ṛgveda**. A riddle occuring in the famous **Ṛgveda** (IV.58.3) describes a mighty bull, with three feet (*pādas*). Here the image of *pāda* occurs in the context of a cosmic view.

चत्वारि शृङ्गा त्रयो अस्य पादा द्वे शीर्षे सप्त हस्तासो अस्य ।
त्रिधा बद्धो वृषभो रोरवीति महो देवो मर्त्यां आ विवेश ॥

ṚV IV.58.3

Four are his horns, three are the feet that bear him;
his heads are two, his hands are seven in number.
Bound with a triple bond the Steer roars
loudly: the mighty God hath entered into mortals.
(Tr. R.T.H. Griffith)

According to Yāska (Nir XIII.7) four horns are four Vedas, three feet are three *savanas*, seven *hastas* mean seven metres and so on. After Yāska this *mantra* has been interpreted by Patañjali and Rājaśekhara in altogether different contexts. Patañjali finds the description of various parts of speech in it and Rājaśekhara applies it for the description of *kāvyapuruṣa*(*belles lettres* as a man).

In an enigmatic *mantra* of the **Ṛgveda** the term *pāda* is recorded to denote season while compounded with the number *pañca*.

पञ्चपादं पितरं द्वादशाकृतिं दिव आहुः परे अर्धे पुरीषिणम् ।
अथेमे अन्य उपरे विचक्षणं सप्तचक्रे षळर आहुरर्पितम् ॥

ṚV I.164.12

The five-footed father, having twelve faces, is said to exist in the upper half of heaven, having wealth of water-stores.
These others speak of him as on high with distant vision, mounted on the seven-wheeled and six-spoken car below.
(Tr. V.S. Agrawala)

Sāyaṇa explains the term *pañcapāda* as five seasons of a year (*pañcapādaṃ pañcasaṃkhyākartvātmaka pādopetam* – ṚV I.164.12).

The image of Puruṣa and *pāda* recur in the Ṛgveda in the celebrated Puruṣasūkta (X.90). The Sūkta says:

एतावानस्य महिमाऽतो ज्यायाँश्च पूरुषः ।

पादोऽस्य विश्वा भूतानि त्रिपादस्यामृतं दिवि ॥
त्रिपादूर्ध्व उदैत् पुरुषः पादोऽस्येहाभवत् पुनः ।

ṚV X.90.3–4ab

That all the worlds are said to be the *pāda* (one-fourth) of Him while three fourth of His — the eternal life— remains in heaven; and that the Pūruṣa went up with three fourth (*tripāda*) of His while the one fourth (*pāda*) remained here.

Pāda here means the fourth part. The same idea is also noticed in the **Atharvaveda** with some variation: *tribhiḥ padbhir dyāmarohat pādasyehābhavat punaḥ* (AV XIX.6.2). Metaphorically, the part sometimes becomes the whole. The **Āśvalāyana Śrauta-Sūtra** prescribes this as injunction: *ṛcaṃ pādagrahaṇe* (ĀśvaŚrSū I.1.17) – if a *pāda* or quarter of a *ṛk* is quoted, it indicates the whole of it, and in rituals the whole *ṛk* should be recited wherever a quarter of it is quoted.

The three strides of Viṣṇu are described in the Viṣṇu-sūkta. They are replete with honey, never coming to an end and auspicious:

यस्य त्री पूर्णा मधुना पदान्यक्षीयमाणा स्वधया मदन्ति ।
य उ त्रिधातु पृथिवीमुत द्यामेको दाधार भुवनानि विश्वा ॥

ṚV I.154.4

Him whose three places that are filled with sweetness, imperishable, joy as it may list them,

Who verily alone upholds the three-fold, the earth, the heaven, and all living creatures. (Tr. R.T.H. Griffith)

Western scholars have seen these three strides as indicative of the sun in the morning, in the noon and in the evening. Obviously the connotation of *pāda* in the sense of rays has led to the linkage of the stride to the position of the sun. Also, the relation of *pāda* or the feet to strides connects them with movement finally adjusting this relationship in time and space. The idea of this relationship has led to the development of myth of Vāmana (the dwarf incarnation of Viṣṇu) and His three strides. Vāmana who was given a piece of land equal to His three strides by the demon king Bali, measured all the worlds in one stride, then the heaven in second stride. He thus vanquished Bali by his third stride.

In the **Yajurveda**, the concept of *pāda* is noticed in the sense of foot of a Vedic *mantra.* Verse division or quarters of a stanza (*pada* or *pāda*) takes an important role to formulate a *nivid mantra,* i.e. a short detached formula of invocation.

अर्ध ऋचैरुक्थानां रूपं पदैराप्नोति निविद: ।
प्रणवै: शस्त्राणां रूपं पयसा सोम आप्यते ॥

YV XIX.25

By verse-halves comes the Ukthas' type Nivids by *pada*s he obtains.
The type of *śastra*s is obtained by *praṇava*-s, Soma by milk.
(Tr. R.T.H. Griffith)

The **Atharvaveda**, while quoting two Ṛgvedic verses (I.164.41–42) in one *mantra*, on thousand-syllabled speech in the highest heaven shows the use of the term *pada* as a string of five epithets: *ekapadī, dvipadī, catuṣpadī, aṣṭāpadī* and *navapadī*. *Pada* denotes motion and *ekapadī* means undivided motion which refers the principle of stasis or rest. But *dvipadī* means a motion in speech. Similarly *catuṣpadī* etc. are also not for the numerical manifestation rather these symbolizes four stages of speech, eight forms of speech and nine syllabled speech, etc.

गौरिन्मिमाय सलिलानि तक्षत्येकपदी द्विपदी सा चतुष्पदी ।
अष्टापदी नवपदी बभूवुषी सहस्राक्षरा भुवनस्य पङ्क्तिस्तस्या:
समुद्रा अधि वि क्षरन्ति ॥

AV IX.10.21

Forming the waterfloods the cow hereself hath lowed, one-footed or two-footed or four-footed, she, who hath become eight-footed or acquired nine feet, the universe's thousand syllabled *paṅkti*. From her descend in streams the seas of water. (Tr. R.T.H. Griffith)

A Ṛgvedic *mantra* (I.2.20) containing the term *pada* is also noticed in the **Taittirīya Saṃhitā** in the context of sprinkling water to the victim for Agni and Soma tied in an erected post.

तद्विष्णो: परमं पदं सदा पश्यन्ति सूरय: । दिवीव चक्षुराततम् ॥

TSam I.3.6.2

That highest step of Viṣṇu, the singers ever gaze upon, like an eye stretched in the sky. (Tr. A.B. Keith)

The term *pāda* is used in the sense of a unit of measurement in the **Śatapatha Brāhmaṇa**.

पादमात्र्यो भवन्ति । अधस्पदमेव तत्पाप्मानं निर्ऋतिं कुरुते ... ।

ŚBr VII.2.1.7

They measure a foot (square): he thus treads evil, corruption, under foot. (Tr. J. Eggeling)

Four parts of a *brahmacārin*'s existence during *brahmacarya* (the studenthood/celibacy) have been nicely expressed in the **Śatapatha Brāhmaṇa** by using the term *pāda* meaning 'one-fourth part'. First three of which are *agnimpadā*, i.e. the quarter sucked by fire, *mṛtyumpadā*, i.e. the quarter sucked by death and *ācāryampadā*, i.e. the quarter delivered to his preceptor, which should be regained by the student by rendering three types of duties, viz. service to the fire, begging of alms and service to the teacher.

> चतुर्द्धा भूतानि प्रविशति । अग्निम्पदा मृत्युम्पदाऽऽचार्यम्पदाऽऽत्मन्येवास्य चतुर्थः पादः परिशिष्यते ॥
>
> ŚBr XI.3.3.3
>
> (When a *brāhmaṇa* enters on a *brahmacārin*'s life) – he enters beings in four parts; with one fourth part (he enters) the fire, with another part death, with another part his religious teacher; and his fourth part remains in his own self. (Tr. J. Eggeling)

In the **Aitareya Brāhmaṇa** quarter hemistich of verse is meant by the term *pāda* in the context of Vedic metres.

> यत्त्रिपदा तेनोष्णिहा गायत्र्यौ, यदस्या एकादशाक्षराणि पदानि तेन त्रिष्टुभ्, यत्त्रयस्त्रिंशदक्षरा तेनानुष्टुभ् .... ।
>
> AitBr I.6
>
> In that it has three *padas* it is the Uṣṇiḥ and Gāyatrī, in that its *padas* have eleven syllables, it is the Triṣṭubh, in that it has thirty-three syllables, it is the Anuṣṭubh. (Tr. A.B. Keith)

The term *pāda* means quarter or one-fourth because of the concept of four-footed cattle (*catuṣpādaḥ paśavaḥ, paśūn evāvarundhe* – PraBr II.1).

In the **Lāṭyāyana Śrauta-Sūtra** *pāda* takes a fundamental role in forming *nidhanas*, a place of cessation or rest in chanting. The *padastobha sāman* shows that all the quarters of the basic verse are individually regarded as *nidhanas*, i.e. the final parts to be chanted by all the chanters.

> चतुर्थस्य प्रथमः पादस्त्र्यक्षराणि चत्वारि निधनानि ॥
>
> LāṭŚrSū VII.7.7.
>
> For the fourth *padastobha sāman* the first quarter of the basic verse is divided into four parts of three syllables each and these parts form the four *nidhanas*. (Tr. H.G. Ranade)

The **Kātyāyana Śulba-Sūtra** uses the term *pada* as a unit of measurement. In the Varuṇapraghāsaparvan of *cāturmāsya* sacrifice, the northern altar in a square having an area of ten square *padas*.

पदं तिर्यङ्मानी त्रिपदा पार्श्वमानी तस्याक्ष्णया रज्जुर्दशकरणी ॥

KātŚulSū II.8

In a right angled triangle, whose side is one *pada*, and the other side is three *padas*, its hypotenuse will produce an area of ten square *padas*. (Tr. S.D. Khadilkar)

In the **Gautama Dharma-Sūtra** the term *pāda* is used in connection with the relation of teacher and student. It is the duty of the disciple to touch his teacher's feet before and after the Vedic recitation, which is the ancient *gurukula* tradition, through which the relation between *guru* and *śisya* are well maintained even to-day in our society. It is also auspicious to touch the feet of the teacher in early morning.

गुरोः पादोपसंग्रहणं प्रातः ॥

GauDhSū I.1.53

(Every) morning the feet of the teacher must be embraced (by the pupil). (Tr. G. Bühler)

The concept of *pāda* as an important organ in physical structure led to the attachment of another meaning – one section or part in a conceptual framework. The **Chāndogya Upaniṣad** talks of the *pādas* of Brahman at two levels– *ādhyātmika* and the *ādhidaivika*. *Vāk, prāṇa, cakṣus* and *śrotra* are its *pādas* at *ādhyātmika* level, whereas, fire (Agni), wind (Vāyu), sun (Āditya) and directions (Diśaḥ) form its *pādas* at the *ādhidaivika* level:

तदेतच्चतुष्पाद् ब्रह्म । वाक्पादः प्राणः पादश्चक्षुः पादः श्रोत्रं पादः । इत्यध्यात्मम्। अथाधिदैवतम् । अग्निः पादो वायुः पाद आदित्यः पादो दिशः पादः । इत्युभयमेवादिष्टं भवत्यध्यात्मं चैवाधिदैवतं च ।

ChUp III.18.2

That Brahma has four quarters. One quarter is speech. One quarter is breath. One quarter is the eye. One quarter is the ear. Thus with reference to the self.

Now with reference to the divinities. One quarter is Agni (fire). One quarter is Vāyu (wind). One quarter is Āditya (the sun). One quarter is the quarters of heaven.

This is the twofold instruction with reference to the self and with reference to the divinities. (Tr. R.E. Hume)

Sections of a discourse, a shastric or a philosophical text could also be called *pādas*. In the same Upaniṣad Satyakāma has been told by a bull that a part of the knowledge (*pāda*) will be revealed to you by fire (Agni), another part *pāda*) will be told by a swan (*haṃsa*) and yet another by a diver bird (*madgu*). The bull explains that the four directions form the four *kalās* of the foot (*pāda*) of Brahman; while the fire identifies the earth, the space, the heaven and the ocean as the four parts (*kalās*) of Brahman; for the swan these *kalās* are the fire, the sun, the moon and the lightning; and for the diver bird they are the vital force (*prāṇa*), the eye and the ear and the mind.

> ब्रह्मणश्च ते पादं ब्रवाणीति । ... एष वै सोम्य चतुष्कलः पादो ब्रह्मणः प्रकाशवान्नाम ॥
> ... अग्निष्टे पादं वक्तेति । ... एष वै सोम्य चतुष्कलः पादो ब्रह्मणोऽनन्तवान्नाम ॥
> ... हंसस्ते पादं वक्तेति । ... एष वै सोम्य चतुष्कलः पादो ब्रह्मणो ज्योतिष्मान्नाम ॥
> ... मद्गुष्टे पादं वक्तेति । ... एष वै सोम्य चतुष्कलः पादो ब्रह्मण आयतनवान्नाम ॥
>
> ChUp IV.5.2–IV.8.3
>
> And let me tell you a quarter of Brahma. ... This, verily, my dear, is the quarter of Brahma, consisting of four sixteenths, named the Shining. ... Fire will tell you a quarter. ... This, verily, my dear, is the quarter of Brahma, consisting of four sixteenths, named the Endless. ... A swan will tell you a quarter. ... This verily, my dear, is the quarter of Brahma, consisting of four sixteenths, named the Luminous. ... A diver-bird will tell you a quarter. ... This, verily, my dear, is the quarter of Brahma, consisting of four sixteenths, named possessing-a-support. (Tr. R.E. Hume)

In the narrative of Aśvapati Kekaya in the same Upaniṣad the earth is said to be the feet of Vaiśvānara Puruṣa (ChUp V.17.1).

In the **Bṛhadāraṇyaka Upaniṣad** a new dimension of *pādanyāsa* or foot-print is hinted at. Here the root *pad-* occurs to mean to trace out something by its foot print.

> तदेतत्पदनीयमस्य सर्वस्य यदयमात्मा। अनेन ह्येतत्सर्वं वेद । यथा ह वै पदेनानुविन्देदेवम् ... ।
>
> BṛUp I.4.7
>
> That same thing, namely, this Self is the trace (*padanīya*) of this All, for by it one knows this All. Just as, verily, one might find by a foot print (*pada*), thus .... (Tr. R. E. Hume)

Śaṅkara, while commenting on the same states that the soul is to be sought through the foot-prints as an animal is recognised by its foot print or hoof-mark.

> तदेतदेव प्रकृतं पदनीयं गमनीयं नान्यत् । ... कथं पुनरेतत्पदनीयमिति । उच्यते-

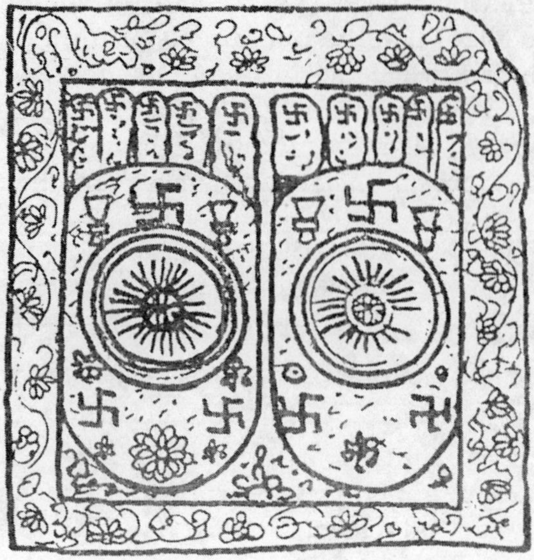

Figure 30: Foot-print of a deity

यथा ह वै लोके पदेन, गवादिखुराङ्कितो देशः पदमित्युच्यते तेन पदेन, नष्टं विवित्सितं पशुं पदेनान्वेषमाणोऽनुविन्देल्लभेत । एवमात्मनि लब्धे सर्वमनुलभत इत्यर्थः ।

ŚBh on BṛUp I.4.7

Of all these, this entity called Self, ... alone should be realised and nothing else. ... How is the Self the one that should be realised? Just as in the world one may get a missing animal that is wanted back by searching it thorough its foot prints — 'foot' etc., similarly when the Self is attained, everything is automatically attained. This is the idea. (Tr. Gambhirananda)

There are numerous references to *pāda* in the **Rāmāyaṇa**. Bharata after the demise of his father when persuaded Rāma to return back and failed in doing so, then he requested Him to gift his wooden sandals, embellished with gold as his representative:

अधिरोहार्य पादाभ्यां पादुके हेमभूषिते ।
एते हि सर्वलोकस्य योगक्षेमं विधास्यतः ॥
सोऽधिरुह्य नरव्याघ्रः पादुके व्यवमुच्य च ।
प्रायच्छत् सुमहातेजा भरताय महात्मने ॥

Rām II.112.21–22

> Stand with your feet on the (pair of) wooden sandals embellished with gold (placed before you), O noble brother! surely this will supply the needs and ensure the safety of men. Placing his feet on the sandals and (immediately) leaving them, Śrī Rāma, a tiger among men, who was endowed with exceptional glory, gave them to the high-souled Bharata. (Tr. Gita Press edn)

Subsequently on his return from Citrakūṭa to Ayodhyā Bharata installed the sandals on the throne and had shown it to the subjects as the embodiment of his elder brother.

> एतद् राज्यं मम भ्रात्रा दत्तं संन्यासमुत्तमम् ।
> योगक्षेमवहे चेमे पादुके हेमभूषिते ॥
> भरतः शिरसा कृत्वा संन्यासं पादुके ततः ।
> अब्रवीद् दुःखसन्तप्तः सर्वं प्रकृतिमण्डलम् ॥
> छत्रं धारयत क्षिप्रमार्यपादाविमौ मतौ ।
> आभ्यां राज्ये स्थितो धर्मः पादुकाभ्यां गुरोर्मम ॥
> भ्रात्रा तु मयि संन्यासो निक्षिप्तः सौहृदादयम् ।
> तमिमं पालयिष्यामि राघवागमनं प्रति ॥
> क्षिप्रं संयोजयित्वा तु राघवस्य पुनः स्वयम् ।
> चरणौ तौ तु रामस्य द्रक्ष्यामि सह पादुकौ ॥
>
> Rām II.115.14–18
>
> This kingdom has been given to me by my (elder) brother (Śrī Rāma) as a foremost sacred trust, as well as these wooden sandals decked with gold, which will supply all our needs and bring security (to us). Having dedicated the sacred trust to the (pair of) wooden sandals with his head bent low, Bharata, who was sore stricken with agony, then spoke (as follows) to the entire body of his ministers: hold the royal umbrella over these sandals; they are considered (by me) to be (as good as) the feet of my elder brother. By these wooden sandals of my elder brother will righteousness be established in the kingdom. From affection alone has this sacred trust been committed to my charge by my (elder) brother. I shall keep this aforesaid trust till the return of Śrī Rāma (a scion of Raghu). Having undoubtedly restored these wooden sandals to Śrī Rāma's feet immediately (on his return to the capital), myself, I for my part shall behold those feet placed on the (wooden) sandals. (Tr. Gita Press edn)

The **Mahābhārata** has recorded the story of Sāvitrī-Satyavān, where Sāvitrī taught Yama the definition of friendship.

प्राहुः सप्तपदं मित्रं बुधास्तत्त्वार्थदर्शिनः ।

MBh III.281.22ab

Wise scholars call him a friend who has stepped seven times together. (Tr. P. Ghosal)

The two meanings of *pāda,* feet and one-fourth sometimes are tagged with one another. In the **Mahābhārata** it is said that without Bhīma, Arjuna cannot come upto the *pāda* of Karṇa.

अजेयो ह्यर्जुनः संख्ये पृष्ठगोपे वृकोदरे।
तमृते फल्गुनो युद्धे राधेयस्य न पादभाक् ॥

MBh I.193.12

Arjuna, O king, is invincible in battle, if Bhīma protects him from behind. Without Bhīma, Arjuna is not equal to even a fourth part of Rādheya (Karṇa). (Tr. P.C. Roy)

The idiomatic expression used here: *phalguno yuddhe rādheyasya na pādabhāk* – may have a double meaning. Arjuna cannot even equal the feet or the one fourth of Karṇa. In the same way, *dharma* is said to be having four *pādas*. In the Śāntiparva of **Mahābhārata** *pāda* denotes the one fourth of the quantity of the virtues and practices under the name of *dharma.*

चतुष्पात् सकलो धर्मो ब्राह्मणानां विधीयते ।
पादावकृष्टो राजन्ये तथा धर्मो विधीयते ॥
तथा वैश्ये च शूद्रे च पादः पादो विधीयते ।
विद्यादेवंविधेनैषां गुरुलाघवनिश्चयम् ॥

MBh XII.35.32–33

All the four *pādas* of *dharma* are to be practised by the *brāhmaṇas*; but the *kṣatriyas* (kings, warriors) can practice one *pāda* (one fourth) less, for the *vaiśyas* (merchants) it is further reduced by one more *pāda,* and still by one more for the *śūdras*. The heaviness or lightness of sins (for purposes of expiation) of each of the four orders, should be determined upon this principle.

However, Śrīmadbhāgavatamāhātmya in the **Padma Purāṇa** presents the metaphor of *dharma,* where *dharma* in the form of a bull stands on all its four feet in Satyayuga, less by one foot in Tretāyuga and so on. Manu says:

पादोऽधर्मस्य कर्त्तारं पादः साक्षिणमृच्छति ।
पादः सभासदः सर्वान् पादो राजानमृच्छति ॥

Manu VIII.18

One quarter (of the guilt of an unjust decision) falls on him who committed (the crime), one quarter on the false witness, one quarter on all the judges and one quarter on the king.
(Tr. G. Bühler)

According to the authors of Sāmudrikaśāstra, the auspicious feet are soft, like lotus inside, their fingers are adjacent to each other, the nails are reddish, the knees are not protruding, they are a little warm and the veins are not visible. Such feet are chatracteristics of kings. On the other hand crooked feet with nails like serpents, dry and white-yellow, with fingers apart; are charcteristics of poverty and sorrow.

शूर्पाकारविरूक्षपाण्डुरनखौ वक्रौ शिरासन्ततौ
संशुष्कौ विरलाङ्गुली च चरणौ दारिद्र्यदुःखप्रदौ ।
मार्गायोत्कटकौ कषायसदृशौ वंशस्य विच्छेददौ
ब्रह्मघ्नौ परिपक्वमृद्द्युतितलौ पीतावगम्यारतौ ॥

BṛSam LXVIII.3

Poverty and grief are produced by feet that have the shape of winnowing baskets, that are very rough, that have white nails, that are crooked or long, that are full of veins, that are very dry and have far-removed toes. Travelling is the effect of having the feet that are raised in the middle; destruction of family is the result of tawny feet; murder of *brāhmaṇas*, of those whose soles have the colour of burnt earth; and cohabitation with forbidden women, of those that are yellow. (Tr. M.R. Bhat)

The term *pāda* has found its due place in the philosophical treatises. The **Dīgha Nikāya** mentions the auspicious marks on the sole of feet of the Buddha which has been termed as '*pādatalacakkatā*':

इमं महापुरिसलक्खणं पटिलभति – हेट्ठापादतलेसु चक्कानि जातानि होन्ति ... ।

DīghNik 148 (PTS) lakkhaṇasutta

He (Buddha) acquires the marks of a *mahāpuruṣa* (Great Man) – having a mark of *cakra* (wheel) on the sole of his foot.
(Tr. N.C. Panda)

In another Buddhist text, i.e. in the **Sutta Nipāta** it is described that a disciple of Buddha deeply intended to pay homage on this auspicious feet.

पादे वीर पसारेहि, सभियो वदन्ति सत्थुनोऽति ॥

SutNip 547

Sabhiya (a disciple of Buddha) requested Lord Buddha for stretching His feet, so that he will (be able to) pay homage on His sacred feet. (Tr. N.C. Panda)

The (Mahānāradakaśyapa) **Jātaka** explains *pāda* as the wheel of a chariot which makes circles and moves ahead. Almost similar is the action of foot.

कायो ते रथसञ्ञातो मनोसारथिको लहु ।
अविहिंसा सारितक्खो संविभागपटिच्छदो ॥
पादसंयम नेमियो हत्थसञ्ञम पक्खरो ।
कुच्छिसञ्ञमनब्भन्तो वाचासञ्ञम कूजनो ॥

Jā VI.544.182–183

Thy body is called a chariot, swift and provided with the mind as a charioteer: having the abstinence from all injury as its axle, liberality as its covering, a careful walk with the feet as the circumference of the wheel, a careful handling with the hands as the side of the carriage; watchfulness over the belly is the nave of the wheel, watchfulness over the tongue is the prevention of the wheel's rattling. (Based on the tr. by E.B. Cowell)

The **Lalitavistara** describes thirty-two auspicious marks of Buddha and one of those, is His foot-print.

आयतपार्ष्णिपादः ।

LVi jp VII, p. 75

Broad heel of the foot (one of thirty-two major marks of Buddha).

According to the **Mīmāṃsā-Sūtra** the division of the hymns of the **Ṛgveda** is based on *pāda*s as per their meanings. This means that the *mantra* is *ṛk* and its division is called feet (*pāda*).

तेषामृग्यत्रार्थवशेन पादव्यवस्था ॥
यत्र पादकृता व्यवस्था स मन्त्र ऋङ्नामा ... ।

MīmSūBh II.1.35

Of these (*mantras*), those are called '*ṛk*' wherein there is division into 'feet' (quarters), on the basis of the meaning.

That is that *mantra* is called '*ṛk*' where there is division into 'feet' ... (Tr. G.N. Jha)

Both Bādarāyaṇa and Patañjali divided their texts, the **Brahma-Sūtra** and the **Yoga-Sūtra** respectively in four *pāda*s each. Bādarāyaṇa in his **Brahma-Sūtra** has pointed out division of *brahman*, consists of four quarter.

बुद्ध्यर्थः पादवत् ॥

BrSū III.2.33

(The statement as to Brahman having size) subserves the purpose of the mind; in the manner of the four feet (quarters).
(Tr. G. Thibaut)

Śaṅkara, while commenting on the **Brahma-Sūtra** has used *pāda* in the sense of metrical foot. For example Gāyatrī metre has four feet each of which consists of six syllables and compared to *catuṣpāt brahma.*

यथा गायत्री चतुष्पदा षडक्षरैः पादैः, तथा ब्रह्म चतुष्पात् ।

BrSūŚBh I.1.25

For just as the Gāyatrī metre has feet consisting of six syllables each, so Brahman also has four feet (i.e. quarters).
(Tr. G. Thibaut)

In Kashmir Śaivism, the feet of Lord have been meditated upon, for spiritual elevation. It is described as the abode of soul.

भगवन्भवदीयपादयोर्निवसन्नन्तर एव निर्भयः ।
भवभूमिषु तासु तास्वहं प्रभुमर्चेयमनर्गलक्रियः ॥

ŚSto XII.8

O Lord, may my permanent abode
Be at your feet
And may I be fearless.
Whatever my station in the world
May I worship you
With actions unrestricted. (Tr. C.R. Bailly)

In another context the devotee desires to shampoo the feet of Lord which may by described as *dāsya,* one of the *navadhā bhakti*:

दासधाम्नि विनियोजितोऽप्यहं स्वेच्छयैव परमेश्वर त्वया ।
दर्शनेन न किमस्मि पात्रितः पादसंवहनकर्मणापि वा ॥

ŚSto XIII.10

Supreme Lord, at Thy own pleasure hast Thou ordained me as Thy servant. Wherefore then am I not made worthy of Thy sight or that of shampooing Thy feet? (Tr. N.K. Kotru)

The same text in another place has concentrated on the lotus feet of Lord.

त्वद्वपुः स्मृतिसुधारसपूर्णे मानसे तव पदाम्बुजयुग्मम् ।
मामके विकसदस्तु सदैव प्रस्रवन्मधु किमप्यतिलोकम् ॥

ŚSto XIX.16

In the *mānasa* lake of my mind, brimming over with the immortal joy of remembrance of Thy form, may the lotuses of Thy feet remain ever abloom emitting sublime nectar. (Tr. N.K. Kotru)

The Classical Sanskrit Literature is stocked with numerous references to *pāda*. Generally the feet of great or senior persons are to be adored. The **Pratimā Nāṭaka** of Bhāsa contains the similar narration, when Lakṣmaṇa desires to worship feet of his elder brother Rāma.

गुरोर्मे पादशुश्रूषां त्वमेका कर्तुमिच्छसि ।
तवैव दक्षिणः पादो मम सव्यो भविष्यति ॥

PraNāṭ I.27

You desire alone to serve the feet of my revered brother: the right foot you alone will have (for serving), while mine will be the left. (Tr. M.R. Kale)

Bharata also intends to stay at Rāma's feet till the completion of vow.

यावद्भविष्यति भवन्नियमावसानं तावद्भवेयमिह ते नृप पादमूले ।

PraNāṭ IV.24ab

Until the condition imposed upon you (or your vow) comes to an end – king, at your feet till then I will abide here. (Tr. M.R. Kale)

The **Buddhacarita** of Aśvaghoṣa describes the auspicious feet of baby Buddha marked with wheel etc.

चक्राङ्कपादं स ततो महर्षिर्जालावनद्धाङ्गुलिपाणिपादम् ।

BudCa I.60ab

Then the great seer wonderingly beheld the prince, the soles of his feet marked with a wheel, the fingers and toes joined by a web. (Tr. E.H. Johnston)

In the **Mṛcchakaṭika** the word *pāda* has been used differently as the demand of occasion. The speed of feet of one person has been compared with another.

किं त्वं पदैर्मम पदानि विशेषयन्ती व्यालीव यासि पतगेन्द्रभयाभिभूता ।
वेगादहं प्रविसृतः पवनं निरुन्ध्यां त्वन्निग्रहे तु वरगात्रि न मे प्रयत्नः ॥

Mṛcch I.22

Why do you, surpassing my steps (i.e. speed) with your own, run away like a female snake overcome with the terror of the lord of birds (the eagle)? Starting off with speed, I can overtake wind itself; but to overtake you, O fair-limbed one, I need make no (special) effort (or, my effort is not for seizing you by force). (Tr. M.R. Kale)

Same has been expressed when one tries to walk in fear:

कुत्र कुत्र सुसभिकविप्रलम्भक पलायसे रे भयपरिवेपिताङ्गक ।
पदे पदे समविषमं स्खलन्कुलं यशोऽतिकृष्णं कुर्वन् ॥

Mṛcch II.4

O you who cheated a good keeper! Where, Oh, where can you run away, with your limbs quaking with fear, stumbling at every step over even as well as uneven ground, and seriously darkening (disgracing) both your family and your good name? (Tr. M.R. Kale)

In another place the action of running of a gambler has been compared with one leg of Viṣṇu, measuring the sky.

पादेनैकेन गगने द्वितीयेन च भूतले ।
तिष्ठाम्युल्लम्बितस्तावद्यावत्तिष्ठति भास्करः ॥

Mṛcch II.11

(What can this poor fellow do to me, who verily) can remain stretched up, so long as the sun stands (in the sky), with one leg in the sky and the other on the ground. (Tr. M.R. Kale)

The celebrated poet Kālidāsa often uses this term indicating auspiciousness. The Rāmagiri hillock has been sanctified by the imprints of the feet of Rāma.

आपृच्छस्व प्रियसखममुं तुङ्गमालिङ्ग्य शैलं
वन्द्यैः पुंसां रघुपतिपदैरङ्कितं मेखलासु ।
काले काले भवति भवतो यस्य संयोगमेत्य
स्नेहव्यक्तिश्चिरविरहजं मुञ्चतो बाष्पमुष्णम् ॥

Megh I.12

Having embraced this lofty mountain, your dear friend, take leave of him who is marked on his slopes with the imprints of Rāma's feet worthy of being adored by men; – of him whose affection for you is evinced, as he, on coming in contact with (meeting) you, every season sheds hot tears due to long separation.
(Tr. M.R. Kale)

At another place reference is made to the colouring of feet of Lady (*yakṣapriyā*) by the natural rock (*dhāturāgaḥ*):

त्वामालिख्य प्रणयकुपितां धातुरागैः शिलाया-
मात्मानं ते चरणपतितं यावदिच्छामि कर्तुम् ।
अस्रैस्तावन्मुहुरुपचितैर्दृष्टिरालुप्यते मे
क्रूरस्तस्मिन्नपि न सहते सङ्गमं नौ कृतान्तः ॥

Megh II.45

The moment I think of portraying myself as fallen at your feet after having painted you, angered in love, on a stone slab with mineral dyes, my sight is obscured by repeatedly gathering tears: cruel fate does not bear (to see) our union even in that (a picture). (Tr. M.R. Kale)

In the **Abhijñānaśākuntala** the word *pādanyāsa* occurs in the sense of trodden with feet as the moon measures the sky with the movement of his feet.

पादन्यासं क्षितिधरगुरोर्मूर्ध्नि कृत्वा सुमेरोः
क्रान्तं येन क्षयिततमसा मध्यमं धाम विष्णोः ।
सोऽयं चन्द्रःपतति गगनादल्पशेषैर्मयूखैः
अत्यारूढिर्भवति महतामप्यपभ्रंशनिष्ठा ॥

AbhŚāk IV.3

The moon who had trodden the mountain Sumeru with his feet and who has also crossed the middle region of Viṣṇu, the same moon now goes down through the sky with very few rays. The too much ascension even of noble personalities is an indication of their downfall. (Tr. R.C. Sharma)

The **Mālavikāgnimitra** uses this term in the sense of foot-work in dance.

अङ्गैरन्तर्निहितवचनैः सूचितः सम्यगर्थः
पादन्यासो लयमनुगतस्तन्मयत्वं रसेषु ।
शाखायोनिर्मृदुरभिनयस्तद्विकल्पानुवृत्तौ
भावो भावं नुदति विषयाद्रागबन्धः स एव ॥

Māla II.8

The meaning was well brought out by her limbs which were eloquent with expression; the placings of her feet were in perfect unison with time; there was complete identification with the sentiments conveyed; the acting made by means of (the movements of) the hands was gentle, while in its successive stages chased away emotion (gave rise to another) from its substratum; still the interest remained just the same. (Tr. M.R. Kale)

At another place the king Agnimitra while describing beauty of Mālavikā, says that her toe of feet are slightly carved.

दीर्घाक्षं शरदिन्दुकान्तिवदनं बाहू नतावंसयो:
संक्षिप्तं निबिडोन्नतस्तनमुरः पार्श्वे प्रमृष्टे इव ।
मध्यः पाणिमितो नितम्बि जघनं पादावरालाङ्गुली
छन्दो नर्तयितुर्यथैव मनसः श्लिष्टं तथास्या वपुः ॥

Māla II.3

Her face has long eyes and the lustre of the autumnal moon; and her two arms are smoothly curved at the shoulders; her chest is compact having close touching elevated breasts; her sides are as if planned off; her waist can be spanned by the hand; her hips are expansive; her feet have toes slightly curved; (her body thus) seems to be moulded just according to the ideal in the mind of the teacher of dancing. (Tr. M.R. Kale)

The **Kumārasambhava** hints to the poetic imagination of blossoming of Aśoka tree when kicked by a damsel.

असूत सद्यः कुसुमान्यशोकः स्कन्धात्प्रभृत्येव सपल्लवानि ।
पादेन नापैक्षत सुन्दरीणां सम्पर्कमासिञ्जितनूपुरेण ॥

Kum III.26

Then the Aśoka tree put forth at once just from its stem flowers together with foliage, and did not wait for a touch from the feet, jingling with anklets, of beautiful ladies. (Tr. M.R. Kale)

In the episode of conversation between Śiva and Pārvatī, Śiva, in the guise of a *brahmacārī* has expressed his desire to know the reason of her penance as after the exchange of seven words they have become friends *(sāptapadīnaṃ sakhyam)*.

प्रयुक्तसत्कारविशेषमात्मना न मां परं संप्रतिपत्तुमर्हसि ।
यतः सतां संनतगात्रि संगतं मनीषिभिः साप्तपदीनमुच्यते ॥

Kum V.39

It does not behove thee to regard me as a stranger, to whom special hospitality was accorded by thee; for, O thou of stooping body, the friendship of good people is declared to be formed after seven words have been exchanged between them (or, after seven steps have been walked together). (Tr. M.R. Kale)

The **Raghuvaṃśa** while describing Rāma's glorious achievements, on His way to Mithilā has informed, that wife of great sage Gautama (i.e. Ahalyā) who was transformed into stone as a consequence of curse of her husband was revived into her original human form by the sanctified dust of feet of Rāma.

प्रत्यपद्यत चिराय यत्पुनश्चारु गौतमवधूः शिलामयी ।
स्वं वपुः स किल किल्बिषच्छिदां रामपादरजसामनुग्रहः ॥

Ragh XI.34

It is said that it was through the favour of the dust of Rāma's feet which destroys sin, that the wife of Gautama changed to stone, did, after a long time again, obtain (was restored to) her own beautiful form. (Tr. G.R. Nandargikar)

In the **Raghuvaṃśa** the feet of Sītā and Bharata have been described as mutually sanctified and worshipful through their respective penances.

लङ्केश्वरप्रणतिभङ्गदृढव्रतं तद्वन्द्यं युगं चरणयोर्जनकात्मजायाः ।
ज्येष्ठानुवृत्तिजटिलं च शिरोऽस्य साधोरन्योन्यपावनमभूदुभयं समेत्य ॥

Ragh XIII.78

That adorable pair of feet of the daughter of Janaka, which had observed the firm vow of spurning the supplications of the Lord of Laṅkā, and the head of the good man, the hair on which had become matted on account of his following the course of his elder brother, coming together, became mutually sanctifying. (Tr. G.R. Nandargikar)

In the same text the word *pāda* occurs to denote rays as well as foot.

जनस्य तस्मिन्समये विगाढे बभूवतुर्द्वौ सविशेषकान्तौ ।
तापापनोदक्षमपादसेवौ स चोदयस्थौ नृपतिः शशी च ॥

Ragh XVI.53

In that excessively hot time of summer two things became (were) greatly agreeable to the people, viz. that king and the moon, – both standing in their rise – the one, the service of whose feet was able to remove misery, the other, the enjoyment of whose rays was able to banish heat (caused by summer). (Tr. G.R. Nandargikar)

In the **Uttararāmacarita,** Bhavabhūti has narrated the scene when Rāma touches and places the feet of Sītā on his head.

देवि देवि अयं पश्चिमस्ते रामशिरसा पादपंकजस्पर्शः ।

UttCa I, after verse 49

(Placing the feet of Sītā on his head). Queen, O my queen, now for the last time Rāma touches your lotus – like feet with his head. (Tr. M.R. Kale)

At the same time Sītā also bows down at the feet of Rāma before departing from Ayodhyā.

नमस्तपोधनेभ्यो नमो रघुकुलदेवताभ्यो नम आर्यपुत्रचरणकमलेभ्यो नमः सकलगुरुजनेभ्यः ।

UttCa I, after verse 51

A bow to those whose wealth is their penance (sages)! My homage to the guardian deities of the Raghu race! My veneration to the lotus-feet of my lord! Reverence to all my elders! (Tr. M.R. Kale)

Again in the context of Candraketu's clash with Lava-Kuśa, Bhavabhūti has prescribed the ethics of battle that a charioteer should not fight with a soldier who is on foot.

न रथिनः पादचारमभियुञ्जन्तीति शास्त्रविदः परिभाषन्ते ।

UttCa V, after verse 20

According to wise, men in chariots do not fight with men on foot. (Tr. C.N. Joshi)

Śrī Harṣa in his **Naiṣadhīyacarita** has described the worshipful lotus-feet of goddess Sarasvatī:

एकैकमद्भुतगुणं धुतदूषणं च हित्वान्यमन्यमुपगत्य परित्यजन्तीम् ।
एनां जगाद जगदञ्चितपादपद्मा पद्मामिवाच्युतभुजान्तरविच्युतां सा ॥

NaiCa XI.57

As she thus, leaving one king and approaching another, was forsaking the latter, too, – each possessing marvellous virtues, and free from blemish – Sarasvatī, whose lotus-feet are worshipped by the world, spake to her who was like Lakṣmī separated from Viṣṇu's bosom. (Tr. K.K. Handiqui)

In the narration of the beauty of Damayantī, her lotus-feet have been described.

प्रिये! वृणीष्वामर भावमस्मदिति त्रपाकृद्वचनं न किं नः ।
त्वत्पादपद्मे शरणं प्रविश्य स्वयं वयं येन जिजीविषाम ॥

NaiCa VIII.103

As we ourselves wish to remain alive by taking shelter under thy louts-feet, will it not be shameful for us to say 'beloved, choose thou immortality from us'? (Tr. K.K. Handiqui)

The **Ratnāvalī** of king Harṣa refers to the jingling of anklets comparable with the striking of feet on the Aśoka tree.

मूले गण्डूषसेकासव इव बकुलैर्वास्यते पुष्पवृष्ट्या
मध्वाताम्रे तरुण्या मुखशशिनि चिराच्चम्पकान्यद्य भान्ति ।
आकर्ण्याशोकपादाहतिषु च रणतां निर्भरं नूपुराणां
झङ्कारस्यानुगीतैरनुरणनमिवारभ्यते भृङ्गसार्थैः ॥

Rat I.18

The wine sprinkled in mouthfuls (and collected) at the root, is, as if, being scented with the shower of their flowers by the Bakula trees; the Campaka flowers smile today after a long time, while the moon-like faces of young females are yet red with the flush of wine; and hearing the jingle of anklets loudly resounding in the act of giving strokes (by ladies) to the Aśoka trees, an imitation of it is begun, as it were, by swarms of bees with their responsive songs. (Tr. M.R. Kale)

At another place the king tries to please and reconcile queen Vāsavadattā by bowing at her feet.

सव्याजैः शपथैः प्रियेण वचसा चित्तानुवृत्याधिकं
वैलक्ष्येण परेण पादपतनैर्वाक्यैः सखीनां मुहुः ।
प्रत्यापत्तिमुपागता न हि तथा देवी रुदत्या यथा
प्रक्षाल्येव तयैव बाष्पसलिलैः कोपोऽपनीतः स्वयम् ॥

Rat IV.1

Not indeed, by equivocal oaths, by endearing words, by ministering to her desire all the more, by the (manifestation of) great sense of shame, by prostrations at her feet, and by the constant exhortations of her friends, did the queen return to herself (her usual genial disposition), as she did, when by her, weeping, anger was removed, of her own motion, having washed it off, as it were, with the waters of her tears. (Tr. M.R. Kale)

The same theme is suggested in Harṣa's another drama the **Priyadarśikā** where the king stands before the queen with folded hand and falls at her feet.

धृष्टः किं पुरतोऽवरुध्य विहसन्गृह्णामि कण्ठे प्रियां
किं वा चाटुशतप्रपञ्चरचनाप्रीतां करिष्यामि ताम् ।
किं तिष्ठामि कृताञ्जलिर्निपतितो देव्याः पुरः पादयोः
सत्यं सत्यमहो न वेद्म्यनुनयो देव्याः कथं स्यादिति ॥

Pri IV.1

Shall I, being bold, obstruct here (course) standing before her and smiling, clasp the dear one at the neck? Or, shall I cause her to be delighted by framing a speech couched in hundreds of flattering expressions? Or, shall I remain with folded hands having fallen before the queen at her feet? Truly, truly, I know not how the queen's conciliation is to be effected. (Tr. M.R. Kale)

Jayadeva in his **Gītagovinda** mentions the episode of measuring the universe by Vāmana in three steps.

छलयसि विक्रमणे बलिमद्भुतवामन ।
पदनखनीरजनितजनपावन ।।
केशव धृतवामनरूप जय जगदीश हरे ॥

Gīta I.9

Wondrous dwarf, when you cheat demon Bali with wide steps,

Water falls from your lotus toenails to purify creatures.

You take form as the Dwarf, Krishna.

Triumph, Hari, Lord of the World! (Tr. B.S. Miller)

There are some references of *pāda* in the collection of popular sayings, e.g. **Mahāsubhāṣita Saṅgraha**, and in one of which the squeezing and stretching of feet or leg has been compared with income and expenditure.

अल्पेन विभवेनैव व्ययाधिक्यं न युक्तितः ।
क्षीणेन वाससाच्छन्ने पादविस्तारणं यथा ॥

MSSaṅg 3207

It is not reasonable to spend much when the income is small; just as the spreading sideways of one's legs when covered with a worn out garment (which will result in the cloth being torn). (Tr. A.A. Ramanathan)

The **Kundamālā** of Diṅnāga suggests the planting of foot one over the other in case of husband and wife.

वामेन नीवारलतां करेण जानुं समालम्ब्य च दक्षिणेन ।
पदे पदे मे पदमादधाना शनैः शनैरेतु मुहूर्त्तमार्या ॥

Kund I.6

Catching hold of the Nīvāra creeper with the left hand and supporting the knee with the right, your ladyship may come slowly, for a while, planting foot upon each of my foot-prints.
(Tr. S.D. Bhanot & Veda Vyas)

In another context the word *pāda* has been combined with *candra* which means rays of moon.

मुक्ताहारा मलयमरुतश्चन्दनं चन्द्रपादाः सीतात्यागात्प्रभृति नितरां तापमेवावहन्ति ।
अद्याकस्माद्रमयति मनो गोमतीतीरवायुर्नूनं तस्यां दिशि निवसति प्रोषिता सा वराकी ॥

Kund III.6

Ever since the abandonment of Sītā, the pearl-necklaces, the Malaya breezes, sandal-pastes and the rays of the moon have caused only extreme torment to me. All of a sudden, today, the breeze from the banks of the Gomatī ravishes the mind. Surely, that poor, exiled creature resides in that direction.
(Tr. S.D. Bhanot & Veda Vyas)

In the poetics, *pāda* has been used in the sense of metrical feet. Daṇḍin in his **Kāvyādarśa** has defined prose:

अपादः पदसन्तानो गद्यम् ... ।

Kāvyād I.23a

Sequence of words which do not fall into metrical feet is *gadyam* (prose). (Tr. V. Narayana)

Manifestation in the Arts

The word *pāda* is used in Vāstuśāstra to denote the lower part of some construction. In the **Mayamata** the term *pāda* is recorded in the context of various dimensions of art and architecture. The architects prescribe *pādabandha* base for four principal castes:

पादबन्धमुदितं तदुच्छ्रये भानुभिर्द्विगुणितांशके कृते ।
देवविप्रनृपवैश्यशूद्रकेष्वेवमुक्तमृषिभिः पुरातनैः ॥

Mayam XIV.20

The height (of the base) is divided into twenty-four parts: such is the *pādabandha* base which is prescribed by the sages for buildings intended for gods, brahmins, kings, *vaiśya* and *śūdra.*
(Tr. Bruno Dagens)

In the description of Śiva's dancing form, various postures related with *pāda* (foot) are shown in the **Mayamata**.

चारुचारीप्रचारेण प्रज्वलच्चरणान्वितम् ॥
दक्षिणं कुञ्चितं पादं वामं जान्वन्तमुद्धृतम् ।
जानुबाह्यादि पार्ष्ण्यन्तमेकादित्रिमुखान्तरम् ॥
तदन्तरेऽष्टभागे तु नवधा निर्गमं मतम् ।
निर्गमं वामपादं तु युक्त्या तत्र प्रयोजयेत् ॥

Mayam XXXVI.69cd–71

His feet are made radiantly beautiful by delicate movement of the steps of the dance. His right leg is bent and his left foot lifted to the height of his (right) knee; the space between the (left) heel and the (right) knee may be three times the value of the height of the face; the displacement of the right leg (in relation to the axis of the image) is nine eighths of the distance indicated above and the displacement of the left leg is to be determined according to circumstance. (Tr. Bruno Dagens)

As a denotation of measurement, the term *pāda* is expressed in many ways showing the difference of measurement in the context of the dimensions of the ornamented frieze in the same text.

दण्डं त्रिपादमर्धं वा प्रत्युत्सेधं तदूर्ध्वतः ॥
स्वोच्चत्रिपाद निष्क्रान्ता प्रतिरर्धेन वा तथा ।
दण्डः सपादः सार्धो वा प्रतिवक्रं विनिर्गमः ॥
तावदूर्ध्वोद्गतिस्तस्याः प्रागुक्तविधिना कुरु ।
सव्याला वा ससिंहेभा ऋज्वी वा स्यात् प्रतेः कृतिः ॥

Mayam XVI.29cd–31

Above this is the frieze with a height of one module or three quarters or half a module and with a projection three quarters or half its height. Or else, the projection of the front of the frieze is one module, one module and a quarter or one module and a half and its height should be that indicated above. This frieze is ornamented with *vyāla*, lions or elephants or it may be bare.
(Tr. Bruno Dagens)

Again, in the description of the ratio of the measurement of the pavillion, walls and pillars, the term *pādona* is used to denote the thickness of the walls as three-quarter or three-fourth.

दारुस्तम्भव्यासात् पादोनं वा त्रिभागमर्धोनम् ।

Mayam XXV.191ab

If the pillars are in wood, the thickness of the walls will be three quarters (3/4), one third (1/3) or half (1/2) their diametre. (Tr. Bruno Dagens)

The alliteration of the term *pāda* in a verse of the **Mayamata** shows the poetic charm while describing the shape of a fillet (*āliṅga*).

आलिङ्गं पादपादोच्चं पादात् पादविनिर्गतम् ।

Mayam XVI.28ab

(Above the cornice) there is a fillet of which the height is a quarter of module and the projection (also) a quarter of a module. (Tr. Bruno Dagens)

Pādavarga means the level of pillars, and *kāyapāda* means the struts. Measurements for all these are prescribed. A particular type of base for a building is called *pādabandha* (Mayam XIV.20). A particular type of pillar is called *śuṇḍapāda* (the pillar with protomes):

युतं तत् कुम्भमण्डिभ्यां शुण्डपादमिति स्मृतम् ॥
मुक्तोत्करणकर्माङ्गं पिण्डिपादं तदेव हि ।

Mayam XV.21cd–22ab

Which is provided with bell capital and abacus is called 'pillar with protomes' (*śuṇḍapāda*), that decorated with pearls throughout its height is called *piṇḍipāda.* (Tr. Bruno Dagens)

In the **Mayamata** *pāda* means a pillar, a pilaster, level of pillars, doorjamb, leg of a seat. The **Mānasāra** holds it as a synonym to *stambha* (pillar) (XV 1-440). The lowest part of a pillar and the flat plinth forming the base for a pillar are also called *pāda*:

द्विभागः स्तंभदण्डोऽपि अपरे पादशीर्षयोः ।
कुंभस्थले पंच छेदे आंक्ष्ये पादश्च कारयेत् ॥

ŚiPrak I.226

Two parts are for the shaft and the remaining two for the base (*pāda*) and the capital (*śīrṣa*). The *kumbha*-part should be divided into five portions (horizontally), in the lowest a flat plinth (*pāda*) should be made. (Tr. A. Boner & S.R. Sarma)

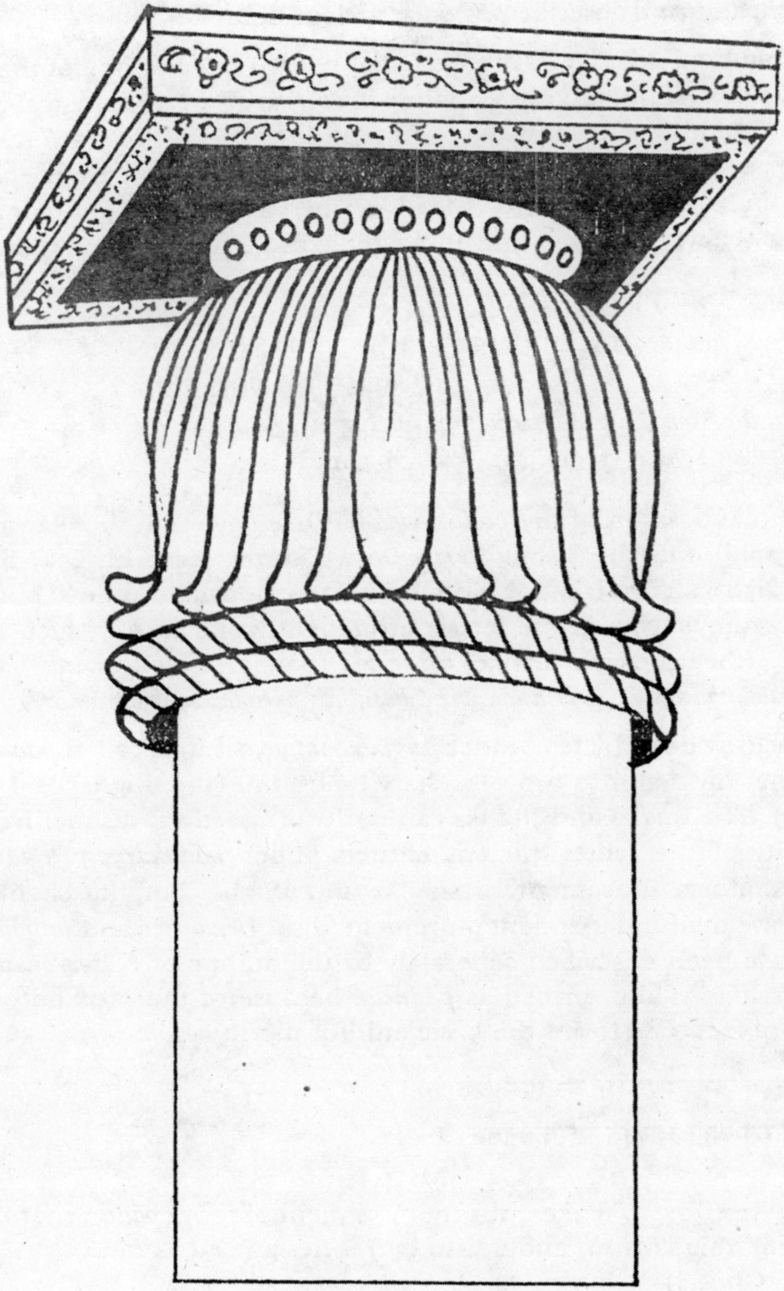

Figure 31: *Śuṇḍa-pāda*: Bell-capital

The **Kāmikāgama** (kp XXXV.28, LIV.47) describes *pāda* in the sense of architrave of the entablature.

In Iconography also, *pāda* invariably occupies an important place, and the texts on *mūrti* and *citra* describe *pādas* for various deities.

In the tradition of **Nāṭya-Śāstra**, *pāda* has been treated as one of the *aṅgas*, the primary limbs of human body applied in *āṅgika abhinaya* (physical gesticulation). The head, hands, chest, sides, hips and the feet – these are the *aṅgas* while eyes, eye-brows, the lower lip, cheeks and chin- these six are the *upāṅgas* (subsidiary limbs). The activity of *pāda* is termed as *pādakarma*. Bharatamuni has also used the word *pāda* in masculine gender as a synonym for *pādakarma*:

उद्घट्टितः समश्चैव तथाग्रतलसञ्चरः ॥
अञ्चितः कुञ्चितश्चैव पादः पञ्चविधः स्मृतः ।

NŚ IX.265cd–266ab

Udghaṭṭita, sama, agratalasañcara, añcita and *kuñcita* – these are the five kinds of *pāda* (feet). (Tr. P.L. Sharma)

A detailed exposition of the *pādakarma* has been given in the **Nāṭya-Śāstra** of Bharatamuni, and the **Viṣṇudharmottara Purāṇa, Agni Purāṇa, Saṅgīta-Ratnākara, Nṛttaratnāvalī** and **Bhāva Prakāśana** normally follow him. The *pādakarma* or the activity of the feet is prominently practised in such categories of *nāṭya* (theatre-performance) or *nṛtya* (dance) as: *aṅgahāras, karaṇas, sthānakas, gatis, maṇḍalas, vartanās, piṇḍībandhas, recakas* and *bhrāmarīs*.

All the activity done by feet under *āṅgika abhinaya* is thus called *pādakarma*. *Pāda* is further divided into two subsidiary limbs: *ūru* (the thighs) and *jaṅghā* (the shanks). The thighs and shanks can perform functions distinct from the whole activity of the feet (which is treated under *pādakarma*). *Pādakarma* consists of uniform movement of shanks and thighs, but the shanks and thighs can have their independent movements also. *Ūrukarma* and *jaṅghākarma* therefore have been described seperately by the author of **Nāṭya-Śāstra** and his followers. *Cārī* is also termed as *pādacārī* because of the proximity of the movements of feet. *Cārī* forms the basic unit for dance.

एवं पादस्य जङ्घाया ऊरोः कट्यास्तथैव च ।
समानकरणे चेष्टा चारीति परिकीर्तिताः ॥

NŚ X.1

Thus, the effort to make uniform movement of foot (*pāda*), shank (*jaṅghā*), thighs (*ūru*) and waist (*kaṭi*) is designated as *cārī*. (Tr. P. Ghosal)

With the induction of movements of hands in *cārī*, *karaṇas* are formed

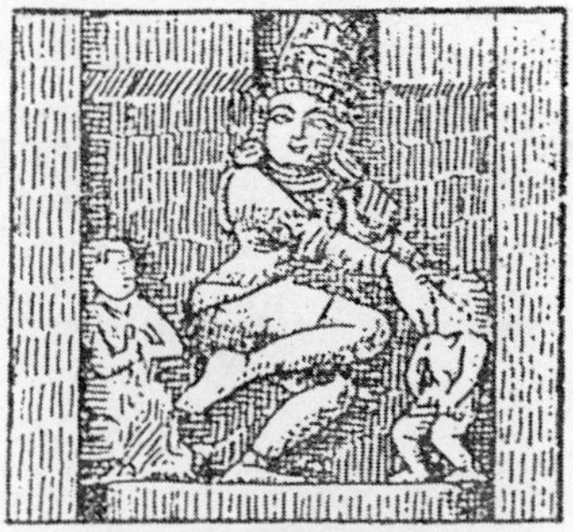

Bhujaṅgatrāsitam

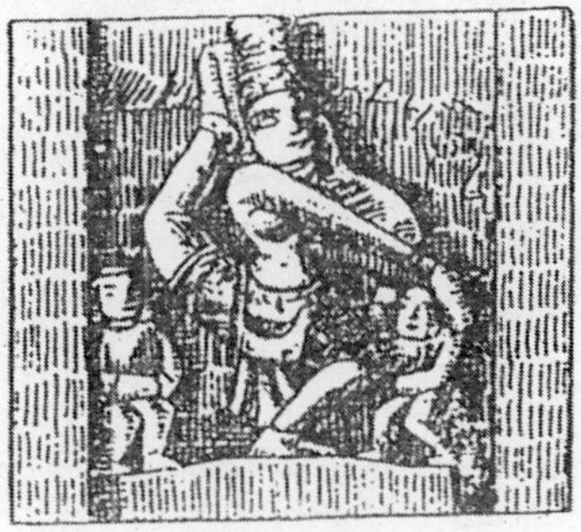

Nikuñcitam

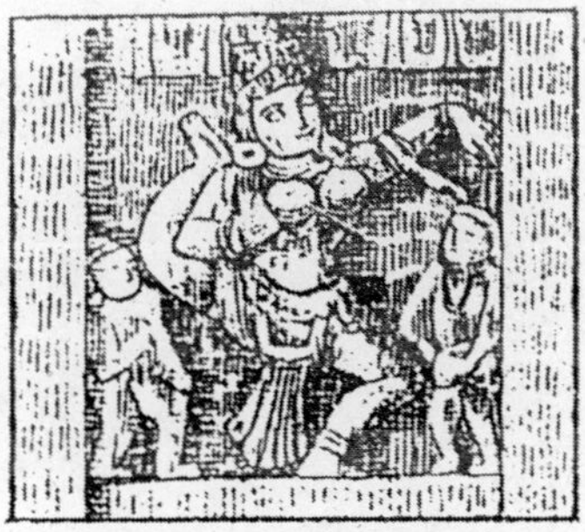

Latāvṛścikam

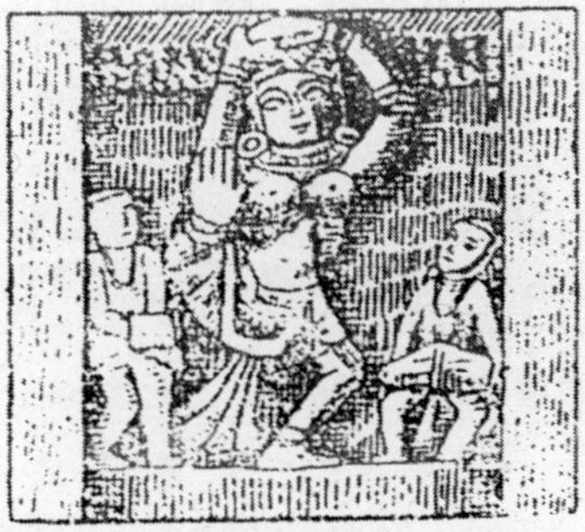

Lalāṭatilakam

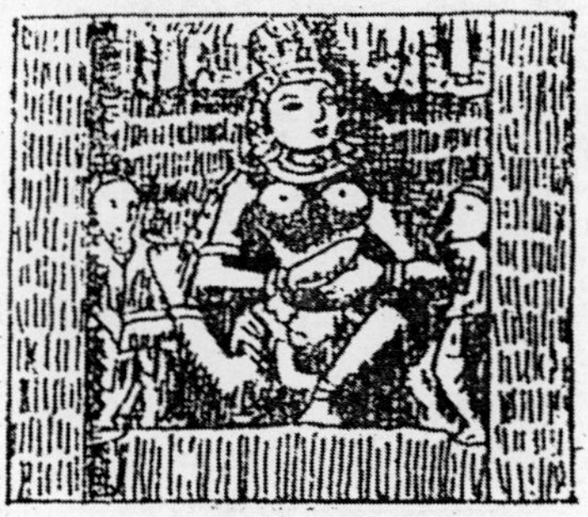

Kuñcitam

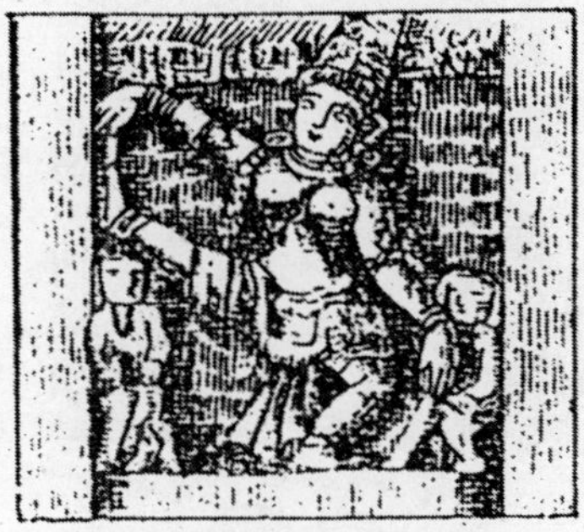

Vikṣiptam

Figure 32: Various types of *pāda-karma*

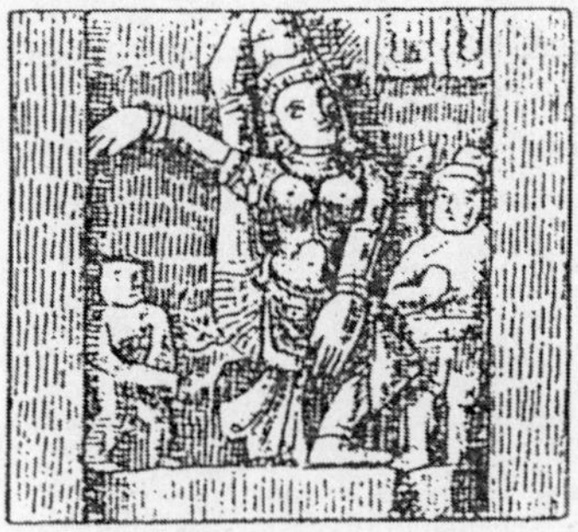

Viddudbhrāntam

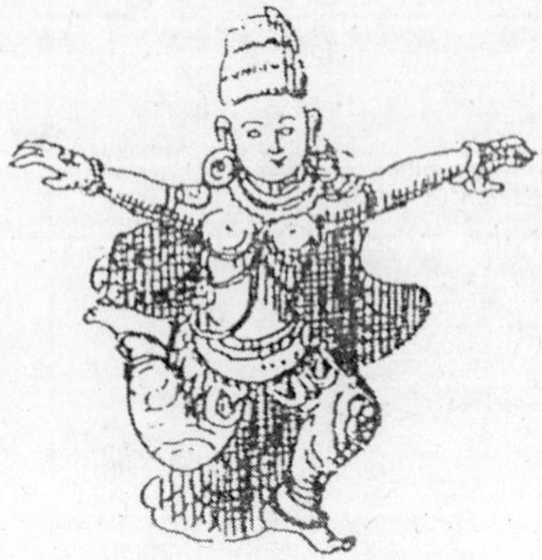

Garuḍaplutakam

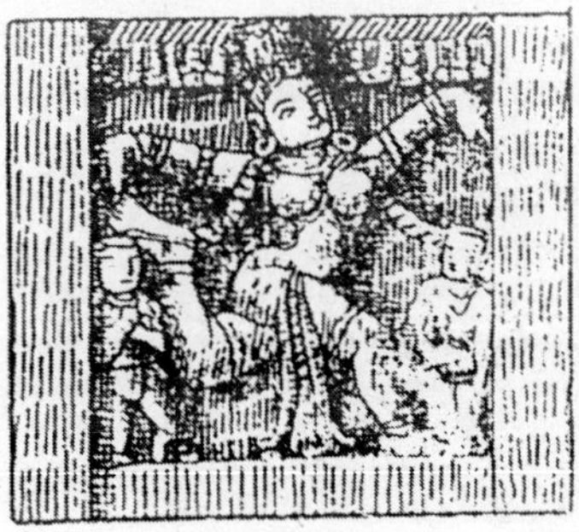

Mayūralalitam

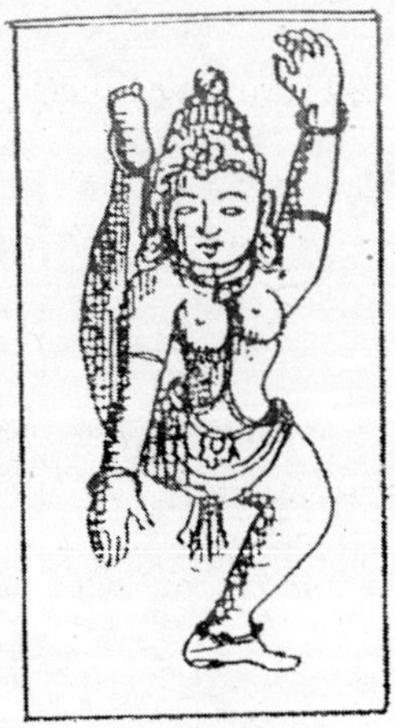

Daṇḍapādam

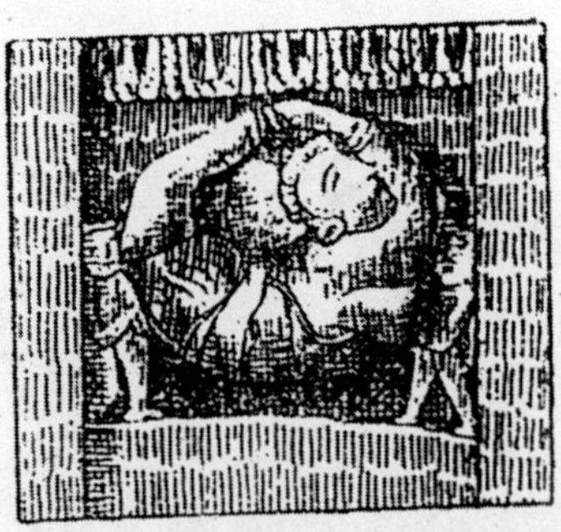

Śakaṭāsyam

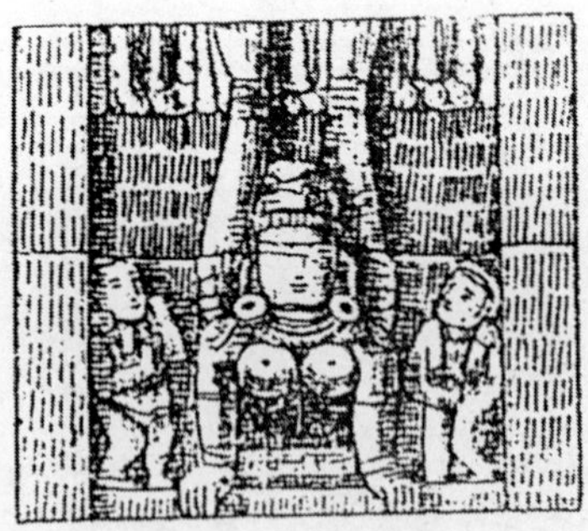

Gaṅgāvataraṇam

Figure 33: Prominent foot-postures

and different combinations of *karaṇas* lead to the formation of *aṅgahāras*.

द्वात्रिंशदङ्गहारा: स्युः करणैर्जनितास्तु ते ।

SUpSā VI.112ab

There are thirty-two *aṅgahāras*. They are created by means of *karaṇas*. (Tr. A. Miner)

According to the **Nāṭya-Śāstra**, the *aṅgahāras*, (thirty-two in number) and the *karaṇas* (108 in number) and the *sthānakas* are formulated basically on the position and action of the feet.

अष्टोत्तरशतं ह्येतत् करणानां मयोदितम् ॥

NŚ IV.55cd

Hence, these one hundred and eight (types of) *karaṇas* have been discussed by me. (Tr. P. Ghosal)

Cārī is basically the movement by one foot, when both the feet are equally employed it becomes a *karaṇa*. Combination of various *karaṇas* forms a *khaṇḍa* and the combination of *khaṇḍas* forms *maṇḍala*. The **Nāṭya-Śāstra** and other texts following it describe ten *bhauma maṇḍalas* and ten *ākāśa maṇḍalas*.

In *karaṇas* like: *pādaviddhaka, ghūrṇita, argala, vivṛtta, vinivṛtta, vidyudbhrānta, vivartita, samunnata, sūcīviddha, apakrānta, ūrdhvajānu, āvarta, dolāpāda, sūcī, viṣṇukrānta* and in *utplutikaraṇas* or *deśīkaraṇas* specific movements and positioning of the feet are required. For example, in *svastikakaraṇa* the legs are placed crossing each other. In *kaṭisama* they are further placed apart; in *samanakha* the feet are placed together; in *dolāpāda* they are kept swinging; in *nivṛtta* they are crossed; in *talasañcara* they strike the ground after the movement for sole.

The practice of *gati* or *gatipracāra* as described in the **Nāṭya-Śāstra**, requires specific employment of feet. So does the *praveśa* (entry of the actor or the dancer on the stage). The pace and grace in *gati* vary according to the type of the character (male or female and *uttama, madhyama* or *adhama*):

धैर्योपपन्ना गतिरुत्तमानां मध्या गतिर्मध्यमसंमतानाम् ।
द्रुता गतिश्च प्रचुराधमानां लयत्रयं सत्त्ववशेन योज्यम् ॥

NŚ XII.13

Three types of (rhythmic) pace should be employed according to serenity or excellence (of the character), the serene and excellent characters (*uttama*) should be shown in calm and slow pace, mediums should be given medium pace, while lower ones' (*adhama*) movement should be swift. (Tr. P. Ghosal)

The standing posture, without movement before and after a *cārī* is called *sthānaka*. The *sthānakas* according to the **Nāṭya-Śāstra** are of two types- *puruṣasthānaka* and *strīsthānaka*. There are six *puruṣasthānakas* and three *strīsthānakas*. Śārṅgadeva adds four more *strīsthānakas* and Jāyasenāpati adds further one more. Both these authors give a detailed account of *deśīsthānakas* also which are 23 in number. These *sthānakas* are formed by the position and distance from each other of the feet. For example, in *vaiṣṇava sthānaka* the feet are placed at a distance of two and half *tālas*, in *samapāda* they are at a distance of one *tāla*.

There are five types of *ūrukarma* : *kampana* (quivering– to be done by raising and putting down the heels repeatedly, *valana* (turning round); by bending the knees inside), *stambhana* (fixity), *udvartana* (springing up by performing *valita* and *āviddha karaṇas*) and *nivartana* (drawing the heels inward).

Of these, *kampana* is used to denote walking by a low character and fear; *valana* is used for circumambulation by ladies, *stambhana* for nervousness and sorrow; *udvartana* for exercise and forceful dance; and *nivartana* for circumambulation in hurry (NŚ IX.252-58).

The **Viṣṇudharmottara Purāṇa** (III.14.44) reads *vivartana* in place of *nivartana*, but does not differ in definition. The **Nāṭya-Śāstra** states:

> आवर्तितं नतं क्षिप्तमुद्वाहितमथापि वा ॥
> परिवृत्तं तथा चैव जङ्घाकर्माणि पञ्चधा ।
>
> NŚ IX.257cd–258ab
>
> *Jaṅghā* (shanks) are of five types: *āvartita* (by keeping the left shank on right and the right one on the left and thus making a cross) , *nata* (bent), *kṣipta* (thrown out), *udvāhita* (raised above) and *parivṛtta* (turned back).

Their applications are: *āvartita* for circumambulation of the Vidūṣaka, *nata* for occupying a seat, sitting and going; *kṣipta* for exercise and forceful dance; *udvāhita* for vigourous walking and *parivṛtta* for *tāṇḍava* dance (NŚ IX.259-65).

Śāradātanaya follows Bharata by accepting these five types, but he refers to an optional set of five other types . They are: *niḥsṛtā* (carried forward), *parāvṛttā* (placing the knee on ground and carrying the shank backward), *tiraścīnā* (placing the outer portion slanted on ground) and *bahirgatā* (expanding in sides) and *kampitā* (shaken). *Parāvṛttā* is used for holy ablutions (*tarpaṇa*) and worship of gods, *tiraścīnā* for taking a seat, and *kampitā* for showing the sound of an instrument called *gharghharikā*.

Jāyasenāpati also follows Bharata by defining his set of five types and like Śārṅgadeva he also adds a set of another five types: *bhrāmita, niḥsṛta, kampa, tiraścīna* and *bahirgata.*

The **Nāṭya-Śāstra** (IX.265cd–266ab) speaks of five types of *pādakarma* as under:

1. *Udghaṭṭita* – It is performed by standing on toes and then letting the heels strike the ground.

Application: *Udghaṭṭita pāda* is employed in practicing *udghaṭṭita karaṇa.*

2. *Sama* – It is performed by placing the feet in natural position on even ground.

Application: *Samapāda* is used in representing natural position of the body, firm nature and in performing various *karaṇas.*

Tryaśra pāda is a variation of *samapāda.* It is practised by keeping the thumb of the feet outside and the heels inside.

3. *Agratalasañcara* – It is performed by throwing the heels up and expanding the thumb and raising the fingers of the feet. It is used in *puṣpapuṭakaraṇa.*

Application: It is employed in inducing- wreaking, remaining in standing posture, hitting up, striking the ground, wandering, casting off something and in various *recaka* movements, walking on the toe to display some injury, wound, etc.

4. *Añcita* – It is performed by keeping the heels rested on ground, raising the toes and keeping them spread. It is used in *unmattakaraṇa.*

Application: It is employed for the representation of some wound in the toe, for showing turning around, for showing the foot struck by something, and various *bhrāmarīs.*

5. *Kuñcita* – The heels are thrown up and the toes are bent forward while the middle parts of the feet are bent.

Application: It is used to show sublimity or grandeur, turning around to right or left.

Definition of an additional *pāda,* named *sucī* is also given in the **Nāṭya-Śāstra** (IX.279cd-281ab) after the description of these above five types of *pādakarma.* Abhinavagupta comments on it: "*sūcīṃ ṣaṣṭhaṃ pādamanye paṭhanti*". Others uphold *sūcī* as the sixth *pāda* by accepting the additional reading. This *pāda* is practiced by raising the heels, and standing on the toe and keeping the left leg in natural position. It is used in *nṛtta* and in tying the anklets.

The **Saṅgītopaniṣat-sāroddhāra** describes only four types of *pāda*: *kuñcita, añcita, recita* and *udghaṭita.*

कुञ्चितश्चाञ्चितश्चैव रेचितोद्धटितौ पदा: ।
नम्रस्तु कुञ्चितो मध्ये द्वितीय: सपदोऽञ्चित: ॥
यत्र भूस्पृग् भवेत् पार्ष्णिरूर्ध्वे चाग्रतले कृते ।
तिर्यक् कृतश्च सूच्यङ्घ्रिर्भ्रमितो रेचितो भुवि ॥
स्थित्वा पादतलाग्रेण पार्ष्ण्या भूमिर्विघट्यते ।
उद्धाटित: स विज्ञेयस्तथैवाग्रतलेन च ॥

SUpSā V.126–128

Kuñcita, añcita, recita, udghaṭita are the foot or leg (major limb) positions. *Kuñcita,* 'contracted' is bent in the middle. The second is bent with the foot.

When the heel touches the ground, and the front part of the sole is raised (and when) the tip of the foot is held at an angle, and revolved on the ground, (that) is *recita* 'turned'.

After setting the front part of the sole of the foot, when the heel strikes the gound, (this) is known as *udghāṭita,* 'manifested'. This is also (done) likewise with the front part of the foot.
(Tr. A. Miner)

Here the definitions of *kuñcita* and *añcita* are also a little different. Accordingly, *kuñcita* is bent in the middle, *añcita* is bent with both feet, *recita* is turned with heels touching the ground, front of the sole raised and the tip of the foot is held and revolved on the ground.

The **Abhinaya Darpaṇa** gives a different set of four types of *pāda*: *maṇḍala, utplavana, bhrāmarī* and *pādacārikā.*

The **Saṅgītopaniṣat-sāroddhāra** also makes a distinction between *pāda* (postures of feet) and *pādakarma* (activity of the feet). The text defines *pādakarma* as the activity done by the heel and the sole of the foot (*pādasya karmāṇi sarvaṃ pārṣṇitalāśrayam* – SUpSā V.130cd). There are seven foot actions according to the same: *urdhvāṅguṣṭha, sthāṇu, ghaṭṭita, ardhaghaṭṭita, recitaghaṭṭita, pariveṣa* and *kuṇḍala.* The **Abhinaya Darpaṇa** further makes a distinction from the point of view of *pādagati* (the movement of feet). It is of four types: *maṇḍala, utplavana, bhrāmarī* and *pādacārikā.*

Śārṅgadeva, besides the *aṅgas* and *upāṅgas* as above, also considers *pārṣṇi* (the heels), *gulpha* (the ankle joint), the fingers of the hands and the feet, the palms, and *pādatala* (sole of the foot) amongst the other *aṅgas* (*aṅgāntara*). He enumerates eight types of *pārṣṇi,* five types of *gulpha* and five types of *pādāṅguli* and six types of *pādatala.* They are as under:

Pārṣṇi (heel) – *utkṣiptā, patitā, utkṣiptapatitā, antargatā, bahirgatā, mithoyuktā, viyuktā* and *aṅgulisaṅgatā.*

Gulpha (ankle joint) – *aṅguṣṭhasaṃśliṣṭa, antaryāta, bahirgata, mithoyukta* and *viyukta.*

Karāṅguli (fingers of hand) – *saṃhatā, viyatā, vakrā, valitā, patitā, kuñcanamūlā* and *prasṛtā.*

Pādāṅguli (fingers of the feet) – *adhaḥkṣipta, utkṣipta, kuñcita, prasārita* and *saṃlagna* (SR VII.522–526).

Conclusion

In fine, it may be said that the word *pāda* conveys several senses in Sanskrit literature. These may be grouped in the following categories:

(i) Basic senses – foot, rays and one fourth of something – these constitute the basic meanings attached to this word. The concept of *pāda* as something physical and perceptible is quite apparent in them.

(ii) Secondary senses – the lowest part, a quarter, the architrave, a pillar, a column, the foot of a cot or a chair, the root of a tree, a measurement, a part or a chapter of a book, a hill near a mountain, a quarter or one line of a verse – these may be taken as the secondary meanings. The range of these secondary meanings opens a wide spectrum and reveal a vista for the development of concepts. Change from 'rays' to 'waves' and from 'one-fourth' to 'a share' are interesting developments.

(iii) Philosophical and metaphorical connotations – these are subtle and symbolical. *Pāda* through them comes to denote the movement and the aim also. The three aspects of life, i.e. *ādhibhautika* (physical), *ādhidaivika* (as perceived by sense organs including the mind) and *ādhyātmika* (the inner or spiritual) – are thus covered in the gamut of various connotations which the term *pāda* gathers in course of conceptual development.

These connotations are related to concepts in biology, philosophy, economics and sociology and are applied in several different disciplines – Sāmudrika, Vāstuśāstra, Pratimāvijñāna, Citra, Nṛtta or Nṛtya and Nāṭya-Śāstra. The last three present the most subtle and aesthetic applications.

Radhavallabh Tripathi

Select Bibliography

Agrawala, V.S.: India as Known to Pāṇini, Varanasi: Prithvi Prakashan, 1963, 2nd rev. edn.

Radhakrishnan, S.: The Principal Upaniṣads, Delhi: Oxford University Press, 1989.

VṚTTI-RĪTI

Overview

The word *vṛtti* (f.) has a long history of various usage. Right from the Upaniṣads and the Vedāṅgas, the word occurs in the Medical treatises, Astrology, Epics, Purāṇas, Dharmaśāstras, Nīti texts, Philosophical literature, Classical Kāvya, Nāṭaka literature, Nāṭyaśāstra, Alaṅkāra treatises, as well as in some texts on Music, Dance and Architecture. In all the above-mentioned areas of knowledge, *vṛtti* has been used to signify different senses, like: existence, mental dispositions, movement, function, behaviour, profession or occupation, maintenance, respectful treatment, commentary or exposition, revolving, a style in composition, customary allowance, manner of thinking, etc. The basic *vṛttis* according to Indian philosophy are three, viz. the *sāttivka*, the *rājasika* and the *tāmasika*. In these three *vṛttis* all human states are covered. The *sāttvika* stands for enlightened state, the *rājasika* stands for the agitated state and the *tāmasika* stands for darkened or selfish state. *Vṛttis* being the state or disposition of mind or of character in general, tend to different modalities of action. These modalities as opposed to the basic state or disposition are to be treated as *rīti* or style of functioning, both mental as well as physical. For example, the hero of a play may be romantic or heroic in nature. All his actions follow different patterns of action according to his attitude (*vṛtti*) of the body, mind or temperament and dialogue. These patterns constitute *rīti* or mode of action according to the basic state of being. Thus, *rīti* is closely related to *vṛtti*, but is different from the same by its practical application. *Vṛtti*, thus, is the internal state of a person, whereas *rīti* is its external exposition.

Etymology and Related Terms

The word *vṛtti* is derived from the root *vṛt-* (*vṛtu vartane*) 'to exist', with the suffix *ktin*. This root is enlisted in the **Dhātupāṭha** thrice (under no. 759) as *bhvādi* class, 'to exist' (under No. 1185) as *divādi* class, meaning 'to choose' (*vṛtu varaṇe*) and again (under No. 1805) along with a long list of verbs, as *curādi* class, 'to elaborate'. The basic senses of all the derivatives of *vṛt-* thus would be associated with the three basic senses of *vartana* (existence), *varaṇa* (selection or choosing) and *bhāṣaṇa* (elaboration or exposition).

The suffixes prescribed are: (1) *ktin* (*striyāṃ ktin* – Pā III.3.94), which gives the form *vṛttiḥ*. The meaning thus signifies existence, occurrence and the state of being; (2) in the same sense the grammar allows another suffix '*kta*' by the *sūtra* – *napuṃsake bhāve kta* (Pā III.3.114), which gives the form '*vṛttam*', in the neuter, signifying 'what has happened or taken place'; also 'character' 'behaviour' (*durvṛtta*) (3) in the same neuter sense another suffix *lyuṭ* is prescribed by '*lyuṭ ca*' (Pā III.3.115), which provides the form *vartanam*, meaning subsistence; (4) the sense of *lyuṭ* has been further widened by the rule – *karaṇādhikaraṇayośca* (Pā III.3.117). Hence, *vartanam* stands for the means of existence, mode or manner of living (instrumental sense) as well as the location of existence, inherence (locative sense) (*śabdasya arthe vṛttiḥ vartanaṃ vā*). This is as per the provision of grammar the following derivatives of *vṛtu* are: (1) *vṛttiḥ*, (2) *vartanam*, and (3) *vṛttam* (character). The usage of *vṛtti* in literature appears to have been based on all these senses – *bhāva* (root sense), *karaṇa* (instrumental sense) and *adhikaraṇa* (locative sense).

Layers of Meaning

The term *vṛtti* has been recorded in several senses and in different contexts in Indian lexicons, viz. the **Amara Kośa, Vaijayantī Kośa, Medinī Kośa, Nānārthamañjarī** and **Viśvaprakāśa Kośa**.

The **Amara Kośa** has five references to *vṛtti* (II.9.1 & 2 and III.3.78), along with *śvavṛtti* (II.9.2) and *liṅgavṛtti* (II.7.54).

(1) *Ājīvo jīvikā vārtā vṛttirvartanajīvane* (AmKo II.9.1). These six are synonyms and denote 'means of livelihood' and profession.

(2) *Striyāṃ kṛṣiḥ pāśupālyaṃ vāṇijyaṃ ceti vṛttayaḥ* (AmKo II.9.2). The following are the professions specifically for the tradesman (*vaiśya*) – agriculture, rearing of animals and trade.

(3) *Kaiśikyādyāśca vṛttayaḥ* (AmKo III.3.73), i.e. *kaiśikī, sāttvatī, ārabhaṭī* and *bhāratī* are the *vṛttis* (emotional disposition and typical to the plays). According to Bharata "*bhāratī sāttvatī caiva kaiśikyārabhaṭī tathā, catasro vṛttayaścaitā yāsu nāṭyaṃ pratiṣṭhitam*" (quoted in Rāmāśramī comm. on AmKo III.20.56). The dramatic art is based on the four *vṛttis*, viz. *bhāratī, sāttvatī, kaiśikī* and *ārabhaṭī. Vṛtti* as such, is derived here as '*vartate asmin*'. It is the typical emotional attitude – romantic, heroic, furious or pathetic, which is fundamental in dramatic representation.

In addition, Amara notes *śvavṛtti* (II.9.2) and *liṅgavṛtti* (II.7.54). Here also the meaning of *vṛtti* is *jīvikā* or means of livelihood or manner. 'The mode of life like a dog' and 'that of an imposter who lives by masquerading as a religious man' are meant by *śvavṛtti* and *liṅgavṛtti* respectively.

Amara's enumeration seems to be based on: (1) basic root sense (*bhāve*) *vṛttiḥ* = *vartanam* = existence; (2) on the instrumental sense (*karaṇa*), *vartate anayā* – means of life, vocation in general and mode or manner of specific life; (3) on the locative sense (*adhikaraṇa*), e.g. *kaiśikī* etc. In the dramatic context *vṛtti* stands for the specific mode of mental or emotional disposition, as opposed to the physical, of the *dramatis personae*. The *brāhmaṇas, kṣatriyas, vaiśyas* and the common people have different ways in a given situation and the four *vṛtti*s relate chiefly to the vocal (*bhāratī*), the romantic (*kaiśikī*), the combative (*ārabhaṭī*) and the heroic (*sāttvatī*) disposition in a play. Since dramatic representation depends on these mental dispositions, these are called *vṛtti*s.

The lexicons have covered almost all the meanings of *vṛtti*. The **Amara Kośa** speaks of livelihood (AmKo II.9.1) and dramatic mode of behaviour as the meanings of *vṛtti* (cf. *kaiśikyādyāśca vṛttayaḥ* – AmKo III.3.73). The **Vaijayantī Kośa** (III.8.1,7) notes the word as meaning '*ājīva*' (livelihood), '*jīvikā*' (profession) and it includes *yājana* etc., i.e. worship or performance of sacrifices as means of livelihood. Apart from referring to the dramatic styles *kaiśikī* etc. (VaiKo III.9.101cd–102a), the **Vaijayantī Kośa** adds *grantha* (composition), e.g. gloss (*ṭīkā*) also as a sense of *vṛtti* (*vṛttirgranthājīvayośca* ... VI.2.36a) as well as *ājīva* (livelihood).

The **Gaṇaratnamahodadhi** speaks of '*dharmadeśanā*' and '*vārtākhyāna*' as the meanings of *vṛtti* (*vārttikaḥ dharmadeśanānipuṇo vārtākhyānanipuṇo vā* – V.336). According to it *vṛtti* has two senses – exposition or instruction of *dharma* and narration of incidents. This sense is covered by *grantha* etc. in the **Vaijayantī Kośa.**

In the **Nānārtha Mañjarī**, the word *vṛtti* denotes several senses or meanings:

> स्याद्वृत्तिर्नाट्येन्द्रजाले कैशिक्यादिकृषीषु च ।
> विचारे स्तम्भने ज्ञाने स्नेहे वर्तनजीवने ।
>
> NāMa 643–44
>
> The term *vṛtti* is used to denote drama, magic, dramatic style or composition (said to be of four kinds), viz. *kaiśikī* etc., agriculture, commentary, the magical art of paralyzing, knowledge, tenderness, and livelihood or profession. (Tr. S. Chattopadhyay)

Reference to drama, in addition to the dramatic style, *indrajāla, stambhana, jñāna* and *sneha* in this lexicon is rather unique. No other lexicon refer to these senses. *Sneha* may mean flow and can be accepted as a sense of *vṛtti*. But *indrajāla*, drama, *stambhana* or *jñāna* do not fit in with the sense of *vṛtti*. Usage have to be sought to justify these senses. Or it may be assumed that *nāṭya* and *indrajāla* stand for *nāṭyavṛtti* and *indrajāla vṛtti*, meaning the profession of acting and profession of a magician respectively. *Vicāra, stambhana, jñāna* and *sneha* are, however, related to the modifications of *citta,* e.g. *vicāravṛtti, sneha-vṛtti,* etc. *Vartana* and *jīvana* are accepted senses of *vṛtti,* as means of living. In addition, in the Rāmāśramī commentary on **Amara Kośa**, the following is quoted from **Viśva Kośa** (LXI.58) to indicate the different senses of *vṛtti* (*vṛttirvivaraṇe jīvye kaiśikyādiṣu ceṣyate*). It means *vṛtti* stands for commentary or exposition, livelihood and the *kaiśikī* etc. In the same commentary (II.9.1) a quotation from **Medinī Kośa** (LVIII.60) is given: *vṛttirvivaraṇājīvakaiśikyādi-pravartane.* Here, an additional sense of *vṛtti* is found as '*pravartana*' (introduction) which, however, is the same as in the **Mahābhāṣya** (Ah. 1, p. 13): *kā punarvṛtti ? śāstrapravṛttiḥ.* So *vṛtti* also stands for introduction and exposition.

Development of the Concept

It would be better to trace the use of *vṛtti* chronologically in the entire Sanskrit literature beginning from the Vedas, since the Vedas are the oldest and foremost basis of the Sanskrit language and literary tradition.

So far as the Saṃhitā portion of the Veda is concerned the word *vṛtti* as such does not figure, although its sense has been touched upon in such expressions as *vartana, jīvana, kṛṣi,* etc. A very long list of profession is also found in the Vedic literature, which proves the concept was very clearly known. More than hundred occupations have been enumerated in the **Yajurveda** (Ch. XVI & XXX) and its Brāhmaṇas, like *pāśupālyam* etc. In addition the root *vṛtu-* can be traced at many places. So, it may be said that the concept of *vṛtti* was clearly perceived by the Vedic seers without any specific use of the word. It may also be noted that this word *vṛtti* is, however, absent in the major Upaniṣads but it has been used in two minor Upaniṣads, viz. **Adhyātma Upaniṣad** and **Kuṇḍika Upaniṣad**. The **Adhyātma Upaniṣad** says:

> वृत्तयस्तु तदानीमप्यज्ञाता आत्मगोचराः ।
> स्मरणादनुमीयन्ते व्युत्थितस्य समुत्थिताः ॥
>
> Adhyātma Upaniṣad 36
>
> During trance the *vṛttis* are not clearly perceived but lie dormant in the soul, which (*vṛttis*) however, can be inferred through its memory after the trance is terminated.

Here *vṛtti* stands for mental disposition, which lie dormant and is not known, but can be inferred mentally by the *yogin* after the trance (*vyutthita*) is over. So the sense of *vṛtti* is here almost same as in the Yoga philosophy, which speaks of *vṛttis* as mental mode.

Another citation of *vṛtti* in this Upaniṣad (*nirvikalpā ca cinmātrā vṛttiḥ prajñeti kathyate* ... 44) defines *prajñā*. It holds that undisturbed state of pure consciousness is *prajñā* and he, who has it, is to be known as *jīvanmukta*.

While discussing the daily routine of an aspirant it has been observed in the **Kuṇḍikopaniṣad** that one who has controlled over his sense organs, should have the following materials as means of livelihood:

> भिक्षादिवैदलं पात्रं स्नानद्रव्यमवारितम् ।
> एवं वृत्तिमुपासीनो यतेन्द्रियो जपेत्सदा ॥
>
> Kuṇḍikopaniṣad 13
>
> One who has controlled his sense-organs, should accept the following means of livelihood – begging of alms, a pot of cane (for holding things) and any approved available vessel for bathing and go on constantly muttering the *mantra*.

Here it may be noted that the above Upanisadic use of *vṛtti* is clearly based on the basic sense of mode of living or modification of the mind.

In the Vedāṅgas *vṛtti* has been used severally. The **Nirukta** (II.1) notes that *vṛttis* involve doubt '*viśayavatyo hi vṛttayo bhavanti*' and so while determining sense of a word it is not advisable to depend entirely on the derivative sense (*saṃskāra*). *Vṛtti* as accepted by the grammarians stands for *parārthābhidhāna*, which includes five different senses like *kṛt, taddhita, samāsa, sanādyanta* and *ekaśeṣa*.

At another place in the **Nirukta** the word *vṛtti* is used clearly to denote 'means of livelihood'. The text refers to nine means of livelihood during a famine.

> शकटं शाकिनी गावो जालमस्यन्दनं वनम् ।
> उदधिः पर्वतो राजा दुर्भिक्षे नव वृत्तयः ॥
>
> Nir VI.5
>
> Nine are the means of livelihood in famine, i.e. cart, pot-herbs, kine, net, restraining the flow of water, forest, ocean, mountain, and the king. (Tr. L. Sarup)

In the Sūtra literature, *vṛtti* has been referred to differently. In a typical reference to Aśvamedha, Kātyāyana observes that an ignorant priest provides means of livelihood to others.

> ब्राह्मणोऽश्वमेधेऽविद्वान्वृत्तिः स वः ॥
>
> KātŚrSū XX.2.14
>
> (O protectors of the horse) a brahmin on your way, who had no

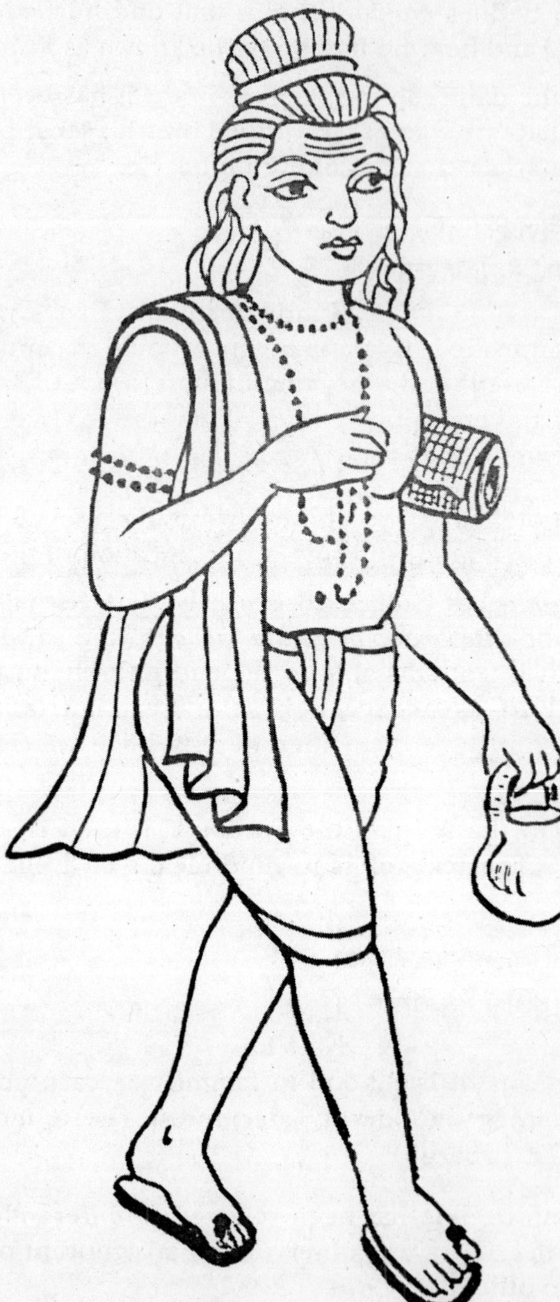

Figure 34: *Yogī* with *vaidala pātra*

introduction (or command over) into the performance of the Aśvamedha sacrifice, deserves becoming the source of your food and maintenance. (Tr. H. G. Ranade)

In the **Mānava Śrauta-Sūtra** the procedure for the conclusion of *gṛhasthadharma*, i.e. handing over the responsibility of the family to the deserving son, it has been said:.

गृहस्थे प्रयोगे। अपत्यमुत्पाद्य दृष्ट्वापत्येऽपत्यानि वा तेषां
वृत्तिं कल्पयित्वा गुणवति पुत्रे कुटुम्बमावेश्याथास्याग्निविनियोगः ॥

MānŚrSū VIII.25.2

For a married brahmin the practice is: after he has procreated and seen his child or the children of his child and has provided for their maintenance and after he has untrusted his family to his virtuous son, he loosens his fires. (Tr. J. M. Van Gelder)

In the sense of vocation, behaviour and means of livelihood *vṛtti* has been used in the **Gautama Dharma-Sūtra**. In relation to *śūdras* Gautama observes that even the vocation of the *śūdras* can be accepted by a brahmin, if no other means be available: "*vṛttiścena nāntareṇa śūdrāt*". As opposed to this prescription Gautama says that a brahmin should never follow the occupation or vocation of a *śūdra*.

सर्वथा वृत्तिरशक्तावशौद्रेण ॥

GauDhSū I.7.22

But if no (other course is) possible (a brahmin) may support himself in any way except by (following the occupations) of a *śūdra*. (Tr. G. Bühler)

For a king Gautama says that he should maintain himself by means of surplus (of income) – '*adhikena vṛtti*' (GauDhSū II.1.30).

In the sense of behaviour the **Gautama Dharma-Sūtra** instructs that a pious *śūdra* should be devoted to his own wife (devotion here means sexual behaviour or conduct: '*svadāravṛttiḥ*' – GauDhSū II.1.56). A further reference to the means of livelihood of the *śūdras* is seen in the text as: '*tebhyo vṛttiṃ lipseta*' (GauDhSū II.1.58). The *sūtrakāra* clearly holds that the *śūdra* should look up to the three upper castes for providing them with the means of livelihood. An alternative vocation, i.e. craft (cottage industries) has especially prescribed for *śūdras* – *śilpavṛttiśca* (GauDhSū II.1.62). The *sūtra* '*gurvabhāve tadapatye vṛtti*' (GauDhSū I.3.7) prescribes that on the said demise of *guru* the disciple should behave with his own son in the same manner.

The root sense of *vṛtti* is 'to exist', i.e. the state of being or continuation.

From this sense the phoneticians have used *vṛtti* to indicate the measure of intonation or pronunciation. The **Yājñavalkya, Pāṇinīya** and **Nāradīya Śikṣā**, all the three have a common verse, which must have been current in tradition. It reads:

अभ्यासार्थे द्रुतां वृत्तिं प्रयोगार्थे तु मध्यमाम् ॥
शिष्याणामुपदेशार्थे कुर्याद् वृत्तिं विलम्बिताम् ।

YājŚik (Sec. on svara) 49cd–50ab
(cf. PāŚik 30, NārŚik I.6.21)

In memorizing the Vedas one should make his reading quick but in applying the same in rituals the recitation should be of medium speed, while at the time of instructing pupils, the Vedic passages should be recited slowly. (Tr. M. Ghosh)

Here the *vṛtti* consists in pointing out the three modes of pronunciation prescribed for different purpose. Practical wisdom of the phoneticians is notable here. When one reads things for own understanding, his mode of repeating the matter is swift or quick. This is being called as *drutavṛtti* – 'swift mode of pronunciation'. When the same person applies the relevant *mantras* for a particular purpose his mode of pronunciation is said to be medium and when as a teacher he teaches his disciples, his mode of pronunciation becomes slow. Thus recitation may have three modes, viz. swift, medium, and slow. It may be noted here that though *vṛtti* does not stand here in the well-known sense of means of livelihood, it easily connotes the phonetic measurement. This idea may again be seen in the context of literature, especially drama, where the actors are supposed to use different modes of pronunciation in giving expression to typical feelings.

The **Bṛhaddevatā** records two uses of *vṛtti*: *jīvāvṛtti* (BṛDev VII.85) and *bhāvavṛtti* (BṛDev VII.135). *Jīvāvṛtti* actually refers to a recalling of life. So *āvṛtti* or recalling of *jīvá*, i.e. life is meant here. *Vṛtti* with the prefix '*ā*' stands for repetition, which may also indicate repetition of words as in *ślokāvṛtti*. In the *bhāvavṛtti*, however *vṛtti* is in the well-known sense of existence. *Bhāvavṛtti* would thus mean one who is endowed with *bhāvas* or feelings. *Vṛtti* thus here indicates mental dispositions.

In another reference to *vṛtti* the **Bṛhaddevatā** speaks of transference of the sense of a word from general to particular.

सामान्यवाचिनः शब्दा विशेषे स्थापिताः क्वचित् ।
पलायने यथा वृत्तिः को नु मर्या इतीषते ॥

BṛDev II.109

The terms (*śabdāḥ*) expressive of a general meaning are occasionally applied in a particular sense (*viśeṣe*); thus (in) 'who, pray, O men' (*ko nu maryāḥ*) the interpretation (of) 'goes' (*īṣate*) is in (the sense of) 'fleeing'. (Tr. A.A. Macdonell)

Śaunaka, the author of the **Bṛhaddevatā** here speaks of the accepted grammatical principle that meaning of a particular word is always to be related with the context. In all the cases general sense may not give the exact meaning as has been exemplified by '*īṣate*', which means 'goes', but not applicable here. It actually means 'fleeing'. This transference from the general sense to the particular sense of 'fleeing' has been referred to as a change in the *vṛtti*.

In grammar also the term *vṛtti* is discussed elaborately. Pāṇini has the following *sūtras* which throw light on the sense of *vṛtti*:

Vṛttisargatāyaneṣu kramaḥ (Pā I.3.38), *jānapadakuṇḍa ... maithunecchākeśaveśeṣu* (IV.1.42) and the *vārttika, 'vṛtteśca'* on the *sūtra: 'prajñāśraddhārcāvṛttibhyo ṇaḥ'* (V.2.101).

(1) *Vṛttisargatāyenaṣu kramaḥ* – in the sense of *vṛtti* etc. the root *kram-* is *ātmanepada*. The *sūtra* says this much. The **Siddhānta Kaumudī** explains *vṛtti* as *vṛttirapratibandhaḥ*, i.e. the word *vṛtti* means without any stoppage or interruption.

(2) *Jānapada* .... – by this *sūtra, ṅīṣ* is prescribed instead of *ṅīp*. The eleven nominal stems beginning with *janapada* and ending with *kabara* take *ṅīṣ* in the senses of livelihood etc. respectively (*janapade bhavā vṛttiḥ, vartate anayeti vṛttirjīvikā*). The suffix *ṅīp*, however, will give the same form (with *ādyudātta*) but will mean 'resident of the countryside'.

(3) In the *sūtra: 'prajñāśraddhārcāvṛttibhyo ṇaḥ'* Pāṇini does not include *vṛtti*, which has been incorporated in the *vārttika, 'vṛtteśca'*. The suffix '*ṇa*' is prescribed for the stems '*prajñā*', '*śraddhā*' and '*arcā*'. The resultant form will be *prājñaḥ, śrāddhaḥ* and *ārcaḥ*. By the inclusion of *vṛtti, vārtaḥ* also can be formed with the suffix '*ṇa*' meaning one who knows the *vṛtti*, relating to *vṛtti*, etc. Here a clarification of the word is provided in the commentary, **Tattvabodhinī**, which observes '*vicchinnasya pratividhānaṃ vṛttiḥ*' – *vṛtti* means 'linking of what is disconnected'.

After Pāṇini, there are some references to *vṛtti* in the **Mahābhāṣya**: (1) in order to justify the enunciation of the alphabet in the form of *śivasūtras*, Patañjali explains the *vārttika 'vṛttisamavāyārtha upadeśaḥ'* and observes that the letters of the alphabet have been enunciated for *vṛtti*. Answering 'what is *vṛtti*', he says – *kā punarvṛttiḥ? śāstrapravṛttiḥ* (Mahābh Āh 1, p. 13) – 'What again is *vṛtti* (in the expression *vṛttisamavāyārthaḥ*)? The application of the science'. Here *vṛtti* stands for the beginning, starting, etc.

(2) The **Mahābhāṣya** observes that letters are divided into three measures.

अवस्थिता वर्णा द्रुतमध्यमविलम्बितासु ।... वक्तुश्चिराचिरवचनाद् वृत्तयो विशिष्यन्ते ।

Mahābh I.1.70

The letters are based on three modes of pronunciation quick, middling and slow. The modes vary accordingly on account of the quick and slow recitation or pronunciation of letters by the speaker. (The ratio of difference from the first to the second, and second to the third is 1 : 3.)

Vṛtti here stands for the mode or manner of pronunciation.

(3) In another place, the **Mahābhāṣya** again observes:

तुल्यः सन्निकर्षो वर्णानां द्रुतमध्यमविलम्बितासु वृत्तिषु ।

Mahābh I.4.109

In the *vṛttis* (modes of recitation and pronunciation) called *drutā, madhyamā* and *vilambitā,* the close contact or contiguity (*sannikarṣa*) of letters is the same. (Tr. R.S. Bhattacharya)

This view clarifies the nature of the *vṛttis* and makes it clear that the modes of pronunciation may vary but that would not affect the order of the letters in a word.

(4) Patañjali provides another technical sense of *vṛtti* almost in the form of an aphorism. He defines *vṛtti* as: *parāthābhidhānaṃ vṛttiḥ,* i.e. *vṛtti* is the function of expressing of a different meaning (compound sense).

So, according to Patañjali, *vṛtti* means: (1) application (beginning); (2) mode of pronunciation (quick, middling and slow); (3) that mode does not affect the basic order of letters (*tulyaḥ sannikarṣo varṇānām*) and (4) the five *vṛttis,* known as: *samāsa, ekaśeṣa, taddhita, kṛt* and *sanādyanta dhātu,* wherein the *vṛtti* indicates (*abhidhāna*) a special type of unified sense. The concluding remark of Patañjali may be quoted as:

अथ ये वृत्तिं वर्तयन्ति किं त आहुः । परार्थाभिधानं वृत्तिरित्याहुः ।

Mahābh II.1.1

They assert that *vṛtti* is the expression of a 'intended meaning', i.e. *vṛtti* is 'expressing a compound sense'.
(Based on the tr. by R.S. Bhattacharya)

Bhartṛhari in his **Vākyapadīya** advocates the atomic theory of evolution of sounds in these words:

अणवः सर्वशक्तित्वाद् भेदसंसर्गवृत्तयः ।
छायातपतमः शब्दभावेन परिणामिनः ॥

Vāk I.110

> Atoms, being endowed with all powers (of combination), function separately or jointly and transforms themselves into shadow, sunlight, darkness and sound.

Here *vṛtti* clearly means function or mode as transformation.

In the Epics, Purāṇas and Dharmaśāstras the word *vṛtti* has been used extensively. In most of the instances *vṛtti* stands for mainly mode of living, vocation or occupation.

In the **Rāmāyaṇa**, Rāma advises Bharata to follow the standard of behaviour followed by the forefathers.

> यां वृत्तिं वर्तते तातो यां च नः प्रपितामहः ।
> तां वृत्तिं वर्तसे कच्चिद् या च सत्पथगा शुभा ॥
>
> Rām II.100.74
>
> Do you follow the way of life which our father treads and which our forefathers trod, nay, which is in accord with the way of the virtuous and which is righteous (in itself)? (Tr. Gita Press edn)

In most of the cases in the **Mahābhārata** *vṛtti* has been used as in the **Rāmāyaṇa** to indicate behaviour in general and standard behaviour in particular. The **Mahābhārata** shows the standard modes of living of the four main castes, viz. *brāhmaṇa, kṣatriya, vaiśya* and *śūdra.* Though there is no reference to *vṛtti* as such *bhaikṣyam, paripālana,* trade and service – these have been variously prescribed as the standard or ideal modes of living (MBh V.130.28).

Similarly, *lokavṛtti* refers to the several conduct of man. A *brāhmaṇa* has been urged to follow such a vocation which is virtuous. At the same time he should follow the ideal of virtuous activities of the righteous persons and avoid injury to others (*satāṃ dharmeṇa varteta ... asaṅkleśena lokasya vṛttiṃ lipseta vai dvija* – MBh III.200.42). These three constitute the high standard of behaviour meant for a *brāhmaṇa.* It has also been said that the *dharma, artha* and *kāma* are the three guiding factors of worldly behaviour (*lokavṛtti*).

> धर्मे चार्थे च कामे च लोकवृत्तिः समाहिता ।
> तेषां गरीयान् कतमो मध्यमः को लघुश्च कः ॥
>
> MBh XII.167.2
>
> The course of the world depends upon virtue, profit and desire. Amongst these three, which is the foremost, which is the second, and which the last, in importance. (Tr. M.N. Dutt)

Slightly away from the standard sense of the mode of behaviour and vocation, *vṛtti* has been used to denote legal judgement. While pointing out the daily duties of the king the **Mahābhārata** refers to direct and indirect judgements made in all the law courts and asks the king to carefully consider these judgements daily (*pratyakṣā ... vṛtterbharataśārdūla nityaṃ caivānvavekṣaṇam* – MBh XII.59.68). *Vṛtti* as behaviour has been extended to mean judgment of the dispensers of law in the classical Sanskrit literature. For example, *vyavahārādhyāya* in the Dharmaśāstras mean the rules of legal judgement.

The **Mahābhārata** also speaks of the relation between *vṛtti* and *karma*. Every *vṛtti* or mode of behaviour must follow the prescribed set of duties, i.e. *karma* for the fulfilment of his mode of behaviour (*anyathā vartamānasya nāsau vṛttiḥ prakalpyate ... tathaiva saḥ* – MBh XII.65.10).

The **Mahābhārata** is clearly of the opinion that every one, whether a householder or a *sanyāsin* must choose the best mode of behaviour, if he desires to attain liberation.

> गृहस्थो ब्रह्मचारी च वानप्रस्थोऽथ वा पुनः ।
> य इच्छेन्मोक्षमास्थातुमुत्तमां वृत्तिमाश्रयेत् ॥
>
> MBh XIV.46.17
>
> A householder, or *brahmacārin*, or forest recluse, who would wish to acquire liberation, should have recourse to that which has been called the best course of conduct. (Tr. M.N. Dutt)

Puranic references to *vṛtti* is chiefly based on the basic sense of the term, i.e. mode of life, means of livelihood or standard behaviour. It has been repeatedly said in the different Purāṇas that definite modes of life should be followed by people of all the *varṇas*. The **Viṣṇu Purāṇa** states:

> कर्षकाणां कृषिर्वृत्तिः पण्यं विपणिजीविनाम् ।
> अस्माकं गौः परा वृत्तिर्वार्त्ताभेदैरियं त्रिभिः ॥
>
> ViPur V.10.29
>
> Agriculture is the subsistence of farmers; buying and selling of traders. These kine are our ultimate support. Thus the knowledge of means of support is threefold. (Tr. H.H. Wilson)

Similar other references are based on the sense of vocation, profession or mode of behaviour. The **Agni Purāṇa** (CCCXL.5), however, refers to the poetic styles as *vṛtti*. *Bhāratī, sāttvatī, kaiśikī* and *ārabhaṭī* are the four accepted styles prescribed especially in the **Nāṭya-Śāstra**. These are related to the representation of different dispositions of the characters such as romantic, heroic, pathetic and furious. Since, these temperamental dispositions constitute specific modes of behaviour, these also are treated as *vṛttis*. The **Agni Purāṇa** also refers to the duties of an ideal king. A king is to provide means of livelihood for his subjects, as well as regulate acquisition and maintenance of their property (*yogakṣemaṃ ca vṛttiṃ ca tathaiva parikalpayet* – AgPur CCXXII.25). *Vṛtti* here clearly means of living or vocation. The famous prayer in the **Mārkaṇḍeya Purāṇa** also refers to the goddess as the dispenser or all the modes of life. The goddess is here conceived as the main source of livelihood of the people.

> या देवी सर्वभूतेषु वृत्तिरूपेण संस्थिता । नमस्तस्यै ... ॥
>
> MārPur LXXXV.27
>
> To the goddess who among all created beings stands firm with the form of activity, reverence to her. (Tr. F.E. Pargiter)

The **Devī Bhāgavata Purāṇa** provides the philosophical concept of *vṛtti.*

> अन्तःकरणमेकं स्याद् वृत्तिभेदाच्चतुर्विधम् ॥
>
> DBhāgPur VII.32.36cd
>
> This *antaḥkaraṇa* is one but on account of difference of modality it is of four kinds (viz. *manas, buddhi, citta* and *ahaṃkāra*). (Tr. Vijnanananda)

Mental mode or mental disposition has been repeatedly indicated by the term *vṛtti* especially in the philosophical literature.

In the **Varāha Purāṇa** the word *vṛtti* is used to denote conduct.

> वृत्तस्था भुञ्जते हीमांश्चतुर्वर्णा न संशयः ।
> ततः सत्यरताः क्षान्ताः दयावन्तः सुधार्मिकाः ॥
>
> VarPur CXCVI.75
>
> It is those persons belonging to the four castes who are settled on good conduct as well as those who adhere to truth, are forbearing, compassionate and pious who really enjoy these (articles of food). (Tr. A. Bhattacharya)

Manu has extensively used the word *vṛtti* in pointing out different modes of livelihood or vocation in his law book. Profession of different people – *brāhmaṇa, kṣatriya, vaiśya, śūdra,* as also a student, a house holder, a *sanyāsin* – all are to follow the prescribed modes of living. Those who follow the right means of livelihood are honoured, whereas those who follow wrong means of livelihood are condemned. Some *vṛtti*s referred to by different Dharmaśāstras may be noted here. The *vṛttis* related to four *varṇas,* viz. *brāhmaṇa-vṛtti, kṣatriya-vṛtti, vaiśya-vṛtti* and *śūdra-vṛtti.* Similarly, the *vṛtti* related to various *āśramas,* like *gṛhastha-vṛtti, sanyāsa-vṛtti,* etc. have also been enumerated. In addition, some *vṛtti*s have been prohibited for the brahmins, e.g. *kusīda-vṛtti* (cf. Manu VIII.151–152), *karṣaka-vṛtti* and *śva-vṛtti* (Manu IV.5–6). Manu has condemned those people who follow *nāstika-vṛtti*:

ये स्तेनपतितक्लीबा ये च नास्तिकवृत्तय: ।
तान्हव्यकव्ययोर्विप्राननर्हान्मनुरब्रवीत् ॥

Manu III.150

Manu has declared that those *brāhmaṇa*s who are thieves, out castes, eunuchs or atheists are unworthy (to partake) of oblations to the gods and manes. (Tr. G. Bühler)

Standard behaviour meant for all the different sects of people have been prescribed and it has been repeatedly said that one should follow that *vṛtti*, which is meant for him without fail. The purpose of Dharmaśāstras is being to regulate the moral life of people. *Vṛtti* or mode of life or life styles have been clearly delineated in all the codes of law, viz. Manu, Yājñavalkya, Nārada, etc.

The **Manu Smṛti** clearly states that a ruler should be a *jitendriya* person, by following the *yāmyayā, yama-vṛtti.* As this *vṛtti* would help the king to rule perfectly (without any prejudice) over his kingdom.

तस्माद्यम इव स्वामी स्वयं हित्वा प्रियाप्रिये ।
वर्तेत याम्यया वृत्त्या जितक्रोधो जितेन्द्रिय: ॥

Manu VIII.173

Let the prince (ruler), therefore, like Yama, not heeding his own likings and dislikings, behave exactly like Yama, suppressing his anger and controlling himself. (Tr. G. Bühler)

The Dharmaśāstras condemn such people who deceive others. The mode of life of such people is called *vaka-vṛtti* or *baiḍāla vrata* (*pāṣaṇḍino vikarmasthān baiḍālavratikāñ chaṭhān, haitukān bakavṛttīṃśca vāṅmātreṇāpi nārcayet* – Manu IV.30). Such impostors are harmful for the society and hence are to be avoided by good men.

The word *vārtā* in the context of mode of life stands for economic profession. *Vārtā* as a discipline concerns itself with the *vṛtti*s of the people and so *vārtā* is also related to *vṛtti* in the sense of occupation, such as agriculture, trade, cattle-rearing, etc. The **Kāmandakīya Nīti Sāra** uses the word *vṛtti* in the above sense as:

पाशुपाल्यं कृषि: पण्यं वार्ता वार्तानुजीविनाम् ।
संपन्नो वार्तया साधुर्न्न वृत्तेर्भयमृच्छति ॥

KāNīSā II.14

Cattle rearing, agriculture and trade constitute the *vārtāśāstra* providing means of occupation or sustenance to the people (i.e. *vārtā* is the sustainer of life). The people, well off (as a result of their success in gainful occupations, *vārtayā*), are never afraid of loss of occupations (during natural calamities). (Tr. S.K. Mitra)

While enumerating the ideal means of livelihood for a *brāhmaṇa* Manu states: *ṛtamuñchaśilaṃ jñeyamamṛtaṃ syādayācitam, mṛtaṃ tu yācitaṃ bhaikṣaṃ pramṛtaṃ karṣaṇaṃ smṛtam* (Manu IV.5). According to this *uñchaśila* or gleaning of corns from the fields, and alms unasked for, begging, and cultivations are the four means of livelihood. It may be noted that these modes of life have been placed in order of merit, i.e. the first – '*uñchaśila vṛtti* is the best, the second – '*ayācita-bhaikṣa-vṛtti*', the third – '*yācita-bhaikṣa-vṛtti*', and the fourth – '*karṣaṇa-vṛtti*' are comparatively less meritorious. The brahmins, who follow gleaning of corn as their means of livelihood are said to follow *śiloñchavṛtti* (cf. Manu IV.10).

The **Nārada Smṛti** speaks about *śiṣya-vṛtti*. The students are advised to give *gurudakṣiṇā*, after completion of their studies, i.e. before returning home, as, through this *śiṣya-vṛtti* the conduct of a pupil has been ascertained (*śiṣyavṛttirudāhṛtā* – NārSm Vyavahārapāda V.15).

In the philosophical context, *vṛtti* mostly stands for: (1) mode of mind, mental disposition, or attitude; (2) existence; (3) permeation besides the other senses.

In the **Tattvārtha-Sūtra** of Jaina philosophy *vṛtti* conveys an attitude or mode of conduct or manner in the following *sūtra*:

तद्विपर्ययो नीचैर्वृत्त्यनुत्सेकौ चोत्तरस्य ॥

TaSū VI.26

The opposites of those mentioned in the previous *sūtra* (censuring others and praising oneself, concealing good qualities present in others and proclaiming good qualities absent in oneself) and humility and modesty cause the influx of *karmas* which determine high status. (Tr. S.A. Jain)

Here the term *nīcairvṛtti* means an attitude of humility towards one's superiors. The same text enumerates the external austerties to be observed by a devout *jaina muni*.

अनशनावमौदर्यवृत्तिपरिसंख्यानरसपरित्यागविविक्तशय्यासनकायक्लेशा बाह्यं तपः ॥

TaSū IX.19

(The external austerities are) fasting, reduced diet, special restrictions for begging food, giving up stimulating and delicious dishes, lonely habitation and mortification of the body. (Tr. S.A. Jain)

Here in '*vṛttiparisaṅkhyāna*' *vṛtti* stands for 'means of living', i.e. taking a mental vow to accept food from a house-holder, only if a certain condition is fulfilled, without letting anyone know about the vow. Hence, a *muni* is to avoid thinking of a particular house for begging his daily meals leading to cessation of desire. The **Sarvārthasiddhi** commentary further adds: '*bhikṣārthino munerekāgārādiviṣayaḥ saṅkalpaḥ cintāvarodho vṛttiparisaṅkhyānamāśānivṛttyartham-avagantavyam*' (SaSi on TaSū IX.19).

In the **Pañcādhyāyī**, *vṛtti* has occurred in a number of places, viz. *sapakṣavṛtti-vipakṣavṛtti* (Pañ I.385), *sādhāraṇīvṛtti* (Pañ II.214, 229), *manovṛttiḥ* (Pañ II.718), *bahirvṛttiḥ* (Pañ II.749), *āvaśyakīvṛttiḥ* (Pañ II.838), *punarvṛtti* (Pañ II.840, 842), *heturdṛgāvṛttiḥ* (Pañ II.928), etc. *Manovṛtti* (Pañ II.718) means mental mode or attitude. The purport being pious and auspicious attitude of all the three – the body, word (*vāk*) and mind, constitute *dharma*. In *āvaśyakī vṛtti* (Pañ II.838), the term *vṛtti* in association with *jñāna* means the form or modification of knowledge, which is typical and uniform with the senses and understanding. In *punarvṛtti* (Pañ II.841), the term is used in the sense of repetition (*vṛtti*).

In the Buddhist philosophy, *vṛtti* is also used in various senses in different texts. The **Abhidharma Kośa** reads the *sūtra* as:

> कर्मान्तेन त्रिभिर्वृत्तिः ... ।
>
> AbhidhKoBh VI.8a
>
> By three is taught the regimen; by the last, activity. (Tr. L.M. Pruden)

It is clear from the above context that people belonging to the *āryavaṃśa*, who have defined *vṛttis*, lasting in *karma*. *Vṛtti* here stands for the basic sense of 'means of livelihood' or *jīvikā*. It may be said that means of livelihood and activities must aim at achieving freedom from all sorts of desire, which is essential for attaining deliverance or *mokṣa*.

Vṛtti in the sense of 'means of living' also found in the **Bodhicaryāvatāra** of Ācārya Śāntideva:

> भवन्त्वक्षयकोशाश्च यावद् गगनगञ्जवत् ।
> निर्द्वन्द्वा निरुपायासाः सन्तु स्वाधीनवृत्तयः ॥
>
> BoCar X.28
>
> May all beings have inexhaustible treasures of riches like the treasury of space. May they be of nature free, devoid of dispute or trouble. (Tr. Paramananda Sharma)

The another text of Śāntideva, **Śikṣāsamuccaya**, which is a famous text on the exposition of the specific conduct of a real Buddhist, who has accepted the three refuges (Dharma, Buddha and Saṅgha) speaks of *tryadhva-vṛtti* in the following verse:

आत्मभावस्य भोगानां त्र्यध्ववृत्तेः शुभस्य च ।
उत्सर्गः सर्वसत्त्वेभ्यस्तद्रक्षा शुद्धिवर्धनम् ॥

ŚikSamu I.4

Give freely for all creatures sake
Thy person, thy enjoyments too,
Thy merit's store, throughout all time
Guard each and grow in holiness. (Tr. C. Bendall & W.H.D. Rouse)

Vṛtti here means conduct or *ācaraṇa* of such persons who have accepted the three *śaraṇas.* The **Śikṣāsamuccaya** also states:

वारमुख्यान् न सेवेत ये चान्ये भोगवृत्तिनः ।
प्रतिसंमोदनं तेभिः सर्वशः परिवर्जयेत् ॥

ŚikSamu III.7

Let him not pay court to choice singers and all others who live by luxury, let him wholly avoid showing any courtesy to these.
(Tr. C. Bendall & W.H.D. Rouse)

Again, in the context of prohibitions to be followed by the initiated (persons) the same text instructs that those who follow the preaching of religious teachers (*dharmabhāṇakas*) should not have any connection with such persons as are involved in all sorts of worldly pleasure. The general term for these people is known here as *bhogavṛtti,* i.e. given to carnal enjoyments of life.

In the **Jātakamālā**, a literary composition relating to the former births of the Bodhisattva, a number of instances of the use of *vṛtti* is found. It is said that *saṃskāras* can be purified through conduct (*śucivṛtti* – Jāmā I.4, prose). Bodhisattvas were more piteous towards all beings and creatures. Their conduct or *vṛtti* was highly impressive and praiseworthy (*sādhujanaḥ svavṛttim* – Jāmā XI.18). *Vṛtti* is also used in the text in the sense of livelihood in various places, viz. *dīnavṛtti* (Jāmā III.10), *durlabhāvṛttiḥ* (VII.5); *sādhuvṛtti* (VIII.37), etc. According to the Śatapatra Jātaka Bodhisottva was so piteous that he left *hiṃsāvṛtti* for maintaining his life and satisfied with simple life by eating fruits, flowers, etc.

बालैः प्रवालैः स महीरुहाणां पुष्पाधिवासैर्मधुभिश्च हृद्यैः ।
फलैश्च नानारसगन्धवर्णैः सन्तोषवृत्तिं बिभरांचकार ॥

Jāmā XXXIV.1

With the young shoots of the trees, with the sweet and delicious flavours of their flowers, and with their fruits of different hue, scent and relish he kept such diet as was dictated by his contentment. (Tr. J.S. Speyer)

The word *vṛtti* is also used in the sense of manner or act in the **Jātakamālā**, e.g. *dviradavṛttimabhipratipadyate* (Jāmā XXXIV.20).

In the Sāṃkhya philosophy *vṛtti* has been defined as *vyāpāra* or function. The **Sāṃkhya-Kārikā** says:

> रूपादिषु पञ्चानामालोचनमात्रमिष्यते वृत्तिः ।
>
> SāṃKā 28ab
>
> The function (namely seeing etc.) of the five sense organs in connection with form and the like is nothing but receiving only. (Tr. R.S. Bhattacharya)

The functions of five action organs are: speech, manipulation, locomotion, excretion and procreation (*vacanādānaviharaṇotsargānandāśca pañcānām* – SāṃKā 28cd). All organs (internal and external) being prompted by mutual impulsion accomplish their respective functions. It is the *puruṣārtha* which is the cause of the functions of organs (*svāṃ svāṃ pratipadyante parasparākūtahetukāṃ vṛttiṃ, puruṣārtha eva hetu* ... – SāṃKā 31). So in the **Sāṃkhya-Kārikā** *vṛtti* specially denotes function.

In the Yoga philosophy *vṛtti* plays primary importance. It has been said that *yoga* aims at the cessation of all the *vṛtti*s. So *vṛtti* means modification or mode or fluctuation of the mind (*yogaścittavṛttinirodhaḥ* – YSū I.2). These *vṛtti*s of the mind are of five kinds and are either hindered (*kliṣṭā*) or unhindered (*akliṣṭā*) (YSū I.5). The *kliṣṭā* has been explained as: *kleśahetukāḥ karmāśayapracaye kṣetrībhūtāḥ kliṣṭāḥ*, – 'the painful are those that are the causes of afflictions in the form of breeding ground for the growth of the vehicle of actions'. While the *akliṣṭā* is elucidated as: *khyātiviṣayā guṇādhikāravirodhinyo'kliṣṭāḥ* – 'the not painful are those that have the sphere of revelation and are adverse to the functions of the energies'. These five kinds of *vṛtti*s are:

> प्रमाण-विपर्यय-विकल्प-निद्रा-स्मृतयः ॥
>
> YSū I.6
>
> Real cognition, perversive cognition, fiction, sleep and memory (are the operations of mind). (Tr. Bangali Baba)

The Yoga philosophy holds that the painful fluctuations of the mind lead to afflictions, whereas the non-painful fluctuations lead to discriminative enlightenment. According to the view point of Yoga all these fluctuations are of the nature of pleasure, pain or stupefaction (*sarvāścaitā vṛttayaḥ sukhaduḥkhamohātmikāḥ* – YSūBh I.11). Fluctuations of the mind give rise to impressions and impressions also give rise to fluctuation. Thus, a cycle of fluctuations and impressions goes on revolving in human life (*evaṃ vṛttisaṃskāracakramaniśamāvartate* – YSūBh I.5). In fact Yoga treats *vṛtti* as fluctuations or dispositions or modes of the mind, which have to be controlled by the *yogin* to attain *yoga*. Practice and non-attachment are said to be the means of restraining the fluctuations of mind (*abhyāsavairāgyābhyāṃ tannirodhaḥ* – YSū I.12).

By the term *cittabhūmi,* Yoga holds the five conditions, viz. *kṣipta* (restless), *mūḍha* (infatuated), *vikṣipta* (distracted), *ekāgra* (concentrated mind), and *niruddha* (restricted) (*kṣiptaṃ mūḍhaṃ, vikṣiptam ekāgraṃ niruddhamiti cittabhūmayaḥ* – YSūBh I.1). Of these the *niruddha* and *ekāgra* condition of the mind are conducive to attain *yoga* or *kaivalya.* It has also been pointed that when all the fluctuation of mind are controlled, the *yogin* attain oneness with the self, otherwise he is identified with the fluctuations only.

According to the **Sarvadarśana-Saṅgraha**, *vṛttis* (modifications) belong to the *dharma* of *citta* and not to the soul (*tasmāt cittasya dharmā vṛttayo nātmanaḥ* – SarDSaṅ, Pātañjala Darśana, p. 352).

According to the Nyāya philosophy, *vṛtti* or significatory function is the relation consisting in either *śakti* 'denotative function' or *lakṣaṇā* 'implication' (*vṛttiśca śaktilakṣaṇānyatarah sambandhaḥ* – Siddhānta Muktāvalī on BhāPari 81). The meaning of a word is known through its function of indicating the sense (*padajanyapadārtha smaraṇam*). This function depends on the utterance of the word which by means of *śakti* (potency), reminds the sense. The word (*pada*) by means of *vṛtti,* which is either *abhidhā śakti*(denotation) or *lakṣaṇā* (implication), brings before mind, the desired sense. Words, as a result, have the power of denoting or implying the senses. This process of reaching at the sense from the word has been accepted widely. The word has power of indicating the sense: *śaktiśca padena saha padārthasya sambandhaḥ* (Siddhānta Muktāvalī on BhāPari 81, p. 371). This relationship between the word and its sense is enumerated in the well-known verse:

> शक्तिग्रहं व्याकरणोपमानात् कोषाप्तवाक्याद् व्यवहारतश्च ।
> वाक्यस्य शेषाद् विवृतेर्वदन्ति सान्निध्यतः सिद्धपदस्य वृद्धाः ॥
>
> Comm. on BhāPari p. 418–419
>
> The elders say that denotative function is apprehended from grammar, comparison, dictionary, statement of trustworthy persons' usage, supplementary statement, para-phrase and the contiguity of a well-known word. (Tr. Madhavananda)

In the **Bhāṣā Pariccheda** of the Nyāya-Vaiśeṣika school a number of references on *vṛtti,* are found, viz. *dravyāditrikavṛttistu* ... (BhāPari 8c), *nityadravyavṛtti* (10c), *pūrvavṛtti* (20a), *jātiryogyavṛtti* (55a), etc. The word has been used here in non-technical sense, but conveys the general sense of the root *vṛt-* 'to be' and hence, inherence or existence. In the verse *dravyāditrikavṛtti* ... it is said that the generic attribute (*jāti*) which inheres in three categories of substance, quality and action is called *parā* (superior) as oppose to the inferior one (*aparā*). The same sense has been uniformly conveyed in other places also.

> समवायिकारणत्वं द्रव्यस्यैवेति विज्ञेयम् ।
> गुणकर्ममात्रवृत्ति ज्ञेयमथाप्यसमवायिहेतुत्वम् ॥
>
> BhāPari 23
>
> Only a substance should be known as being the inherent cause, while the fact of being a non-inherent cause should be known as belonging only to qualities and actions.

The **Tarka Bhāṣā** speaks of *pakṣa, sapakṣa* and *vipakṣa vṛtti*. It means, for being a valid reason (*liṅga*) it is necessary that it should exist in the *pakṣa* and *sapakṣa*, but not in *vipakṣa*. For example, when fire is inferred in a hill, the reason smoke should exist in the hill (*pakṣa*) as well as in the kitchen (*sapakṣa*), but not in a pond, i.e. *vipakṣa*.

Thus, *vṛtti* indicates existence or inherence. Similarly, in other instances also *vṛtti* indicates the existence uniformly (e.g. *pṛthivyāditrayavṛtti* – TaBhā, ch. guṇa; *dravyamātravṛtti* – *ibid.*, ch. karma; *nityadravyavṛtti* – *ibid.*, ch. viśeṣa, etc.).

In the **Nyāya-Sūtra** of Gautama, the view point of Sāṃkhya relating to the unity of *vṛtti* and *vṛttimān* has been refuted (NySū III.2.4). *Vṛtti* in the form of knowledge is the same as knowledge itself. Thus according to the Sāṃkhya view the subject and object of a particular knowledge of a thing are not different, i.e. the same. The sense being matter and its knowledge can not be differentiated, i.e. *ghaṭa* and *ghaṭajñāna* are one and the same. *Ghaṭa* being *vṛtti*, the knowledge of it is to be considered as *vṛttimān*. So both are inseparable. But Gautama refutes this view point of Sāṃkhya. The Vātsyāyana Bhāṣya (III.2.4) on the same may be quoted as: "*vṛttivṛttimatoranyatve vṛttimato'vasthānād vṛttīnāmavasthānamiti* ...". S.C. Vidyabhushana has clarified this as: "The Sāṃkhyas affirm that knowledge is a mode of the permanent intellect from which it is not different. Knowledge, according to them, is nothing but the permanent intellect modified in the shape of an object which is reflected on it through the senses. The Naiyāyikas oppose this view by saying that if knowledge as a mode (*vṛtti*) of the permanent intellect is not different from it, then we must admit various sorts of knowledge to be permanent. But as a fact various sorts of knowledge are not permanent, that is, we can not receive various sorts of knowledge simultaneously. Hence, knowledge is not identical with the permanent intellect" (*The Nyāya Sūtras of Gotama*, pp. 83–84).

In this context it may be noted that *vṛtti* stands for the form or mode or nature of a particular knowledge. This has been further explained by the commentator thus:

> अतीते च प्रत्यभिज्ञाने वृत्तिमानप्यतीत इत्यन्तःकरणस्य विनाशः प्रसज्यते, विपर्यये च नानात्वमिति ।
>
> NySūBh III.2.5
>
> If knowledge as a mode of the intellect is not different from it, then the cessation of recognition which is a kind of knowledge should be followed by the cessation of the intellect.
> (Tr. S.C. Vidyabhushana)

This will upset the conclusion of the Sāṃkhyas that the intellect is permanent. Hence, knowledge is not identical with the intellect.

Kramavṛtti in the *sūtra* '*kramavṛttitvādayugapad grahaṇam*' (NySū III.2.6) means that *vṛtti* or modes of knowledge are not simultaneous, but may be successive as well. The *bhāṣya* (III.2.6) clears it thus: *indriyārthānām, vṛttivṛttimatornānātvamiti, ekatveca prādurbhāvatirobhāvayorabhāva iti.* The elucidation of S.C. Vidyabhushana is quite clear. As he explains it as: "The Naiyāyikas say that if knowledge as a mode of the permanent intellect had been identical with it, then there would have been neither a variety of knowledge nor origination and cessation of it. The different sorts of knowledge do not occur simultaneously because they are produced, according to the Naiyāyikas, by the mind which is atomic in dimension coming in contact with the senses in due succession" (*The Nyāya Sūtras of Gotama*, pp. 84–85).

In the Mīmāṃsā philosophy especially in the **Śabara Bhāṣya** the word *vṛtti* is used in technical grammatical sense of *parārthābhidhāna.* The grammarians accept five functions of words: *kṛt, taddhita, samāsa, sanādyanta-dhātu* and *ekaśeṣa.* The text adds further:

> न चास्मिन्नेव प्रयोगे समासार्थे वृत्तिरिष्यते, एतस्मिन्नेव तद्धितार्थे ।..
>
> MīmSūBh II.1.16
>
> Nor, on the other hand, would it be possible to have the compound by connecting the term '*indra*' with '*mahat*', if the former stood in need of, and were taken along with the nominal suffix.
> (Tr. G.N. Jha)

The practice of the Andhra people of calling every *kṣatriya* as king, even if he does not perform royal duties, viz. looking after the country and the city is referred as *vṛtti*:

> ननु जनपदपुर परिरक्षणवृत्तिमनुपजीवत्यपि क्षत्रिये राजशब्दमान्ध्राः प्रयुञ्जते प्रयोक्तारः ...।
>
> MīmSūBh II.3.3

> But the people of the Andhra country apply the term '*rājā*' to every *kṣatriya*, even if he does not perform the function of protecting the country and the city. (Tr. G.N. Jha)

Here, *vṛtti* refers to the 'conduct' or 'function' or 'life-style', prescribed for a king.

The source of income of a brahmin is prescribed as:

> याजनाध्यापनप्रतिग्रहा ब्राह्मणस्यैव वृत्त्युपाया इति ।
>
> MīmSūBh XII.4.43
>
> Officiating as a priest, teaching and receiving of gifts are the means of livelihood reserved for brahmins only. (Tr. G.N. Jha)

The text here clearly notes that worshipping, teaching and receiving of gifts are the exclusive means of livelihood for brahmin.

In the **Prakaraṇapañcikā** *vṛtti* retains the sense of existence and it raises the question:

> अपि चावयविनः किमवयवेषु प्रत्येकं कात्स्न्येंन वृत्तिः व्यासङ्गेन वा इति चिन्तनीयम् ।
>
> PraPañ p.67
>
> Moreover, it is to be considered whether a whole entirely exists in each of the parts or partly. (Tr. R.S. Bhattacharya)

Netravṛtti in the same text (PraPañ p.183) has used in the sense of function.

In the **Mānameyodaya** the author refers to the function of the word (*śabda vṛtti*) in conveying the conventional sense of the word *paṅkaja* and refers to the view of *guru*, i.e. Prabhākara. According to Prabhākara the word '*paṅkaja*' (lotus) does not indicate the conventional sense as lotus (*rūḍhārtha*), but the sense of lotus is conveyed by the etymology itself. The text says:

> न पंकजादिषु रूढिरस्ति अवयवशक्त्यैव पद्मे वृत्त्युपपत्तेः ।
>
> MāMey, Pramāṇa sec. on Pratyakṣa, para - 19
>
> (Guru says:) in *paṅkaja,* etc. there is no convention, because its application to the lotus is intelligible even through the significance of the parts. (Tr. C.K. Raja & S.S.S. Sastri)

Here, *vṛtti* in this context means function (of the word) in conveying sense.

In the **Ślokavārttika** the use of *vṛtti* has uniformly been in the sense of function, for example: *na rūpe śrotravṛttitā* (ŚlVā sec. on Codanā sūtra 114). It is pointed out here that *śrotra,* ears do not have any function in the matter of visualizing (*rūpa*) form of a thing. At another place it is said:

एवं पदार्थवाक्यार्थसङ्घातैरुपकल्पिताम् ।
विशिष्टां भावनां प्राप्य वृत्तिर्विधिनिषेधयोः ॥

ŚIVā sec. on Vākya 273

Thus, reaching at the specific *bhāvanā* by means of conglomeration of word-meaning and sentence-meaning, injunctions as well as prohibitions function properly.

Here, '*vṛttirvidhiniṣedhayoḥ*' means the function of either *vidhi* or *niṣedha*.

A number of references to the *vṛtti* are found in the **Śaṅkara Bhāṣya** of **Brahma-Sūtra**. Mostly the usage of *vṛtti* is in the sense of *vyāpāra* or function. As the commentary says:

प्राणवृत्तौ अपरिलुप्यमानायाम् इन्द्रियवृत्तयः परिलुप्यन्ते ।

BrSūŚBh I.1.23

While the process of breathing goes on uninterruptedly, the activity of the sense organs is interrupted. (Tr. G. Thibaut)

Here, *prāṇavṛtti* and *indriyavṛtti* both mean the function of *prāṇa*, i.e. breathing and that of physical organs. (While in sleep) vital breath goes on functioning, but the function of the organs remain suspended. Likewise, in other places also the **Brahma-Sūtra Bhāṣya** has uniformly used *vṛtti* in the sense of function or *vyāpāra (vṛttyudbhavābhibhavau tvaprakṛtisamāśrayāvapi dṛśyete* – IV.2.1; and *vṛttidvāreṇaiva sarvāṇīndriyāṇi mano'nuvartante* – IV.2.2).

In the **Pañcadaśī** a large number of verses refer to the term *vṛtti*. The general sense conveyed by *vṛtti* is *vyāpāra* (function). It indicates modification of the mind or the intellect as in *cittavṛtti*, *manovṛtti* (*ibid.*, XV.3), *māyāvṛtti*, i.e. function of *māyā* (*ibid.*, IV.19) and *lakṣaṇāvṛtti*, i.e. function of the word in conveying the implied sense (*ibid.*, VII.73–74). It has also been pointed out that the mind functions in two ways – internally as well as externally. The two functions of the mind follow a succession. The feeling of 'I am' is said to be the internal modification of mind, whereas the knowledge of objects outside is that of external mind.

In Vedānta philosophy *buddhi* or intellect has two ingredients – intellect and the reflection of consciousness in it (*cidābhāsa*). For all empirical knowledge, function of both the aspects of *buddhi* is necessary. The function of *buddhi* is to remove the ignorance relating to the object of knowledge and the function of the reflection of consciousness is to manifest the same.

बुद्धितत्स्थचिदाभासौ द्वावपि व्याप्नुतो घटम् ।
तत्राज्ञानं धिया नश्येदाभासेन घटः स्फुरेत् ॥

ब्रह्मण्यज्ञाननाशाय वृत्तिव्याप्तिरपेक्षिता ।
स्वयं स्फुरणरूपत्वान्नाभास उपयुज्यते ॥

Pañcad VII.91-92

In the perception of a jar the intellect and *cidābhāsa* are both concerned. There the nescience is negated by the intellect and the pot is revealed by *cidābhāsa*. In the cognition of Brahman the modification of the intellect is necessary to remove ignorance; but, as Brahman is self-revealing the help of *cidābhāsa* is not needed to reveal It. (Tr. Swahananda)

In the **Vivekacūḍāmaṇi**, *vṛtti* conveys the sense, as before, the function of mind or organs. While describing the *antaḥkaraṇa* it says:

निगद्यतेऽन्तःकरणं मनोधीरहंकृतिश्चित्तमिति स्ववृत्तिभिः ।
मनस्तु संकल्पविकल्पनादिभिर्बुद्धिः पदार्थाध्यवसायधर्मतः ॥
अत्राभिमानादहमित्यहंकृतिः । स्वार्थानुसन्धानगुणेन चित्तम् ॥

ViCū 93–94

The inner organ (*antaḥkaraṇa*) is called *manas, buddhi,* ego or *citta,* according to their respective functions: *manas,* from its considering the pros and cons of a thing; *buddhi,* from its property of determining the truth of objects; the ego, from its identification with this body as one's own self; and *citta,* from its function of remembering things it is interested in. (Tr. Madhavananda)

It may be noted that mind, intellect and ego constituting *citta* or internal organs – all have their specific functions of consideration of pros and cons, determination and realization of the self-hood respectively.

Similar use of *vṛtti* is seen in the following verse:

अव्यक्तमेतत्त्रिगुणैर्निरुक्तं तत्कारणं नाम शरीरमात्मनः ।
सुषुप्तिरेतस्य विभक्त्यवस्था प्रलीनसर्वेन्द्रियबुद्धिवृत्तिः ॥

ViCū 120

This undifferentiated, spoken of as the compound of the three *guṇas,* is the causal body of the soul. Profound sleep is its special state, in which the functions of the mind and its organs are suspended. (Tr. Madhavananda)

Here, the special state of deep sleep (*suṣupti*) has been defined as the suspension of all the functions of the organs and the mind.

Vṛtti in the **Vedānta-Paribhāṣā** relates to the function, attribute or modification of the mind and also of the entire *antaḥkaraṇa* which includes all the four – *manas, buddhi, citta* and *ahaṃkāra.* Mental modifications are not permanent, but one modification lasts till another modification takes place. This nature of mind has pointed out by Dharmarāja Adhvarīndra in the **Vedānta-Paribhāṣā** as:

> यावद् घटस्फुरणं तावद् घटाकारान्तःकरणवृत्तिरेकैव, न तु नाना, वृत्तेः स्वविरोधिवृत्त्युत्पत्तिपर्यन्तं स्थायित्वाभ्युपगमात् ॥
>
> VedPar Intro. 6
>
> So long as there is the cognition of a jar, the mental state that assumes the form of the jar is just one, and not multiple, for a mental state is admitted to last till another state opposed to it has arisen. (Tr. Madhavananda)

The text while refuting the view that mind is devoid of parts, clearly states that it is not so and modification of mind occurs naturally.

> ननु निरवयवस्यान्तःकरणस्य परिणामात्मिका वृत्तिः कथम् ?
> इत्थम् । न तावदन्तःकरणं निरवयवं, सादिद्रव्यत्वेन सावयवत्वात् ।
>
> VedPar I.5–6
>
> Now, in the case of the partless, internal organ, how can there be psychosis, which is of the nature of a modification?
>
> It is thus: the internal organ is not partless, since, being a substance with beginning, it has parts. (Tr. S.S.S. Sastri)

The process of modification of mind has been exemplified picturesquely with the simile of water running out of a hole and passing through a channel and entering into plots of different shapes. The water is thus flowing out (and) takes the form of a rectangle or square as the plot is. The mind also following the sense organs reaches out to the objects and become subject of modification (*yathā taḍāgodakaṃ chidrānnirgatya ... sa eva pariṇāmo vṛttirityucyate* – VedPar I.18). This is known as *vṛtti* or modification of mind.

That the *antaḥkaraṇa* assumes four forms according to its four fold function (*vṛtti*) of doubting (*saṃśaya*), determination (*niścaya*), ego (*garvaḥ*), and memorising (*smaraṇa*) (VedPar I.58). Owing to this diversity of states, the mind though one, is designated as the manas, the intellect, the ego and the *citta* (*vṛttibhedena ekamapi antaḥkaraṇaṃ mana iti buddhiriti ahaṅkāra iti cittamiti cākhyāyate* – VedPar I.58).

In the **Mahānirvāṇa Tantra**, *vrata* and *vṛtta* have been used in the sense of *vṛtti*, i.e. means of livelihood or profession. The Tantra holds that all the four *varṇas* should normally follow the prescribed profession enumerated in the Dharmaśāstras. They however, may follow trade or service if they are unable to practice the same. The following verse clarify the Tantric position in this respect.

अध्यापनं याजनं च विप्राणां व्रतमुत्तमम् ।
अशक्तौ क्षत्रियविशां वृत्तैर्निर्वाहमाचरेत् ॥

MNT VIII.110

Teaching and the performance of sacrifices are the proper duties of a *brāhmaṇa.* But if he be incapable of these, he may earn his livelihood by following the profession of *kṣatriya* or *vaiśya.*
(Tr. John Woodroffe)

Regarding the profession of *kṣatriyas* and *śūdras* the text further adds:

राजन्यानां च सद्वृत्तं संग्रामो भूमिशासनम् ।
अत्राशक्तौ वणिग्वृत्तं शूद्रवृत्तमथाश्रयेत् ॥
वाणिज्याशक्तवैश्यानां शूद्रवृत्तमदूषणम् ।
शूद्राणां परमेशानि सेवावृत्तिं विधीयते ॥

MNT VIII.111–112

The proper occupation of a *kṣatriya* is that of fighting and ruling. But if he be incapable of these, he may earn his livelihood by following the profession of a *vaiśya* or *śūdra.*

If a *vaiśya* cannot trade, then for him the following of the profession of a *śūdra* involves no blame. For a *śūdra,* O sovereign Queen! (*parameśāni*) service is the prescribed means of livelihood.
(Tr. John Woodroffe)

Hence, *vṛtti* in the above quotations is used in the sense of profession or occupation.

In the context of Kashmir Śaivism *vṛtti* has been used variously in different context. The main sense however, is the modification of the mind, condition of the self (*suṣupti,* etc.), function of the sense organs (*indriya vṛtti,* etc.) as well as attitude or disposition in general. According to specific stand point of Kashmir Śaiva philosophy the Ultimate Reality is Śiva alone. Even if it is so, the entire universe is the creation of Śakti, which is indivisible constituent of Śiva. Everything comes down in the form of all the worldly objects. That is why, the concept of unified Śiva and Śakti is both immanent and transcendent in as much as everything in this world is basically one with Śiva (*śivātmaka*) and transcends its limited 'it-ness' as well. The **Tantrāloka** explains the *śivātmikā-vṛtti* and says that *vṛtti* descends from the Śiva, but maintains its oneness with Him and remains unchanged. *Vṛtti* here clearly stands for the state or condition of Śakti in its course of descent from Śiva.

निस्तरङ्गावतीर्णा सा वृत्तिरेका शिवात्मिका ॥

TĀl V.89cd

The One modification of Śiva descends from the Ultimate, which is unperturbed.

Here, in the modification of Śiva is conceived as an unchanged entity. The idea is that though Śiva and its modification (*vṛtti*) comes down but does not undergo any change, so far as its essence is considered. The Śaiva philosophy of Kashmir tradition holds that Śiva and His Śakti (*vṛtti*) are both immanent and transcendent.

The mental states have to be eliminated by all the aspirants as the **Vijñāna Bhairava** prescribes the following method.

यथा तथा यत्र तत्र द्वादशान्ते मनः क्षिपेत् ।
प्रतिक्षणं क्षीणवृत्तेर्वैलक्षण्यं दिनैर्भवेत् ॥

ViBhai 51

In whatsoever manner and wheresoever place, one should fix his mind at *dvādaśānta*. By doing so repeatedly the fluctuation of the mind will diminish and within a few days one will achieve an extraordinary distinction.

Here, *dvādaśānta* is explained in different ways. Some of them are: (1) it stands for the top of *sahasrāra*, which is at a distance of twelve fingers from the tip of the nose; (2) *bindu, ardhacandra, nirodhikā, nāda, nādānta, śakti, vyāpinī, samanā, unmanā,* and the three states: *jāgrat, svapna* and *suṣupti* represented by '*a, u, m*' are considered to be twelve in number, the end of it is meant by *dvādaśānta*; (3) the span of the vital breath is measured as twelve fingers from the nose, the end of that is the *dvādaśānta*.

An alternative method of concentration has been referred to in the **Vijñāna Bhairava** as:

निर्वृक्षगिरिभित्त्यादि-देशे दृष्टिं विनिक्षिपेत् ।
विलीने मानसे भावे वृत्तिक्षीणः प्रजायते ॥

ViBhai 60

One should fix his gaze on the floor of a mountain, or such other places, which are bereft of all growth (trees and plants). When all the mental feelings will cease (die out), modification of the mind will diminish.

In this verse *mānasabhāva* and *vṛtti* both stand for modification of mind.

Vṛtti in the sense of *vyāpāra* both internal and external activities is mentioned in the **Pratyabhijñā-Kārikā**. While defining *suṣupti* the author says:

साक्षाणामान्तरी वृत्तिः प्राणादिप्रेरिका मता ।
जीवनाख्याथवा प्राणेऽहन्ता पुर्यष्टकात्मिका ॥

PrKā III.2.14

In the *śūnya*, there is the internal activity of senses, which sets the vital airs, etc. in motion, and that which is the so-called life; or it is the subjectiveness (ego) arrogated to one's vital airs – *prāṇas* and which consists of the group of eight (*pūryaṣṭakātmikā*).
(Tr. R.K. Kaw)

Here, the deep sleep '*suṣupti*' is the state of rest of the conscious thinking subject in the *prāṇa* (vital air) which is in the state of *śūnya* (void). In this context *vṛtti* means function or the activity of senses.

In the **Parātrīśikā Vivaraṇa** of Abhinavagupta, *vṛtti* is used in the sense of function of the mind (*cittavṛttīnāṃ vaiṣamyam* – PTrīVi pp. 40–41).

It has already been noted that the root *vṛt-* initially means existence (*vartanam*). Hence, *vṛtti* indicates or implies a large number of senses associated with the basic sense of existence. Thus, *vṛtti* may indicate the means of existence, mode of behaviour, different modes of livelihood and even qualities and actions related to specific modes of existence. Mode or manner or disposition or livelihood, duties prescribed for different types of people as well as different disposition of the mind – all are covered by the term *vṛtti*. In literature, both Kāvya and Nāṭya, the poets have used *vṛtti* in all these senses. A survey of the Kāvya and the Nāṭya literature will show up the wide range of meanings of the term. Everywhere, however, the sense of mode or manner is intrinsic. Some examples culled out from the standard classical Kāvyas and Nāṭakas, would be beneficial in ascertaining the concept of *vṛtti*.

Aśvaghoṣa in his **Buddhacarita** has used *vṛtti* in various places. While describing the effect of the noble advice of Buddha given to Āmrapālī, a famous beautiful prostitute, the poet says:

श्रुत्वा धर्म्यं मुनेर्वाक्यं जहौ कामं मनोगतम् ।
स्त्रीभावं तुच्छमाज्ञाय स्ववृत्तौ त्वकरोद् घृणाम् ॥

BudCa XXII.50

Hearing the preaching of piety delivered by the sage (Buddha), she (Āmrapālī) cast aside her attachment to lust and considering womenhood as very trivial, despised her own profession (prostitution).

In another place the poet uses *vṛtti* as sustenance (means of maintenance).

While describing the mode of maintenance of the bee the poet observes thus:

> भ्रमरो रसमादत्ते भिन्ते छिन्ते न कर्हिचित् ।
> तथा न पीडयेत्कश्चिद् वृत्तिं मात्रामिवार्जयन् ॥
>
> BudCa XXVI.43
>
> As the bees do not injure the flowers in sipping their juice in the garden, so also you should (practise to) collect such a quantum of food, so that no one would be troubled for it.

Mādhukarī vṛtti or the means of living followed by a bee has been praised and prescribed to be followed by the saintly people. The above verse has a reference to this harmless manner of maintaining one's own life.

In Kālidāsa, the greatest of the poets *vṛtti* occurs in different contexts and senses. Describing Śiva in trance (*samādhi*) the poet says:

> मनो नवद्वारनिषिद्धवृत्ति हृदि व्यवस्थाप्य समाधिवश्यम् ।
> यमक्षरं क्षेत्रविदो विदुस्तमात्मानमात्मन्यवलोकयन्तम् ॥
>
> Kum III.50
>
> Having withdrawn the mind from the nine openings of the sense organs and placing it in the heart by means of concentration, he was visualizing his own soul in himself, whom the ascetics (*kṣetravid*) known as the Ultimate Eternal Being.

This verse is an example of Kālidāsa's versatile genious and speaks of his great understanding of the methods of yogic *sādhanā*. *Vṛtti* in '*navadvāra-niṣiddhavṛtti*' has the sense of running towards movements or *sañcāra* as explained by Mallinātha in his commentary. The tendency of the mind running to the worldly objects constitute the typical function of the mind. This tendency has been expressed as *vṛtti* by Kālidāsa. The same mental tendency has again been touched by the poet to describe the stunning effect on Rati at the burning of Madana. By means of the figure of speech (*utprekṣā*) the poet says that Rati falls unconscious as a result of the terrible effect of the sudden action and was as if benefited by this unconsciousness, because she did not realize the demise of her husband. This was due to stunning of her sense-organs, cursed by the terrible event (*tīvrābhiṣaṅgaprabhaveṇa vṛttiṃ mohena .... ratirbabhūva* – Kum III.73). Her sense-organs ceased to function. This cessation of the sense organ has been denoted by *vṛtti* here.

Vṛtti in the sense of *jīvanopāya* – 'means of subsistence' has been used at various places. Describing Pārvatī's penance the poet says that she followed the means of living peculiar to the trees. *Vṛkṣa-vṛtti* or the mode of living of a tree has been referred to the mode of living followed by Pārvatī at the time of her severe penance.

अयाचितोपस्थितमम्बु केवलं रसात्मकस्योडुपतेश्च रश्मयः ।
बभूव तस्याः किल पारणाविधिर्न वृक्षवृत्तिव्यतिरिक्तसाधनः ॥

Kum V.22

Only the water that came to her without any effort on her part and the rays of the moon (Lord of the constellations), full of nectar, broke her fast, the means being not different from those by which trees subsist. (Tr. M.R. Kale)

Exactly in the same sense another verse is recorded in the **Kumārasambhava** (V.28), viz. '*svayaṃviśīrṇadrumaparṇavṛttitā parā hi kāṣṭhā tapasas tayā punaḥ, tad apyapākīrṇam ataḥ priyaṃvadāṃ vadantyaparṇeti ca tāṃ purāvidaḥ*'. Here *drumaparṇa-vṛttitā* means living on dried up leaves of trees, which fall down automatically. Kālidāsa here provides a charming derivative sense of '*aparṇā*'. He says the ascetics live on only such leaves, but Pārvatī was a still higher ascetic as she rejected such leaves also for her maintenance.

In the context of the dialogue between Śiva in disguise and Pārvatī, Kālidāsa uses *anuvṛtti, pāpavṛtti, āśopahatātmavṛtti* and *kāmavṛtti,* mainly in the sense of 'modes of behaviour'. Disparaging Śiva as the desired bridegroom the disguised Śiva says "I full well know this Śiva, whom you have choosen as your beloved. Since I know his attachment to things inauspicious, I do not feel enthused to approve of thy desire" (*amaṅgalābhyāsaratiṃ vicintya taṃ tavānuvṛttiṃ na ca kartumutsahe* – Kum V.65cd). *Vṛtti* being *vyavahāra, anuvṛtti* means to ditto the same. Approval of a particular behaviour is the sense of *anuvṛtti* here.

The mode of behaviour or *ācaraṇa* is the sense of *pāpavṛtti, kāmavṛtti, ātmavṛtti,* etc. Hence the mode behaviour typical to a sinner (*pāpavṛtti* – Kum V.36), a self-willed man (*kāmavṛtti* – Kum V.82) and that of one who is a slave to various desires (*āśopahatātmavṛtti* – Kum V.76) have been conveyed in these expressions. It may be noted that *ātmavṛtti* and *manovṛtti* mean the same thing. *Manovṛtti* or modification of the mind means idea, notion, or disposition relating to the mind. So *vṛtti* as such is to be repeated as the notion or attitude.

In the seventh canto of **Kumārasambhava**, Kālidāsa describes the conjugal life of Śiva and Pārvatī. He refers to their witnessing of a play enacted by the *apsaras* for the delectation of the couple Śiva and Pārvatī. Modes of temperamental behaviour known as *kaiśikī, sāttvatī,* etc. typical to the drama have been referred by *vṛtti* in the following verse:

तौ सन्धिषु व्यञ्जितवृत्तिभेदं रसान्तरेषु प्रतिबद्धरागम् ।
अपश्यतामप्सरसां मुहूर्तं प्रयोगमाद्यं ललिताङ्गहारम् ॥

Kum VII.91

They saw, for a while, the first representation (of a play), in the combination of the different incidents of which the styles of description were properly brought out, in which the different sentiments were delineated by proper modes of music, and in which there were graceful bodily movements (i.e. gesticulations).
(Tr. M.R. Kale)

In the **Raghuvaṃśa** the use of *vṛtti* (*āvṛtti* and *anuvṛtti*) figure in many places. In most places *vṛtti* stands for mode of behaviour, means of livelihood, *āhāra* or food in an extended sense. Sage Vasiṣṭha orders Dilīpa to serve his cow 'Nandinī' in the following manner:

वन्यवृत्तिरिमां शश्वदात्मानुगमनेन गाम् ।
विद्यामभ्यसनेनेव प्रसादयितुमर्हसि ॥

Ragh I.88

Living upon forest fare you should try to propitiate this cow by your constant (personal) attendance upon her; as one acquires learning by constant application. (Tr. G.R. Nandargikar)

The king is enjoined by the *guru* to constantly attend the cow subsisting on whatever food is available in the forest (*vanyavṛtti*).

Vṛtti as action or function plays a role in *āvṛtti*. The movement of the cow towards the forest is her *vṛtti* and when she comes back from her journey in the evening it is denoted by *āvṛtti* or return:

आपीनभारोद्वहनप्रयत्नाद्गृष्टिर्गुरुत्वाद्वपुषो नरेन्द्रः ।
उभावलंचक्रतुरञ्चिताभ्यां तपोवनावृत्तिपथं गताभ्याम् ॥

Ragh II.18

On account of the labour of bearing the burden of the udders the cow which had only one calf, and the king by reason of his bodily heaviness both decorated the way by which they returned from the sacred forest with their graceful gaits.
(Tr. G.R. Nandargikar)

Here, *tapovanāvṛttipatham* means the way by which they (king and the cow) returned from the sacred forest to the hermitage. In the context of Aja's marriage (seventh canto) the poet beautifully describes the mutual impact of love on the bride as well as bride-groom. He says:

आसीद्वरः कण्टकितप्रकोष्ठः स्विन्नाङ्गुलिः संववृते कुमारी ।
वृत्तिस्तयोः पाणिसमागमेन समं विभक्तेव मनोभवस्य ॥

Ragh VII.22

The hair on the wrist of the bride-groom stood erect and the fingers of the princess became wet with perspiration; thus by the joining of their hands the action of love was, as it were, equally divided in them at that moment. (Tr. G.R. Nandargikar)

The physical reaction of the lovers on touching each other has been very beautifully described with the help of the figure, *utprekṣā.* The horripilation of Aja and sweating of the palms of Indumatī have been imagined as it were as the simultaneous impact of the god of love. Here *vṛtti* in the sense of *vartana* (existence) is meant, which includes in its sphere, the quality and action (*guṇa* and *karma*) as well.

Anuvṛtti in the sense of 'following the pattern or mode' is seen in the expression. Bharata's head which was full of matted hair due to his decision of following the mode of behaviour of his elder brother is conveyed by this epithet of his head.

लङ्केश्वरप्रणतिभङ्गदृढव्रतं तद्
वन्द्यं युगं चरणयोर्जनकात्मजायाः ।
ज्येष्ठानुवृत्तिजटिलं च शिरोऽस्य साधो-
रन्योन्यपावनमभूदुभयं समेत्य ॥

Ragh XIII.78

The adorable pair of feet of the daughter of Janaka, which had observed the firm vow of spurning the supplications of the Lord of Laṅkā, and the head of the good man, the hair on which had become matted on account of following the course of his elder brother, coming together, became mutually sanctifying.
(Tr. G.R. Nandargikar)

Keeping *abhidhā* or function of the word in mind Kālidāsa has cleverly pointed out two different senses of the word Rāma. Sage Paraśurāma says that sofar the word Rāma denoted him alone, while after the rise of Rāma, the son of Daśaratha, the same word now denotes another person, which is disgraceful to him. This extension of denotation has been referred to as *vyasta vṛtti* – conveyance of different sense.

अन्यदा जगति राम इत्ययं शब्द उच्चरित एव मामगात् ।
व्रीडमावहति मे स संप्रति व्यस्तवृत्तिरुदयोन्मुखे त्वयि ॥

Ragh XI.73

At other times than the present the epithet Rāma being pronounced in the world was applicable to (signified) me alone. Now that you are rising to importance the same name with its signification being changed (i.e. proper force or meaning being divided) puts me to shame! (Tr. G.R. Nandargikar)

A very psychological depiction of Rāma's mind by Kālidāsa is seen in the verse: '*kimātmanirvādakathāmupekṣai .... dolācalacittavṛttiḥ*' (Ragh XIV.34). Rāma was as if facing a horn of dilemma on hearing the slanderous comments about the chastity of Sītā. Whether he should neglect these accusation or abandon her (Sītā) who was free from, all blemishes, were the two alternatives available to him. The poet says that not being able to accept either of the two alternatives Rāma's mental state (*citta vṛtti*) was just like a swing, touching two points in its motion.

In the **Meghadūta**, *vṛtti* is used in a number of places (*anyathā vṛtti* – I.3, *pratihatatamo-vṛtti* –II.3 and *karuṇā-vṛtti* – II.33). In the first instance *vṛtti* means *vyāpāra.* The poet says that seeing a vast cloud the mind of even happy persons behave differently (*anyathā vṛtti*), i.e. disposition of the mind undergoes a change, which is the effect of rising cloud. While describing the unique conditions of Alakā the poet in the **Meghadūta** (II.3) says that at every evening the Alakā is bright with permanent moonlight. It is so due to the fact that in this unique city the moon shines everyday, irrespective of the division of dark half and bright half. The poetic expression is '*nityajyotsnāḥ pratihatatamovṛttiramyāḥ pradoṣāḥ*' (Megh II.3d). *Tamovṛtti* means 'spread of darkness', which does not take place in the evening at this divine city. So, *vṛtti* as *sañcāra,* covering or spreading all around is meant here. In *karuṇāvṛtti* (Megh II.33) *karuṇā* or sympathy is a mental disposition. The poet generalizes that the persons whose inner mind is soft and compassionate have sympathetic dispositions for others in distress (*prāyaḥ sarvo bhavati karuṇāvṛttirārdrāntarātmā*).

Bhāravi, a great poet, has used *vṛtti* at various places in his **Kirātārjunīyam**. Mode of mind or disposition is uniformly notable, when the poet speaks of the conduct of the king in relation to his subjects, he mentions *prajāsu vṛtti* (Kir I.1), i.e. conduct. *Cittavṛtti* (Kir I.37), *antaḥkaraṇa vṛtti* (Kir III.3), *sama vṛtti* (Kir II.38-39), etc. also represent mental mode in general or manner of treatment. In *sambhāvitavṛtti* (Kir II.7) *vṛtti* means existence. The prowess (*pauruṣa*) existing in Yudhiṣṭhira was highly appreciated by all the gods. *Śamaika vṛtti* means 'exclusively peaceful mentality', which is described in the following verse:

विधाय विध्वंसमनात्मनीनं शमैकवृत्तेर्भवतश्छलेन ।
प्रकाशितत्वन्मतिशीलसाराः कृतोपकारा इव विद्विषस्ते ॥

Kir III.16

Working ruin upon you who always act peacefully by means of a fraudulent scheme, but to their own detriment your enemies, in as much as they have prominently brought into light the excellence of your wisdom and character, have, as it were, conferred an obligation upon you. (Tr. M.R. Kale)

Bhaṭṭi uses *vṛtti* in the sense of *vyāpāra,* i.e. function or vocation:

ततोऽभ्यगाद् गाधिसुतः क्षितीन्द्रं रक्षोभिरभ्याहतकर्मवृत्तिः ।
रामं वरीतुं परिरक्षणाऽर्थं राजाऽऽर्जिहत् तं मधुपर्कपाणिः ॥

BhaKā I.17

Later, Viśvāmitra whose performance of sacrifices had been hampered by demons, approached that king to seek Rāma for the protection (of the sacrifices). The king, honoured him with *madhuparka* offerings in his hand.
(Tr. M.A. Karandikar & Mrs. S. Karandikar)

For another instance the spirited statement of Sītā regarding her abduction and sojourn at Rāvaṇa's capital may be mentioned. She says that her heart existed always in Rāma. Although her body was overpowered by the demons. This truth is known to all the gods, who are the knower of the real truth.

चेतसस्त्वयि वृत्तिर्मे शरीरं रक्षसा हृतम् ।
विदांकुर्वन्तु सम्यञ्चो देवाः सत्यमिदं वचः ॥

BhaKā XX.28

The activity of my mind rests on you; (only) the body was abducted by the demon; let the equanimous gods, verify this true statement. (Tr. M.A. Karandikar & Mrs. S. Karandikar)

Karma-vṛtti and *citta-vṛtti (cetaso-vṛtti)* here and *bhinna-vṛtti* (BhaKā I.16), *rājanya-vṛtti* (BhaKā II.35), *viśvajanīna-vṛtti* (BhaKā II.48) convey the sense of function or *vyāpāra* uniformly. In the last of the five great court epics, viz. the **Naiṣadhīyacarita**, the use of *vṛtti* can now be considered by the way of concluding our survey of the Mahākāvyas. Here also the highly talented and scholarly reputed poet Śrīharṣa uses the word to convey the prevalent sense of function, nature, livelihood and disposition of the mind. For example, in the **Naiṣadhīyacarita** (VIII.42) the word *śiloñcha vṛtti* clearly stands for vocation or means of livelihood of a noble/ideal *brāhmaṇa.* The use of *citta-vṛtti* (NaiCa VIII.45 and XI.8) stands for mode or disposition of the mind.

In the following verse the poet underlines the fact that the fire does not hurt a chaste women. This behaviour of fire has been conveyed by *satīṣu-vṛtti,* i.e. conduct of fire in relation to the chaste ladies.

त्वयैकसत्या तनुतापशङ्कया ततो निवर्त्यं न मनः कथंचन ।
हिमोपमा तस्य परीक्षणक्षणे सतीषु वृत्तिः शततो निरूपिता ॥

NaiCa IX.55

Thou who art the one devoted woman shouldst not turn back thy mind at any cost from the god of fire, for fear of thy body being burnt; at the moment of ordeal his snowlike action on women that are chaste hath been a hundred times proved.
(Tr. K.K. Handiqui)

By the way of concluding the literary field we may take of the use of *vṛtti* in the prose text of the **Hitopadeśa**. In the didactic tales comprising the **Hitopadeśa**, *vṛtti* has been variously used. *Vṛtti* as *jīvikā* is seen in the verse: '*yasmindeśe na sammāno na vṛttir na ca bāndhavaḥ*' (Hit I.105ab) etc. Of course *vṛtti* would mean here not merely vocation but an honourable one. Similarly, in the verse: '*vṛttyartham nāticeṣṭeta sā hi dhātraiva nirmitā*' (Hit I.179ab) etc. the author cautions that one should not hanker after a vocation too much as vocations are more or less ordained by fate. *Vṛtti* in the following verse however, indicates *vartana* or position. The idea is that a really wise man has only two positions in the society – either to be honoured by all or to die neglected just like a bunch of flowers.

कुसुमस्तबकस्येव द्वे वृत्ती तु मनस्विनः ।
सर्वेषां मूर्ध्नि वा तिष्ठेद्विशीर्येत वनेऽथवा ॥

Hit I.134

The course of action of a wise man, like that of a bunch of flowers, is two-fold, viz. either to stand at (on) the head of all, or to die (wither) away in a forest. (Tr. M.R. Kale)

In the **Abhijñānaśākuntala** *vṛtti* has been variously used by the poet Kālidāsa. The disposition of mind or condition of mind is known as *vṛtti* in the following quotation:

अहो चेष्टाप्रतिरूपिका कामिजनमनोवृत्तिः ।

AbhŚāk I (prose), after verse 25

Ah, how similar to action is the working of a lover's mind?
(Tr. M.R. Kale)

At another place, *vṛtti* is used to denote 'the function of eyes'.

उत्पक्ष्मणोर्नयनयोरुपरुद्धवृत्तिं बाष्पं कुरु स्थिरतया विरतानुबन्धम् ।
अस्मिन्नलक्षितनतोन्नतभूमिभागे मार्गे पदानि खलु ते विषमीभवन्ति ॥

AbhŚāk IV.15

Do you, with firmness, check the continuity of your tears which obstruct the function of your eyes with up-turned, protruding eyelashes. Your foot-steps are indeed falling unevenly on the road, the ups and downs of which are not being noticed by you. (Tr. M.R. Kale)

In one of the best *ślokas* of **Abhijñānaśākuntala,** Maharṣi Kaṇva advises Śakuntalā on the duties of a wife and a daughter in law.

शुश्रूषस्व गुरून्कुरु प्रियसखीवृत्तिं सपत्नीजने ।

AbhŚāk IV.18ab

Serve your elders and treat your co-wives as your dear friends.

Here, *vṛtti* means conduct or behaviour. According to the laws of Maharṣi Manu (Manu VII.130–132, cf. Ragh V.8) a king was authorized to take one sixth part (or eighth or one twelfth, according to the productivity of the land) of grain, etc. Likewise, according to the **Abhijñānaśākuntala**, the means of existence of a king has been prescribed as one sixth share collected from his subjects (*ṣaṣṭhāṃśavṛtterapi dharma eṣa* – AbhŚāk V.4d). So *vṛtti* here denotes *jīvikā* or livelihood.

The sage Mārica is described as supporting life on air which is the highest degree of spirituality reached by an ascetic (*prāṇānāmanilena vṛttirucitā* – AbhŚāk VII.12). Thus *vṛtti* stands for 'means of livelihood' as the sage depends only on air for his maintenance, nothing else.

In the **Veṇīsaṃhāra** *vṛtti* is used to denote 'means of livelihood', Yudhiṣṭhira says to Bhīma that you have supported yourself always with the remnants of eatables left over by me, as such your *vṛtti* or means of livelihood is dependent on me.

मया पीतं पीतं तदनु भवताम्बास्तनयुगं
मदुच्छिष्टैर्वृत्तिं जनयसि रसैर्वत्सलतया ।

Veṇī VI.31ab

I sucked my mother's breasts and thereafter you sucked them; through affection you lived on juicy articles that remained after I had partaken of them. (Tr. M.R. Kale)

In the **Uttararāmacarita** Bhavabhūti explains *vṛtti* in the sense of behaviour or conduct, i.e. a conduct full of affection.

प्रियप्राया वृत्तिर्विनयमधुरो वाचि नियमः प्रकृत्या कल्याणी मतिरनवगीतः परिचयः ।
पुरो वा पश्चाद्वा तदिदमविपर्यासितरसं रहस्यं साधूनामनुपधि विशुद्धं विजयते ॥

UttCa II.2

A behaviour full of kindness, a restraint over speech pleasing by its modesty, a mind naturally prone to do good, and a friendship irreproachable – triumphant is this secret of the life of the good, of a sweetness not altered by time past or future, guiltless and pure. (Tr. M.R. Kale)

Vṛtti is used in the sense of 'movement' in the **Mālatīmādhava** of Bhavabhūti.

विष्वग्वृत्तिर्जटानां प्रचलति निबिडग्रन्थिबद्धोऽपि भार:
संस्कारक्वाणदीर्घं पटु रटति कृतावृत्तिखट्वाङ्गघण्टा ।
ऊर्ध्वं धूनोति वायुर्विवृतशवशिर: श्रोणिकुञ्जेषु गुञ्ज-
न्नुत्ताल: किंकिणीनामनवरतरणत्कारहेतु: पताका: ॥

MālMā V.4

The mass of my matted hair though tied together by a tight knot shakes forcibly moving in all directions; the bell attached to my *khaṭvā* (a sort of club) moving circuitously makes a piercing sound, prolonged by its continuous tinkle, and the howling wind, the cause of the incessant tinkling of the bells and resounding through the hollows of the lines of the bare skulls of dead bodies, shakes upwards the banners. (Tr. M.R. Kale)

So here *viṣvakvṛtti* means 'movement' (of hair) in different directions.

In the **Nāgānanda**, *vṛtti* denotes conduct or behaviour.

नृपस्यानुकरोमि वृत्तिम् ॥

Nāgā IV.1d

I am imitating the conduct of the king.

So in the dramas *vṛtti* is used in different senses.

Manifestation in the Arts

Vṛtti plays an important role in literature in general and the dramatic art in particular. If we trace the use of *vṛtti* in the **Nāṭya-Śāstra** which happens to be the earliest treats of the entire literary tradition. Bharata, in addition to many references to it devotes a full chapter (XX) on the *vṛtti*.

The **Nāṭya-Śāstra** treats of *vṛtti* as a fundamental principle of dramatic art. It speaks of the four *vṛtti*s, viz. *bhāratī, kaiśikī, sāttvatī* and *ārabhaṭī* for the first time and observes that dramatic art is based on these four *vṛttis.* And at the same time Bharata relates these four *vṛttis* with the four Vedas to emphasize their importance.

ऋग्वेदाद्भारती क्षिप्ता यजुर्वेदाच्च सात्त्वती ।
कैशिकी सामवेदाच्च शेषा चाथर्वणादपि ॥

NŚ XX.25

The *bhāratī vṛtti* was extracted from the Ṛgveda, the *sāttvatī* from the Yajurveda, the *kaiśikī* from the Sāmaveda and the last one, i.e. the *ārabhaṭī vṛtti* from the Atharvaveda.

This verse easily reminds us of another verse in the **Nāṭya-Śāstra**, which holds that dialogue, songs, acting and *rasa*, were collected respectively from the Ṛk, Sāman, Yajus and the Atharvan.

जग्राह पाठ्यमृग्वेदात्सामभ्यो गीतमेव च ।
यजुर्वेदादभिनयान् रसानाथर्वणादपि ॥

NŚ I.17

He took *pāṭhyam* (recitals) from the Ṛgveda, *gītam* (music) from the Sāmans; *abhinayas* (histrionic and gestural representation) from the Yajurveda and *rasas* (sentiments) from the Atharvaveda. (Tr. A Board of Scholars)

In addition to this Bharata has given an elaborate account of the origin and special features of each *vṛtti* with a reference to the fight of Viṣṇu with Madhu and Kaiṭabha (cf. NŚ chapter XX).

As has already been noted *vṛtti* in context of dramatic art means special modes of behaviour of the *dramatis personae* under the impact of different types of temperaments. Modes of romantic temperaments is called *kaiśikī*; that of heroic temperaments is called *sāttvatī*; and that of combative temperaments is called *ārabhaṭī*; whereas the basic vocal representation is considered as *bhāratī*.

Kaiśikī etc. can also be directly related to the basic sense of the root *vṛt-* 'to exist'. The meaning of existence can also indicate inherence. As such *kaiśikī* etc. are also *vṛttis* as dramatic art inherent in these *vṛttis*. When we say the *vṛtti* or behaviour of a *brāhmaṇa*, the qualities meant are inherent in that *vṛtti*. Four fold *abhinaya*, i.e. *āṅgika, vācika, āhārya* and *sāttvika* – all are inherent in *naṭavṛtti*. In this sense, applications of *vṛtti* to indicate *kaiśikī* etc. is fully justified.

The **Bhāva Prakāśana** which happens to be a comprehensive compilation of all the different views on drama and related literature, also refers to the *vṛtti*. The *vṛttis* are enumerated in the text as:

वृत्तिश्चतुर्विधा ऋग्यजुस्सामाथर्वसम्भवा ॥
भारती सात्त्वती चैव कैशिक्यारभटीति च ।
औद्भटाः पञ्चमीमर्थवृत्तिं च प्रतिजानते ॥
अर्थवृत्तेरभावात्तु विश्रान्तां पञ्चमीं परे ।

BhPrak I.86

Vṛttis (modes) are of four types on account of its being originated from Ṛk, Sāma, Yajur and Atharva Vedas, viz. *bhāratī, sāttvatī, kaiśikī* and *ārabhaṭī*. Udbhaṭācārya – recognised a fifth *vṛtti*, named *arthavṛtti*. But another scholar, (i.e. Bhoja) considered *viśrāntā* as fifth *vṛtti* instead of *arthavṛtti*. (Tr. P. Ghosal)

Apart from these dramatic *vṛttis* Śāradātanaya refers to *manovṛtti* (*īdṛśī ca rasotpattiḥ manovṛttiśca śāśvatī* – BhPrak II.55) and *ahaṅkāravṛtti* (*ahaṅkārasya vṛttiryā so'bhimānaḥ prakīrtitaḥ* – BhPrak II.46). Here *vṛtti* stands for mental mode or modification of mind or *antaḥkaraṇa*.

In later dramatic treatises this very basic concept of *vṛtti* has been variously elaborated, of course on the lines of **Nāṭya-Śāstra.** The **Daśarūpaka** for example refers to the four *vṛttis* and points out their uses in different sentiments (*yadvyāpārātmikā vṛttiścaturdhā* – DaRū II.47). The text further speaks about the nature of different *vṛttis* as:

शृङ्गारे कैशिकी, वीरे सात्त्वत्यारभटी पुनः ।
रसे रौद्रे च बीभत्से, वृत्तिः सर्वत्र भारती ॥

DaRū II.62

Kaiśikī vṛtti is employed to show *śṛṅgāra rasa* (erotic sentiment), in sphere of *vīrarasa* (heroic sentiment) *sāttvatī* is employed, further *ārabhaṭī* is used in case of *raudra rasa* (furious) and *bībhatsa* (disgustful), while *bhāratī* (on account of its being oral expression) may be employed to show all the sentiments. (Tr. P. Ghosal)

In the Alaṅkāra literature *vṛtti* figures mainly in three contexts. For the first time it was the *dhvanivādins* who discussed three functions of words, viz. *abhidhā, lakṣaṇā* and *vyañjanā*. These three (in the original sense) were not noted as *vṛttis*. Ānandavardhana, Abhinavagupta and following them Mammaṭa also discuss these three as *śabda-vyāpāra*, i.e. function of the words. Mammaṭa clearly states: "*sa mukhyo'rthastatra mukhyo vyāpāro'syābhidhocyate*" (KāPrak II.8). To explain *abhidhā*; "*mukhyārthabādhe tadyoge rūḍhito'tha prayojanāt/anyo'rtho lakṣyate yat sā lakṣaṇāropitā kriyā*" (KāPrak II.9). To explain *lakṣaṇā*: "*anekārthasya śabdasya vācakatve niyantrite, saṃyogādyair avācyārthadhīkṛd vyāpṛtir añjanam*" (KāPrak II.19). It may be noted that following the *dhvani* tradition Mammaṭa refers to all those functions as *vyāpāra* or function of the word. *Vṛtti* in the sense of *vyāpāra* was first referred to by Viśvanātha, when he uses *śakti* as well as *vṛtti* to denote the functions of the words.

> वाच्योऽर्थोऽभिधया बोध्यो लक्ष्यो लक्षणया मत: ।
> व्यङ्ग्यो व्यञ्जनया ता: स्युस्तिस्र: शब्दस्य शक्तय: ॥
>
> SāDar II.6
>
> The indicated sense is conveyed by indication (*abhidhā*), the implied sense is conveyed by implication (*lakṣaṇā*), the suggestive sense is conveyed by suggestion (*vyañjanā*). These are the three functions (*vṛtti*) of three types of words.

In the same sense Viśvanātha later clarified these functions as *vṛtti*s. In his statement:

> विरतास्वभिधाद्यासु ययार्थो बोध्यतेऽपर: ।
> सा वृत्तिर्व्यञ्जना नाम शब्दस्यार्थादिकस्य च ॥
>
> SāDar II.19
>
> When the function of indicative and implicative words are over, the *vṛtti* that brings about the suggestive sense is to be known as *vyañjanā* of both the words and sense.

It may be noted here that the basic sense of *vyāpāra* has been taken to mean *vṛtti*, which however is fully justified. *Vṛtti* as behaviour involves function as well. It may also be said that since the *vyāpāra* or the function inheres in the words, their functions are designated as *vṛtti*s.

In this context the *tātparya vṛtti* can also be explained, which has been defined by Viśvanātha as:

> तात्पर्याख्यां वृत्तिमाहु: पदार्थान्वयबोधने ।
>
> SāDar II.27ab
>
> In the matter of providing a unified sense of all the words in a sentence the function of *tātparya* is resorted.

On *tātparya vṛtti* the commentary of **Sāhitya-Darpaṇa** further adds:

> अभिधाया एकैकपदार्थबोधनविरमात् वाक्यार्थरूपस्य पदार्थान्वयस्य बोधिका तात्पर्यं नाम वृत्ति: ।
>
> Comm. on SāDar II.27
>
> When the power of denotation ceases, after conveying the meanings of individual words, then arises the function entitled purport, which leads a man to apprehend the comprehensive meaning of a complete sentence. (Tr. P. Ghosal)

Tātparya is a technical term used specifically by the school of Mīmāṃsā known as '*abhihitānvayavāda*'. They hold that meaning of individual words are conveyed by *abhidhā*. But for the correlation of the senses of all independent words in a sentence is provided by a separate function of the word, which is known as *tātparya*. Thus *vṛtti* and *vyāpāra* have become interchangeable.

So far as the function of words is concerned three functions have been accepted by literary critics, especially by the *dhvanivādins*. In their view, *abhidhā* or indicative function of the word is the primary function. When this is obstructed, the secondary function, i.e. implicative power brings about the meaning. *Abhidhā* and *lakṣaṇā* are thus treated as primary (*mukhyā*) and secondary (*gauṇī*) *vṛttis*. Along with these two, *tātparya* or correlative power (the function of providing *anvaya* – correlation) is also accepted for the understanding of the complete sense of a sentence. *Vyañjanā* or the suggestive power is thus the fourth *vṛtti* accepted by he *dhvani-vādins*, who reverentially bows to it saying: '*turyāṃ vṛttimupāsmahe*' – we bow down to the fourth *vṛtti*.

Apart from these four *vṛttis* we come across *vṛtti* in the pre-*dhvani* schools of poetics. They hold that *vṛtti* signifies alliteration, i.e. repetition (*āvṛtti*) of the same types of letters in a poetic composition. *Anuprāsa* thus stands for a *vṛtti* or function aiming at adding peculiar charm to the poetic composition. Such *vṛttis* are counted mainly as three *upanāgarikā, paruṣā* and *komalā*. All these are treated as *vṛttis*, because they exist in the different enumerated modes of expression. This idea of *vṛtti* as forms of alliteration are relegated to the background by the *dhvanivādins*. According to them these *vṛttis* actually signify the different styles of composition (*rīti*) known as *vaidarbhī, gauḍī, pāñcālī*, etc. The observation of Acharya Mammaṭa on this point may be quoted: (i) *mādhuryavyañjakairvarṇairupanāgarikocyate;* (ii) *ojaḥprakāśakaistaistu paruṣā*; (iii) *komalā paraiḥ* (KāPrak IX.80). *Upanāgarikā vṛtti* is constituted by the letters suggestive of *mādhurya*, while *paruṣā* is constituted by letters suggestive of *ojas* and *komalā* is constituted by other letters (suggestive of *prasāda*). This being the view of the *dhvanivādins, vṛttis* have been incorporated in the so-called *rītis* or styles of composition, viz. *vaidarbhī* etc. The styles of composition or *rītis* were originally conceived as *rīti* or *mārga*. But later on according to *dhvani* theorists these were classified as the *vaidarbhī, gauḍī* and *pāñcālī* styles. Modes of composition being the basic sense, *rīti* is here related to *vṛtti* as well.

In all sorts of literary compositions dramatic or narrative, *rasa*, more exactly the suggestion of the sentiments is the ultimate according to *dhvanivādins*. Ānandavardhana (DhvĀl III.33), Abhinavagupta and following them Mammaṭa and Viśvanātha (*rasaviṣayavyāpāravatī varṇaracanā vṛtti* – comm. on SāDar X.5), all have pointed out in their respective treatises the supreme position of *rasa*. The fourfold dramatic modes of representation, viz. *kaiśikī* etc. as well as styles of composition in the narrative literature known as *vaidarbhī, gauḍī*, etc. are all *vṛttis* as these inhere in the composition of the poets. *Vṛtti* as behaviour involves mode of procedure as well. One who behaves in a particular manner definitely follows a mode of action, that is why *rīti* and *vṛtti* may be treated as related concepts.

Having surveyed the basic concept of *vṛtti* and its varieties in the context of dramatic and literary treatises it may be pointed out that the following are the senses conveyed by *vṛtti*. In the **Nāṭya-Śāstra** tradition *vṛtti* has been accepted as one of the basic concepts of drama. *Vṛtti* here stands for the histrionic arts (*abhinaya*) which is dependent on patterns of set ways of acting. Thus, *kaiśikī, sāttvatī, ārabhaṭī* and *bhāratī* are *vṛttis* in the sense of modes of temperamental behaviour and dialogue. *Vṛtti* as such is a special feature that distinguishes drama from literature in general. All the *vṛttis* are thus indicative of modes of behaviour.

It may be noted that Dhanañjaya presents his view in a different physiology but all his ideas are basically Bharatan.

Similarly, the **Nāṭakalakṣaṇaratna Kośa** explains the Bharatan term *caturvṛtti* as *bahuvrīhi* compound and holds that all the four *vṛttis* constitute the drama. His justification for calling them *vṛttis* may be quoted as:

> नेपथ्यगीतवादित्ररसभावाभिनयनृत्यजातीनां क्वापि विशेषे वर्तनमिति वृत्तिःकथिता ।
>
> NLRKo under 109
>
> *Vṛtti* is so called because it inheres any of those make-up, song, orchestra (musical instruments), sentiments, emotion, acting and different types of dances in a special manner.

In other words *vṛtti* is the manner of presenting grandeur (of the theme) (cf. *vilāsa vinyāsakramo vṛtti* – NLRKo under 109).

In the context of Alaṅkāra literature *vṛtti* has been used mainly in three senses, viz. (1) *abhidhā* etc., which are function of the words; (2) *upanāgarikā* etc., which are the use of specific letters and words in literary compositions; (3) *vaidarbhī* etc., which though are called *rītis*, but actually are the styles or modes of composition. All these three varieties of *vṛttis* are linked with the basic sense of mode of behaviour or rules of behaviour. *Vṛtti* also has been defined as *vyāpārātmikā*, i.e. *vṛtti* involves certain functions. All these aforementioned *vṛttis* are indicative of certain functions. *Abhidhā* etc. are the *vṛttis* because they are conceived as the function of the word in conveying a particular sense.

The Alaṅkāra schools, prior to Ānandavardhana conceived of these *vṛttis* as varieties of usages of letters and words which are capable of effecting a peculiar charm to the poetic diction. Taking the clue from the *guṇa-rīti vādins,* viz. Daṇḍin and Vāmana, who hold *mārga* or way or style and special construction of words (*viśiṣṭā padaracanā rīti* – KāvyālSū II.7) respectively, the later *dhvanivādins* concluded that these three *vṛtti*s should be treated as three styles of compositions based on the three *guṇa*s. Mammaṭa says, and is echoed by Viśvanātha that *upanāgarikā* is based on letters suggestive of the quality of sweetness (*mādhurya*) and *paruṣā* is based on those which are suggestive of the quality of harshness (*ojaḥ*) and *komalā* is constituted by the remaining letters suggestive of the quality of simplicity (*prasāda*). They have enumerated these letters in their respective treatises.

माधुर्यव्यञ्जकैर्वर्णैरुपनागरिकोच्यते ।
ओजःप्रकाशकैस्तैस्तु परुषा कोमला परैः ॥
केषाञ्चिदेता वैदर्भी प्रमुखा रीतयो मताः ।

KāPrak IX.80–81ab

That (diction) which is characterised by consonants suggestive of sweetness is called '*upanāgarikā*'– 'polished' and that which is characterised by consonants suggestive of floridity is called '*paruṣā*' – harsh. That characterised by others is called '*komalā*' – 'soft'. By some people these styles of diction have been called the *vaidarbhī* and the rest. (Tr. G.N. Jha)

According to others, i.e. Vāmana and his followers, the three styles of diction just described have been called respectively, *vaidarbhī, gauḍī* and *pāñcālī*. *Mārga* and *rīti* both mean a mode of poetic diction and so *rīti* is as mode or style of composition may also be treated as *vṛtti*s.

Style of composition has also been defined by Rājaśekhara and others as *vacanavinyāsakrama*, i.e. arrangement of poetic diction or style, which fits in with the general conception of the mode or style.

In other treatises on Alaṅkāra references to *vṛtti* and *rīti* are found separately. It may be noted that *rīti* has been defined by Vāmana as: '*viśiṣṭā pada racanā*', which stands for mode of poetic style. In this sense it has been equated with *vṛtti* in later literature. The number of *rīti*s has been elaborately pointed out with proper illustrations. But everywhere (it) being indicative of mode or style, *rīti* may be treated as *vṛtti*.

Daṇḍin in his **Kāvyādarśa** uses this word to define the figure of speech known as *utprekṣā*. He states:

अन्यथैव स्थिता वृत्तिश्चेतनस्येतरस्य वा ।
अन्यथोत्प्रेक्ष्यते यत्र तामुत्प्रेक्षां विदुर्यथा ॥

Kāvyād II.221

When the condition or action of an animate or inanimate object is in a particular manner and it is fancied (by the poet) in a different manner, they call that (figure of speech) *utprekṣā* (or conceit). (Tr. V. Narayana & J.V. Bhattacharya)

In the above verse *vṛtti* means the mode of quality and action. So when the different modes of quality and action pertaining to the animate or inanimate objects are imagined differently, that is known as *utprekṣā*. So here *vṛtti* stands for simply as mode.

Rājaśekhara in his **Kāvya-Mīmāṃsā** (III, p. 22) refers to *vṛtti* as: '*vilāsavinyāsakrama*', *rīti* as: '*vacanavinyāsakrama*' and *pravṛtti* as: *veśavinyāsakrama*. This expression '*veśavīnyāsakrama pravṛtti*' clearly indicates that *pravṛtti* is the prevalent mode or fashion of dressing, found in different regions. The **Viṣṇudharmottara Purāṇa** states:

वेशभाषानुकरणं तथाचारप्रवर्तनम् ॥
प्रवृत्तिरिति विख्याता वृत्तीनामाश्रयास्तु ताः ।

VDhPur III.20.59cd–60ab

Pravṛtti is imitating the dress, language and culture [of a particular region] and depends on *vṛtti*. (Tr. M. Bose)

Here also *vṛtti* is indicative of a mode of procedure either of specific behaviour or specific style of expression. In another context Rājaśekhara gives a definition of the works known as *vṛtti*: *sūtrāṇām sakalasāravivaraṇam vṛttiḥ* (KāMīm II, p.12). *Vṛtti* as *vivaraṇa* or elucidation is well known. In the lexicons also this sense has been enumerated. Since such *vṛtti*s follow a particular *sūtra* it can be thought of as *anuvṛtti* or exposition in continuity.

Kuntaka who is also the initiator of the theory of 'artistic turn of speech' (*vakrokti*) as opposed to 'plain narration' as the essential feature of poetry. He has enumerated mainly six varieties of such artistic 'turns of speech', which are further sub-divided in many other varieties. *Vṛtti vaicitrya vakratā* or artistic turn of speech based on the use of compound as one of these sub-varieties. He uses *vṛtti* in the technical grammatical sense. *Vṛtti* according to grammar stands for '*parārthābhidhāna*' and they speak of five such *vṛtti*s, which are: *kṛt, taddhita, samāsa, sanādyanta-dhātu* and *ekaśeṣa*. In this regard Kuntaka observes:

अव्ययीभावमुख्यानां वृत्तीनां रमणीयता ।
यत्रोल्लसति सा ज्ञेया वृत्तिवैचित्र्यवक्रता ॥

VaJī II.19

A usage where beauty of word – forms such as adverbial compounds shines forth may be deemed as an instance of beauty of '*vṛtti*'. (Tr. K. Krishnamoorthy)

Bhoja in his **Śṛṅgāra Prakāśa** uses *vṛtti* in the several sense as mode of behaviour (cf. *ceṣṭā-viśeṣa-vinyāsakramaḥ vṛtti* – ŚṛPrak XII, p. 486). He observes that the mind (*citta*) undergoes four dispositions under the impact of overpowering emotions. These four are: upliftment (*vikāsa*), perturbance (*vikṣepa*), expansion (*vistāra*) and contraction (*saṅkoca*). With regards to the *vṛttis* Bhoja gives two numbers. The emotional *vṛttis* are six and the temperamental *vṛttis* are five. The emotional *vṛttis* are: *kaiśikī, ārabhaṭī, bhāratī, sāttvatī, madhyamārabhaṭī* and *madhyamakaiśikī* (*vṛttiḥ sā ṣoḍhā*) – ŚṛPrak X, p. 373). Bhoja here adds two additional *vṛttis*, viz. *madhyamārabhaṭī* and *madhyamakaiśikī*, to the list of four *vṛttis* accepted by Bharata in his **Nāṭya-Śāstra**. Similarly, in another place Bhoja regards the *vṛttis* as the modes of action of the dramatic characters. In the list of temperamental *vṛttis* Bhoja adds *vimiśrā* as an additional *vṛtti* along with the four Bharatan *vṛttis* (*mukhādisandhiṣu ca vyāpriyamāṇā nāyakopanāyakādīnāṃ manovāk-kāyakarmanibandhanāḥ pañcavṛttayo bhavanti, bhāratī, ārabhaṭī, sāttvatī, kaiśikī, vimiśrā ceti* – ŚṛPrak XII, p. 485). In both these cases the concept of *vṛtti* is based on mode of behaviour physical or mental and as such no new notion plays any role here, only the number varies.

In the texts on music, the **Saṅgīta Dāmodara**, the **Saṅgītopaniṣad Sāroddhāra** and the other texts as well *vṛtti* has been refered to in different contexts. The **Saṅgīta Dāmodara** speaks of four modes of temperamental representation, known as *kaiśikī, ārabhaṭī, sāttvattī* and *bhāratī*, as four *vṛttis*, which are the basis of drama.

कैशिक्यारभटी चैव सात्त्वती भारती तथा ।
चतस्रो वृत्तयः प्रोक्ता नाट्यसम्भवकारिकाः ॥

SDām p. 73

Kaiśikī, ārabhaṭī, sāttvatī and *bhāratī* – these are the four *vṛttis*, which make the dramas possible.

The **Saṅgītopaniṣad Sāroddhāra** (V.58cd–60) however, describes twenty movements of the hand apparently meant for a dancer or an actor. These twenty include in them *vṛtti, pravṛtti* and *udvṛtti. Vṛtti* here appears to mean the basic condition or status (*vartanam*) and *pravṛtti* means the movement indicating beginning of an action, whereas *udvṛtti* indicates an upward movement.

In the domain of Art and Architecture (Vāstu) the use of *vṛtti* figures in many places. The **Vāstusūtra Upaniṣad**, though a late work, deals with *vṛtti* in the context of conception of forms (*rūpabhāvanā*) and with reference to image-making, i.e. sculpture. In the *sūtra* (V.3) the idea is: *vṛttis* or fluctuations are a matter of the mind and are many. For example: by looking at a woman the mind develops the disposition of sexual enjoyments as well as such other dispositions. This is the general way of development of mental fluctuations in all human beings. The reference to *vṛtti* here is associated with the function of mind. The text and its *vṛtti* make this point more clear.

> मनसि वृत्तिर्बहुधा प्रजायते । तदा भिन्नभिन्नरसाद्रूपं नैकं भवति ॥
>
> VSUp V.3
>
> Many fluctuations arise in the mind, by their different *rasas* forms assume many types. (Tr. A. Boner)

Under different situation the human mind undergoes various modifications. The commentary on the *sūtra* may be quoted thus:

> यथा मोहान्नारीं प्रति मैथुनेच्छा प्रभवति तद् जीवमात्रस्य सत्यम् ।
>
> Comm. on VSUp V.3
>
> Just as (on seeing a woman) due to infatuation there arises a desire to unite with her. This is the common truth of all living beings. (Tr. A. Boner)

This view has been corroborated by another statement: *sarvasya vṛttirasti* – all have their different attitude (tr. A. Boner, VSUp V.17). Here, in this context *vṛtti* has a double meaning: it is at the same time the mental modification or state of mind which gives rise to the conception of these beings, and their attitude or mode of activity.

In another *sūtra* the importance of *vṛtti* has been underlined by saying :

> मनुष्याणां वृत्तिर्मुख्येति ॥
>
> VSUp V.18
>
> Of humans it is the mental modification (*vṛtti*) which is important. (Tr. A. Boner)

The purport of this statement may be said to point the fact that sentiments are related to human mental dispositions, which lead to respective actions.

> वृत्तेर्निष्कल-सकल-भावा उपजायन्त इति मार्गः क्रियायाः परिणाम इति ।
>
> Comm. on VSUp V.18
>
> From the mental modification arise inactive and active sentiments, this is the way resulting an action. (Tr. A. Boner)

It is said that the conception of god-head is also dependent on the specific mental dispositions.

The idea or the conception of a Divine Being is that which causes change in the representation of that Being.

वृत्त्या दैवचिन्तने भेदः सञ्जायते ॥

VSUp VI.2

According to the (differences of) mental modification (*vṛtti*) a difference arises in the conception of divinities. (Tr. A. Boner)

That the *rūpa* or form also gives rise to a specific *vṛtti* is also noted. While considering the image making constant contemplation of a form (*rūpadhārā*) gives rise to the proper attitude of the artists. For a sculptor, the contemplation of form is essential in making an image. Image is a reproduction of the mental attitude.

रूपधाराया वृत्तिरिति श्रेष्ठा ॥

अथ रूपधारायाः शृणु वृत्तिभेदान् । यथा वृत्त्याः परिणामः ।
प्राजापत्यप्रथमवृत्तिर्मनः । मनसो वृत्तिः प्राणः । प्राणस्य वृत्तिः क्रिया ।

VSUp VI.24

From the sequence of forms comes the condition (of the mind) this procedure) is the best.

Now hear about the different attitudes derived from the flow of the form, how the transformation of the attitudes takes place. Prajāpati's first state of creation was mind ('Prajāpati verily is like mind', as said in the Taittirīya Brāhmaṇa II.2.1,2). From the mind developed life-breath, the evolution of life-breath is action. (Tr. A. Boner)

So *vṛtti* is here known as condition of the mind.

While the **Vāstusūtra Upaniṣad** discusses the position of *vṛtti* or mental disposition in relation to representation of forms the **Śilpa Prakāśa** discusses the methodology of specific architectural designs. The purpose being different and more practical, i.e. related to the actual practice of the artists, the text does not deal with *vṛtti* but speaks of *rīti*, i.e. the style or method of procedure for the artist (*śilpin*). *Rīti* as style or mode of expression is well known in the context of literature, whereas *vaidarbhī, gauḍī*, etc. are accepted as different styles of literary composition. In architecture *rīti* stands for the same style or methodology.

In the context of temple architecture the **Śilpa Prakāśa** mentions the following methods (*rīti*) and designs. It appears that relating to the top of a temple or pillar represented by a *kumbha* and the base of the same (*khura* or *nimnabhāga*), the style of construction differs. The same difference of style is also prescribed for designing the *vajramastaka,* i.e. prominent ornament on the *khura* (base) and other parts.

कुंभे खुरे निम्नभागे पृथग् रीतिस्तु जायते ।
शृणु भेदान् तथा वज्रमस्तके रेखानिश्चयम् ॥

ŚiPrak I.130

On the *kumbha* (*khura*) and on the lower portions it is done in a different way. Hear about the various designs of *vajramastakas*. (Tr. A. Boner)

RĪTI

In the context of *vṛtti* a survey of *rīti* is also called for. *Rīti* also may be synonymous with *vṛtti* in the sense of natural property, *svabhāva* and *prakṛti* (*svabhāvaḥ prakṛtī rītiḥ* – VaiKo V.22). So natural property, characteristic feature or the original form of a thing or person is clearly covered by *vṛtti*, meaning existence or mode of existence. *Rīti*, however, has a different sense in the context of metallurgy. The **Vaijayantī Kośa** (VI.2.30cd) gives three senses: (1) *dagdha suvarṇādimala*, (2) *sthiti*, and (3) *ārakūṭa* (scoria/oxide formed on metals like gold etc. due to exposure to heat, original condition (of the metal and pale-brass). The same view is corroborated in the **Nānārtha Mañjarī** as:

रीतिः प्रचारे स्यन्दे च प्रकारे लोहकीटके । आरकूटे ... । रीतिः स्वभावे स्रवणे ... ।

Nāma 629–30, 637

The term *rīti* (f.) is used to denote going fourth, flowing (stream), method, rust of iron, a kind of brass, etc. The term in feminine gender also means nature and stream. (Tr. S. Chattopadhyay)

In the context of *rīti*, the **Medinī Kośa** notes it as a feminine word (*rītiḥ striyāṃ syandapracārayoḥ, pittale lohakiṭṭe ca* – MedKo XVI.51) meaning a stream, usage or practice, brass (*pittala*) and rust of iron. Here also the overlapping of senses may be noted in the first two senses of *rīti* – *syanda* = unhindered flow and *pracāra* = the mode of movement, can very easily be conveyed by *vṛtti*. Brass and rust of iron are typical to *rīti* in the context of metallurgy.

There is a subtle relationship between the concepts of *vṛtti* and *rīti*. *Vṛtti* as has already been noted etymologically is derived from *vṛt-* 'to exist', whereas *rīti* is derived from the root *ṛ-* or *rī-* 'to go' or 'to flow'. Related with the basic sense of existence *vṛtti* stands for various senses, viz. means of existence, modification or attitude of the mind, function, modes of emotional representation and such others. All these cognate senses are related basically with the sense of being or existence. The differences in the sense are due to mode or means or status as such. Thus, we have words like *jīvikā* (means of livelihood), *cittavṛtti* and mere existence. If *vṛtti* is basically the mode of various existence, *rīti* comes to denote the pattern or manner of that existence. *Cittavṛtti* for example provides the idea of a particular mode of the mind, whereas *rīti* denotes the manner or the pattern of functioning of that *vṛtti*. Thus, *vṛtti* is the mode of function, whereas *rīti* stands for the manner or procedure of the same. It may be said that a particular *cittavṛtti* has a certain pattern which is indicated by *rīti*. The formula of *rīti* thus is related with the *vṛtti*s. *Vṛtti* is static, whereas *rīti* is the moving principle – that brings out the specific nature of different *vṛtti*s. *Rīti* is the manner or method of outer expression of *vṛtti*, which basically is an inner state of the human beings.

The etymological primary sense of *rīti* is '*gati*' or flow. This primary sense of gait connotes not mere gait, but special or characteristic gait, i.e. manner, norm or style of the basic movements. *Rīti* thus provides all these senses along with the sense of flow or *pravāha*. In addition, *rīti* is also used in a purely technical sense in the context of metallurgy as brass (cf. MedKo XVI.51).

In the available literature the **Rāmāyaṇa** uses *rīti* in the sense of 'mere flow' or 'stream'.

पीड्यमानस्तु बलिना महेन्द्रस्तेन पर्वतः ।
रीतोर्निर्वर्तयामास काञ्चनाञ्जनराजतीः ॥

Rām V.1.15

Being praised by that mighty one Hanumat, the mount Mahendra let loose the streams of having the hues of gold, antimony and silver.

In the literary context the relation between *vṛtti* and *rīti* has already been hinted at. The verbal style of presenting the internal feelings has been accepted as *rīti* or style of composition. Following Rājaśekhara we come across the definitions of *vṛtti*, *rīti* and *pravṛtti* in the **Agni Purāṇa** and **Bhāva Prakāśana**. The manner or style of expression to indicate the internal feeling has universally been accepted as *rīti*. When Vāmana says: '*rītirātmā kāvyasya*' and '*viśiṣṭā padaracanā rītiḥ*'. He is pointing out the fact that specific styles of composition constitute different *rīti*s and style is the soul of poetry. The poeticians have spoken of four to six different styles to be followed by the poets, viz. *vaidarbhī*, *pāñcālī*, *gauḍī*, *lāṭī*, *saurāṣṭrī* and *drāviḍī*. The same sense of *rīti* as: '*vacana vinyāsa krama*' is used in the different texts. In the **Śṛṅgāra Prakāśa** Bhoja defines *rīti* as:

विदर्भादीनां वाक्यरचनावर्त्म रीतिः । सा षोढा, वैदर्भी, पांचाली, गौडीया, आवन्तिका, लाटीया, मागधी च ।

ŚṛPrak X, p. 373

Rīti is the manner (*vartma*), i.e. way of expression followed by the people reacting in places like Vidarbha etc. These are six distinct styles of literary expressions, viz. *vaidarbhī, pāñcālī, gauḍīyā, āvantikā, lāṭīyā* and *māgadhī.*

The **Bhāva Prakāśana** speaks of *rīti* as: '*buddhyārambhānubhāveṣu rītiḥ prathamamucyate*' (BhPrak I.84). *Rīti* or the style of expression is the first of all the intellectual resultants following a *vibhāva* (determinant). The idea is that of all the *anubhāvas*, the mode of expression is of utmost important. Under the impact of a particular feeling the verbal reaction of a person is technically known as *rīti*. Actually it is the verbal expression that reflects the basic mental feeling. As the text accepts the basic sense of literary style as: '*vacana-vinyāsakrama*' (I.84b), i.e. the manner or style of specific order of verbal expression typical to different regions.

The **Bhāva Prakāśana** however, speaks of four primary *rītis*, viz. *vaidarbhī, pāñcālī, lāṭī* and *gauḍī*. Two more *rītis* have been added to the list, i.e. *saurāṣṭrī* and *drāviḍī* (*tatra vaidarbhapāñcālalāṭagauḍavibhāgataḥ, saurāṣṭrī drāviḍī ceti rītidvayamudāhṛtam* – BhPrak I.84cd).

The **Agni Purāṇa** further adds:

बोधाय एष व्यापारः सुबुद्ध्यारम्भ इष्यते ।
तस्य भेदास्त्रयस्ते च रीतिवृत्तिप्रवृत्तयः ॥

AgPur CCCXXXIX.54

The function (of *vāc, manas* and *śarīra*) in accordance with the advice of intelligence is called *buddhyārambha* (one of the aspects of *anubhāva*). It has three varieties, viz. *rīti* (connected with *vāc*), *vṛtti* (connected with *manas*) and *pravṛtti* (connected with *śarīra*).

In the **Caraka Saṃhitā** and **Bṛhat Saṃhitā** the metallurgical sense of *rīti* as brass or rust of iron has been used. Caraka prescribes the metals to be used for the preparation of tongue-scrapers.

सुवर्णरूप्यताम्राणि त्रपुरीतिमयानि च ॥
जिह्वानिर्लेखनानि स्युरतीक्ष्णान्यनृजूनि च ।

CarSamSūSthā V.74cd–75ab

Tongue-scrapers should be made of gold, silver, copper, tin and brass and should be non-sharp and curved. (Tr. P.V. Sharma)

The **Bṛhat Saṃhitā** prescribes a compound of metals known as *vajra-saṅghāta* and mentioned the use of lead, bell-metal and brass or rust of iron in different proportions for the same.

अष्टौ सीसकभागाः कांसस्य द्वौ तु रीतिकाभागः ।

मयकथितो योगोऽयं विज्ञेयो वज्रसंघातः ॥

BṛSam LVII.8

A compound of eight parts of lead, two of bell-metal, and one of iron rust, has been mentioned by Maya and is to be known as *vajra-saṅghāta* (adamantine compound). (Tr. M.R. Bhat)

A text on *nṛtyābhinaya* known as **Śrīhasta Muktāvalī** points out the manner of movements of hand by a danseuse as opposed to male dancers. Though the context is different, *rīti* means manner or method of movement of hands.

दक्षिणेनैव हस्तेन पुंसामभिनयो मतः ।
वामेन प्रायशः स्त्रीणामिति रीतिः पुरातनी ॥

ŚHMu 10

Men are to be indicated with the right hand and women mostly by the left. This is an old custom. (Tr. M. Neog)

So, *rīti* has also a wider meaning and use in different texts of Indian culture.

PRAVṚTTI

Pravṛtti commonly means a tendency or a beginning, whereas *nivṛtti* stands for withdrawal or cessation. Moral Philosophy, especially the Upaniṣads, Vedānta, the Epic literature as well as **Bhagavad-Gītā** have pointed out that the whole of human life is directed by two basic urges; one of which is designated as *pravṛtti* and the other as *nivṛtti.* Acceptance of worldly life leading to happiness in this world as well as felicity in the other are the goal of *pravṛtti. Bhoga* and *svarga* can be had by following the path of worldly life which is known as *pravṛtti mārga.* As opposed to this, there is the other viewpoint especially of the Upaniṣads that the *summum bonum* of human life is to attain the ultimate Reality by negating everything mundane. This path of renunciation or negation has been eulogised as *nivṛtti-mārga* or the process of negating everything other than the Brahman (*neti neti,* cf. BṛUp II.3.6). This idea is exemplified by the statement of Maitreyī when She rejects everything worldly and opts for the Ultimate (cf. *yenāhaṃ nāmṛtā syāṃ kimahaṃ tena kuryām* — BṛUp IV.5.4). This Upaniṣadic view peculiarly finds a reflection in the Buddhist thought of Nirvāṇa. It should however be noted that *pravṛtti-mārga* does not stand for a licentious way of life, although it advocates following of the *varṇāśrama* pattern of human life to achieve *dharma, artha, kāma* and *mokṣa* – the four *puruṣārthas.* The house holders and the *sannyāsins* represent the two paths, known as *pravṛtti-mārga* and *nivṛtti-mārga.*

The nature of *pravṛtti* and *nivṛtti* has been well defined in the following verse of the **Kūrma Purāṇa**.

तस्माज्ज्ञानेन सहितं कर्मयोगं समाश्रयेत् ।
प्रवृत्तञ्च निवृत्तञ्च द्विविधं कर्म वैदिकम् ॥
ज्ञानपूर्वं निवृत्तं स्यात्प्रवृत्तं यदतोऽन्यथा ।
निवृत्तं सेवमानस्तु याति तत्परमं पदम् ॥
तस्मान्निवृत्तं संसेव्यमन्यथा संसरेत्पुनः ।

KūrPur I.2.63–65ab

Hence, one should resort to *karmayoga* (the path of disinterested action) accompanied by *jñāna* (spiritual knowledge). The Vedic *karma* is of two types, viz. the *pravṛtta* (*karma* that causes continuation in *saṃsāra*) and the *nivṛtta* (*karma* causing cessation of mundane existence).

The act which is based on spiritual knowledge is the *nivṛtta karma* and that which is other than this, is called *pravṛtta karma.* He who resorts to the *nivṛtta* type of *karma* attains to the highest region, viz. *mokṣa.* Hence one should follow the *nivṛtta* type of *karma*, otherwise one shall have to undergo the sufferings of worldly existences again and again. (Tr. G.V. Tagare)

The **Bhagavad Gītā**, while discussing the basic difference between the divine and the demoniac wealth, observes:

प्रवृत्तिं च निवृत्तिं च जना न विदुरासुराः ।
न शौचं नापि चाचारो न सत्यं तेषु विद्यते ॥

BhG XVI.7

Of creative action and its return to rest the devilish folk know nothing; in them there is no purity, no morality, no truth. (Tr. R.C. Zaehner)

People of demoniac character are not capable of comprehending what should be done (*pravṛtti*) and what should not be done (*nivṛtti*). They don't have any sense of purity, nor of morality and there is no appreciation of truth in them.

Here *pravṛtti* stands for the right attitude to life, i.e. ideal standard of moral behaviour.

Manu considers *pravṛtti* to be the general principle guiding human life, whereas *nivṛtti* grants greater merit to all human activity (cf. *pravṛttireṣā bhūtānāṃ nivṛttistu mahāphalā* – Manu V.56cd).

Conclusion

To conclude it may be said that *vṛtti* stands for a state of mind or a physical state. It may be noted that *vṛtti*, derived from the root *vṛt-*, actually conveys the sense of the root *sthā-* as well. This state can be of various types, sometimes mental, sometimes physical. This *vṛtti* or *sthiti* however, follows different manner or pattern, which is pointed out by *rīti*. That is why, the statement: *vilāsavinyāsa-krama* is very appropriate for understanding *vṛtti*, whereas *vacanavinyāsa-krama*, in wider sense is true so far as *rīti* is concerned.

The other senses of *vṛtti* as *parārthāvidhāna* (in Vyākaraṇa), explanation or exposition, etc., are also extended sense of *vṛtti*. The metallurgical sense of *rīti* is also to be explained as a technical variation of *rīti*. Thus, *vṛtti* and *rīti* are subtly related as per the context. By the way of pointing out the close relationship as well as the difference between *vṛtti* and *rīti*, it can be said that *vṛtti* represents a mental state, whereas the *rīti* or style relates to the specific expression of that feeling either by words or action. Thus, temperamental mode is the *vṛtti*, whereas specific verbal expression of that mode is called *rīti*.

Biswanath Bhattacharya
Narasingha Charan Panda

Select Bibliography

Bhattacharya, Biswanath: Sanskrit Drama and Dramaturgy. Delhi: Sarada Publishing House, 2nd edition, 1994.

Vidyabhusana, M.M. Satisa Chandra: The Nyāya Sūtras of Gotama, Allahabad: The Panini office, Bhuvaneswari Ashrama, Bahadurganj, 1913.

BIBLIOGRAPHY

A

Abhidhānacintāmaṇi Kośa of Hemacandra: ed. by H.K. Javeri, M.M. Chokasi. Surat: Jain Pustakoddhara Samstha, 1946.

Abhidharma Kośa of Vasubandhu: ed. by Swami Dvarikadas Sastri. Varanasi: Bauddha-Bharati, 1987.

— tr. into Eng. by Subhadra Jha. Patna: Kashi Prasad Jayaswal Research Institute, 1983.

Abhidharma Kośa Bhāṣya: by Louis de lavallee Poussin, tr. into Eng. by L.M. Pruden. Berkeley: Asian Humanities Press, 1988, 4 Vols.

Abhidharma Samuccaya: ed. by Prahlada Pradhan. Santiniketan: Visva Bharati, 1950.

— Le Compendium de la Super-Doctrine (Philosophie) (Abhidharmasamuccaya) d'Asaṅga, traduit et annoté par Walpola-Rahula. Paris: Ecole Française D'Extrême Orient, 1971.

Abhijñānaśākuntalam of Kālidāsa: with the Comm. Arthadyotanikā of Rāghava Bhaṭṭa, ed. by N.B. Godbole; Revised by W.L. Shastri Panasikar. Bombay: Tukaram Jawaji, Nirnayasagar Press, 6th edn, 1913.

— ed. and tr. into Eng. by M.R. Kale. Delhi: Motilal Banarsidass, 1987.

Abhilaṣitārthacintāmaṇi of Someśvara Deva: ed. by R. Samasastry. Mysore: University of Mysore, 1926.

Abhinaya Darpaṇa of Nandikeśvara: tr. into Eng. by A.K. Coomaraswamy & G.K. Duggirala. Cambridge: Harvard University press, 1917.

Adhyayanasūtra: ed.by Muni Puṇyavijaya. Jainagama Granthamala-15. Bombay: Sri Mahavir Jain Mahavidyalaya, 1977.

Āgamaprāmāṇya of Yāmunācārya: ed. by R.N. Narasimhacharya. Baroda: Baroda Oriental Institute, 1976.

Aghoraśivācāryapaddhati (Kriyākramadyotikā): with Prabhā Comm. of Nirmalamani, ed. by K. Krishna Sastri and P. Rama Sastri. Tamilnadu, 1927.

Agni Purāṇa: Ananda Ashram Sanskrit Granthavali-41. Poona: Ananda Ashram, 1957.

Āgniveśya Gṛhya Sūtra: ed. by L.A. Ravi Varma. Trivendrum Sanskrit Series-44, Trivendrum, 1940.

Ahirbudhnya Saṃhitā: ed. by M.D. Rāmānujācārya. Madras: Adyar Library, 1966.

Aitareya Āraṇyakam: with the Comm. of Sāyaṇācārya, ed. by Kashinatha Sastri. Ananda Ashram Sanskrit Granthavali-32. Poona: Ananda Ashram, 1979, 2 Vols.

— ed. and tr. into Eng. by A.B. Keith. Oxford: Oxford University, 1909.

Aitareya Brāhmaṇa of the Rigveda: ed. and tr. into Eng. by Martin Haug. London: Trubner and Co., 1863, 2 Vols.

— Rigveda Brāhmaṇa: The Aitareya and Kauṣītaki Brāhmaṇas of the Rigveda: tr. into Eng. by A.B. Keith. Harvard Oriental Series-25. Delhi: Motilal Banarsidass, 1981, Reprint.

Ajitāgama: ed. by N.R. Bhatt. Pondicherry: Institut Français d'Indologie, 1964, 1967, 2 Vols.

Amarakośa of Amarasiṃha: with Comm., of Ācārya Kṛṣṇamitra, ed. by Satyadeva Misra. Patna: Indira Prakashan, 1972.

Amṛtodaya of Gokulanātha: ed. by M.M. Sivadatta. Bombay: Nirnayasagar Press, 1897.

Anekārthasaṃgraha of Hemachandra: ed. by S.P. Jagannath Shastri Hoshing. Varanasi: Chowkhamba Sanskrit Series, 1969.

Aparājitapṛcchā of Bhuvana Deva: ed. by Popatbhai Ambashankar Mankad. Baroda: Baroda Oriental Institute, 1950.

Āpastamba Dharmasūtra: ed. by G. Bühler. Bombay Sanskrit Series-44, 50. Bombay: The Department of Public Construction, 3rd edn, 1932.

Āpastamba Gṛhyasūtra: ed. by A. Chinnaswami Sastri, and U.C. Pandey. Kashi Sanskrit Series-59. Varanasi: Chowkhamba, 1971.

Āpastamba Śrautasūtra: ed. by T.T. Srinivasagopalachary. Oriental Research Institute Publications Sanskrit Series-98. Mysore: University of Mysore, 1953, Vol. II.

— ed. by A. Srinivasaraghavacharya. Oriental Research Institute Publications Sanskrit Series-104. Mysore: University of Mysore, 1960, Vol. III.

Āpastamba Śulbasūtra: ed. by Satya Prakash and R.S. Sharma. Ratna Kumari Pub. Series-5. Delhi: Mahalakshmi Pub. House, 1968.

Arthaśāstra of Kauṭilya: ed. and tr. into Eng. by R.P. Kangle. Delhi: Motilal Banarsidass, 1986, 3 Vols.

Arthaviniścayasūtra: Patna: K.P. Jayaswal Research Institute, 1971.

Āryabhaṭīya of Āryabhaṭṭa: ed. by Kripa Shankar Shukla. New Delhi: The Indian National Science Academy, 1976.

Āryamañjuśrīmūlakalpa: ed. by M.M.T. Ganapati Sastri. Sri Satguru Publications. Delhi: Indian Books Centre, 2nd edn, 1989, 3 Vols.

Āścaryacūḍāmaṇi of Śaktibhadra: with an Introduction by S.Kuppuswami Sastri. Shri Balamanorama Series-9. Madras: Sri Balamanorama Press, 1926.

Aṣṭādhyāyī of Pāṇini: tr. into Eng. by S.M. Katre. Delhi: Motilal Banarsidass, 1987.

— ed. & tr into Eng. by S.C. Basu. Varanasi: Motilal Banarsidass, 1988.

Aṣṭaprakaraṇa: ed. by V.V. Dwivedi. Varanasi: Sampurnananda Sanskrit University, 1988.

Aṣṭasāhasrikā Prajñā Pāramitā: ed. by Rajendralal Mitra. Bibliotheca Indica, A Collection of Oriental Works. Calcutta: The Asiatic Society, 1888.

— tr. by Edward Conze. Bibliotheca Indica, A Collection of Oriental Works No.284. Calcutta: The Asiatic Society, 1970.

— Prajñāpāramitā and Related Systems: ed. by Lewis. Buddhist Studies Series. Lancaster, Berkeley, 1977.

Āśvalāyana Gṛhyasūtra: ed. and tr. into Eng. by N.N. Sharma. Delhi: Eastern Book Linkers, 1976.

Āśvalāyana Śrautasūtra: tr. into Eng. and ed. by H.G. Ranade. Ranade Publication Series-2, 4. Poona, 1981, 1986, 2 Vols.

Atharvaveda Pariśiṣṭa: ed. by J.M. Balling and J.V. Negelein, with Hindi Notes by Ram Kumar Rai. Varanasi: Chaukhamba Orientalia, 1976.

Atharvaveda Saṃhitā: ed. by Sripada Damodar Satvalekar. Paradi: Svadhyaya Mandala, 1985, 4 Vols.

— The Hymns of the Atharvaveda: tr. into Eng. by R.T.H. Griffith. The Chowkhamba Sanskrit Studies-66. Varanasi: Chowkhamba Publication, 1968, 2 Vols.

— Paippalāda Saṃhitā of the Atharvaveda: ed. by Durgamohan Bhattacharya. Calcutta: Sanskrit College, 1970.

Aṭṭhasālinī (on Dhammasaṅgaṇi): ed. by P.V. Bapat and R.D. Vadekar. Poona: Bhandarkar Oriental Research Institute, 1942.

— The Expositor: tr. into Eng. by Pe Maung Tin, ed. by Mrs. R. Davids. London: Luzac and Co. Ltd., 1958.

Aucityavicāracarcā of Kṣemendra: ed. by R.S. Tripathi. Chowkhamba Sanskrit Series. Varanasi, 1982.

Avadāna Śataka: ed. by P.L. Vaidya. Darbhanga: Mithila Institute, 1958.

Āvaśyaka Niryukti: Bhavanagar: Yasovijaya Granthamālā, w.d.

B

Baudhāyana Dharmasūtra: ed. by A. Chinnaswami Shastri. Kashi Sanskrit Series-104. Varanasi: Chowkhamba Sanskrit Sansthan, 1972.

Baudhāyana Gṛhyasūtra: ed. by R. Shamasastry. New Delhi: Meharchand Lachhmandas, 1982.

Baudhāyana Śrautasūtra: ed. by W. Caland. New Delhi: Munshiram Manoharlal, 1982, 3 Vols.

Baudhāyana Śulbasūtra: with Sanskrit Comm. by Dwarka Nath Yajvan, Eng. tr. by G. Thibaut, ed. by Satya Prakash and Ram Swarup Sharma. New Delhi: The Research Institute of Ancient Scientific Studies, 1968.

— Śulba Sūtras of Baudhāyana, Āpastamba, Kātyāyana and Mānava: ed. and tr. by S.N. Sen and A.K. Bag. New Delhi: Indian National Science Academy, 1983.

Bhagavadgītā: with Śāṅkarabhāṣya. Gorakhpur: Gita Press, 1967.

— with Commentaries ed. by W.L.S. Panasikar. Varanasi: Indological Book House, 1984.

— with Sarvatobhadra Comm. of Rājānaka Rāmakaṇṭha. Kashmir Series of Texts and Studies-64. Srinagar: Research Department, Jammu and Kashmir State, 1943.

— tr. into Eng. by R.C. Zaehner. London: Oxford University Press, 1981.

— tr. into Eng. by Swami Gambhirananda. Calcutta: Advaita Ashrama, 2nd edn, 1991.

— tr. into Eng. by A.M. Sastry. Madras: Samata Books, 1995, Reprint.

Bhāgavata-Purāṇa of Kṛṣṇa Dvaipāyana Vyāsa: ed. and tr. by A.C. Bhaktivedanta Swami Prabhupada. Manila: Bhaktivedanta Book Trust, 1982.

Bhaktirasāmṛtasindhu of Rūpagosvāmin: with 'Durgāsaṅgamanī' Comm. of Jīvagosvāmin and "Bhaktisārapradarśinī" Comm. of Visvanatha Chakravarti, ed. by Shyamdas. Vrindavan, 1981.

— tr. into Hindi. P.L. Sharma. Delhi: Indira Gandhi National Centre for the Arts and Motilal Banarsidass, 1998.

Bhaktirasāyana of Madhusūdana Sarasvatī: ed. by Janardana Shastri Pandey. Varanasi, 1976.

Bhāradvāja Gṛhyasūtra: ed. by H.J.W. Salomons. New Delhi: Meharchand Lachhmandas, 1981.

Bharata-Bhāṣya of Nānyadeva: ed. by Chaitanya P. Desai. Khairagarh: Indira Kala Sangita Visvavidyalaya, 1961, 1976, 2 parts.

Bhāsanāṭakacakram: ed. by C.R. Devadhara. Delhi: Motilal Banarsidass, 1987.

Bhāṣāpariccheda: Swami Madhavananda. Calcutta: Advaita Ashrama, 2nd edn, 1954.

Bhāskarīya – Bījagaṇita: with the Comm. Navāṅkurā of Kṛṣṇa Daivajña, ed. by V.G. Apte. Ananda Ashram Sanskrit Series-90. Poona, 1930.

Bhāṭṭacintāmaṇi of Gāgā Bhaṭṭa: Varanasi: Chowkhamba, 1933.

Bhāvanākramaḥ of Acarya Kamalaśīla: ed. by Acarya Gyaltsen Namdol. Sarnath: Central Institute of Higher Tibetan Studies, 1985.

Bhāvaprakāśana of Śāradātanaya: ed. by Yatiraja Swami and K.S. Ramaswami Sastri. Baroda: Baroda Oriental Institute, 1986, Reprint.

Bhoja Prabandha: with the Comm. on Kedarnath Sharma. Varanasi: Chowkhamba Vidyabhawan, 3rd edn, 1970.

Bodhicaryāvatāra of Śāntideva: ed. by P.L. Vaidya. Darbhanga: The Mithila Institute, 1960.

— tr. into Eng. by Paramananda Sharma. New Delhi: Aditya Prakashan, 1990, 2 Vols.

Brahma Mahā Purāṇam: ed. by Pt. Nagasharan Singh. Delhi: Nag Publishers, 1985.

Brāhmasphuṭasiddhānta of Brahmagupta: ed. by Ram Swarup Sharma. New Delhi: The Indian Institute of Astronomical and Sanskrit Research, 1966, 4 Vols.

Brahmasūtra: with Śāṅkarabhāṣya. Bombay: Nirnayasagar Press, 1948.

– with Śāṅkarabhāṣya. Delhi: Motilal Banarsidass, 1985.

– tr. into Eng. by G. Thibaut. Sacred Books of the East Series-34,38. Delhi: Motilal Banarsidass, 1890, 1896, 2 Vols.

– ed. and tr. into Eng. by Swami Gambhirananda. Calcutta: Advaita Ashrama, 1983.

– Brahmasūtra-Śrībhāṣya of Rāmānuja: ed. by Uttamur Vira Raghavacharya. Ubhaya Vedant Granthamala. Madras, 1963.

— Vedāntasūtra of Bādarāyaṇa: with the Comm. of Baladeva, tr. into Eng. by Srisa Chandra Vasu. Delhi: Oriental Books Reprint Corporation, 1979.

— Vedāntasūtra: with the Comm. of Rāmānujācārya, tr. into Eng. by G. Thibaut. Sacred Books of the East Series-48. Delhi: Motilal Banarsidass, 1984.

Bṛhaddeśī of Mataṅga Muni: ed. by K. Sāmbaśiva Śāstrī. Trivandrum Sanskrit Series-94. Trivandrum, 1928.

— ed. and tr. into Eng. by Prem Lata Sharma. Kalāmūlaśāstra. Series – 8 and 10. Delhi: Indira Gandhi National Centre for the Arts and Motilal Banarsidass, 1992–1994, 2 Vols.

Bṛhaddevatā of Śaunaka: A Summary of the details and myths of the Ṛgveda, ed. by A.A. Macdonell. Delhi: Motilal Banarsidass, 1965, 2 Vols.

Bṛhat Jātaka of Varāhamihira: ed. by B.V. Raman and tr. into Eng. by B.S. Rao. Delhi: Motilal Banarsidass Publishers, 1998, Reprint.

Bṛhat Saṃhitā of Varāhamihira: ed. and tr. into Eng. by M. Ramakrishna Bhat. Delhi: Motilal Banarsidass, 1981, 1982, 2 Vols.

Buddhacarita of Aśvaghoṣa: ed. and tr. into Hindi by Suryanarayana Chaudhuri. Bihar: Samskrta Bhavana, 1948.

— tr. into Eng. by E.H. Johnston. Delhi: Motilal Banarsidass, 1992.

Buddha-Pratimā Lakṣaṇa: ed. by Haridas Mitra. Benaras, 1993.

C

Campūbhāratam (Bharatacampū) of Ananta: with the Comm. of Ramachandrabudhendra, ed. by Kashinath Pandurang Parab. Bombay: Nirnayasagar Press, 1930.

Campūrāmāyaṇa (Rāmāyaṇa Campū) of Bhoja: with the Comm. of Rāmacandrabudhendra, ed. by K.P. Parab. Bombay: Nirnayasagar Press, 1898.

Carakasaṃhitā: tr. into Eng. by P.V. Sharma. Varanasi: Chaukhamba Orientalia, 1981, 1983, 1985, 3 Vols.

— with the "Āyurveda Dīpikā" Comm. of Cakrapāṇidatta, ed. by Jadavji Trikamji Acarya. Delhi: Munshiram Manoharlal, 4th edn, 1981.

Chandas Śāstram: Śrī Piṅgalācārya with Comm. Mṛtasañjīvanī, by Śrī Halāyudha Bhaṭṭa: ed. by Pt. Kedaranatha, M.M. Pt. Durgaprasada and Wasudeva Laxmana Shastri Panashikara. Varanasi: Chaukhamba Orientalia, 1986, Reprint.

Chandomañjarī of Gaṅgādāsa: ed. with Sanskrit and Hindi Commentaries by Brahmananda Tripathi. Varanasi: Chaukhamba Surabharati Prakashan, 1997.

Citralakṣaṇa: ed. & tr. into Eng. by Asok K. Bhattacharya. Calcutta: Saraswat Library, 1974.

D

Daśabhūmikasūtra: ed. by P.L. Vaidya: Buddhist Sanskrit Text Series-7. Darbhanga: Mithila Institute of Post-Graduate Studies and Research, 1967.

Daśarūpaka of Dhanañjaya: with Comm. of Dhanika, ed. and tr. into Hindi by Bholasankara Vyasa. Varanasi: Chaukhamba Vidyabhavan, 4th edn, 1973.

Daśavaikālika Sūtra: tr. into Eng. by K.C. Lalwani. Delhi: Motilal Banarsidass, 1973.

Dattilam of Dattila: ed. by Sambasiva Sastri. Trivandrum Sanskrit Series-102. Trivandrum, 1930.

— ed. and tr. into Eng. by Mukund Lath. Delhi: Indira Gandhi National Centre for the Arts and Motilal Banarsidass, 1988.

Devatāmūrtiprakaraṇa of Sūtradhāra Maṇḍana: ed. by U.M. Sankhyatirtha. Calcutta Sanskrit Series – 12. Calcutta, 1936.

Devī Bhāgavatam: ed. by Maunalal Abhimanyu. Varanasi: Sanskrit Pustakalaya, 1955.

— tr. into Eng. Swami Vijnanananda. New Delhi: Munshiram Manoharlal Pvt. Ltd., 1921, 4th edn, 1992.

Dhammapada: Pali text, Eng. tr. and notes, ed. by S. Radhakrishnan. Delhi: Oxford University Press, 1950, 8th edn, 1984.

— tr. into Eng. by C. Kunhan Raja. Adyar: Theosophical Publishing House, 1956.

Dhammasaṅgaṇi: ed. by P.V. Bapat & R.D. Vadekar. Poona: Bhandarkar Oriental Research Institute, 1940.

– tr. into Eng. by C.A.F. Rhys Davids. London: The Pali Text Society, 3rd edn, 1974.

Dhvanyāloka of Ānandavardhana: ed. by Pattabhirama Sastri. Varanasi:

Chaukhamba Sanskrit Series Office, 1940.

— Dhvanyāloka or Theory of Suggestion in Poetry: tr. into Eng. by K. Krishnamoorthy. Poona Oriental Series-92. Poona: Oriental Book Agency, 1955.

Dīgha Nikāya Pāli: ed. & tr. into Hindi by Swami Dwarikadas Shastri. Varanasi: Bauddha Bharati, 1996, 3 Vols.

Dravya Saṃgraha: Nemichandra Siddhanta Chakravartti, ed. by S.C. Ghoshal. Delhi: Motilal Banarsidass, 1989, Reprint.

G

Gāthā Saptaśatī of King Hāla: ed. and tr. into Eng. by Radhagovinda Basak. Calcutta: The Asiatic Society, 1971.

— The Gāhākośa of Hāla (Sātavāhana): Part II, ed. by M.V. Patwardhan. Delhi: Bhogilal Leherchand Institute of Indology, 1988.

Gaṇaratnamahodadhi of Vasubandhu: ed. by J. Eggeling. Delhi: Motilal Banarsidass, 1968, Reprint.

Gobhila Gṛhyasūtra: with Bhaṭṭanārāyaṇa's Comm., ed. by Chintamani Bhattacharya. Delhi: Munshiram Manoharlal, 2nd edn, 1982.

Gommaṭasāra Jīva-Kāṇḍa of Nemichandra Siddhanta Chakravartti: ed. with tr. into Eng. and Comm. by J.L. Jaini. New Delhi: Today and Tomorrow's Printers & Publishers, 1990, Reprint.

Gopatha Brāhmaṇam: ed. by Vijayapala Vidyavaridhi. Calcutta: Savitri Devi Bagadia Trust, 1980.

Gṛhya Sūtras: tr. into Eng. by H. Oldenberg and F. Max Müller. Sacred Books of the East-29–30. Delhi: Motilal Banarsidass, 1981, 1989, 2 Vols, Reprint.

Guhyasamāja Tantra: ed. by B. Bhattacharya. Baroda: Baroda Oriental Institute, 1967, Reprint.

H

Halāyudhakośa: ed. by Jaya Shankar Joshi. Lucknow: Uttar Pradesh Hindi Samsthan, 3rd edn, 1993.

Haṭhayogapradīpikā: with Jyotsnā Comm. of Brahmānanda, ed. and tr. into

Eng. by Srinivasa Iyangar. Madras: Adyar Library, 1975, Reprint.

Hevajra Tantra: A Critical Study, with Yogaratnamālā Comm. of Kanhapada, ed. by D.L. Snellgrove. London: Oxford University Press, 1980, 2 Vols, Reprint.

I

Īśānaśivagurudevapaddhati: ed. by T. Ganapati Sastri. Delhi: Bharatiya Vidya Prakashan, 1988, 4 Vols.

Īśvarapratyabhijñā Kārikā of Utpaladeva: with Vimarśinī by Abhinavagupta, ed. by M.S. Kaul. Kashmir Series of Texts and Studies. Srinagar: Research Department, Jammu and Kashmir State, 1918, 1921, 2 Vols.

Īśvarapratyabhijñāvimarśinī of Abhinavagupta: with the Comm. Bhāskarī, ed. by K.A. Subramaniya Iyer and K.C. Pandey and tr. into Eng. by K.C. Pandey. Delhi: Motilal Banarsidass, 1986, 3 Vols.

J

Jaiminīya Brāhmaṇa: ed. by Raghu Vira and Lokesh Chandra. Delhi: Motilal Banarsidass, 2nd rev. edn, 1986.

Jātaka: ed. by V. Fausboll. Pali Text Society. London: Messrs Luzac & Company Ltd., 1962–1964, 7 Vols, Reprint.

Jātakamālā: ed. & tr. into Hindi by S.N. Chaudhari. Delhi: Motilal Banarsidass, 1991, Reprint.

— tr. into Eng. by J.S. Speyer. Delhi: Motilal Banarsidass, 1971.

Jayākhya Saṃhitā of Pāñcarātra Āgama: ed. by Embar Krishnamacharya. Baroda: Baroda Oriental Institute, 1967.

Jñānārṇava of Śrī Śubhachandāchārya: Published by Śrī Paramaśruta Prabhāvaka Maṇḍala, Śrīmad Rājachandra Āshram, Beriya, Gujarat, 5th edn, 1981.

K

Kalpadrukośa of Keśava: Baroda: Baroda Oriental Institute, 1932.

Kāmakalāvilāsa: with the Comm. of Naṭānandanātha, tr. into Eng. by Arthur Avalon. Madras: Ganesh and Comp. Ltd., 1953.

Kāmasūtra of Vātsyāyana: ed. by Gosvami Damodar Shastri. Banaras: Chowkhamba Sanskrit Series Office, 1929.

Kapiṣṭhala-Kaṭha Saṃhitā: A Text of the Black Yajurveda, ed. by Raghuvira. Delhi: Meharchand Lachhmandas, 1968.

— Kāṭhaka Die Saṃhitā der Kaṭha Śākhā: ed. by Leopold von Schroeder. Wiesbaden: Franz Steiner Verlag, 1970, 2 Vols.

— Yajurvedīya Kāṭhaka Saṃhitā: ed. by Sripada Damodara Satvalekar. Paradi: Svadhyaya Mandala, 1985.

Kātyāyana Śrautasūtra: tr. into Eng. by H.G. Ranade, Ranade Publication Series. Pune: 1978.

— The Śrautasūtra of Kātyāyana: with extracts from the Comm. of Karka and Yājñikadeva, ed. by Albrecht Weber. Chowkhamba Sanskrit Series. Varanasi: 1972.

Kātyāyana Śulbasūtra: ed. and tr. into Eng. by S.D. Khadilakar. Poona: Vaidika Samsodhana Mandala, 1974.

Kauṣītaki Brāhmaṇa: ed. by E.R. Sree Krishna Ṣarma. Wiesbaden: Franz Steiner Verlag, 1968, 3 Vols.

Kāvyādarśa of Daṇḍin: with Comm. of Jīvānanda Vidyāsāgara Bhaṭṭācārya, tr. into Eng. by V. Narayana Iyer. Madras, 1952.

Kāvyālaṅkāra of Bhāmaha: ed. and tr. into Eng. by P.V. Naganatha Sastri. Delhi: Motilal Banarsidass, 1991.

Kāvyālaṅkārasūtra of Vāmana: ed. by Narayana Ram Acharya. Varanasi: Motilal Banarsidass, 1983.

Kāvyamīmāṃsā of Rājaśekhara: ed. by S.D. Dalal and R.A. Sastry. Gaekwad's Oriental Series-1. Baroda: Baroda Oriental Institute, 1934.

— with Comm. "Prakāśa", ed. and tr. into Eng. by Ganga Sagar Roy. Varanasi: Chaukhamba Vidyabhavan, 1964.

Kāvyaprakāśa of Mammaṭa: tr. into Eng. by Ganganatha Jha. Varanasi: Bharatiya Vidya Prakashan, 1967.

— with Comm. of Vaman Jhalakikar. Pune: Bhandarkar Oriental Research Institute, 1921.

— with Comm. "Saṅketa". Pune: Ananda Ashrama, 1921.

Khādiragṛhya Sūtra (or Drāhyāyaṇa Gṛhya Sūtra): ed. with Hindi Comm. by

Thakur U.N. Singh. Delhi: Chaukhamba Sanskrit Pratisthan, 1991, Reprint.

Kiraṇāvalī of Udayanācārya: ed. and tr. into Bengali by Gaurinath Shastri, Vol. 2, Calcutta, 1990.

Kulārṇava Tantra: ed. by Tārānātha Vidyāratna with Introduction of Arthur Avalon and Readings of M.P. Pandit. Delhi: Motilal Banarsidass, 1984, Reprint.

Kumārasambhava of Kālidāsa: with Comm. of Mallinātha on 1-8 Cantos, and Comm. of Sitaram on 8-17 Cantos, ed. by Wasudev Laxman Shastri Panasikar. Bombay: Nirnayasagar Press, 1961.

— ed. by M.R. Kale. Delhi: Motilal Banarsidass, 1986.

L

Laghu Yogavāsiṣṭha of Abhinanda: with "Vasiṣṭha Candrikā" Comm., ed. by Wasudeva Laxman Shastri Panasikar. Delhi: Motilal Banarsidass, 1985, Reprint.

Lakṣmī Tantra: Pāñcarātra Āgama, ed. by V. Krishnamacarya. Adyar Library Series-87. Madras: Adyar Library and Research Centre, 1975, Reprint.

Lakṣmī Tantra: A Pāñcarātra Text, tr. into Eng. with notes by Sanjukta Gupta. Leiden: E.J. Brill, 1972.

Lalitavistara: ed. by P.L. Vaidya. Darbhanga: Mithila Institute, 1985.

Laṅkāvatāra Sūtra: ed. by P.L. Vaidya. Darbhanga: Mithila Institute, w.d.

– Tr. into Eng. by D.T. Suzuki. London: Routledge & Kegan Paul Ltd., 1956, Reprint.

Liṅga Purāṇa: ed. by J.L. Shastri. Delhi: Motilal Banarsidass, 1985, Reprint.

M

Mādhavīyā Dhātuvṛtti: by Sāyaṇācārya; ed. by Swami Dwarikadas Shastri. Varanasi: Tara Book Agency, 1983.

Madhyamaka Śāstra of Nāgārjuna: with the Comm. Prasannapadā by Candrakirti; ed. by P.L. Vaidya. Darbhanga: Mithila Institute, 1960.

Mahābhārata: ed. by V.S. Sukhthankar. Poona: Bhandarkar Oriental Research Institute, 1971, 1974, 19 Vols.

— tr. into Eng. by M.N. Dutt. Delhi: Parimal Publications, 1988, 7 Vols.

— tr. into Eng. and ed. by J.A.B. Van Buitenen. Chicago: The University of Chicago Press, 1980, 1981, 1978, 3 Vols.

— tr. into Bengali and ed. by Haridas Siddhantavagisha with the Comm. of "Bhāratabhāvadīpa" and "Bhārata Kaumudī". Calcutta: Vishvavani Prakashani, 1976–93, 43 Vols.

Mahābhāṣya of Patañjali: ed. by F. Kielhorn, revised by K.U. Abhyankar. Poona: Bhandarkar Oriental Research Institute, 1985, 1965, 1972, 3 Vols.

— Paspaśāhnika: tr. into Eng. by K.C. Chatterji. Calcutta, 1957.

La Mahā Nārāyaṇa Upaniṣad: ed. critique, tr. Française... en annexe La Prāṇāgnihotra Upaniṣad per Jean Varenne. Paris: De Boccard, 2nd edn, 1986.

Mahāpurāṇe Ādipurāṇa of Acharya Jinasena: ed. and tr. into Eng. by Pt. Pannalal Jain. New Delhi: Bharatiya Jnanapith Publication, Part I and II, Part I, 4th edn, 1993 and Part II, 3rd edn, 1988.

Mahāpurāṇe Uttarapurāṇa of Acharya Guṇabhadra: ed. and tr. into Eng. by Pt. Pannalal Jain. New Delhi: Bharatiya Jnanapith Publication, 4th edn, 1993.

Mahārthamañjarī of Maheśvarānanda: with the Comm. Parimala, ed. by V.V. Dvivedi. Varanasi: Varanaseya Sanskrit Visvavidyalaya, 1972.

Mahāsubhāṣita Saṅgraha of Ludwig Sternbach: ed. by S. Bhaskaran Nair. Vishveshvarananda Indological Series-71 (New revised edn, 1986 ff.). Hoshiarpur: V.V.R.I., 1977, 5 Vols.

Mahāvīracarita of Bhavabhūti: with Vīrarāghava Comm., ed. by T.R. Ratnam Iyar, S. Rangachariar and K.P. Parab. Bombay: Nirnayasagar Press, 1901.

Mahāyānasūtrālaṅkāra of Ārya Asaṅga: ed. by Swami Dwarikadas Shastri. Varanasi: Bauddha Bharati, 1985.

Mahāyānaviṃśaka of Nāgārjuna: ed. with tr. into Eng. by Pt. Vidhushekhara Bhattacharya. Vishva Bharati Studies-1. Calcutta: Vishvabharati, 1931.

Maitrāyaṇī Saṃhitā: ed. by Sripada Damodar Satavalekar. Paradi: Svadhyaya Mandala, 1942.

— Die Saṃhitā der Maitrāyaṇīya Śākhā, Herausgegeben von Leopold von Schroeder. Wiesbaden: Franz Steiner Verlag GMBH, 1970, 3 Vols.

Majjhima Nikāya: ed. by Rahula Sankrityayana, Vol. II. Nalanda: Bihar Pali Publication Board, 1958.

– ed. & tr. into Hindi by Swami Dwarika Das Shastri. Varanasi: Bauddha Bharati, 1989–1993, 5 Vols.

Mālatīmādhava of Bhavabhūti: with Comm. of Jagaddhara, ed. and Eng. tr. by M.R. Kale. Delhi: Motilal Banarsidass, 3rd edn, 1967.

Mālavikāgnimitram of Kālidāsa: with Comm. of Kāṭayavema, ed. by K.P. Parab. Bombay: Nirnayasagar Press, 5th edn, 1918.

Mālinīvijayottara Tantra: ed. by Madhusūdana Kaul Shastri. Kashmir Series of Texts and Studies-37. Bombay: Research Department, Jammu and Kashmir State, 1922.

Mānameyodaya of Nārāyaṇa: ed. with tr. into Eng. by C. Kunhan Raja and S.S. Suryanarayana Shastri. Madras: Theosophical Publishing House, Adyar, 1933.

– tr. in Hindi by Swami Yogindrananda. Varanasi: Chaukhamba Vidya Bhawan, 2nd edn, 1996.

Mānasāra: tr. into Eng. by P.K. Acharya. Allahabad: Oxford University Press, 1933.

Mānasollāsa of Someśvara: ed. by G.K. Shirgondekar. Gaekwad's Oriental Series. Baroda: Baroda Oriental Institute, 1967, 1939, 1961, 3 Vols.

Manusmṛti of Manu: ed. by J.L. Shastri. Delhi: Motilal Banarsidass, 1983.

— The Laws of Manu: tr. into Eng.by G. Bühler. Sacred Books of the East Series-25. Delhi: Motilal Banarsidass, 1964, Reprint.

Mataṅga Pārameśvarāgama: with Comm. of Bhaṭṭa Rāmakaṇṭha, ed. by N.R. Bhatt. Pondicherry: Institut Français d'Indologie, 1982.

Matsya Purāṇa of Vyāsa: Bombay: Laksmi Venkatesvara Press, 1980.

— ed. by Nag Sharan Singh. Delhi: Nag Publishers, 1983, 2 Vols.

Mayamata: critically ed. and tr. into French by Bruno Dagens. Pondicherry: Institut Français d'Indologie, 1976.

— tr. into Eng. by B. Dagens. Delhi: Indira Gandhi National Centre for the Arts and Motilal Banarsidass, 1994, 1985, 2 Vols.

Meghadūta of Kālidāsa: with Comm. of Mallinātha, ed. and tr. into Eng.by M.R. Kale. Delhi: Motilal Banarsidass, 1987.

Medinīkośa of Medinikara: ed. by J.S. Hoshing. Varanasi: Chowkhamba Sanskrit Series Office, 1968.

Milindapañha Pāli: ed. and Hindi tr. by Swami Dwarikadas Shastri. Varanasi: Bauddha Bharati, 1990.

Mīmāṃsāsūtra of Jaimini: with Śābara Bhāṣya, ed. by Ratna Gopal Bhatta. Varanasi: Chaukhamba Publications, 1910.

— ed. by Ganesh Shastri Joshi. Poona: Ananda Ashram Sanskrit Granthavali – 97. Ananda Ashram, 1981, 6 Vols.

Mṛcchakaṭika of Śūdraka: with the Comm. of Pṛthvīdhara, ed. and tr. into Eng. by M.R. Kale. Bombay: Booksellers Publishing Co., 1962.

Mṛgendrāgama (Kriyāpāda and Caryāpāda): with the Comm. by Bhaṭṭa Nārāyaṇa Kaṇṭha, ed. by N.R. Bhatt. Pondicherry: Institut Français d'Indologie, 1962.

— (Vidyāpāda and Yogapāda): ed. by Madhusudan Kaul Sastri. Kashmir Series of Texts and Studies-50. Srinagar: Research Department, Jammu and Kashmir State, 1930.

Mudrārākṣasa of Viśākhadatta: critically ed. and Eng. tr. by K.H. Dhruva. Poona: Oriental Book Agency, 2nd edn, 1923.

Mūlācāra of Ācārya Vaṭṭakera: with Ācārā Vṛtti – Sanskrit Comm. of Vasunandi Siddhanta Chakravarty, ed. by Pt. Kailashchandra Sastri, Pt. Jaganmohanlal Sastri and Pt. (Dr.) Pannalal Jain., Part - I, 1st edn, 1984, Part - II, 2nd edn, New Delhi: Bharatiya Jnanapitha Publication, 1992.

N

Nāgānanda of Harṣa: ed. by J.M. Ashar. Bhavanagar: Students Publishing Co., w.d.

— tr. into Eng. by Bak Kun Bae. Delhi: Motilal Banarsidass, 1st Indian edn, 1992.

Ṇāṇasāra of Śrī Padmasingh Munirāj: ed. by Pt. T. Jain. Surat: Mulchand Kisandas Kapadiya, Digambara Jaina Pustakalaya, Vira Samvat 2470.

Nārada Bhaktisūtra: ed. and tr. into Eng. by Swami Chinmayananda. Bombay: Chinmaya Mission Trust, 1982.

Nāradīya Śikṣā: with the Comm. of Bhaṭṭa Śobhākar, ed. and tr. into Eng. by Usha R. Bhise. Poona: Bhandarkar Oriental Research Institute, 1986.

Nartananirṇaya of Paṇḍarīka Viṭṭhala: ed. and tr. into Eng. by R. Sathyanarayana. Kalāmūlaśāstra Series-17. Delhi: Indira Gandhi National Centre for the Arts and Motilal Banarsidass, 1994–1998, 3 Vols.

Nāṭyaśāstra of Bharata: with Abhinava Bhāratī Comm., ed. by M. Ramakrishna Kavi and J.S. Pade. Gaekwad's Oriental Series-36, 68, 104-105. Baroda:

Baroda Oriental Institute, 4 Vols (Vol. I-Chapts 1-7, 1956; II-Chapts 8-18, 1934; III-Chapts 19-27, 1954; IV-Chapts 28-37, 1964).

Netra Tantra: with the Comm. by Kṣemarāja, ed. by Madhusudana Kaul Shastri. Kashmir Series of Texts and Studies. Bombay: Research Department Jammu and Kashmir State, 1926, 1936, 2 Vols.

Nighaṇṭu and the Nirukta of Yāska: ed. and tr. into Eng. by Lakshman Sarup. Delhi: Motilal Banarsidass, 1984, Reprint.

— Niruktam (in Bengali): Yāska's Nirukta, ed. by Amareswara Thakur. Calcutta: University of Calcutta, 1955, 1960, 1963, 1970, 4 Vols.

Niṣpannayogāvalī of Abhayākargupta: ed. by B. Bhattacharya. Baroda: Baroda Oriental Institute, 2nd edn, 1972.

Nīti and Vairāgya Śatakas of Bhartṛhari: ed. and tr. into Eng. by M.R. Kale. Delhi: Motilal Banarsidass, 1971.

Nyāya Kusumāñjali of Udayanācārya: ed. & tr. into Eng. by E.B. Cowell. Delhi: Caxston Publishers, 1983, Reprint.

Nyāya Sūtra of Gautama: with Bhāṣya of Vātsyāyana, tr. into Eng. by Ganganatha Jha. Delhi: Motilal Banarsidass, 1984, Reprint.

— tr. into Eng. by Mrinalkanti Gangopadhyaya. Calcutta: Indian Studies, 1982.

P

Padacandrikā (comm. on Amar Kośa): ed. by Kali Kumar Dutta. Calcutta: Sanskrit College, Vol. I – 1966, Vol. II – 1973, Vol. III – 1978.

Padmānanda MahāKāvya of Aṃarachandra Kavi: ed. by H.R. Kapadia. Baroda: Baroda Oriental Institute, 1932.

Pañcadaśī: tr. into Eng. by Swami Svahananda. Madras: Sri Rama Krishna Math, 4th imp., 1967.

Pañcāstikāyasāra of A. Chakravartinayanar: ed. by A.N. Upadhye. New Delhi: Bharatiya Jnanapith Publication, 1st edn, 1975.

Pāṇinīyaśikṣā: ed. by Man Mohan Ghosh. Delhi: Asian Humanities Press, 1986.

Parānanda Sūtra: ed. by Swami Trivikrama Tirtha. Baroda: Baroda Oriental Institute, 1931.

Parātrīśikā Vivaraṇa of Abhinavagupta: ed. by M.S. Kaul Shastri. Kashmir

Series of Texts and Studies-18. Srinagar: Research Department, Jammu and Kashmir State, w.d.

— ed. by B. Bäumer, tr. into Eng. by Jaideva Singh. Delhi: Motilal Banarsidass, 1988.

Pauṣkara Saṃhitā: ed. by P.P Apte. Tirupati: Rashtriya Sanskrit Vidyapeetha, 1st edn, 1991.

Prabodha Candrodaya of Kṛṣṇamiśrayati: with the Nāṭakābharaṇa of Govindāmṛta, ed. by K. Sambasiva Sastri. Trivandrum Sanskrit Series-22. Trivandrum, 1936.

Prakaraṇa Pañcikā of Śālikanātha Miśra: ed. by A. Subramaniyam Shastri. Darśana Series-4. Varanasi: Banaras Hindu University, 1961.

Prapañcasāra Tantra of Śaṅkarācārya: revised by A. Avalon, ed. by Atalananda Sarasvati. Tantric Text Series-19. Delhi: Motilal Banarsidass, 2 parts in one Vol., 1989, Reprint.

Prāsāda Maṇḍana: ed. & tr. into Hindi by Bhagawan Das Jaina. Jayapur: B.S. Sharma, 1963.

Praśamaratiprakaraṇa of Umāsvāti: ed. by Rajkumar. Bombay: Sri Paramasrutaprabhavakamandala, 1950.

Prasthāna Ratnākara of Puruṣottama Gosvāmin: Varanasi: Vidyavilasa Press, 1909.

Pratimālakṣaṇa of Viṣṇudharmottara: ed. & tr. into Eng. by D.C. Bhattacharya. New Delhi: Harman Publishing House, 1991.

Pratimānāṭakam of Bhāsa: with Eng. tr. by M.R. Kale. Bombay: Motilal Banarsidass, 1930, New Delhi: 1991, Reprint.

Pratiṣṭhālakṣaṇa-Sāra-Samuccaya: ed. by Damodara Sharma. Nepal: Rajakiya Pustakalaya, 1st edn, 2023–2025 V.S., 2 Vols.

Pratyabhijñā Hṛdayam of Kṣemarāja: ed. and tr. into Eng. by Jaideva Singh. Delhi: Motilal Banarsidass, 1973.

Priyadarśikā of Śrīharṣa: ed. by R.V. Krishnamachariar. Sri Vani Vilas Sanskrit Series-3. Madras, 1906.

Puggalapaññati: ed. by Bhikkhu J. Kasyap. Nalanda Devanagari Pali Series. Nalanda: Pali Publication Board, Bihar Government, 1960.

— Designation of Human Types (Puggalapaññati): tr. by Bimala Candra Law. London: Messrs Luzac and Company Ltd., 1969.

R

Raghuvaṃśa of Kālidāsa: with Mallinātha Comm., ed. and Eng. tr. by G.R. Nandargikar. Delhi: Motilal Banarsidass, 1982.

Rājataraṅgiṇī of Kalhaṇa: tr. into Eng. and ed. by M.A. Stein. Delhi: Motilal Banarsidass, 1979, 3 Vols.

Rājavārtika (Tattvārthavārtika) of Shri Akalaṅka Deva: ed. by Prof. Mahendra Kumar Jain. Varanasi: Bharatiya Jnanapitha Kashi, Part I, 1953; Part II, 1957.

Rāmāyaṇa of Vālmīki: with the Tilaka Comm. of Rama, ed. by Wasudev Lakshman Shastri Panasikar. Delhi: Indological Book House, 1983, 2 Vols.

— tr. into Eng. by M.N. Dutt. Patna: Eastern Book House, 1987, 4 Vols, Reprint.

— tr. into Hindi by Dwarka Prasad Sharma. Allahabad: Ram Narayan Lal, 1950.

Rasagaṅgādhara of Jagannātha: with the Comm. of Nāgeśa Bhaṭṭa, ed. by Mathuranatha Sastri. Kāvyamālā Series-12. Bombay: Nirnayasagar Press, 6th edn, 1947.

Ratnāvalī of Śrīharṣa: ed. and Eng. tr. by M.R. Kale. Bombay: Booksellers Publishing Company, 3rd edn, 1964.

Rauravāgama: ed. by N.R. Bhatt. Pondicherry: Institut Français d'Indologie, 1961, 1972, 2 Vols.

Ṛgveda Saṃhitā: ed. by Sripada Damodara Satavalekara. Paradi: Svadhyaya Mandala, 1985, 4 Vols.

— The Hymns of the Rigvedá: tr. into Eng. with Comm. by R.T.H. Griffith. Varanasi: Chaukhamba Sanskrit Series Office, 1971, 2 Vols.

Ṛtusaṃhāra of Kālidāsa: with "Haripriyā" Comm., ed. by Laksmiprapannacharya. Varanasi: Chaukhamba Amarabharati Prakashan, 1977.

Rūpamaṇḍana: ed. & tr. into Hindi by Balaram Srivastav. Varanasi: Motilal Banarsidass, 1992, Reprint.

S

Saddharmapuṇḍarīka: ed. with Hindi tr. by Ram Mohan Das. Patna: Bihar Rastrabhasha Parishad, 1966.

– ed. by P.L. Vaidya. Darbhanga: Mithila Institute, 1960.

— The Lotus of the True Law: tr. into Eng. by H. Kern. Sacred Book of the East Series-21, 1884. Delhi: Motilal Banarsidass, 1986, Reprint.

Sāhitya Darpaṇa of Viśvanātha: with Kusumapratibhā Comm., ed. by Haridas Bhattacharya. Calcutta: Hemacandra Bhattacharya, 1945.

Sakalādhikāra: ed. by V. Gopal Iyengar. T.S.M.S. No. – 141. Tanjavur, 1973.

Samarāṅgaṇa Sūtradhāra of Bhoja: ed. by V.S. Agrawala. Gaekwad's Oriental Series-25. Baroda: Baroda Oriental Institute, 1966.

Sāmaveda: ed. and tr. into Eng. by Devi Chand. Delhi: Munshiram Manoharlal, 1980.

Sāṃkhya Kārikā of Īśvarakṛṣṇa: with Yuktidīpikā Comm., ed. by Ram Chandra Pandeya. Delhi: Motilal Banarsidass, 1967.

Sāṃkhya Sūtra: with Pravacanabhāṣya of Vijñāna Bhikṣu, ed. by R.S. Bhattacharya. Varanasi: Bharatiya Vidya Prakasana, 1977.

— The Sāṃkhya Philosophy: containing Sāṃkhya Pravacana Sūtram, with the Vṛtti of Aniruddha, and the Bhāṣya of Vijñāna Bhikṣu and extracts from the Vṛttisāra of Mahādeva Vedāntin; Tattva Samāsa; Sāṃkhya Kārikā; Pañcaśikha Sūtram, tr. into Eng. by Nandlal Sinha. Delhi: Oriental Books Reprint Corporation, 1979, Reprint.

Samūrtārcanādhikaraṇa: ed. by V. Raghunatha Chakravarti Bhattacharya. Tirupati: Sri Venkatesvara Sanskrit Kala Shala, 1943.

Saṅgītaratnākara of Śārṅgadeva: with Comm. of Siṃhabhūpāla and Kallinātha, ed. by S. Subramanya Sastri. Madras: Adyar Library and Research Centre, 4 Vols, Vol. I. Chapt. I, 1943; II Chapts II-IV, 1944; III Chapts V, VI, 1986; IV Chapt. VII, 1953.

— ed. and Eng. tr. by R.K. Shringy and Prem Lata Sharma. Delhi: Motilal Banarsidass, 1978, Vol. I.

— ed. and Eng. tr. by R.K. Shringy. Delhi: Munshiram Manoharlal Pub. Pvt. Ltd., 1989, Vol. II. and forthcoming Vol. III.

Saṅkalpa Sūryodaya of Veṅkaṭanātha (Vedānta Deśika): with Sanskrit Comm., ed. and Tamil tr. by T. Viraraghavacharya. Madras: India Printing Works, w.d.

Śāṅkhāyana Āraṇyaka: ed. by Sridhar Pathak. Poona: Anand Ashrama, 1987.

— tr. into Eng. by A.B. Keith. London: The Royal Asiatic Society, 1908.

Śāṅkhāyana Brāhmaṇa: ed. by Gulabrao Vajesankara Ojha. Poona: Anand Ashrama, 1977.

Śāṅkhāyana Śrautasūtra: with Comm. of Varadattasutra Ānartīya and Govinda, ed. by A. Hillebrandt. Delhi: Meharchand Lacchmandas, 1981, 4 Vols.

— tr. into Eng. by W. Caland and ed. by Lokesh Chandra. Delhi: Motilal Banarsidass, 1980, Reprint.

Śāradā Tilaka of Lakṣmaṇa Deśikendra: ed. by Arthur Avalon. Varanasi: Motilal Banarsidass, 1933.

Sarasvatīkaṇṭhābharaṇa: ed. by B. Bhattacharya. Varanasi: Banaras Hindu University, 1979.

— ed. by Anundoram Barooah. Assam Publication Board, 1969, Reprint.

Sarvadarśana Saṅgraha of Sāyaṇa - Mādhava: ed. by T.G. Mainkar. Poona: Bhandarkar Oriental Research Institute, 1978.

– tr. into Hindi by Uma Shankar Sharma. Varanasi: Chowkhamba Vidya Bhawan, 1984.

– tr. into Eng. by E.B. Cowell & A.E. Gough. Delhi: Motilal Banarsidass, 1996.

Sarvārthasiddhi of Pūjyapāda: ed. and tr. by Pt. Phoolchandra Shastri. New Delhi: Bharatiya Jnanapith Publication, 5th edn, 1991.

Śatapatha Brāhmaṇa of the White Yajurveda in the Mādhyandina Recension: ed. by A. Chinnaswami Sastri, Pattabhirama Sastri and Ramanatha Diksita. Varanasi: Chaukhamba Sanskrit Sansthan, 1984.

— according to the Mādhyandina recension with the Vedārthaprakāśa Bhāṣya of Sāyaṇācārya, supplemented by the Comm. of Harisvaini. Delhi: Gian Publishing House, 1987, 5 Vols.

— according to the text of Mādhyandina recension, tr. into Eng. by Julius Eggeling. Sacred Books of the East Series-12, 26, 41, 43, 44. Delhi: Motilal Banarsidass, 1986, Reprint.

Ṣaṭcakranirūpaṇam: ed. by Tārānātha Vidyāratna and tr. into Eng. by A. Avalon (The Serpent Power), Madras: Ganesh & Co., 3rd rev. edn, 1931.

Ṣaṭkhaṇḍāgama of Puṣpadanta and Bhūtabali: with the Comm. Dhavalā of Vīrasena, Vol. IV, Kṣetra-Sparśana-Kālānugama, ed. by Hiralal Jain. Amraoti, Berar: Published by Shrimanta Seth Shitabrai Laxmichandra, Jaina Sāhitya Uddhāraka Fund Kāryālaya, 1942.

Ṣaṭtriṃśattattva-Sandoha: ed. & tr. into Eng. by D. B. Sensharma. Kurukshetra: B. N. Chakraborty University, 1977.

Sātvata Saṃhitā: ed. by V.V. Dvivedi. Varanasi: Sampurnananda Sanskrit University, 1982.

Saundarananda of Aśvaghoṣa: ed. and tr. into Eng. by E.H. Johnston. Delhi: Motilal Banarsidass, 1975.

Saundaryalaharī of Śaṅkarācārya: ed. and tr. into Eng. by W. Norman Brown. Cambridge: Harvard University Press, 1958.

Siddhāntaleśa Saṅgraha of Sri Appaya Dīkṣita: ed. with the comm. by Jivananda Vidyasagar. Varanasi: Chowkhamba Vidyabhawan, 1992, Reprint.

Siddhāntaśekhara of Śrīpati: with the Comm. of Makki Bhaṭṭa and Babuaji Misra, ed. by Babuaji Misra, Calcutta: University of Calcutta, 1947, 2 Parts.

Śilpa Prakāśa of Rāmacandra Kaulācāra: ed. and tr. into Eng. by Alice Boner and Sadasiva Rath Sarma. Leiden: E.J. Brill, 1966.

Śilparatna of Śrīkumāra: Part II, ed. by K. Sambasiva Sastri. Trivandrum: Deptt. of Publication, Govt. of Travancore, 1929.

Śilparatnakośa of Sthāpaka Nirañjana Mahāpātra: ed. and tr. into Eng. by B. Bäumer and R.P. Das. Kalāmūlaśāstra Series-16. Delhi: Indira Gandhi National Centre for the Arts and Motilal Banarsidass, 1994.

Śiśupālavadha of Māgha: with Comm. of Vallabhadeva, ed. by Ram Chandra Kak and Harabhatta Shastri. Delhi: Bharatiya Book Corporation, 1990.

Śivadṛṣṭi of Śrī Somānandanātha: with the Vṛtti by Utpaladeva, ed. by M.S. Kaul Shastri. Kashmir Series of Texts and Studies-54. Srinagar: Research Department Jammu and Kashmir State, 1934.

Śivamahimnastotra of Puṣpadanta: with the Comm. of Jagannātha Chakravarty, ed. and tr. into Eng. by Arthur Avalon. Madras: Ganesh and Co., 3rd edn, 1953.

Śiva Purāṇa: ed. by Ramtej Pandey. Varanasi: Chowkhamba Vidyabhavana, 1986.

— tr. into Eng. by J.L. Śhastri. Ancient Indian Tradition and Mythology Series-1-4. Varanasi: Motilal Banarsidass, 1981-1988, 4 Vols, Reprint.

Śivastotrāvalī of Utpaladeva: tr. into Eng. by N.K. Kotru. Delhi: Motilal Banarsidass, 1985.

Śiva Sūtras: The Yoga of Supreme Identity, ed. and tr. into Eng. by Jaideva Singh. Delhi: Motilal Banarsidass, 1979.

Śivasūtravimarśinī of Kṣemarāja: ed. by J.C. Chatterjee. Kashmir Series of Texts and Studies-1. Srinagar: Research Department of Jammu and Kashmir State, 1911.

Śivatattvaratnākara of Basavarāja of Keladi: ed. by R. Rama Shastry. Mysore

Series – 108 & 112, Mysore: Oriental Research Institute, 1964, 1969, 2 Vols.

Skanda Purāṇa: Calcutta: Manasukharai Mor Prakashan, Vol. I, 1965.

Ślokavārttika of Kumārila Bhaṭṭa: with Comm. "Kāśikā" of Sucarita Misra and Nyāya Ratnākara of Parthasarathi Mishra, ed. and Eng. tr. by Ganganatha Jha. Delhi: Satguru Publications, 1979.

— ed. and tr. into Eng. by Durgadhar Jha. Darbhanga: Kameshvar Singh Darbhanga Sanskrit Visvavidyalaya Prakashan, 1979.

Smṛtitattva of Raghunandana Bhattacharya: ed. by Jivananda Vidya Sagar Bhattacharya. Calcutta, 2nd edn, 1895, 2 Vols.

Somaśambhupaddhati: ed. and tr. into French by Helene Brunner Lachaux. Pondicherry: Institut Français d'Indologie, 1963.

Spandakārikā: The Divine Creative Pulsation, The Kārikās and the Spanda Nirṇaya of Kṣemarāja, ed. and tr. into Eng. by Jaideva Singh. Delhi: Motilal Banarsidass, 1980.

Śrautakośa: ed. by R.N. Dandekar. Pune: Vaidika Saṃśodhana Maṇḍala, Vol. I, Part I and II, Vol. II, Part I and II, 1962.

Śrītattvacintāmaṇi of Pūrṇānanda: ed. with Comm. and by Bhuvanamohan Sankhyatirtha and Chintamani Bhattacharya. Calcutta: Metropolitan Printing and Publishing House Ltd., 1936.

Śṛṅgāramañjarī Kathā of Bhoja: ed. by Kalpalata Munshi. Singhi Jaina Series – 30. Bombay: Bharatiya Vidya Bhawana, 1959.

Śṛṅgāra Prakāśa of Bhoja: ed. by G.R. Josyer. Mysore: International Academy of Sanskrit Research, 1955, 1963,1969, 1977, 4 Vols.

Stavamālā: ed. by Bhavadatta Sastri and Sivadatta. Bombay: Nirnayasagar Press, 1903.

Śukranītisāra: tr. by Jagadishvarananda Saraswati. Sonipat: Rishidevi Rupalal Kapur Dharmartha Trust, 1983.

Sūryasiddhānta: ed. by Phanindralal Gangooly. Delhi: Motilal Banarsidass, 1989.

Suśruta Saṃhitā: with "Nibandhasaṅgraha" Comm. of Śrī Ḍalhaṇācārya and Nyāyacandrikā Pañjikā of Gayadāsācārya on Nidānasthāna, ed. by Jadavji Trikamji Acharya. Varanasi: Chaukhamba Orientalia, 1980, Reprint.

— ed. with Eng. tr. by K.L. Bhishagratna. Varanasi: Chowkhamba Sanskrit Series Office, 3rd edn, 1981, 3 Vols.

Suttanipāta: ed. by P.V. Bapat. Delhi: Sri Satguru Publications, 2nd edn, 1990.

Suvarṇa Prabhāsa sūtra: ed. by S. Bagchi. Darbhanga: The Mithila Institute of Post-Graduate Studies & Research in sanskrit Learning, 1967.

Svacchanda Tantra: with the Comm. of Kṣemarāja, ed. by Madhusudana Kaul Sastri. Kashmir Series of Texts and Studies-31, 38, 44, 48, 51, 53, 56. Srinagar: Research Department, Jammu and Kashmir State, 1921-35, 7 Vols.

T

Taittirīya Āraṇyaka: with the Comm. of Bhaṭṭa Bhāskara Miśra, ed. by A. Mahadeva Sastri and K. Rangacarya. Delhi: Motilal Banarsidass, 1985.

Taittirīya Brāhmaṇa: with the Comm. of Sāyaṇācārya, ed. by Narayanasastri Godbole. Sanskrit Granthavali-37. Poona: Ananda Ashram, 3 Vols.

— with the Comm. of Bhaṭṭa Bhāskara Miśra. Delhi: Motilal Banarsidass, 1985, 4 Vols.

Taittirīya Prātiśākhya: with the Comm. Tribhāṣyaratna, ed. by W.D. Whitney. Delhi: Motilal Banarsidass, 1973.

— ed. by R. Samasastri and K. Rangacarya. Delhi: Motilal Banarsidass, 1985.

Taittirīya Saṃhitā of the Black Yajurveda: with the Comm. of Bhaṭṭa Bhāskara Miśra, ed. by A. Mahadevasastri and K. Rangacarya. Delhi: Motilal Banarsidass, 1986, 10 Vols.

— Kṛṣṇayajurvedīya Taittirīya Saṃhitā: ed. by Sripada Damodar Satavalekar. Paradi: Svadhyaya Mandala, 4th edn, 1958.

— Veda of the Black Yajus School entitled Taittirīya Saṃhitā: tr. into Eng. by A.B. Keith. Harvard Oriental Series-18–19. Delhi: Motilal Banarsidass, 1967, 2 Vols.

Tāṇḍyamahābrāhmaṇa: with the Comm. of Sāyaṇācārya, ed. by A. Chinnaswami Sastri. Kashi Sanskrit Granthamala-105. Varanasi: Chaukhamba Sanskrit Series Office, 2nd edn, 1987, 2 Vols.

Tantrāloka of Abhinavagupta: with the Comm. "Viveka" by Rājānaka Jayaratha; ed. by M.R. Sastri and M.S. Kaul. Kashmir Series of Texts and Studies. Srinagar: Research Department, Jammu and Kashmir State, 12 Vols, Vol. I, 1981; II, III, IV, 1921; V, VI, 1922; VII 1924; VIII 1926; IX 1933;X 1936; XI and XII 1938.

— with the Comm. "Viveka" by Rājānaka Jayaratha, ed. by R.C. Dwivedi and

Navajivana Rastogi. Delhi: Motilal Banarsidass, 1987, 8 Vols, Reprint.

Tantrasaṅgraha: ed. by M.M. Gopinath Kaviraj. Varanasi: Varanaseya Sanskrit Visvavidyalaya, 1970, 2 Vols.

Tantrasāra of Abhinavagupta: ed. by M.S. Kaul. Kashmir Series of Texts and Studies-17. Srinagar: Research Department, Jammu and Kashmir State, 1981.

Tantravārttika: tr. into Eng. by M.M.G.N. Jha, Delhi: Sri Satguru Publications, 2nd edn, 1983.

Tarkasaṅgraha of Annambhaṭṭa: tr. into Eng. by M.R. Bodas. Bombay Sanskrit Series-45. Bombay: The Department of Public Instruction, 1930.

Tattvacintāmaṇi of Gaṅgeśa Upādhyāya: with Comm. "Prakāśa". Darbhanga: Mithila Vidyapith, 1957.

Tattvārthādhigama Sūtra of Umāsvātivācakācārya: ed. by Pt. Motilal Ladhaji. Pune, Vira Samvat 2453.

Tattvasaṅgraha of Śāntarakṣita: with the Comm. of Kamalaśīla, ed. by Embar Krishnamacharya. Baroda: Baroda Central Library, 1926, 2 Vols.

— tr. into Eng. by Ganganatha Jha. Baroda: Baroda Oriental Institute, 1937, 1939, 2 Vols.

Tilakamañjarī of Dhanapala: Kāvyamala No. 85. Bombay: Nirnaya Sagar Press, 1938.

Tiloya Paṇṇattī: ed. by A.N. Upadhye & Hiralal Jain. Sholapur: Solapuriyo Jaina-Samskriti Samraksaka Samgha, 1956, 2 Vols.

Trikaṇḍaśeṣa Kośa: ed. by R.S. Bhattacharya, Varanasi: Ratna Publications, 1995.

U

Ubhayābhisārikā of Vararuci: ed. by V.S. Agrawala and Moti Chandra. Bombay: Hindi Grantha Ratnakara Karyalay, 1959.

Udāna: ed. by Paul Steinthal. London: Oxford University Press, 1948, Reprint.

Udayasundarī Kathā: ed. by C. D. Dalal & E. Krishnamacharya. Baroda: Baroda Oriental Institute, 1920.

Ujjvalanīlamaṇi of Rūpa Gosvāmin: Delhi: Chaukhamba Sanskrit Pratisthan, 1984.

Upaniṣads:

— Upaniṣatsaṅgraha: ed. by J.L. Shastri. Delhi: Motilal Banarsidass, 1970.

— Eighteen Principal Upaniṣads (Aṣṭādaśa Upaniṣadaḥ): ed. by V.P. Limaye and R.D. Vadekar. Poona: Vaidika Saṃśodhana Maṇḍala, 1958.

— Thirteen Principal Upanishads: tr. into Eng. by R.E. Hume. Delhi: Oxford University Press, 1983, Reprint.

Uttararāmacarita of Bhavabhūti: with the Comm. of Ghanaśyāma, ed. by P.V. Kane and C.N. Joshi. Delhi: Motilal Banarsidass, 1962.

– With the Comm. of Vīrarāghava, ed. and tr. into Eng. by M.R. Kale. Delhi: Motilal Banarsidass, 1993, Reprint.

Uvāsagadasāo: ed. by N.A. Gore. Poona, 1953.

V

Vaijayantīkośa of Śrī Yādavaprakāśācārya: ed. by Pt. Haragovinda Shastri Mishra. Varanasi: Chowkhamba Sanskrit Series Office, 1971.

Vaiśeṣika Sūtra Bhāṣya: tr. into Eng. by M.M.G.N. Jha, 1915. Benares: Chowkhamba Orientalia, 1982, Reprint.

Vaiśeṣika Sūtra of Kaṇāda: with Bhāṣya of Praśastapāda and Comm. 'Upaskāra', ed. by Dhundhiraja Sastri. Varanasi: Chaukhamba, 1923.

Vaitānasūtra: The Ritual of the Atharvaveda, ed. by R. Garbe. New Delhi: Mahalaksmi Publication House, 1982.

Vakroktijīvita of Rājānaka Kuntaka: ed. by Sushil Kumar De. Calcutta: Firma K.L. Mukhopadhyay, 3rd edn, 1961.

Vākyapadīya of Bhartṛhari: with the Comm. of Puṇyarāja and Vṛtti, ed. by K.A. Subramania Iyer. Delhi: Motilal Banarsidass, 1966.

Vāmana Mahāpurāṇam: ed. by Pt. Nagasharan Singh. Delhi: Nag Publishers, 1983.

Vāstusūtra Upaniṣad: The Essence of Form in Sacred Art, ed. and tr. into Eng. by Alice Boner, Bettina Bäumer and Sadasiva Rath Sharma. Delhi: Motilal Banarsidass, 1982.

Vedānta Paribhāṣā: tr. into Eng. by Swami Madhavananda. Howrah: Ramakrishna Mission Sharada Pitha, Belur Math, 1963.

Vedānta Sāra: ed. by Nikhilananda Swami. Calcutta: Advaita Ashrama, 1974.

Veṇīsaṃhāra of Bhaṭṭa Nārāyaṇa: ed. and tr. into Eng. by R.S. Venkatarama Sastri. Madras: Malati Trades, 1943.

Vibhaṅga Pāli: ed. by Bhikkhu J. Kashyap. Nalanda: Pali Publication Board, Bihar Government, 1960.

— The Book of Analysis: ed. and tr. into Eng. by P.A. Thiṭṭila. London: Luzac and Company Limited, 1969.

Vijñānabhairava: ed. and Eng. tr. by Jaideva Singh. Delhi: Motilal Banarsidass, 1979.

— with the Comm. of Kṣemarāja and Śivopādhyāya, ed. by M.R. Shastri. Kashmir Series of Texts and Studies-8. Srinagar: Research Department, Jammu and Kashmir, 1918.

Vijñaptimātratāsiddhi: ed. and tr. into Eng. by K.N. Chatterjee. Varanasi: Kishor Vidya Niketana, 1980.

Vikramorvaśīyaṃ of Kālidāsa: ed. by Surendra Nath Shastri. Bombay: Nirnayasagar Press, 1942.

Vimalaprabhā of Kalki Śrī Puṇḍarīka: A Comm. on Śrī Laghukālacakratantrarāja of Śrī Mañjuśrīyaśa, Vol. I, ed. by Jagannatha Upadhyaya. Bibliotheca Indo-Tibetica Series 11, Vol. II–III, ed. by V. Dwivedi and S.S. Bahulkar, Rare Buddhist Text Series 12–13. Varanasi: C.I.H.T.S., 1986, 1994.

Vinaya Piṭaka: ed. by J. Takakusu and Makoto Nagai. London: Pali Text Society, 1947.

Viṣṇudharmottara Purāṇa: ed. by Priyabala Shah. Gaekwad's Oriental Series. Baroda: Baroda Oriental Institute, 1958, 1961, 2 Vols.

Viṣṇu Purāṇa: Gorakhpur: Gita Press, 1961.

— tr. into Eng. by H.H. Wilson. London: Trubner and Co., 1864, 4 Vols.

Viṣṇusmṛti with Keśavavaijayantī Ṭīkā: ed. by Pt. V. Krishnamacharya. Adyar Library Series-93-94. Madras: Adyar Library and Research Centre, 1964, 2 Vols.

Visuddhimaggạ: ed. by Dharmananda Kosambi. Bombay: Bharatiya Vidya Bhawan, 1940, 2 Vols.

— ed. by Revatdhamma. Varanasi: Varanaseya Sanskrit University, 1962.

— The Path of Purification: tr. into Eng. by Bhikkhu Ñyāṇamoli. Srilanka: Buddhist Publication Society, 1979, 2 Vols. Reprint.

Viśvāmitra Saṃhitā: ed. by U.S. Bhatta. Tirupati: Rashtriya Sanskrit Vidyapeetha, 2nd edn, 1991.

Vṛttaratnākara: ed. by Aryendra Sharma. Hyderabad: Sanskrit Academy, Osmania University, 1969.

Vyaktiviveka of Rājānakamahimabhaṭṭa: with the Comm. of Rājānaka Ruyyaka, ed. by Madhusudana Mishra. Haridas Sanskrit Granthamala-121. Benaras: Chowkhamba Sanskrit Series, 1936.

Y

Yājñavalkya Śikṣā: with the Comm. "Śikṣāvallī", ed. by Amaranath Sastri. Kashi: Padmanabha Sharma Diksit, 1937.

Yājñavalkyasmṛti of Yājñavalkya: with Mitākṣarā Comm. of Vijñāneśvara, ed. by Umesh Chandra Pandey. Varanasi: Chowkhamba Sanskrit Sansthana, 1983, 2 Vols.

— with Mitākṣarā Comm., tr. by Srisa Chandra Vidyarnava. Allahabad: Panini Office, 1918, Book I.

Yajurveda Saṃhitā: ed. by S.D. Satavalekara. Paradi: Svadhyaya Mandala, 1957.

— The Text of the White Yajurveda, tr. into Eng. with Comm. by R.T.H. Griffith. Banaras: E.J. Lazarus and Co., 1957.

Yogasārasaṅgraha of Vijñānabhikṣu: tr. into Eng. by Ganganatha Jha. New Delhi: Akay Book Corporation, 1986.

Yogasūtra of Patañjali: with the Comm. of Vyāsa and Gloss of Vācaspatimiśra, tr. into Eng. by Rama Prasada. Allahabad: Panini Office, 1924.

— tr. into Eng. by J.H. Woods. Delhi: Motilal Banarsidass, 1988, Reprint.

— with the Vyāsa Bhāṣya, tr. into Eng. by Bangali Baba. Delhi: Motilal Banarsidass, 1982, Reprint.

Yoginī Hṛdaya: with "Dīpikā" Comm. of Amṛtānanda and "Setubandha" of Bhāskarācārya, ed. by M.M. Gopinath Kaviraj. Banaras: Govt. Sanskrit Library, Saraswati Bhavan, 1923.

— ed. by Vrajavallabha Dwivedi. Varanasi: Motilal Banarsidass, 1988.

Reference Works

Bharatakośa: A dictionary of technical terms with definitions collected from the work on Music and Dramaturgy by Bharata and others, ed. by M. Ramakrishna Kavi. Delhi: Munshiram Manoharlal, 1983.

Bhāratīya Vyāvahāra Kośa: ed. by V.D. Narawane. Pune: Meheta Publishing

House, 3rd edn, 1993.

Buddhist Hybrid Sanskrit Grammar and Dictionary: ed. F. Edgerton. New Haven, U.S.A.: 1953.

Concordance to the Principal Upanishads and Bhagavadgītā: ed. by G.A. Jacob. Delhi: Motilal Banarsidass, 1985.

A Dictionary of Hinduism: Its Mythology, Folklore and Development 1500 B.C.–A.D. 1500, ed. by Margaret and James Stutley. London: Routledge & Kegan Paul, 1985, Reprint.

Dictionary of Indology: complied by A.K. Roy and N.N. Gidwani. Delhi: Oxford & IBH Comm., 1983, 4 Vols.

Encyclopaedia Indica – Hindi Viśvakośa: ed. by Nagendra Nath Vasu. Delhi: B.R. Publishing, 1986, 25 Vols., Reprint.

Encyclopaedia of Indian Literature: Chief editor Amaresh Datta. New Delhi: Sahitya Akademi, 1987, 1988, 1989, 3 Vols.

Encyclopaedia of Indian Philosophies: Gen. ed. Karl H. Potter. Delhi: Motilal Banarsidass, 1970–1999, 8 Vols.

Encyclopedia of Indian Temple Architecture, South India: ed. by M.A. Dhaky, Vol.I, Part 3. New Delhi: AIIS and IGNCA, 1996.

Encyclopaedia of Puranic Beliefs and Practices: ed. by Sadashiv Ambadas Dange. 3 Vols; Vol. I-A-C. 1986; Vol. II-D-G. 1987; Vol. III-H-N., 1987. Delhi: Navarang.

Encyclopaedia of Religion: ed. by Mircea Eliade. New York: MacMillan Publication Company, 1987, 16 Vols.

Encyclopaedia of Religion and Ethics: ed. by James Hastings. Edinburgh: T & T Clark, 1979, 12 Vols.

Encyclopaedia of the Upaniṣads: ed. by N.S. Subrahmanin. Delhi: Sterling Publishers, 1985.

An Encyclopaedic Dictionary of Sanskrit on Historical Principles: Gen. editors A.M. Ghatage & S.D. Joshi. Poona: Deccan College Postgraduate and Research Institute, 1976–1995, 5 Vols.

A Glossary of Indian Figures of Speech: ed. by Edwin Gerow. Paris: Mouton, 1971.

Hindi Viśvakośa: ed. by Nagari Pracharini Sabha. Varanasi: 1986, 12 Vols.

Hindu World: An Encyclopaedic Survey of Hinduism: ed. by Benjamin Walker. Delhi: Munshiram Manoharlal, 1983, 2 Vols.

A History of Indian Literature: ed. by J. Gonda (Chief editor). Wiesbaden: Otto Harassowitz, Several Vols.

Iconographic Dictionary of the Indian Religions – Hinduism – Buddhism – Jainism: ed. by Gösta Lievert. Delhi: Sri Satguru Publications, 1986.

The Illustrated Dictionary of Hindu Iconography: ed. by Margaret Stutley. London: Routledge & Kegan Paul, 1985.

Jainendra Siddhānta Kośa of Jinendra Varni: New Delhi: Bharatiya Jnanapith Publication, 4 Vols, Vol. I. 4th edn, 1993, Vol. II. 3rd edn, 1992, Vol. III. 2nd edn, 1987, Vol. IV. 2nd edn, 1988.

Kalātattvakośa: Gen. ed. Kapila Vatsyayan. New Delhi: Indira Gandhi National Centre for the Arts and Motilal Banarsidass Publishers Pvt. Ltd., 1988, 1992, 1996, 1999, 4 Vols.

Kurzgefasstes Etymololgiches Wörterbuch des Altindischen: A Concise Etymological Sanskrit Dictionary: ed. by Manfred Mayrhofer. Heidelberg: Universitätsverlag, 1956, 4 Vols (New revised edn, 1987 ff.).

Pali-English Dictionary: ed. by T.W. Rhys Davids and William Stede. New Delhi: Munshiram Manoharlal Publishers Pvt. Ltd., 1989, Reprint.

Pauranic Kośa: ed. by Rana Prasad Sharma. Varanasi: Jñāna Maṇḍala, 1950.

Puranic Encyclopaedia: ed. by Vettam Mani. Harvard Oriental Series-10. Delhi: Motilal Banarsidass, 1964, Reprint.

The Practical Sanskrit-English Dictionary: V.S. Apte. Delhi: Motilal Banarsidass, 1992, Reprint.

The Sanskrit-English Dictionary: M. Monier-Williams. Oxford University Press, 1986, Reprint.

Sanskrit-Wörterbuch: O. Böhtlingk, & R. Roth. 7 Vols (1855–1875).Delhi: Motilal Banarsidass, 1990, Reprint.

Vedic Experience: Mantramañjarī: An Anthology of the Vedas for Modern Man and Contemporary Celebration: ed. by R. Panikkar. Delhi: Motilal Banarsidass, 1983.

Vedic Index of Names and Subjects: ed. by A.A. Macdonell & A.B. Keith. Delhi: Motilal Banarsidass, 1982, 2 Vols.

Wörterbuch zum Rig-Veda: H. Grassmann. Wiesbaden: Otto Harrassowitz, 5th edn, 1976.

INDEX

A

B

D

E

F

G

H

I

J

K

L

M

N

O

P

Q

S

T

V

W

Y

Z